From the reviews

"John Boswell restores one's faith in scholarship as the union of erudition, analysis and moral vision. I would not hesitate to call his book revolutionary, for it tells of things heretofore unimagined and sets a standard of excellence that one would have thought impossible in the treatment of an issue so large, uncharted and vexed. . . . His knowledge of the relevant scholarly literature is remarkable, and his book displays the sweep and control that one finds only in the work of a major historian. . . . The book's argument is of such richness—its empirical base so broad, its reasoning so fierce—that it succeeds in making one think the unthinkable. It forces us to re-examine even the most fixed notions about our moral and cultural heritage. . . . He has also mastered one of the rarest of skills: the ability to write about sex with genuine wit. Improbable as it might seem, this work of unrelenting scholarship and high intellectual drama is also thoroughly entertaining."—Paul Robinson, *New York Times Book Review*

"*Christianity, Social Tolerance, and Homosexuality* is one of the most critical and probing studies yet to appear. For Mr. Boswell has emerged with an interpretation which looks distinctly new. His argument is that intolerance of homosexuality was not an essential feature of Christianity itself, but only became the dominant attitude after nearly twelve hundred years of Church history. . . . Mr. Boswell's scholarly and painstaking analysis will bring academic respectability to what has hitherto been regarded as a faintly murky subject. It may even do something to foster more tolerant attitudes."—Keith Thomas, *New York Review of Books*

"To characterize this analysis as revolutionary—in its implications for historical studies, for Christianity, for the current debate over sexual mores—is to state the obvious. Boswell's study is indubitably one of the most profound, explosive works of scholarship to appear within recent memory. His book will inaugurate controversies bound to rage for years. . . . Even now it is safe to say that *Christianity, Social Tolerance, and Homosexuality* is that rare item—a truly ground-breaking study. With an abundance of skill and daring, John Boswell has opened up a vast historical terrain for reassessment, some of it never before explored, much of it marked for far too long by barricaded, sealed borders."—Martin Bauml Duberman, *New Republic*

"An astonishing work of scholarship that ranges with ease over fourteen centuries, almost as many languages, characters as diverse as Socrates, Ovid, Caesar, Richard the Lion-Hearted, King Edward II and Saint Thomas Aquinas, and the history of social tolerance. What makes this work so exciting is not simply its content—fascinating though that is—but its revolutionary challenge to some of Western culture's most familiar moral assumptions."—*Newsweek*

Christianity, Social Tolerance, and Homosexuality

John Boswell

Christianity, Social Tolerance, and Homosexuality

Gay People in Western Europe

from the Beginning of the Christian Era

to the Fourteenth Century

The University of Chicago Press

Chicago and London

Publication of this volume has been assisted by a grant
from the National Endowment for the Humanities.

The University of Chicago Press, Chicago 60637
The University of Chicago Press, Ltd., London
© 1980 by The University of Chicago
All rights reserved. Published 1980
Paperback edition 1981
Printed in the United States of America

03 02 01 00 99 98 97 96 95 94   11 12 13 14 15

Library of Congress Cataloging in Publication Data
Boswell, John.
   Christianity, social tolerance, and homosexuality.
   Bibliography: p.
   Includes indexes.
   1. Homosexuality—Europe—History.   2. Homosexuality
and Christianity—History.   I. Title.
HQ76.3.E8B67   301.41'57'094   79–11171
ISBN 0–226–06711–4 (paper)

This book is printed on acid-free paper.

To my parents for their love and example,

and to Ralph for his help

Love is not a crime; if it were a crime to love,
God would not have bound even the divine with love.

    Carmina Burana

Because of the diverse conditions of humans, it happens that some acts are
virtuous to some people, as appropriate and suitable to them, while the same
acts are immoral for others, as inappropriate to them.

    Saint Thomas Aquinas, *Summa theologiae*

We can easily reduce our detractors to absurdity and show them their hostility
is groundless. But what does this prove? That their hatred is *real*. When every
slander has been rebutted, every misconception cleared up, every false opinion
about us overcome, intolerance itself will remain finally irrefutable.

    Moritz Goldstein, "Deutsch-jüdischer Parnass"

Contents

Illustrations

Abbreviations

AL	*Anthologia Latina*
AP	*Anthologia Palatina* (or *Greek Anthology*)
BM	British Museum
BN	Bibliothèque nationale
CSEL	*Corpus scriptorum ecclesiasticorum Latinorum*
EI	*Encyclopedia of Islam*
JB	Jerusalem Bible
KJV	King James or Authorized Version
LC	Loeb Classical Library
LSJ	*Greek–English Lexicon*, ed. H. G. Liddell and Robert Scott, 9th ed., rev. H. Stuart Jones
LXX	Septuagint
Mansi	J. D. Mansi, *Sacrorum conciliorum nova et amplissima collectio*
MGH	*Monumenta Germaniae historica*
NEB	New English Bible
NT	New Testament
OBMLV	*Oxford Book of Medieval Latin Verse*, ed. F. J. Raby
OCD	*Oxford Classical Dictionary*, 2d ed.
OED	*Oxford English Dictionary*
OT	Old Testament
PG	*Patrologiae cursus completus, Series Graeca*
PL	*Patrologiae cursus completus, Series Latina*
Poetae	*Poetae Latini medii aevi* (in MGH)
PW	*Paulys Real-Encyclopädie der classischen Altertumswissenschaft*
Settimane	*Settimane di studi del Centro italiano di studi sull'alto medioevo* (Spoleto)
SS	*Scriptores* (in MGH)
SS.RR.MM.	*Scriptores rerum Merovingicarum* (in MGH)
ZFDA	*Zeitschrift für deutsches Altertum*
[ ] or Pseudo-	Indicates spurious attribution

Preface

It is not possible to write history in a vacuum. No matter how much historians and their readers may wish to avoid contaminating their understanding of the past with the values of the present, they cannot ignore the fact that both writer and reader are inevitably affected by the assumptions and beliefs of the age(s) in which they write and read. Because very many of the issues addressed in this book as historical problems are viewed today chiefly as moral questions, and because their social importance is generally supposed to result from the moral traditions regarding them, it would be impossible to present a persuasive argument for the essentially social significance of such phenomena without examining, at some length, the moral texts and opinions thought to have been determinative in establishing Western attitudes toward them. Very widespread preconceptions regarding historical causations must be addressed in detail; they cannot be refined or altered by judicious silence or a simple assertion to the contrary. If religious texts are widely supposed to have been the origin of a medieval prejudice, their role in determining the attitude in question must be carefully examined; if it is assumed that scholastic opinions on a subject were an inevitable response to the force of the preceding Christian tradition, a historian who wishes to present an alternative explanation must examine the force of the previous tradition in minute detail. Only if he can demonstrate that it is insufficient explanation for the opinions in question can he expect his alternative explanation to carry much weight.

It is, on the other hand, the province of the historian not to praise or blame but merely to record and explain. This book is not intended as support or criticism of any particular contemporary points of view—scientific or moral— regarding homosexuality. Where extended discussion of arguments against homosexual behavior has been presented, the aim has been twofold: to demonstrate that what may seem to have been the origin of popular antipathy in the past often was not, and to clarify crucial differences between ostensibly analogous ancient and modern objections to homosexuality. The analysis of ideas about the "unnaturalness" and "nonreproductivity" of homosexuality presented in Chapter 1, for instance, is aimed not at defending it from such criticism but at providing a clearer perspective on the most common specific objections employed against it by ancient and medieval writers (as, e.g., in a text on medieval alchemical ideas one might employ current scientific data to demonstrate the feasibility of alchemical theories or procedures). What will strike some readers as a partisan point of view is chiefly the absence of the negative attitudes on this subject ubiquitous in the modern West; after a long, loud noise, a sudden silence may seem deafening.

*   *   *

Because the material considered in this volume comprises both a very broad geographical and temporal expanse and many very detailed and technical issues, it has been somewhat difficult to provide a scholarly apparatus of use to all who might desire it and still make the book accessible to the general reader. Specialists may be surprised at explanations of facts or material which seem perfectly obvious, and nonspecialists may find it difficult to wade through dense, recondite notes. Few who are interested in the niceties of biblical lexicography will be familiar with the nuances of Hispano-Arab poetry, and many people quite interested in the general areas of intolerance or homosexuality may have very limited acquaintance with medieval history of any sort. Every effort has been made to keep the text readable, self-explanatory, and focused on central issues. As far as possible, all purely technical and linguistic considerations have been placed in footnotes or appendices. Brief introductions to relevant aspects of some of the periods and cultures involved have been provided, in the hope that whatever ennui or amusement they provide historians will be offset by the help they offer readers from other disciplines.

Citations have been particularly troublesome in this regard, since inconsistencies which might bother specialists may enable those less familiar with the same literature to locate passages with greater ease.[1] Most works are cited for this reason in their most familiar or recognizable form, even where this has required erratic use of foreign or English titles for the same author (e.g., Plutarch), and many convenient editions (e.g., the *Patrologia*) have been preferred to better or more modern versions of the same texts.

---

1. For example, it is impossible to be entirely consistent in transliterating Persian and Arabic in a work of this nature, because many names and some titles are cited from works in other languages which employ differing systems of transliteration, and because many names have become familiar in forms which do not correspond to a specific system. Where I have transliterated and was not limited by a tradition or published version, I have used a slightly modified version of the system employed by the editors of the EI, which will, I think, provide no difficulty to readers of Arabic and Persian.

Only where the text itself bears on the historical issues have efforts been made to address textual problems.

For reasons outlined below, it has seemed essential to consult all sources in their original, even when modern translations exist. All translations provided in the text, except where specifically noted, are my own, and every effort has been made to effect them as accurately and candidly as possible, even to the point of employing obscene language. Perhaps the medieval dictum that "to cite heresy is not to be a heretic" may be modified in this context to urge that to cite obscenity is not to be obscene. It would at any rate be arrogant to assume that readers could not judge such material for themselves without the intervention of censorship by historians. Renderings of literary material, including poetry, have been effected with clarity and literal accuracy the paramount considerations; no effort has been made to reflect literary nuances unless these provide insight into the questions at hand.

*   *   *

A word of explanation may be appropriate regarding the relative absence of materials relating to women. Most of the sources for this (as for nearly all) history were written by men about men, and where they deal with women, they do so peripherally. Wherever possible, examples involving women have been cited, and an effort has been made to consider the feminine correlates of scientific, philosophical, religious, and social aspects of male homosexuality, but no one could offset the overwhelming disproportion of data regarding male and female sexuality without deliberate distortion.

*   *   *

The research for this book was begun nearly a decade ago, and it would be impossible now to recall all those who contributed in some way to its preparation. An incalculable debt is owed Ralph Hexter, who rendered practical assistance at every stage of the endeavor, read the entire manuscript several times and offered valuable critical advice, and provided information on many matters; in the realm of literature, for example, he brought to my attention the existence of the poems "Ganymede and Hebe" and "Married Clergy," published here for the first time. No words of thanks could suffice to express my gratitude for his assistance or to apprise readers of the extent of his contributions.

Several colleagues, notably James Weinrich of Harvard, Douglas Roby of Brooklyn College, and John Winkler and James Rodman of Yale, have contributed generously of their time and knowledge, and I am grateful to them. I am equally indebted to my students at Yale, both graduate and undergraduate, especially to Ruth Mazo for her sensitive and erudite study of Aelred of Rievaulx, Richard Styche for his work on Icelandic law, and

Frances Terpak and Vasanti Kupfer for their advice and assistance in locating materials relating to medieval art.

I also wish to thank David Frusti and Libby Berkeley for more practical but no less important help; the Council on the Humanities of Yale University for a grant through the A. Whitney Griswold Faculty Research Fund; and the librarians and archivists of the Bayerische Staatsbibliothek of Munich, Karl Marx Universität in Leipzig, Gonville and Caius College of Cambridge University, the Bodleian library of Oxford University, and the Archive of the Crown of Aragon in Barcelona.

I   Points of Departure

1 Introduction

"All those whose lives are spent searching for truth are well aware that the glimpses they catch of it are necessarily fleeting, glittering for an instant only to make way for new and still more dazzling insights. The scholar's work, in marked contrast to that of the artist, is inevitably provisional. He knows this and rejoices in it, for the rapid obsolescence of his books is the very proof of the progress of scholarship."[1]

Between the beginning of the Christian Era and the end of the Middle Ages, European attitudes toward a number of minorities underwent profound transformations. Many groups of people passed from constituting undistinguished parts of the mainstream of society to comprising segregated, despised, and sometimes severely oppressed fringe groups. Indeed the Middle Ages are often imagined to have been a time of almost universal intolerance of nonconformity, and the adjective "medieval" is not infrequently used as a synonym for "narrow-minded," "oppressive," or "intolerant" in the context of behavior or attitudes. It is not, however, accurate or useful to picture medieval Europe and its institutions as singularly and characteristically intolerant. Many other periods have been equally if not more prone to social intolerance:[2] most European minorities fared worse during the "Renaissance"

1. "Tous ceux dont la vie se passe à chercher la vérité savent bien que les images qu'ils en saisissent sont nécessairement fugitives. Elles brillent un instant pour faire place à des clartés nouvelles et toujours plus éblouissantes. Bien différente de celle de l'artiste, l'oeuvre du savant est fatalement provisoire. Il le sait et s'en réjouit, puisque la rapide vieillesse de ses livres est la preuve même du progrès de la science": Henri Pirenne, cited in Georges Gérardy, *Henri Pirenne, 1862–1935*, Ministère de l'éducation nationale et de la culture, Administration des services educatifs (Brussels, 1962), p. 4.

2. "Social" tolerance or intolerance is used in this study to refer to public acceptance of personal variation or idiosyncrasy in matters of appearance, life-style, personality, or belief. "Social" is implicit even when, to avoid repetition, it is not used to modify "tolerance" or "intolerance." "Social tolerance" is thus distinguished from "approval." A society may well "tolerate" diversity of life-style or belief even when a majority of its members do not personally approve of the variant beliefs or behavior; this is indeed the essence of "social tolerance," since no "tolerance" is involved in accepting approved behavior or belief. Non-acceptance of disapproved behavior or traits does not of course necessarily constitute

3

than during the "Dark Ages," and no other century has witnessed anti-Semitism of such destructive virulence as that of the twentieth. Moreover, treating these two subjects—intolerance and medieval Europe—as if each were in some sense a historical explanation of the other almost wholly precludes understanding of either one. The social history of medieval Europe and, perhaps even more, the historical origins and operations of intolerance as a social phenomenon require far subtler analysis.

This study is offered as a contribution to better understanding of both the social history of Europe in the Middle Ages and intolerance as a historical force, in the form of an investigation of their interaction in a single case.[3] It would obviously be foolhardy to attempt any broader approach to the first; it may be slightly less obvious why there is no general treatment of the second in the study which follows.

In the first place, it would be extremely difficult to define the boundaries of such a general study. Although intolerance has weighed heavily on

---

intolerance: it could be a defensive response to persons whose variation from the norm threatens social well-being, or a response to religious imperatives which explicitly transcend the value of "tolerance." Both of these issues are taken up below in relation to gay people in the Middle Ages.

3. In a previous study (*The Royal Treasure: Muslim Communities under the Crown of Aragon in the Fourteenth Century* [New Haven, 1977]) I have addressed this issue from the perspective of Muslim communities in Christian Spain in the later Middle Ages. So little scholarly work on the subject of gay people in history is presently extant that it would be premature to attempt anything in the way of a bibliographical essay. With few exceptions, no modern studies have been useful for the present investigation. Almost all modern historical research on gay people in the Christian West has been dependent on the pioneering study of Derrick Sherwin Bailey, *Homosexuality and the Western Christian Tradition* (London, 1955). This work suffers from an emphasis on negative sanctions which gives a wholly misleading picture of medieval practice, ignores almost all positive evidence on the subject, is limited primarily to data regarding France and Britain, and has been superseded even in its major focus, biblical analysis. Nonetheless, it remains the best single work on the subject in print, and it is for this reason that I have been at pains throughout the following chapters to expand on or disagree with those portions of it related to this study. No other studies of homosexuality in general can be recommended without severe reservation. The first well-known overview of the subject was a sketch by Richard Burton, appended as the "Terminal Essay: D. Pederasty" in his 1885 translation of the *Arabian Nights* (reprinted in *Sexual Heretics: Male Homosexuality in English Literature, 1850–1900,* ed. Brian Reade [New York, 1970], pp. 158–93). Raymond de Becker's *L'érotisme d'en face* (Paris, 1964; trans. M. Crosland and A. Daventry as *The Other Face of Love* [New York, 1969]) is pleasant and readable and contains many entertaining illustrations (some of dubious relation to the text). Although the scientific speculation which composes pt. 1 is now completely outdated and pt. 2 (on the Middle Ages) should be ignored, pt. 3—on modern Europe—is still useful. Thorkil Vanggaard's *Phallos: A Symbol and Its History in the Male World* (London, 1972) has been probably deservedly largely ignored by scholars, as have Arno Karlen's *Sexuality and Homosexuality* (New York, 1971) and Vern Bullough's *Sexual Variance in Society and History* (New York, 1976), which superseded it with substantial but not sufficient improvement. For the sake of completeness alone I mention A. L. Rowse's *Homosexuals in History* (New York, 1977).

the conscience of the twentieth century, so little is known about its nature, extent, origins, and effects in a historical context that merely delineating the outlines and proportions of the problem would require a study of considerably greater length than the present one. The writer would need not only to be familiar with the techniques and findings of a host of specialized fields—anthropology, psychology, sociology, etc.—but also to have some means of adjudicating the validity of their competing claims and assessing their relative importance. Arbitrarily pursuing some and excluding others would be perilous in so understudied a field.[4]

Moreover, even if the problem could be defined, it would not be possible to write about a subject as comprehensive and far-reaching as intolerance with the degree of historical detail provided in this study except in a work of encyclopedic proportions. From the historian's point of view, however, general theories are of little value unless rooted in and supported by specific studies of particular cases, and since there are so few of these at present to substantiate ideas regarding intolerance, it has seemed more useful to provide data for eventual synthetic analysis by others than to embark prematurely on the analysis itself. This appoach has the egregious disadvantage of producing, in effect, an elaborate description of a single piece of an unassembled puzzle, but given the extreme difficulty of even identifying, much less assembling, all the other pieces, it appears to be the most constructive effort possible at present. It has, moreover, the compensating advantage of allowing the data assembled to be employed within any larger theoretical framework, historical or scientific, current or subsequent, since there is little built-in theoretical bias.

Of the various groups which became the objects of intolerance in Europe during the Middle Ages, gay people[5] are the most useful for this study for a number of reasons. Some of these are relatively obvious. Unlike Jews and Muslims, they were dispersed throughout the general population everywhere in Europe; they constituted a substantial minority in every age[6]—rather than in a few periods, like heretics or witches—but they were never (unlike the poor, for instance) more than a minority of the population. Intolerance of gay people cannot for the most part be confused with medical treatment, as in the case of lepers or the insane, or with protective surveillance, as in the case of the deaf or, in some societies, women. Moreover, hostility to gay people provides

---

4. This study is thus "social history" not in its most modern sense—i.e., application of the findings and conventions of social sciences to history—but only in an older and more prosaic sense: the history of social phenomena rather than of politics or ideas.

5. The word "gay" is consciously employed in this text with connotations somewhat different from "homosexual." The distinction and the reasons for employing a word which has not yet become a part of most scholars' vocabulary are discussed at length in chap. 2.

6. For estimates of the numbers of gay people in the past (and the present) see below, pp. 53–58.

singularly revealing examples of the confusion of religious beliefs with popular prejudice. Apprehension of this confusion is fundamental to understanding many kinds of intolerance, but it is not usually possible until either the prejudice or the religious beliefs have become so attenuated that it is difficult to imagine there was ever any integral connection between them. As long as the religious beliefs which support a particular prejudice are generally held by a population, it is virtually impossible to separate the two; once the beliefs are abandoned, the separation may be so complete that the original connection becomes all but incomprehensible. For example, it is now as much an article of faith in most European countries that Jews should not be oppressed because of their religious beliefs as it was in the fourteenth century that they should be; what seemed to many Christians of premodern Europe a cardinal religious duty—the conversion of Jews—would seem to most adherents of the same religious tradition today an unconscionable invasion of the privacy of their country-men. The intermingling of religious principles and prejudice against the Jews in the fourteenth century was so thorough that very few Christians could distinguish them at all; in the twentieth century the separation effected on the issue has become so pronounced that most modern Christians question the sincerity of medieval oppression based on religious conviction. Only during a period in which the confusion of religion and bigotry persisted but was not ubiquitous or unchallenged would it be easy to analyze the organic relation of the two in a convincing and accessible way.

The modern West appears to be in just such a period of transition regarding various groups distinguished sexually, and gay people provide a particularly useful focus for the study of the history of such attitudes.[7] Since they are still the objects of severe proscriptive legislation, widespread public hostility, and various civil restraints, all with ostensibly religious justification, it is far easier to elucidate the confusion of religion and intolerance in their case than in that of blacks, moneylenders, Jews, divorced persons, or others whose status in society has so completely ceased to be associated with religious conviction that the correlation—even if demonstrated at length—now seems limited, tenuous, or accidental.

Much of the present volume, on the other hand, is specifically intended to rebut the common idea that religious belief—Christian or other—has been the *cause* of intolerance in regard to gay people. Religious beliefs may cloak or incorporate intolerance, especially among adherents of revealed religions

7. The order in which societies come to grips with categories of invidious discrimination may reveal much about their social structure. It is interesting that in the modern West public attention has been focused on intolerance related to sexuality only long after com-parable issues involving race or religious belief have been addressed, whereas in most ancient cities gay people achieved toleration long before religious nonconformists, and race (in its modern sense) was never an issue.

which specifically reject rationality as an ultimate criterion of judgment or tolerance as a major goal in human relations. But careful analysis can almost always differentiate between conscientious application of religious ethics and the use of religious precepts as justification for personal animosity or prejudice. If religious strictures are used to justify oppression by people who regularly disregard precepts of equal gravity from the same moral code, or if prohibitions which restrain a disliked minority are upheld in their most literal sense as absolutely inviolable while comparable precepts affecting the majority are relaxed or reinterpreted, one must suspect something other than religious belief as the motivating cause of the oppression.

In the particular case at issue, the belief that the hostility of the Christian Scriptures to homosexuality caused Western society to turn against it should not require any elaborate refutation. The very same books which are thought to condemn homosexual acts condemn hypocrisy in the most strident terms, and on greater authority: and yet Western society did not create any social taboos against hypocrisy, did not claim that hypocrites were "unnatural," did not segregate them into an oppressed minority, did not enact laws punishing their sin with castration or death. No Christian state, in fact, has passed laws against hypocrisy per se, despite its continual and explicit condemnation by Jesus and the church. In the very same list which has been claimed to exclude from the kingdom of heaven those guilty of homosexual practices, the greedy are also excluded. And yet no medieval states burned the greedy at the stake. Obviously some factors beyond biblical precedent were at work in late medieval states which licensed prostitutes[8] but burned gay people: by any objective standard, there is far more objurgation of prostitution in the New Testament than of homosexuality. Biblical strictures have been employed with great selectivity by all Christian states, and in a historical context what determines the selection is clearly the crucial issue.

Another advantage in employing gay people as the focus of this study is the continued vitality of ideas about the "danger" they pose to society. Almost all prejudice purports to be a rational response to some threat or danger: every despised group is claimed to threaten those who despise it; but it is usually easy to show that even if some danger exists, it is not the origin of the prejudice. The "threat" posed by most groups previously oppressed by Christian society (e.g., "witches," moneylenders), however, now seems so illusory that it is difficult for modern readers to imagine that intelligent people of the past could actually have been troubled by such anxieties. In fact one is apt to dismiss such imagined dangers out of hand as willful misrepresentations

8. Many European monarchies of the later Middle Ages licensed prostitutes: for England, see John Bellamy, *Crime and Public Order in England in the Later Middle Ages* (London, 1973) p. 60; for Spain, see Boswell, *The Royal Treasure*, pp. 70–71, 348ff.; see also chap. 2 below.

flagrantly employed to justify oppression. Not only is this untrue; it obscures the more important realities of the relationship between intolerance and fear.

No such skepticism obscures this relationship in the case of gay people. The belief that they constitute some sort of threat is still so widespread that an assumption to the contrary may appear partisan in some circles, and those who subscribe to the notion that gay people are in some way dangerous may argue that for this very reason they are not typical victims of intolerance.

It should be noted that whether a group actually threatens society or not is not directly relevant to the issue of intolerance unless the hostility the group experiences can be shown to stem from a rational apprehension of that threat. Traveling gypsies may actually have been at some point a hazard to isolated communities if they carried infections and diseases to which local residents had no immunity, but it would be injudicious to assume that it was this threat which resulted in antipathy toward them, particularly when it can be shown that such hostility antedates by centuries any realization of the communicability of most infections and when the content of antigypsy rhetoric bears no relation to disease at all.

The claims about the precise nature of the threat posed by gay people have varied extravagantly over time, sometimes contradicting each other directly and almost invariably entailing striking internal inconsistencies. Many of these are considered in detail below, but it may be worth alluding here to two of the most persistent.

The first is the ancient claim that societies tolerating or approving homosexual behavior do so to their own manifest detriment, since if all their members engaged in such behavior, these societies would die out. This argument assumes—curiously—that all humans would become exclusively homosexual if given the chance. There seems to be no reason to make such an assumption: a great deal of evidence contradicts it. It is possible that the abandonment of social sanctions against homosexuality occasions some increase in overt homosexual behavior, even among persons who would not otherwise try it; it is even conceivable (though not at all certain) that more people will adopt exclusively homosexual life-styles in societies with tolerant attitudes. But the fact that a characteristic increases does not demonstrate its danger to the society; many characteristics which, if adopted universally, would presumably redound to the disadvantage of society (e.g., voluntary celibacy, self-sacrifice) may nonetheless increase over periods of time without causing harm and are often highly valued by a culture precisely because of their statistical rarity. To assume that any characteristic which increases under favorable conditions will in the course of time eliminate all competing characteristics is bad biology and bad history. No current scientific theories regarding the etiology of homosexuality suggest that social tolerance determines

its incidence. Even purely biological theories uniformly assume that it would
be a minority preference under any conditions, no matter how favorable.[9]

Moreover, there is no compelling reason to assume that homosexual
desire induces nonreproductivity in individuals or population groups.[10] No
evidence supports the common idea that homosexual and heterosexual
behavior are incompatible; much data suggests the contrary.[11] The fact that

9. In the late nineteenth century, when the issue of homosexuality first began to exercise
the minds of scientists, most authorities assumed that homosexual inclinations were congenital, and differed only on whether they were a defect (Krafft-Ebing) or a part of the
normal range of human variation (Hirschfeld). The triumph of psychoanalytical approaches
to human sexual phenomena resulted in general abandonment of this approach in favor
of psychological explanations, but in 1959 G. E. Hutchinson published a paper speculating
on the possible genetic significance of "nonreproductive" sexuality (which he labeled
"paraphilia"), including homosexuality ("A Speculative Consideration of Certain
Possible Forms of Sexual Selection in Man," *American Naturalist* 93 [1959]: 81–91). In the
1970s a great deal of speculation has followed on the issue of the evolutionary significance
of homosexuality, much of it agreeing on the essential likelihood of genetic viability for
homosexual feelings through one selection mechanism or another. A theory based on
parent-offspring conflict as a mechanism for producing homosexuality was published in 1974
by R. L. Trivers ("Parent-Offspring Conflict," *American Zoologist* 14 [1974]: 249–64). In
1975 E. O. Wilson (*Sociobiology: The New Synthesis* [Cambridge, Mass., 1975]) suggested that
homosexuality might involve a form of genetic altruism, through which gay people benefit
those closely related to them and offset their own lowered reproductivity (see pp. 22, 229–31,
281, 311, 343–44, and esp. 555). This argument was expanded and simplified in "Human
Decency Is Animal," *New York Times Magazine* (October 12, 1975), pp. 38ff. and in *On Human
Nature* (Cambridge, Mass., 1978), pp. 142–47. The most detailed and comprehensive study of
this subject to date, examining nearly all modern theories for the etiology of homosexuality,
is that of James D. Weinrich, "Human Reproductive Strategy: The Importance of Income
Unpredictability and the Evolution of Non-Reproduction," pt. 2, "Homosexuality and
Non-Reproduction: Some Evolutionary Models" (Ph.D. diss., Harvard University, 1976).
An extraordinarily lucid and readable summary of previous biological approaches, with
provocative original speculations, appeared in John Kirsch and James Rodman, "The
Natural History of Homosexuality," *Yale Scientific Magazine* 51, no. 3 (1977): 7–13.

10. This is certainly not to suggest that there may not be groups of persons whose sexual
inclinations are essentially nonreproductive or that some of these persons might not qualify
as "gay." As noted below, the homosexual/heterosexual distinction is a crude one and may
obscure more significant sexual differences. Men who primarily desire to be passive, for
instance, would probably leave fewer offspring than men whose principal erotic pleasure is
derived from penetration of others. The former would necessarily be chiefly aroused by
other men, and persons of this sort may in fact comprise the nonreproductive "caste"
theorized by Wilson and Weinrich, along with women who chiefly desire to arouse women
(or men) with parts of their anatomy other than those involved in reproduction. The extent
to which a person's "sexuality" is composed of such desires for specific behavior, and the
biological input involved, are almost wholly unknown.

11. The phobic theory of the origin of homosexuality (i.e., the idea that gay people prefer
sexual contact with their own gender because they are frightened of such contact with the
opposite sex) has been largely discredited (at least for males) by modern research. For a particularly interesting example of such disproof, see Kurt Freund, Ron Langevin, et al., "The
Phobic Theory of Male Homosexuality," *Archives of Internal Medicine* 134 (1974): 495–99; see
also Freund's earlier article, using the same clinical method (penile plethysmography),
"The Female Child as Surrogate Object," *Archives of Sexual Behavior* 2 (1972): 119–33.

gay people (definitionally) prefer erotic contact with their own gender would imply a lower overall rate of reproductive success for them only if it could be shown that in human populations sexual desire is a major factor in such success. Intuition notwithstanding, this does not appear to be the case.

Only in societies like modern industrial nations which insist that erotic energy be focused exclusively on one's permanent legal spouse would most gay people be expected to marry and produce offspring less often than their nongay counterparts, and it appears that even in these cultures a significant proportion of gay people—possibly a majority—do marry and have children. In other societies (probably most literate premodern cultures), where procreation is separable from erotic commitment and rewarded by enhanced status or economic advantages (or is simply a common personal ambition), there would be no reason for gay people not to reproduce.[12] With the exception of the clergy, most of the gay people discussed in the present study were married and had children. The persistence of the belief in the nonreproductivity of gay people must be ascribed to a tendency to notice and remember what is unusual about individuals rather than what is expected. Far fewer people are aware that Oscar Wilde was a husband and father than that he was gay and had a male lover. Socrates' relationship with Alcibiades attracts more attention than his relationship with his wife and children. The love of Edward II of England for his four children is scarcely mentioned in texts which dwell at length on his passion for Piers Gaveston. To a certain extent such emphasis is accurate: the persons in question obviously devoted the bulk (if not the entirety) of their erotic interest to persons of their own gender. But the fact remains that they married and had children, and fascination with their statistically less common characteristics should not give rise to fanciful explanations of these traits—or of popular hostility to them—which overlook or contradict the more ordinary aspects of their lives.[13]

12. The sexual investment required for a male to produce offspring can hardly be imagined to be so great as to preclude other outlets; the much greater parental investment required of females has been offset reproductively in most such societies by the fact that women had less choice about their marital status and suffered a much greater loss of prestige and freedom if they did not marry and reproduce.

13. Viewed in this light, homosexual behavior cannot be presumed to entail significant social disadvantages. On the contrary, since pair-bonding of various sorts, erotic and non-erotic, is manifestly advantageous to most human societies (providing as it does mechanisms for social organization, mutual assistance, care of offspring in the event of a parent's death, etc.), homosexual attachments and relations are no more peculiar biologically than friendships. If one took the extreme view that only sexual or emotional activities directly conducive to reproduction would be favored in human evolution, one would be constrained to reject the majority of human erotic behavior as "unnatural." Homosexuality cannot be shown to diminish reproductive success any more than friendship, which is assumed to be ubiquitous in human societies, or masturbation, which some 90 percent of American males practice.

The second threat which might be adduced as explanation of intolerance of homosexuality relates to its "naturalness." May it not be that human society reacts with hostility to gay people because their preferences are inherently "unnatural"? So much space in this volume is devoted to assessing the precise meaning of "natural" and "unnatural" in various philosophical and historical contexts that it may be worth devoting several pages here to some preliminary observations on this subject. It should be noted, in the first place, that the meanings of "natural" and "unnatural" will vary according to the concept of "nature" to which they are related.

1. Some ideas of "nature" are primarily "realistic," i.e., related to the physical world and observations of it. For example, (i) one may speak of "nature" as the character or essence of something (the "nature" of love, "human nature"). "Unnatural," as opposed to this concept, means "uncharacteristic," as "to do otherwise would be 'unnatural' to him." (ii) In a broader sense, "nature" may be used for all of the "natures" (properties and principles) of all things, or the observable universe ("death is part of 'nature'"; the laws of "nature").[14] As the negation of this sense, "unnatural" refers to what is not part of the scientifically observable world, e.g., ghosts or miracles.[15] (iii) In a less consistent way,[16] "nature" is opposed to humans and their efforts, to designate what does or would occur without human intervention (man-made elements not found in "nature"). Here "unnatural" either means characteristic only of humans, as "hunting for sport rather than food is 'unnatural,'" or simply artificial, like "unnatural" (or "nonnatural") fibers, foodstuffs, etc.[17]

14. The "laws of nature" under this schematization refer only to this sense (ii). "Natural law"—an entirely different concept—has some relation to the "nature" of humans (i) and to "nature" minus humans (iii) but is chiefly a moral concept (2), as discussed below.

15. No philosophical systems make cogent distinctions among "nonnatural," "supernatural," and "unnatural." These words appear to be used chiefly in response to emotional nuances: "supernatural" referring to what is not "natural" but is therefore admired; "unnatural" to what is not "natural" and therefore feared or disdained; "nonnatural" to what is not "natural" but evokes no emotional response. It is striking, for instance, that synthetic fibers, which do not occur in "nature" (sense iii) are "nonnatural," while homosexuality, which is (erroneously) supposed not to occur in the same sense of "nature," is "unnatural."

16. Originally the exclusion of human ingenuity and artifice from the "natural" may have been the result of a belief in the "supernatural" or divine attributes of intelligence as a function of the soul, but in a modern frame of reference there seems very little justification for considering what is uniquely human any less "natural" than what is uniquely canine or uniquely bovine. This categorization raises enormous conceptual difficulties.

17. This popular concept of "nature," which had a profound impact on Western thought, is hereafter discussed as either "nature minus human intervention" or as "animal nature," since (nonhuman) animal behavior has been the most common "control" for assessing the operations of "nature" without the interference of humans. It need scarcely be pointed out that this procedure rests on the most perplexing notion of what constitutes an "animal" and leaves ambiguous such questions as whether plants cultivated by animals, or animals in

Although "realistic" categories of "natural" and "unnatural" are used with great imprecision,[18] two major assumptions may be mentioned as underlying the belief that homosexuality is "unnatural" in comparatively "realistic" conceptions of "nature." The most recent of these, the idea that behavior which is inherently nonreproductive is "unnatural" in an evolutionary sense, is probably applied to gay people inaccurately. Nonreproductivity can in any case hardly be imagined to have induced intolerance of gay people in ancient societies which idealized celibacy or in modern ones which consider masturbation perfectly "natural," since both of these practices have reproductive consequences identical with those of homosexual activity. This objection is clearly a justification rather than a cause of prejudice.

The second assumption is that homosexuality does not occur among animals other than humans. In the first place, this is demonstrably false: homosexual behavior, sometimes involving pair-bonding, has been observed among many animal species in the wild as well as in captivity.[19] This has been recognized since the time of Aristotle and, incredible as it seems, has been accepted by people who *still* objected to homosexual behavior as unknown to other animals. In the second place, it is predicated on another assumption—that uniquely human behavior is not "natural"—which is fundamentally unsupportable in almost any context, biological or philosophical. Many animals in fact engage in behavior which is unique to their species, but no one imagines that such behavior is "unnatural"; on the contrary, it is regarded as part of the "nature" of the species in question and is useful to taxonomists in distinguishing the species from other types of organisms. If man were the

---

captivity to other animals (both common among ants, e.g.), are "natural." Are humans the only species whose intervention in the lives of other animals disrupts "nature," or are all symbiotic relations which alter the life patterns of one of the species "unnatural"?

18. Two people may agree that the dyed hair of a third looks "unnatural," when one person means only that it does not suit the person in question (i) and the other means that artificial hair color is inherently unaesthetic or undesirable (iii). Laboratory conditions are "unnatural" situations for animals under observation both because they are not the "characteristic" environments of the creatures (i) and because they involve human intervention (iii). Extremes of evil or good are sometimes thought of as "unnatural" in senses (i): not characteristic of the individuals in question or of humans in general and (ii): so unusual as to require supernatural explanation. The "nature" which "abhors a vacuum" touches all bases, being predicated on the conflated notions that (i) a vacuum is uncharacteristic of or uncommon in the material world, (ii) an absolute vacuum—i.e., a space with absolutely nothing in it—cannot exist (except perhaps through miraculous intervention), and (iii) the most familiar approximations to a vacuum are created by human intervention.

19. Much material has come to light since Wainwright Churchill published his *Homosexual Behavior among Males: A Cross-Cultural and Cross-Species Investigation* (New York, 1967). References are collected in Weinrich, pp. 145–56 and passim; and in Kirsch and Rodman. For more recent material, see George Hunt and Molly Hunt, "Female-Female Pairing in Western Gulls (*Larus occidentalis*) in Southern California," *Science* 196 (1977): 81–83.

only species to demonstrate homosexual desires and behavior, this would hardly be grounds for categorizing them as "unnatural." Most of the behavior which human societies most admire is unique to humans: this is indeed the main reason it is respected. No one imagines that human society "naturally" resists literacy because it is unknown among other animals.

2. An entirely separate category of "natural/unnatural" opposition depends on what might be termed "ideal nature." [20] Although concepts of "ideal nature" resemble and are strongly influenced by meanings of "real nature," they differ significantly from the latter in explicitly presupposing that "nature" is "good." [21] Whether "ideal nature" is understood to include all physical things or simply the nonhuman, it is always believed to operate to the "good." Some "natural" things may be sad or distressing, may even give the appearance of evil, but all can be shown to result in something which is desirable or worthwhile in the long run or on a grand scale. Anything which is truly vicious or evil must be "unnatural," since "nature" could not produce evil on its own. Concepts of "ideal nature" are strongly conditioned by observation of the real world, but they are ultimately determined by cultural values. This is particularly notable in the case of "unnatural," which becomes in such a system a vehement circumlocution for "bad" or "unacceptable." Behavior which is ideologically so alien or personally so disgusting to those affected by "ideal nature" that it appears to have no redeeming qualities whatever will be labeled "unnatural," regardless of whether it occurs in ("real") nature never or often, or among humans or lower animals, because it will be assumed that a "good" nature could not under any circumstances have produced it.

Not surprisingly, adherents of "ideal" concepts of nature frequently characterize as "unnatural" sexual behavior to which they object on religious or personal grounds. What is surprising is the extent to which those who consciously reject "ideal" nature are nonetheless affected by such derogation. This confusion, like that of religious conviction and personal antipathy, is particularly well illustrated in the case of attitudes toward gay people.

The idea that homosexuality is "unnatural" (perhaps introduced by a chance remark of Plato) [22] became widespread in the ancient world due to

---

20. The Latin "Natura" is used by some scholars to designate idealized concepts of nature, especially in imperial Roman or medieval literature, but this usage begs the question of the precise meaning of "nature" in such writings, whose attitudes varied widely on the issue of "real" vs. "ideal" attributes of *Natura*.

21. Those employing "real" concepts of "nature" also probably imagine that "nature" is "good" but do not make it an article of faith. The distinction is not overly subtle: if confronted with overt cruelty in animals, a "realist" about "nature" would conclude that "nature is cruel." An "idealist" would insist that cruelty is "unnatural."

22. In his last work, the *Laws* (636B–C; 825E–842), Plato characterizes homosexual

the triumph of "ideal" concepts of nature over "realistic" ones.[23] Especially during the centuries immediately following the rise of Christianity, philosophical schools of thought using idealized "nature" as the touchstone of human ethics exercised a profound influence on Western thought and popularized the notion that all nonprocreative sexuality was "unnatural." Although this argument subsequently fell into disfavor, it was revived by Scholastics in the thirteenth century and came to be a decisive, even con-

---

relations as "παρὰ φύσιν," a phrase traditionally rendered "against nature." This is extremely perplexing, since sexual desire as discussed in all Plato's earlier works is "almost exclusively homosexual" (K. J. Dover, ed., Aristophanes' *Clouds* [Oxford, 1968], p. lxiv) and entirely "natural." The *Laws* are atypical of Plato's thought in a great many ways, and this may simply be part of a general change in his thinking, but his comment should in any case be interpreted as accurately as possible. Probably all he meant by "παρὰ φύσιν" was "unrelated to birth" or "nonprocreative," not "unnatural" in the sense of contravention of some overriding moral or physical law. "Physis" was probably originally derived from "φύω," "to grow" or "to be born," and Plato himself had distinguished in an earlier work (*Republic* 381A) between the "man-made" ("τέχνῃ") and the "natural" ("φύσει"), the latter in the sense of "what is born" as opposed to what is "constructed." This paronomastic relation of "physis" as "birth" to a broader concept of "nature" survived among later Platonists in the tautology "Τὸ δὲ μὴ εἰς παίδων γονὴν συνιέναι ἐνυβρίζειν ἐστι τῇ φύσει" ("to have sex for any purpose other than to have children is to injure birth," i.e., nature), and is obviously responsible in part for the intuitive appeal of the dictum. (It is impossible to convey in English the various subtleties involved; "ἐνυβρίζειν" is also paronomastic.) It would certainly not have been missed by Greek-speaking Christians of later centuries, since the same ambiguity underlies many NT uses of "physis" (e.g., Gal. 2:15). Many different meanings of "physis" are implied by the Athenian stranger's remarks on this and other issues in the *Laws*, and I do not suggest that "birth" is the only meaning present even in the specific passages cited. Plato delighted in paranomastic and multifaceted uses of "physis," as his exasperated interlocutor in the *Gorgias* (482D) points out. What I do mean to emphasize is that the most direct and immediate associations for Athenian contemporaries would have been different from those present in the minds of later readers. Plato describes as "completely unconvincing" the argument that since animals do not engage in homosexual relations, humans should not (836C), and very strongly suggests that human behavior is inherently superior to that of animals, even when he idealizes ornithological chastity (840D–E). At the outset of the discussion in question he states that, far from being a response to "nature," the prohibitions of homosexual activity he recommends are efforts to make "reason" (*logos*) into law (*nomos*) (835E). Moreover, the subject of the passage is the damage occasioned by sexual pleasure in general; homosexual acts are introduced as subsidiary to heterosexual promiscuity, which is derogated throughout, and the discussion is predicated on the ubiquity of homosexual attraction and desire. (Indeed one of the advantages the lawgiver hopes would accrue from his plan to limit sexual pleasure to procreation, where pleasure is unavoidable, would be men's learning to love their wives, 839B.) In his first mention of the subject (636C) Plato even introduces the idea of the "unnaturalness" of homosexual acts as something of a joke ("καὶ εἴτε παίζοντα εἴτε σπουδάζοντα").

23. The transition from Platonic-Aristotelian concepts of the "naturalness" of homosexuality to the ideas of its "unnaturalness" evinced by middle Platonists like Philo and the Alexandrian school has not been studied, although there is a wealth of material available. See, e.g., Robert Bloch, *De Pseudo-Luciani amoribus*, in *Dissertationes philologicae Argentoratenses*, 12.3 (Strasbourg, 1907), esp. pp. 13–19, 23–42; see also Gustav Gerhard, *Phoinix von Kolophon* (Leipzig, 1909), esp. pp. 51ff., 140–55.

trolling concept in all branches of learning, from the technical sciences to dogmatic theology. The scientific, philosophical, and even moral considerations which underlay this approach have since been almost wholly discredited and are consciously rejected by most educated persons, but the emotional impact of terms like "unnatural" and "against nature" persists. Although the idea that gay people are "violating nature" predates by as much as two millennia the rise of modern science and is based on concepts wholly alien to it, many people unthinkingly transfer the ancient prejudice to an imagined scientific frame of reference, without recognizing the extreme contradictions involved, and conclude that homosexual behavior violates the "nature" described by modern scientists rather than the "nature" idealized by ancient philosophers.

Even at the level of personal morality, the persistence of the concept of "unnatural" in this context, when it has been abandoned in nearly all others, is a significant index of the prejudice which actually inspires it. Historical ethical systems based on "nature" opposed shaving, growing flowers indoors, dyeing garments, regular bathing, birth control, and scores of other activities performed daily by the same people who use the term "unnatural" to justify their antipathy toward gay people. The objection that homosexuality is "unnatural" appears, in short, to be neither scientifically nor morally cogent and probably represents nothing more than a derogatory epithet of unusual emotional impact due to a confluence of historically sanctioned prejudices and ill-informed ideas about "nature." Like "illiberal," "unenlightened," "un-American," and various other imprecise negations, it may provide a rallying point for hostility but can hardly be imagined to constitute the origin of the emotions involved.

In addition to casting a clearer light on the relationship of intolerance and religious beliefs and imaginary dangers to society, the study of prejudice against gay people affords, as the final advantage to be discussed here, revealing insights into the similarities and differences of intolerance toward many different groups and characteristics. In a number of ways the separate histories of Europe's minorities are the same story, and many parallels have been drawn in this study with groups whose histories relate to or reflect the history of gay people. Most societies, for instance, which freely tolerate religious diversity also accept sexual variation, and the fate of Jews and gay people has been almost identical throughout European history, from early Christian hostility to extermination in concentration camps. The same laws which oppressed Jews oppressed gay people; the same groups bent on eliminating Jews tried to wipe out homosexuality; the same periods of European history which could not make room for Jewish distinctiveness reacted violently against sexual nonconformity; the same countries which insisted on religious uniformity imposed majority standards of sexual conduct; and even the same methods of propaganda were used against Jews and gay people—picturing them as animals bent on the destruction of the children of the majority.[24]

But there are significant differences, and these bear heavily on the present analysis. Judaism, for example, is consciously passed from parents to children, and it has been able to transmit, along with its ethical precepts, political wisdom gleaned from centuries of oppression and harassment: advice about how to placate, reason with, or avoid hostile majorities; how and when to maintain a low profile; when to make public gestures; how to conduct business with potential enemies. Moreover, it has been able to offer its adherents at least the solace of solidarity in the face of oppression. Although European ghettos kept the Jews in, they also kept the Gentiles out; and Jewish family life flourished as the main social outlet for a group cut off from the majority at many points in its history, imparting to individual Jews a sense not only of community in the present but of belonging to the long and hallowed traditions of those who went before.

Gay people are for the most part not born into gay families. They suffer oppression individually and alone, without benefit of advice or frequently even emotional support from relatives or friends. This makes their case more comparable in some ways to that of the blind or left-handed, who are also dispersed in the general population rather than segregated by heritage and who also are in many cultures the victims of intolerance. Gay people are even more revealing than most such dispersed minorities, however, because they are usually socialized through adulthood as ordinary members of society, since parents rarely realize that children are gay until they are fully grown. Their reactions and the reactions of those hostile to them thus illustrate intolerance in a relatively uncomplicated form, with no extraneous variable such as atypical socialization, inability to contribute to society, or even visible abnormality. In every way but one, most gay people are just like those around them, and antipathy toward them is for this reason an unusually illuminating instance of intolerance.

Only when social attitudes are favorable do gay people tend to form visible subcultures. In hostile societies they become invisible, a luxury afforded them by the essentially private nature of their variation from the norm, but one which greatly increases their isolation and drastically reduces their lobbying effectiveness. When good times return, there is no mechanism to encourage

24. For a bibliography on medieval anti-Semitism in general, see chaps. 7, 10 below. For imagery in particular, see Isaiah Schachar, The "Judensau": A Medieval Anti-Jewish Motif and Its History (London, 1974); and Bernhard Blumenkranz, Le juif médiéval au miroir de l'art chrétien (Paris, 1966).

steps to prevent a recurrence of oppression: no gay grandparents who remember the pogroms, no gay exile literature to remind the living of the fate of the dead, no liturgical commemorations of times of crisis and suffering. Relatively✶ few gay people today are aware of the great variety of positions in which time has placed their kind, and in previous societies almost none seem to have had such awareness.

✶Because of this, except in cases where they happen to wield considerable authority, gay people have been all but totally dependent on popular attitudes toward them for freedom, a sense of identity, and in many cases survival. The history of public reactions to homosexuality is thus in some measure a history of social tolerance generally.

It is only fair to point out that in addition to the advantages of using gay people to study intolerance, there are several salient disadvantages. The most fundamental of these is the fact that the longevity of prejudice against gay people and their sexuality has resulted in the deliberate falsification of historical records concerning them well into the present century, rendering accurate reconstruction of their history particularly difficult. Distortion on this issue was little known in the ancient world [25] but became more widespread with the dramatic shift in public morality following the fall of the

25. In contrast to the meager offerings on the history of gay people in general, homosexuality in ancient Greece has been thoroughly and at times very well examined by many researchers, making it especially useful as a point of comparison for later, less documented periods. Only a sampling of the material available can be considered here. The earliest (and still fundamental) work in this area is the article by M. H. E. Meier, "Paederastia," in *Allgemeine Encyclopädie der Wissenschaften und Kunsten*, ed. J. S. Ersch and J. J. Gruber (Leipzig, 1837), 3.9.149–88. This was translated into French and considerably expanded almost a century later by L.-R. de Pogey-Castries as *Histoire de l'amour grec dans l'antiquité* (Paris, 1930; hereafter cited as Meier/de Pogey-Castries) and is better consulted in this version. In the meantime John Addington Symonds had written, independently of Meier but with similar results, the first thorough account of the subject in English, "A Problem in Greek Ethics," which he printed privately in 1873 and then included as app. A to *Sexual Inversion* (1897; reprint ed., New York, 1975), coauthored with Havelock Ellis as vol. 1 of Ellis's *Studies in the Psychology of Sex*. In 1925–28 the renowned classicist Paul Brandt published, under the pseudonym Hans Licht, his *Sittengeschichte Griechenlands*, containing an excellent discussion of homosexuality (and most other aspects of Greek life) as portrayed in Attic and Hellenistic literature. It was translated into English by J. H. Freese as *Sexual Life in Ancient Greece* (London, 1932). David Robinson and Edward Fluck used nonliterary materials for their *Study of Greek Love-Names, Including a Discussion of Paederasty and a Prosopographia* (Baltimore, 1937), a work brimming with sound judgment, erudition, and good sense and sadly neglected by scholars. During the last two decades a good deal of less substantial writing has appeared, some of it regrettable (e.g., Robert Flacelière, *L'amour en Grèce* [Paris, 1960]; and G. Devereux, "Greek Pseudo-Homosexuality and the 'Greek Miracle,'" *Symbolae Osloenses* 42 [1967]: 69–92); some worthwhile, especially the writings of K. J. Dover: e.g., "Eros and Nomos," *Bulletin of Classical Studies* 11 (1964): 31–42; *Greek Popular Morality* (Oxford, 1975); and "Classical Greek Attitudes to Sexual Behavior," *Arethusa* 6 (1973): 69–73. Even Dover's scattered comments in editions (e.g., of *Clouds*) are helpful,

Roman Empire in the West. Ignorance was the major force behind the loss of information on this subject in medieval Europe—with Alcibiades occasionally appearing in medieval literature as a female companion to Socrates[26]—but the heavy hand of the censor was also evident. In a manuscript of Ovid's *Art of Love*, for example, a phrase which originally read, "A boy's love appealed to me less" was emended by a medieval moralist to read, "A boy's love appealed to me not at all," and a marginal note informed the reader, "Thus you may be sure that Ovid was not a sodomite."[27]

Crudities of this sort are of course easily detected, and more modern ages devised subtler means of disguising gay sentiments and sexuality. Changing the gender of pronouns has been popular at least since Michelangelo's grand-nephew employed this means to render his uncle's sonnets more acceptable to the public;[28] and scholars have continued the ruse even where no one's reputation was involved: when the Persian moral fables of Sa'di were translated into English in the early nineteenth century, Francis Gladwin conscientiously transformed each story about gay love into a heterosexual romance by altering the offending pronouns.[29] As late as the mid-twentieth century, the *ghazels* of Hafiz were still being falsified in this way.[30]

honest, and much to be preferred to the reticent and misleading approaches of other modern scholars, although his tendency to contradict himself from one work to another makes it necessary to compare his more recent works carefully with earlier writings (e.g., compare his comments on vase depiction of homosexual coitus in *Greek Popular Morality*, p. 214, with those of "Classical Greek Attitudes," p. 67). *Greek Homosexuality* (Cambridge, Mass., 1978), his major work on this subject, appeared as this study was going to press, and it was not possible to take account of its findings.

26. E.g., in Rémi of Auxelle's commentary on the *Consolatio philosophiae* of Boethius, where Alcibiades is identified as "a woman famous for her beauty, said to have been the mother of Hercules" (see Pierre Courcelle, *La consolation de philosophie* [Paris, 1967], p. 280; cf. p. 258, n. 4, where the same [?] quotation occurs in different form). Odo of Cluny, adopting this error, then glosses *Consolatio* 3, prose 8, as referring to women ("sicut lyncei in Boetia [*sic*] cernere interiora feruntur, mulieres videre nausearent," Courcelle, p. 258). Courcelle regards this feminine Alcibiades as the real identity of the mysterious Archipiada in most texts of Villon's "Ballade des dames du temps jadis." Iolaus, Hercules' beloved, also appears in medieval poetry as a female: see "Olim sudor Herculis," in George Whicher, *The Goliard Poets* (New York, 1949), pp. 36–41.

27. Originally "Hoc est quod pueri tangar amore minus" (*Ars amatoria* 2.684), altered to read, "Hoc est quod pueri tangar amore nihil" and accompanied in the margin by "Ex hoc nota quod Ovidius non fuerit Sodomita." See Domenico Comparetti, *Vergilio nel medio evo* (Leghorn, 1872), 1: 115, n. 1.

28. Almost all modern editions restore the original genders. Symonds was one of the first to translate them into English.

29. Francis Gladwin, trans., *The Gulistan* (London, 1822). An accurate translation by Edward Rehatsek is now available (*The Gulistan or Rose Garden* [London, 1964]). Note esp. nos. 14, 17, 18, 20. The earlier translation by Richard Burton, *Tales from the Gulistán, or Rose Garden of Sheikh Sa'di of Shiráz* (London, 1928), is reasonably frank.

30. E.g., in *Fifty Poems of Hafiz*, ed. A. J. Arberry (Cambridge, Mass., 1947). Arberry does print the Persian texts, but this is of little help to most English readers and only heightens

A more honest though hardly more edifying approach is deletion. This may range from the omission of a single word which indicates gender (as is common where the original would reveal that the love object in the *Rubaiyat* is in fact male)[31] to an entire work, like the *Amores* (*Affairs of the Heart*) of Pseudo-Lucian, which Thomas Francklin excised from his translation because it contained a dispute about which sex was preferable as erotic focus for males: "But as this is a point which, at least in this nation, has been long since determined in favour of the ladies, it stands in need of no farther discussion: the Dialogue is therefore, for this, as well as some other still more material reasons, which will occur to those who are acquainted with the original, entirely omitted."[32] (The more material reasons may now be consulted in a reasonably frank translation by M. D. MacLeod in vol. 8 of the LC edition of the works of Lucian.)

Even hostile accounts of gay sexuality are often expurgated in English translations,[33] and the suppression of details related to homosexuality affects historical accounts which can hardly be considered lurid or titillating, as when the *Oxford Classical Dictionary* observes that the Attic lovers Harmodius and Aristogiton were "provoked by private differences" to kill the tyrant Hippias.[34]

Probably the most entertaining efforts to conceal homosexuality from the public have been undertaken by the editors of the Loeb Classics, the standard collection of Greek and Latin classical texts with English translation. Until

---

the absurdity for those familiar with Persian. (The contrast between the text and translation of no. 3 is esp. remarkable.) Earlier editions in English (e.g., *Ghazels from the Divan of Hafiz*, trans. J. H. McCarthy [New York, 1893]) were even worse. Twentieth-century French scholars have provided the most reliable renderings (e.g., Arthur Guy, *Les poèmes érotiques ou ghazels de Chems Ed Dîn Mohammed Hâfiz* [Paris, 1927], with helpful analysis of the ambiguous relationship between the "beloved" and the "Divine" in the poems [esp. pp. xxii–xxiv]; cf. Vincent Monteuil, "Neuf qazal de Hâfiz," *Revue des études islamiques* [1954], pp. 21–57, with facing transliteration of the Persian). There is of course no substitute for the original.

31. E.g., 49.29 and 102.156, ambiguously rendered in many English versions. The French translation by Guy, *Les robaï* (Paris, 1935), includes helpful comments on this issue (pp. 26–27). As recently as 1969 the noted orientalist Charles Pellat explained that "decency forbids us to translate" an influential work of Jāhiz because of its frankness about homosexuality (*The Life and Works of Jāhiz*, trans. D. M. Hawke [London, 1969], p. 270). Fortunately "decency" did not prevent Pellat from editing the Arabic original (a debate on the relative merits of male and female slaves as sex objects). Even in the Arabic, however, he felt constrained to apologize for publishing a work on this subject: see al-Jāhiz, *Kitāb mufākharāt al-jawārī wa'l-ghilmān*, ed. Charles Pellat (Beirut, 1957), pp. 5–7.

32. *The Works of Lucian* (London, 1781), 1:xxxvii–xxxviii. This work is no longer attributed to Lucian.

33. E.g., in H. von E. Scott and C. C. Swinton Bland's translation of the dialogues of Caesar of Heisterbach, *The Dialogues on Miracles* (London, 1929), various details of the punishment inflicted on a dead priest for homosexual acts are suppressed (pp. 157–59); cf. the original cited in chap. 7, n. 46 below.

34. OCD, s.v. "Aristogiton"; for a franker discussion, see Plato's comments, chap. 2 below.

very recently many sections of Greek works in this series dealing with overt homosexuality were translated not into English but Latin, and some explicit passages in Latin found their way into Italian.[35] In addition to the ambiguous comment this procedure makes on the morals of Italian readers, it has the curious effect of highlighting every salacious passage in the major classics, since the interested reader (with appropriate linguistic skills) has only to skim the English translation looking for Latin or Italian. The practice applied equally to profane and sacred writers: even Christian condemnations of homosexual acts were deemed too provocative for English readers.[36]

As in most matters, half-truths are more misleading than whole lies, and the historian's greatest difficulties are presented by slight twists of meaning in translations which appear to be complete and frank. A wealth of information is concealed by the English translation of a line in Cornelius Nepos which reads, "In Crete it is thought praiseworthy for young men to have the greatest number of love affairs."[37] In a climate of opinion which did not automatically assume that references to love affairs implied heterosexuality, this translation would only be too loose; for modern English readers, it is tantamount to falsehood. The original sense of the comment is "In Crete it is considered praiseworthy for a young man to have as many [male] lovers as possible."[38]

Sometimes their anxiety to reinterpret or disguise accounts of homosexuality has induced translators to inject wholly new concepts into texts, as

35. The most recent LC edition of Martial (1968) provides English translations of passages printed in Italian in previous editions. In personal correspondence the editor, G. P. Goold, informed me that the new English portions were "editorial." There is no indication in the text itself of the authorship of the newly translated passages. For an example of Greek, see below, or editions of Diogenes Laertius; for Latin examples see LC Martial, Juvenal, Suetonius, Catullus, et al.

36. As in the LC Epistle of Barnabas (in *The Apostolic Fathers*) at 10:6–8 (1:377; cf. original on p. 376). The Latin is often inaccurate: see p. 141, below. In *Fathers of the Second Century*, the Ante-Nicene Fathers, vol. 2, ed. C. Coxe (New York, 1885) portions of Clement of Alexandria's *Paedagogus* are given in Latin rather than English (e.g., pp. 259, 260–62). A complete translation is available in the Fathers of the Church series.

37. Cornelius Nepos, *On the Great Generals*, trans. J. Rolfe (New York, 1929), praef. 4, p. 369.

38. "Laudi in Creta ducitur adulescentulis quam plurimos habuisse amatores," ibid., p. 368. An entirely misleading impression is also conveyed by the LC translation of a line from the Elder Seneca, which implies that a freedman was tried on charges of homosexuality: "while defending a freedman who was charged with being his patron's lover" (*Controversiae* 4.10, trans. M. Winterbottom [London, 1974], p. 431). The word rendered "lover" here in fact means "concubine" and is used in Latin literature to designate a slave officially employed for sexual release. Criticism of a freed person's being employed in this capacity is no more an objection to homosexuality than criticism of female prostitution is an objection to heterosexuality. Moreover, in the Latin it is not all clear that homosexuality has anything to do with the charges brought against the freedman: the most likely interpretation would be that it was simply brought up as a "reproach" during the course of a trial on other charges.

when the translators of a Hittite law apparently regulating homosexual marriage insert words which completely alter its meaning [39] or when Graves "translates" a nonexistent clause in Suetonius to suggest that a law prohibits homosexual acts. In many cases such distortions directly contradict other portions of the same text: in the Loeb translation of Ovid's *Metamorphoses* the Latin "inpia virgo" ("shameless girl") becomes, by virtue of its occurrence in a homosexual context, "unnatural girl," even though her desires have been specifically characterized as "natural" by Ovid only a few lines above. [40]

It is little wonder that accurate analysis of gay people in a historical context is so rare when such formidable barriers oppose access to the sources for anyone not proficient in ancient and medieval languages. Even those who have taken the trouble to learn the requisite tongues find that most lexical aids decline to comment on the meaning of terms related to acts of which the lexicographers disapprove; [41] only painstaking collation and very extensive

39. For the law and interpolation, see E. Neufeld, *The Hittite Laws* (London, 1951), pp. 10–11; also J. B. Pritchard, *Ancient Near Eastern Texts Relating to the Old Testament* (Princeton, N.J., 1950), p. 194. For dissenting views, see J. Pedersen, *Israel* (Oxford: 1926), 1:66; D. R. Mace, *Hebrew Marriage* (London, 1953), p. 224; and Bailey, pp. 35–36. The Hittites also had a law specifically forbidding father-son incest (Table 2, 189), a restriction one would hardly expect in a society where homosexuality was not well known and (at least in some contexts) legal.

40. Ovid *Metamorphoses* 10.345, trans. Frank Miller (1916; reprint ed., Cambridge, Mass., 1976), 2:89, contradicted by lines 324ff., esp. 330–31. "Unnatural" is a favorite anachronism or insertion for translators convinced that all ages have regarded homosexual behavior through the lens of modern prejudices. Hundreds of instances could be cited. H. Rackham renders the Greek "ἄτοπος" (perhaps "unseemly") as "unnatural" in the LC *Nicomachean Ethics* (New York, 1926), 7.5.3, even though Aristotle specifically considered such behavior "natural" and criticized it himself as being "animal" (e.g., θηριώδεις). The NEB also inserts this concept into Jer. 5:25 ("Your wrongdoing has upset nature's order"), although the Hebrew "עֲוֹנֹתֵיכֶם הִטּוּ־אֵלֶּה" makes no mention of "nature," and the concept was unknown to the author of Jeremiah. (Even the LXX, whose authors probably were familiar with such a concept, rendered the passage without reference to "nature"; the KJV has "Your iniquities have turned away these things".) In contrast, the NEB does not include the concept "nature" in its translation of Jude 10, even though it is present in the Greek.

41. E.g., in the standard lexicon of classical Greek (LSJ), under the very common Greek word "πυγίζειν" one finds, rather than an English equivalent, the Latin "paedico." And if one then consults the standard Latin lexicon, *A Latin Dictionary*, ed. C. T. Lewis and Charles Short (Oxford, 1879), to find out what "paedico" means, one finds "to practice unnatural vice." In fact both these words very specifically mean "to penetrate the anus," a concept which admittedly cannot be rendered agreeable to many sensibilities but which might be approximated much more closely than "to practice unnatural vice." The precise meaning of "πυγίζειν" and "paedico" is often crucial in classical texts. For an even more misleading example, see ibid., s.v. "irrumo," an interesting Latin word with no equivalent in any European language. Lewis and Short say it means "to treat in a foul or shameful manner, to abuse, deceive," and cite Catullus as the source. In this passage in Catullus, as elsewhere, the word means "to offer the penis for sucking," and it is a pity that the unique significance of this word should be concealed from the public. Even the identity of parts of the body is withheld from the English-speaking public: Lewis and Short give for "mentula"

reading in the sources enables the investigator to uncover with any degree of accuracy the actions and attitudes of previous cultures which have not suited the tastes of modern scholarship. Until a new generation of translators has removed the fig leaves, research on a large scale will be difficult.

A second difficulty in investigating this type of intolerance is presented by the fact that it concerns sexual and emotional matters which are essentially personal[42] and would tend not to occur in official documents except in societies characterized by hostility to such feelings, where legal measures have been taken to suppress them. Even this sort of record, however, is treacherous: it would certainly be a mistake to draw conclusions about the position of gay people in most American cities from the legal strictures theoretically affecting them, and previous studies of this subject have doubtless erred in laying too much stress on the existence of restrictive statutes. Simply noting that something is illegal may be grossly misleading if one does not also comment on the extent to which such laws are honored, supported, or generally approved.

The monuments of love are principally literary: what bills of sale and tax records are to economic history, poems and letters are to the history of personal relations and attitudes toward them. As a consequence, this study has relied rather more than most historical texts on literary sources. Such works often concentrate on the unusual and may present the bizarre rather than the ordinary, but this is also true of more conventional historical sources, which usually record events of note rather than common occurrences. Especially during the Middle Ages—when the outcome of military ventures might be communicated through poetry of a rather fanciful nature, and sober historians informed their readers of miraculous events which even contemporaries found droll—there was no clear division between historical and literary sources, so this is less of a problem than it might seem.

Literary sources do, however, present special problems. Most of these are discussed below individually as they occur, but one general issue deserves advance notice: the questioning of such sources as historical records on the basis of what might be termed the "historical theory of literary emanation." According to this approach, if something can be shown to have had some

---

(which means "cock" or "prick") "membrum virile." For Greek an excellent scholarly tool has recently been published by Jeffrey Henderson, *The Maculate Muse: Obscene Language in Attic Comedy* (New Haven, 1975), although unfortunately the sections dealing with homosexuality leave much to be desired in accuracy and objectivity. There is no equivalent for Latin.

42. But not necessarily *private*: Athenians and Romans were quite open about homosexual feelings, and gay relationships were "public" in the sense of being frankly acknowledged and generally accepted. They did not, however, require the supervision or regulation of the state in the same way that heterosexual relationships did, and records of their existence are therefore fewer and more personal. Aeschines vs. Timarchus, Demosthenes' *Erotikos*, and a few other public orations on the subject constitute rare exceptions to this.

literary antecedent in a previous culture, its appearance in a later one is no longer significant in any context other than that of artistic derivation. If Roman writers imitate Greek homosexual poetry, for instance, one is assured that such verses are simply imitations and that they do not represent real feelings. One supposes that if Greeks could be shown to have imitated earlier forms, they would not have experienced homosexual feelings either, and the real enterprise of historical scholarship must be to discover the original people who alone experienced real emotions, bequeathing to the rest of the human race the motifs which are mechanically imitated in all subsequent literature.

Obviously, imitation of homosexual themes is itself a significant fact. In most modern Western cultures prior to the mid-twentieth century one could not publish homosexual poetry of any sort without danger of prosecution, although the homosexual interests of the Greeks were recognized, and their poetry was studied and admired. That Roman authors published a great deal of homosexual poetry—with or without ostensible Hellenic influence—is evidence of a significant difference between Roman society and later ones.

There are a limited number of ways to express erotic attraction and an even more limited number of genders as objects of that attraction. Seizing on the fact that an author is attracted to both genders as proof of derivation from Ovid, or on pederastic sentiments as proof of imitation of Greek sources, is laughable. Anyone erotically stimulated by boys may sincerely write pederastic verse, despite the fact that Greeks did it first.

It is notable in this context that (*a*) it is never suggested that imitations of heterosexual lyric verse are proof that writers in question did not experience heterosexual attraction, a theory equally likely under the "historical emanation" approach; and (*b*) the fact that later Christian writers regularly imitated the literary styles of the fathers of the church is hardly considered evidence of insincerity on their part: on the contrary, consciously maintaining a literary tradition in this context is taken as proof of the persistence of the sentiments which gave rise to the tradition in the first place.

A final disadvantage, the difficulty of avoiding anachronistic stereotypes, is a much more serious scholarly problem for both the author and the readers of a study of this type. It is unlikely that at any time in Western history have gay people been the victims of more widespread and vehement intolerance than during the first half of the twentieth century, and drawing inferences about homosexuality from observations of gay people in modern Western nations cannot be expected to yield generalizations more accurate or objective than inferences made about Jews in Nazi Germany or blacks in the antebellum South. Until very recently only the tiniest percentage of gay people have been willing to identify themselves publicly, and such persons, given the reactions they could reasonably expect, must have been atypical.

As a consequence, one must be extremely cautious about projecting onto historical data ideas about gay people inferred from modern samples which may be entirely atypical. The idea that gay men are less masculine, for instance, and gay women less feminine is almost certainly the result of antipathy to homosexuality rather than empirical observation. The universal expectation in cultures intolerant of gay people that males will be erotically affected only by what the culture regards as feminine—and females only by culturally defined masculinity—leads inevitably to the anticipation that males who wish to attract other males will be "feminine" and females erotically interested in females will be "masculine." Atypical conformity to gender expectations appears in fact to be randomly distributed in most populations, completely independent of sexual preference; but if even a very small percentage of gay women are more masculine or a very few gay men more feminine than their nongay counterparts, they will corroborate the stereotype in the mind of a public predisposed to believe it and usually possessed of no large sampling as a control. (Effeminate nongay men or masculine heterosexual women are ignored, if possible, or considered part of the normal range of human adaptation.)

It must not be supposed, however, that such stereotypes affected more tolerant societies, or that any connection between homosexuality and "inappropriate" gender behavior[43] was assumed. On the contrary, among ancient peoples who acknowledged the likelihood and propriety of erotic interest between persons of the same gender it was often assumed that men who loved other men would be more masculine than their heterosexual counterparts, by the logical (if unconvincing) argument that men who loved men would emulate them and try to be like them, while men who loved women would become like women, i.e., "effeminate." (The obverse would presumably be true of women, but in every age anxiety about female gender roles seems to have been less acute.) Aristophanes' speech in the *Symposium* of Plato is probably the most blatant example of this counterprejudice. "Those who love men and rejoice to lie with and be embraced by men are also the finest boys and young men, being naturally the most manly. The people who accuse them of shamelessness lie; they do this not from shamelessness but from courage, manliness, and virility, embracing what is like them. A clear proof of this is the fact that as adults they alone acquit themselves as men in public careers" (192A; cf. Phaedrus's speech. This passage may be a caricature, but it is no less revealing for that).

43. This is particularly true of "effeminacy" in males. The use of femininity as a measure of undesirability or weakness more properly belongs in a study of misogyny, and the other senses of "effeminate," e.g., "cowardly," "weak," "morally inferior," no more relevant to gay than to nongay males, are excluded from consideration here.

An equation of homosexuality with effeminacy in men would hardly have occurred to people whose history, art, popular literature, and religious myths were all filled with the homosexual exploits of such archetypally masculine figures as Zeus, Hercules, Achilles, et al.[44] Plato argued that pairs of homosexual lovers would make the best soldiers (*Symposium* 178E–179; cf. Aristotle *Politics* 2.6.6), and the Thebans actually formed an army of such pairs in what turned out to an extraordinarily successful experiment.[45] In Greek debates about the relative merits of homosexuality and heterosexuality for men, advocates of the latter are sometimes stigmatized as "effeminate," but never those who favor the former (for such debates, see chap. 5 below).

Romans inherited Greek attitudes on this subject and were in any case familiar with the homosexual interests of such thoroughly masculine public figures as Sulla and Hadrian. Long after public idealization of gay males disappeared in the West, they continued to distinguish themselves in traditionally masculine enterprises. Richard Lion Heart, Edward II, the Duc d'Orléans, the Prince de la Roche sur Yon, the Grande Condé, the Maréchal de Vendôme[46]—all these men noted for martial skill or valor were also noted for being gay, and it would have been difficult to foment in the minds of their contemporaries any necessary association of effeminacy and homosexuality in men.

Likewise, one must avoid transposing across temporal boundaries ideas about gay relationships which are highly culture-related, such as the expectation that they must parallel or imitate heterosexual relationships (e.g., with one partner adopting a "male" and one a "female" role). Where gay relations are approved and open, imitations of this sort are generally neither expected nor evident. Especially where someone may be acceptably involved in gay and heterosexual relationships simultaneously, one would expect the two to be independent; overlap or imitation might occur, but there is no reason to assume a priori that it would be in one direction only. Many Greek writers use homosexual love as an ideal to which heterosexual lovers might aspire. Even in other oppressive cultures one must be cautious: gay couples may imitate nongay ones, but the nature of heterosexual marriage varies

---

44. With Hercules alone more than fourteen male lovers are associated: see, e.g., the list in Meier/de Pogey-Castries, p. 37. Xenophon (*Symposium* 8.31) claimed that the relationship between Achilles and Patroclus was not erotic, but most Greeks disagreed with him: Plato records Phaedrus on the same occasion as having voiced the opposite opinion. The idea that the two were lovers was at least as old as Aeschylus (*Myrmidons* fr. 135–36) and persisted through the fourteenth century A.D. (Aeschines *Against Timarchus* 142; Plutarch *Erotikos* 751C; Philostratus *Epistles* 5, 8; [Lucian] *Amores* 54; Athenaeus 13.601; cf. Martial 11.44).

45. Plutarch *Pelopidas* 18–20; Athenaeus 13.561E; Polyaenus 2.5.1.

46. Medieval figures are discussed below. For early modern generals (e.g., the last four cited here), see Marc Daniel, *Hommes du grand siècle* (Paris, n.d.).

widely by the time and place, and gay unions must be studied in relation to the customs of their day, not in terms of modern expectations.

To insist, for instance, that in order to constitute "marriages" homosexual unions of the past must emulate modern heterosexual marriage is to defy history. No marriages in ancient societies closely match their modern equivalents. Most were vastly more informal; some were more rigid. Most cultures regard marriage as a private arrangement negotiated between two families; supervision of its niceties depends on the heads of the families. No precise criteria could be specified as constituting a "legal" marriage during most of the period of this study: two people who lived together permanently and whose union was recognized by the community were "married." Even early Christian theology recognized the difficulties of deciding who was and was not married; Augustine was willing to designate as a "wife" any woman who intended to be permanently faithful to the man she lived with (*De bono conjugali* 5.5 [PL, 40:376–77]).

Where homosexual relationships are described by contemporaries as "marriages"[47] or where laws imply that such unions enjoyed social sanction, there can be no reason to reject this information, and there is no reason to regard such relationships as inherently unlikely.[48]

Related to this is the question of whether gay relationships may be inherently different from heterosexual ones. Most modern Westerners, even many gay people, tend to think of gay love affairs as being more transitory and physical in nature than their (often idealized) heterosexual equivalents. Whether or not this is true, it must be viewed in conjunction with the variable of social hostility. It is obviously very much to a gay person's advantage in hostile environments not to be part of a permanent relationship: the longer lasting and more intimate a relationship between two persons of the same gender, the more likely it is to incur suspicion where homosexuality is

---

47. This seems, for instance, to be what Xenophon is suggesting in *Constitution of Sparta* 2:12: "Οἱ μὲν τοίνυν ἄλλοι Ἕλληνες ἢ ὥσπερ Βοιωτοὶ ἀνὴρ καὶ παῖς συζυγέντες ὁμιλοῦσιν" ("Among the other Greeks, like the Boeotians, man and boy live joined together"). Of course "marriage" may be used in an ironic or sarcastic sense, but such usage is usually easy to identify (e.g., in Lucian *Dialogues of the Gods* 8.4., where Hera jibes at Zeus that perhaps he will "marry" Ganymede, "Εἴθε καὶ γαμήσειας αὐτὸν ἐμοῦ γε οὕνεκα").

48. The Talmud credits the Gentiles with three observances of the commandments given the sons of Noah: they do not draw up a *kethubah* (marriage deed?) for males; they do not weigh the flesh of the dead in the market; and they respect the Torah (Hullin 92b). The first of the three is as puzzling as the last; homosexual marriages were well known in the Roman world, and most Jews were familiar with such aspects of Roman life. Two explanations seem likely: (1) the Talmud assumes that the absence of legal documents for such relationships demonstrates inferior status (ignoring the generally looser structure of all Gentile marriages); or (2) *kethubah* refers not to the legalization of the marriage but to a particular aspect of it, probably the dowry agreement (see, e.g., Maimonides, *The Guide of the Perplexed*, trans. M. Friedlander [New York, n.d.], 3:49).

oppressed. Canny gay people may circumvent this, but the most effective defense against oppression will lie in fleeting and clandestine relationships which do not attract attention or provoke suspicion.

Where there is public admiration for gay people and their love, on the other hand, one would not expect any such syndrome to evolve for protection, and indeed one does not find anything of the sort in more tolerant societies. Many Greeks represented gay love as the only form of eroticism which could be lasting, pure, and truly spiritual. The origin of the concept of "Platonic love" (which postdates Plato by several centuries) was not Plato's belief that sex should be absent from gay affairs but his conviction that only love between persons of the same gender could transcend sex. The Attic lawgiver Solon considered homosexual eroticism too lofty for slaves and prohibited it to them. In the idealistic world of the Hellenistic romances, gay people figured prominently as star-crossed lovers whose passions were no less enduring or spiritual than those of their nongay friends. In Rome Hadrian's undying devotion to his dead lover Antinous was one of the most familiar artistic expressions of erotic fidelity. In Islamic Sufi literature homosexual eroticism was a major metaphorical expression of the spiritual relationship between God and man,[49] and much Persian poetry and fiction providing examples of moral love used gay relationships. Among the ancient Chinese the most popular literary expression for gay love was "the love of the cut sleeve," referring to the selfless devotion of the last emperor of the Han dynasty, Ai-Ti, who cut off his sleeve when called to an audience rather than wake his lover, Tung Hsien, who had fallen asleep across it.[50] Even among primitive peoples some connection is often assumed between spirituality or mysticism and homosexuality.[51] Only in comparatively recent times have homosexual feelings come to be associated with moral looseness.

If the difficulties of historical research about intolerance of gay people could be resolved by simply avoiding anachronistic projections of modern

---

49. See, *inter alia*, A. J. Arberry, *Sufism* (London, 1956); R. A. Nicholson, *The Mystics of Islam* (London, 1914); and R. W. J. Austin, *Sufis of Andalusia* (London, 1971). By the fourteenth century such "sufic" literature appears to be principally erotic, although mysticism is still involved. As Guy points out in the case of Hâfiz (*Les poèmes érotiques*, p. xxv), "it is difficult to apply to God 'curly locks, ruby lips, a figure like a young cypress, etc.'"

50. See G. H. Van Gulik, *Sexual Life in Ancient China* (Leiden, 1961), p. 63.

51. For the subject in general, see the early but still useful study by Edward Carpenter *Intermediate Types among Primitive Folk* (London, 1914), pt. 1; or his "On the Connexion between Homosexuality and Divination, and the Importance of the Intermediate Sexes Generally in Early Civilizations," *Revue d'ethnographie et de sociologie* 11–12 (1910): 310–16. See also the material below on the *berdache*, often supposed to have magical qualities. Associations of this sort may have been at least partly responsible for OT strictures against homosexuality, and the idea that gay people are disproportionately represented in the service of religion has often had negative impact on the intolerant.

myths and stereotypes, the task would be far simpler than it is. Unfortunately, an equally distorting and even more seductive danger for the historian is posed by the tendency to exaggerate the differences between homosexuality in previous societies and modern ones.

One example of this tendency is the common idea that gay relationships in the ancient world differed from their modern counterparts in that they always involved persons of different ages: an older man (the lover) and a young boy (the beloved).[52] Some scholars even propose that such age-differentiated relationships cannot be considered examples of "real homosexuality." One must immediately wonder whether heterosexual relations between men and girls are any less heterosexual for the difference in age. The whole point of the homosexual/heterosexual distinction, it would seem, is to subsume all varieties of erotic interest into categories of gender relation; if the term "homosexual" has any significance at all, it clearly includes relations between men and boys no less than between men and men or boys and boys.

On the other hand, it does not seem likely that, with a few exceptions, the apparent prevalence of erotic relationships between adults and boys in the past corresponded to reality.[53] It was, rather, an idealized cultural convention. It is useful to note here that in modern European and American

52. The distinction is consistently drawn only in Greek, as "ἐραστής" and "ἐρώμενος"; it may only correspond to conceptual peculiarities of the Athenians. Whether these terms resulted from some sort of definite role expectation is difficult to assess at this distance. It is apparent that the roles were not predetermined, since there was often uncertainty about which person played which part, even when their respective ages were known (see, e.g., Plato's *Symposium* 180B). The same person, moreover, might be both lover and beloved of different persons at the same time (Xenophon *Symposium* 4.23). It is clear that in many cases it was superior beauty which earned one the position of beloved, not inferior age: while Socrates, known for his homeliness, always appears as the lover of others, Alcibiades, equally famous for his beauty, was a beloved all his life. In any event, one did not have to be young in any accepted sense: Euripides was the lover of Agathon when Euripides was seventy-two and Agathon forty; Parmenides and Zenon were in love when the former was sixty-five and the latter forty; Alcibiades was already full bearded when Socrates fell in love with him. According to Plutarch ("Bruta animalia ratione uti, sive Gryllus," *Moralia* 990E), Achilles was a beloved when he was a father. In the discussion in Plato's *Symposium* about whether Aeschylus properly assigned the roles of lover and beloved to Achilles and Patroclus, age is only one of several characteristics mentioned as criteria. Romans used only Greek words to distinguish between "lover" and "beloved," and it seems quite possible that during the time covered by this study the distinction was purely a semantic nicety, with few real social implications. The fact that they adopted Greek terms in this instance does not, however, indicate that Romans imported stylized homosexual relationships or that homosexuality or the distinction implied by the terms was new to them. English appears to have no real equivalent for the French term "fiancé," but this is certainly no indication that the idea of heterosexual engagement was unknown in the British Isles prior to its adoption. Why foreign words for social relations ("protégé," "gigolo," "madame," etc.) catch on and supplant indigenous terms is a complex issue; the notion that the phenomena they describe were unknown before importation of the word belongs among the least likely explanations.

53. See Dover, "Eros and Nomos" (as above, n. 25), p. 31.

culture teenaged girls are ubiquitously standards of feminine beauty: advertisements, popular literature, pornography, movies and television, even vulgar humor (e.g., "traveling salesman" jokes) assume the sixteen–twenty-year-old female as an archetype of feminine beauty. It would certainly be wrong, however, to infer from this that most men either wish to or do have sexual relations with women in this age group. It is not even clear that this is the age group most attractive to all men.

English terminology is also misleading on this point. "Girl," while technically denoting a preadult female, is in fact used to denote any woman seen as a sex object, even if she is twenty or more years beyond "girlhood." An adult male will frequently speak of his adult female lover as his "girlfriend," and she will likewise characterize him as her "boyfriend," even if he is much older than she. This peculiar use of words suggesting youth appears to be related to two general tendencies of Western society. The first is an equation of youth and physical beauty. Although the age with which maximum beauty is associated varies culturally, it is nearly always a young one.

Related to this is a tendency to use diminutives in speaking to or of persons to whom one is drawn by affection or desire. Lovers will address each other as "baby," "sweetie," "cutie," or various other terms associated with infants as a sign of love and affection; the same words applied to strangers would be absurd or insulting. Even among friends suggestions of youth imply intimacy: until the word acquired unfavorable connotations, many adult women in the United States would refer to their female friends as "the girls," even if they were fifty years old. A "night out with the boys" says nothing of the age of the parties but does imply friendship among those involved.

The same was manifestly the case with erotic relations in the past. Beautiful men were "boys" to the Greeks just as beautiful women are "girls" to modern Europeans and Americans.[54] The actual age of the male involved may have mattered to some Greeks; to others it obviously did not.[55] Plato carefully

54. Although beauty was not considered exclusively in terms of youth: "For just as a boy may be beautiful, so may a young man, an adult, or an old man. This is shown by the fact that as garland bearers for Athena old men are often chosen, demonstrating that there is beauty in every stage of life" (Xenophon *Symposium* 4.17). The fact that women in Attic literature were less often depicted in terms of youth probably reflects the more general use of males as objects of erotic attention, especially in literature. The obverse disparity is observable in the Modern West, where women are far more frequently sex objects, and the use of terms of affection implying youth is much commoner in relation to them: describing a male as a "boy" would rarely have the same erotic significance as describing a woman as a "girl."

55. In some cases differences in taste may have been only incidentally related to age. Preference for or against beards or other body hair, for instance, would be related to age in the case of some males and not for others, since some men are never very hairy. Athenaeus suggests that the lack of body hair among the Etruscans accounted for their predilection for older youths and the extreme frequency of homosexuality among them (12.517–18). The question of body hair and the beard has been a common theme in male homosexual

distinguishes in his dialogues between men who are attracted to boys and those who are attracted to other men,[56] but few ancient writers were so careful. Most used terms which suggested erotic attraction for young men and for older males interchangeably,[57] clearly implying that age was not a consideration. The term "pederasty" frequently has no more relation to the age of the objects of desire than "girl chasing."[58]

The convention of using terms implying youthfulness to express affection or intimacy survived throughout the Middle Ages. The persistence of Ganymede as a symbol of the gay male as well as Christian symbolic filial relations (e.g., between monks and their abbot or "father") enriched the tradition even further. Alcuin addresses a cleric he loves as "beautiful boy"; Walafrid Strabo writes to a fellow monk as "little boy" or "little lad"; Saint Aelred refers to Simon, his lover and contemporary, as a "boy" and calls him "son"; Marbod, Bishop of Rennes, even refers to himself as a "boy" in a letter to his lover.

It is, naturally, the author's hope that the difficulties of avoiding anachronistic projections of this sort—and all the disadvantages discussed here in regard to using gay people as a case study of intolerance—will be outweighed

---

literature in almost every culture. Gay men, of course, are not necessarily exclusive in their tastes on the matter: Philostratus argues at some times that the arrival of a boy's beard will spoil his looks (e.g., *Epistles* 13) and at others that it will make him even more beautiful, since a beard is a sign of masculinity (15).

56. E.g., *Symposium* 192: "Ὁ τοιοῦτος παιδεραστής τε καὶ φιλεραστὴς γίγνεται; ὁ παιδεραστὴς καὶ ἄλλος πᾶς" (note that heterosexual males are "φιλογύναικες," heterosexual females "φίλανδροι," gay women "ἑταιρίστριαι"; Plato is the only ancient author to make such comprehensive semantic distinctions on the basis of object choice, although Pollianus [second century A.D.] uses a word which appears to mean a heterosexual male: "γυναικεραστής," AP, 3.68, 70). Cf. LSJ, s.v. φιλογυναίης.

57. E.g., Plutarch *Moralia* 751B: "Δούλοις μὲν γὰρ ἐρᾶν ἀρρένων παίδων ἀπεῖπε καὶ ξηραλοιφεῖν"; John Chrysostom *Commentaria in Epistolam ad Titum* 5.4: "Ἔσφαξε τοὺς παῖδας ἐκείνους," where the variant reading has "τοὺς ἄνδρας"; Pseudo-Lucian, *Affairs of the Heart* (*Amores*), quoted below.

58. Often the beloved in a discussion of "pederasty" will be designated with a word which refers to an adult (e.g., Pseudo-Lucian, *Affairs of the Heart*, where in a discussion introduced under the rubric παιδεραστία, the general designation for the passions involved is "τὰς ἄρρενας ἐπιθυμίας" or "ἐρώτων τοὺς ἄρρενας"); and in very many cases where both parties are known to be full grown the words used imply youthfulness on the part of the beloved (e.g., Dio Cassius 59.11.1). In the majority of instances homosexual relations are described as occurring between fully grown persons, and no disparity in age is implied or stated (e.g., Plutarch *Moralia* 751; Clement of Alexandria *Paedagogus* 3; Chrysostom *In Epistolam ad Romanos* 4.3; etc.; for a more exhaustive listing of such terms, see below, app. 1). When ancient writers speak of "youths," moreover, they almost certainly do not mean young boys. An official Roman document of the second century refers (in a specifically homosexual context) to a "boy" ("παῖς") who is seventeen (*Oxyrhynchus papyri*, ed. B. Grenfell and A. Hunt [London, 1903], pt. 3, no. 471, p. 148, lines 49–51). Philo cites a definition of a "youth" as between fifteen and twenty (*De mundi opificio* 18C), and the word is used to describe persons serving in the Roman army.

by the advantages treated earlier. To a large extent the success of the enterprise will depend on eventual increases in understanding of intolerance as a general phenomenon. Such broad analysis, as noted previously, lies beyond the scope of the present study and even outside the range of these general introductory remarks. However, since some attention has been devoted here to considering what is probably not responsible for intolerance of homosexuality, it may be useful to provide some idea of the types of factors which *could* be responsible for it.

Of a great many examples which a more theoretical analysis might examine, only two will be considered here, and these are described in the spirit of commonsense deductions rather than scientific extrapolations with predictive certainty. Moreover, the first is advanced with many reservations: it is at most useful for understanding some of the changes in public tolerance treated in parts II and III of this volume. It is by no means a sufficient or comprehensive explanation even for these changes and is wholly irrelevant to (if not contradicted by) the social changes characterized in part IV. Both are intended chiefly as suggestions for areas of further inquiry and investigation where there is at present almost no analytical apparatus.

The first of the two factors is the relation of social organization to sexual morality and tolerance. In several places in this volume two general types of social organization are contrasted under the headings "urban" and "rural": it should be clear from the outset that such designations represent gross oversimplifications and are intended only as abbreviations of much more complicated concepts. By "rural" is meant social organization structured primarily around extended family units, in which political loyalty does not transcend blood relation and kinship structures are chief means of maintaining order and providing social services. As an ideal type, "rural" societies would exist principally among preindustrial agrarian peoples with little political organization; to a lesser extent such characteristics are found in rural areas even of industrialized countries.

In a "rural" social structure, extended family relations are crucial to the individual's survival: throughout his life they provide education, sustenance, work, marriage partners and accoutrements, moral values, and safety. It is ✳ the family in such cultures which allots labor roles, providing a work force for harvesting and planting, shepherding and building, etc.; which supervises care of the young and old and the sick; which arranges marriages and provides child care for parents who must work outside the home; which sees that orphans or widows are cared for; which passes on wisdom and moral values from one generation to another and guarantees property rights and traditional divisions of land and resources; which provides for the individual a place in society psychologically as well as physically.

A salient characteristic of "rural" societies is reliance on the family to administer punishment to persons (within or without the family) who cause harm to family members. Blood feuds and tribal or family vendettas are particularly associated with rural areas and groups, where political units either do not exist or are not trusted to administer justice, and abstract justice (if known) is consciously subordinated to family loyalty. In the early Middle Ages a principal difficulty in establishing friendly relations between urban Romans and the rural barbarians was the type of family justice based on blood feuds among the latter,[59] which the Romans regarded as atavistic and uncivilized.

Where social status, power, emotional security, and even survival are dependent on clearly defined positions within an extended family structure, the definition of such positions becomes a chief function of ethics, mores, and laws, much as access to citizenship and government position is a primary function of such forces in politically regulated societies. A very great proportion of social and moral taboos in kinship-structured communities is directed toward regulating legitimate procreation and discouraging forms of sexuality which would complicate social organization by producing persons with ambiguous claims to a position within the family. Such efforts usually bear little relation to superficially similar concerns which underlie sexual morality in politically organized societies. Divorce may be quite easy (for males), for instance, and polygamy common, while extramarital sexuality is punished by death; free-born women may be ruined (or even killed) for a single sexual indiscretion, while their male relatives or husbands have recourse to slaves or prostitutes with impunity; widows may be required to remain celibate until death, while males may have dozens of concubines and several wives all at once. The rationale behind such strictures is clearly not related either to sexual purity in any abstract sense or to safeguarding any affective aspects of family life. It is not even an effort to maximize reproduction, since illegitimate children will at best be afforded no guarantees of social protection and at worst be actually put to death.

On the contrary, the interest behind these seemingly capricious and unrelated taboos and strictures is apparently the limitation of access to position and privilege within the family. Although this motivation is only

59. Actually many of the barbarian groups which invaded the Roman Empire either had reached or quickly reached under Roman influence an intermediate stage of justice, in which one tribe did not simply inflict damage on another one in retribution for injuries sustained by one of its members but, rather, demanded payment of a fixed sum (*wergild*) agreed upon with regard to the nature of the injury and the social standing of the victim. The family was still the arbiter and guarantor of justice, and this arrangement strongly supported the rural sexual ethos described below, but it was not so primitive as the unrestrained vendetta common among some nomadic peoples.

subliminally present in many communities, highly developed ethical codes of essentially rural origin may be quite conscious of it.

> Perfect love, brotherhood, and mutual assistance is only found among those near to each other by relationship. The members of a family united by common descent from the same grandfather, or even from some more distant ancestor, have towards each other a certain feeling of love, help each other, and sympathize with each other. . . . To effect the great boon that all men should know their relationship to each other, prostitutes were not tolerated, and sexual intercourse was only permitted when man has chosen a certain female, and married her openly.[60]

The creation of moral sanctions of sufficient gravity, simplicity, and comprehensiveness to achieve this goal usually results in the exclusion or condemnation of much sexual activity which is not in fact detrimental to the extended family structure but which could not be allowed without blurring the focus of the general code or undermining a principle which has been enunciated in justification of it.[61] If such behavior is quite common—e.g., masturbation—it may be tacitly allowed as long as the code is not questioned by those who privately indulge in it. If it seems unusual—e.g., homosexuality—it will often be more severely repressed, since its irrelevance to the concerns underlying the common morality will seem even more suspicious in light of its statistical oddity. Deviance in sexual matters in cultures organized by sexually created relationships is much like heresy in theologically dominated societies or political dissent in politically organized communities. Gay people seem as dangerous in kinship societies as heretics once did in Catholic Europe or as socialists more recently in Western democracies. In all such cases dissent or deviance may appear to be treason at first;[62] only time, familiarity, and

---

60. Maimonides, on the purpose of the sexual regulations of Jewish law, in *The Guide of the Perplexed*, trans. Friedlander, 3:49, pp. 256–57. This relationship has been noted by prominent modern Jewish scholars as well: see, e.g., S. D. Goitein, *Jews and Arabs: Their Contacts through the Ages* (New York, 1955), esp. pp. 37–43. Note that although Goitein does not make the connection explicit, there is also a correlation in his thought between rural (or at least sedentary agricultural) family-oriented social organization and hostility to homosexuality: pp. 14–15. Compare Plutarch's ranking of the four types of human love: (1) familial, (2) hospitable, (3) friendly, (4) erotic (*Moralia* 758D).

61. Particularly revealing examples of this are constituted by Maimonides' comments on the relationship of the central purpose of the sexual laws to such seemingly capricious prohibitions as those against an unmarried man holding his penis (even to urinate), a man watching women bending over their work, or anyone at all looking at animals mating.

62. A fascinating example of this is celibacy, which is condemned in most rural ethical codes (see, e.g., *The Code of Maimonides, Book 5: The Book of Holiness*, trans. Louis Rabinowitz and Philip Grossman, Yale Judaica Series, vol. 16 [New York, 1965], 21.26) as counter to the purposes of the moral system (i.e., the maintenance of extended-family units with

education can make room for harmless nonconformity and enable the majority to distinguish between those forms of atypical behavior which actually are destructive of the social order and those which are not.[63]

In contrast, "urban" societies are characteristically organized in political units which explicitly transcend kinship ties. Urban communities can afford to effect a transition to a larger realm of moral concern because more sophisticated social organization in cities removes from the family unit much of the burden of social welfare and organization, providing schools, divisions of labor, jobs, marital opportunities, religious institutions, safety and personal protection, and care for widows, orphans, and the sick—all independent of one's position in an extended family. Nuclear families remain a basic element of social organization in such cultures and are consciously protected, but moral codes in urban environments tend to emphasize civic, abstract, or divinely revealed concepts of right and wrong as specifically superior to ethics based primarily on private considerations, such as family loyalty.[64] Most urban communities, for instance, consciously discourage personal or family justice, especially in serious matters, and seek to substitute for it

---

clearly defined relationships), but which is sometimes discovered to be actually beneficial when socially regulated. The exemption of the celibate from all reproductive pressure in rural value systems is a salient and innovative characteristic of Catholicism as a religion, imposed on it, at least in the view of Catholics, by Jesus.

63. Some rural societies, for instance, do recognize homosexual marriages, as long as one partner agrees to play the role of wife. Often, though not always, this involves transvestism and cross-gender behavior in addition to such formal matters as dowry. This adaptation, plus the atypical aspects of their social organization, would seem to account for the common institution of the *berdache* (a respected gay person with clearly defined roles) among American Indians; see esp. Donald Forey, "The Institution of Berdache among the North American Plains Indians," *Journal of Sex Research* 11 (1975): 1–15; W. Hill, "The Status of the Hermaphrodite and Transvestite in Navaho Culture," *American Anthropologist* 37 (1935): 273–79; and "Note on the Pima Berdache," ibid. 40 (1938): 338–39; A. Métraux, "Le shamanisme araucan," *Revista del Instituto de antropología* 2 (1942): 309–62; and N. O. Lurie, "Winnebago Berdache," *American Anthropologist* 55 (1953): 708–12.

64. In a number of historical incidences, one can observe a conscious effort on the part of a society to effect a transfer in the popular consciousness from family or tribal loyalty to civic loyalty, often by propaganda efforts in which sacrifice of close relatives for the state is lavishly praised and idealized. A good example of this at Rome is the congeries of legends surrounding the first consul, Lucius Junius Brutus, who expelled the last king. When his own sons joined the king's effort to return, Brutus had them executed (see Livy 2.5). Vergil, a great patriot writing at Rome's urban zenith, comments on this that "love of country and a great desire for praise will triumph" ("vincet amor patriae laudumque immensa cupido," *Aeneid* 6.823); but Servius, commenting on this line in an age of increasing reversion to a more rural ethos, disapproved: "Love for one's country ought not to displace the force of nature" ("Non extorquere vim naturae debet amor patriae"); the textual tradition of Servius's commentaries is unusually complex. I have used the incomplete Harvard edition, *Servianorum in Vergilii carmina commentariorum*, ed. E. K. Rand et al. [Lancaster, Pa., 1946–65]).

concepts of abstract justice administered impartially by the state for the welfare of all.

Likewise, urban sexual morality is often directed toward goals other than legitimate position within an extended family. Although the family remains the object of legal safeguards and public concern, quality of upbringing for children and the strength of affective bonds within the family are considered more important than the number or status of offspring. Polygamy is rarely allowed in urban environments, and more attention is paid in ethical writings to the quality of the relationship between man and wife than to legalistic concerns of legitimacy or subordination. Illegitimate children usually suffer fewer disadvantages in cities, since their skills make them valuable in a social structure which accommodates laborers not related to a particular blood line. Prostitution is usually seen simply as a form of self-indulgence, possibly demeaning to the individuals involved but not civilly punishable. (The state often intervenes only to prevent exploitation of the unwilling or to tax the practice for the common good.) Most sexual matters are considered outside the proper purview of the state; moral codes of sexuality in cities tend to emphasize personal purity and the importance of fidelity and nonexploitative relations between social equals rather than procreation and legitimacy.

Homosexuality is usually tolerated and often idealized in highly urban societies. At worst it is seen as a harmless by-product of civilization and leisure, causing no damage to the city and possibly enriching it through art, commerce, or taxes related to amorous pursuits. At best, it is seen as an expression of precisely that sort of spiritual loyalty, independent of the constraints of blood relation, which creates and maintains municipalities and civilizations, a more intense form of the love and devotion which should exist between citizens regardless of biological accident or particulars of kinship. It is perhaps more than mere coincidence that most Athenians attributed the establishment of their democracy to a pair of gay lovers and that the Western societies most noted for favoring gay sexuality—Athens and Rome—were also those most closely associated with urban democracy.[65] "For people

65. The "urban-rural" dichotomy is further defined by factors which may be only incidentally related to social organization. Marriage in urban environments, for instance, is often perceived as a luxury rather than a necessity, a refinement of life which must be earned. Those amenities which in the country only a wife is thought to provide and the support for which rural women are often completely dependent on men, are provided to both in cities by social services and specialized labor. Only men with sufficient means to support a family properly are able to court and marry women in many urban cultures. While it is extremely unlikely that such conditions alter the proportion of gay men or women in such communities—or even substantially affect the incidence of homosexual behavior—it is quite likely that they result in the recognition and approval of many life-styles other than marriage as fulfilling and responsible and thus increase tolerance of gay relationships. Similarly, urban children are exposed to a variety of ethical codes from an

will abandon tribesmen and relatives and even—by God—parents and children. But no one has ever come between lover and beloved, who are inspired by God, nor has any enemy triumphed over them" (Plutarch *Moralia* 761C).

These generalizations must be viewed with extreme caution. Exceptions to these broad categories will immediately present themselves. Nomadic rural societies—e.g., Bedouins and American Indians—are generally favorable to gay people, and urban societies characterized by extreme concern with conformity are often hostile to them.[66] The complexity of human existence must inevitably frustrate efforts at logical analysis,[67] and no effort will be made here to defend these inferences against the many valid objections which might be raised. It may be more useful to reiterate their stated limitations and to emphasize that the designations "rural" and "urban" should not be understood as more than abbreviations for complex phenomena

---

early age. Unlike rural children, who are for the most part given a choice between their parents' morality and "immorality," urban young people recognize early that many people whose mores are different from their own family's may nonetheless be living what is regarded by others as a "moral" life. Large urban communities are forced, in fact, to make more distinctions between public and private morality, conformity and ethics, personal judgment and civil obedience, etc., than small rural ones, and this pressure has traditionally operated to the advantage of many minority groups, including gay people. Even physical differences between urban and rural environments may redound to the benefit of gay people: in the greater anonymity of cities, hostile attitudes toward homosexuality can be circumvented with greater ease than in small rural communities.

66. One may observe that this dichotomy might have been more directly addressed by employing the headings "kin based" and "political" in place of "rural" and "urban." I have chosen not to do so principally because the former terms are even more misleading in some important ways and because they lend themselves to polemical abuse in suggesting that societies in the second category are less concerned with the family than those in the first. This is not true—most adherents of larger political structures imagine that greater social organization is the best means of strengthening and protecting their families.

67. A salient difficulty of analysis on this basis is that the phenomena to which it relates are both subjective and fluid: the degree to which individual members of a society organize their lives around family relations rather than political ones would be extremely difficult to quantify and is doubtless in constant flux. This does not argue against the reality or importance of the effects of such differences but greatly hampers construction of persuasive arguments about them. For an effort in this direction, see Jacques Heers, *Le clan familial au Moyen Age* (Paris, 1974). Few other works of medieval history address this issue directly, although the writings of David Herlihy approach it indirectly very sensibly: e.g., "Land, Family, and Women in Continental Europe, 701–1200," in *Women in Medieval Society*, ed. S. Stuard (Philadelphia, 1976), pp. 13–46; or "The Tuscan Town in the Quattrocento: A Demographic Profile," *Medievalia et humanistica: Studies in Medieval and Renaissance Culture*, n.s., 1 (1970): 81–111; and those of Georges Duby provide invaluable background: e.g., *Rural Economy and Country Life in the Medieval West*, trans. Cynthia Postan (Columbia, S.C. 1968). Studies of the medieval family itself are relatively recent and of uneven quality; for a recent collection, see R. Forster and O. Ranum, eds., *Family and Society: Selections from "Annales: économies, sociétés, civilisations"* (Baltimore, 1976).

defying easy categorization. It should also be noted that such distinctions, even where clearly influential, would affect differences in popular attitudes, not individual behavior.[68] The small amount of extant empirical data regarding the incidence of homosexual behavior (and all extramarital sexuality) does indicate a significant difference in urban and rural mores,[69] but it also demonstrates that homosexuality is by no means unknown in rural environments.

This idea about "urban-rural" differences is advanced only to suggest to readers ways of understanding some of the changes in popular attitudes detailed below. The aim is not to establish its certainty or even great likelihood but, rather, to propose it as one among many possible working hypotheses. At best it would account for only a small portion of the phenomena to which it relates, and many other factors will have to be discovered and analyzed before its relative importance can be determined.

In many cases it clearly has no bearing at all. Even if the extent to which a society is "rural" or "urban" has some effect on public tolerance regarding sexuality, it is often completely overridden by other aspects of social organization. The transition from tolerance to hostility which occupies the latter chapters of this book had little if anything to do with the dichotomy described above; it was almost wholly the consequence of the rise of corporate states and institutions with the power and desire to regulate increasingly personal aspects of human life. Minorities in states invested with substantial power over the private lives of citizens inevitably fare only as well as the central authority wishes. Although the period of greatest urbanization in Rome took place under the Empire, gay people were actually safer under the Republic, before the state had the authority or means to control aspects of the citizenry's personal lives. Any government with the power, desire, and means to control such individual matters as religious belief may also regulate sexuality, and since gay people appear to be always a minority, the chance that their interests will carry great weight is relatively slight.

68. Note that even in regard to stated attitudes, these descriptions of urban vs. rural ethics are intended to clarify the behavior not of individuals but only of groups. A person from the provinces may move to the city and be horrified by what he sees there, as appears to have been the case with many early Christian writers (e.g., Augustine, Jerome, Ambrose), or he may go to the city in search of a social freedom not available in the country and be ecstatic at having found it (e.g., Martial). But individual leaders probably cannot dramatically change group moral opinions. Even radical religious revolutions like Christianity and Islam largely involve the incorporation of traditional mores into a new theological framework, and hostility to minorities based on moral considerations can usually only work if it draws on some sort of popular feeling.

69. See Alfred Kinsey, Wardell Pomeroy, and Clyde Martin, *Sexual Behavior in the Human Male* (Philadelphia, 1948), chap. 12; and *Sexual Behavior in the Human Female* (Philadelphia, 1953), chap. 1.

Even in democratic states political conditions vary extravagantly. Governments which pride themselves on protecting the rights of minorities—e.g., European cities of the twelfth century—will frequently protect gay people. In many democracies, however, the practical impetus for statehood—subordination of private rights for the common good—becomes an article of quasi-religious faith, and those lowest-common-denominator areas upon which the majority is able to agree take on an aspect of sanctity rather than utility. In the Middle Ages this development was captured in the shibboleth *Vox populi vox Dei*—"The voice of the people is the voice of God." An extremely effective means of inculcating absolute loyalty to a government "of the people," this principle also proved fatal to persons—like Jews, gay people, and "witches"—whose life-styles differed from those of the majority: a voice not in harmony with that of "the people" was ipso facto out of harmony with God and hence punishable. The preferences of a majority of the people came to be equated with God's preferences, and if a majority of people disliked gay people, then so did God. This was not of course the official teaching of the church, and it was explicitly rejected by many theologians; but it was exploited by propagandists of various causes, including intolerance of several minorities, and came to seem self-evident in many contexts.

A tendency of humans to dislike or mistrust what is different or unusual adds a certain visceral force to this belief in the rightness of majority sentiment. Especially when difficulties beset a population already inclined to value conformity for its own sake, those who are perceived as willfully different are apt to be viewed not only as mistaken (or "unnatural") but as potentially dangerous. It seems to have been fatally easy throughout most of Western history to explain catastrophe as the result of the evil machinations of some group distinct from the majority; and even when no specific connection could be suggested, angry or anxious peoples have repeatedly vented their negative emotions on the odd, the idiosyncratic, and the statistically deviant. In the vibrant Rome of the first century or the bustling Paris of the twelfth, Jewish or gay nonconformists apparently struck their contemporaries as part of the variegated fabric of life, contributing their distinctive portions to a happy whole; but in the collapsing and insecure Rome of the sixth century or Paris in the later fourteenth, any deviation from the norm took on a sinister and alarming mien and was viewed as part of the constellation of evil forces bringing about the destruction of the familiar world order.

Tracing the course of intolerance reveals much about the landscape it traverses, and for this reason alone it deserves to be studied. Perhaps it is not too much to hope that its examination will yield beyond this insights of use to those who might wish to reduce or eradicate the suffering associated with it. On the other hand, the social topography of medieval Europe remains so unexplored that studies of any aspect of it are largely pioneering and hence provisional. Later generations will certainly recognize many wrong turns, false leads, and dead ends mistakenly pursued by those who had no trails to follow, whose only landmarks were those they themselves posted. Once the terrain has been better mapped, it will be possible to improve initial surveys very substantially; early studies may appear in retrospect absurdly round-about or wholly useless. To this ineluctable hazard of early research is added the difficulty in the case at issue that a great many people believe they already know where the trails *ought* to lead, and they will blame the investigator not only for the inevitable errors of first explorations but also for the extent to which his results, however tentative and well intentioned, do not accord with their preconceptions on the subject. Of such critics the writer can ask only that before condemning too harshly the placement of his signposts they first experience for themselves the difficulty of the terrain.

2 Definitions

Although the word "gay" is now regularly used in English and numerous other modern languages[1] to designate a person who prefers erotic contact with his or her own gender, its use in scholarly circles has so far been resisted. The reasons for this opposition are not obvious. It is not, after all, as if "homosexual" were such a satisfactory alternative. Compounded macaronically of a Greek prefix and Latin root, its most obvious meaning is "of one sex" (as "homogeneous," "of one kind"). This definition is quite adequate in reference to a relationship or sexual act: a sexual relation involving two parties "of one sex" is indeed a homosexual one. But what is a "homosexual" person? Is this someone "of one sex"? By extension, one supposes, a "homosexual" person is one given to "homosexual" acts. But in just how many such acts must one indulge before becoming "homosexual"—one, two, ten, four hundred? And what of the person who only dreams of committing the act but never realizes the ambition? Is he or she "homosexual"?

Alfred Kinsey[2] posited a seven-point scale on which a person of exclusively

1. "Gay" (or "gai") is now widely used in French, Dutch, Danish, Japanese, Swedish, and Catalan with the same sense as the English. It is coming into use in Germany and among the English-speaking upper classes of many cosmopolitan areas in other countries. Very few languages have an equivalent term. The Castilian "entendido" is probably the closest equivalent to a nonopprobrious designation used by gay people themselves. The German "Warmbruder" or "schwul" is less derogatory than the French "tante" or "comme ça," but not quite the equivalent of "gay." Because the idea of a homosexual/heterosexual dichotomy is relatively infrequent, few other languages even have an equivalent of "homosexual." The Hebrew "mishchav zachur," while used to mean "homosexual," is etymologically quite distinct from the psychological implications of the latter. Arabs use "lūtī" (a follower of Lot? see chap. 7, n. 95), but this has only the implications of the English word "sodomite": i.e., specifically sexual, not emotional and not necessarily homosexual; a husband and a wife may commit "sodomy." Modern Greek "ὁμοφυλόφιλος" is a new word, coined in imitation of "homosexual," and unknown in classical or patristic Greek.

2. Kinsey et al., *Sexual Behavior in the Human Male*, pp. 638–41. A Kinsey 1 is "predominantly heterosexual, only incidentally homosexual"; a 2, predominantly heterosexual, but more than incidentally homosexual"; 4 and 5 the obverse.

heterosexual experience would represent 0, a person of exclusively homosexual experience 6, a person of equal experience of both kinds 3, and so on.
Although Kinsey tried to account for fantasy in addition to behavior, this
scale is not useful in characterizing human beings for whom one does not
have a substantial case history.

There is no conceivable way of quantifying the homosexual versus
heterosexual experience of most historical personages, and such analysis
would indicate little even if it were possible. If, for instance, Alexander
the Great had sexual relations with hundreds of women and only two men,
but one of the men (Bagoas) was unquestionably the erotic center of his life,
the statistics would give us a highly misleading picture. If Tiberius invited
more men than women to his orgies on Capri, this is hardly grounds for
assuming that he had more homosexual than heterosexual interest. Social
factors may play a crucial role in sexual experience, as evidenced by the
fact that an enormous number of gay persons in highly repressive cultures
never express their sexual feelings at all.[3]

Given such difficulties—many of them quite troublesome to researchers in
the field—it seems likely that scholarly disinclination to employ the word
"gay" is due less to enthusiasm about "homosexual" than to a general reluctance on the part of academics to employ popular neologisms. However
justifiable this tendency may be generally, it is somewhat misguided in this
particular case. The word "homosexual," despite its air of antiquity, was
actually coined in the late nineteenth century by German psychologists,
introduced into English only at the beginning of the present century,[4] and

3. It can be well argued that the homosexual/heterosexual dichotomy is not a real one,
and this would have been the response of most ancient authorities. At best these categories
group together according to one arbitrarily chosen aspect of sexual actions—the genders of the
parties involved—varieties of sexual behavior which may be more dissimilar than similar.
"Heterosexuality" runs the gamut from the fevered orgies of the Marquis de Sade to the
restraint of Queen Victoria, from boot fetishes to the love between the Brownings.
Moreover, it is not clear that in most humans it is the gender of the other party which
makes the sexual act desirable or not: many people are apparently more aroused by the acts
themselves (penetration, oral stimulation, etc.) than by the persons involved, and some
people respond only to blonds or to people with blue eyes. Such objections are cogent but
serve only to demonstrate the inevitable weakness of taxonomic arrangement of human
behavior: the homosexual/heterosexual dichotomy is crude and imprecise and often
obscures more than it clarifies; but it does nonetheless correspond to types of actions
and feelings which can be distinguished by this criterion, and the fact that they could also
be arranged in different ways does not undermine the limited validity of the division.

4. Probably by John Addington Symonds, who referred to "homosexual instincts" in *A
Problem in Modern Ethics* in 1891, six years before the first occurrence cited in the OED. This
essay is excerpted in Reade, pp. 248–85. When the "Hod-Horizontal" volume of the OED
was published in March 1899, the word "homosexual" was not well enough known to be
included. It first appeared in the supplement (p. 407) published some forty years later.

vehemently opposed for decades after its appearance precisely because of its bastard origin and vague connotations.[5]

In contrast, "gay" (in the sense under discussion) probably antedates "homosexual" by several centuries[6] and has generally been employed with far greater precision: most speakers use "gay" to describe persons who are conscious of erotic preference for their own gender. This obviates the most urgent defect of "homosexual" (i.e., who is and who is not) by making the category one which is principally self-assigned. In a prison, for example,

---

Prior to this, English had employed "sodomite" to describe those who engaged in homosexual acts, but this word did not suggest erotic preference, a concept largely unknown when it was coined. In the late nineteenth century, the terms "Uranian" and "urning" had been popular among male gay writers and those sympathetic to them. The former was derived from the speech of Phaedrus in Plato's *Symposium*, in which gay love is described as "heavenly" ("οὐράνιος") and heterosexual passions as "vulgar." "Urning" was presumably a corruption of this. Terms like "inversion," "intermediate sex," "third sex," "homogenic love," etc., were all used for "homosexuality" before the latter became acceptable in English, replacing all previous terminology by the 1930s.

5. In 1897 Havelock Ellis employed "homosexuality" (*Studies in the Psychology of Sex*, 1:1) but observed that "'homosexual' is a barbarously hybrid word, and I claim no responsibility for it."

6. No scholarly work has been done on the origins of "gay" in the sense under discussion, and an embarrassment of riches complicates its history. The Provençal word "gai" was used in the thirteenth and fourteenth centuries in reference to courtly love and its literature and persists in Catalan—Provençal's closest living relative—as a designation for the "art of poesy" ("gai saber"), for a "lover" ("gaiol"), and for an openly homosexual person. It is by no means clear that the last-named use is not borrowed from English, but such contamination would not constitute proof that "gai" had not meant "homosexual" at some earlier point. The cult of courtly love was most popular in the south of France, an area noted for gay sexuality, and some troubadour poetry was explicitly homosexual. Moreover, both troubadour poetry and courtly love were closely associated with southern French heretical movements, especially the Albigensians, who were internationally suspected of favoring homosexuality. Possibly "gai" also acquired homosexual connotations outside areas familiar with the full range of troubadour eroticism. Bruce Rodgers, *The Queen's Vernacular* (San Francisco, 1972), s.v. "gay," opines that the derivation is from "16th-century French gaie = homosexual man" but offers no substantiation, and I have discovered none. Numerous European languages use "gay" or its cognates, however, in reference to sexual looseness. Grimm, *Deutsches Wörterbuch* (Leipzig, 1878), s.v. "gähe" (4), gives "irrational," or "ill-considered," reminiscent of the medieval application of "ἀλογευσάμενοι" ("irrational") to gay people; but more obviously relevant parallels are to be found in the Castilian "gaya" and older English "gay," both used in reference to female prostitutes or the life-style of the men who resort to them (for English usage, see OED, s.v. "gay," A.2.a,b). Although the popular association of prostitution with homosexuality is apparently unfounded (see, e.g., Paul Gebhard, "Misconceptions about Female Prostitutes," *Medical Aspects of Human Sexuality* 3, no. 3 [1969]: 24–30), it is ancient and pervasive. One may in any event easily imagine a transference of the idea of the sexual looseness of prostitution to the immorality attributed to homosexual persons in hostile environments. In the early twentieth century "gay" was common in the English homosexual subculture as a sort of password or code. Its first public use in the United States outside of pornographic fiction appears to have been in the 1939 movie *Bringing up Baby*, when Cary Grant, wearing a dress, exclaimed that he had "gone gay."

many persons may be involved in homosexual acts or even relationships without thinking of themselves as "gay." Well over one-third of the adult male population of the United States has participated in a homosexual act,[7] but this same percentage of men would probably not describe themselves as gay.[8]

In this study, therefore, "homosexual"—used only as an adjective—occurs either in its original sense of "all of one sex" (as in "a homosexual marriage") or elliptically to mean "of predominantly homosexual erotic interest" ("a homosexual person"). "Homosexuality" refers to the general phenomenon of same-sex eroticism and is therefore the broadest of the categories employed; it comprises all sexual phenomena between persons of the same gender, whether the result of conscious preference, subliminal desire, or circumstantial exigency. "Gay," in contrast, refers to persons who are conscious of erotic inclination toward their own gender as a distinguishing characteristic or, loosely, to things associated with such people, as "gay poetry." "Gay sexuality" refers only to eroticism associated with a conscious preference. This book is primarily concerned with gay people and their sexuality, but it must necessarily deal at length with other forms of homosexuality, because it is often impossible to make clear distinctions in such matters and because many societies have failed to recognize any distinctions at all.

7. The best available statistics for the incidence of homosexual behavior are still those published in the pioneering studies of Kinsey et al. (*Sexual Behavior in the Human Male*, *Sexual Behavior in the Human Female*), and the reader is encouraged to consult the chapters entitled "Homosexual Outlet" in each. These studies are unfortunately more often cited than read: the statistics must be consulted in their original context to be understood properly. I have relied for the most part on the slightly reinterpreted totals provided by Paul Gebhard's "Incidence of Overt Homosexuality in the United States and Western Europe," in *National Institute of Mental Health Task Force on Homosexuality: Final Report and Background Papers*, DHEW Publication no. 72–9116 (Washington, DC.: Government Printing Office, 1972), pp. 22–30.

8. It is doubtless true that many persons would be unsure whether they are gay or not gay or might deny that they are either. This does not obviate the advantages of the dichotomy. That many persons cannot be classified as either strictly blond or strictly brunet does not demonstrate that "blonds" and "brunets" do not exist. It merely substantiates the wisdom of accepting all classifications of living beings as imperfect. Kinsey believed (like Freud) that humans are born with a capacity to respond erotically to either sex and that social factors dispose most people to prefer one to the other (see, e.g., his "Homosexuality: A Criteria for a Hormonal Explanation of the Homosexual," *Journal of Clinical Endocrinology* 1, no. 5 [1941]: 424–28; or "The Causes of Homosexuality: A Symposium," *Sexology* 21, no. 9 [1955]: 558–62). In this view, homosexual and heterosexual persons are representatives not of distinct types but simply of the end points on a sliding scale ranging from exclusive heterosexuality to exclusive homosexuality, with the majority of humans occurring at midpoints and capable of responding to either sex (but often constrained by circumstances to limit their responses to a single partner for much of their lives). If this view is correct, then "gay" people are those far enough toward the homosexual end of the Kinsey scale to think of themselves as chiefly homosexual.

The opposite of "homosexual" is "heterosexual," and it is used throughout as its obverse: "heterosexuality" comprises all sexual phenomena between persons of different genders, whether preferential, circumstantial, or subliminal. In common parlance the opposite of "gay" is "straight." This word is less defensible than "gay" on almost any grounds: it has no demonstrable history;[9] its connotations are even less specific than those of "heterosexual" (since it may refer to persons who are generally stodgy or who do not take drugs, etc.); and it appears to entail negative implications for its opposite.[10] Therefore, "gay" has been contrasted in this study with "nongay," an expression which may startle some readers but which is no less justifiable than "non-Jewish", "non-Catholic," "non-German," or "non-" anything else which comprises the focus of attention.

This terminology has advantages beyond semantic precision. The word "homosexual" implicitly suggests that the primary distinguishing characteristic of gay people is their sexuality. There does not seem to be any evidence that gay people are any more or less sexual than others, and from the historian's point of view, tacitly suggesting such a thing is unwarranted. "Gay" allows the reader to draw his own conclusions about the relative importance of love, affection, devotion, romance, eroticism, or overt sexuality in the lives of the persons so designated. Sexual interest and expression vary dramatically in the human population, and a person's sexual interest may be slight without precluding the realization that he or she is attracted to persons of the same gender and hence distinct in some way from the majority.

Moreover, "homosexual" has come to be associated with males more than females. The phrase "lesbians and homosexuals" now appears frequently in print, and the use of "gay people" in this study is more clearly inclusive. (It should also be observed, in this context, that it is not at all certain that minors do not have clearly defined erotic preferences, and the term "gay people" comes closer to recognizing this than "homosexuals," which generally evokes mental images of adults.)

It might also be noted that gay people appear to prefer the term "gay," which they have chosen to apply to themselves, to "homosexual," which was coined and popularized in the context of pathology. There can be no more justification for retaining a designation out of favor with gay people than for continuing to use "Negro" when it has ceased to be acceptable to blacks. One cannot of course please everyone, but it does seem that a reasonable

9. Presumably "straight" is derived from "straight arrow," a slang term suggesting adherence to conventional values.

10. In the sense that "not straight" implies a deliberate flouting of those values which are upheld by "straight" persons, rather than an involuntary sexual preference.

concession of speech is an effort which scholars can make at very small cost to themselves.[11]

A related though less specific semantic difficulty is presented by the supposed dichotomy between "friendship" and "love." In an intellectual tradition characterized by polarizing logic and mutually exclusive categories, failure to distinguish clearly between these areas of human emotion may seem quite serious, but from the scholar's point of view, any distinction between "friendship" and "love" must be extremely arbitrary. No scientific differentiation has ever been proposed, nor is it easy to conceive of an experiment which might be performed to determine whether one person's love for another was friendly or erotic. From a phenomenological point of view, it seems likely that "friendship" and "love" are simply different points on a scale measuring a constellation of psychological and physiological responses to other humans.

From a historical point of view, the task of effecting such a division seems almost hopeless, since there is confusion and doubt not only in the historian's own frame of reference but also in that of the sources he uses. The popular notion, for example, that ancient Greek neatly expressed discrete categories of emotion under the headings φιλία, ἔρως, and ἀγάπη is mistaken; there was very considerable overlap and ambiguity in the uses of all three. The verb "φιλέω" may refer equally to a love which is quite passionless or to a torrid kiss. Only context and judicious inference can suggest which is meant in a particular case.

In Latin the ambiguity is simpler and more extreme. "Amicus," or "friend," and "amans," "lover," are derived from the same verb—"amo," "to love"—and are very largely interchangeable. Personal intuition or prevailing attitudes often predispose translators to render "amica" in a heterosexual context as "girlfriend" or "loved one," and "amicus" in a homosexual context as "friend," or "companion," but there is little a priori justification for such a distinction.[12] "Amicitia," "friendship," certainly refers to a category

---

11. Readers familiar with modern gay terminology may be struck by the absence from a book dealing with antigay prejudice of the popular term "homophobia," used to designate an irrational fear of gay people and their sexuality. "Homophobia," unlike "homosexual," is properly derived from Greek by exact analogy with many other English words; according to the mode of its derivation and the obvious relation of its parts, however, it should mean "fear of what is similar," not "fear of homosexuality" (which would be—assuming the present macaronism is ineradicable—"homosexophobia"). The former meaning is not alien to the current use of "homophobia," since it does connote fear of sexual contact with one's own gender as well as fear of those who favor such contact. But the relation of these two meanings remains ambiguous, and the general appeal of "homophobia" seems to be based on a superficial similarity to "homosexual."

12. Cf. in Greek the masculine "ἑταῖρος," translated as "companion," while the feminine "ἑταίρα" is a courtesan or prostitute.

distinct in some way from "amor," "love," but in precisely what way and with what relation to modern ideas of "friendship" as opposed to "love" is not generically determinable. Especially among Latin writers affected by Greek ideals it may in fact more closely resemble "romance" in a modern context than "friendship."

It is thus often impossible on the basis of words alone to discern whether a particular figure in Greek or Latin sources "loved" or "was in love with" another person. This confusion is probably not accidental. It is likely in fact that ancient societies recognized fewer boundaries between "friendship" and "romance" than modern ones, and for the researcher to suggest that a clear dichotomy existed or to place a particular relationship on one side of it is usually anachronistic and inaccurate.

Exterior evidence of the erotic nature of relationships varies widely by culture and time, and one must regard as crucial the anticipated responses of contemporaries to expression or representations of love. It was not necessary in classical Attic literary works to specify the erotic content of an intense relationship between two males: that it was a love relationship was assumed. (Aeschines observes that Homer refrained from specifying the erotic nature of the friendship between Achilles and Patroclus "because he thought that the intensity of their affection would be obvious to the educated in his audience" [*Against Timarchus* 142]). In contrast, it would have evoked surprise if eroticism had been absent; many readers fail to grasp this as the point of Alcibiades' story in the *Symposium* (216C–219) about spending the night with Socrates and arising "as if he had spent the night with his father or elder brother." Socrates' behavior was obviously not at all what his hearers expected and astounds them with its extraordinary restraint, unanticipated even by Alcibiades.

Since the Greek tradition powerfully affected Roman writing, one must regard as likely the expectation on the part of many imperial writers that depictions of intense love between males would be taken as indicating more than simple friendship. After the disappearance of this tradition in the West, however, and the rise of hostility toward same-sex eroticism, much more caution must be exercised in assessing effusive romantic expressions between persons of the same gender, which may be hyperbolic manifestations of distinctly nonerotic friendships or even of simple charity.

Throughout this essay every effort has been made, therefore, to submit dubious cases to the reader's own judgment: to provide sufficient context and description of the relationship in question to allow for independent private judgment on the reader's part. Wherever possible the subject's own description of his feelings has been cited. Inferences about relations for which little direct evidence survives have been made with primary attention to historical context rather than modern expectations. In some cases parallels have been drawn between romantic literary effusion on the part of writers who probably did not think of themselves as gay and persons who probably did. The point of such juxtapositions is not to suggest that the former were "latently homosexual" but, rather, to clarify the emotional frame of reference in which the homosexual feelings of the latter would have been judged. For example, a comparison of literary descriptions of John of Salisbury's feelings for Pope Hadrian IV and Richard Lion Heart's love for Philip of France is intended not to hint that because the second appears to have been a gay relationship the first must also have been but, rather, to suggest that John and Hadrian, who conceived of their love for each other in terms very like those used to describe the passion between the two kings, would have reacted somewhat differently to homosexual sentiments than modern churchmen, who would not describe their friendships with men in such terms. To insist that because John and Hadrian were churchmen there is perforce *no* similarity between the two relationships, despite the literary parallel, would be as much a distortion as to leap at such similarities as proof of some equation between the two.

It is, moreover, essential to bear in mind the limitations of conscientious scholarship. One cannot expect and should not demand from historical sources "proof" of emotional states. Considering that even the individuals involved are often not absolutely certain whether their relationship is erotic or not, it is unrealistic to expect that ancient and medieval records will be able to offer some sure means of distinguishing between friends and lovers. Even for such urgent and quantifiable matters as the population of ancient cities historians must content themselves with very rough probabilities; it is hardly fair to demand more of emotional states which even modern science cannot measure or discriminate.

It would be useful if a discussion of the etiology, phenomenology, and extent of gay sexuality in present-day populations could be appended to these semantic preliminaries as preparation for the historical material which follows, but the present climate of opinion on the subject has so hampered objective investigation of such matters that most of the factual data which might have comprised such an introduction is either wanting or disputed to the point of uselessness. Indeed, historical data may prove to be of some value to modern researchers in this regard, since records from more tolerant ancient societies probably provide a more accurate—if less detailed—picture of gay sexuality than those from highly oppressive modern cultures.

In regard to the question of etiology, it should be noted that what "causes" homosexuality is an issue of importance only to societies which regard gay people as bizarre or anomalous.[13] Most people do not wonder what "causes" statistically ordinary characteristics, like heterosexual desire or right-handedness; "causes" are sought only for personal attributes which are assumed to be outside the ordinary pattern of life. Since very few people in the ancient world considered homosexual behavior odd or abnormal, comments about its etiology were quite rare.

There are in fact no explanations in any classical literature for homosexual desire, which everyone apparently considered ubiquitous and entirely ordinary. Aristophanes, who ridiculed every aspect of human behavior, often made fun of prominent gay Athenians but nonetheless characterized homosexual desire as a "natural necessity" like heterosexual desire, eating, drinking, and laughing.[14] Xenophon expressed the opinion of most Greeks of his day when he commented that homosexuality was a part of "human nature."[15] All of the Platonic discussions of love are predicated on the ubiquity of homosexual attraction, and heterosexuality appears in some of them as a somewhat inferior preference.[16] Centuries later Philostratus complains that a youth who will not respond to his affections is "opposing the commands of nature."[17]

Despite some inconsistency on the subject,[18] Aristotle apparently considered a homosexual disposition perfectly "natural": "This disposition

13. An enormous amount of writing—in great disproportion to the amount of knowledge supporting it—has appeared on the psychological, psychiatric, and medical aspects of homosexuality in the past two or three decades. This material (up to 1968) is conveniently arranged and abstracted in Martin Weinberg and Alan Bell, *Homosexuality: An Annotated Bibliography* (New York, 1972). More recent material may be located by consulting the quarterly bibliography published in the *Journal of Homosexuality*.

14. *Clouds* 1075: "Πάρειμ' ἐντεῦθεν ἐς τὰς τῆς φύσεως ἀνάγκας." The vexed question of the author's sympathies in this passage is irrelevant: the actions alluded to by "ἐντεῦθεν" (παίδων, γυναικῶν, κοττάβων, ὄψων, πότων, κιχλισμῶν) are so universal that it is scarcely possible that Aristophanes intended this point to be controversial, much less mistaken. It does not seem likely that if he had intended Wrong's point to be taken ironically, he would have included heterosexuality, eating, drinking, and laughing.

15. *Hiero* 1.33: "'Εγὼ γὰρ δὴ ἐρῶ μὲν Δαϊλόχου ὧνπερ ἴσως ἀναγκάζει ἡ φύσις ἀνθρώπων δεῖσθαι παρὰ τῶν καλῶν."

16. E.g., *Symposium* 181B, 191E–92. Even in the *Laws*, where homosexuality is disparaged, there is no suggestion that it is anything less than ubiquitous.

17. *Epistles* 64: "ἀντίπαλον τῶν φύσεως ἐπιταγμάτων."

18. In the *Nicomachean Ethics* (7.5.3ss) he uses the word "θηριώδεις" to describe homosexual relations, and this word has sometimes been translated as "morbid propensities" or "unhealthy passions," but such translations are ill-advised; fingernail biting is included in the same category and hardly justifies terms like "morbid" or "unhealthy." At the very most "bad habit" may be implied, but even this is suspect, since elsewhere in the same work Aristotle represents homosexuality as quite normal and healthy (e.g., 8.4.1–2). "Quirk" or "idiosyncrasy" is probably the most accurate understanding of the meaning here, and it may be intended only to refer to passive desires in men rather than homosexuality per se.

occurs in some people naturally [φύσει]. . . . When nature is responsible, no one would call such persons immoral, any more than they would women because they are passive in intercourse rather than active. . . . And whether the individual so disposed conquers or yields to it is not properly a moral issue." [19] Even those aspects of homosexual behavior which Aristotle considered most unusual and least "normal" (e.g., passivity in males) [20] struck him as "natural," since it was "nature" in Aristotle's thought which created the statistically less common as well as the ordinary. [21]

Plutarch not only implies throughout his writings but makes explicit at many points his conviction that all humans are attracted to both sexes:

> The noble lover of beauty engages in love wherever he sees
> excellence and splendid natural endowment without regard for any
> difference in physiological detail. . . . The lover of human beauty [will]
> be fairly and equally disposed toward both sexes, instead of

19. Ibid. 7.5.3–5. This passage affected many later views on the subject: see below, chap. 11. Note that this is a good example of the original "realistic" sense of "nature" in Greek, with no attendant idealization even in a comment on the morality of homosexual behavior.

20. The terms "active" and "passive" in the context of homosexual behavior may cause some confusion. Since sexual terminology is less often a subject of scholarly study than most areas of vocabulary, it is sometimes difficult to apprehend or demonstrate fine shades of meaning in regard to words for sexual acts. It is striking evidence of the difference in cultural attitudes toward sexuality that the English language cannot even name acts which are common subjects of Latin literature. Without elaborate circumlocution it is virtually impossible to translate words like "irrumo," "paedico," "ceveo," etc., and one must therefore attempt to subsume such distinctions under the much less precise English dichotomy between "active" and "passive" sexual behavior. On the basis of modern informal usage, comparable ancient designations, and persistent sexual stereotypes at many points in history, I use these terms throughout with the understanding that "active" refers to the individual in a male homosexual liaison who inserts his penis into his partner, either orally or anally, and that "passive" refers to the party so entered. I do not mean to suggest anything about the psychological aspects either of the acts involved (e.g., "passive" should not be interpreted as "uninterested," "coerced," "unwilling," "effeminate," etc.) or of the relationship: a very aggressive, socially dominant person may prefer what—for want of better terms—is here called "passive" sexual behavior. This dichotomy sometimes, though less often, occurs in historical documents in reference to women (gay or nongay) and in such cases should be understood in a sense analogous to its application to men: a woman who takes the "active" part enters her partner, either with some portion of her body or with an object; her "passive" partner—male or female—is entered. (Such comments about women may be more a projection of male sexual feelings than observation of female ones.) This whole area of speech is awkward and troubling; these efforts to clarify are the best I can offer, but far from satisfactory.

21. *Problems* 4.26 [880A]: "Τὰ μέντοι πολλὰ καὶ τὸ ἔθος ὥσπερ πεφυκόσι γίνεται." (The *Problems* are probably not genuine, but the ideas evident in this passage parallel those expressed in authentic Aristotelian works: see the discussion of Aristotle's influence on Aquinas in chap. 11 below.)

supposing that males and females are as different in the matter of love as they are in their clothes.[22]

Ancient writers were much more apt to comment on homosexuality as a public phenomenon than as a private practice. They recognized that its public manifestations varied widely by time and place and remarked on the significance of this. At Athens, not surprisingly, it was regarded as a political matter. In the *Symposium* Plato specifically equated acceptance of homosexuality with democracy.

> It is regarded as shameful by the Ionians and many others under foreign domination. It is shameful to barbarians because of their despotic government, just as philosophy and athletics are, since it is apparently not in the best interests of such rulers to have great ideas engendered in their subjects, or powerful friendships or physical unions, all of which love is particularly apt to produce. Our own tyrants learned this lesson through bitter experience, when the love between Aristogiton and Harmodius grew so strong that it shattered their power.[23]
>
> Wherever, therefore, it has been established that it is shameful to be involved in homosexual relationships [literally, "to gratify lovers," χαρίζεσθαι ἐρασταῖς], this is due to evil on the part of the legislators, to despotism on the part of the rulers, and to cowardice on the part of the governed. [*Symposium* 182B–D]

It is not clear from this whether Plato considers Athenian democratic acceptance of homosexual behavior more "normal" than despotic intolerance, but in the *Laws* he implies that homosexual acts would be extremely difficult, if not impossible, to prohibit effectively in any society; and Plutarch (*Moralia* 760C) suggests that tyrannicide was the result of interference in gay love in several other cities as well.

Aristotle represents encouragement of homosexuality as the deliberate purpose of Cretan lawmakers, a means of regulating population (*Politics* 2.7.5), and considers that the "public honor" accorded gay sexuality among the barbarians, particularly the Celts, had the effect of reducing attachment to wealth (2.6.6). He considered his teacher Plato's suggestions about prohibiting or discouraging homosexual behavior "ridiculous" ("ἄτοπος," 2.4). Philo (*De Abrahamo* 26) claimed that an increase in homosexual

22. Plutarch, *Dialogue on Love* ["*Amatorius*"], trans. W. C. Helmhold (Cambridge, Mass., 1961), p. 415 (= *Moralia* 767).

23. Aristogiton and Harmodius plotted to assassinate the sixth-century tyrant Hippias when he attempted to come between them. Their plot failed, but it inspired universal admiration among later Greeks, many of whom falsely attributed the founding of the Athenian democracy to their efforts. Cf. Plutarch *Moralia* 760C.

behavior was the result of excessive food production, Theodoret of Cyrus that homosexuality was ordinarily a "custom" which some men turned into a "permanent way of life" for reasons he did not specify. Plutarch—probably facetiously—had one character in his *Erotikos* maintain that nudity in the *gymnasia* popularized homosexuality (*Moralia* 751).

One common notion was that homosexual behavior was "learned" through cross-cultural contact; this has remained a favorite. As early as the fifth century B.C. Herodotus claimed that the Persians learned homosexual behavior from the Greeks,[24] an opinion still known to Athenaeus some 700 years later,[25] but apparently disbelieved by Quintus Curtius Rufus (first century A.D.), who claimed that homosexual relations were not known among Persians.[26] Such ideas persisted throughout the Middle Ages: crusaders were thought to have brought homosexual behavior back to Europe from the Middle East. Walther of Châtillon claimed young men learned it in cities. Giraldus Cambrensis thought that the English picked it up from the Normans, who in their turn had gotten it from the French.[27]

Late antique astrology contributed various theories about zodiacal constellations which would produce one sexual proclivity or another.[28] Varieties of homosexual behavior are mentioned—e.g., pederasty (apparently in a technical sense), passivity, male prostitution—but no word occurs which might mean "gay" or "homosexual" generically. Certain relations of Venus and Mars at the moment of birth, however, were thought to cause heterosexuality.[29]

Behavior which is disapproved or considered singularly idiosyncratic is often dismissed under the rubric of "disease": heresy was a "disease" to the

24. 1.135: "ἀπ' Ἑλλήνων μαθόντες, παισὶ μίσγονται."

25. 12.603a: "Πέρσας δὲ παρ' Ἑλλήνων φησιν Ἡρόδοτος μαθεῖν τὸ παισὶν χρῆσθαι."

26. 10.1.26: "nec moris esse Persis mares ducere qui stupro effeminarentur." This comment would appear to apply literally only to promiscuous, passive males, but it was made of Bagoas, Alexander's lifelong faithful companion. It is almost certainly erroneous.

27. *De vita Galfridi archiepiscopi Eboracensis* 2, in *Opera*, ed. J. S. Brewer (London, 1873), 4:423.

28. See, e.g., Julius Firmicus Maternus, *Matheseos libri VIII*, ed. W. Kroll and F. S. Kutsch (Stuttgart, 1967), 6.30.16, p. 144: "Si vero sine testimonio Iovis Venus fuerit cum his inventa, omne vitium inpudicae inpuritatis indicitur. Tunc viri spontaneo furoris ardore muliebra patiuntur, tunc inpura facinora ardore vitiosae libidinis exequuntur." Most of this information is to be found in Greek in the series *Catalogus codicum astrologorum Graecorum* (Brussels, 1898). The excerpts published from the sixth-century work of Rhetorius Aegyptius are particularly valuable (vols. 1, ed. Alexander Olivieri [1898], pp. 140–73; 7, ed. Francis Boll [1908], pp. 194–230; 8.4, ed. Pierre Boudreaux and Franz Cumont [1921], pp. 115–253). In several chapters (8.4, 66–68, pp. 194–99) a variety of astrological causes are propounded for producing pederasts, incontinent women, passive men, anally obsessed women, men given to incontinence with their tongues, male prostitutes, men who prefer "dirty" (?) sex, eunuchs, hermaphrodites, transsexuals, etc.

29. Rhetorius Aegyptius 8.4.68, p. 198: "Ἀφροδίτη ἐπίκεντρος καὶ ἐν θηλυκῷ ζῳδίῳ ὑπὸ Ἄρεως θεωρουμένη δίχα Ἑρμοῦ φιλογυναίους ποιεῖ, μάλιστα δὲ ἑσπέριος."

later Middle Ages,[30] and many nonconformists are labeled "sick" in modern societies. No ancient writers appear to have considered homosexual attraction itself pathological, but some did regard passive sexual behavior in adult males as "sick," possibly due to their attitudes toward female sexuality. The *Problems* attributed to Aristotle speculated on the cause of this condition,[31] and Philo opined that a male's passivity, though voluntary at first, would eventually result in sterility and an incurable "female disease."[32] The fifth-century Roman physician Caelius Aurelianus grouped passivity and opposite-gender identification together as a mental disorder, although he noted that persons suffering from this "disease" experienced no "impairment" of mental faculties. He presented two theories on etiology: it was either the result of a birth defect (improper mingling of sperm and egg) or an inherited disease.[33]

Patristic and medieval writers on the subject rarely speculated on the provenance of homosexual feelings. Most limited themselves to phenomenological observations or moral commentary. Albertus Magnus, however, considered homosexuality a contagious disease, especially common among the wealthy and extremely difficult to cure. Saint Thomas Aquinas, following Aristotle's opinion on passivity, regarded it as a genetic defect.

In contrast to these few indications of ancient ideas about homosexuality's origins, there are practically no data at all about the number of gay people in the past. The population of the United States is apparently the only one which has ever been surveyed to determine the number of its gay people.[34] The results of this research (conducted in the late 1940s by Kinsey) are now well known: about 13 percent of the adult male and 7 percent of the adult

30. For one of many studies on this subject, see the recent article by R. I. Moore, "Heresy as Disease," in *The Concept of Heresy in the Middle Ages (11th–13th Centuries): Proceedings of the International Conference, Louvain, May 13–16, 1973 (Medievalia Lovaniensia, Series I, Studia IV)* (Louvain, 1976).

31. If the normal passageway through the penis were congenitally blocked, he suggests, the semen would attempt to exit through the anus, and the male would wish to have intercourse through the anal opening. Some men, he theorized, might have only a partial defect and would enjoy both roles in intercourse; others might be genetically normal but become used to the passive role: *Problems* 4.24–26. This may have been an effort to account for the role of the prostate in anal intercourse with males.

32. "Θηλεία νόσος": *De Abrahamo* 26; cf. *De specialibus legibus* 3.7.

33. *Tardarum passionum* 4.9, trans. and ed. I. E. Drabkin (Chicago, 1950), pp. 900–905. In the *Celerum vel acutarum passionum* (in the same volume) he characterizes *active* homosexual desires as perfectly healthy and normal.

34. Some evidence from earlier periods is available for Germany (see M. Hirschfeld, "Das Ergebnis der statistischen Untersuchungen über den Prozentsatz der Homosexuellen," *Jahrbuch für sexuelle Zwischenstufen* 6 [1904]: 109–78), and some European countries have small samplings, but no evidence from any other nation compares in methodology or scale to the Kinsey studies.

female population are primarily or exclusively homosexual for at least a part of their lives; nearly 40 percent of the male and 20 percent of the female population have had some overt homosexual experience after puberty.[35]

In the present state of knowledge, it is impossible to know whether these figures represent historical constants or were even accurate for their day. It is evident from psychological evidence that many people are unaware of their own sexual feelings, and the phenomenon known to gay people as "coming out of the closet" often occurs quite late in life. Moreover, the bulk of the Kinsey statistics were gathered during a period of great difficulty for gay people and may not represent typical conditions even in the United States.[36]

In the myth about the origins of love in Plato's *Symposium* (189–93), Aristophanes seems to suggest that the proportions of gay and nongay men and women are roughly equal. The point is not introduced as if it were controversial, and none of his hearers seems to find it questionable.[37] In much classical literature gay and nongay desires and actions are juxtaposed as equally likely options; this may not justify the inference that the writers consider their contemporaries equally divided in the matter, but it does seem to indicate a public familiarity with gay people and their sexuality far greater than that in modern countries. Philostratus writes to an unresponsive young man that his disinterest in gay sexuality shows that he could not come from Sparta, Thessaly, Athens, Ionia, or Crete and must be from a barbarian land[38]—implying, doubtless with exaggeration, that homosexual feelings were universal in civilized states (*Epistles* 5).

Much evidence from the ancient world, however, is either contradictory or indicative of wide variation from one population to another: the fact that males not "married" to other males in Crete were socially disadvantaged would seem to imply that gay relationships involved a majority of the male population,[39] while the elitist aspect of the sacred band of Thebes seems to imply that gay relationships were a minority preference. The vast amount of homoerotic cultural paraphernalia at Athens—sculpture, painting, vase inscriptions, graffiti, terminology, law, literature, etc.—makes it seem that a majority (if not almost the whole) of the adult male population was involved in homosexual relationships and feelings.

35. The extraordinary furor the Kinsey figures caused at the time of their publication has now been generally forgotten but is conveniently summarized in C. A. Tripp, *The Homosexual Matrix* (New York, 1975), pp. 232–40. Harold Dodds, president of Princeton University, referred to them in print as "toilet-wall inscriptions."

36. Within a decade of publication of these findings, for instance, the United States witnessed the McCarthy investigations and the trials in Boise, Idaho, which led to the ruin of many individuals suspected of homosexuality.

37. Not even Phaedrus, who has characterized heterosexuality as πάνδημος.

38. "Scythia," i.e., beyond the Black Sea, in the wilds of Asia.

39. Conveniently discussed in Meier/de Pogey-Castries, pp. 42–46.

In Rome gay feelings do not seem to have been more than a part of the erotic life of the population. It is obvious that some people focused their affections and desires primarily on their own sex, but it is not at all clear how many did so, since the categories "homosexual" and "heterosexual" almost never occur in Latin literature. External observers of Roman mores give the impression that homosexuality was extremely common at all levels of society. Some, like Philo, imagined that it could be so widespread as to be demographically devastating. Saint John Chrysostom suggests very strongly that in fourth-century Antioch heterosexual persons were in a small minority, but his contemporary in the west, Caelius Aurelianus, thought some people might find it "hard to believe" that certain men would be passive in intercourse.

At many points in the Middle Ages gay people seem to have been rare to the point of exciting wonder—although people seem to have known what they were when they encountered them—and at other times heterosexual writers expressed concern that gay people were taking over the world. Late twelfth-century writers compare them to "the sands of the shore" and see Europe as "awash" with them. In the fourteenth century Arnald de Vernhola solemnly assured the inquisitor Jacques Fournier that if he attempted to catch all the people involved in homosexual activity in Pamiers "he would have enough to do, since there were more than 3,000 there."[40] This figure must have represented well over half the population of the town, and although it is undoubtedly an extreme exaggeration, it does hint at a rather large gay population.

One demographic consideration regarding gay people has often given rise to misleading speculations and deserves comment here. Some writers have claimed or hinted that homosexuality in the ancient world was limited to the upper classes. This supposition may be very obliquely related to reality: Kinsey and other researchers have discovered real differences in sexual behavior related to social class, wealth, and educational level.[41] Most sexual taboos, especially against aspects of sexuality related more to pleasure than to procreation, are more pronounced among persons of lower socioeconomic status and less education.

These differences have not been shown, however, to relate to erotic interest or desire, but only to resistance to or disregard of taboos against specific activities. That is, there is no evidence that homosexual desire varies

40. "Dicebat etiam quod satis haberet facere dictus dominus episcopus si omnes qui sunt in Appamiis infecti nunc de dicto crimine caperet, quia ibi plures erant quam mille ter," *Le régistre d'inquisition de Jacques Fournier, évêque de Pamiers*, ed. Jean Duvernoy (Toulouse, 1965), 3:32.

41. See, e.g., Kinsey et al., *Sexual Behavior in the Human Male*, "Social Level and Sexual Outlet"; Weinrich, pt. 1; see below, chap. 5, for further discussion.

by social class, only data to suggest that among the upper classes gay people are more apt to resist or ignore social sanctions against the sort of behavior to which they are inclined. Any form of unconventional behavior is usually more noticeable in a privileged class, since its members have less reason to fear censure or punishment and since their activities generally attract more attention than those of the masses.

In societies which have no taboos against homosexual behavior, however, such differential resistance to pressure would be irrelevant. Powerful prejudices against specific acts (especially oral intercourse) were known in the Mediterranean cities of antiquity, but these applied to both genders and to any combination thereof; they would have had no effect on homosexual behavior per se.

Evidence from these and other societies which tends to imply that homosexuality was the exclusive prerogative of the upper classes must be viewed with caution. Often such indications are the result of biased recording; vastly more evidence of every sort survives about the wealthy and powerful in ancient societies than about the poor and socially unimportant. This applies to heterosexuality, friendship, child rearing, religious sentiment, education, and personal finances—every aspect of life about which records tend to be personal and literary. Arguments about the nonexistence of such phenomena among the lower classes based exclusively on the silence of the sources must be rejected. There is no more reason to believe that homosexuality in Athens was limited to persons of Plato's social class than that friendship at Rome was known only to those of Cicero's rank. It is no more likely that only literate clerics experienced homosexual feelings in twelfth-century France than that only literate clerics felt delight at the approach of spring. These groups simply chanced to record their feelings, while lower-level groups did not.

Even more direct evidence must often be disregarded. A number of ancient and medieval commentators on gay sexuality specifically claimed that it is characteristic of the upper classes. Sometimes this was simply the result of the greater attention paid to the foibles of the powerful; sometimes it was mudslinging. Occasionally it was snobbery: in several debates about the relative merits of homosexuality and heterosexuality, the gay side claimed that gay sexuality is an aspect of aristocratic mores. Such claims were responses to the heterosexual charge that homosexuality is unknown among animals; the gay side argued that homosexual passions arise only among the wealthy classes with leisure to devise refinements of the baser biological drives. Neither of these assertions appears to be true, and there is no more reason to accept one than the other.

Moreover, there is a great deal of historical material suggesting that homosexuality was known among all classes. Many records of homosexual passion are not particularly literate. Vase paintings depicting homosexual eroticism may have been designed to please the wealthy,[42] but there is no reason to assume that this is true of the inscriptions of one male's love for another which are found all over the Mediterranean on such everyday objects as sling stones and roof tiles[43] or scribbled on the walls of temples and buildings from Athens to Pompeii.[44]

Nor do literary accounts themselves generally support the idea of exclusivity in such matters. Most (but not all) "lovers" in ancient literature are aristocratic. Even in upper-class literature, however, the objects of affection are very often of lesser social standing, frequently slaves and freedmen. Philostratus (*Epistles* 7) writes at length to a boy about the advantages of accepting as a lover a man who is not wealthy and powerful. Solon's proscription of love affairs between slaves and free youths would have been pointless if homosexuality were unknown or infrequent among the lower class. In Roman literature no class consciousness seems to intrude on erotic interests: emperors sleep with actors,[45] kings with soldiers, senators with slaves. Tacitus records an instance of the murder of the prefect of the city by his slave as a consequence of their rivalry in love for the same male prostitute.[46] Fiction of the time (e.g., the *Satyricon*) depicts gay people of every condition,

42. W. Klein (*Die griechischen Vasen mit Lieblingsinschriften* [Leipzig, 1898]) knew more than 550 vases with erotic inscriptions (some addressed to females) in Greek; Robinson and Fluck refined his research and included non-Attic vases as well. No substantial treatment of vases with erotic painting has appeared. The finest collection of Greek vases with depictions of homosexual eroticism on public display in the United States is that of the Boston Museum of Fine Arts. Most museums subtly disguise or do not exhibit such material (even in the Boston museum an unguent vase in the shape of the male genitalia has been turned to the wall so that its form is not recognizable and labeled—through reticence or ignorance— "Ascribed to the artist Priapos"). Vases of this sort were not limited to Hellas: for an Etruscan example, see Michael Grant, *Eros in Pompeii* (New York, 1975), p. 103.

43. See the list of such objects in Robinson and Fluck, p. 47.

44. These cover a very broad temporal expanse as well as a wide geographical distribution. The famous early Greek inscriptions at Thera (see *Corpus inscriptionum Graecarum*, vol. 12, fasc. 3, *Inscriptiones Graecae insularum*, ed. Friedrich Hiller von Gärtringen [Berlin, 1898], pp. 126ff.) scribbled on rocks outside the gymnasium range from discreet praise for another male's beauty to frank admissions of coitus. Those at Pompeii (see *Corpus inscriptionum Latinarum*, 4. *Inscriptiones parietariae Pompeianae*, ed. Karl Zangemeister [Berlin, 1871], and *Supplementum*, 2 [Berlin, 1909]) are nearly all praise of the sexual prowess of a local male ("Phoebus the perfume maker fucks excellently," no. 2184, taken as homosexual by virtue of no. 2194, q.v.), expressions of desire ("I want to fuck a male" ["Piidicarii volo"], no. 2210), or references to coitus effected near the spot ("Auctus fucked Quintius here," *Suppl.*, no. 4818). See also nos, 1882, 2176, 2185, 2188, 2192, 2193, 2247, 2253 (in Greek), 2254, 2357, etc.; and *Suppl.* nos. 3938, 4818, etc.

45. A despised group in most of the ancient world and indeed well into the present century.

46. *Annals* 14.42. Alternatively, Tacitus suggests, it may have been because the prefect would not allow the slave to buy his freedom.

and more serious analyses of sexuality and its manifestations never claim any class difference in the incidence of homosexual desire or behavior, even when they conclude that only the noble of birth or character will be capable of truly ideal relationships.[47] In Plutarch's dialogue "Beasts Are Rational" the porcine critic of human behavior notes that "there is a good deal of homosexuality among your brightest and best, not to mention the more common lot."[48]

Few classicists have doubted that homosexuality occupied a prominent and respected position in most Greek and Roman cities at all levels of society and among a substantial portion of the population. Indeed familiarity with the literature of antiquity raises one very perplexing problem for the scholar which will not have occurred to most persons unacquainted with the classics: whether the dichotomy suggested by the terms "homosexual" and "heterosexual" corresponds to any reality at all. Terms for these categories appear extremely rarely in ancient literature, which nonetheless contains abundant descriptions and accounts of homosexual and heterosexual activity. It is apparent that the majority of residents of the ancient world were unconscious of any such categories.

This fact is disturbing. How can a dichotomy so obvious to modern society, so morally troublesome, so urgent in the lives of many individuals, have been unknown in societies where homosexual behavior was even more familiar than it is today? It is not as if indifference in sexual matters produced a general dearth of distinctions about erotic interests. Most other terms for sexual acts or predilections are in fact based on distinctions recognized and named in Greece or Rome ("pedophilia," "narcissism," "incest," "fellatio," etc.).[49]

47. Neither should one make the mistake of imagining that the poorer classes in the ancient world viewed their social superiors in the same way that the poor in modern industrial societies view the rich. Where some connection was assumed between superior status and superior character; where only the prosperous were educated, only they could vote, they alone regulated religious functions, only they supported and protected the poor and needy; and where the rich and powerful controlled a very large proportion of the lower classes directly (slaves) or indirectly (clients), the attitudes of the wealthy were enormously more important in determining public opinion than they would be in modern states.

48. Plutarch "Bruta animalia," *Moralia* 990D: "῞Οθεν οὔτ᾽ ἄρρενος πρὸς ἄρρεν οὔτε θήλεος πρὸς θῆλυ μῖξιν αἱ τῶν θηρίων ἐπιθυμίαι μέχρι γε νῦν ἐνηνόχασιν. ὑμῶν δὲ πολλὰ τοιαῦτα τῶν σεμνῶν καὶ ἀγαθῶν· ἐῶ γὰρ τοὺς οὐδενὸς ἀξίους."

49. With the notable exception of the term "sadomasochism," a dichotomy which might seem to be parallel to that of homosexuality/heterosexuality. But few people imagine that everyone is *either* a sadist or a masochist, whereas the general presumption in the modern West is that everyone is either homosexual, heterosexual, or a combination of both. It is not imagined, as in the case of sadism/masochism, that most people would fit in neither category.

The answer to this question appears to relate less to the incidence or reality of homosexuality than to the perception of it. Awareness of grounds of distinction appears to follow on the desire to distinguish. The issue of who is "black" or "colored" or "mulatto" is only vexing to societies affected by racial prejudice; such differentiations, if present, are much looser in cultures not concerned to categorize people by skin color. To non-Christians, the standard Christian division of the world's religions into Christian and non-Christian must seem pointless and silly: why not categorize religions on the basis of some other criterion (e.g., mono- or polytheistic, mystical or theological, eschatological or present-oriented)? Majorities, in other words, create minorities, in one very real sense, by deciding to categorize them. Left-handed people may be statistically less numerous in all human societies, but they are really a minority only where manual preference takes on social significance and people make it their business to categorize their countrymen on that basis.

In the ancient world so few people cared to categorize their contemporaries on the basis of the gender to which they were erotically attracted that no dichotomy to express this distinction was in common use. People were thought of as "chaste" or "unchaste," "romantic" or "unromantic," "married" or "single," even "active" or "passive," but no one thought it useful or important to distinguish on the basis of genders alone, and the categories "homosexual" and "heterosexual" simply did not intrude on the consciousness of most Greeks or—as will be seen—Romans.

Why some societies make invidious distinctions on the basis of race, religious belief, sexual preference, or other personal idiosyncrasies while others do not is a complex matter still awaiting elucidation. The following study is intended to make a small contribution in that direction.

3 Rome:

The Foundation

In a now famous remark, Edward Gibbon observed that "of the first fifteen⭐ emperors Claudius was the only one whose taste in love was entirely correct," meaning heterosexual.[1] If Gibbon was right,[2] the Roman Empire was ruled for almost 200 consecutive years by men whose homosexual interests, if not exclusive, were sufficiently noteworthy to be recorded for posterity.

Homosexuality and attitudes toward it among the Romans—unlike their counterparts among Greeks—have not received comprehensive scholarly attention.[3] This is due in part to the extreme diffusion of material on the

---

1. "But," added W. C. Firebaugh, "Claudius was a moron" (*The Satyricon of Petronius Arbiter* [New York, 1966], p. 228). In the 1789 edition of Gibbon's *History of the Decline and Fall of the Roman Empire*, the observation is made in 1:78, n. 40. In the more common version edited by Dean Milman, M. Guizot, and W. Smith (London, 1898), it is in 1:313, n. 40. The comment occurs in connection with Hadrian's love for Antinous and clearly refers to homosexuality.

2. If Gibbon intended Julius Caesar to be understood as the first emperor, he was certainly correct; if not, I am curious as to what evidence he had about Antoninus Pius, who is fifteenth in the usual reckoning.

3. Of the many studies in print concerning Roman social life and mores, none can be recommended without severe reservations regarding their treatment of gay people. Otto Kiefer's *Sexual Life in Ancient Rome* (London, 1934; translated from the German, *Kulturgeschichte Roms unter besonderer Berücksichtigung der römischen Sitten*) is particularly inaccurate and misinformed, despite its apparent popularity and constant reprinting. The discussions of Rome in the few general histories of homosexuality are useless: it will suffice here to cite Bullough's opinion that "a general denunciation of such 'immorality' [i.e., homosexuality] is a constant theme of Roman literature" (p. 151) and his invocation, as proof, of the authority of "Suidas" and Gibbon (p. 137). F. C. Forberg's *De figuris veneris*, anonymously translated into English as *The Manual of Classical Erotology* (privately printed 1844; reprint ed., New York, 1966), collects many Latin passages dealing with less common aspects of Roman sexuality but is, especially in the English version, inaccurate in citation and detail and provides no analysis or insight. A. E. Housman's brief "Praefanda," *Hermes* 66 (1931) 402–12 (reprinted in *The Classical Papers of A. E. Housman*, ed. J. Diggle and F. R. D. Goodyear, vol. 3, *1915–1936* [Cambridge, Eng., 1972], pp. 1175–84) is in the same anecdotal vein, though more accurate and sophisticated. The appendix on Rome at the end of Meier/de Pogey-Castries is accurate, if brief. A few articles may be recommended with enthusiasm. Among these the most general is Wilhelm Kroll's "Römische Erotik,"

61

subject. With the exception of Hellenistic debates (see chap. 5), no single republican or imperial writer treated gay sexuality in an analytical way. References to it are ubiquitous but matter-of-fact, and hence extremely difficult to compile and interpret. This chapter will attempt only to provide an introductory acquaintance with Roman attitudes and practices; even more than other chapters, it should be considered provocative rather than definitive.

Since Romans were extraordinarily dispassionate about sexuality,[4] Latin writers were under no pressure either to idealize or to suppress accounts of homosexual passion, and Latin literature provides an unusually valuable source of information about gay people and gayness in a cultural setting which included little if any intolerance of them. Unfortunately, most people have access to this data only as filtered through the alembic of the distinct prejudices of modern historians. Its value is thus vitiated, if not wholly

---

Zeitschrift für Sexualwissenschaft und Sexualpolitik 17, no. 3 (1930–31): 145–78; his *Kultur der Ciceronischen Zeit* (Leipzig, 1933), pp. 177ff., is also excellent but more limited. Jasper Griffin's "Augustan Poetry and the Life of Luxury," *Journal of Roman Studies* 66 (1976): 87–105, is outstanding as far as it goes, although the author's conclusions differ from my own in regard to the *Lex Scantinia* (cf. below). An excellent discussion of Roman sexuality and morality, as well as the family and the general position of women, is available in Sarah Pomeroy, *Goddesses, Whores, Wives, and Slaves: Women in Classical Antiquity* (New York, 1975).

4. Sexual (as opposed to romantic) issues for Romans were primarily proprietary: Romans were concerned to see that their rights over their spouses and children (of either sex) were not violated, that their offspring married into situations which enhanced their prestige (or wealth), and that they themselves avoided any overt violations of the rights of others which might be unjust (or incur retribution). Apart from these simple, if compelling, interests, Roman sexuality was virtually untrammeled. Proven adultery was theoretically a hazard even for the powerful, but Latin literature abounds with accounts and accusations of infidelity. Most such cases clearly went unpunished; some took place with the connivance of the spouse. Marriage for the upper classes was largely dynastic, political, and economic; it was arranged, at least for females, by the father and often could be dissolved by him. Amicable divorce was common. For the lower classes practical considerations also constituted the principal issue in deciding upon marriage: propinquity, financial feasibility, family wishes, etc., were paramount. Among no group of people would concepts of romantic love parallel to those common today have been the operative factors in arranging marriage: "love" between husband and wife was something expected to develop as a consequence of marriage, not to occasion it. It consisted of fair treatment, respect, and mutual consideration and often corresponded more to paternal affections in the modern world (e.g., Catullus 72: "Dilexi tum te non tantum ut vulgus amicam/Sed pater ut natos diligit et generos . . . "); age differences may have contributed to this. The concept of "fidelity" applied only to married or marriageable women, since only in their case was legitimate succession—and hence proprietary interest—inevitably involved. For males of any social class sexual morality was largely personal and ranged from severe asceticism to extreme promiscuity. Wives often encouraged husbands to employ slaves (of either gender) for sexual release, and the attitude of Antony on the subject of heterosexual relations is probably typical of Roman males: in a letter to Augustus (who, like Antony himself, was married at the time) he asked, "Can it matter where or in whom you put it?" (Suetonius *Augustus* 69: "An refert, ubi et in qua arrigas?"; cf. Martial 11.20).

negated, and before beginning a fresh analysis the first order of business must be to discuss at least two major distortions which modern historiography has foisted on the public.

The first of these regards the legality of homosexual practices in Rome. One might suppose that this would be a matter of little uncertainty, considering the organization and legal sophistication of the Roman state and the considerable scholarship which has been devoted to studying Roman law during recent centuries. In fact, however, the issue is clouded by great uncertainty, despite the fact that it would be rather a simple matter to collect the known texts which relate to the legality of homosexual acts.[5]

Valerius Maximus, writing in the first half of the first century A.D., mentions a number of cases of criminal prosecutions for sexual crimes under the Republic. At least six of these involve homosexual relations (6.1.6,7,9–12; cf. 1.5), and this fact has sometimes been used as evidence for the illegality of such acts in Republican Rome. Such a conclusion is unjustified. The incidents involved are listed among and interspersed with accounts of heterosexual "crimes," and no distinction is suggested between the two.[6] The common theme of all the cases is abuse of a free-born Roman citizen; gender is irrelevant. As Valerius himself observes, the senate "wished chastity to be safe in Roman blood in whatever position it might be placed."[7] In each of the incidents which are clearly homosexual, the defendant is either an adult who tried to assault or seduce the minor son of a Roman citizen or a civil or military official who attempted to force a subordinate to gratify him.[8]

The most celebrated of the cases involved a young soldier in the army of Gaius Marius who killed a tribune when the latter tried to coerce him into a sexual relation.[9] There was no question about the reason for the slaying, but

5. The specific issue of Roman law and homosexual behavior has been discussed in detail by Bailey, pp. 64–66, and more recently by Jérome Bernay-Vilbert in "La répression de l'homosexualité dans la Rome antique," *Arcadie: revue littéraire et scientifique* 250 (October 1974): 443–56. My conclusions differ markedly from those of Bailey and only slightly less from those of Bernay-Vilbert, both of whom assume greater certainty about the *Lex Scantinia* than seems to me justified, although both admit an "aura of uncertainty" surrounding it. Cf. Griffin's sensible views.

6. Note that in 6.1.8 a man is prosecuted simply for the *intention* of seducing a free-born woman.

7. "In qualicumque enim statu positam Romano sanguini pudicitiam tutam esse uoluit," 6.1.9.

8. 6.1.7 (the case of C. Scantinius Capitolinus) is mentioned below, as is 6.1.9; 6.1.10 recounts the prosecution of a decorated veteran who had "defiled" a free-born youth ("ingenuus adulescentulus"); 6.1.11 is the case of a tribune who attempted to seduce a subordinate and was condemned because "he had tried to corrupt the virtue of someone for whom he should have been setting an example."

9. 6.1.12. The same story is told in Plutarch *Life of Gaius Marius* 14.3–5, and Quintilian *Declamationes maiores* 3, 3B; a somewhat garbled version appears in Dionysius of Halicarnassus 16.4.8 (the obvious borrowing from Valerius Maximus in the section immediately

the youth was brought to trial and had to prove that he had not previously accepted favors from the tribune or accepted the advances of others. Plutarch states that not a single witness would testify on behalf of the soldier (*Marius* 14.5). Even when a complete lack of complicity had been established, there was considerable question about the right of a subordinate to slay a superior who sexually abused him; Marius's decision to acquit the youth became famous, and the popularity of the story among Roman writers is evidence of the wonder it inspired.[10] (It was not until several centuries later that Roman law unequivocally upheld the right of a male to kill to defend himself from sexual violence: *Digest* 48.8.1.4 [rescript of Hadrian].)

In no account is it stated that a sexual liaison between males was itself illegal, and the suggestion that the tribune could rightly have coerced him if the soldier had ever accepted advances in the past would seem to exclude this possibility categorically. Livy recounts a remarkably similar story about a barbarian queen who slew the Roman centurion assigned to guard her when he assaulted her sexually (38.24). The suggestion is not that heterosexual practices were considered reprehensible but that sexual assaults on the unwilling invited retribution from either the victim or the state.

Another famous case involved a young Roman enslaved for debt and cruelly beaten by his master when he would not submit to the latter's advances.[11] A near riot ensued when his mistreatment became known, and a special session of the senate had to be convened. The legislation enacted as a result of the incident, however, had nothing to do with sexuality; it prohibited the enslavement of Roman citizens for debt. In each of the accounts of this case, the Roman populace was stirred to anger not by learning that

---

following makes it unlikely that this passage is independent). The date and authorship of the *Declamationes* are uncertain. Quintilian wrote at the end of the first century A.D.; the *Declamationes* may be as late as the fourth century, although it is not clear that no part of them is due to Quintilian. It is a great pity that they cannot be dated even approximately, since they contain a good deal of material for assessing attitudes toward the sexual offenses involved in the case. The author of 3 emphasizes the inopportune timing of the tribune, who decided to satisfy his desires at the moment of battle (3.6), the potential hazards for military discipline if superiors were allowed to command their subordinates to comply in such matters (3.16–17), and the glory which would accrue to Marius if he upheld the innocence of the soldier against the tribune, who was a relative of his (3.18). The writer of 3B considers the charge against the tribune to have been trumped up, and his prosecution implies very strongly that only force is reprehensible in such cases ("Miles armatus erat et fortior, et ei vim irrogare tribunus voluit imbecillis?").

10. E.g., [Quintilian]: "Suum quisque habeat fortasse judicium: mea sententia non satis pudicus est miles qui armatus tantum negat." Many apparently felt that Marius's blood relation to the tribune required him to avenge his death regardless of the circumstances. His failure to do so no doubt heightened the controversy about the events.

11. Valerius Maximus, 6.1.9; Livy, 8.28; Dionysius of Halicarnassus, 16.9 (doubtless derived from Valerius Maximus). The incident took place in the fourth century B.C.

the master had any sexual interest in the boy but by seeing the whip marks on the back of a Roman citizen;[12] it was clearly the physical abuse of a citizen which invited retribution.[13]

Moreover, when Calidius Bonboniensis, a man of no rank or family connections, was caught in the room with a married woman at night, his fate as an adulterer seemed sealed: "The place was suspicious, the hour was suspicious, the woman herself was suspect, and his own youthfulness was incriminating" (Valerius Maximus 8.1.12).[14] But he got off scot-free by claiming that he was in the room "on account of his passion for a slave boy."[15] Thus "his confession of overwhelming desire freed him from any suspicion of crime."[16] If homosexual relations themselves had been illegal, it hardly seems likely that Bonboniensis would have clung to his story, as Valerius observes, like a shipwrecked man clinging to a plank,[17] or that the judges would have acquitted him entirely.

Indeed, in one case reported by Valerius Maximus (6.1.10), the accused freely admitted that he had committed a homosexual act, asserting that no crime had occurred, since the youth involved was a prostitute; obviously it was not the gender of the parties which rendered an act questionable.[18]

The only law which might have regulated any homosexual practices in the Republic or under the early emperors was the *Lex Sca[n]tinia*, probably enacted around 226 B.C.[19] No text of this law survives, and it is impossible to conclude with any certainty what it regulated. It has hitherto been assumed by most authorities to have prohibited homosexual behavior, on the basis of some or all of the following considerations: (1) Both Plutarch[20] and Valerius Maximus (5.1.7) record an incident involving one C. Scantinius Capitolinus who made lewd advances to the son of M. Claudius Marcellus; it is supposed

12. Livy comments, "Et cum consules tumultu repentino coacti senatum vocarent, introentibus in curiam patribus lacertum iuvenis tergum, procumbentes ad singulorum pedes, ostentabant" ("And when the consuls, constrained by the sudden uproar, convened the senate, [the mob] threw themselves at the feet of each of the senators entering the curia and pointed to the lacerated back of the youth"), 8.28.7.

13. Livy, the better authority, mentions no penalty inflicted on the master; Valerius Maximus (and hence Dionysius) states that he was imprisoned.

14. "Suspectus erat locus, suspectum tempus, suspecta matris familiae persona, suspecta etiam adulescentia ipsius."

15. "Adfirmat enim se ob amorem pueri servi eo esse perductum."

16. "Crimen libidinis confessio intemperantiae liberauit."

17. "Tamquam fragmentum naufragii leue admodum genus defensionis amplexus."

18. The man died in prison, but his conviction had nothing to do with homosexuality: "Non putarunt enim tribuni pl[ebis] rem publicam nostram cum fortibus uiris pacisci oportere, ut externis periculis domesticas delicias emerent."

19. So little is known about this law that even the proper spelling is disputed. "Scantinia" is preferred, but "Scatinia" occurs.

20. *Life of Marcellus* 2.

that from the prosecution of this case the law in question arose; (2) in a passage relating to sexual license, Suetonius observes that the emperor Domitian "sentenced certain members of both orders under the Scantinian law" (*Domitian* 8);[21] (3) Quintilian refers to a legal penalty involved in a homosexual offense of his day (*Institutiones oratoriae* 6.2.69);[22] (4) Juvenal specifically associated the Scantinian law with homosexual practices, and although he described it as "sleeping," he described the *Lex Julia de adulteriis coercendis* in the same way, implying that it was in effect, if not enforced vigorously (2.44); (5) Sextus Empiricus stated categorically that homosexual activity (ἀρρενομιξία) was forbidden by law among the Romans (*Outlines of Pyrrhonism* 1.152); (6) Saint Cyprian and other Christian writers of the later Empire refer to homosexual activity as a "crime."

As regards these points, the following must be observed:

1. There is absolutely no demonstrable connection between the case mentioned by Plutarch and Valerius Maximus and the mysterious *Lex Scantinia*. Neither makes any such connection, and the two disagree on such important matters as the rank of Scantinius himself.[23] It is, moreover, extremely unlikely that a law outlawing a practice would bear the name of a notorious *defendant* in such a case.[24]

If there were a connection between this incident and the *Lex Scantinia*, the latter's provisions would certainly have applied to the attempted seduction of minors—the issue in question—but it is virtually certain that no such law existed under the Empire, since the *Lex Julia de adulteriis* later had to be extended to cover such cases.

2. Nothing in Suetonius's remark about Domitian's proscription suggests that the crime was related to homosexuality. Comments in the *Epigrams* of Martial, if taken to apply to Domitian's use of the *Lex Scantinia*, would tend

21. "Quosdam ex utroque ordine lege Scantinia condemnauit." There is absolutely no justification for the misleading translation of this offered by Robert Graves, who renders it "and sentenced many members of both Orders under the Scantinian Law, which was directed against unnatural practices" (*The Twelve Caesars* [London, 1957], p. 300). Even if "quosdam" could properly be translated "many" (which is doubtful), the clause beginning "which" is wholly the product of Graves's imagination.

22. "Ingenuum stuprauit et stupratus se suspendit, non tamen ideo stuprator capite ut causa mortis punietur, sed decem milia, quae poena stupratori constituta est, dabit." Cf. 7.4.42, where the issue of the stuprator's responsibility for the youth's death seems less certain.

23. Valerius Maximus calls him a tribune of the plebs; Plutarch designates him co-aedile. The name of the law may not even be the same as the name of the man, depending on which is the proper spelling.

24. Roman laws were named after the proposer of the law. Plutarch describes in detail the process brought by Marcellus and what he did with the money awarded him by the senate as damages, but he does not mention any legislation connected with the case. The argument that Scantinius may have proposed the law himself to clear his family name is purely conjectural, and without parallel in such cases.

to suggest that it protected minor and infant males from involuntary prostitution or castration (e.g., 9.6, 8),[25] but it is not credible that Domitian could have desired or would have been able to prosecute anyone for homosexual relations. A prominent ex-praetor, Claudius Pollio, possessed and displayed a letter in Domitian's own handwriting containing an offer to engage in homosexual acts with him (Suetonius *Domitian* 1),[26] and Martial (and others) published poems describing the emperor's homosexual relationship with the boy Earinos in volumes intended to flatter him (Martial 9.11–13, 16, 36).[27]

3. The case referred to by Quintilian is almost certainly one of rape (it is hard to imagine the boy's hanging himself if he had cooperated). The *Lex Scantinia* is not mentioned in the account, but if this is a reference to it, it is very good evidence that the law was aimed at the protection of minors, since the victim is specified as such.

4. Juvenal undermines his own credibility severely by implying that the Scantinian law was dormant, since it had in fact been invoked during his own lifetime on a large scale.[28] In any case, no inferences about the precise nature of the law could be drawn from his passing remark, since it occurs in a satire objurgating everything from cosmetics to gluttony. The immediately proximate complaint, the one which seems to elicit the demand for revival of the *Lex Scantinia*, is against a man's wearing perfume. As an example of "effeminacy," this would fit well with the conjecture that the law protected minor citizens from prostitution or castration, both perceived as emasculating. Homosexuality itself was not associated with "effeminacy" in males, as has been noted.

5. Sextus Empiricus, Athenian by birth and upbringing, was a physician, not an expert on Roman law, and claimed moreover that homosexual acts were against the law among Greeks as well, which they were not (*Outlines of Pyrrhonism* 3.199).[29]

6. There is no reason to believe that Cyprian, Prudentius, or any other Christians writing more than 400 years after the supposed passage of the *Lex Scantinia* had any greater knowledge of it than we now have. None of them

25. Castration of young male slaves was practiced on a very large scale by traders, to the disgust of many Romans, and may well have come under the provisions of the law by Domitian's time. Petronius has Eumolpus mockingly harangue against it (119), but genuine outrage of this sort is expressed by Seneca and others.

26. If this incident is untrustworthy on the sole authority of Suetonius, so is the reference to the *Lex Scantinia*, for the same reason.

27. In 6.39 Martial states categorically that it is not a crime for a father to have homosexual relations with his son ("Percide, si vis, filium: nefas non est"), but this is probably only a comment on the absolute powers of the paterfamilias.

28. By Domitian: point (2) above. It had also been invoked in Cicero's time by both parties in a dispute over money: *Epistulae ad familiares* 8.12.13, 14.4.

29. Cf. n. 30 below.

quotes it or specifies its contents, and it is mentioned in widely varying contexts. Furthermore, the majority of Christian comments about homosexual behavior among the Romans insist that it was not only legal but unanimously approved. Minucius Felix says that homosexual relations were "the Roman religion" (*Octavius* 28); Tatian that pederasty was held in "preeminent esteem by the Romans" (*Adversus Graecos* 28 ff.); Lactantius adds that Romans considered homosexual acts "trivial and virtually admirable." (*Institutiones divinae* 6.23.10). Clement of Alexandria states that in his day homosexual acts were legal among the Romans, although they had been prohibited "among the ancients" (*Paedagogus* 3.3 [PG, 8:585]).[30]

Of the few Latin writers who stigmatized homosexuality, none maintained that it was illegal. Most who objected, like Cornelius Nepos (Praef. 4 [Rolfe, p. 369]), described it as dishonorable ("partim humilia atque ab honestate remota") or shameful, and a few called it "criminal," but only metaphorically: no one invoked the authority of law to condemn it.[31]

It is hardly possible, in fact, that homosexual relations could have been illegal in the later Republic. Cato made a public speech complaining that in his day (second century B.C.) the value of male prostitutes exceeded that of farm lands (Polybius 31.25). He did not suggest that anything illegal was involved in the purchase of males for sexual relations but simply implied that the disparity in price between such concubines and farms constituted a serious economic disproportion.[32]

The former consul Lucius Quinctius Flamininus was expelled from the senate in 184 B.C.—only forty years after the enactment of the mysterious *Lex Scantinia*—for having someone murdered at a banquet to entertain his lover. Two versions of the story survive: in one, the lover is a male prostitute of noble birth (Livy 39.42.5 ff.); in the other, a female courtesan.[33] Livy

---

30. "Ταῦτα οἱ σοφοὶ τῶν νόμων ἐπιτρέπουσιν· ἔξεστιν αὐτοῖς ἁμαρτεῖν κατὰ νόμων." Like Sextus Empiricus, Clement was probably Athenian, and faith in his veracity on this point must be tempered by his rather fanciful understanding of the practice of "the ancient Roman lawmakers," who he thought buried those guilty of homosexuality alive ("ἀνδρόγυνον ἐμίσησαν ἐπιτήδευσιν οὗτοι, καὶ τοῦ σώματος τὴν πρὸς τὸ θῆλυ κοινωνίαν παρὰ τὸν τῆς φύσεως νόμον ὀρύγματος κατηξίωσαν κατὰ τὸν τῆς δικαιοσύνης νόμον," ibid.). Patristic Greek used "ἀνδρόγυνος" more frequently in the sense of "effeminate" than in its original sense of "hermaphrodite." This may have led Clement to conflate "hermaphrodite," "effeminate," and "homosexual" (such inaccuracy would hardly be unique among those hostile to homosexuality) and to confuse the Roman harshness in dealing with children born as hermaphrodites, which were regarded as evil omens (see Livy 31.12), with Roman attitudes toward homosexual persons or acts.

31. Except possibly Juvenal; see below.

32. He compares it directly with the disproportion between the cost of a jar of caviar and that of a plowman, suggesting that male prostitutes were a legal luxury like caviar.

33. Ibid. 43.1ff., and in Valerius Maximus 2.9.3. Cf. Cicero *Cato Maior* 42. Theoretically Livy's phrase could mean "notorious prostitute" rather than "noble," since in his time

observes that the two versions are "alike in lust and cruelty." Nothing in his comments on the homosexual relationship implies that it was illegal. Valerius Maximus, writing after him, used only the heterosexual version. It is extremely unlikely that subsequent recorders of Flamininus's misdeeds would fail to mention an accusation of homosexuality certainly known to them if such behavior in itself constituted a violation of Roman law.[34]

Indeed, if there was a law against homosexual relations, no one in Cicero's day knew anything about it, including Cicero himself, whose knowledge of Roman law was exhaustive. Catiline's lover—a consul—interceded for him with Cicero,[35] and Sulla publicly flaunted his affair with Metrobios.[36] Cicero himself, notoriously upright, persuaded Curio the Elder to honor the debts his son had incurred on behalf of Antonius, to whom the younger Curio was, in Cicero's words, "united in a stable and permanent marriage, just as if he had given him a matron's *stola*."[37] Although the father objected to the relationship, there was no intimation of illegality, and Cicero himself seems to have considered paying off the debts the only legal course of action.

Cicero ridicules several prominent male citizens as having been prostitutes in their youth[38] but never suggests that such activity was illegal, and in defending Cnaeus Plancius from the charge that he had taken a male lover into the country to have sex with him, Cicero states categorically that "this is not a crime."[39]

There is, on the other hand, no doubt that Cicero was familiar with the *Lex Scantinia*,[40] whatever it was, and the only conclusion would seem to be that this law did not prohibit homosexual relations.

Nor does it seem that any law did so. Tacitus considers it irrelevant whether the slave of the prefect Pedanius Secundus murdered his master as a result of a homosexual love triangle in which both were involved or as a consequence of the master's having refused to let the slave buy his freedom

---

nobilis meant both "well born" and "well known," but a similar usage in Valerius Maximus (9.1.8), where *nobilis* must mean "noble," argues for this meaning here as well.

34. Clearly only Flamininus's cruelty was against the law and worthy of censure. Livy specifies that "whichever way it occurred," the murder was "savage and horrible," and it was for this reason alone that the consul was expelled (39.43.4–5).

35. *Post reditum in senatu* 4, "Alter a me Catilinam, amatorem suum, multis audientibus, . . . reposcebat."

36. See, e.g., Plutarch *Life of Sulla* 2, 36.

37. *Philippic*, 2.18.45: "Te a meretricio quaestu abduxit et, tamquam stolam dedisset, in matrimonio stabili et certo collocavit." The *stola* was the distinctive garb of a married Roman woman.

38. E.g., Antonius and the tribune Gabinus, *Post reditum* 5; cf. *Pro Sestio* 8.

39. *Pro Cnaeo Plancio* 12.30, "Quod non crimen est."

40. *Epistulae ad familiares* 8.12.3, 14.4. The tone in which Caelius mentions to Cicero his own prosecution under this law makes it appear that its provisions were considered trivial.

(14.42).[41] In the debate in the senate over whether to punish the other household slaves for not having prevented the crime, there is not a hint that the situation which led to the murder was in any way illegal or even shameful: on the contrary, some of those present argued that the slave/murderer might have been justified in killing his master if the latter had tried to take away his lover (14.43).[42]

Homosexual acts could hardly have been illegal in Augustan Rome, where the government not only taxed homosexual prostitution[43] but accorded boy prostitutes a legal holiday;[44] and it is virtually impossible to imagine any law regulating homosexual activities in the Rome in which Martial wrote: not only does he mention by name numerous prominent citizens having homosexual affairs, often listing their partners, but he frankly admits to engaging in such activities himself. (That some of his epigrams were designed to please the emperor and that he made his living by selling his books argue almost irresistibly against a double standard in the matter between public and private mores.)[45]

A second-century complaint against a provincial official describes in detail his liaison with a seventeen-year-old boy. The official obviously made no effort whatever to disguise the nature of this relationship, even from the boy's father, who apparently approved, and there is no suggestion in the document that the relationship was in any way illegal; the complaint is against the favoritism shown the boy as a result of the official's interest (*Oxyrhynchus papyri* 147).[46]

Moreover, the rise of Roman legal actions against homosexual behavior can be dated precisely to the third century A.D., when a series of laws was

41. "Seu negata libertate cui pretium pepigerat, siue amore exoleti incensus et dominum aemulum non tolerans."

42. "An, ut quidam fingere non erubescunt, iniurias suas ultus est interfector, quia de paterna pecunia transegerat aut auitum mancipium detrahebatur?"

43. This tax was collected by all emperors, Christian and non-Christian, well into the sixth century. That it guaranteed the legality of homosexual relations—at least with prostitutes—is stated explicitly by Lampridius for the West (*Historia Augusta, Elagabalus* 32.5–6) and Evagrius for the East (*Ecclesiastical History*, PG, 86: 2680).

44. *Corpus inscriptionum Latinarum*, 1.2.236 (A.D. 6–9); cited by Griffin, p. 102.

45. Martial disclaims his books as an accurate representation of his own morals (1.4, 11.15; but cf. 12.65, etc.), but his anxiety to protect his reputation is certainly related to the instances of dishonesty and fraud in his works rather than his sexual proclivities.

46. "'Ημεῖς δ' οὐκ εἰληφέναι σε μισθὸν [ἀλλὰ δε]δωκέναι φαμέν." The exact objections of the plaintiffs to the relationship are not perfectly clear. The favors to the boy are juxtaposed with the prefect's niggardliness to others, especially the poor, and the boy's own behavior is regarded as shameful; but considering that the document was effected under the reign of Hadrian (see below) or shortly after, it is scarcely credible that any derogation of homosexual activities in general would be included in what appears to be a complaint to the emperor. The whole affair is highly reminiscent of heterosexual political scandals in the modern West.

enacted regulating various aspects of homosexual relations, ranging from the statutory rape of minors to gay marriages.[47] Not only would such laws have been superfluous if homosexual relations were already illegal, but it is certain that homosexual acts not covered by the particular laws in question remained legal until the sixth century, when by all accounts homosexual relations were categorically prohibited by Roman law for the first time.[48]

The second major distortion in modern treatments of Roman homosexuality is the idea that tolerance of or indifference toward homosexual practices was associated with the decline of Rome. Several varieties of this theory exist, some claiming that it was homosexuality and general immorality which *caused* the decline of Rome, others that such sexual license was a concomitant of imperial decadence. All are agreed that under the democratic and robust days of the Republic no such moral decadence was tolerated.

The only historical basis for these notions is the relatively greater occurrence of references to homosexual behavior in imperial than in republican literature. Information about almost every single aspect of Roman life survives in greater abundance from the Empire than from the Republic. It cannot be shown that *proportionally* more evidence survives from imperial than republican Rome regarding gay people and acts. Moreover, if one wished to compare the *quality* of such testimony, several of the preimperial sources (e.g., Polybius, Cicero) are far more reliable than most of the later ones (e.g., Lampridius, Suetonius).

It is characteristic of economically complex and socially sophisticated societies to remember their humble origins nostalgically or to envy the simpler life of country dwellers; this tendency is observable in almost every urban society from ninth-century Baghdad to twentieth-century America. Romans writing under the Empire often indulged in such feelings regarding the smaller and simpler Rome of the Republic and imagined that it had been a time of "purity" in politics and personal morality. Ignoring the fact that such ideas and claims are a commonplace of urban literature, even conscientious historians have frequently echoed this sentiment and painted the Republic as a time of strict sexual mores and rigid concepts of decency, as contrasted with the hedonism and moral anarchy of the Empire. This

47. On the statutory rape of minors, consult *Digest* 47.11.1.2; 48.5.6.1, 34.1; 50.16.101. This material is discussed by Bailey (pp. 68–70), but he fails to grasp the significance of the facts he presents (i.e., that extensions of the *Lex Julia de adulteriis coercendis* to protect freeborn boys would hardly be necessary if there were some law in effect against homosexual relations per se).

48. Procopius *Anecdota*, 11.34–36; Joannes Malalas *Chronographia* 18.168; Justinian *Institutes* 4.18.4; Theophanes *Chronographia* A.C.521. Evagrius stated explicitly that homosexual relations were legal only a few years before, at the time Anastasius abolished the imperial tax on prostitution: see chap. 7.

picture is at variance with the facts. Indeed, insofar as it is due to a projection of the personal standards of imperial writers, it suggests, if anything, a tightening of morality under the Empire.

Although there were certainly changes under the Empire and probably a certain relaxation of hitherto more rigid ethical codes, most of these changes related to political integrity and public service. Very little change is evident in standards of personal morality, which continued to vary from the ascetic to the wildly self-indulgent. Marcus Aurelius was as chaste as Scipio Africanus, and many of the same activities satirized by the imperial writer Juvenal are described or implied by republican authors.

There is no change in the documents regarding homosexual activities. Homosexual behavior is recorded in the fourth century B.C. Polybius, a historian of rare objectivity and unparalleled reliability, records that during the heyday of the Republic—two centuries before the Empire—"moderation" in sexual matters was virtually impossible for young men in Rome, since nearly all of them were having affairs with courtesans or other young men. There is no hint of disapproval based on gender; what Polybius criticized was the fiscal extravagance of the "many men who have spent a talent [about $2,000] for a male lover or 300 drachmas for a jar of caviar from the Black Sea" (31.25.5).[49] Cicero mentions that the jurors in a famous case of his day were bribed with the favors of women and young men of noble lineage (*Letters to Atticus* 1.16.5).[50] Homosexual prostitution was common under the Republic, and Cicero states that Clodius always had a number of male prostitutes with him (*Pro Milone* 21 [55]; see also the case of L. Quinctius Flamininus above).[51] Writers of erotic literature during the Republic (e.g., Catullus) treat homosexual passion with absolute candor and complete moral indifference; and under Augustus, Vergil, Tibullus, Horace, and Ovid all speak of erotic love (or physical acts) between men without the slightest hint that such things might be suspect. When Lucretius writes of a man's love, it involves "either a boy . . . or a woman" (*De rerum natura* 4.1052–54).[52] Nowhere is there any indication that such passions or acts might be illegal or disapproved until the time of Juvenal—an imperial writer.

49. "Καὶ τηλικαύτη τις ἐνεπεπτώκει περὶ τὰ τοιαῦτα τῶν ἔργων ἀκρασία τοῖς νέοις ὥστε πολλοὺς μὲν ἐρώμενον ἠγορακέναι ταλάντου, πολλοὺς δὲ ταρίχου Ποντικοῦ κεράμιον τριακοσίων δραχμῶν." (Possibly it was just salt fish instead of caviar; the Greek is ambiguous.)

50. "Iam vero (o di boni, rem perditam!) etiam noctes certarum mulierum atque adulescentulorum nobilium introductiones non nullis iudicibus pro mercedis cumulo fuerunt." Cf. 1.18, where he suggests that such "introductions" led to something ("constuprato").

51. "Semper secum scorta, semper exoletos, semper lupas duceret."

52. "Sic igitur Veneris qui telis accipit ictus,/sive puer membris muliebribus hunc iaculatur/seu mulier toto iactans e corpore amorem . . . "

It is worth noting in this context that the period of greatest output of gay literature was not during the decay of the Empire at all—homosexual writings from the third century on became increasingly rare—but from the first two centuries of the Empire, when Rome was at the zenith of its power and prestige. Petronius, Juvenal, Martial, Plutarch (*Erotikos*), Achilles Tatius, Lucian, and many of the later Greek poets—all worked not in the collapsing Empire of the third and fourth centuries but in the thriving, vital Empire of the first and second, following the traditions of Vergil, Catullus, et al. who had written even earlier. By the time the Empire was clearly in decline, very little literature dealt with homosexual themes, and that which did—like the *Affairs of the Heart*—depicted a society in which tolerance of homosexuality was declining as rapidly as political stability.

In a sense, then, early imperial Rome may be viewed as the "base period" for social tolerance of gayness in the West. Neither the Roman religion nor Roman law recognized homosexual eroticism as distinct from—much less inferior to—heterosexual eroticism. Prejudices affecting sexual behavior, roles, or decorum generally affected all persons uniformly. Roman society almost unanimously assumed that adult males would be capable of, if not interested in, sexual relations with both sexes. It is extremely difficult to convey to modern audiences the absolute indifference of most Latin authors to the question of gender. Catullus writes of two male friends enamored of a Veronese brother and sister, "Caelius is crazy about Aufilenus and Quintius about Aufilena, the flower of Veronese youths—the former for the brother, the latter for the sister" (100)[53] and jokes with his friend Cato about surprising a boy and girl in the act of love, whereupon—"to please Venus"— he inserted himself into the boy (56).[54] Martial insists to his "wife"[55] that both homosexual and heterosexual outlets are necessary and that neither can replace the other ("You use your part, let the boys use theirs," 12.96, cf. 11.43) but generally betrays complete indifference as to the gender of the object of his attentions.[56] Of some fifty-five love letters by Philostratus, twenty-three

---

53. "Caelius Aufilenum et Quintius Aufilenam,/Flos Veronensum depereunt iuuenum,/ hic fratrem, ille sororem . . . ." When pressed to support one, Catullus opted for the gay couple. For a translation, see Peter Whigham, *The Poems of Catullus* (Berkeley, 1969), p. 212. Many editions of Catullus do not translate the homosexual verses; a recent Oxford school edition (trans. C. J. Fordyce, 1961) does not even print them. Whigham's is the only really accurate translation into English. Martial published a less refined comment on two brothers of different sexual persuasions (3.87).

54. Whigham translates, "Just now I found a young boy/stuffing his girl,/I rose, naturally, and/(with a nod to Venus)/fell and transfixed him there/with a good stiff prick, like his own."

55. Most scholars consider this term rhetorical: Martial was probably unmarried.

56. Epigrams illustrating the bisexuality of the time: 2.47, 62; 6.16, 54; 8.46, 73; 9.32, 56; 11 passim, esp. 45, 46. Cf. AP, bks. 5, 11.

are to males, thirty to females; the two groups are so similar in tone that some manuscripts reverse the genders of the addressees.[57]

Most imperial discussions of love juxtapose gay and nongay passions as equal sides of the same coin.[58]

> Zeus came as an eagle to god-like Ganymede, as a swan came he to the fair-haired mother of Helen.
> So there is no comparison between the two things; one person likes one, another likes the other; I like both.[59]

Nor were any exaggerated claims made for homosexual passion: it was not imagined to be the only noble form of love, and its adherents were not thought to possess any special genius.

This is certainly not to imply that there were no sexual prejudices or taboos in Roman society but simply that none was directly related to homosexual relations as a class. It is virtually impossible to speak with authority on Roman prejudices, however, since they so often occur in satirical or ironical contexts. For instance, what is one to make of Martial's satirizing someone for masturbation with traditional Stoic moral outrage (9.41: "What you are losing in your fingers, Ponticus, is a human being!") when he has casually admitted to masturbating himself in various other epigrams (e.g., 2.43, 11.73)? Obviously Stoics as well as Ponticus are the objects of ridicule, but neither Martial's own beliefs nor those of his contemporaries emerge clearly from evidence of this sort.

A very strong bias appears to have existed against passive sexual behavior on the part of an adult male citizen.[60] Noncitizen adults (e.g., foreigners, slaves) could engage in such behavior without loss of status, as could Roman youths, provided the relationship was voluntary and nonmercenary. Such persons might in fact considerably improve their position in life through liaisons of this type. But if an adult citizen openly indulged in such behavior, he was viewed with scorn. Apart from general questions of gender expectations and sexual differentiation, the major cause of this prejudice appears to have been a popular association of sexual passivity with political impotence. Those who most commonly played the passive role in intercourse were boys, women, and slaves—all persons excluded from the power structure. Often they did so under duress, economic or physical; and the idea that a Roman

57. See *Epistles*, ed. A. R. Benner and F. H. Fobes, in LC (Cambridge, Mass., 1949).

58. E.g., Horace *Epodes* 1.18, 70–75; Athenaeus 13.601–5.

59. AP, 1.65, trans. W. R. Paton.

60. An interesting instance of this prejudice is suggested by Livy's account of the Bacchanalian initiation rites, which were administered only to those under the age of twenty, "captari aetatis et erroris et stupri patientes" (39.13.14). The incident in question was supposed to have occurred in 186 B.C., but Livy recorded it a century and a half later.

citizen should be exploited in this way evoked a particular horror among Romans who prided themselves on their control of the world around them.[61] A male who voluntarily adopted the sexual role of the powerless partook of the inferior status they occupied.[62] He did not actually forfeit his position,[63] but he invited scorn in metaphorically abdicating the power and responsibility of citizenhood.

This prejudice is especially evident in the poetry of Catullus (d. 54 B.C.), who bragged at length about his conquests of boys as manly and praiseworthy but would threaten to perform the same act on an adult citizen as if doing so would subject his victim to the absolute depths of degradation and infamy.[64] Julius Caesar incurred considerable disrespect for his relations with Nicomedes, king of Bithynia, because he was widely rumored to have been passive. Suetonius says that Dolabella called Caesar "the queen's rival"; his partner in the consulship described him in an edict as "the queen of Bithynia"; his soldiers at the triumph held in honor of his conquest of Gaul chanted, "Caesar conquered Gaul; Nicomedes, Caesar"; Curio the Elder called him "every man's wife and every woman's husband" (*Julius* 49, 51–52).[65] In contrast, the charge that Augustus had *as a boy* submitted to Caesar in the same way seems never to have done him much harm (*Augustus* 68).

Under the early Empire, prejudice of this sort declined considerably, possibly because some emperors were known as or admitted to being passive.[66] Although Martial jibes at the passivity of some friends, they remain nonetheless friends, and there is no hint in Juvenal's satire on Virro that it is scandalous for an adult citizen to be employing an *active* prostitute.

Efforts were later made, however, not only to revive the prejudice but to enact it as law. It does not seem that they met with much success before the end of classical Roman civilization.[67] The emperor Elagabalus, known to

61. Accounts of homosexual rape of citizens were favorite themes of moral history, as evidenced in the stories told by Valerius Maximus. Legislation enacted under the later Empire against passivity on the part of citizens specifically exempted those who suffered violation by brigands or enemies (*Digest* 3.1.1.6: "Si quis tamen vi praedonum vel hostium stupratus est, non debet notari").

62. The attitude evinced toward Giton in Petronius's *Satyricon* by the men who fight over his favors is particularly revealing of this relationship.

63. By the third century there were legal penalties, but these seem to have been universally ignored.

64. See esp. 16 (cf. Martial 6.44). Catullus's poetry is a sociological gold mine; notable homoerotic poems are 15,16, 21, 24, 33, 56, 57, 81, and 100.

65. It is not important whether the charges were true: what is significant is the reaction of the populace. Cf. Catullus 57, where he characterizes Caesar as *cinaedus* and *pathicus*.

66. E.g., Caligula and Nero.

67. By the fifth century the Roman physician Caelius Aurelianus could remark that many people would find it hard to believe that passive males even existed (*Tardarum passionum* 4.9) and characterized their predilections as an inherited and incurable disease, although

prefer a passive role in intercourse himself, exiled the jurist who suggested a penalty for passive sexual behavior by citizens.

Many Roman writers stigmatize behavior which they consider inappropriate to the gender of the party under discussion, but such characterizations must be read with caution. Sexual-object choice is almost never the issue. Words translated as "effeminacy" imply "unmanliness" in the sense of weakness or self-indulgence rather than gender roles or sexual behavior. It was probably not the passivity of the *cinaedi*, for instance, which inspired hostility to them but, rather, their promiscuity and debauchery, which were taken as a sign of moral weakness. Many were apparently heterosexual.[68]

The Latin word "mollis" ("soft") was often used as a term of derogation, and it is frequently assumed that it refers to passivity or "effeminacy." Even where this is the most obvious inference, it is often not the correct one: Martial, who frequently does poke fun at the "effeminacy" of friends, uses the word in an epigram to describe Otho the emperor—who was indeed considered "effeminate" by contemporaries of Martial[69]—but the sense of the comment leaves no doubt that "mollis" refers to Otho's tendencies toward political pacifism rather than sexual passivity (6.32).[70]

Really gender-related concepts of decorum and behavior were, as in most cultures, dependent on cultural and temporal variables. New styles of clothing were often derogated as "effeminate,"[71] as were habits of grooming which were novel or extravagant. Such charges were leveled at obviously heterosexual persons as well as apparently gay ones, and it is clear that the stigma had no relation to sexual preference.[72]

---

elsewhere he alludes to active homosexual desires as perfectly normal and healthy (*Celerum vel acutarum passionum* 3.8: "Do not admit visitors, and particularly young women and boys. For the attractiveness of such visitors would again kindle the feeling of desire in the patient. Indeed even healthy persons, seeing them, would in many cases seek sexual gratification," Drabkin trans., p. 413). Apparently not catching the import of this passage, Drabkin erroneously labeled the discussion of passivity in men (and active desires in women) as referring to "homosexuality," as if the author regarded same-sex desires as generically unhealthy. The women in this section are manifestly not simply lesbian, since they indulge their "unhealthy" desires with men as well as women ("quod utrumque venerem exerceant, mulieribus magis quam viris").

68. See, e.g., Martial 7.58; Epictetus 3.1.32.

69. On Otho's "effeminacy," see Juvenal 2.99: "Ille tenet speculum pathici gestamen Othonis." Cf. Suetonius *Otho* 2.

70. Note that this word's supposed sexual connotations have misled translators of "μαλακός" as well; see below.

71. See, e.g., Aulus Gellius *Attic Nights* 6.12; the Elder Seneca *Controversiae* 1, praef. 8–10.

72. Indeed, the extreme inconsistency of many writers on such points renders their testimony valueless. Martial pillories as "effeminate" beauty and ugliness, slovenly appearance and fastidious vanity, body odor and perfumed scent, depilation and hairiness, smooth cheeks and beards—in short, any characteristic a person whom he dislikes may exhibit. Almost all Stoics objurgate shaving or depilating the body as "unnatural" and "effeminate":

On the other hand, a few writers do mock behavior which is strikingly like the inversions of gender expectations one occasionally encounters in modern gay subcultures. Martial, for instance, describes a lesbian who can outdrink and outeat any man, plays at male sports, wrestles, can lift heavier weights than a man, and who "puts it to" eleven girls a day (7.67).[73] Lucian portrays Megilla as shaving her head and boasting that she is "a man in every way" (*Dialogues of the Courtesans* 5.3).[74]

In addition to taboos regarding passivity, very strong opprobrium attached to male citizens who became prostitutes,[75] due to the facts that (1) prostitution represented the bottom level of a profession already viewed with disdain by well-born Romans, i.e., commerce; and (2) anyone—citizen or slave—could avail himself of the services of a prostitute. The prospect of a Roman citizen servicing a slave sexually and for money was certain to invite contempt and disgust.

No stigma whatever resulted from the use of such prostitutes, however, and Romans were free to prostitute anyone but minor citizens until the fourth century.[76] Very large numbers of prostitutes were recruited from the lower classes and among foreigners and slaves. They were highly visible, and prominent persons not only had recourse to but even fell in love with them. Both Tibullus (1.4, 8–9)[77] and Catullus (24, 48, 81, 99) were in love with prostitutes, as were the consul Flamininus and several emperors. Philostratus (*Epistles* 19) praises a boy prostitute as being like the stars, which belong to all, or the sun, which is a common blessing. Prostitution was taxed and provided a considerable revenue for the state. Male prostitutes had their own legal holiday. In addition to male brothels, male prostitutes frequented alleyways or the arches of buildings, where female prostitutes also plied their trade. Many public places in Rome were pickup locations for male and female prostitutes, and male prostitutes frequented the public baths to meet

---

see, e.g., the Elder Seneca 1, praef. 10; Epictetus 3.1.28 ff.; Seneca *Naturales quaestiones* 7.31.2, *Epistles* 47, 122; Aulus Gellius 3.6; Martial 2.62, 29; Juvenal 2.11–13. But none suggests that it was characteristic of gay males, and it was the notably gay emperor Hadrian who revived the custom of wearing a beard in the Roman world. Early Christians vehemently opposed shaving and depilation (see, e.g., Clement of Alexandria *Paedagogus* 3.3). Most historians ignore the moral and social significance attached to facial and body hair in the ancient and medieval world. A comprehensive study is badly needed.

73. Cf. below for lesbians in particular and for the caution with which accounts by male writers should be taken. These attitudes may reflect only the projections of Roman males.

74. "Τὸ πᾶν ἀνήρ εἰμι."

75. But note Valerius Maximus 9.1.8, and the case of Flamininus.

76. But cf. n. 25 above.

77. Discussed by Meier/de Pogey-Castries, pp. 192–93.

customers.[78] Colors and styles of clothing appear to have been used as symbols both for availability as prostitutes and for the role preferred.[79]

Owners of slaves could prostitute them or use them for their own sexual purposes.[80] There is reason to believe that many Roman gentlemen customarily employed a particular male slave for sexual release prior to marriage,[81] and the testimony of Latin literature makes clear that in the households of the wealthy large numbers of slaves were frequently employed sexually.[82] Martial even complains of a friend who will not lend his (male) slaves for this purpose (2.43).[83]

The rights and duties of freedmen in this regard are less clear. The Elder Seneca records a case (*Controversiae* 4) in which a freedman is criticized for being his patron's concubine,[84] but his lawyer responds that "sexual service is an offense for the free born, a necessity for the slave, and a duty for the freedman,"[85] thus giving rise to a spate of jokes on the order of "You aren't doing your 'duty' by me" and "He has become very 'dutiful' toward so-and-so."[86]

Although data for chronological analysis are wanting, it was probably under the early Empire that prostitution underwent its most elaborate development. In the early Republic the neuter word "scortum" had been

78. For meeting places, see Juvenal 9.22–24; and Martial 1.34, 62; 2.14. On the baths, see Petronius 92; and Martial 1.23, 96; 2.70; 11.47; 12.18.

79. Martial 1.96; Aulus Gellius 6.12.

80. This was clearly not regarded as adultery, at least for men. Scipio Africanus, noted for his moral probity, favored one of his female slaves, apparently with his wife's consent and approval (Pomeroy, p. 192). At least by the third century there were, however, laws against the use of force in obtaining sexual favors from slaves. Ulpian opines, "Sed et si serui pudicitia adtemptata sit, inuriarum locum habet" (*Digest* 47.10.9.4). A rescript of Pius had forbidden this in Baetica as early as the second century (ibid. 1.6.2), but there is no evidence that either law had much effect before the fourth century. On the subject of slavery in general at Rome, see Heinrich Chantraine, *Freigelassene und Sklaven im Dienst der römischen Kaiser* (Wiesbaden, 1967); Moses Finley, *Slavery in Classical Antiquity* (Cambridge, 1968); William W. Buckland, *The Roman Law of Slavery* (1908; reprint ed., Cambridge, 1970); et al.

81. Most specifically suggested by Catullus 61 ("Epithalamium") and Martial 8.44; cf. discussion in Symonds, "Notes on the Concubinus," app. E in Symonds and Ellis.

82. It would be impossible to catalog all the mentions of slaves used homosexually in classical literature. The single most useful source is Martial (esp. 1.58; 2.43; 5.46; 7.80; 8.52; 9.21, 22, 25, 59, 73; 10.66, 98; 11.23, 56, 70; 12.16, 17, 23, 64, 86); cf. Seneca *Epistles* 47.7, 95.24; the Elder Seneca 10.4.17; Horace *Satires* 1.2, 117; and the discussion following.

83. "Grex tuus Iliaco poterat certare cinaedo:/at mihi succurrit pro Ganymede manus."

84. I.e., the slave used for sexual release. It was doubtless the demeaning nature of this particular position which prompted the reproach and Haterius's qualification of the behavior as *inpudicitia*. Homosexuality per se was not a subject of controversy. (Objecting to a woman's being a concubine could hardly be construed as a comment on heterosexuality.)

85. "Inpudicitia in ingenuo crimen est, in servo necessitas, in liberto officium."

86. "Non facis mihi officium"; "multum ille huic in officiis versatur."

used to denote prostitutes of both genders, but by the first century A.D. Latin had developed distinctions of terminology corresponding to the discrimination of prostitutes according to gender, age, role played in intercourse, and various aspects of their persons. The most common distinction was between active and passive male prostitutes: *catamiti* were passive, *exoleti* active.[87] The development of the latter class signals the decline (though not the disappearance) of the earlier prejudice against adults playing the passive role in homosexual coitus. Several emperors were known to have favored *exoleti* (Nero and Elagabalus in particular).

Juvenal's ninth satire consists of a conversation with an active male prostitute (Naevolus) about the latter's client, Virro, who is extremely wealthy (and apparently a Roman citizen). Naevolus also services women, including Virro's wife,[88] and claims to have sired two children for him. He is bitter about Virro's niggardliness, and although Juvenal has fun at Naevolus's expense, the satire is mainly directed at his employer. There is no hint of outrage on the speaker's part at Naevolus's profession, and Juvenal assures him at one point that he should not fear for his job: "As long as these hills are still standing and sound, you will never lack a passive friend; they will come from everywhere, by carriage and ship" (130–32).[89]

Public hostility toward free males engaging in prostitution may also have declined at the beginning of the Christian era; Juventius, the prostitute loved by Catullus, came of a good family, and Augustus himself was rumored to

87. "Catamitus" is supposedly derived from "Γανυμήδης," the name of the Greek youth raped by Zeus. "Exoletus" is the past participle of "exolesco," "to grow up," "to come to maturity." That the "full-grown" should be considered generally active indicates some prejudice, ironic because they were presumably employed by other full-grown men. On the function of *exoleti*, see Lampridius 13.4, 26.4, 31.6; cf. Martial 12.91, etc.; Suetonius *Galba* 21; Meier/de Pogey-Castries, p. 195. Some confusion arises because several Latin authors use either term generically for "male prostitute" or even "concubine": e.g., the Elder Seneca 10.4.17; cf. Cicero *Pro Milone* 21 (55). The niceties of the distinction between types of prostitutes probably escaped those who did not actually avail themselves of their services. Many other terms indicate a similar distinction in function: e.g., "pueri," "cinaedi," "pathici" for passives; "drauci," "paedicatores," "glabri" for those playing an active role.

88. Cf. Martial 12.91.

89. "Ne trepida, numquam pathicus tibi derit amicus,/stantibus et salvis his collibus: undique ad illos/convenient et carpentis et navibus omnes. . . ." Few translations do justice to Juvenal's extremely colorful Latin. Peter Green's translation, *The Sixteen Satires* (Baltimore, 1967), is probably the best, although Green's attitude toward gay people and their sexuality is hostile or at least ill informed. In addition to referring to homosexual intercourse as "unnatural practices," he uses such terms as "fags," "queers," and "pansies" to render Latin terms of derogation for male prostitutes. While some of these terms do require a sense of opprobrium in their translation, the disapproval intended by Juvenal had nothing to do with the gender of the parties involved but only with peculiarities of the relationships. There was no word in Latin for "homosexual," and certainly none which corresponded to the epithets used in modern societies characterized by intense hostility to gay people.

have sold his favors to the governor-general of Spain (Suetonius *Augustus* 68). Tiberius had to take stringent measures to stop well-born women from taking up the trade (*Tiberius* 35).

Homosexual interest and the activities of the gay minority in Roman society occur everywhere in Latin literature. Large genital endowment among males elicits much more comment among Roman writers than unusual breast development in women,[90] and some of the sexual preferences of prominent citizens which were apparently common knowledge in their own day could not even have been committed to print in the West during most of the twentieth century.[91] Many emperors were believed or rumored to have obtained power by submitting to the advances of the preceding ruler (e.g., Augustus by gratifying Julius, Otho through his relationship with Nero, Hadrian because of Trajan's love for him).

On the other hand, it is eminently likely that the more extreme and sensational aspects of Roman sexuality were emphasized by writers like Suetonius precisely to make their works lively and exciting, and that the majority of Romans—gay or not—led lives of more restrained passions and activities. It would be quite wrong to imagine that Roman society in general tolerated sexual behavior which was viewed as harmful either to individuals or society. Slaves could, it is true, be exploited rather ruthlessly, but slavery and its attendant inhumanities have been characteristic of almost all Western societies, including extremely puritanical ones like the colonial Americas.

90. A play about a man obsessed with large penises was performed in Seneca's day (*Naturales quaestiones* 1.16). The main claim to fame of Juvenal's *exoletus* appears to have been his enormous proportions ("destiny lies in those parts which the clothes conceal," 9.32–6, 92). Martial wrote many epigrams on the subject of large penile development (e.g., "Your member is so long, Papylus, and your nose so big, that whenever you get it up you must be able to smell it!" 6.36; cf. 9.33; 10.55; 11.51, 63). Petronius relates an incident in a public bath where a crowd gathers around a particularly ample male and applauds (92; cf. Martial 9.33). The emperor Elagabalus is said to have sent out emissaries all over the Empire to seek out men "hung like mules" ("onobeloi," the Greek equivalent of a common Latin expression: cf. Juvenal on Naevolus above). He also opened previously private baths to the public so that he could inspect the men who frequented them and combed the docks at night, like Faustina; see Lampridius 5, 8. Female interest in this subject is of course an ancient *topos*, possibly as old as the Hebrew Scriptures (Ezek. 16:26).

91. Even allowing for exaggeration, which is certainly present, some of the accounts in Suetonius and Lampridius are astonishing. Tiberius set an example few of his successors could equal by popularizing *spintriae*—chains of persons joined front and back in sexual unions; by training children to gratify him while he swam (he called them his "minnows"); and generally making of his retirement palace on Capri a center of every sort of imaginative sexuality (Suetonius *Tiberius* 43–44). Nero is possibly the sole classical example of a person indulging in what is now called sadomasochism. He would have himself released from a "den" dressed in the skins of wild animals and "attack" the private parts of men and women who were bound to stakes (*Nero* 28–29). Elagabalus delighted in forcing his friends into awkwardly sexual circumstances such as shutting them up for the night with old black women or young boys (Lampridius 32.5–6).

Romans made strenuous efforts to protect free-born children from sexual abuse. Since homosexuality and heterosexuality were generally regarded as equal alternatives, this concern applied to both male and female offspring. Most writers specifically equate the modesty of children of both sexes as a precious commodity,[92] and rape of minors was severely punished. Seduction seems to have been viewed somewhat more leniently. This is possibly because in the ancient world children were often regarded as small adults and assumed to have erotic feelings themselves, an aspect which Petronius emphasizes with considerable humor (85–87). Horace praised his father for having protected him as a boy from "losing his virtue or even being suspected of it" (Satires 1.6. 81–88);[93] but when he grew up he frankly declared himself a lover of both boys and girls (Epodes 11).[94] It is likely that "boy" and "girl" in such cases should not be taken in too literal a sense; in terms of sexual adulthood persons were still classed as "boys" by Roman writers when they were serving in the Roman army.[95] What is probably intended by "boy" in such cases is a suggestion of youthful beauty rather than chronological minority. Writers of other nationalities specifically criticize Roman men for limiting their eroticism to older youths.[96]

The rather sensational sexuality of the Empire also obscures a deeper and more spiritual love between persons of the same sex which was equally common. This love is celebrated along with bawdier elements throughout Latin literature and finds a place in historical accounts as well. Whether or not one would consider Encolpius and Giton in the Satyricon models of faithful affection, there could hardly be more romantic accounts of love than those represented between homosexual lovers by Ovid or Vergil; and Horace and even the racy Catullus penned lines of deep feeling.[97] Martial does not seem to have had one lover, but a number of his epigrams evince deep sensibility to spiritual love (esp. 1.46, 88), and he suggests in 10.20 that it was a boyhood lover who drew him back to Spain after living in Rome for many years.

By the time of the early Empire the stereotyped roles of "lover" and "beloved" no longer seem to be the only model for homosexual lovers, and even emperors abandoned traditional sexual roles for more reciprocal erotic

92. E.g., Achilles Tatius Leucippe and Clitophon 1.10.

93. Cf. Juvenal 10.295–309. This sort of protection is doubtless what made the bribe offered the jurors in Cicero's time so attractive (see above, p. 72).

94. "Amore qui me praeter omnes expetit /mollibus in pueris aut in puellis urere."

95. E.g., see Dionysius of Halicarnassus 16.4.

96. E.g., Boadicea of Britain, who characterizes Romans as "profligate" because they "bathe in warm water, eat artificial dainties, drink unmixed wine, anoint themselves with myrrh, and sleep on soft couches with boys for bedfellows—boys past their prime at that!" (Dio Cassius 62.6.4; cf. Dio's own comment on Seneca's preference for older boys at 61.10).

97. Ovid Metamorphoses 10 (Apollo and Hyacinth); Vergil Eclogues 2; Horace Odes 4.1; Catullus, esp. the lines to Quintius (82) and Caelius (100); cf. those to Juventius (48, 99).

relations.[98] Many homosexual relationships were permanent and exclusive. Among the lower classes informal unions like that of Giton and Encolpius may have predominated, but marriages between males or between females were legal and familiar among the upper classes. Even under the Republic, as has been noted, Cicero regarded the younger Curio's relationship with another man as a marriage, and by the time of the early Empire references to gay marriages are commonplace. The biographer of Elagabalus maintains that after the emperor's marriage to an athlete from Smyrna, any male who wished to advance at the imperial court either had to have a husband or pretend that he did (Lampridius 10–11).[99] Martial and Juvenal both mention public ceremonies involving the families, dowries, and legal niceties.[100] It is not clear that only aristocrats were involved: a cornet player is mentioned by Juvenal. Martial points out (11.42) that both men involved in one ceremony were thoroughly masculine ("The bearded Callistratus married the rugged Afer")[101] and that the marriage took place under the same law which regulated marriage between men and women.

Nero married two men in succession, both in public ceremonies with the ritual appropriate to legal marriage. At least one of these unions was recognized by Greeks and Romans, and the spouse was accorded the honors of an empress. (Suetonius reports a popular joke of the day to the effect that if Nero's father had married that sort of wife, the world would have been a happier place; *Nero* 28–29.) One of the men, Sporus, accompanied Nero to public functions, where the emperor would embrace him affectionately. He remained with Nero throughout his reign and stood by him as he died.[102]

Accounts of lesbian love do not survive from Rome on the same scale as male homosexual passions. This is rather obviously due to the fact that almost all Roman writers were male; if they were gay, they wrote of men as lovers; if not, of women. There may also, however, have been some legal ambiguity about lesbianism as a form of adultery on the part of married women: both the Elder Seneca and Martial refer to lesbian activities as adultery, the former suggesting that the death penalty was appropriate when

98. Caligula, for instance, is carefully designated as both lover and beloved of Marcus Lepidus (Dio Cassius 59.2.1; cf. Suetonius *Caligula* 36).

99. Although Lampridius's authority is hardly above question, this passage occurs in the section of the work which is generally considered most accurate. The disgust affected by the writer in recounting other details of Elagabalus's sexual foibles seems to be wanting in the account of his mariage to Zoticus.

100. Juvenal 2.117–42; Martial 1.24, 11.42.

101. "Barbatus rigido nupsit Callistratus Afro."

102. Although the authority for the marriage of Elagabalus might be impugned, that for Nero can hardly be questioned: it is mentioned at length by Suetonius (*Nero* 28–29), Tacitus (15.37), and Dio Cassius (61.28, 62.12) and briefly by Aurelius Victor, Orosius, and others.

the two were discovered in the act by a husband.[103] Ovid tells a story of erotic love between two women, but one is thought to be a man by the other and is eventually transformed into a male by the gods (*Metamorphoses* 9.666–797).[104] It is striking that Ovid has this character expatiate on the extreme oddness of lesbian passions,[105] whereas he appears to regard homosexual love between males as perfectly normal (e.g., 10.78–215).[106] (On the other hand, the moral prejudices evidenced in the *Metamorphoses* are often simply rhetorical.)[107]

Lucian (and his audience?) evinced less surprise and greater familiarity with female homosexuality in the fifth of his *Dialogues of the Courtesans*,[108] where a woman from Lesbos is pictured as having fallen in love with and seduced Leaena, another of the characters in the dialogue. The other speaker, Clonarium, has heard that in Lesbos there are many such women (5.2), but the phenomenon is clearly not geographically limited: the woman in question, Megilla, is married to a woman from Corinth (5.3).[109] Leaena is somewhat embarrassed about the whole thing and refers to it as "bizarre" (5.1),[110] although she is apparently living with Megilla (and her wife?) at the time of the discussion.[111] Clonarium, on the other hand, is fascinated and cannot pry enough details from her reticent friend.

Lucian's own attitude may account for the very stereotypical picture of Megilla, who seems quite male-oriented, although it is possible that gay women in the Empire did sometimes adopt stereotypically opposite-gender behavior

103. Martial 1.90; 7.67, 70; the Elder Seneca, 1.2.23. A Roman would of course also have the right to kill a male caught in bed with his wife.

104. This story (Iphis and Ianthe) was cited in later ages as a comment on lesbianism.

105. See below, p. 152; cf. Juvenal 2.47–49.

106. At one point in the *Ars amatoria* (1.524) Ovid seems to deprecate homosexual desires ("siquis male vir quaerit habere virum"), but the point of the comment is imprecise. It is probably intended only to derogate men who seek to have other men by deceit ("male habere" rather than "male quaerit"), since it occurs in the context of a condemnation of women who go to excess in beautifying themselves. Elsewhere in the same work (2. 684) Ovid casually admits to homosexual experience himself. (The contrast between Ovid's treatment of male and female homosexuality provides the subject of a medieval poem, translated on p. 237 below).

107. Caelius Aurelianus, *Tardarum passionum* 4.9, also discusses lesbian activity at some length, but this discussion is less interesting since it is the specific activity which is at issue, not the gender of the parties or their feelings, and since the discussion is probably not original.

108. Courtesans are also represented in what might be regarded as lesbian activity in Alciphron *Letters of Courtesans* 14.

109. "Γεγάμηκα πρόπαλαι ταύτην τὴν Δημώνασσαν, καὶ ἔστιν ἐμὴ γυνή."

110. "Αἰσχύνομαι δέ, ἀλλόκοτον γὰρ τί ἐστι." By no stretch of the imagination can M. D. MacLeod's translation (LC, vol. 7 [London, 1961]) of "ἀλλόκοτον" here as "unnatural" be justified. See above, p. 21.

111. To Clonarium's question about whether Leaena is living with Megilla, Leaena answers, "It's true," 5.1.

in a way that gay men did not. The evidence of literature written by and for males is poor grounds for conjecture on this point.

Lucian's contemporary Iamblichus included in his novel, the *Babyloniaca*, a subplot about the queen of Egypt, Berenice, and her passion for the beautiful Mesopotamia. The story survives only in the summary by the patriarch Photius,[112] who explains that it contains

> a digression about Berenice, the daughter of the king of Egypt, and her wild and inordinate passions,[113] and how she slept with Mesopotamia, who was afterward taken by Saka and led away to Garmos with her brother, Euphrates. . . . But [Berenice's servant] Zobaras, having drunk from the spring of love and seized with passion for Mesopotamia, rescued her and returned her to Berenice, from whom she had been taken, and who had become the queen of Egypt after her father's death. Berenice married Mesopotamia,[114] and there was war between Garmos[115] and Berenice on her account.[116]

Probably the most famous pair of lovers in the Roman world were Hadrian and Antinous. Hadrian (r. 117–38) was the most outstanding of the "five good emperors";[117] his rule was peaceful and productive, and he was the first emperor since Tiberius to retire in peace rather than succumb to assassination or death in battle. He appears to have been exclusively gay.[118]

112. Photius *Bibliotheca* 94, most conveniently edited in the Budé Series by Réné Henry, *Photius: Bibliothèque*, 2 vols. (Paris, 1960); but I have used the Teubner edition by Elmar Habrich, *Iamblichi Babyloniacorum reliquiae* (Leipzig, 1960). Although Photius wrote in the ninth century, his *Bibliotheca* (or *Myriobiblion*) is a major and for the most part extremely reliable source for late Hellenistic prose: see Tomas Hägg, *Photius als Vermittler antiker Literatur: Untersuchungen zur Technik des Referierens und Exzerptierens in der Bibliotheke* (Uppsala, 1975).

113. Henry's translation of "ἐκθέσμων" as "contre nature" (p. 44) is entirely unjustified; it suggests an attitude which Iamblichus could hardly have evinced (see below) and which Photius would not have been likely to impute to him.

114. In my judgment, this is the only possible translation for the odd Greek expression "Καὶ γάμους Μεσοποταμίας ἡ Βερενίκη ποιεῖται." Henry renders it "Bérénice fait célébrer le mariage de Mesopotamia," which is more literal but no clearer. Since Berenice is the only person in the story (other than her servant) erotically interested in Mesopotamia, there seems to be no reason to assume that she celebrated the latter's marriage to anyone else. On the contrary, given her feelings, it seems eminently unlikely that she would even allow Mesopotamia's marriage to someone else, much less bring it about. Marriage between men was common in the ancient world, but this is one of extremely few instances of its occurrence between women and is notable for the very official form it seems to have taken.

115. Garmos was not in love with Mesopotamia, as this excerpt seems to suggest, but was seeking to kill her because she had impersonated the heroine of the story.

116. Translated from Habrich, 17, p. 58, and 20, p. 64; Henry, pp. 44, 46.

117. I.e., Nerva, Trajan, Hadrian, Antoninus Pius, and Marcus Aurelius.

118. In sources of Hadrian's life only men are romantically or erotically associated with him (see Spartianus 1.7.23; cf. Gibbon [1898], 1:313) and none seriously except Antinous. He was so uninterested in the woman to whom he was officially married that there were

Little is known of Antinous, the young Greek with whom Hadrian fell deeply in love, except that the affection the emperor displayed toward him excited wonder and admiration even in the passion-sodden early Empire. Antinous was drowned while crossing the Nile with Hadrian in 130.[119] The emperor was heartbroken and wept "like a woman."[120]

Hadrian had Antinous deified and established an oracle in his name at Mantinea, with yearly mysteries and a festival every four years. Games were established in his name at Athens, Eleusis, and Argos and were still being celebrated more than 200 years after his death. The emperor also founded a city on the Nile (halfway between Memphis and Thebes) to honor him and had great roads built to it to ensure that it would thrive. Dio Cassius relates that Hadrian erected statues in honor of Antinous "throughout the entire world" (69.11), and his image survives today in Hellenistic sculpture, architecture, painting, coinage, and literature: "The loftiest and most typical development of the Hadrianic period was the creation of the character of Antinous."[121]

The enormous appeal of the love between Hadrian and Antinous may have been due in some part to the prevalence of same-sex couples in popular romantic literature of the time. Everywhere in the fiction of the Empire—from lyric poetry to popular novels—gay couples and their love appear on a

---

rumors after her death that he had poisoned her (Spartianus, ibid.). These are rejected by historians, as are the tales that Hadrian was responsible for the death of his lover by either sacrificing him or inducing him to sacrifice himself in response to a prediction that the emperor would die (Dio Cassius 69.11).

119. For historical accounts of Hadrian and Antinous, see Spartianus *Hadrian* 14.5; Dio Cassius 69.11, Ammianus Marcellinus 22.16.2. Modern accounts do or do not recount the affair with Antinous, depending on the attitude and frankness of the author. A reasonably objective version is provided by Bernard W. Henderson, *The Life and Principate of the Emperor Hadrian, A.D. 76–138* (London, 1923), pp. 130–34 (see esp. p. 130, n. 4, where he cites later commentary by ancient authors). Cf. Paul MacKendrick, *The Mute Stones Speak* (New York, 1960). MacKendrick sees almost everything Hadrian did after meeting Antinous as an expression of love for him: see pp. 283–84.

120. "Antinoum suum, dum per Nilum navigat, perdidit, quem muliebriter flevit" (Spartianus, *Hadrian* 14.5).

121. Eugenia Strong, *La scultura romana da Augusto a Costantino*, rev. and trans. G. Gianelli (Florence, 1926; from the earlier English version of 1907), 2:228: "Il piu alto e più caratteristico prodotto del periodo adrianeo fu la creazione del tipo dell'Antinoo." Henderson (pp. 131–32) waxes eloquent on the subject of Antinous in art: "So wonderful a human beauty, the romance of his pathetic death and the Emperor's bitter grief for him, these wrought in such wise upon the artists and sculptors of the day that Roman art attained its highest achievements in the portrayal of this youth." For other accounts of Antinous in epigraphy, etc., see PW, s.v. "Antinous"; Gibbon (1898), 1:313, n. 40; etc. The relationship between Hadrian and Antinous scandalized a few antigay Christian writers, elicited a stony silence from the self-consciously heterosexual Marcus Aurelius (who did not even list Antinous among the friends of the man who had raised him to power), and seems to have amused the more relaxed emperor Julian. Cf. Henderson, p. 131, n. 4.

completely equal footing with their heterosexual counterparts.[122] The example of the lesbian couple in the *Babyloniaca* has been noted already. In the *Ephesiaca*, a novel by Xenophon of Ephesus,[123] Hippothoos is consecutively in love with a male of his own age, an older woman, and a younger man. The first love of Dionysos, the hero of the *Dionysiaca* by Nonnos of Panopolis, is Ampelos, another male (10.175–12.397).[124]

In Plutarch's *Amatorius* a handsome young man is being courted by males and females; his mother leaves the decision about whether he should marry to his older cousin and "the most responsible of his lovers" (749F).[125] The *Affairs of the Heart*, like other dialogues of the time, constantly juxtaposes love for "women at their fairest and young men in the flower of manhood" as two sides of the same coin.[126]

In *Clitophon and Leucippe*,[127] a novel read not only by Romans of the third century but by Christian monks for centuries thereafter,[128] homosexual and heterosexual romantic love appear as absolutely indistinguishable except for the accident of gender. A heterosexual male goes to his older gay cousin for advice on love; the cousin helps him escape with the woman he loves; three men meeting on a ship are all bereft halves of star-crossed couples: two have tragically lost male lovers and one a female. When Charicles is killed riding a horse given him by his lover, Clinias, a servant of the family rushes immediately to inform Clinias of the former's death, and Charicles' father and lover weep together over his bier. Nor are such relations portrayed as

122. This material has not received broad scholarly attention, and it would be impossible here to offer the nonspecialist an introduction to Greek popular literature of the later Empire. Dating, authorship, distribution, and even textual questions remain unresolved for many important texts; and the historical significance of crucial works is often ill understood. A reading of the AP (most accessible in the LC), bk. 12, will give the interested reader a fair comprehension of gay passions as they appear in the poetry read (though not necessarily written) by Romans. Some of the major novels or "romances" are discussed below.

123. Conveniently translated by Moses Hadas in *Three Greek Romances* (New York, 1953).

124. W. Rouse's 1940 LC edition of this work (with translation) has been superseded by the text edited by R. Keydell (Berlin, 1959). Nonnos was apparently also the author of a paraphrase of the Gospel of John.

125. "'Ο δὲ Πεισίας αὐστηρότατος τῶν ἐραστῶν."

126. Ed. and trans. M. D. MacLeod (London, 1967) as vol. 8 of the LC Lucian, although it is not a genuine work of Lucian (ca. A.D. 125–80); it is now considered to date from the early fourth century.

127. Edited with an old but readable translation by S. Gaselee in the LC (1917; rev. ed., London, 1969). This novel is an extremely useful introduction to the romantic ethos of the period. That its attitudes were typical is unquestioned: Suidas comments that it "is in all respects like that of the other writers of love-romances" (quoted by Gaselee, p. ix.).

128. According to Suidas, Achilles Tatius was himself a bishop (see discussion by Gaselee or the fuller treatment in the introduction of E. Vilborg's edition of *Clitophon and Leucippe* [Stockholm, 1955]); but the ninth-century Byzantine patriarch Photius, who had read the novel, considered it "shameless and disgusting" (94).

unique to the upper classes: in Hellenistic romances gay affections are felt by pirates and brigands as much as by aristocrats and philosophers.

Greek literature of the Empire was doubtless the product of the educated urban elite and was constructed as escapist fantasy: its particulars can hardly be invoked as historical evidence. But novels of this sort addressed to the general reading public were the closest ancient parallel to popular literature; the fact that permanent and exclusive homosexual relationships appear in them without any suggestion of oddity and are considered only as interesting as heterosexual relationships speaks eloquently of the climate of opinion in Mediterranean cities in the centuries following the birth of Christ.

Roman society is universally regarded as the cultural matrix of western Europe; almost every aspect of culture and social organization among the peoples who used the ruins of its Empire as the foundations of new societies shows Roman influence or inspiration. This dependence makes it all the more odd that there could be such enormous differences between Romans and their heirs on matters as basic as sexuality and tolerance.

The common impression that Roman society was characterized by loveless hedonism, moral anarchy, and utter lack of restraint is as false as most sweeping derogations of whole peoples; it is the result of extrapolations from literature dealing with sensational rather than typical behavior, which was calculated to shock or titillate Romans themselves. Most citizens of Roman cities appear to have been as sensitive to issues and feelings of love, fidelity, and familial devotion as people before or after them, and Roman society as a whole entertained a complex set of moral and civil strictures regarding sexuality and its use.

But Roman society was strikingly different from the nations which eventually grew out of it in that none of its laws, strictures, or taboos regulating love or sexuality was intended to penalize gay people or their sexuality; and intolerance on this issue was rare to the point of insignificance in its great urban centers. Gay people were in a strict sense a minority, but neither they nor their contemporaries regarded their inclinations as harmful, bizarre, immoral, or threatening, and they were fully integrated into Roman life and culture at every level.

This attitude did not for the most part pass to the heirs of Roman civilization. Charlemagne not only imitated but tried to revive the Roman Empire culturally as well as politically, but his attitudes toward homosexuality could hardly have been more different from those of the emperors he admired. Renaissance Italians who strove to be like their forebears in the smallest details of language and all the minutiae of art execrated feelings which classical Rome had immortalized in public sculpture, mythology, and literature of every sort. How this startling and highly selective transition took place and what motivated it are the subjects of the following chapters.

II The Christian Tradition

4　The Scriptures

Although it is hard to imagine a more profound change in popular morality than that which took place between the time of the later Roman Empire and the early Middle Ages, relatively little attention has been focused on either the causes or the exact nature of this crucial transition in Western history. Indeed the silence on this seemingly major historical problem is deafening. The transformation of the almost limitless tolerance of Roman mores into the narrowness which characterized, for example, Visigothic Spain—a nation racked by violence and hostility against Jews, heretics, political dissidents, gay people, and other nonconformists—must have been caused, one is left to infer, either by the total disappearance of the Roman population or by the advent of one or both of the two forces which replaced Roman hegemony, Christianity and the barbarians.

Since the Roman population did not in fact disappear, it seems safe enough to discount the first possibility. The barbarians did alter European social structures profoundly, although not deliberately, by destroying many of the major urban centers in the West and ruining the communications systems which had linked the capitals of Roman Europe. This severely reduced urban hegemony in the area and reintroduced to most of the continent a predominantly rural pattern of life. As the urban-rural dichotomy proposed above would suggest, this may have had some impact on popular morality, especially in regard to gay people, and this is discussed at some length in chap. 7.

Christianity also had a major effect on the shift in mores, but its influence on attitudes toward homosexuality was probably less important than is commonly supposed and was certainly more complex and varied than has hitherto been recognized. It is discussed here and in the following two chapters under three headings: (1) the importance of the scriptural tradition (i.e., writings received or written by the first generation of Christian leaders); (2) social and intellectual factors relating to early Christian opinion on the subject; and (3) the precise nature of theological objections to homosexuality among the church fathers.

In considering the supposed influence of certain biblical passages on Western attitudes toward homosexual behavior, one must first relinquish the concept of a single book containing a uniform corpus of writings accepted as morally authoritative. The "Bible" was not disseminated in the early church under the form in which it came to be known later. Early Christians read and venerated many books now rejected as apocryphal (e.g., the Epistle of Barnabas, part of the text of the most famous codex of the Bible) and did not generally recognize some which are now regarded as authentic (e.g., the Apocalypse).[1] Roman Catholicism did not officially establish the canon of the Bible until the Council of Trent in 1546, although there had been general agreement on the contents of the New Testament at least since the eighth century.

The Bible was not the only or even the principal source of early Christian ethics, and the biblical passages purportedly relating to homosexuality had little to do with early Christian misgivings on the subject. Very few influential theologians based objections to homosexual practices on the New Testament passages now claimed to derogate such behavior, and those who did invoked them only as support for arguments based primarily on other authorities. It is, moreover, quite clear that nothing in the Bible would have categorically precluded homosexual relations among early Christians. In spite of misleading English translations which may imply the contrary, the word "homosexual" does not occur in the Bible: no extant text or manuscript, Hebrew, Greek, Syriac, or Aramaic, contains such a word. In fact none of these languages ever contained a word corresponding to the English "homosexual," nor did any languages have such a term before the late nineteenth century. Neither Hebrew nor Arabic has such a word today, nor does modern Greek, except as they coin words by analogy with the pseudo-Latin "homosexual." There are of course ways to get around the lack of a specific word in a language, and an action may be condemned without being named, but it is doubtful in this particular case whether a concept of homosexual behavior as a *class* existed at all.

The idea that homosexual behavior is condemned in the Old Testament stems from several passages. Probably the most well known, certainly the most influential, is the account of Sodom in Genesis 19. Sodom in fact gave

1. It is assumed throughout this study that the books of the Bible were composed by those to whom they are commonly attributed. This is of course an extremely simplistic approach to a very complex problem, but it seems not only justified but demanded by the circumstances. It was on this assumption that all patristic and medieval biblical exegesis was based, that medieval moral theology was devised, and that Bible-based legislation was enacted. What is at issue here is not how modern Jews and Christians interpret the Bible but how ancient and medieval ones did, and twentieth-century criticism is manifestly irrelevant to the development of patristic and medieval moral theology.

its name to homosexual relations in the Latin language,[2] and throughout the Middle Ages the closest word to "homosexual" in Latin or any vernacular was "sodomita." A purely homosexual interpretation of this story is, however, relatively recent. None of the many Old Testament passages which refer to Sodom's wickedness suggests any homosexual offenses, and the rise of homosexual associations can be traced to social trends and literature of a much later period. It is not likely that such associations played a large role in determining early Christian attitudes.

On the basis of the text alone, there would seem to be four inferences one could make about the destruction of Sodom: (1) the Sodomites were destroyed for the general wickedness which had prompted the Lord to send angels to the city to investigate in the first place; (2) the city was destroyed because the people of Sodom had tried to rape the angels; (3) the city was destroyed because the men of Sodom had tried to engage in homosexual intercourse with the angels (note that this is not the same as [2]: rape and homosexual intercourse are separably punishable offenses in Jewish law); (4) the city was destroyed for inhospitable treatment of visitors sent from the Lord.

Although it is the most obvious of the four, the second possibility has been largely ignored by biblical scholars both ancient and modern, probably due to ambiguities surrounding homosexual rape. Since 1955 modern scholarship has increasingly favored interpretation (4), emphasizing that the sexual overtones to the story are minor, if present, and that the original moral impact of the passage had to do with hospitality.[3] Briefly put, the thesis of this trend in scholarship is that Lot was violating the custom of Sodom (where he was himself not a citizen but only a "sojourner") by entertaining

2. Wherever possible the term "sodomy" ("sodomia") has been excluded from this study, since it is so vague and ambiguous as to be virtually useless in a text of this sort. Its etymology is probably a misprision of history, and it has connoted in various times and places everything from ordinary heterosexual intercourse in an atypical position to oral sexual contact with animals. At some points in history it has referred almost exclusively to male homosexuality and at others almost exclusively to heterosexual excess. Every effort has been made herein to specify what is meant in documents which employ "sodomy" or its equivalent. In certain circumstances, however, its unqualified use has been unavoidable. If a law, for instance, prohibits "sodomy" without further clarification and there is no secondary evidence to suggest what the legists meant by the term, there is no recourse but to discuss the law as opposing "sodomy." Or if a popular satirist vituperates against "sodomy" in a treatise which specifically derogates many forms of sexuality, it would be misleading and unjustified to assume a priori that "sodomy" referred to a particular one of these, and it is more accurate to retain its imprecision directly.

3. This theory was most prominently expounded by Bailey but has been taken up subsequently by many writers, with varying degrees of acceptance: see John McNeill, *The Church and the Homosexual* (Kansas City, Mo., 1976), pp. 42–50; and Marvin Pope, in *The Interpreter's Dictionary of the Bible, Supplementary Volume* (Nashville, Tenn., 1976), pp. 415–17.

unknown guests within the city walls at night without obtaining the permission of the elders of the city. When the men of Sodom gathered around to demand that the strangers be brought out to them, "that they might *know* them," they meant no more than to "know" who they were, and the city was consequently destroyed not for sexual immorality but for the sin of inhospitality to strangers.

Numerous considerations lend this argument credibility. As Bailey pointed out,[4] the Hebrew verb "to know" (יָדַע) is very rarely used in a sexual sense in the Bible (despite popular opinion to the contrary): in only ten of its 943 occurrences in the Old Testament does it have the sense of carnal knowledge. The passage on Sodom is the only place in the Old Testament where it is generally believed to refer to homosexual relations.

Jesus himself apparently believed that Sodom was destroyed for the sin of inhospitality: "Whosoever shall not receive you, nor hear your words, when ye depart out of that house or city, shake off the dust of your feet. Verily I say unto you, it shall be more tolerable for the land of Sodom and Gomorrah in the day of judgment, than for that city" (Matt. 10:14–15, KJV; cf. Luke 10:10–12).

There are, moreover, numerous other references in the Old Testament to Sodom and its fate, and scholars have failed to accord this facet of the controversy the importance it deserves. Sodom is used as a symbol of evil in dozens of places,[5] but not in a single instance is the sin of the Sodomites specified as homosexuality.[6] Other sins, on the other hand, are explicitly mentioned. Ecclesiasticus says that God abhorred the Sodomites for their pride (16:8), and the book of Wisdom advances the same theory (19:13–14) that Bailey and others have more recently propounded.[7] In Ezekiel the sins of Sodom are not only listed categorically but contrasted with the sexual sins of Jerusalem as less serious: "As I live, saith the Lord God, Sodom thy sister hath not done . . . as thou hast done. . . . Behold, this was the iniquity of thy

4. Bailey, pp. 2–3. The LXX makes no implication of carnal knowledge but uses a Greek expression connoting simply "making the acquaintance of," "becoming familiar with": "συγγενώμεθα αὐτοῖς"; this is in marked contrast to the verbs employed in reference to Lot's daughters ("ἔγνωσαν" and "χρήσασθε"), which clearly refer to sexual behavior.

5. E.g., Deut. 29:23, 32:32; Isa. 3:9, 13:19; Jer. 23:14, 49:18, 50:40; Lam. 4:6; Ezek. 16:46–48; Amos 4:11; Zeph. 2:9; Matt. 10:15; Luke 17:29; Rom. 9:29; 2 Pet. 2:6; Jude 7. Considering the number of references to the "wickedness" of Sodom in subsequent Scripture, it is rather difficult to believe that none of them would have placed the "wickedness" squarely in a homosexual context if such were indeed the understanding of it.

6. Some authors mistakenly interpret Jude 7 as a homosexual allusion, but there is absolutely no justification for this: see below, p. 97.

7. Ecclesiasticus and Wisdom are considered apocryphal by Protestants and Jews. Regardless of the dispute over the OT canon, these works certainly antedate the tradition of Sodom's homosexuality and indicate a more ancient tradition.

sister Sodom, pride, fulness of bread, and abundance of idleness was in her and her daughters, neither did she strengthen the hand of the poor and the needy" (16:48–49, KJV).

One must also bear in mind that such Old Testament writers were responding to the same story which some modern interpreters still claim "obviously" refers to "homosexuality" and that they were on a far more intimate footing than modern writers with both the language and life-style of the people involved. Their refusal to see the account as a moral about homosexual behavior cannot be lightly disregarded, especially in the face of so little evidence to support a homosexual interpretation.

Indeed only one argument can be advanced to demonstrate any sexual desire on the part of the Sodomites: that Lot's offering his daughters to the men must suggest some anticipation on their part of sexual satisfaction. This argument, however, does not stand close scrutiny. Bailey comments, "Its connection with the purpose (whatever it was) for which the citizens demanded the production of his guests is purely imaginary. No doubt the surrender of his daughters was simply the most tempting bribe Lot could offer on the spur of the moment to appease the hostile crowd. . . ."[8]

This action, almost unthinkable in modern Western society, was consonant with the very low status of female children at the time and was not without its parallels even in the more "civilized" Roman world: Ammianus Marcellinus recounts (19.10) a similar instance where the Roman consul Tertullus offers his children to an angry crowd to save himself. There is no sexual interest of any sort in the incident.

Even more striking is a passage in Judges (19:22ff.) obviously strongly influenced by, if not modeled on, Genesis 19. In this story the Levite of Ephraim and his concubine are unable to find hospitality in Gibeah until an old man—a "foreign resident" just like Lot (19:16)—takes them into his home. The subsequent outrage perpetrated by the men of Gibeah exactly parallels what happened in Sodom—they not only gather around the door of the old man's house but use the same words as the Sodomites: "Bring the man out that we may *know* him"[9]—and the old man even offers his daughter as a bribe. But Jews and Christians have overwhelmingly failed to interpret this story as one of homosexuality,[10] correctly assessing it as a moral about

8. P. 6. The *Bible de Jérusalem* observes that "the honor of a woman was at that time of less value than the sacred duty of hospitality" ("l'honneur d'une femme avait alors moins de prix que le devoir sacré de l'hospitalité").

9. "Nedaenu"; the LXX renders it "γνῶμεν," the Vulgate "abutamur."

10. In the Middle Ages "sodomy" was occasionally imputed to the Benjaminites on the basis of Judges 19, as in the documents of the Council of Paris of A.D. 829, which also attributed the Flood to "sodomy" (see MGH, *Legum*, sec. 3, *Concilia*, 2, 2, p. 634, capitulum 34). As noted, however, "sodomy" at the time covered a multitude of sins.

inhospitality, as did the Levite himself, who recounted the incident to the Israelites he called upon to avenge him without any hint of sexual interest (in him) on the part of the men of Gibeah.[11]

Moreover, it is anachronistic to imagine that the sexual preoccupations of later ages were major issues in such Old Testament stories as that of Sodom. The parallel story in Joshua 6 is eloquent testimony to the paramount importance of hospitality in relation to sexual offenses: the city of Jericho, like Sodom, was completely destroyed by the Lord, and the one person spared was a prostitute—though prostitution is prohibited in both Leviticus (19:29) and Deuteronomy (23:17)—because she offered hospitality to the messengers of Joshua.

Some modern readers may have difficulty imagining that a breach of hospitality could be so serious an offense as to warrant the destruction of a city. According to Genesis, of course, the Lord was already inclined to punish the Sodomites before the angels arrived there (which is why they were sent). It should be remembered, moreover, that in the ancient world inns were rare outside of urban centers, and travelers were dependent on the hospitality and goodwill of strangers not just for comfort but for physical survival. Ethical codes almost invariably enjoined hospitality on their adherents as a sacred obligation. Among the Greeks Zeus himself was the protector of guests, as the epithet "Ζεὺς Ξένιος" testifies:[12] "For Zeus's care is every stranger...."[13]

Stories of divine testing of human piety by dispatching beggars or wayfarers to demand the sacred right of hospitality ("theoxeny") are a commonplace of folklore in many cultures and occur elsewhere in the Old Testament as well (e.g., immediately before the Sodom story in Gen. 18; cf. Deut. 23:3–4 [KJV]: "An Ammonite or Moabite shall not enter into the congregation of the Lord: even to their tenth generation they shall not enter into the congregation of the Lord for ever: because they met you not with bread and water in the way, when ye came forth out of Egypt"). In nearly all such stories evil persons appear either as neighbors or other townsfolk who do not fulfill their obligation and are punished, violently or by exclusion from some divine benefice, while the solitary upright family is rewarded with a gift or a prophecy of misfortunes to come.[14] Genesis 19 obviously belongs in this context,

11. "And the men of Gibeah rose against me, and beset the house round about upon me by night, and thought to have slain me: and my concubine have they forced, that she is dead" (KJV). The *Bible de Jérusalem* notes, "Ici encore le devoir sacré de l'hospitalité passe avant le respect de l'honneur d'une femme."

12. *Iliad* 13.625; *Odyssey* 9.271; Aeschylus *Agamemnon* 61–62, 362, etc.

13. *Odyssey* 6.207ff., 14.57ff. In discussing the types of human love Plutarch places hospitality (τὸ ξενικόν) toward strangers second after love for family, and before friendship (*Moralia* 758D).

14. For modern readers the most familiar example of the sacred duty of hospitality may be that of Hunding and Siegmund in Wagner's *Die Walküre*, where the former feels bound

no matter how many modern commentators may have ignored it, and a sexual element, if present at all, was probably intended only as the concrete expression of the Sodomites' lack of hospitality.[15] "On the sinners, however, punishments rained down not without violent thunder as early warning; and deservedly they suffered for their crimes, since they evinced such bitter hatred towards strangers. Others had refused to welcome unknown men on their arrival, but these had made slaves of guests and benefactors" (Wisd. 19:13–14, JB).

Although the original understanding of the story of Sodom survived in some circles until well into the Middle Ages, the increasing emphasis of Hellenistic Jewish and Christian moralists on sexual purity gave rise in late Jewish apocrypha and early Christian writings to associations of Sodom with sexual excesses of various sorts. Thus the Epistle of Jude: "Even as Sodom and Gomorrah, and the cities about them in like manner, giving themselves over to fornication, and going after strange flesh, are set forth for an example, suffering the vengeance of eternal fire" (7, KJV). In these early accretions to the story there is no hint of homosexuality: "strange flesh" hardly suggests homoeroticism. The Jewish tradition to which Jude alludes was a legend that the *women* of Sodom had intercourse with the angels.[16]

But in an intellectual environment vehemently opposed to the casual hedonism of the Hellenistic world, many issues which had not been specifically sexual became so; this was the case with marital questions such as adultery and onanism and with homosexuality.[17] It was a short step for those predisposed to object to Graeco-Roman gender blindness from the "strange flesh" ("σαρκὸς ἑτέρας") of the Sodom story to the "alien intercourse" ("μίξις ἄθεσμος," homosexual relations) which some early fathers vociferously condemned.

On the other hand, Genesis 19 was not a principal source of early Christian hostility to homosexual relations, although it eventually gave a name to those who took part in them. This was partly due to misgivings about the Old Testament's authority, especially among Christians of non-Jewish ancestry, and partly due to the survival of more authentic interpretations of

---

to provide hospitality to the latter despite the enmity between them. For the gods as wayfarers, a classic example is provided by Ovid in the story of Baucis and Philemon (*Metamorphoses* 8). Far Eastern parallels are provided by the author of the article in the *Encyclopedia Biblica*, s.v. "Sodom and Gomorrah." See also Jakob Grimm, *Deutsche Mythologie* (Göttingen, 1835), pp. xxxiv–xxxvii, 312–14.

15. Cf. the *Encyclopedia Judaica*, s.v. "Sodom and Gomorrah"; *The Jewish Encyclopedia*, s.v. "Sodom."

16. Bailey, pp. 11–16.

17. For one example of this, see John Noonan, *Contraception: A History of Its Treatment by the Catholic Theologians and Canonists* (Cambridge, Mass., 1965), pp. 33ff.; cf. chaps. 5, 6 below.

the story's meaning. The extremely ascetic and antisexual Origen, for instance, who allegedly castrated himself to avoid sexual temptation, nonetheless refrained from any comments about homosexuality when analyzing the story, seeing it simply in terms of hospitality: "Hear this, you who close your homes to guests! Hear this, you who shun the traveler as an enemy! Lot lived among the Sodomites. We do not read of any other good deeds of his: . . . he escaped the flames, escaped the fire, on account of one thing only. He opened his home to guests. The angels entered the hospitable household; the flames entered those homes closed to guests" (*Homilia V in Genesim* [PG, 12:188–89]).[18] The only sexual matter relating to Lot which the influential theologian chose to comment on was the incestuous behavior of Lot's daughters, and he wrote at some length on whether or not this could be justified (189ff.). Likewise Saint Ambrose, although he believed there was sexual interest on the part of the Sodomites, saw the moral issue as primarily one of hospitality: Lot "placed the hospitality of his house—sacred even among a barbarous people—above the modesty [of his daughters]."[19] John Cassian rejected or ignored the supposed homosexual import of Sodom's fall and claimed that it was occasioned by gluttony,[20] and many subsequent Christian authors completely ignored any sexual implications of Sodom's fate (e.g., Saint Isidore of Seville, in his *Sententiae* 42.2 [PL, 83:647]). As late as the fourteenth century *Piers Plowman* voiced the opinion that "the awful catastrophe that came on the Sodomites was due to overplenty and to pure sloth."[21]

The word "sodomite" occurs twice in the King James translation of the Old Testament in contexts which imply sexual sins.[22] Even if these were accurate translations, the word would not necessarily imply homosexuality, since by the early seventeenth century "sodomy" referred to "unnatural" sex acts of any type and included certain relations between heterosexuals— anal intercourse, for instance. But in fact these are simply mistranslations of

18. Cf. Chrysostom's commentary (PG, 54:405): "Τοῦ δὲ δικαίου τούτου τὴν φιλοξενίαν ζηλώσωμεν καὶ τὴν ἄλλην ἀρετήν."

19. "Praeferebat domus suae verecundiae hospitalem gratiam, etiam apud barbaras gentes inviolabilem," *De Abrahamo* 1.6.52 (PL, 14:440).

20. Doubtless influenced by Ezek. 16:49: "Sodomitis causa subversionis atque luxuriae, non vini crapula, sed saturitas exstitit panis," *De coenobiorum institutis* 5.6 (PL, 49:217–18). Cf. Augustine *De nuptiis et concupiscentia* 2.19 (PL, 44:456), and the comments of Peter Cantor, app. 2 below.

21. *Piers the Plowman*, passus 14, lines 75–78, trans. Margaret Williams (New York, 1971), p. 230.

22. Deut. 23:17: "There shall be no whore of the daughters of Israel, nor a sodomite of the sons of Israel." 1 Kings 14:24: "And there were also sodomites in the land: and they did according to all the abominations of the nations which the Lord cast out before the children of Israel."

a Hebrew word for temple prostitute. The word "kadash" (plural "ka-dēshim") literally means "hallowed" or "sacred," referring to prostitutes in pagan temples. There is no reason to assume that such prostitutes serviced persons of their own sex. The word itself implies no such thing, and there is so little evidence about practices of the time that inferences from history are moot.

Mistranslations of this word began very early. The Jewish scholars who effected the Septuagint translation into Greek in the third and second centuries B.C. apparently had considerable difficulty in rendering "kadash" in Greek: they employed no fewer than six different terms to translate the one Hebrew word.[23] The uncertainty of the Jewish translators themselves is further reflected in the imprecision of many of the Greek words they chose[24] and the fact that in at least one case they misrepresented the gender of the Hebrew.[25]

None of the terms which appear in the Septuagint as translations for "kadash" would have suggested homosexuality to the theologians of the early church, who relied almost exclusively on the Greek translation of the Old Testament. The Vulgate rendered the terms as "effeminati" and "scortator."[26] Only the former could be taken as relating to gay sexuality, but in fact almost no theologians invoked these passages as condemnations of homosexual behavior until after the mistranslation of the words into English. They are wholly irrelevant to the development of attitudes toward homosexuality in medieval Christendom.[27]

23. Deut. 23:18: "οὐκ ἔσται πορνεύων"; 1 (LXX: 3) Kings 14:24: "καὶ σύνδεσμος ἐγενήθη," 15:12: "καὶ ἀφεῖλεν τὰς τελετάς" (the Hebrew indicates masculine here), 22:47: "καὶ πέρισσον τοῦ ἐνδιηλλαγμένου"; 2 (4) Kings 23:7: "καὶ καθεῖλεν τὸν οἶκον τῶν καδησιμ" (the Hebrew is simply transliterated here); Hos. 4:14: "καὶ μετὰ τῶν τετελεσμένων ἔθυον."

24. E.g., the transliteration of 2 (4) Kings 23:7, or the hapax legomenon, now virtually untranslatable except by comparison with the Hebrew, of 1 (3) Kings 22:47.

25. 1 (3) Kings 15:12, feminine in the Greek, is masculine in the Hebrew. In Hosea the Greek renders a Hebrew feminine form ("kadeshot") ambiguously; Jerome, apparently having only the Greek text, put this into Latin as "effeminati"—inadvertently stigmatizing persons who were in fact female for being feminine.

26. Precisely what is meant by "effeminati" is indeterminable. The word is used for all but one (Deut. 23:18; 17 in the Vulgate) of the occurrences of "kadash" in the Vulgate. "Whoremonger" is probably the meaning of "scortator" here (Deut. 23:17), although the Greek is ambiguous and could refer either to a man who had recourse to or was himself a prostitute.

27. In a very few cases writers cited one of these passages as corroboration of antihomosexual feelings, but never as authority for them. Clement of Alexandria, for instance, did refer to Deut. 23:18 in the Paedagogus (see app. 2), but he also invoked passages which no one else regarded as related in any way to homosexuality (e.g., Jer. 12:9); and it was his animal argument, not his exegesis, which was repeated by those under his influence.

The only place in the Old Testament where homosexual acts per se are mentioned is Leviticus:

Thou shalt not lie with mankind, as with womankind: it is abomination. [18:22]

If a man also lie with mankind, as he lieth with a woman, both of them have committed an abomination: they shall surely be put to death; their blood shall be upon them. [20:13, KJV][28]

The Hebrew word "toevah" (תּוֹעֵבָה), here translated "abomination,"[29] does not usually signify something intrinsically evil, like rape or theft (discussed elsewhere in Leviticus), but something which is ritually unclean for Jews, like eating pork or engaging in intercourse during menstruation, both of which are prohibited in these same chapters. It is used throughout the Old Testament to designate those Jewish sins which involve ethnic contamination or idolatry and very frequently occurs as part of the stock phrase "toevah ha-goyim," "the uncleanness of the Gentiles" (e.g., 2 [4] Kings 16:3). For example, in condemnations of temple prostitution involving idolatry, "toevah" is employed (e.g., 1 [3] Kings 14:24), while in prohibitions of prostitution in general a different word, "zimah," appears (e.g., Lev. 19:29). Often "toevah" specifically means "idol,"[30] and its connection with idolatry is patent even within the context of the passages regarding homosexual acts. Leviticus 18 is specifically designed to distinguish the Jews from the pagans among whom they had been living, or would live, as its opening remarks make clear—"After the doings of the land of Egypt, wherein ye dwelt, shall ye not do: and after the doings of the land of Canaan, whither I shall bring you, shall ye not do: neither shall ye walk in their ordinances" (3, KJV). And the prohibition of homosexual acts follows immediately upon a prohibition of idolatrous sexuality (also "toevah"):[31] "And thou shalt not let any of thy seed pass through the fire to Molech, neither shalt thou profane the name of thy God. . ." (21, KJV).

Chapter 20 begins with a prohibition of sexual idolatry almost identical with this, and like 18, its manifest (and stated: 20:3-4) purpose is to elaborate a system of ritual "cleanliness" whereby the Jews will be distinguished from neighboring peoples. Although both chapters also contain prohibitions (e.g., against incest and adultery) which might seem to stem from moral absolutes,

28. LXX: "Καὶ μετὰ ἄρσενος οὐ κοιμηθήσῃ κοίτην γυναικός· βδέλυγμα γάρ ἐστιν" (18:22); "Καὶ ὃς ἂν κοιμηθῇ μετὰ ἄρσενος κοίτην γυναικός, βδέλυγμα ἐποίησαν ἀμφότεροι· θανατούσθωσαν, ἔνοχοί εἰσιν" (20:13).

29. The connotations of this word, alien to both the Hebrew and Greek originals, have greater significance than may be immediately apparent.

30. E.g., Isa. 44:19; Ezek. 7:20, 16:36; Jer. 16:18; cf. Deut. 7:25-26.

31. See 2 (4) Kings 16:3, where this practice is specifically condemned as תַּעֲבוֹת הַגּוֹיִם.

their function in the context of Leviticus 18 and 20 seems to be as symbols of Jewish distinctiveness.[32] This was certainly the interpretation given them by later Jewish commentaries, for example, that of Maimonides.[33] As moral imperatives the same matters are taken up elsewhere in the Old Testament (e.g., in Exod. 20 or Deut. 4 and 10) without the ritualistic concerns which appear to underlie these chapters.[34]

The distinction between intrinsic wrong and ritual impurity is even more finely drawn by the Greek translation, which distinguishes in "toevah" itself the separate categories of violations of law or justice ($\dot{a}\nu o\mu\dot{\iota}a$) and infringements of ritual purity or monotheistic worship ($\beta\delta\dot{\epsilon}\lambda\nu\gamma\mu a$).[35] The Levitical proscriptions of homosexual behavior fall in the latter category.[36]

In the Greek, then, the Levitical enactments against homosexual behavior

32. The argument that the invocation of the death penalty for the acts in question is significant of their unique enormity is unconvincing. It presupposes that the relation of the penalty to severity of the crime in OT strictures may be determined with sufficient consistency to outweigh the obvious import of the distinction between *toevah* and other sorts of crimes. The tradition of Jewish exegesis argues against this: the Mishnah generally ignores the occurrence or nonoccurrence of specific penalties in the OT and comments on the gravity of offenses according to their similarity to other forbidden activities. Thus incest, bestiality, blasphemy, soothsaying, violation of the Sabbath laws, intercourse with a betrothed virgin, cursing one's parents, sorcery, and filial disobedience are all listed in the Talmud, Sanhedrin 7.4, as deserving the death penalty, although only two or three specifically incur such punishment in the OT. Obviously the Jewish commentary did not regard the stated punishment (or lack thereof) as an index of moral gravity. Cf. Noonan, p. 50. Although Philo and other Hellenized Jews regarded homosexual acts as singularly reprehensible, the general exegetical tradition is much better exemplified by the Mishnah's attitude, which regarded male homosexuality as punishable along with all other idolatrous or ritually impure behavior; and by such later authorities as Maimonides, who specifically and repeatedly equated homosexual acts with matters like the hybridization of cattle, which had long since become morally indifferent in the Christian tradition.

33. See, e.g., *The Code of Maimonides*, bk. 5, *The Book of Holiness*, 21.8.

34. It might also be observed that there is considerable room for doubt about precisely what is being prohibited. The Hebrew reads literally, "You shall not sleep the sleep of a woman with a man." Jewish moralists have debated for a millennium about exactly what constitutes "the sleep of a woman" and who is technically a "man": see, e.g., in the Talmud, Sanhedrin 7.4.53A; and Maimonides' commentary in the *Code* 5.1.14. Moreover, since the actions of the *kadeshim* were specifically labeled as *toevah* (e.g., in 1 [3] Kings 14:24), one might well infer that the condemnations in Leviticus were in fact aimed at curbing temple prostitution in particular rather than homosexual behavior in general. This was not the usual understanding of the later Jewish tradition, but it is suggested by the LXX, upon which Christian moralists drew.

35. See LXX translations of Deut. 7:25–26, 3 Kings 14:24; 4 Kings 16:3; Isa. 44:19, Jer. 16:18 ("toavot" here, being more general and serious than the preceding "nivlat shikutz," is rendered "$\dot{a}\nu o\mu\dot{\iota}a$," "$\beta\delta\dot{\epsilon}\lambda\nu\gamma\mu a$" then being used to render the preceding term), and Ezek. 7:20; cf. the rendering in Ezek. 16:36 and the juxtaposition in 8:6 and 9.

36. This division is maintained in the NT: Saint Paul uses "$\dot{a}\nu o\mu\dot{\iota}a$" to designate sin or injustice in general—e.g., Rom. 2:12, 4:7; 2 Cor. 6:14; 2 Thess. 2:7; Heb. 1:9—and "$\beta\delta\dot{\epsilon}\lambda\nu\gamma\mu a$" or its derivatives in reference to idolatry or violations of Jewish ritual purity in particular—Rom. 2:22; Titus 1:16.

characterize it unequivocally as ceremonially unclean rather than inherently evil. This was not lost on Greek-speaking theologians, many of whom considered that such behavior had been forbidden the Jews as part of their distinctive ethical heritage or because it was associated with idolatry,[37] not as part of the law regarding sexuality and marriage, which was thought to be of wider application. The irrelevance of the verses was further emphasized by the teaching of both Jesus and Paul that under the new dispensation it was not the physical violation of Levitical precepts which constituted "abomination" ("βδέλυγμα")[38] but the interior infidelity of the soul.

Even where such subtleties were not well understood, however, the Levitical proscriptions were not likely to have much effect on early Christian morality. Within a few generations of the first disciples, the majority of converts to Christianity were not Jews, and their attitude toward Jewish law was to say the least ambivalent. Most Christians regarded the Old Testament as an elaborate metaphor for Christian revelation; extremely few considered it morally binding in particular details. Romans and Greeks found Jewish dietary customs distasteful and squalid and had so profound an aversion to circumcision, the cornerstone of Mosaic law, that large and often bloody conflicts resulted from their efforts to extirpate it.[39] It would have been difficult to justify the imposition of only those portions of Leviticus which supported personal prejudices, and even without circumcision it is difficult to imagine the wholesale adoption by the Graeco-Roman world of Levitical laws which prohibited the consumption of pork, shellfish, rabbit—all staples of Mediterranean diet—or of meats containing blood or fat. Thorough reaping and gleaning of fields, hybridization, clothing of more than one type of fabric, cutting of the beard or hair[40]—all were condemned under Jewish law, and all were integral parts of life under the Empire. Viewed through the lenses of powerful modern taboos on the subject, the prohibition of homosexual relations may seem to have been of a different order: to those conditioned by social prejudice to regard homosexual behavior as uniquely enormous, the Levitical comments on this subject may seem to be of far

37. E.g., Eusebius of Caesaria *Praeparationis evangelicae libri quindecim* 4.16 ("De antiqua hominum immolandorum consuetudine," PG, 21:276); and the *Apostolic Constitutions* (as below).

38. Luke 16:15, Rom. 2:22, Titus 1:10–16.

39. For a brief but judicious summary of Roman anti-Semitism, see A. N. Sherwin-White, *Racial Prejudice in Imperial Rome* (Cambridge, 1967). For a recent review of the vast literature on this subject, see K. R. Stow, "The Church and the Jews," in *Bibliographical Essays in Medieval Jewish Studies* (New York, 1976), esp. pp. 114–17.

40. It was in fact about the time that the Christian religion became popular that the custom of shaving became universal in the Roman world, and beards were not popular again until the reign of Hadrian. Some Christian writers, notably Clement of Alexandria, did object to shaving, but none made much fuss about cutting the hair of the head.

greater weight than the proscriptions surrounding them. But the ancient world, as has been shown, knew no such hostility to homosexuality. The Old Testament strictures against same-sex behavior would have seemed to most Roman citizens as arbitrary as the prohibition of cutting the beard, and they would have had no reason to assume that it should receive any more attention than the latter.

In fact non-Jewish converts to Christianity found most of the provisions of Jewish law extremely burdensome, if not intolerable, and a fierce dispute racked the early church over whether Christians should be bound by it or not. The issue was finally resolved at the Council of Jerusalem (ca. A.D. 49; see Acts 15). After long and bitter debate within the highest ranks of the Christian community, it was decided that pagan converts to the Christian faith would not be bound by any requirements of the Mosaic law—including circumcision—with four exceptions: they were to "abstain from pollutions of idols, from blood, from things strangled, and from fornication."[41] An apostolic letter was sent to Gentile Christians informing them of this decision and specifically censuring efforts of Jewish Christians to impose Jewish law on them beyond these matters.

Neither "pollutions of idols" nor "fornication" was or could be interpreted as referring to homosexuality. The former alluded to food which had been sacrificed to idols and was afterward often served at meals in pagan homes, as is made clear in the apostolic letter itself (v. 29) and elsewhere in the New Testament (e.g., Acts 21:25, 1 Cor. 8:10). Although there is some ambiguity about the Greek word "πορνεία" here translated "fornication," it is clearly distinct from the term "βδέλυγμα," under which the Levitical proscriptions of homosexuality are comprised. Homosexuality is nearly always distinguished from "fornication" in patristic literature,[42] although sometimes subsumed under "adultery" ("μοιχεία"). In the New Testament itself (e.g., 1 Cor. 6:9 and 1 Tim. 1:10) each of the latter is listed as a category

41. "'Απέχεσθαι εἰδωλοθύτων καὶ αἵματος καὶ πνικτῶν καὶ πορνείας" (15:29; cf. 20).

42. See, e.g., *Apostolic Constitutions* 28 (PG, 1:984), where such a distinction is carefully drawn: ἡ Σοδόμων ἁμαρτία is classified as βδελυκτή, while πορνεία is discussed in a completely separate category, ἀδικία. (Cf. the common triple prohibition: "οὐ πορνεύσεις, οὐ μοιχεύσεις, οὐ παιδοφθορήσεις," which occurs in the Epistle of Barnabas, Clement's *Paedagogus*, the *Apostolic Constitutions*, etc. See also Damascene *Sacra parallela* 2.11 [PG, 96:248]: "περὶ πορνείας, καὶ μοιχείας, καὶ ἀρσενοκοιτίας.") In Latin the same distinction was maintained: *fornicatio* referred only to heterosexual indulgence; *sodomia* or *peccatum contra naturam* either constituted a form of *adulterium* or an *abominatio*. Beginning in the eighth century some prominent theologians did subsume homosexual behavior under *fornicatio*, but by the period of the Scholastics the older use again prevailed. For a particularly clear Scholastic definition of the various terms, see Albertus Magnus *Summa theologiae*, 2.28.122.1.4, in *Opera*, ed. August Borgnet (Paris, 1895), 33:400. Aquinas also distinguished *fornicatio* from *vitia contra naturam*, considering the generic name for such sins to be *luxuria*: see his *Summa theologiae* 2a.2ae.154.11.

quite separate from the words which modern translators have taken to refer to homosexuality,[43] and the word "πορνεία" occurs in discussions of sexual immorality as a specific type of behavior, not as the general designation for such activity.[44]

It can be argued, moreover, that even the four exceptions listed in Acts were imposed upon new Christians not by way of moral judgment on the acts involved but simply to facilitate interaction between pagan-born and Jewish members of Christian communities (by encouraging the former to eschew behavior whose profanity might particularly offend Jews adhering to Levitical precepts).[45] This point of view is supported by scriptural evidence (e.g., 1 Cor. 10:32) as well as by the almost complete silence on the issue of strangled meat and blood in subsequent Christian moral teaching[46]—a silence which would be perplexing if the church had considered the exceptions mentioned at the Council of Jerusalem to be binding moral judgments.

The struggle over the issue of Gentile Christians and the Mosaic law was such a profound trauma for the early church that once it was resolved there was no thought of trying to bind new Christians—even converts from Judaism—by its proscriptions. Saint Paul urged Christians not to be "entangled again with the yoke of bondage" (Gal. 5:1–2) or to give "heed to Jewish fables, and commandments of men, that turn from the truth," for "unto the pure all things are pure" (Titus 1:14–15). In fact he went so far as to assert that "if ye be circumcised, Christ shall profit you nothing" (Gal. 5:2).

Almost no early Christian writers appealed to Leviticus as authority against homosexual acts.[47] A few patristic sources invoked Levitical prece-

43. The most common Latin gloss of the Middle Ages regarded *immunditia* (e.g., in 2 Cor. 12:21) as the generic designation for "unnatural" sins and distinguished it specifically from *fornicatio* (PL, 192:89). Cf. commentary by Aquinas in *Summa* as above (n. 42).

44. E.g., 2 Cor. 12:21: "ἀκαθαρσίᾳ καὶ πορνείᾳ καὶ ἀσελγείᾳ"; Gal. 5:19: "πορνεία, ἀκαθαρσία, ἀσέλγεια." For a medieval understanding of these terms, see Aquinas *Summa* 2a.2ae.154.1.5–6.

45. See esp. the notes to the very clear JB translation of the passage in Acts. This was certainly the medieval understanding; see, e.g., Aquinas *Summa* 2a.2ae.154.2.1.

46. But see below, p. 365.

47. Clement of Alexandria is an exception to this as to most generalizations, as are the *Apostolic Constitutions*, a fourth-century work whose influence in the matter was minimal, since they were hortatory rather than preceptive, never enjoyed wide acceptance as apostolic, and were not known in the West until the sixteenth century. A fascinating effort to demonstrate the common basis of Mosaic and Roman law is preserved in a manuscript edited by M. Hyamson, *Mosaicarum et Romanarum legum collatio* (London, 1913), useful as a text for Roman law; but its influence on the Christian community was negligible (only three manuscripts survive, and Hincmar of Reims is the only theologian of note to cite it). It is highly selective in its use of Levitical material. Other medieval uses of Leviticus are equally misleading. Isidore of Seville (*Origines* 6.8) claimed Mosaic law was the origin of Western law, but he lived in a country which punished observance of the fundamental precepts of that law—circumcision and dietary proscriptions—with death.

dents about eating certain animals in relation to homosexuality, but they did so incorrectly and offered the Levitical law only as a symbol of how God felt about the animals. They did not suggest for a minute that the dietary laws be observed in their entirety. It would simply not have occurred to most early Christians to invoke the authority of the old law to justify the morality of the new: the Levitical regulations had no hold on Christians and are manifestly irrelevant in explaining Christian hostility to gay sexuality. Even in the case of the exceptional Christian theologians who did refer to Leviticus 18:22 or 20:13, the opinions therein cannot be seen as the origin of their attitudes, since they rejected the vast majority of Levitical precepts, retaining only those which suited their personal prejudice. Their extreme selectivity in approaching the huge corpus of Levitical law is clear evidence that it was not their respect for the law which created their hostility to homosexuality but their hostility to homosexuality which led them to retain a few passages from a law code largely discarded.

If the Old Testament had no specific positive role in creating early Christian attitudes toward homosexual acts, may it not have had a negative role? Would not the complete silence on the subject of gay sexuality and the predication of all Old Testament moral legislation on a heterosexual model have predisposed Christians to reject homosexuality as alien to God's plan, no matter how they viewed the authority of Jewish law? The assumption that the creation of humankind through heterosexual union in Genesis and the subsequent emphasis on marriage throughout the Old Testament demonstrates tacit rejection of gay sexuality is insupportable in a modern context, and it does not seem to have occurred to early Christians. It does not figure in any polemic on the subject and would have constituted an extremely weak argument if it had. In fact intense love relations between persons of the same gender figure prominently in the Old Testament—e.g., Saul and David, David and Jonathan, Ruth and Naomi—and were celebrated throughout the Middle Ages in both ecclesiastical and popular literature as examples of extraordinary devotion, sometimes with distinctly erotic overtones. Moreover, in an age which employed symbols and myths to explain all its fundamental truths, it would have been obvious even to the most naive that in order to account for the origins of the human race the writer of Genesis would inevitably describe the creation of the separate sexes which produce offspring and would comment on the nature of the union which brings about procreation. One would no more expect an account of gay love than of friendship in Genesis: neither could produce offspring, neither had and neither would contribute to the story of the peopling of the earth.

Moral codes are generally silent on the subject of homosexuality, for reasons described at length above. The laws of Rome have no more to say about homosexual relations than those of Israel, and they regulate marriage as thoroughly, if with different purposes and assumptions. Yet no one would imagine that this silence in Roman law betokened the absence of interest or knowledge regarding homosexual behavior. If all that survived of Roman literature were laws ambiguously denigrating homosexual liaisons of some sort and a wealth of regulations safeguarding the purity of marriage, historians might well imagine that gay sexuality was unknown or severely repressed in Rome. Such an inference would be wholly wrong in the case of Rome and has scant justification in analysis of societies from which little erotic literature survives.

What is more to the point is the fallacy of selective inference which underlies this approach. Certainly opposition to homosexual behavior was not seen by most non-Jews as the hallmark of the Jewish religion: Jews were most noted for their dietary and ritual distinctiveness and for the practice of circumcision. Since all three of these were abandoned wholesale by the Christian community within less than 100 years of the inception of the religion, it seems hardly likely that lingering prejudice against this or that particular action could be ascribed to the overwhelming force of the Jewish tradition.

Saint Paul, whose commitment to Jewish law had taken up most of his life, never suggested that there was any historical or legal reason to oppose homosexual behavior: if he did in fact object to it, it was purely on the basis of functional, contemporary moral standards.

There are three passages in the writings of Paul which have been supposed to deal with homosexual relations. Two words in 1 Corinthians 6:9 and one in 1 Timothy 1:10 have been taken at least since the early twentieth century to indicate that "homosexuals" will be excluded from the kingdom of heaven.[48]

The first of the two, "μαλακός" (basically, "soft"), is an extremely common Greek word; it occurs elsewhere in the New Testament with the meaning "sick"[49] and in patristic writings with senses as varied as "liquid," "cowardly," "refined," "weak willed," "delicate," "gentle," and "debauched."[50] In a specifically moral context it very frequently means "licentious," "loose," or "wanting in self-control."[51] At a broad level, it

48. For a more detailed examination of the significance of the words in question, see app. 1.

49. E.g., Matt. 11:8; cf. 4:23, 9:35, 10:1.

50. Dio Chrysostom, e.g., applies it to the demoralizing effect wrongly presumed to attend learning (66.25); in Vettius Valens (113.22) it refers to general licentiousness; Epictetus, a contemporary of Paul, used it to describe those too "softheaded" to absorb true philosophy (*Discourses* 3.9).

51. Note that Aristotle explains exactly what he understands to be the moral significance

might be translated as either "unrestrained" or "wanton," but to assume that either of these concepts necessarily applies to gay people is wholly gratuitous. The word is never used in Greek to designate gay people as a group or even in reference to homosexual acts generically, and it often occurs in writings contemporary with the Pauline epistles in reference to heterosexual persons or activity.[52]

What is more to the point, the unanimous tradition of the church through the Reformation, and of Catholicism until well into the twentieth century,[53] has been that this word applied to masturbation. This was the interpretation not only of native Greek speakers in the early Middle Ages[54] but of the very theologians who most contributed to the stigmatization of homosexuality.[55] No new textual data effected the twentieth-century change in translation of this word: only a shift in popular morality. Since few people any longer regard masturbation as the sort of activity which would preclude entrance to heaven, the condemnation has simply been transferred to a group still so widely despised that their exclusion does not trouble translators or theologians.

The second word, "ἀρσενοκοῖται," is quite rare, and its application to homosexuality in particular is more understandable. The best evidence, however, suggests very strongly that it did not connote homosexuality to Paul or his contemporaries but meant "male prostitute" until well into the fourth century, after which it became confused with a variety of words for disapproved sexual activity and was often equated with homosexuality.

The remaining passage, Romans 1:26–27, does not suffer from mistranslation, although little attention has been paid to the ramifications of its wording: "For this cause God gave them up unto vile affections: for even their women did change the natural use into that which is against nature: And likewise, also the men, leaving the natural use of the woman, burned in their lust one toward another; men with men working that which is

---

of μαλακός in the *Nicomachean Ethics* 7.4.4—"unrestraint" in respect to bodily pleasures, a moral defect hardly peculiar to gay people in the eyes of Aristotle or anyone else in the ancient world.

52. E.g., in Plutarch's *Erotikos* 753; cf. 751, where even "μαλθακός"—a word with clearer relation to passive sexuality in men (see chap. 3: Caelius Aurelianus, a late imperial physician, called passive men "malthacoe")—is applied to heterosexuality.

53. See, e.g., H. Noldin, *Summa theologiae moralis scholarum usui* (Leipzig, 1940), "De sexto praecepto," 1:29; cf. the *Catholic Encyclopedia* (1967 ed.), s.v. "masturbation."

54. See, e.g., Jejunator *Poenitentiale* (PG, 88:1893): "Ὡσαύτως καὶ περὶ μαλακίας, ἧς δύω εἰσὶν αἱ διαφοραί· μία μὲν ἡ διὰ οἰκείας χειρὸς ἐνεργουμένη· ἑτέρα δὲ ἡ δι' ἀλλοτρίας."

55. At least from the time of Aquinas on, all moral theologians defined "mollitia" or "mollicies" (the Latin equivalent of "μαλακία") as masturbation: see *Summa theologiae* 2.2.154.11, Resp., and Vincent of Beauvais *Speculum doctrinale* 4.162.

unseemly, and receiving in themselves that recompense of their error which was meet" (KJV).[56]

It is sometimes argued that the significance of the passage lies in its connection with idolatry: i.e., that Paul censures the sexual behavior of the Romans because he associates such behavior with orgiastic pagan rites in honor of false gods.[57] This might seem to be suggested by the Old Testament condemnations of temple prostitution. Paul may have been familiar with temple prostitution, both homosexual and heterosexual, and it is reasonable to conjecture that he is here warning the Romans against the immorality of the *kadeshim*. The fact that the overall structure of the chapter juxtaposes the sexual activities in question with the superstitious beliefs of the Romans adds further credence to this theory, as do possible Old Testament echoes.

Under closer examination, however, this argument proves to be inadequate. First of all, there is no reason to believe that homosexual temple prostitution was more prevalent than heterosexual or that Paul, had he been addressing himself to such practices, would have limited his comments to the former. Second, it is clear that the sexual behavior itself is objectionable to Paul, not merely its associations. Third, and possibly most important, Paul is not describing cold-blooded, dispassionate acts performed in the interest of ritual or ceremony: he states very clearly that the parties involved "burned in their lust one toward another" ("ἐξεκαύθησαν ἐν τῇ ὀρέξει αὐτῶν εἰς ἀλλήλους"). It is unreasonable to infer from the passage that there was any motive for the behavior other than sexual desire.

On the other hand, it should be recognized that the point of the passage is not to stigmatize sexual behavior of any sort but to condemn the Gentiles for their general infidelity. There was a time, Paul implies, when monotheism was offered to or known by the Romans, but they rejected it (vv. 19–23).[58] The reference to homosexuality is simply a mundane analogy to this theological

---

56. Although Paul does not invoke or explicitly allude to any previous scriptural attitudes toward homosexuality, these verses resemble or echo a number of other passages (in addition to the *Testament of Naphtali*: see below, n. 65). A general similarity to Wis. 12:23–27 is often pointed out, but glosses and commentators have generally failed to notice that v. 26 is remarkably similar to a passage in Ezek. 7:20: "Ἕνεκεν τούτου δέδωκα αὐτὰ αὐτοῖς εἰς ἀκαθαρσίαν." This line in Ezekiel relates to idolatry and may be an indication that there is some connotation of temple prostitution involved in Paul's comments, although no such deduction is necessary.

57. E.g., by Herman van de Spijker, *Die gleichgeschlechtliche Zuneigung* (Freiburg, 1968), pp. 82ff.

58. The idea that pagans had once had a chance at salvation is a commonplace of Semitic religious polemic: see the Qur'an 11:33. All subsequent exegesis assumed that the pagans could have known the truth if they had wished to (e.g., Theodoret: "Εἰ γὰρ δὴ γνῶναι αὐτὸν ἐβουλήθησαν τοῖς θείοις ἂν ἠκολούθησαν νόμοις," *Interpretatio Epistolae ad Romanos* 1 [PG, 82:63]).

sin; it is patently not the crux of this argument. Once the point has been made, the subject of homosexuality is quickly dropped and the major argument resumed (vv. 28ff.).

What is even more important, the persons Paul condemns are manifestly not homosexual: what he derogates are homosexual acts committed by apparently heterosexual persons. The whole point of Romans 1, in fact, is to stigmatize persons who have rejected their calling, gotten off the true path they were once on. It would completely undermine the thrust of the argument if the persons in question were not "naturally" inclined to the opposite sex in the same way they were "naturally" inclined to monotheism. What caused the Romans to sin was not that they *lacked* what Paul considered proper inclinations but that they *had* them: they held the truth, but "in unrighteousness" (v. 18), because "they did not see fit to retain Him in their knowledge" (v. 28).

This aspect of the verses, overlooked by modern scholarship, did not escape the attention of early Christian writers. Noting that Paul carefully characterized the persons in question as having *abandoned* the "natural use," Saint John Chrysostom commented that Paul thus

> deprives them of any excuse, . . . observing of their women that they "did change the natural use." No one can claim, he points out, that she came to this because she was precluded from lawful intercourse or that because she was unable to satisfy her desire she fell into this monstrous depravity. Only those possessing something can change it . . . .
>
> Again, he points out the same thing about the men, in a different way, saying they "left the natural use of the woman." Likewise he casts aside with these words every excuse, charging that they not only had [legitimate] enjoyment and abandoned it, going after a different one, but that spurning the natural they pursued the unnatural.[59]

Although the idea that homosexuality represented a congenital physical characteristic was widespread in the Hellenistic world[60]—and undoubtedly well known to Chrysostom—it is not clear that Paul distinguished in his thoughts or writings between gay persons (in the sense of permanent sexual preference) and heterosexuals who simply engaged in periodic homosexual behavior. It is in fact unlikely that many Jews of his day recognized such a distinction, but it is quite apparent that—whether or not he was aware of their existence—Paul did not discuss gay *persons* but only homosexual *acts* committed by heterosexual persons.

59. Chrysostom *In Epistolam ad Romanos*, homily 4 (PG, 60:415–22).
60. Plato and Aristotle had both suggested variations on this idea, and it was a commonplace of Roman medicine.

There is, however, no clear condemnation of homosexual acts in the verses in question. The expression "against nature" is the standard English equivalent of Paul's Greek phrase "παρὰ φύσιν," which was first used in this context by Plato. Its original sense has been almost wholly obscured by 2,000 years of repetition in stock phrases and by the accretion of associations inculcated by social taboos, patristic and Reformation theology, Freudian psychology, and personal misgivings.

The concept of "natural law" was not fully developed until more than a millennium after Paul's death,[61] and it is anachronistic to read it into his words. For Paul, "nature" was not a question of universal law or truth but, rather, a matter of the *character* of some person or group of persons, a character which was largely ethnic and entirely human: Jews are Jews "by nature," just as Gentiles are Gentiles "by nature."[62] "Nature" is not a moral force for Paul: men may be evil or good "by nature," depending on their own disposition.[63] A possessive is always understood with "nature" in

61. Philo Judaeus and a few of the Greek fathers clearly entertained some notion of over-riding laws of "nature," violation of which was inherently sinful even for those ignorant of the law of God. Even in Philo, however, there is considerable overlap of divine law, "natural law," human legislation, and other sources of moral insight: see H. A. Wolfson, *Philo: Foundations of Religious Philosophy in Judaism, Christianity, and Islam* (Cambridge, Mass., 1947), 2:303ff. Among the fathers influenced by or familiar with Philo's (or similar) ideas the confusion was increased rather than diminished, and in the West there was little clear apprehension of the concept until the High Middle Ages. The writings attributed to Paul show no familiarity with such associations of "nature," and if some familiarity had been present, it would indicate little about Paul's attitude, since the tradition itself was so confused. A strikingly similar passage in Plutarch (*Moralia* 751), for instance, uses "παρὰ φύσιν" and "ἀσχήμων" together in discussing homosexuality, but it is hardly illuminating. The latter term is juxtaposed with "ἀναφρόδιτος," an expression which would have been meaningless to Paul, and "παρὰ φύσιν" is used later in the same work (761E) to describe—with obvious approbation—courage in women. Cf. 755C: "Ἡ γὰρ φύσις παρανομεῖται γυναικοκρατουμένη."

62. Gal. 2:15: "ἡμεῖς φύσει Ἰουδαῖοι"; Rom. 2:27: "ἐκ φύσεως ἀκροβυστία" (literally, "uncircumcision by nature").

63. Eph. 2:3: "τέκνα φύσει ὀργῆς"; Rom. 2:14: "φύσει τὰ τοῦ νόμου ποιῶσιν." The only instance in which "nature" seems to have a moral significance for Paul greater than simply "human nature" is 1 Cor. 11:14 (KJV): "Doth not even nature itself teach you, that, if a man have long hair, it is a shame unto him?" But it would be fatuous to imagine that "nature" even in the most idealized sense could have an effect on the length of a man's hair. Idealized natural ethical systems would be more apt to prohibit cutting one's hair than to invoke "nature" as proof of the desirability of short hair. Clearly Paul here uses "nature" in the sense of custom, tradition, or ethical heritage, ignoring (or rejecting) the usual dichotomy in Greek between custom and nature (χρῆσις and φύσις; e.g., in Ignatius to the Trallians: "οὐ κατὰ χρῆσιν ἀλλὰ κατὰ φύσιν," 1:1). He thus fuses the concept of mores with that of innate character. The enormously complicated question of the relationship between φύσις and νόμος enters into this discussion as well. By Paul's time much of the earlier meaning of "νόμος" had been—somewhat illogically—subsumed under "φύσις." Biblical scholars have barely begun to wrestle with what NT writers understood by these terms, whose meaning even

Pauline writings: it is not "nature" in the abstract but *someone's* "nature," the Jews' "nature" or the Gentiles' "nature" or even the pagan gods' "nature" ("When ye knew not God, ye did service unto them which by nature [i.e., by *their* nature] are no gods," Gal. 4:8, KJV).[64]

"Nature" in Romans 1:26, then, should be understood as the *personal* nature of the pagans in question. This is made even clearer by the strikingly similar passage in the *Testament of Naphtali*, a roughly contemporary document whose comment on this subject was obviously influenced by (if not an influence on) Paul's remarks.[65] "The Gentiles, deceived and having abandoned the Lord, changed their order. . . . [Be ye not therefore] like Sodom, which changed the order of its nature. Likewise also the Watchers[66] changed the order of their nature . . ." (3.3.4–5).[67]

"Against" is, moreover, a somewhat misleading translation of the preposition "παρά." In New Testament usage "παρά" connotes not "in opposition to" (expressed by "κατά")[68] but, rather, "more than," "in excess of"; immediately before the passage in question, for example, what the King James renders as "more than" (the creator) is the same preposition.[69]

---

in Attic is hotly disputed. For illuminating studies, see W. J. Beardslee, *The Use of ΦΥΣΙΣ in Fifth-Century Greek Literature* (Chicago, 1918); A. W. H. Adkins, *Moral Values and Political Behavior in Ancient Greece* (London, 1972); and André Pellicer, *Natura: étude sémantique et historique du mot latin* (Paris, 1966), pp. 17–35.

64. "Ἐδουλεύσατε τοῖς φύσει μὴ οὖσιν θεοῖς." Note the theme of infidelity, parallel to that in Rom. 1:26–27.

65. The date and the origin of the *Testament of Naphtali* are the subject of lively controversy. Opinions range from those favoring Jewish authorship possibly as early as the third century B.C. to those suggesting Christian composition by a disciple of Saint Paul. Since the discovery of Semitic fragments of Naphtali in the caves at Qumran, some connection with the Essene community there has been generally assumed, but the looseness of the relationship between the Semitic fragments and the Greek text, as well as the numerous Christian elements in the Greek, make more precise identification difficult. Marc Philonenko made a strong case for Essene authorship with few Christian additions (*Les interpolations chrétiennes des Testaments des Douze Patriarches et les Manuscrits de Qumran* [Paris, 1960]) but was superseded by the more restrained arguments of Jürgen Becker (*Untersuchungen zur Enstehungsgeschichte der Testamente der Zwölf Patriarchen* [Leiden, 1970]). Probably the issue will not be solved without further documentation, and the best that can be argued at present is that there is some connection between the Pauline writings and the testament.

66. See Bailey, pp. 12–21.

67. "Ἔθνη πλανηθέντα καὶ ἀφέντα Κύριου ἠλλοίωσαν τὴν τάξιν αὐτῶν. . . . Μὴ γένησθε ὡς Σόδομα, ἥτις ἐνήλλαξε τάξιν φύσεως αὐτῆς. Ὁμοίως δὲ καὶ οἱ Ἐγρήγοροι ἐνήλλαξαν τάξιν φύσεως αὐτῶν. . . ," in *The Greek Versions of the Testaments of the Twelve Patriarchs*, ed. R. H. Charles (Oxford, 1908), pp. 149–50 (this edition should be supplemented with that of M. de Jonge, *Testamenta XII Patriarcharum* [Leiden, 1964], p. 54). The similarity of wording and context down to such details as the use of "πλανέω" and "ἀφέντα" would hardly seem to admit of coincidence.

68. This is, e.g., the word Jesus uses in observing that "he that is not against you [καθ' ὑμῶν] is for you," Luke 9:50; cf. 11:23, κατ' ἐμοῦ.

69. Although in certain stock phrases such as "παρὰ δόξαν" "contrary to" may be the

Finally, this exact same phrase—"παρὰ φύσιν"—is used later in the same epistle to describe the activity of God in saving the Gentiles: "For if thou wert cut out of the olive tree which is wild by nature, and wert graffed contrary to nature [παρὰ φύσιν] into a good olive tree: how much more shall these, which be the natural branches, be graffed into their own olive tree?" (Rom. 11:24, KJV). Since God himself is here described as acting "against nature," it is inconceivable that this phrase necessarily connotes moral turpitude. Rather, it signifies behavior which is unexpected, unusual, or different from what would occur in the normal order of things: "beyond nature," perhaps, but not "immoral." There is no implication of the contravening of "natural law" in Paul's use of this phrase,[70] and for Christians familiar with all of the books which now comprise the New Testament the phrase may have had no negative implications at all; in 2 Peter 2:12, for example, a similar passage employs "natural" as a term of derogation.[71]

Paul believed that the Gentiles knew of the truth of God but rejected it and likewise rejected their true "nature" as regarded their sexual appetites, going beyond what was "natural" for them and what was approved for the Jews. It cannot be inferred from this that Paul considered mere homoerotic attraction or practice morally reprehensible,[72] since the passage strongly implies that he was not discussing persons who were by inclination gay and

---

best rendering of "παρά" with the accusative, this is a much less frequent usage than the meaning of "more than" or "beyond." In the majority of the twenty-four occurrences of "παρά" with the accusative in the Pauline epistles "beyond" is the only possible translation, and in all of them it is quite as admissible as "against." This very phrase is in fact frequently translated into Latin as "beyond" nature rather than "against" it: Rufinus quotes Origen as giving "extra naturam" rather than "contra" (*Commentaria in Epistolam ad Romanos* 4.474–75), and the Codex Boerneriani translates the Greek as "secus naturam." Cf. Tertullian's "et in sexus ultra naturae" (PL, 2:987).

70. The English "extralegal" offers some parallel, in that it implies not *violation* of the law but, rather, lack of reference to it.

71. See discussion below. The resemblance between "τὴν ἀντιμισθίαν ἣν ἔδει τῆς πλάνης" at Rom. 1:27 and "ἀδικούμενοι μισθὸν ἀδικίας" at 2 Pet. 2:13 would probably have been noticed by those familiar with both epistles.

72. Beyond this phrase there is certainly very little in the passage to justify the horror and severe censure that homosexuality has often elicited from the Christian community. The words translated by the KJV as "vile affections"—"πάθη ἀτιμίας"—are words of very broad interpretation. The term "πάθος" can apply to almost any human activity—a feeling, an experience, an endeavor—and has no moral coloration whatever. On the other hand, "ἀτιμία" clearly refers to dishonor. The question is, Whence arises the dishonor—from the act itself, from God's attitude toward it, or from the attitude of the community? Without attempting to demonstrate the relevance of classical usage, which tends overwhelmingly to the last of the three, it is possible to get a good cross-reference from the Pauline writings themselves: in 2 Cor. 6:8 "ἀτιμία" is employed in the sense of ill repute in *contrast*

since he carefully observed, in regard to both the women and the men, that they changed or abandoned the "natural use" to engage in homosexual activities.

In sum, there is only one place in the writings which eventually became the Christian Bible where homosexual relations per se are clearly prohibited—Leviticus—and the context in which this prohibition occurred rendered it inapplicable to the Christian community, at least as moral law. It is almost never cited as grounds for objection to homosexual acts (except allegorically; see chap. 6). The notion that Genesis 19—the account of Sodom's destruction—condemned homosexual relations was the result of

---

to wickedness. It refers in fact to the servants of God, who are thought ill of by the world. In 1 Cor. 15:43 the same meaning occurs—"What is sown in dishonor rises in glory"—and the pejorative sense is as ironic as in the first passage. In 2 Cor. 11:21 the sense again requires that it is "the others" who consider the Christians worthy of reproach. In 1 Cor. 11:14 it is a question of a man's wearing his hair long, which is seen as a "shame." It is possible that this constitutes a case of the shame being inherent in the act, but it seems more likely that the "shame" is the opprobrium of the community. Rom. 9:21 and 2 Tim. 2:20 both use the word in reference to pots. Probably the best interpretation of the phrase "pots made for dishonor" is that they are chamber pots. Few people would be prepared to assert that chamber pots are morally reprehensible, so again "ἀτιμία" refers to human values. People find chamber pots unpleasant, and they are therefore considered "ignoble." The passions, therefore, to which God has given over the pagans are most probably "degrading" rather than evil, in that they incur the disrespect of society (cf. v. 24: they "dishonor their own bodies among themselves"). This is confirmed by the otherwise mysterious reference at the end of this discussion to the "recompense" such men receive "in themselves," "which was meet." Moreover, Jerome clearly understood the word in this sense (he translated it as "ignominia"), as did subsequent Greek exegetes. Theodoret observes that "ignominy is the ultimate punishment" ("Τιμωρία γὰρ ἐσχάτη . . . ἡ ἀτιμία," PG, 82:63). There are only two other words of possible moral value in the passage. One is "πλάνη," translated accurately by the KJV as "error." This word occurs in NT eleven times, four of them in the writings ascribed to Paul. It is patent that Paul uses it only in the sense of a mistake, never with any associations of moral turpitude. The other word is "ἀσχημοσύνη," charmingly rendered in the KJV as "that which is unseemly." "Ἀσχημοσύνη" occurs in the LXX as a noun, but in the NT only a related verb and adjective appear. In 1 Cor. 12:23 it appears in reference to the "uncomely" parts of the body, which nevertheless have "more abundant comeliness." In 1 Cor. 13:5 the verb "ἀσχημονεῖ" is translated by Jerome as "est ambitiosa," by the KJV "behave itself unseemly," by the RSV "is arrogant," by the Confraternity (following the Douay) "is ambitious." (A negative has been deleted from both the Greek and the English to avoid confusion.) 1 Cor. 7:36 offers in the KJV "behaveth himself uncomely." The allusion is to a father who does not give his virgin daughter in marriage, and there can certainly be no question of moral failure here, despite Jerome's translation as "turpem se videri." The matter could be better viewed in terms of what is most becoming or seemly. In point of fact the noun in question is merely a privative of "σχῆμα," which has many meanings, all revolving around the basic concept of appearance or form. As has been observed, Paul does not associate it with any clearly discernible moral concept, and it has here, as elsewhere in his works, the idea that what is going on does not make a good appearance—completing the idea that pagans render themselves liable to social opprobrium by engaging in such activities.

myths popularized during the early centuries of the Christian era but not universally accepted until much later and only erratically invoked in discussions of the morality of gay sexuality. Many patristic authors concluded that the point of the story was to condemn inhospitality to strangers; others understood it to condemn rape; most interpreted it in broadly allegorical terms, only tangentially related to sexuality. There was no word in classical Hebrew or Greek for "homosexual," and there is no evidence, linguistic or historical, to suggest that either the *kadēshim* of the Old Testament or the ἀρσενοκοῖται of the New were gay people or particularly given to homosexual practices. On the contrary, it is clear that these words merely designated types of prostitutes: in the case of the former, those associated with pagan temples; in that of the latter, active (as opposed to passive) male prostitutes servicing either sex.

Romans 1 did not condemn homosexual behavior as "against nature" in the sense of the violation of "natural law." No clear idea of "natural law" existed in Paul's time or for many centuries thereafter. To Paul, the activities in question were *beyond* nature in the sense of "extraordinary, peculiar," as was the salvation of the Gentiles, described with the same phrase. Moreover, the persons referred to were considered by influential early Christian theologians to have been necessarily heterosexual (i.e., "naturally" attracted to the opposite sex). There was no implication in the passage that homosexual acts, much less homosexual persons, were *necessarily* sinful.

It might be urged that the general thrust of New Testament sexuality would preclude licit homosexual relations for Christians regardless of specific prohibitions. Any arguments which could be made in support of this position however, would be anachronistic; on the basis of the text of the Bible alone no such conclusion is warranted. Sexuality appears to have been largely a matter of indifference to Jesus. His comments on sexual mores are extremely few, especially in comparison with the frequency of his observations on such matters as wealth and demonic possession, which were largely ignored by later Christians. Even where sexuality is specifically mentioned, the aim is generally to make a larger point: e.g., using the example of committing adultery "in one's heart" to point out that it was the intent which constituted sin (Matt. 5:28). Although he insisted on the indissolubility of the marriage bond, he was widely thought to have advocated celibacy (Matt. 19:10–12; some of his followers, notably Origen, took this quite literally), and he certainly rejected the position of paramount importance accorded the family under Mosaic law and Judaic culture (Matt. 8:21–22, 10:35–37, 12:46–50, 19:29; Luke 9:59–60, 14:26–27; etc.). When confronted with adulterers, he recommended no punishment and clearly suggested that the sins anyone else might have committed were of equal gravity (John 8:3–11;

cf. 4:16–19).[73] He pronounced no condemnations of sexuality among the unmarried[74] and said nothing which bore any relation to homosexuality. The only sexual issue of importance to Jesus appears to have been fidelity: he did not mention the procreation or rearing of children in connection with marriage but only its permanence, and he prohibited divorce except in cases of infidelity.[75] He was apparently celibate himself, and the only persons with whom the Gospels suggest he had any special relationship were men, especially Saint John, who carefully describes himself throughout his gospel as the disciple whom Jesus loved.[76]

While Saint Paul did not specifically comment on gay feelings or lifestyles, he would have disapproved of any form of sexuality which had as its end purely sexual pleasure, and he might have disapproved of relationships directed chiefly at the expression of erotic passion. He did not, however, suggest any connection between sexuality and procreation—a link created by a later age—and he clearly regarded licit sexuality as that contained within a permanent and monogamous relationship. He not only permitted but urged Christians to satisfy the sexual needs of their spouses ("Do not refuse each other except by mutual consent, and then only for an agreed time, to leave yourselves free for prayer," 1 Cor. 7:5, JB). In recommending celibacy, and sexual abstinence even for the married, he did not adduce the evils of sexual pleasure or concupiscence as arguments against the liceity of sex but clearly indicated as the reason for Christian restraint in such matters the impending arrival of the Kingdom of God, before which *all* earthly concerns should seem secondary: "But this I say, brethren, the time is short: it remaineth, that both they that have wives be as though they had none; and they that weep, as though they wept not; ... and they that buy, as though they possessed not" (1 Cor. 7:29–30, KJV).

For Paul, Christian sexuality had little to do with "purity" of seed ("All things are lawful unto me," 1 Cor. 6:12) or of procreative justification for sexual pleasure ("To avoid fornication, let every man have his own wife," 7:2) but was, rather, a question of good stewardship—of using sexuality in a way that was not obsessive ("All things are lawful for me, but I will not be

73. The latter passage must be read in Greek to understand its potential ambiguity. The Greek does not distinguish between "man" and "husband," both being expressed by "ἀνήρ," so that it is impossible to tell whether Jesus considers the five "men" with whom the woman has lived to have been her "husbands" or not.

74. Matt. 15:19 (Mark 7:21) might be an exception to this, but neither the text nor the context makes clear that Jesus intends to comment on the morality of extramarital sexuality in general. The exact meaning of "πορνεία" in NT writings is unclear, and the word occurs only four times in statements of Jesus; in two of these the meaning is clearly what later ages would call "adultery" (Matt. 5:32, 19:9).

75. Matt. 5:32, 19:9; Mark 10:11–12 does not admit this exception.

76. This was not lost on gay Christians of later ages: see below, pp. 225–26.

brought under the power of any," 6:12), did not cause scandal, and did not distract Christians from the service of the Lord ("that ye may attend upon the Lord without distraction," 7:35, all KJV).

There is no inherent reason why unions between persons of the same sex could not have met these moral criteria, but it may well be argued that the complete silence of Christian writers on the subject and the exclusively heterosexual focus of New Testament comments on sexuality reflect general disapproval of homosexuality on the part of Jesus or the early church. Such a conclusion fails to take cognizance of the historical circumstances surrounding the formulation of early Christian sexual ethics. It is hardly surprising that Jesus and Paul, in responding to questions put to them regarding marriage, the family, and divorce, would frame their answers in terms of heterosexual relationships. Their intent was manifestly not to explain or legislate on the whole range of human affections, and they made no pretense of providing moral guidance on all forms of love. They simply answered troublesome questions about heterosexual marriage submitted to them by persons attempting to establish a new sexual morality in societies where there were no social services for the widowed or orphaned; no legal guarantees of protection for unwed mothers or alimony for divorcees; no effective means of birth control except abstinence, abortion, or abandonment of unwanted children.

Gay relationships, whether sexual or not, occasioned no legal difficulties, left no one defenseless or unprovided for, created no unwanted pregnancies or illegitimate offspring, and were not even likely to produce property-settlement problems. That early Christian writers did not feel called upon to comment explicitly on such relationships is no more surprising than their failure to mention household pets and is at least comparable to, if not subsumed under, the complete absence from their literature of references to the type of romantic passion which is the basis for marriage in all industrialized societies. Few Christian theologians before the twelfth century made any references to what is today called "falling in love"; the phenomenon would *seem* to have been completely unknown to Jesus and his followers and to most of the church until the rise of what is loosely termed "courtly love" in the twelfth century. The Greek word for romantic love ($\xi\rho\omega\varsigma$)—one of the most common words among Greek speakers throughout the ancient world—does not occur in the New Testament.

It does not, however, seem likely that the founders of the Christian church did not know of "romantic love," or that they rejected it as immoral. It appears in fact overwhelmingly probable that they considered it irrelevant to basic questions of Christian doctrine, something which those who accepted the teachings of Jesus would be able to regulate for themselves without causing harm to others or being insensitive to the needs of weaker or legally disadvantaged members of society. Chrysostom carefully notes that in derogating homosexual behavior among the pagans Saint Paul did not describe people who "had fallen in love and were drawn to each other by passion" but only those who "burned in their lust one toward another."[77] Enduring love between persons of the same gender, albeit erotic, may have seemed quite a different matter.

The New Testament offered only an outline of social action. In general only the most pressing moral questions are addressed by its authors. Details of life appear only to illustrate larger points. No effort is made to elaborate a comprehensive sexual ethic: Jesus and his followers simply responded to situations and questions requiring immediate attention. They did not comment extensively on friendship, although Jesus apparently considered it the highest form of human commitment (John 15:13–14),[78] and of the few comments in the Gospels on human familial love many appear to be negative.

The New Testament takes no demonstrable position on homosexuality. To suggest that Paul's references to excesses of sexual indulgence involving homosexual behavior are indicative of a general position in opposition to same-sex eroticism is as unfounded as arguing that his condemnation of drunkenness implies opposition to the drinking of wine. At the very most, the effect of Christian Scripture on attitudes toward homosexuality could be described as moot. The most judicious historical perspective might be that it had no effect at all. The source of antigay feelings among Christians must be sought elsewhere.

77. *In Epistolam ad Romanos*, homily 4 (translated in app. 2): "Οὐ γὰρ εἶπειν, ὅτι ἠρασθήσαν καὶ ἐπεθύμησαν ἀλλήλων, ἀλλ' ἐξεκαύθησαν ἐν τῇ ὀρέξει αὐτῶν εἰς ἀλλήλους."

78. The relationship between this sort of "friendship," which appears to refer to the "friendship" that all good men should extend to each other and the personal attachments Jesus felt for such Gospel figures as Lazarus and Saint John, is unclear.

5 Christians and Social Change

Christianity came to power in the Roman world during a period of profound crisis. It is very difficult at this distance to distinguish the extent to which the new religion was responsible for, responsive to, or incidentally coordinate with the various transformations occurring in the Graeco-Roman world during the early centuries of what is now called the Christian Era. It is even more difficult to account for the apparent devolution, especially in the West, of a brilliant and complex civilization into a comparatively much less advanced state of organization and culture.

Two aspects of these changes may be closely related to the decline of Roman tolerance on sexual issues, but it is impossible at present to do more than characterize their possible effects. Their actual influence, their relation to each other, and their relative importance as compared with other factors can not be determined. Conjectures about changes of this magnitude in areas so little understood will inevitably be unsatisfactory to a very large extent; the dramatic alterations in sexual mores which accompanied the disintegration of the Roman state and the rise of the barbarian kingdoms are clearly vastly more complex than any brief approach to a single aspect of the problem can indicate, and they may eventually be shown to result from social phenomena as yet wholly unstudied.

One factor which may have had some impact was the increasing ruralization of the formerly urban cultural centers of Roman civilization. The exhaustion of the urban elite was already noticeable in the second century and grew steadily worse in the third and fourth as political instability, economic change, social disruptions, natural disasters, and the lower birthrate of the wealthy wiped out large numbers of Rome's noble families. The ranks of the upper classes were replenished by the emperors largely by the appointment to noble orders of wealthy provincials, whose fortunes (and attitudes) had in many cases been less affected by economic conditions in Rome than those of the urban patriciate.

During this same period the control of the Empire passed almost entirely into the hands of armies and generals, who made and unmade emperors with dizzying celerity and determined to a large extent the policies of those in power. After the first century A.D. few citizens of the city of Rome served in its armies, and by the middle of the third century most soldiers were not even recruited from rural Italy. Provincials (granted citizenship by Caracalla in 212 partly for this very purpose) and barbarian allies now made up the bulk of the army; even officers were more and more often provincials or barbarians who had been promoted through the ranks. From Julian's time half the officers were Germans, and with the admission of the Goths in the fourth century the Roman army ceased to be "Roman" in any aspect save nomenclature.

Nor were the men placed on the imperial throne by these armies any more "Roman" in outlook. Few of the emperors after the first century were born in Rome; some were never even in the city. At the end of the fourth century the poet Claudian lamented that only three emperors had even set foot in Rome during the past century. The imperial court, as if consciously symbolizing the steady ruralization of Roman society, moved first to Milan and then to Ravenna.[1]

Eventually external forces stormed and took the city of Rome itself, not content to allow it to decay at its own pace, and imposed their own value systems on it from without. But profound changes in the traditional values of the city had begun centuries before the barbarians breached the city walls. These changes took many forms: the importation of foreign religious cults, especially those emphasizing magic and mystery; increased fascination with foreign cultures and languages, especially those of Greece and Egypt; the formulation of escapist philosophies focused more on the spiritual world than the perceptible one; increasing dependence by most of society on a state imagined and claiming to be omnipotent, and the consequent extension of the power of the state into increasingly minor and personal aspects of people's lives; the rise or revitalization of ethical codes, such as Stoicism and some branches of Christianity, that emphasized sexual morality and self-denial rather than civic virtue or social contributions (and whose intellectual leaders were often from provincial areas of the Empire).

As the upper echelons of Roman government—civil and ecclesiastical—became increasingly dominated by rural outlooks, official attitudes toward Roman social mores were considerably altered.[2] Traditional Roman ideas of sexual propriety, based on marital fidelity, the protection of minors, and the

---

1. These were of course cities, but enormously less sophisticated and traditionally urban than Rome, the only real metropolis of the West.

2. With some exceptions, notably Elagabalus. Although born in the provinces (Emesa, in what is now Syria), he does not seem to have espoused a traditional rural morality.

nuclear family, gave way to much more rigid categorization of legitimate sexual outlets, the exclusion of sexual pleasure as a positive good, and general intolerance of sexual deviation. How far official rhetoric on these matters, whether civil or religious, corresponded to social reality is extremely difficult to gauge. Though most later emperors and many prominent Christian leaders came from the provinces, much of their constituency remained urban. There is considerable evidence that urban Christians did not share the narrow sexual views of famous ascetics, and among all religions demographic considerations may have played a major role, not yet analyzed in detail.

A second factor, which may have had less effect on popular mores but was even more important from an institutional point of view, was the increasing absolutism of Roman government. The gradual abandonment of the myth of the diarchy—joint rule by the emperor and the senate—and a general abdication, through coercion and apathy, of individual responsibility and power resulted in greater and greater totalitarian control over personal aspects of Romans' lives. By the late fourth century many citizens could no longer choose their religion, their occupation, their place of residence, or even their favorite athletic team without imperial interference. Public aspects of religion and morals had always been the object of some governmental supervision, but the increasingly theocratic despotism of the later Empire often led to intervention in matters such as personal religious conviction or private sexual expression which would have been considered entirely individual under the early emperors. At the end of the second century the emperor Marcus Aurelius (from a Spanish family) wrote that he had learned from his father "to suppress all passion for young men"[3] but limited his official action to his refusal to list Antinous among the friends of his predecessor, Hadrian. A subsequent claimant to the imperial throne, however, was noted for active persecution of gay people.[4] The third-century emperor Severus Alexander, born in North Africa, considered outlawing the *exoleti* but finally thought better of it, realizing that he could not actually end the practice and by forbidding it would only drive it underground (Lampridius *Severus Alexander* 24, 4).[5] He limited himself, therefore, to assuaging his misgiving by diverting the tax on male prostitution to public works instead of his own imperial treasury (ibid. 3). One of his successors, Philip (born in Arabia), did outlaw the *exoleti* in the West in the mid-third century, but

3. "Καὶ τὸ παῦσαι τὰ περὶ τοὺς ἔρωτας τῶν μειρακίων," *Meditations* 1.16.
4. Clodius Albinus, "aversae Veneris semper ignarus et talium persecutor" (Capitolinus 11.7).
5. "Habuit in animo ut exsoletos vetaret, quod postea Philippus fecit, sed veritus est ne prohibens publicum dedecus in privatas cupiditates converteret, cum homines inlicita magis prohibita poscant furore iactati." Possibly "exoleti" refers to male prostitutes of any type.

more than 100 years later they still flourished, and it is unlikely that there was any popular support for the measure.[6] (Homosexual prostitution was not abolished in the Eastern Empire until the sixth century.)

The third century also witnessed a theoretical broadening of the definition of the legal term "stuprum" to include some varieties of homosexual behavior. The basic meaning of "stuprum" is "defilement," and in this sense it was used by Roman jurists to describe sexual behavior—either active or passive—which was unbecoming the status of a Roman citizen and not covered under another legal rubric such as rape, adultery, etc.[7]

In early law the popular prejudice against an adult male citizen's passivity in sexual relations does not seem to have found official expression, but by the third century it had become a form of *stuprum*. The jurist Paulus opined in his *Sententiae* (2.27.12), collected around 300, that a male who voluntarily underwent *stuprum* (i.e., was passive to another male) should lose half his estate.[8]

6. "Usum virilis scorti removendum honestissime consultavit" (Aurelius Victor *Liber de Caesaribus* 28.6, supposedly inspired by seeing a young man who looked like his son standing in front of a male brothel). When Aurelius Victor observes that such prostitution "yet remains," he is writing about 360 A.D.

7. If an unmarried female citizen had sexual relations with a man to whom she was not married, this constituted *stuprum*, as long as it was not a case of rape and she was not a prostitute. (In the latter case no sexual behavior would be unbecoming to her status, and she could not seek redress or be prosecuted under any law regarding *stuprum*.) Similarly, if a husband had relations with a married woman other than his wife, it was adultery, but if he did so with an unmarried woman, he was guilty of *stuprum*. No form of sexual activity with slaves, foreigners, or prostitutes of either sex constituted *stuprum*, but the seduction, rape, or prostitution of free-born minors of either gender were all *stupra*, regardless of the consent of the minor involved: e.g., in regard to boys, *Digest* 47.10.9.4, 47.11.1.2, 48.6.3.4. Literary use of the term was somewhat looser. Most extralegal sources use "stuprum" to describe immoral sexual conduct regardless of legal niceties of responsibility or fault: e.g., Livy 39.8.7, "Stupra promiscua ingenuorum feminarumque errant"; see also 39.13.10, "Plura virorum inter sese quam feminarum esse stupra." Note that in these instances there is no moral distinction made or implied on the basis of gender. None of the published studies on Roman law and homosexuality discusses *stuprum* in any detail, but Bailey's treatment is better than others.

8. "Qui voluntate sua stuprum, flagitiumque patitur, dimidia parte honorum suorum multatur; nec testamentum ei ex majore parte facere licet." The *Digest* also repeated an edict barring men who voluntarily underwent *stuprum* from bringing suits on behalf of others (3.1.1.6: "Removet autem a postulando pro aliis et eum, qui corpore suo muliebria passus est"). It is not suggested that they could not bring legal action on their own behalf, and the point of the provision seems to be the exclusion from legal practice of men known to be pathics. No historical source records any instance of the invocation of this edict, and it was common knowledge that a number of emperors were passive in sexual relations with men. The Elder Seneca cites an earlier law which prohibits an "unchaste man" from public speaking (*Controversiae* 6, *Inpudicus contione prohibeatur*), but "inpudicus" has no specifically homosexual connotations, and the case from which Seneca cites the law is so bizarre that it is next to impossible to discover what role (if any) homosexual acts played in it—a hand-

Whether this opinion had any force of law before its inclusion in Justinian's legal compilation of the sixth century is doubtful. Paulus was exiled by Elagabalus, noted for his predilection for passive homosexual behavior, and even after his recall (by Severus Alexander) there is no indication that this attitude enjoyed official sanction.

In 342 gay marriages, which had hitherto been legal (at least de facto) and well known, were outlawed in a curiously phrased statute which some authors have regarded as entirely facetious.[9] The highly propagandistic nature of the law and lack of any penalty for noncompliance probably indicate that its imperial drafter(s) expected it to meet with popular opposition or neglect.[10]

---

some young man, on a bet, went out in public in women's clothes, was raped by ten youths, had them convicted of rape, was then barred by a magistrate from speaking publicly, and sued the magistrate for damages. The *Mosaicarum et Romanarum legum collatio* compiled in the late fourth century conflates the opinion of Paulus and the praetorian edict (Hyamson ed., p. 82) and prefixes them to a prohibition of homosexual prostitution. The *Collatio*, however, is not reflective of actual legal practice. Hyamson (ibid., note to ll. 8–10) attributes the edict confiscating half the estate of pathics to Severus, on the basis of a comment by Zosimus: "'Ἐγένετο μὲν περὶ τοὺς ἁμαρτάνοντας ἀπαραίτητος, τῶν ἐπὶ τοῖς ἀτόποις εὐθυνομένων δημοσίας ποιῶν τὰς οὐσίας"(*Historia* 1.8, ed. Ludwig Mendelssohn [Leipzig, 1887], p. 8), but the equation seems tenuous.

9. Theodosian Code 9.7.3. Bailey (p. 70) unaccountably refuses to accept the obvious reading of this law and insists that it does not refer to marriages between males. Why he does so is unclear; he admits that such unions were well known in the later Empire, though he minimizes their frequency and importance. He inserts words into the text to justify his claim, adding an "and" which the lawmakers would surely have included had they intended it. But even after taking this liberty, he is left wondering what the law actually prohibited, half-heartedly suggesting that the whole statute might be facetious. (He has the same trouble with a Hittite law regarding homosexual marriage and inserts words into its text, p. 35.) It is clear what the law regulates: "nubere" refers to marriage, either directly or by analogy, and is in fact the very verb used by the Latin writers who describe gay marriages (see chap. 3). An epigram of Martial depends entirely on this use of "nubere" (1.24; see also 8.12), and Martial specifies the legality of such marriages. (Indeed this law seems almost a direct response to his epigrams.) The best-known translator of the code, Clyde Pharr (*The Theodosian Code and Novels and the Sirmondian Constitutions* [Princeton, N.J., 1952], pp. 231–32), understood the statute to apply to gay marriages and cited as cross-references accounts of such by Latin writers. It is true, as Bailey observes, that Pharr gives "porrecturam" in the opening sentence a rather unusual construction, but it is not at all necessary to insert any words to correct this: "quum vir nubit in feminam viris porrecturam" undoubtedly means "when a man marries as a woman who offers herself to men." This is quite a common use of "in" (see, e.g., Lewis and Short, s.v. "in") and corresponds exactly to the nuance of "nubere," which is the word used to describe a woman's part of heterosexual marriage ("ducere" being used to describe the man's role). Neither the best text (T. Mommsen, ed., *Theodosiani libri xvi cum constitutionibus Sirmondianis* [Berlin, 1905]) nor any of the variant readings (for which see the annotated edition of Gustav Haenel [Leipzig, 1842]) justify the translation suggested by Bailey.

10. The translation of this law is inevitably affected by one's opinion about the *Lex Scantinia*. Since there is no definite article in Latin, where the author of this statute writes

The first corporal penalty for an act related to homosexuality was imposed in 390 for forcing or selling males into prostitution.[11] The death penalty prescribed in this statute may be an indication of the horror with which the emperor Theodosius (born in Spain) regarded the practice,[12] but its promulgation as law does not demonstrate anything about the attitude of the populace. The Theodosian Code also insisted on death for offering sacrifices to pagan deities, although this had been completely legal only decades before and was widely practiced for centuries after.[13]

Autocratic oppression and increasingly rural ethics were only two aspects of a much more complicated phenomenon. Moreover, it should not be imagined that the transition to a less tolerant social ambience was effected without opposition. In response to the rising tide of intolerance, gay people began to defend their preferences and criticize their opponents in various literary genres. Poses of partisan sexuality were already a commonplace of Hellenistic verse, and facetious interchanges such as that between Meleager ("I do not have a heart obsessed with men. What pleasure can there be, love, in mounting males, if you wish to get without giving anything?") and an ardent devotee of gay love ("There is no desire for women in my soul, but the glow of males has set me on fire")[14] were a staple of Roman literary

---

"iubemus insurgere leges" one might (like Pharr) translate either "we order the laws to arise," implying that laws against such behavior were already in existence but not enforced, or "we order that laws arise," suggesting that laws should be passed against it. It is obvious that no subsequent authors knew of any law which antedated this one, nor, considering the history of Roman law and homosexuality, does it seem at all likely that the drafter of the statute believed any such law existed. The following phrase, "we order the laws to be armed" only heightens the ambiguity.

11. Efforts to read into this law general antigay legislation (e.g., Bailey, p. 72) are doomed to failure. Bailey was unaware of a longer version of the statute, preserved in the *Mosaicarum et Romanarum legum collatio*, in which it is specified that the persons guilty of this offense are to be dragged out of the brothels in which they worked ("omnibus eductos, pudet dicere, uirorum lupanaribus," Hyamson ed., p. 82). The date of the *Collatio* is uncertain, but its readings are generally meticulous and cannot be dismissed. Haenel comments extensively on the relationship between the two versions (cols. 845–46). Note that the *Collatio* does not repeat the law of 342. The broadest justifiable interpretation would be condemnation of all those involved in passive prostitution, i.e., the panderers and the prostitutes, but "damnare" seems to militate against this.

12. But both this and the outlawing of sacrifice may have been imposed on the emperor as penance by Ambrose, bishop of Milan, who had refused him communion after a massacre at Thessalonica in 390. It would not be surprising if Ambrose was hostile to gay sexuality.

13. 16.10.4. Note that this statute uses the very same phrase ("gladio ultore") in regard to the death penalty as the edict against prostitution, suggesting that they were part of the same campaign. For the persistence of pagan sacrifice, see J. N. Hillgarth, *The Conversion of Western Europe, 350–750* (Englewood Cliffs, N.J., 1969); and S. MacKenna, *Paganism and Pagan Survivals in Spain up to the Fall of the Visigothic Kingdom* (Washington, D.C., 1938).

14. AP, 5.208, 12.17. The first poem is ironic, since Meleager was noted for his erotic poetry to young men. It seems to pillory the lack of reciprocity in heterosexual relations,

fare. Under the early Empire such poetry had represented little more than a facetious approach to the pansexuality of the time, whose tolerant mores accommodated every style of life, but under the influence of increasingly narrow sexual attitudes in the declining later Empire, these arguments became acrid and vehement, and the basis of objections to homosexual acts shifted from personal preference to moral absolutes and prudery. (Athenaeus even deprecated Plato himself, calling his dialogues on love "indecent" and claiming that he compiled them "in utter contempt of his future readers," 11.508d.)

Complex debates on the subject became common, examining (or purporting to examine) the validity, morality, and aesthetic desirability of the two kinds of love (for men, at least).[15] Around the beginning of the second century A.D., Plutarch had devoted a book of his *Moralia* to such an argument and had the proponent of gay love deprecate heterosexual passion in strident terms:

> True love has nothing to do with women's quarters, nor will I agree that you have ever felt *love* for women or girls, any more than flies feel love for milk. . . . [750C][16]
>
> But if this [heterosexual] passion must also be called "love," it is an effeminate and illegitimate one. . . . The one true love is the love of youths . . . . That other soft and domestic passion that whiles away its time on the laps and beds of women, constantly seeking indulgence and emasculating itself with unmanly, unloving, and uninspiring pleasure— it deserves to be banished, as Solon did in fact banish it. . . . Love is beautiful and decorous; pleasure is vulgar and servile. For this reason it is considered uncouth for a free man to be in love with slaves, since this sort of passion is merely sexual, like relations with women. . . . [751]

The advocate of heterosexual love was no less emphatic:

> If unnatural relations with men do not preclude or impede a loving relationship, then it is much more likely that the love of men and women, which happens according to nature, will give rise to love through fondness. . . . If, then, we really examine the truth . . ., we see that both the passion for youths and that for women are one type of love. But if you want to make distinctions for the sake of argument,

especially in the third line ("ἁ χεῖρ γὰρ τὰν χεῖρα . . ./ἔρροι πᾶς ἄρσην ἀρσενικαῖς λαβίσιν"); cf. 12.7 ("τὸ δὲ μεῖζον ἐκεῖνο,/ οὐκ ἔστιν πού θῆς τὴν χέρα πλαζομένην"), 23, 52, etc. The chronological relationship between Meleager's poem and that of his opponent is not certain; Meleager may have been the respondent.

15. Since women's feelings and desires are not explicitly represented in any of these discussions, the desirability of lesbianism is left entirely moot.

16. Cf. Plutarch's *De communibus notitis* 28 (*Moralia* 1073), where a similar image is used.

you will see that this male love does not play fair but that, as one come
late and untimely to the world, illegitimate and ill-favored, it drives
out the legitimate and older love. . . . [751–52][17]

A later[18] dialogue in a novel by Achilles Tatius treats the controversy in
similar fashion, but with greater sophistication and less invective. The
opponent of gay love compares it to the tortures of Tantalus, saying that
the beauty of young men has no sooner appeared than it fades, leaving the
lover unsatisfied and still thirsty for love (2.35). The advocate of gay love
responds that true pleasure lies in desire, not satiety (2.36), and that gay love
is heavenly (as in Plato's *Symposium*), as is clearly evidenced by the fact that
Zeus carried off to heaven not a woman but a youth, Ganymede, to replace
his wife. His antagonist replies with counterexamples from mythology,
attempting to demonstrate that it is the love of women which is heavenly.
The argument grows heated. The gay side derides women as the artificial
creations of makeup and unguents, while the beauty of boys is simple and
unaffected. The argument is not concluded, although the gay spokesman has
the last word.

The dialogue *Affairs of the Heart* is undoubtedly the subtlest of the genre,
with elaborate historical speculations on the biological necessity of marriage
and the social factors giving rise to homosexual relations. The proponent of
gay love admits that marriage is necessary but does not feel this makes it
desirable: "Marriages were devised as a means of insuring succession, which
was necessary, but only the love of men is a noble undertaking of the philosopher's soul" (33).

Let no one expect love of males in early times. For intercourse with
women was necessary so that our race might not utterly perish for lack
of seed. . . . Do not then, Charicles, again censure this discovery as
worthless because it wasn't made earlier, nor, because intercourse with
women can be credited with greater antiquity than the love of boys,
must you think love of boys inferior. No, we must consider the pursuits

17. It is rather difficult to tell where Plutarch's sympathies lie in this dialogue. There is
certainly more invective against the gay position, but after the real argument has been
broken off, one of the formerly antigay speakers delivers a long encomium of love drawing
almost entirely on examples of famous gay lovers (758ff.); and throughout the dialogue
nongay speakers constantly use gay love as the model for erotic relations (e.g., 758C: "Nor
is there any contest or competition more fitting for a god to watch over and supervise than the
pursuit and courting of beautiful young men by their lovers"; also 754D: "The nurse
governs the baby, the teacher the boy, the gymnasiarch the youth, the lover the young
man"). Many of Plutarch's ostensibly antihomosexual remarks, moreover, are patently
ironic.

18. The date is arguable; current opinion tends to place its composition in the later
second century.

that are old to be necessary, but assess as superior the later additions invented by human life when it had leisure for thought. [Macleod trans., p. 205]

The gay side proposes not an end to relations with women but merely that they be limited to what is physically necessary for the survival of the race. True love, it insists, is possible only between men. A series of misogynistic comments follows about the natural unattractiveness of women and the artifices to which they must resort to make themselves fetching to men. Then the gay speaker points out that gay love is not an "exotic indulgence of the time" but a hallowed and lawful heritage. He concludes by recommending restraint in attachment, counseling that none squander permanent affection for the sake of a brief pleasure. (It is not clear that the chaste relations commended by the gay speaker in the major debate are idealized by the author of the text, since a subsequent speaker, Theomnestus, argues eloquently that such restraint is undesirable, if not impossible.)

This debate, unlike the preceding ones, is officially judged. "Marriage is a boon and a blessing to men when it meets with good fortune, while the love of boys, that pays court to the hallowed dues of friendship, I consider to be the privilege only of philosophy. Therefore all men should marry, but let only the wise be permitted to love boys, for perfect virtue grows least of all among women" (ibid., p. 229). The verdict is conciliatory, but the gay speaker has the final word in the debate, and his arguments are then praised by another gay speaker. Moreover, the heterosexual debater is pictured as dejected, while his opponent celebrates by hosting a banquet. The narrator specifically praises the heterosexual speaker for making a good case for "the more awkward cause" (ibid., p. 231).[19]

The legal status of gay people and their relations was not to be officially denied until the sixth century, but the tide was already turning against them by the beginning of the fourth century, and this did not escape the notice of some observers at the time. In view of what history had in store for them in later years, there is considerable poignancy in the remark by the author of *Affairs of the Heart* that gay people are already "strangers cut off in a foreign land" and his assertion that "we shall not, all the same, be overcome by fear and betray the truth" (31, my trans.).[20]

Since Christianity was the official religion of the Roman Empire from the fourth century on and was the only organized force to survive the final disintegration of Roman institutions in the West after the barbarian invasions of the fifth century, it became the conduit through which the narrower morality

19. "Ὅτι δυσχερεστέρῳ μέρει δυνατῶς συνηγόρησεν."
20. "Ξένοι τε ἐπ᾽ ἀλλοτρίας γῆς ἀπειλήμμεθα . . . , ὅμως τἀληθὲς οὐ προδώσομεν νικηθέντες ὄκνῳ."

of the later Empire reached Europe. It was not, however, the author of this morality. The dissolution of the urban society of Rome and the ascendance of less tolerant political and ethical leadership occasioned a steady restriction of sexual freedom which transcended credal boundaries. This is not to deny that Christian synods and princes enacted penalties against homosexual relations during the period. But execution is different from authorship, and it is misleading to characterize Christianity as somehow peculiarly liable to antigay feelings or doctrines. All the organized philosophical traditions of the West grew increasingly intolerant of sexual pleasure under the later Empire, and it is often impossible to distinguish Christian ethical precepts from those of pagan philosophy during the period. Most contemporary religious movements were struggling with moral concerns similar to those of early Christians.

There is, moreover, no evidence that Christians in general were much affected by the narrow sexual attitudes of some of their leaders. Individual Christians had to face such urgent and traumatic moral problems as whether to accept martyrdom at the hands of imperial officials, whether to adopt children exposed by pagans, how to limit their own families, etc. Homosexuality must have seemed a minor concern. Inadequate material survives for assessing the responses of communities to the question. Early councils were preoccupied with such fundamental theological issues as the nature of Christ, the authority of the church, the efficacy of the sacraments, etc., and were not at leisure to formulate a detailed code of sexual ethics. (The first "general" council to deal with homosexuality was Lateran III, in 1179.)

Some Christian theorists addressed the issue, but these were relatively few and generally those representing schools of extreme asceticism. It does not seem likely that their attitudes were typical; and the inconsistent, contradictory, and often illogical arguments they adduced probably did little to establish a general attitude toward homosexuality among rank-and-file Christians, the majority of whom were illiterate and unable to appreciate such speculation in any event.

None of the philosophical traditions upon which Christianity is known to have drawn would necessarily have precluded homosexual behavior as an option for Christians. Aside from the Bible, three specific moral traditions had major impacts on early Christian sexual attitudes: the Judaeo-Platonist schools of Alexandria, discussed below (chap. 6), dualist aversion to the body and its pleasures, and Stoic concepts of "natural" sexuality.

Dualism—i.e., the philosophy that there are good and evil forces warring for control of man's soul—was extremely influential in the early church. Saint Augustine had been a member of a dualist sect, the Manicheans, for many years before his conversion to Christianity, and many Christian moralists were consciously or unconsciously affected by the powerful dualist intellectual currents of the later Empire. Dualists deprecated all forms of sexuality as weapons of the evil forces against the good, arguing that all pleasures distract the soul from spiritual ends and that sexual pleasures, as more powerful than most, are more dangerous than most. Most Manicheans opposed all forms of sexuality equally. Homosexual pleasures were seen by some as worse than heterosexual ones, since they did not even accord with the design of the Creator in regenerating the human race. But they were seen by many as less serious than heterosexual acts since (a) they did not partake of the false aura of sanctity which marital sexuality used to seduce the unwary into lives of self-indulgence, and (b) they did not entrap souls in matter, as heterosexual intercourse did when children resulted. Dualist influence was thus ambivalent on the subject of homosexuality and could have pushed Christians affected by it in either direction. Augustine seems to have been aiming his comments about homosexual acts in the *Confessions* at Manicheans; medieval dualists were almost unanimously accused of *favoring* homosexual relations.[21]

Western Neoplatonism often exhibited dualist tendencies in its rejection of the physical as gross, if not bad, but this input into Christian thought was also ambivalent on the subject of homosexual behavior. Plotinus, for instance, regarded homosexuality as a straying from the path to perfection, like heterosexual activity with pleasure as its end, but considered that it arose from "natural principles."[22] Certainly his attitude would not have produced a public reaction to homosexuality notably different from attitudes toward heterosexual pleasure.

It is often supposed that the profound impact of Stoicism on early Christian morality[23] in some way affected Christian attitudes toward gay sexuality, but few of the most important antihomosexual texts of the early church clearly incorporate Stoic ideas,[24] and what is supposed to have been the major contribution of Stoicism to Christian sexual morality—the idea that the sole "natural" (and hence moral) use of sexuality was procreation—was in fact a common belief of many philosophies of the day. It was espoused by persons vehemently opposed to Stoicism, like Plutarch,[25] and it probably entered

---

21. But see chap. 10 below.

22. "Οἱ δ' ἂν ἐν παρανόμῳ καὶ παρὰ τὴν φύσιν ἐθέλωσι γεννᾶν, ἐκ τῆς κατὰ φύσιν πορείας ποιησάμενοι τὰς ἀρχὰς γενόμενοι παράφοροι ἐκ ταύτης οἷον ὁδοῦ ὀλισθήσαντες κεῖνται πεσόντες," *Plotini Enneades* 3.5.1, ed. Hermann Mueller (Berlin, 1878), p. 208.

23. Concisely illustrated in Moses Hadas, *Hellenistic Culture* (New York, 1959), chap. 18. It is notable that Seneca, perhaps the foremost exponent of Stoic morality in the Latin West, was born in one of the most rural areas of the Roman Empire, Spain, whose provincial mores had severely depressed the more urban Martial.

24. John of Salisbury, one of the few late medieval authors influenced by Stoicism, had somewhat unclear feelings about homosexuality: see chap. 8.

25. Plutarch was the author of at least nine treatises against the Stoics, yet he wrote that "anyone who takes a woman not for the sake of children but for pleasure is clearly dis-

Christian schools of thought primarily through the influence of the Alexandrian Platonists. The fact that philosophical systems which agreed in no other point came to the same conclusions regarding procreation as the "end" of sexuality would seem to indicate that this was a sufficiently common notion not to require any specific philosophical derivation; it was probably more a social phenomenon than an intellectual one.

Moreover, it is far from clear that the Stoics themselves disapproved of homosexual activity: Zeno—the founder of Stoicism—recommended that sexual partners be chosen without regard to gender ("Do not make invidious comparisons between gay and nongay, male and female"; "You make distinctions about love objects? I do not") [26] and was reputed to have had intercourse only with other males. [27] Most prominent exponents of Stoic thought apparently considered homosexuality morally neutral. [28] Epictetus spoke of homosexual and heterosexual attraction in terms of complete equality [29] and urged his followers not to be judgmental toward those given to sexual indulgence (*Encheiridion* 33[8]).

Seneca, the most influential Stoic in the West, was rumored not only to have indulged in homosexuality himself but to have inspired his pupil Nero to do so as well. [30] Whether or not the story is true, it does not seem that Western Stoicism would have opposed homosexual acts unless they involved excess. Seneca devoted a long passage in his *Naturales quaestiones* (1.16) to

---

regarding the good of marriage and . . . has made his children's birth a reproach to them" (*Solon* 22.4: "῾Ο γὰρ ἐν γάμῳ παρορῶν τὸ καλὸν οὐ τέκνων ἕνεκα δῆλός ἐστιν, ἀλλ᾽ ἡδονῆς ἀγόμενος γυναῖκα, τόν τε μισθὸν ἀπέχει, καὶ παρρησίαν αὐτῷ πρὸς τοὺς γενομένους οὐκ ἀπολέλοιπεν, οἷς αὐτὸ τὸ γενέσθαι πεποίηκεν ὄνειδος").

26. "Διαμηρίζειν μηδὲν μᾶλλον μηδὲ ἧσσον παιδικὰ ἢ μὴ παιδικὰ μηδὲ θήλεα ἢ ἄρρενα," in Sextus Empiricus *Outlines of Pyrrhonism* 3.245; Διαμεμήρικας τὸν ἐρώμενον; οὐκ ἔγωγε," in Sextus Empiricus *Adversus mathematicos* 11.190.

27. Athenaeus 13.563E: "Ζήνωνα τὸν Φοίνικα, ὃς οὐδεπώποτε γυναικὶ ἐχρήσατο, παιδικοῖς δ᾽ ἀεί." Athenaeus is not a particularly trustworthy authority, but this information conforms to the general impression of Zeno in the ancient world: see Diogenes Laertius 7.129; Plutarch *Quaestiones conviviales* 3.6.1. (653E); Johann von Arnim, *Stoicorum vetera fragmenta* (Leipzig, 1905), 1:58–59, nos. 247–253; and Seneca *Epistles* 123.15: "Qui nos sub specie Stoicae sectae hortantur ad vitia. . . . Quaeramus, ad quam usque aetatem iuvenes amandi sint."

28. "The followers of Zeno, Cleanthes, and Chrysippus say this is indifferent," Sextus Empiricus *Outlines of Pyrrhonism* 3.200.

29. E.g., *Encheiridion* 10: "᾽Εὰν καλὸν ἴδῃς ἢ καλήν, εὑρήσεις δύναμιν πρὸς ταῦτα ἐγκράτειαν"; see also *Discourses* 4.11.19.

30. "Καὶ μειρακίοις ἐξώροις ἔχαιρε, καὶ τοῦτο καὶ τὸν Νέρωνα ποιεῖν ἐδίδαξε," Dio Cassius 61.10. Although Dio obviously considered it noteworthy that Seneca preferred adult males, this may have been more moral in Seneca's eyes than having sexual relations with children. Although Dio is generally an excellent authority for the Empire, this passage occurs only in an epitome of his work and cannot be accorded the authority of portions which survive in their entirety.

describing the dissolute life-style of a man much given to homosexual relations. The point of the story, however, is not to make a comment on any sort of sexual behavior but to condemn the man's fascination with mirrors. "Nature" is invoked to demonstrate the real function of mirrors (1, passim, esp. 17), but not to provide any insight about gender choice, and there is the distinct suggestion that everyone has at one time or another participated in the sort of activity the man favored ("quaeque sibi quisque fecisse se negat"). All vices, in Seneca's view, violated nature, none more than others.[31]

Prevailing social conditions and the attitudes of those in power may have predisposed inhabitants of many parts of the Empire to look upon homosexual acts with suspicion or hostility, but in large cities like Rome or Constantinople the range of opinion was much greater, and there is no evidence that general Christian behavior was markedly different from that of non-Christian citizens. Homosexual prostitution was not only tolerated but actually taxed by Christian emperors in Eastern cities for nearly two centuries after Christianity had become the state religion.

Many pagan writers objected to Christianity precisely because of what they claimed was sexual looseness on the part of its adherents,[32] and much Christian apologetic was aimed at defending Christians against the common belief that they were given to every form of sexual indulgence—including homosexual acts.[33] This belief seems to have been at least partly rooted in fact. Even Chrysostom had to admit that gay sexuality was absolutely rampant in the Christian society of fourth-century Antioch from the highest level on down.

> Those very people who have been nourished by godly doctrine, who instruct others in what they ought and ought not to do, who have heard the Scriptures brought down from heaven, these do not consort with prostitutes as fearlessly as they do with young men.
>
> The fathers of the young men take this in silence: they do not try to sequester their sons, nor do they seek any remedy for this evil.
>
> None is ashamed, no one blushes, but, rather, they take pride in their little game; the chaste seem to be the odd ones, and the disapproving the ones in error. If these [disapprovers] are insignificant, they are

31. "Omnia vitia contra naturam pugnant, omnia debitum ordinem deserunt," *Epistles* 122. This epistle contains a list of activities Seneca considers "unnatural": they include swimming in heated pools, growing plants indoors, trying to look youthful, and drinking on an empty stomach.

32. E.g., Tacitus *Annals* 15.44; Pliny *Epistles* 10.96.

33. An especially interesting example of this is Minucius Felix's *Octavius*, a defense of Christians against extravagant charges of immorality, including ceremonial fellatio and temple prostitution; see esp. chap. 28. For Christian immorality (real and pretended) in general, see Noonan, esp. chaps. 3 and 4.

intimidated; if they are powerful, they are mocked, laughed at, refuted with a thousand arguments. The courts are powerless, the laws,[34] instructors, parents, friends, teachers—all are helpless.

If any avoid such practices they will find it difficult to escape the bad reputation of those involved, first of all because they are very few and will be easily lost in the great throng of the evil livers . . . .

Indeed, . . . there is some danger that womankind will become unnecessary in the future, with young men instead fulfilling all the needs women used to. . . .[35]

Since Chrysostom was, for reasons discussed elsewhere in this volume, personally disturbed by homosexuality, he regarded this situation as scandalous, but it seems reasonable to infer that those Christians "with a thousand arguments" ready to justify their life-style entertained rather different opinions about the morality of homosexual relationships, and it is striking that by Chrysostom's own admission this group included not only the respectable establishment of the city but the leadership of the Christian community itself, "those very people who have been nourished by godly doctrine, who instruct others in what they ought and ought not to do, who have heard the Scriptures brought down from heaven." Though not necessarily defending his own behavior, Theodoret of Cyrus evinced an attitude toward gay sexuality strikingly similar to Plato's, deprecating passion only insofar as it was obsessive or addictive: "I myself think that those *excessively* [λίαν] addicted to [these] pleasure passions do not recommend the passion but in time become slaves, making a habit into a way of life."[36] There is no appeal to procreation-based sexuality, or indeed any suggestion that nonobsessive homosexuality would be un-Christian. A Christian contemporary in the West, Ausonius, kept in his library volumes of homosexual literature which were considered scandalous even by Roman standards[37] and took delight in translating from Greek to Latin such tidbits as Strato's puzzle about four sex acts being performed simultaneously by three men.[38]

34. Chrysostom is probably referring to laws protecting minors.

35. *Adversus oppugnatores vitae monasticae* 3.8, translated in part in app. 2. For the accuracy of his comments on Antioch, see the works of the contemporary pagan writer Libanius; and A. J. Festugière, *Antioche paienne et chrétienne* (Paris, 1959), pp. 195–209.

36. Theodoret of Cyrus, *Thérapeutique des maladies helléniques* [*Graecarum affectionum curatio*], ed. and trans. Pierre Canivet (Paris, 1958), pp. 352–53: (9.53–54): "'Εγὼ γὰρ οἶμαι καὶ τοὺς λίαν ἡδυπαθείαις δουλεύοντας οὐκ ἐπαινεῖν τὸ πάθος, ἀλλὰ δουλεύειν τῷ χρόνῳ, τὸ ἔθος ἕξιν ἐργασαμένους." Perhaps the translation should be "become slaves to time," i.e., to the world of the flesh rather than that of the spirit.

37. Epistle 13, in the MGH, *Auctores*, 5.2, p. 173.

38. Ibid., *Epigrams*, 59. The Greek original occurs in two versions in the AP: 11.225 and 12.210. The latter version is the better one:

Ausonius was passionately loved by Saint Paulinus, bishop of Nola, and their relationship found expression in poetry of exquisite tenderness, setting the tone for much of the love literature of medieval Europe.

> Through all that life may allot
> Or assign to mortals,
> As long as I am held within this prison body,
> In whatever world I am found,
> I shall hold you fast,
> Grafted onto my being,
> Not divided by distant shores or suns.
> Everywhere you shall be with me,
> I will see with my heart
> And embrace you with my loving spirit.[39]

There is no evidence that the relationship between the two men was a sexual one (nor any indication that it was not), but it represents a trend in early Christian sexual morality which was both significant and influential. Their friendship can scarcely be called anything but passionate; whether or not physical eroticism was involved, it was certainly a relationship involving *eros* in the Greek sense, or what more recent ages have called "romantic love." No one seems to have considered the attraction "unnatural," nor did Saint Paulinus's ardent love for a man trouble his conscience in regard to either its object or its intensity. Far from dissuading him—as it had dissuaded Saint Paul and Origen—from surrendering to terrestrial loves, the prospect of eternity only deepened his passion.

> And when, freed from my body's jail
> I fly from earth,

Count as three all those on a bed, of whom two are active
And two are passive. I seem to relate a marvel,
Yet it is not a falsehood: the one in the middle performs doubly,
Pleasing in the back and being pleased in the front.

H. G. Evelyn White, the LC translator of Ausonius's *Epigrams* (Cambridge, Mass., 1919–21), does not mention this version, although there is no way to be certain which of the two Ausonius was translating (or if he knew both). The use of the word "stuprum" in the epigram should be interpreted cautiously; its ramifications are probably juridical rather than moral.

39. *Carmen* 11, ll. 49–68, in the CSEL (Vienna, 1894), 30:41–42; and in the OBMLV, pp. 31–32 (no. 24). These lines were translated and reprinted by Helen Waddell in *Medieval Latin Lyrics* (New York, 1948), pp. 36–37. The translation is excellent; I have provided my own only for the sake of clarity, since poetic considerations are secondary in the present study. Waddell provides an extremely moving account of the relationship between the two men in her notes to the poem (pp. 289–94). Waddell's book is indispensable for anyone interested in medieval love poetry.

Wherever in heaven our Father shall direct me,
There also shall I bear you in my heart.
Nor will that end,
That frees me from my flesh,
Release me from your love.

This type of relationship—passionate or "erotic" friendship between males—was the source of some of the most affecting poetry of the Middle Ages. Although it probably rarely involved conscious sensuality, it borrowed heavily from the language of sexual relations and often deliberately imitated the homosexual literature of antiquity.[40] It is best to avoid oversimplification in such matters, but it seems fair to say that the authors of such sentiments were expressing, at the very least, gay sensibilities, since the primary focus of their love relationships was confined to their own gender, and since the passion animating the friendships far exceeds what would be considered "normal" between heterosexual friends in societies which distinguish between homosexual and heterosexual feelings.[41] Paulinus's society was only beginning to make such distinctions, and with or without physical expression, these clerical relationships were certainly more like those existing today between lovers than between friends of the same sex.

It would be inaccurate to suggest any exact parallel between such relationships and modern phenomena—as it is to compare medieval marriage with its modern counterpart. But to suggest that this difference is due simply to changing concepts of friendship and not related to the status of homo-

40. The literary relationship between Marcus Aurelius and Fronto is an especially clear example of this: see, in the LC edition by C. R. Haines (London, 1919), 1.20–30, 30–33; 2.120–26. Marcus Aurelius was personally opposed to homosexuality, but to any modern reader these would seem to be passionate love letters.

41. C. S. Lewis, e.g., probably knew the love literature of antiquity and the Middle Ages as well as any other modern scholar, lived in an age which certainly distinguished between "homosexual" and "heterosexual," and was himself anxious to preclude any imputation of homosexuality to medieval love literature; but his efforts to differentiate between "friendship" and "love" clearly leave relationships like those between Ausonius and Paulinus in the latter category: friendship "has least commerce with our nerves; there is nothing throaty about it; nothing that quickens the pulse or turns you red and pale. . . . Lovers are always talking to each other about their Love; Friends hardly ever about their Friendship. Lovers are normally face to face, absorbed in each other; Friends, side by side, absorbed in some common interest. Above all, Eros [while it lasts] is necessarily between two only," The Four Loves (New York, 1960), pp. 88ff. Probably the most detailed recent discussion of the difficulties of separating Christian amicitia, with its exaggerated literary conventions, from romance or eroticism is that of Peter Dronke, Medieval Latin and the Rise of European Love Lyric, 2d ed. (Oxford, 1968), esp. 1:192–220. This generally judicious treatment must, however, be read in context: it is in the interest of Dronke's central thesis (about the relatively late emergence of erotic lyric) to emphasize the conventional aspects of early medieval love poetry.

sexuality is to beg the question: the erotic content of "friendship" in antiquity was due in no small measure to the fact that homosexuality was conventional in many ancient societies and could have been part of the relationship; friends of the same sex borrowed from the standard vocabulary of homosexual love to express their feelings in erotic terms.

The popularity of the story of Saints Perpetua and Felicitas, for instance, was largely due to the appeal of the love between the two women. Five Christians were martyred together at Carthage on March 7, 203, suffering death at the hands of wild animals and the sword, but only Perpetua and Felicitas captured the fancy of the Christian community, apparently because the tale of the two women comforting each other in jail, suffering martyrdom together as friends, and bestowing upon each other the kiss of peace as they met their end, charmed the tastes of the age.[42]

Saint Augustine himself, writing in this tradition, expressed the love he felt for a friend of his youth, whose death so desolated him that he was driven to God in unbearable pain: "For I felt that my soul and his were one soul in two bodies, and therefore life was a horror to me, since I did not want to live as a half; and yet I was also afraid to die lest he, whom I had loved so much, would completely die" (*Confessions* 4.6). Unlike many of his Christian contemporaries, Augustine bitterly regretted the sexual aspect of such passions ("Thus I contaminated the spring of friendship with the dirt of lust and darkened its brightness with the blackness of desire," 3.1)[43] and rejected as an adult the possibility of licit homosexual relationships. In the thirteenth century his opinion was to gain ascendancy in Christian circles, but only after vigorous opposition at many points in Christian history.

Not only does there appear to have been no general prejudice against gay people among early Christians; there does not seem to have been any reason for Christianity to adopt a hostile attitude toward homosexual behavior. Many prominent and respected Christians—some canonized—were involved in relationships which would almost certainly be considered homosexual in cultures hostile to same-sex eroticism. Antierotic pressure from government and more ascetic schools of sexual ethics was in time to achieve the supression of most public aspects of gay sexuality and ultimately to induce a violently hostile reaction from Christianity itself, but this process took a very long time and cannot be ascribed to widespread attitudes or prejudices among early adherents of the Christian religion. To a contemporary observer of social

42. The story was written by contemporaries in Latin and (perhaps subsequently) in Greek; the two versions are printed together by J. A. Robinson in *The Passion of St. Perpetua* (Cambridge, 1891).

43. "Venam igitur amicitiae coinquinabam sordibus concupiscentiae, candoremque eius obnubilabam de tartaro libidinis."

trends, it would probably have seemed that the examples of Ausonius and Paulinus or Perpetua and Felicitas would in the end triumph over the hostility of Ambrose or Augustine, and that Christian sexual attitudes would be focused on the quality of love, not the gender of the parties involved or the biological function of their affection.

6 Theological Traditions

Although the attitudes of Christian ascetics probably affected only a small portion of the early church, they were eventually to provide the official justification for the oppression of gay people in many Christian states, and they deserve to be considered here. They can be subsumed under four headings: (1) animal behavior, (2) unsavory associations, (3) concepts of "nature," and (4) gender expectations.

Of the four, only the last was designed to disparage homosexual behavior in particular. The other three were originally condemnations of behavior which involved homosexuality only incidentally—and only to the extent that they involved heterosexuality—but came, through misinterpretation and selective inference, to be applied to gay people in particular.

Animal behavior.   The earliest and most influential of all arguments used by Christian theologians opposed to homosexual behavior were those derived from animal behavior. The Epistle of Barnabas, probably composed during the first century A.D., is now considered apocryphal but was accepted as Scripture by most early Christians familiar with it. It forms part of the text of the most famous surviving manuscript of the Bible, the Codex Sinaiticus, and its influence can be traced for centuries in the writings of many prominent fathers of the church (Clement, Origen, Eusebius, et al.). The author of the work equated Mosaic prohibitions of eating certain animals with various sexual sins:

> [Moses said,] You shall not eat the hare [cf. Lev. 11:5]. Why? So that, he said, you may not become a boy-molester[1] or be made like

---

1. The Greek word here, "παιδόφθορος," should actually refer to child-molesting in general, regardless of the gender of the child, but since subsequent writers influenced by Barnabas apparently understood the term to apply to the abuse of boys by men, I have translated the word as "boy-molester." Possibly the alleged anal proclivities of the hare suggested male homosexual relations more strongly than any other type of sexual behavior. Many patristic authorities confused pederasty with homosexuality, but even given this frequent conflation, the association here of the boy-molester with an animal possessing many anuses is an extremely illogical metathesis of ideas: surely it should be the boy whose anus is the object of attention, not the molester's.

these. For the hare grows a new anal opening each year, so that however many years he has lived, he has that many anuses.[2]

Nor should you eat the hyena, he said, so that you may not become an adulterer or a seducer, or like them. Why? Because this animal changes its gender annually and is one year a male and the next a female.[3]

And he also rightly despised the weasel [cf. Lev. 11:29]. You shall not, he said, become as these, who we hear commit uncleanness with their mouths, nor shall you be joined to those women who have committed illicit acts orally with the unclean. For this animal conceives through its mouth.[4]

The opinions of this text and the errors involved in applying them to homosexuality involve so many and such complex misunderstandings that only the barest summary can be provided here. Moses did not, of course, attribute these bizarre characteristics to the animals in question, nor did he in fact even prohibit the eating of the hyena,[5] but few early Christians knew

2. No one has traced the origins of this notion, but it is probably derived from Aristotle's observation that hares are retromingent (*Historia animalium* 6.33), an idea repeated by Aristophanes of Byzantium: see *Excerptorum Constantini De natura animalium libri duo: Aristophanis Historiae animalium epitome, subjunctis Aeliani Timothei aliorum eclogis*, ed. Spyridon Lambros, in *Supplementum Aristotelicum*, 1.1.409 (Berlin, 1885), p. 116. Pliny ascribes it to Archelaus but also upholds its veracity himself: "Archelaus auctor est quot sint corporis cavernae ad excrementa lepori totidem annos esse aetatis: varius certe numerus reperitur," *Natural History* 8.81.218. In the *Hieroglyphics* of Horapollo the hieroglyph for the hare is said to represent an "opening," though no sexual allusion is made: see *The Hieroglyphics of Horapollo Nilous*, ed. and trans. Alexander T. Cory (London, 1840), p. 48. There is no way to determine at present what is original in Horapollo's work and what is an interpolation by his Christian translator, Philip, who was probably familiar with the Epistle of Barnabas.

3. Male and female hyenas resemble each other genitally in a curious way: for a modern biological interpretation, see Wilson, p. 229; cf. the comments by A. L. Peck in the LC edition (Cambridge, Mass., 1960) of Aristotle's *On the Generation of Animals*, pp. 565–66.

4. Aristotle specifically refuted this notion, alleged by Anaxagoras and already common in his day; he suggested that it had arisen because the female weasel carried her young in her mouth. "How," he asked, "would the embryo make its way from the uterus to the mouth?" (*On the Generation of Animals* 3.6). Aristophanes followed Aristotle in rejecting oral birth among weasels but claimed that weasels (like pigeons) did have oral intercourse: "Οὐ γὰρ ὀχεύει, ἀλλὰ τιθασεύει ὡς ἡ περιστερά" (*Excerptorum*, p. 110). Many birds were thought by the ancients to have intercourse orally: e.g., Aristotle *On the Generation of Animals* 3.6.

5. The hyena is not specifically mentioned in Leviticus. In Deut. 14:8 the word used in the LXX to express the prohibition against eating pork ["ὖς," in the accusative "ὖν"] resembles the word for "hyena" ("ὕαινα"), and the two are etymologically related. Both the emphasis in Deuteronomy on the impurity of doubleness (cloven-hoofed animals) and the classification of the ὖς as "βδέλυγμα" (the designation for homosexual acts in Leviticus) may have contributed to the conflation of popular animal lore with the Mosaic law. In the *Physiologus* (see below), which may derive its discussion of the hyena from Barnabas, the

the text of Leviticus well enough to recognize the distortion, and it was at any rate the fashion among Christians to extrapolate rather fancifully from the Mosaic law. Moreover, these strange notions about animal behavior were all but universally accepted in the ancient world. The legend about the hyena was already widely believed in Aristotle's day, and although he refuted it (*Historia animalium* 6.32, *On the Generation of Animals* 3.6), by the time of the natural historian Aelian (second or third century A.D.) all serious zoological treatises again accepted it as fact,[6] and both Ovid (*Metamorphoses* 15.408–9) and Oppian (*Cynegetica* 3.289–92) used the story in popular fables. The idea about the hare was equally ubiquitous—at about the same time Barnabas was writing, Pliny included it in his natural history and embellished it with even more extravagant stories.[7] No less a figure than Plutarch introduced his readers to the supposed sexual aberrations of the weasel (*Isis and Osiris* 74 [31B]), and Ovid even created a myth to explain how the weasel came to be associated with oral birth (*Metamorphoses* 9.322–23).

Barnabas's use of this popular zoological tradition in a moral context was a decisive influence on many Christians, who not only adopted but expanded his prejudices and misprisions. Whether Barnabas intended his prohibition to apply to both sexes of children or not, it was certainly addressed to the issue of sexual relations with minors,[8] and this understanding survived through the fourth century.[9] But by the time of the *Apostolic*

---

word "ἀλλάσσειν" is used for "change" of sex. This might be an echo of Wis. 14:26 ("γενέσεως ἐναλλαγή") and would suggest another source of the biblical-scientific conflation of hyena stories.

6. "Should you this year set eyes on a male hyena, next year you will see the same creature as a female; conversely, if you see a female now, this time next year you will see a male. They share the attributes of both sexes and are both husband and wife, changing their sex year by year," Aelian *On the Characteristics of Animals* 1.25, trans. A. F. Scholfield (Cambridge, Mass., 1958–59).

7. Pliny (8.81.218) cites Archelaus as stating that rabbits are hermaphroditic and that they conceive while pregnant ("superfetation"). Aelian (*On Animals* 13.12) relates that the male hare bears young and "has a share in both sexes."

8. There is no indication of what constituted a "child" in terms of age. Cotelerius cites Joannes Monachus's definition of "παιδοφθορία" as the corruption of a child under the age of twelve: "Τὸ κόρην παρθένον νεᾶνιν πρὸ τῆς ἥβης, ἤγουν πρὸ τῶν δώδεκα χρόνων διαφθαρῆναι" (PG, 1:999, n. 15).

9. In the *Didache* (2.2), e.g., it appears in its original form: "Δευτέρα δὲ ἐντολὴ τῆς διδαχῆς· οὐ φονεύσεις· οὐ μοιχεύσεις· οὐ παιδοφθορήσεις." The relationship between the *Didache* (also called *The Teaching of the Twelve Apostles*) and the Epistle of Barnabas is much disputed and too complex to be dealt with here. Readers who wish to form their own opinion may consult the translations of both published in vol. 1 of the Fathers of the Church series. (The injunction of the *Apostolic Constitutions* is almost certainly derived from the *Didache*.) Older translations (e.g., that of Kirsopp Lake in the LC edition of *Apostolic Fathers* [Cambridge, Mass., 1912]) often incorrectly rendered "οὐ παιδοφθορήσεις" as "thou shalt not commit sodomy," but more recent scholars (e.g., C. Richardson in the 1953

Constitutions of that century, his comments were already being applied to all sexual activity between persons of the same gender (or to all nonprocreative sexuality between any persons).[10] This was doubtless due in large measure to its adoption by Clement of Alexandria as the backbone of his argument against homosexuality in the *Paedagogus*, an extremely popular manual of instruction for Christian parents. Although Clement was one of the earliest Christian theologians to invoke the "Alexandrian rule" (that sexual intercourse must be directed toward procreation in order to be moral) in discussing homosexuality, his deprecation of homosexual relations was based primarily on the animal arguments of Barnabas. Moses, he observed, had rejected "fruitless sowings" by forbidding eating hyena and hare, since "these animals are quite obsessed with sexual intercourse."[11] Clement had obviously read Aristotle (or an epitome) and was aware that naturalists of his day were wrong in attributing to the hyena the ability to change gender, but he believed that male hyenas regularly mounted each other rather than the female and inferred that Moses' supposed prohibition against eating them must be a specific condemnation of homosexual relations. He buttressed his arguments with the comments of Paul in Romans and quotations from Plato taken out of context, and he maintained that Plato had objected to homosexual behavior on the basis of his reading of the Bible.

It is easy to deride Clement's ignorance, but his attitudes on this point were influential. In an age when his argument that the only lawful end of sexual pleasure was procreation had not yet won universal acceptance, his other objections were ultimately persuasive, especially since they followed the Epistle of Barnabas, which both Clement and his readers considered apostolic, and since they were addressed to the sensitive issue of the proper rearing of children.[12]

In the West, where fanciful zoology was equally popular and where the particular foibles of the hare, hyena, and weasel had been introduced into

---

edition in the Library of Christian Classics [Philadelphia]) have adhered more faithfully to the original sense and translated the words as "do not corrupt boys" (*Early Christian Fathers*, 1 : 172). See also the Council of Elvira of 305, which condemned "stupratores puerorum."

10. *Apostolic Constitutions* 7.2 (PG, 1 : 1000): "Οὐ παιδοφθορήσεις· παρὰ φύσιν γὰρ τὸ κακὸν ἐκ Σοδόμων φυέν, ἥτις πυρὸς θεηλάτου παρανάλωμα γέγονεν."

11. This and all subsequent quotations from the *Paedogogus* are from the translation printed in app. 2.

12. The *Commentary on the Hexaemeron* traditionally attributed to Eustathius, e.g., derives its material on the hyena directly from Clement and draws the same moral conclusions about the "unnaturalness" of its behavior: " Ἐν ἀλλήλοις τὴν παρὰ φύσιν μίξιν ἐργάζονται," PG, 18 : 744, although surprisingly the author also appears to have drawn on Achilles Tatius (see Friedrich Zoepfl, *Der Kommentar des Pseudo-Eustathios zum Hexaëmeron* [*sic*], in *Alttestamentliche Abhandlungen*, ed. Alfons Schulz [Münster, 1927], 10 : 48). The work, composed in the late fourth or early fifth century, was almost certainly not by Eustathius.

literature of all types, a Latin translation of Barnabas acquainted Christians with the moral implications of such behavior.[13] Novatian, obviously affected by this idea, wrote that "in animals the law has established a sort of mirror of human life.[14] . . . For what does the law intend when it says, 'You shall not eat . . . the hare'? It condemns those men who have made themselves women."[15]

The persistence and ubiquity of this tradition were assured by the incorporation of the sexual inferences about the animals in question into the single most popular work of natural science of the Middle Ages, one of the most widely read treatises of any sort prior to the seventeenth century.[16] The *Physiologus* was a collection of anecdotes about animals—some more or less accurate, some wildly fanciful—in which a Christian moral was extracted from various aspects of animal behavior. It first appeared in Greek a little after the Epistle of Barnabas and quickly made its way into Latin, where its popularity gave rise to dozens of different versions.[17] During the Middle Ages it was translated into almost every medieval vernacular from Icelandic to Arabic.[18] Its influence was incalculable, particularly during the High Middle Ages. Available in every Romance language as "the bestiary," it served as a manual of piety, a primer of zoology, and a form of

13. This translation appears to have been rather loose: cf. the Latin and Greek versions of the prohibition of eating the weasel in the LC Barnabas. Only one complete text is extant.

14. Note that the fifth-century physician Caelius Aurelianus cites animals as "nature's mirrors" while claiming that homosexuality is *not* known among them (*Tardarum passionum* 4.9. [Drabkin ed., pp. 904–5]).

15. Novatian, *De cibis Judaicis* (PL, 3:957–58): "In animalibus, per legem quasi quoddam humanae vitae speculum constitutum est. . . . Quid enim vult sibi lex cum dicit . . . leporem non manducabis? Accusat deformatos in feminam viros." Considerable controversy attaches to the proper reading of "deformatos," but it is not germane to the question at hand. Cf. Tertullian on the hyena: *De pallio* 3.2 (PL, 2:1091).

16. E. P. Evans opines that "perhaps no book except the Bible has ever been so widely diffused among so many people for so many centuries" (quoted in T. H. White, *The Bestiary: A Book of Beasts* [New York, 1954], p. 232.) Many hundreds of manuscripts are known in Latin and Romance, Germanic, and Semitic languages.

17. The literature on the *Physiologus* is vast, but many crucial problems regarding it (such as its origins) remain unsolved. The most recent study (Nikolas Henkel, *Studien zum Physiologus im Mittelalter* [Tübingen, 1976]) provides a brief summary of the complexities involved with the Greek and Latin texts, as well as an overview of the Romance and Germanic works derived from them, but several earlier studies are more thorough and detailed: e.g., that of Friedrich Lauchert, *Geschichte des Physiologus* (Strasbourg, 1889), pp. 229–79. Lauchert's Greek text is the most convenient one, since the better edition by Francesco Sbordone (Milan, 1936) which I have used is not available in American libraries. There is no critical edition.

18. One of several Arabic versions has been partly edited by J. Land in *Anecdota Syriaca* (Leiden, 1875), vol. 4; for an Icelandic version, see that of Halldor Hermannson (Ithaca; N.Y., 1938).

entertainment. Even many modern bits of animal lore owe their popularity to the influence of the *Physiologus* and bestiaries derived from it.

Whether or not they were partly derived from Barnabas or Clement,[19] early Greek and Latin versions of the *Physiologus* made exactly the same fanciful connection between the colorful legends about animal sexuality and Mosaic law.

> The law says, "You shall not eat the weasel or anything like it." The Physiologus has written of it that it has this trait: the female receives from the male in her mouth, becomes pregnant, and gives birth through her ears. . . .[20] The law says, "You shall not eat the hyena or anything like it." The Physiologus has written of it that it is male-female;[21] that is, at one time male and at another female. It is therefore an unclean animal, because of this sex change. This is why Jeremiah says, "Never will the den of the hyena be my inheritance."[22]
>
> You must not, therefore, become like the hyena, taking first the male and then the female nature; these, he says, the holy Apostle reproached when he spoke of "men with men doing that which is unseemly."[23]

These associations profoundly affected subsequent attitudes toward homosexual behavior.[24] Half a millennium after Barnabas, the bishop of Pavia could make fun of a gay male by comparing him to a hare,[25] and a

19. The application of the passages from Jeremiah and Rom. 1:26–27 to the behavior of the hyena seem to be derived from Clement; neither is used by Barnabas, and they are sufficiently rare in subsequent treatments of the material to justify the assumption that they were not obvious associations. It is not in fact inconceivable that Clement could be the author of a Greek form of the *Physiologus*.

20. In the Latin tradition it was often added that if the offspring were born from the right ear, they would be male; if from the left, female ("Si autem per aurem dexteram contigerit ut generit, masculus erit; si vero per sinistram, femina," "Physiologus Latinus versio Y," ed. Francis Carmody, *University of California Publications in Classical Philology* 12, no. 7 [1941]: 127).

21. Ἀρρενόθηλυ. This word may have been associated with the Pauline "ἀρσενοκοῖται" among later Greek speakers.

22. In the LXX this passage occurs in Jer. 12:9: "Μὴ σπήλαιον ὑαίνης ἡ κληρονομία μου ἐμοί." The Vulgate renders the Hebrew more accurately as a reference to a type of speckled bird, but the Vetus Latina must have followed the LXX; at least one Latin tradition includes this passage: "Hieremias dixit: Numquid spelunca beluae hereditas mea mihi" (Carmody, p. 129).

23. Sbordone, pp. 76–77, 85–86. Cf. Lauchert, pp. 253–54, 256, chaps. 21, 24. (The chapter headings of the *Physiologus* vary extravagantly from one edition to another and are of little assistance in checking citations.)

24. And possibly toward the rabbit: one wonders if the obscene pun suggested by the Hispanic Latin term for rabbit, "cuniculus," was an etymological accident.

25. Ennodius *Epigrammata* 52 (PL, 63:344): "Vir facie, mulier gestu, sed crure quod ambo, / Jurgia naturae nullo descrimine solvens, / Es lepus, et tanti conculcas colla leonis." (Epigrams 51–55 all deal with the same subject.) This epigram had some effect on moral treatises of the High Middle Ages: see chap. 11 below.

thousand years later Bernard of Cluny could assail homosexual relations with the simple observation that a man who thus "dishonors his maleness" is "just like a hyena."[26] There was no need to explain such references; medieval writers could be sure that their audiences were familiar with one or more of the dozens of bestiaries available in nearly every European language which explained the offensive practices of the hare, hyena, and weasel.[27]

In the Greek East the legends about these animals not only persisted but expanded. In the sixth-century version of Timothy of Gaza not only the hyena but also the hare changed gender annually, and the weasel could drop its young through the ear or the mouth;[28] in the Greek version of the *Hieroglyphics* of Horapollo, hyenas had magical properties as well as sex changes, and the female weasel had the male organ of her species.[29] These confused legends passed into Arabic lore as well, whence they were eventually to reenter the Western tradition in altered form.[30]

Unsavory associations.   At least three types of unsavory associations colored the view some Christian writers took of homosexuality. The association of homosexuality with child molesting, noticeable by the fourth century, was due partly to increasing semantic imprecision (or deliberate conflation)[31] and partly to the extreme prevalence of an ancient custom which is execrated by modern industrialized cultures but was an accepted part of the social

26. *De contemptu mundi*, in *The Anglo-Latin Satirical Poets and Epigrammatists*, ed. Thomas Wright (London, 1872), 2:80: "Mas maris immemor, o furor! o tremor! est ut hyaena."

27. Illustrations may have had equal or greater influence on popular attitudes. In the eleventh- or twelfth-century illustrated *Physiologus* of Smyrna (see Josef Strzygowski, *Der Bilderkreis des griechischen Physiologus* [Leipzig, 1899]) the illustration for the hyena is a representation of Lot greeting the angelic visitors to Sodom (pl. 13; the manuscript was destroyed in the early twentieth century, and Strzygowski's plates are all that remain of it). Several Western manuscripts pictured two hyenas—presumably both male—embracing each other (see pls. 9 and 12 in this text); others portrayed the hyena devouring corpses— hardly a flattering image (pl. 10).

28. Timothy of Gaza, *De animalibus* 4.1; 18.2; 39.1, ed. M. Haupt ("Excerpta ex Timothei Gazaei libris De animalibus," *Hermes* 3 [1869]: 1–30).

29. Horapollo 36, 69, 70–72.

30. By the ninth century the legends about the hyena's sex change were already widely known in the Arab world: see ᶜAmr ibn Baḥr al-Jāḥiz, *Kitāb al-Ḥayawān* (Cairo, 1945–47), 7:168–69; see also 5:117, 484; 6:46, 450.

31. Philo, whose writings influenced many early Christian writers, seems to have conflated the concepts of pederasty and homosexual relations consciously. It is clear that he understood "παιδεραστεῖν" to refer to relations between persons of differing ages, since he observes that the love in such cases is one of "ἀνδρῶν ἄρρεσιν ἡλικίᾳ μόνον διαφέρουσι" (*De vita contemplativa* 59; and 52: "Μειρακία πρωτογένεια . . . ἀθύρματα πρὸ μικροῦ παιδεραστῶν γεγονότες"), and since he complains of the effect on a boy's youth of having a lover (6off.). But in passages such as the *De Abrahamo* 135–38, the *De specialibus legibus* 3.37– 42, etc., he consistently fails to make any distinction on the basis of age, using such terms as "ἀνδρόγυνοι," "παιδικά," "παιδεραστεῖν," "ἄνδρες ὄντες ἄρρεσιν ἐπιβαίνοντες," etc., interchangeably.

context in which Christian attitudes toward varieties of sexual behavior were forged. This was the abandonment of unwanted children to be sold into slavery. A very large percentage of such children were used for sexual purposes, at least from adolescence until they were old enough to be employed as laborers. The testimony of both pagan writers and Christian apologists bear witness to the ubiquity of this practice. Justin Martyr explains that "we have been taught that it is wrong to expose even the newborn . . . because we have observed that nearly all such children, boys as well as girls, will be used as prostitutes."[32] Clement describes how boys being sold as slaves were "beautified" to attract potential buyers (*Paedagogus* 3.3).

Aside from (sometimes instead of) the obvious moral issues of involuntary prostitution and the sexual exploitation of minors, Christian writers were profoundly disturbed by the possibility of accidental incest presented by this aspect of the slave trade. Justin enjoins against recourse to male prostitutes because a man availing himself of such services might be unwittingly committing incest with his son, brother, or another close relative (1 *Apology* 27 [PG, 6:372]). Tertullian argues against exposing or offering for adoption children who may ultimately engage in incestuous relations with parents they cannot recognize;[33] and Clement laments "the countless unknown tragedies occasioned by casual sexual encounters. How many fathers, forgetting the children they abandoned, unknowingly have sexual relations with a son who is a prostitute or a daughter become a harlot?"[34] The public sale of children as slaves clearly persisted for centuries after the Roman world had become Christian: in his account of the evangelization of England, Saint Bede pictures Pope Gregory the Great as encountering beautiful English boys for sale in the public market of Rome itself in the sixth century.[35]

Associations of homosexuality with paganism may also have roused suspicion against it, although in general the objections of Christian moralists to pagan sexuality applied to both inclinations. When Justin Martyr

32. "'Εκτιθέναι καὶ τὰ γεννώμενα, πονηρῶν εἶναι δεδιδάγμεθα· πρῶτον μὲν, ὅτι τοὺς πάντας σχεδὸν ὁρῶμεν ἐπὶ πορνείᾳ προάγοντας οὐ μόνον τὰς κόρας, ἀλλὰ καὶ τοὺς ἄρσενας," 1 *Apology* 27 (PG, 6:369).

33. *Apology* 9 (PL, 1:325–26); cf. *Ad nationes* 1.16 (PL, 1:653–54).

34. *Paedagogus* 3.3 (PG, 8:585). Note that Clement, apparently considering it fruitless to attack the slave trade itself, suggests that Christians should avoid casual sexuality in order to prevent such incestuous unions.

35. *Historia ecclesiastica* 2.1. Gregory found the English boys so beautiful that he called their appearance "angelic" (a pun on the Latin "anglicus") and opined that such loveliness deserved the reward of heaven. In the anonymous *Vita antiquissima* of Whitby, the English are full-grown men visiting Rome voluntarily (chap. 9), but regardless of the authenticity of the story, it is significant that Bede accepted the likelihood of English boys being sold into slavery in Rome only a century before him.

assailed the sexual exploits of the gods, he did not discriminate between gay and nongay: "We have dedicated ourselves to God, who was not born and does not suffer, and who we believe did not come upon Antiope or other women with desire, or upon Ganymede.[36]

Homosexual acts were sometimes criticized as one of many symptoms of hedonistic sexuality or as involving some activity in itself objectionable, like male prostitution.[37] Although neither oral nor anal intercourse was specifically condemned in the Jewish or Christian Scriptures, the former was the object of considerable contempt among citizens of the ancient world, and popular antipathy to both animated much prejudice against homosexual behavior.[38] At the theoretical level, of course, opposition to either would apply to common forms of heterosexual intercourse as well, but in the arena of public debate the visceral force of such hostility seems to have been directed chiefly against gay people, perhaps because it was easier to condemn such behavior as a characteristic of an increasingly unpopular minority than to question the private lives of the majority. Christian revulsion against social ills such as the abuse of children, originally perceived as the evils of a generally sinful society, gradually came to focus more and more on particular unpopular groups—barbarians, heretics, Jews, gay people.

Concepts of "nature." The word "nature" does not occur in the Gospels; insofar as these documents represent an accurate record of Jesus's comments and instructions, he never uttered a word about "nature." Nor was "nature" in the abstract a concern for Saint Paul: apart from one or two ambiguous references,[39] the word "nature" occurs in the Pauline writings only in the sense of the "nature" *of* something—the Jews, the Gentiles, the pagan gods, trees, etc. In the Epistles of Peter and Jude[40] the "natural" is specifically

---

36. "Θεῷ δὲ τῷ ἀγενήτῳ καὶ ἀπαθεῖ ἑαυτοὺς ἀνεθήκαμεν, ὃν οὔτε ἐπ' Ἀντιόπην καὶ τὰς ἄλλας ὁμοίως, οὐδὲ ἐπὶ Γανυμήδην δι' οἶστρον ἐληλυθέναι πειθόμεθα," 1 *Apology* 25 (PG, 6:365), and 1.29 and 2 *Apology* 12.5. See also Chrysostom *In Epistolam ad Titum* 5.4, and Arnobius *Adversus gentes* 4.26, 5.6–7. Note that Arnobius is stunningly ignorant of the actual classical tradition.

37. Minutius Felix 28 (PL, 3:344–45).

38. Clement of Alexandria *Paedagogus* 2.10 (PG, 8:500ff.). Clement calls it "λίχνος πόρνος, πυγῇ ἀγαλλόμενος" and recommends that those who practice it be barred from the city.

39. The only occurrence of "nature" in an Aristotelian sense in the Pauline writings is almost certain proof that the author did not draw the same moral inferences from "unnatural" that his Jewish and Greek contemporaries often did: see p. 110 above.

40. 2 Peter 2:12: "But these, as natural brute beasts, made to be taken and destroyed, speak evil of the things that they understand not; and shall utterly perish in their own corruption" (KJV). The force of "natural" is stronger in Greek ("Οὗτοι δὲ, ὡς ἄλογα ζῷα γεγεννημένα φυσικά") and more generic in the Latin version known to the Middle Ages ("Hi vero velut irrationabilia pecora naturaliter in captionem et in perniciem . . . peribunt");

opposed to the righteous and characterized as destructive. There was hardly a sound scriptural basis for Christian concern with "nature" as a moral principle.

But Christianity passed its infancy in a society profoundly affected by late versions of Platonic and Aristotelian concepts of "ideal nature," and some of its early adherents were much affected by them. Stoics tautologically inferred from "natural" processes what was "natural" and made this their ethical norm. It was "natural," they assumed, to eat moderately, only as much as necessary for nourishment, so the intent of "nature" must be that humans eat only as much as needed for this purpose; anything beyond this would be "unnatural." (Of course they could have assumed that eating had two "natural" functions—sustenance and enjoyment—but they did not.)

Stoic concepts of "natural" morality were already widespread in the Roman world before Christianity entered it, and the similarity at the practical level of Stoic and Christian ethics probably greatly facilitated the success of the latter.[41] The correspondence between the moral teachings of Seneca and Saint Paul on some points was so striking that later ages were to invent an actual "correspondence" (i.e., a set of letters) between them.[42] Many followers of Saint Paul easily adopted the prejudices of Seneca regarding "nature," despite their irrelevance to Christian teaching.

Platonists viewed "nature" either explicitly or implicitly as the semi-divine force that transformed the "ideal" into the "real" and considered its dictates to have the force of moral law. Hellenized Jews, strongly influenced by both Stoic morality and Platonism, invoked the "natural" as a corollary of divine law, the earthly reflection of the will of God, and used it to provide a philosophical justification for Old Testament morality. The idea that the only "natural" use of sexuality was procreation, for instance, could be made, with some sleight of logic, to seem the foundation of Mosaic sexual legislation.

The Judaeo-Platonist schools of the East, especially in Alexandria, greatly influenced some early Christians, since they combined the authority of classical learning with a tradition of Old Testament scholarship (responsible

---

Jude 10: "But what they know naturally, as brute beasts, in those things they corrupt themselves" (KJV). This seems more generic in the Greek ("Ὅσα δὲ φυσικῶς τὰ ἄλογα ζῷα ἐπίστανται, ἐν τούτοις φθείρονται"); cf. the Latin: "Quaecumque autem naturaliter tamquam muta animalia norunt, in his corrumpuntur." These sections of Peter and Jude are obviously related, and most authorities consider 2 Peter dependent on Jude.

41. But note the attitude of Stoicism to homosexuality, discussed above, chap. 5.

42. Mentioned by Jerome De viris illustribus 12 (PL, 23:629) as "read by many." Seneca and Saint Paul lived in Rome at the same time: contact between them was not impossible, though efforts to demonstrate such a connection have not met with acceptance, and the eight letters alluded to by Jerome are universally judged spurious by modern scholarship.

for the Septuagint translation which most Christians used). The intellectual hegemony of these schools among Greek-speaking Jews and the fact that many Greek Christians studied in Alexandria greatly enhanced the apparent —though misleading—similarities between the Platonic and Pauline concepts of "natural" and had much to do with the eventual triumph of the so-called Alexandrian rule. In the third century Clement of Alexandria could assert dramatically that "to have sex for any purpose other than to produce children is to violate nature,"[43] just as if Christ had instructed his disciples to obey "nature"; and the *Apostolic Constitutions* could divide all actions into those on "the way of life," which is "according to nature," and those on "the way of death."[44] Even in the West, where Judaeo-Platonist influence was less pronounced, Saint Augustine could enunciate as a Christian principle that "in order to be sinless an act must not violate nature, custom, or law"[45]—criteria with no discernible relationship to the moral principles of the New Testament.

The doctrine of the Manicheans that the "natural" world was inherently evil also elicited from many Christians—especially those like Saint Augustine who had once been Manicheans—resounding defenses of "nature" and the "natural" as basically good.

It would, however, be quite wrong to assume that such concepts of "nature" were determinative in the formation of Christian sexual ethics or that Christians subscribed to the theological and philosophical premises underlying the "natural morality" which they casually invoked. In fact the principal effect of these philosophies on Christian thought was simply the elimination of any "real" concepts of "nature" from Christian philosophy; no consistent principles of "ideal nature" replaced them until the thirteenth century. Bits and pieces of "natural" philosophies entered Christian thought at many points and sometimes lodged permanently in some niche in the framework of Christian theology, but the difficulties involved in reconciling

43. "Τὸ δὲ μὴ εἰς παίδων γονὴν συνιέναι ἐνυβρίζειν ἐστι τῇ φύσει," *Paedagogus* 2.10 (PG, 8:512). There is an untranslatable pun in the sentence, obvious to a Greek speaker, which considerably mitigates the seeming absoluteness of the dictum. "Ὑβρίζειν" is the Greek equivalent of the Latin "stuprare," and one of its meanings is "to have sex illicitly." In this sense Clement's statement is tautological, and its force is descriptive rather than prescriptive. To contemporaries it probably suggested hedonism ("to fornicate with nature") rather than the violation of universal order. The *Paedagogus* is filled with ambiguities of language which bear directly on the moral import of the text; unfortunately most of them are untranslatable.

44. PG, I : 992. The "two ways" probably predate Christianity as a framework for moral teaching. Their origins and transmission in various Christian didactic works (e.g., Barnabas and the *Didache*) are much disputed. "Nature," however, appears only in relatively late versions.

45. *De bono conjugali* 25 (PL, 40:395).

"nature" with New Testament concerns and the illogical and inconsistent philosophical bases of "natural morality" precluded any general or systematic appeals to "nature" for Christians.

Even at the most practical level, Christians found difficulty in accommodating popular concepts of "nature" to the demands of Christ and his apostles. For Platonist Jews like Philo, any use of human sexuality, potential or actual, which did not produce legitimate offspring violated "nature": all moral issues were subordinate to the primary duty of males to procreate. Celibacy was as "unnatural" as homosexuality,[46] failure to divorce a barren wife as "unnatural" as masturbation.[47]

No matter how appealing Christians found Alexandrian concepts of the "natural," they could not accept these basic premises. In stark contrast to Philo's belief that procreation was the ultimate and necessary use of human sexuality, the New Testament clearly and consistently taught that celibacy was the highest response to human eroticism, that not only was there no imperative to procreate, it was in fact morally better not to do so. Marriage in the New Testament was not "nature's" way of peopling the world, but man's way of avoiding fornication by compromising with the awesome forces of uncontrolled sexual desires. Christians were bound, moreover, by absolute commands which directly precluded the adoption of Judaeo-Platonist norms of "natural" sexuality aimed exclusively at procreation: Jesus's prohibition of divorce,[48] for instance, which was taken to apply even to barren wives, and Paul's insistence on fulfillment of the "marriage debt" with no reference to procreative purpose (1 Cor. 7:4–6).

The best that could result for Christians pursuing "natural" ethical norms was a forced suspension of immiscible elements. Augustine's approach to marriage, for example, was influenced to a certain extent by "natural" concerns. Wherever he followed these most faithfully, he was constrained to adopt positions either unrelated or in opposition to New Testament teachings. Whereas Paul, unaffected by "nature," commanded Christians to satisfy their spouses' sexual needs, Augustine considered intercourse undertaken for any purpose other than procreation to be inherently, if venially, sinful. Neither the Old Testament nor the New prohibited any particular

46. Philo's comments on homosexuality are in *De specialibus legibus* 3.7.37–42; *De Abrahamo* 26.133–37; *De vita contemplativa* 6.48–53, 7.59–64; *On Genesis* 4.38.

47. For Philo's sexual ethics, see esp. *De specialibus legibus* 3; see also Wolfson, as cited in chap. 4, n. 61 above. The Judaeo-Platonist tradition was not the only Judaic sexual ethic; several are represented in the OT and others in Talmudic and later writings. The attitude toward sexuality of writings like the Song of Solomon seems markedly hedonistic, although many later schools of thought—Jewish and Christian—have been at pains to argue the contrary.

48. Matt. 5:31–32, 19:3–9 (Mark 10:2–12). No exception is suggested for barrenness, which put Christians squarely in opposition to Philo's approach.

sexual activities within marriage, but both condemned prostitution absolutely and in no uncertain terms.[49] Augustine's horror of "unnatural" (i.e., non-procreative) sex acts was so great that he not only forbade them absolutely to married persons but actually instructed Christian women to have their husbands perform such acts with prostitutes (who were a "natural" and necessary part of life, in his view)[50] if they felt a need for them.[51]

At higher theological levels, "nature" could not be accommodated in a Christian frame of reference at all. In the East, although it persisted in popular moral treatises, prominent theologians rejected it altogether. Saint Basil wrote that "he who follows nature in these matters condemns himself, in that he has not yet completely conquered nature and is still ruled by the flesh."[52]

In the West, ideal "nature" is notably absent from serious theological works. This was partly due to the concept of "nature" among Latin speakers, whose use of "natura" centered around "innate characteristics," i.e., the nature *of* something. (Lucretius's *De rerum natura* dealt with the whole of "nature," but it was the "rerum"—"of things"—which suggested to Latin readers what modern speakers mean by "nature.")[53] When the Greek "against nature" was translated into Latin as "contra naturam," it probably suggested something more like "uncharacteristic" or "atypical" to most Roman Christians.

Moreover, the Western philosophical tradition regarding "nature" was unrelated, if not opposed, to most Christian moral issues. Most "natural morals" schools were not opposed to homosexual behavior, but the term "unnatural" was applied to everything from postnatal child support to legal contracts between friends.[54] Even Seneca, who condemned many urban extravagances as "unnatural" (see esp. *Epistles* 47, 122; and *De brevitate vitae* 12.5), did not imagine that "nature" could be a source of

49. Nor did subsequent Jewish teaching place any restrictions on marital sexual practices: e.g., Maimonides specifically allowed any sexual use of a wife by her husband, though he discouraged nonprocreative ones (*Code*, 5.21.9). For prostitution in the OT, see above, chap. 4; in the NT, see 1 Cor. 6:15–20.

50. "Remove prostitutes from human affairs, and you will destroy everything with lust" ("Aufer meretrices de rebus humanis, turbaveris omnia libidinibus," *De ordine* 11.4.12 [PL, 32:1000]).

51. *De bono conjugali* 11. Paul could hardly have approved this recommendation.

52. "Ὁ γὰρ ἐν τούτοις τῇ φύσει ἀκολουθῶν κατηγορεῖ ἑαυτοῦ, ὅτι οὔπω τελείως ἀπέστη τῆς φύσεως, ἀλλ' ἔτι ὑπὸ σαρκὸς διοικεῖται," *Sermo* 2.235E (PG, 31:885). But cf. *Homilia in hexaemeron* 9.6 (PG, 29:204).

53. The phrase may itself have had moral force, however: e.g., see Martial 9.41 ("Ipsam credi tibi naturam dicere rerum").

54. E.g., for the former, see Plutarch *De sollertia animalium* 964E, and for the latter, Aristotle *Eudemian Ethics* 7.10.17.

consistent ethics: "Nature does not bestow virtue; it is an art to become good."[55]

Where "nature" does occur in early Christian theology, as in the writings of Augustine, its use is quite different from that common among popular moralists or the Alexandrian school. For Augustine as for Paul, "nature" referred to the characteristics of individuals or things rather than to an ideal concept. He wrote of the "nature of good" or of "human nature," and even when he seems to treat of "nature" in the abstract ("On Nature and Grace"), it turns out to be human nature that he is discussing. The abstraction which later ages would call "nature" was usually "order" ("ordo") in Augustine's works—an amoral force which supported evil as well as good. (The treatise De ordine is entirely devoted to this concept: PL, 32.) Where "nature" occurs in a broader sense, it means "all that is," as in The City of God (16.8), where he suggests that whatever exists is perforce "natural" and part of the divine plan.

It is true that many of Augustine's statements about morals closely resemble Stoic arguments about "nature,"[56] and that the subsequent popularity of "natural" sexuality can be traced in part to his enormous influence and the recurrence in his writings of phrases like "the natural use" or "against nature." But he was ultimately unconcerned about "nature" itself, and these phrases reflect contemporary linguistic conventions rather than consistent philosophical constructs. It was not, after all, "nature" which saved anyone or gave value to his actions, but grace. "Nature" was the old dispensation; grace the new. "Nature" could be flouted—for example, by voluntary celibacy, even to the point of wrecking its designs and bringing about the physical end of the human race (De bono conjugali 10 [PL, 40:381])—and this would still accord with the will of God, who had created all things "natural."

The "natural use" for Augustine was not that decreed by an omnipotent "nature" but the "characteristic," "native," or "normal" use. This is particularly evident in the case of his objections to homosexual behavior, which he stigmatizes specifically as "incongruous" and "contrary to human custom," that is, not characteristic of the human sexuality familiar to him.[57]

55. "Non enim dat natura virtutem; ars est bonum fieri," Epistles 90:45. Note also 123:16: "Nemo est casu bonus. Discenda virtus est."

56. E.g., De bono conjugali 16.18 (PL, 40:385): "What food is to the health of a man, that sex is to the health of the race, and neither is without some carnal pleasure. But if this is moderate and directed by the restraint of temperance only to the natural use, it cannot be [called] lust." Augustine later repudiated this statement (Retractiones 22.2); cf. Contra Julianum 4.14.67 (PL, 44:771) and the discussion in Noonan, pp. 127–31.

57. Confessions 3.8 (PL, 32:689–90): "Itaque flagitia quae sunt contra naturam, ubique ac semper detestanda atque punienda sunt, qualia Sodomitarum fuerunt. Quae si omnes gentes

Although he refers to it as "against nature," he leaves no doubt that he means the individual human natures of the persons involved in such activity, who "corrupt and pervert *their* natures" ("corrumpendo ac pervertendo naturam suam"). He does not suggest that such actions violate a "law of nature" but states explicitly that it is divine law which "has not made men to use one another thus," although no such law is cited. In the end, as the thrust of his discussion makes evident, it is conformity which is at issue. Augustine objects to the behavior in question because it is odd and unfamiliar and admits this quite frankly: "Every part which does not fit into its environment is wrong."[58]

It is not surprising that Augustine, having grown up in and retired to rural North Africa, where homosexuality was probably clandestine and publicly denigrated, should have considered it bizarre and alien. It is striking that the major treatment of homosexual relations per se in his writings[59] occurs in his description of his first sojourn in a great city, where he abandoned himself to urban pleasures with an enthusiasm he was later to regret bitterly. There is a hint that he was surprised at the large numbers of persons involved in what he had previously considered extremely rare behavior.[60]

It is in fact typical of theologians born in the provinces—like Jerome, from what is now Yugoslavia, or Ambrose, from southwest Germany— to derogate homosexual behavior with the casual assumption that it is so bizarre as scarcely to require comment, while writing at great length on abuses of

---

facerent, eodem criminis reatu divina lege tenerentur, quae non sic fecit homines ut se illo uterentur modo. Violatur quippe ipsa societas quae cum Deo nobis esse debet, cum eadem natura, cujus ille auctor est, libidinis perversitate polluitur. Quae autem contra mores hominum sunt flagitia, pro morum diversitate vitanda sunt. . . ." That the "nature" polluted by "desire" is the specific "nature" of the individual persons involved rather than "nature" in the abstract is clear from logical analysis as well as subsequent reference; if it were not so, the relation ("societas") between God and man would be always and everywhere in permanent rupture, since by Augustine's own admission it is all but impossible even for the married to live without carnal desire.

58. Several decades later, in his *City of God* (16.8), Augustine adopted a much humbler and less conformist stance, opining that "someone who cannot see the whole may be offended by the deformity of one part, not knowing to what it conforms or how it fits in" ("qui totum inspicere non potest, tanquam deformitate partis offenditur; quoniam cui congruat, et quo referatur, ignorat," PL, 41:486). Since there is little comment on homosexuality in the *City of God*, there is no way to know whether this constitutes a retraction of the position in the *Confessions*.

59. I.e., that in the *Confessions*. Most of Augustine's comments on the subject are extremely brief, e.g., *Contra mendacium* 17.34 (PL, 40:542); *City of God* 16.30.

60. "Quae si omnes gentes facerent, eodem" seems to imply either that someone had argued to Augustine that it was not so rare as he imagined or that he himself was surprised at how many persons were involved.

heterosexuality. In contrast, theologians in large urban centers like Alexandria, Antioch, or Constantinople, whose flocks were exposed to open and traditionally accepted gay life-styles, had to elaborate much more complex arguments if they wished to discourage gay sexuality. They could hardly hope to convince Christians who daily encountered unabashed gay people that homosexuality was "against human nature," so they had to appeal to a "nature" other than the human one and to cite—with selectivity— animals as demonstration of the workings of "nature" in regard to sexuality.

Such appeals may have had rhetorical force in popular declamations and were often cited by those familiar with Stoic or Judaeo-Platonic idealizations of "nature"; they persisted well into the Middle Ages and were consciously revived by Scholastics. But they could hardly be incorporated into any consistent Christian moral philosophy, especially during the formative centuries of Christian thought. By the time of the early Christian fathers, almost all zoologists considered some animals homosexual,[61] and some were even thought to have homosexual attractions to humans—a curious twist on "bestiality."[62] Ovid had a lesbian character lament the oddness of her passions in the ninth book of his *Metamorphoses* by comparing them with animal "nature":

> Cows do not burn with love for cows, nor mares for mares;
> The ram is hot for the ewe, the doe follows the stag.
> So also do birds mate, and among all the animals
> No female is seized with desire for a female.[63]

But in the next book he had to concede that animal ways do not always provide an apt model for human sexuality:

> The other animals mate indiscriminately;
> It is not considered shameful for a heifer
> To be mounted by her father; his own daughter may become a stallion's
>   mate,

---

61. In addition to the instances cited above, see Aelian *Varia historia* 1.15, where lesbian activity among pigeons is reported: "*Καὶ αἱ θήλειαι ἀλλήλας ἀναβαίνουσιν, ὅταν τῆς πρὸς ἄρρενα μίξεως ἀτυχήσωσι.*"

62. Aelian *On the Characteristics of Animals* 12.37; cf. Plutarch *De sollertia animalium* (*Moralia* 972D–F). This must have been part of vulgar lore as well: see the striking graffiti reproduced in "Graffiti in the Athenian Agora," in *Excavations of the Athenian Agora*, Picture Book 14, no. 30 (Princeton, N.J. 1974).

63. Nec vaccam vaccae, nec equas amor urit equarum:
    Urit oves aries, sequitur sua femina cervum.
    Sic et aves coeunt, interque animalia cuncta
    Femina femineo conrepta cupidine nulla est. [731–34]
Cf. 758–59: "At non vult natura, potentior omnibus istis [i.e., humans] / Quae mihi sola nocet."

The goat goes into the flocks he has fathered, and a female
Bird will conceive by him from whom she herself was conceived.[64]

Gay people had, moreover, raised pointed objections to arguments against them based on animal behavior.

Is it any wonder that, since animals have been condemned by nature not to receive from the bounty of Providence any of the gifts afforded by intellect, they have with all else also been deprived of gay desires? Lions do not have such a love, because they are not philosophers either. Bears have no such love, because they are ignorant of the beauty that comes from friendship. But for humans wisdom coupled with knowledge has after frequent experiments chosen what is best, and has formed the opinion that gay love is the most stable of loves.[65]

Some gay writers even took the offensive in denigrating heterosexuality precisely because it was so common among animals:

All irrational animals merely copulate,[66] but we rational ones
Are superior in this regard to all other animals:
We discovered homosexual intercourse.[67] Men under the sway of women
Are no better than dumb animals.[68]

Even in a heterosexual context, classical thought through the Augustan period was more apt to censure than praise sexual acts imitative of animal behavior. "Let us not," Petronius wrote, "leap into it in a blind rush, like

64.   . . . Coeunt animalia nullo
      Cetera dilectu, nec habetur turpe iuvencae
      Ferre patrem tergo, fit equo sua filia coniunx,
      Quasque creavit init pecudes caper, ipsaque, cuius
      Semine concepta est, ex illo concipit ales. [324–27]
Actually the character speaking these lines approves of "nature's" tolerance of incest and juxtaposes it with "spiteful laws" among humans which condemn it.
      65. Pseudo-Lucian *Affairs of the Heart* 36. I have paraphrased the generally reliable translation of Macleod (p. 207), substituting "human" for "man" and "gay love" for "love between males," since it is not certain that the speaker wished to limit his comments to men only, and the Greek expressions Macleod translates as masculine may have been stock phrases without significant relation to gender. The case could be made that the gay speaker considers women also to have been deprived of the gifts of the intellect and therefore to be incapable of the loves he praises, but it is by no means a foregone conclusion, and the Platonic tradition would seem to militate against this inference.
      66. Βινεῖ, i.e., to mount the female.
      67. Πυγίζειν, i.e., to mount a male (from the rear).
      68. Πᾶν ἄλογον ζῶον βινεῖ μόνον· οἱ λογικοὶ δὲ
            Τῶν ἄλλων ζώων τοῦτ' ἔχομεν τὸ πλέον,
      Πυγίζειν εὑρόντες, ὅσοι δὲ γυναιξὶ κρατοῦνται,
            Τῶν ἀλόγων ζώων οὐδὲν ἔχουσι πλέον. [AP, 12.245]

animals in heat."[69] Many writers criticized Stoic philosophy precisely for the illogic of its appeals to animal behavior.[70] "It is ridiculous," Plutarch observed, "to cite the behavior of irrational animals in one place as an example and to reject it as irrelevant in another place."[71] In his dialogue on the two kinds of love, he mocked such conventions by having the gay side use Stoic arguments to demonstrate the immorality and "unnaturalness" of heterosexuality (*Moralia* 750C–D). Moreover, some prominent Stoics were quite conscious of the inadequacy of animal behavior as a model for humans. Seneca, for example, did not entertain any lofty notions about animal virtue: "Pleasure is a vulgar thing, petty and unworthy of respect, common to dumb animals—something to which the smallest and most contemptible of them fly."[72]

From a religious vantage, the fact that the gods had intercourse with humans in the form of animals—both homosexually and heterosexually— complicated the issue for pagans (AP, 1.15), and for Christians and Jews the Old Testament's position was vague and contradictory.[73] Leviticus forbade human intervention in animal sexuality (i.e., hybridization)[74] or recourse to animals for sexual pleasure (bestiality, Lev. 18:23, 19:19), but the Scriptures hardly presented animals as models of wholesome sexuality—adulterers were compared to horses (Jer. 5:8) and whores to dogs (Deut. 23:18).

69. "Non ergo ut pecudes libidinosae, caeci protinus irruamus illuc," *Poetae Latini minores*, ed. Emil Baehrens (Leipzig, 1848) 4:101.

70. The ideas of urban Stoics about "nature" and the "natural world" were often hilariously inaccurate: in a nonsexual context, see Epictetus *Discourses* 4.11.1 and the notes in the LC edition of W. A. Oldfather (London, 1926–28), pp. 388–89, 408.

71. "Ἄτοπον μὲν οὖν τὸ ἐκεῖ μὲν εὔκαιρον τὴν τῶν ἀλόγων ζῴων ἀποθηρίωσιν, ἐνταῦθα δ᾽ ἀπόλογον," *De stoicorum repugnantiis* 22; see also 34–35. Plutarch's own opinion in the matter of animals and homosexuality is confused by the many opinions expressed by characters in his writings, but in light of this statement and his general philosophy it does not seem likely that he would have considered animal behavior a relevant datum for either side. The claim that homosexual behavior is unknown among animals made in *Bruta animalia* 990D must be regarded as insincere, since it is followed immediately by counter examples (990E; see also *De sollertia animalium* 972F) and since most of the claims of animal superiority in this treatise are denied elsewhere in Plutarch's writings (e.g., the claim that animals do not lust after humans, 990F–991A, is contradicted at length by *De sollertia animalium* 972Dff.).

72. *Epistles* 123.16: "Voluptas humilis res et pusilla est et in nullo habenda pretio, communi cum mutis animalibus, ad quam minima et contemptissima advolant."

73. God had of course created all the animals and observed of his work that it was "good" but then declared many animals "unclean." The snake introduced humans to evil and appears irredeemable by the end of Genesis, but it is obliquely praised by Jesus for its "wisdom" (Matt. 10:16). Wolves are generally negative examples of savagery and deception, and doves usually figure as positive illustrations of peace and love, but other animals play more ambivalent roles: foxes, for instance, spoil the vine (Song of Sol. 2:15) and provide Jesus with a negative metaphor for Herod (Luke 13:32) but are pictured by Ezekiel (13:4) as innocent victims like the Hebrew prophets.

74. Which Jacob apparently used to trick Laban (Gen. 30:31–42).

Popular folklore among Jews and Christians held that many animals were ritually "unclean" because of their sexual irregularities.[75]

The most prominent Jewish exponent of "natural" morality, Philo, reflected these inconsistencies. Although he condemned homosexuals for not following the "laws of nature," he execrated men who married sterile women precisely because of the similarity of their behavior to that of animals: "Those who woo women who have been shown to be barren with other husbands are simply mounting them in the manner of pigs or goats and should be listed among the impious as enemies of God."[76]

Christian heirs to the tradition had even greater difficulties with it. In the East, Clement struggled vainly to explain how the "nature" which he claimed directed sexuality exclusively toward procreation could have created homosexual animals like the hyena, and he paradoxically cited ordinary animal sexuality as both positive and negative examples.[77] In the West, conscientious theologians eschewed animals altogether as sources of moral guidance. Saint Jerome used the adjective "animal" in his translation of the New Testament to characterize humans not on the path to salvation,[78] and when Augustine invoked the example of birds to justify Christian sexual morality, his inference was not that their behavior showed something about the operations or intentions of "nature" but that they were individually exemplifying the "nature" of marriage.[79] Animal behavior could hardly have been held up as ideal by someone who believed that "every act of an animal's life is either the seeking of bodily pleasure or the avoidance of pain."[80]

Even at the popular level of Barnabas, Clement, or the *Physiologus* it is obvious that animal behavior was a convenient—if inconsistent—justification for prejudice against gay people rather than the origin of it. The fact that most animals practice incest did not inspire Philo or Clement to infer that incest was one of "nature's purposes" in sexual relations, nor did the

75. Many authorities, e.g., considered that some animals "naturally" committed adultery of various sorts. See Basil *Homilia in hexaemeron* 7.6 (PG, 29:160), or John Damascene, *Sacra parallela* 2.11 (PG, 96:254).

76. *De specialibus legibus* 3.36: "῞Οσοι δὲ προδεδοκομασμένας ἑτέροις ἀνδράσιν ὡς εἰσὶν ἄγονοι μνῶνται συῶν τρόπον ἢ τράγων ὀχεύοντες αὐτὸ μόνον, ἐν ἀσεβῶν στήλαις ἐγγραφέσθωσαν ὡς ἀντίπαλοι θεοῦ."

77. E.g., in a passage devoted to demonstrating that "nature" could not approve of homosexuality, he refers to it as "bestial" and to those who practice it as "quadrupeds": see *Paedagogus*, quoted in app. 2.

78. 1 Cor. 2:14: "Animalis autem homo non percipit ea, quae sunt Spiritus Dei." The Greek has "ψυχικὸς δὲ ἄνθρωπος." Note the confusing relation this suggests to the "two ways" mentioned above.

79. E.g., *De nuptiis et concupiscentia* 1.4.5; *De adulterinis conjugiis* 2.12.12.

80. "Jam vero appetere voluptates corporis, et vitare molestias, ferinae vitae omnis actio est," *De libero arbitrio* 1.8.18 (PL, 32:1231).

knowledge that females of most mammal species allow many males to mount them during their fertile period prompt them to approve female promiscuity as "natural." Indeed their reverence for "nature" as exemplified by animals was so clearly subordinate to their personal hostility toward homosexuality that they could characterize gay sexuality as "unnatural" in spite of the fact that most of them believed several species of animals to be innately homosexual.[81] Whether or not "nature" is in fact responsible for homosexual inclinations, it was certainly not responsible for Christian condemnations of them.

Gender expectations.   The one patristic authority who commented at length on homosexuality itself and whose objections seem to have been directly related to the gender of the parties involved (rather than their age, procreative purpose, or pagan associations, etc.), was Saint John Chrysostom, but his antipathy was so inconsistent that it had little impact on subsequent theology.

Chrysostom was influenced both by Manichean opposition to pleasure and Stoic reverence for nature, and this led him into the paradoxical position of condemning sexual pleasure ("The passions in fact are all dishonorable")[82] while at the same time denouncing homosexual acts for not providing pleasure: "Sins against nature . . . are more difficult and less rewarding, so much so that they cannot even claim to provide pleasure, since real pleasure is only in accordance with nature."[83] Like Paul, he alleged that immoral homosexual acts arose not from "perversion" but from excess of desire (i.e., not as a replacement for heterosexual outlets but *in addition* to them). Since, however, he realized that many people were inclined to limit themselves to one sex or the other, Chrysostom had difficulty explaining why some should

81. Clement, having argued that "nature" designed sexual organs for heterosexual, procreative functions, is unable to explain why the hyena has an orifice apparently specifically created by "nature" to facilitate homosexual activity. He does point out that the hyena's activity should not serve as a model for human behavior, since (*a*) he believed Moses prohibited eating it and (*b*) it is not actually anal intercourse practiced by hyenas, since the passage employed is one designed specifically for this purpose rather than for some other use. This leaves unanswered the most interesting question of all: Why does "nature" cause hyenas to employ coitus between members of the same gender, and for nonreproductive purposes?

82. *In Epistolam ad Romanos*, homily 4 (PG, 60:415 ff.). There is no corpus of translations of Chrysostom's writings, although some major treatises appear in the Nicene and Post-Nicene Christian Fathers series. These translations are outdated, however, and in places bowdlerized. Several important passages appear in English in app. 2 below. M. L. Laistner published a useful translation of the *De inani gloria* (see n. 98) in *Christianity and Pagan Culture in the Later Roman Empire* (Ithaca, 1951), pp. 85–123.

83. Saint Cyprian also objected that homosexual activities "could not be pleasing to those who commit them," "fiunt quae nec illis possunt placere qui faciunt," *Epistles* 1 (PL, 4:216).

fall into this trap while others did not. The excess of desire, he concluded, must be a result of God's abandonment of the people in question because of some heinous sin. And what was the sin? Excess desire.[84] In one discussion he recognized the respectable ancestry of gay passions among the earlier Greeks, whom he admired intensely, but in another work he described such passions as a "new and illicit love, a new and insufferable crime."[85] At one point he announced that "whatever sin you mention, you will not name one which is the equal of this. . . . There is nothing, absolutely nothing more demented or noxious than this wickedness" (*In Epistolam ad Romanos*, homily 4); in two other places, however, he remarked that "there are ten thousand sins equal to or worse than this one."[86]

Beneath Chrysostom's contradictory diatribes a single powerful hostility seems to be responsible for his feelings about homosexual acts, a profound horror of what he considered to be the degradation of one man's passivity to another. "If those who *suffer it* [my emphasis] really perceived what was being done to them, they would rather die a thousand deaths than undergo this. . . . For I maintain that not only are you made [by it] into a woman, but you also cease to be a man; yet neither are you changed into that nature, nor do you retain the one you had" (*In Epist. ad Rom.* 4.2, 3, in app. 2).

In the West both Saint Augustine and Lactantius expressed feelings of disgust similar to Chrysostom's in regard to a man allowing his body to be used "as that of a woman" since, in Augustine's words, "the body of a man is as superior to that of a woman as the soul is to the body."[87] Cassian relates with astonishment the terrible sufferings of a young monk who "burned in an intolerable heat of passion with the desire to submit to rather than commit an 'unnatural' act."[88] In many cases this mysogynistic revulsion from males doing anything "feminine" had little to do with sexuality: Saint Cyprian thought it obscene that men should even play the role of women on the stage (*Epistles* 1 [PL, 4:211]). That the anxieties of Chrysostom (and many other fathers) about homosexual acts were largely responses to

84. Plutarch (*Moralia* 750) uses this argument against heterosexual passions. Scholastics were to regard *all* sexual desire as a consequence of sin, a position which would completely undermine Chrysostom's argument on Rom. 1:26–27.

85. *Adversus oppugnatores vitae monasticae* 3.8 (in app. 2)

86. "Νῦν δὲ μυρία καὶ ἴσα καὶ χαλεπώτερα γίνεται," *De perfecta caritate* 7 (PG, 56:288). The same statement occurs in *In Epistolam I ad Thessalonicas* 3, homily 8 (PG, 62:433).

87. Augustine *Contra mendacium* 7.10 (PL, 40:496): "Quanto diligentius atque constantius animi castitatis in veritate servanda est, cum verius ipse corpori suo, quam corpus virile femineo corpori praeferatur." Lactantius *Institutiones divinae* 5.9: "Qui denique immemores, quid nati sint, cum foeminis patientia certent."

88. *Institutes* 12.20 (PL, 49:457): "Nam contra usum naturae desiderio patiendi magis quam inferendi ignominiam intolerabili aestu libidinis urebatur." I am grateful to Mr. Douglass Roby for bringing this to my attention.

violations of gender expectations rather than the outgrowth of a systematic approach to sexual morality is further demonstrated by the almost complete absence of comments about homosexual relations between women in patristic sources, despite the fact that lesbianism was well known in the Hellenistic world. Augustine wrote to nuns that love between them should be spiritual rather than carnal and that married women and virgins should refrain from the "shameless playing with each other" in which women "with no regard for modesty" indulged.[89] But apart from this and one or two other comments, the fathers' silence is marked; a more typical approach is the opinion attributed to Anastasius regarding Romans 1:26, which discounts the possibility of lesbianism altogether: "Clearly [the women] do not mount each other but, rather, offer themselves to the men."[90]

All but one of these attitudes relating (sometimes unintentionally) to homosexual acts had powerful opponents within the Christian community. Only the authority of Barnabas was unassailed, and it became a dead issue for most theologians when the text was lost in the West, although its prejudices survived in popular scientific writings and folklore.

The other arguments were often as controversial as the behavior they were intended to disparage. Appropriate gender behavior, for instance, was considered by many to be an essentially improper concern for Christians. Jesus had hinted that at least some of his followers were called to be "eunuchs for the kingdom of heaven's sake" (Matt. 19:12), and Paul had asserted that in Christ there was "neither male nor female; for you are all one in Christ Jesus" (Gal. 3:28). In light of such texts, insistence on certain modes of sexual behavior seemed counter to Christian teaching. The influential "Egyptian Gospel" emphasized again and again the necessity of terminating traditional patterns of sexuality, expecially childbearing, and asserted that the Apocalypse would not occur until "the two [genders] become one, and man and woman are neither male nor female."[91]

89. *Epistles* 211 (PL, 33:964): "Non autem carnalis, sed spiritualis inter vos debet esse dilectio: nam quae faciunt pudoris immemores, etiam feminis feminae, jocando turpiter et ludendo, non solum a viduis et intactis ancillis Christi in sancto proposito constitutis, sed omnino nec a mulieribus nec a virginibus sunt facienda nupturis."

90. Mentioned by marginal glosses in two manuscripts of the *Paedagogus* of Clement: "Οὐκ ἀλλήλαις βαίνουσι δηλαδή, ἀλλὰ τοῖς ἀνδράσι παρέχουσιν ἑαυτάς," PG, 8:501, n. 9. Saint Augustine also seems to have interpreted the passage as applying to "unnatural" heterosexual use: see *De nuptiis et concupiscentia* 2.20 (PL, 44:456–57).

91. "Πυνθανομένης τῆς Σαλώμης, πότε γνωσθήσεται τὰ περὶ ὧν ἤρετο, ἔφη ὁ κύριος· ὅταν τὸ τῆς αἰσχύνης ἔνδυμα πατήσητε καὶ ὅταν γένηται τὰ δύο ἓν καὶ τὸ ἄρρεν μετὰ τῆς θηλείας οὔτε ἄρρεν οὔτε θῆλυ," Clement *Stromateis* 3.13.92 (PG, 8:1192–93). Note that Clement's admiration for the "Egyptian Gospel" precluded his making the sort of sex-role argument Chrysostom used a major part of his argument. Somewhat parallel feelings, however, are expressed in the *Paedagogus* 3.3.

Associations of homosexuality with pagan antiquity worked in more than one direction as well, since many Christians had reverence for the cultural inheritance of Rome and Greece and since the fathers often flatly contradicted each other in commenting on the classical tradition. While Clement, for instance, had written that Plato was inspired by Holy Scripture to oppose homosexual relations, Theodoret of Cyrus thought Plato had considered gay persons happy on earth and blessed in heaven.

> "No longer [according to Plato] is there a law consigning to the shadows and an underground journey those [gay people] already embarked on a journey heavenward; instead, they lead shining lives and travel in blessedness together, taking flight by virtue of their love." He concludes by exclaiming, "O youth! Such heavenly rewards will a man's love bestow on you!" And he makes these observations not in regard to chaste lovers but unrestrained ones, as can be easily discerned in his dialogues. . . . [92]

Even Chrysostom was troubled by the Greek attitude toward gay relationships, and in the later Middle Ages classical admiration for homosexuality was effectively used to defuse the moral issue altogether.

The various prototypes of the "natural law" theory were widely opposed and often mutually contradictory. The "Alexandrian rule" was rejected by Chrysostom and remained controversial through the early Middle Ages; as late as the eighth century Saint John Damascene and his disciples placed sexual pleasure first among the ends of marriage.[93] Moreover, most Christians considered homosexual *attraction* perfectly natural; even if they objected to genital expression of gay feelings, they would not have done so on the basis of arguments from "nature."

Saint Basil wrote to contemporaries following a monastic ideal,

> It is frequently the case with young men that even when rigorous self-restraint is exercised, the glowing complexion of youth still blossoms forth and becomes a source of desire to those around them. If, therefore, anyone is youthful and physically beautiful, let him keep his attractiveness hidden until his appearance reaches a suitable state.[94]

92. Theodoret of Cyrus *Thérapeutique des maladies helléniques* [*Graecarum affectionum curatio*] 9.53–54 (Canivet ed., pp. 352–53): "Εἰς γὰρ σκότον καὶ τὴν ὑπὸ γῆς πορείαν οὐ νόμος ἐστιν ἔτι ἐλθεῖν τοῖς κατηργμένοις ἤδη τῆς ὑπουρανίου πορείας, ἀλλὰ φανὸν βίον διάγοντας εὐδαιμονεῖν μετ' ἀλλήλων πορευομένους καὶ ὁμοπτέρους ἔρωτος χάριν. Τούτοις δὲ ἐπιλέγει ταῦτα· Ὦ παῖ, καὶ οὕτω σοι θεία δωρήσεται ἡ παρ' ἐραστοῦ φιλία. Καὶ ταῦτα οὐ περὶ τῶν σωφρόνως, ἀλλὰ περὶ τῶν ἀκολάστως ἐρώντων ἔφη· καὶ ῥάδιον ἐκ τῶν ἐκείνου διαλόγων ταῦτα μαθεῖν. . . ."

93. E.g., *Sacra parallela* 2.11 (PG, 96:256): "Ἔχεις γυναῖκα· ἔχεις μετὰ ἀσφαλείας ἡδονήν"; cf. Theodore Abucara, in PG, 97:1556.

94. *De renuntiatione saeculi* 6 (PG, 31:640). W. K. L. Clarke (*The Ascetic Works of St. Basil*

Sit in a chair far from such a youth; in sleep do not allow your
clothing to touch his but, rather, have an old man between you.[95]
When he is speaking to you or singing opposite you, look down as you
respond to him, so that you do not by gazing at his face take the seed
of desire from the enemy sower and bring forth harvests of corruption
and loss. Do not be found with him either indoors or where no one can
see what you do, either for studying the prophecies of Holy Scripture or
for any other purpose, no matter how necessary.[96]

Obviously Basil did not consider erotic attractions between males "unnatural"; he assumed that the men to whom he was writing were susceptible
to the physical charms of other men. Because the persons in question were
following a monastic ideal of celibacy, he cautioned them strongly against
succumbing to these charms, but he did not imply that any such lapse would
be particularly heinous: the first passage is followed by recommendations
that monks nod yes or no rather than swear with oaths, and the second by
admonitions against gluttony—hardly the sort of contexts to suggest the
matter was a grave one.

Despite his violent rhetoric against homosexual practices, Saint John
Chrysostom himself obviously considered homosexual *attraction* perfectly
normal and constantly juxtaposed homosexual and heterosexual desires as
two faces of the same coin. In complaining, for instance, about sinful motivations for entering the temple of the Lord, he mentions in terms of equal
likelihood a man's desire to view the beauty of women or of young men who
frequent the sanctuaries;[97] and in warning parents about the difficulty of
restraining the sexual desires of adolescents, he emphasizes that the danger

---

[London, 1925], p. 9) argues that this work is not by Basil. The opposite opinion is
maintained by others, but which way the issue is resolved is not really important to the
present discussion. The comments are certainly those of a contemporary of Basil's and were
believed to be his.

95. It was common for men, especially in communal life, to share beds in the ancient
world. This was forbidden to monks by Benedict and others, apparently due to the same
fears which troubled Basil.

96. *Sermo asceticus* 323 (PG, 32:880).

97. "Πολλοὶ εἰσίασι κάλλη γυναικῶν περιβλέποντες· ἄλλοι παίδων ὥρας περιεργαζό-
μενοι," *Homilia in Matthaeum* 73.3 (PG, 58:677). Van de Spijker's comment that "der Kompa-
rativ 'curiosus,' 'mit noch grösserer Neugier,' weist auf einen stärkeren Vorwurf hin" (p. 254,
n. 128) is silly: "curiosus" occurs only in the Latin translation he uses; there is no such word
in the original Greek. Moreover, he could have avoided this error by simply reading further
in the Latin, where the word "curiose" occurs a few lines below in regard to women ("For-
mam mulierum curiose respicis?"). A similar mistake is made by George Prevost in his
translation of the work, *The Homilies of St. John Chrysostom, Archbishop of Constantinople, on the
Gospel of St. Matthew* (New York, 1888), p. 443. An echo of Chrysostom's complaint appears

is twofold, since the "beast" of lust may impel the youth either to being debauched by men or to debauching women.[98]

It may be objected that the general thrust of early Christian sexual ethics would have precluded homosexual intercourse regardless of the particular objections brought against it. This argument deserves attention. It should be noted in the first place that whether or not early opponents of gay sexuality could have deduced the sinfulness of homosexual behavior from general systems of sexuality, they did not. Saint Augustine, for example, who more than any other single writer determined the sexual attitudes of the Christian West, never related homosexual activities to heterosexual ones, and discussions of homosexual acts are conspicuously absent from the treatises in which he expounded his system of sexual morality. Even when he appealed to Paul's comments in Romans to justify his objurgation of "unnatural" sex practices, he addressed himself to heterosexual intercourse.[99] When he deprecated homosexuality itself, he used specific arguments completely unrelated to his general theories on sexuality.

What early Christian sexual ethics actually had in common with these schools of thought was a social matrix profoundly different from most modern ones, which must be appreciated in order to see why many late Roman systems of sexual morality might emphasize or insist upon procreative purpose in heterosexual relations without espousing any particular attitude toward homosexual ones. In the absence of any effective chemical, mechanical, or biological means of contraception, every completed heterosexual coupling in the ancient world had to be viewed as the potential creation of a child. Only the interruption of coitus, which was difficult and thought by Christians (probably wrongly) to have been specifically forbidden in the Bible, or abortion, regarded by many as murder, could prevent the birth of a child. The fate of abandoned or illegitimate children was often ghastly by

---

in the "ordinary gloss" to the *Decretum* of Gratian, but significantly it has a purely heterosexual focus: see James Brundage, "Prostitution in the Medieval Canon Law," *Signs: Journal of Women in Culture and Society* 1 (1976): 835, n. 51.

98. *De inani gloria* 76, ed. Anne-Marie Malingrey (Paris, 1972): "῍Ωρα δὴ λοιπὸν ἐπὶ τὴν ἐπιθυμίαν ἰέναι. ᾿Εκεῖ καὶ διπλῆ ἡ σωφροσύνη καὶ διπλῆ ἡ βλάβη, οἶμαι, ὥστε μήτε αὐτὸν καταπορνεύεσθαι μήτε πορνεύειν εἰς κόρας."

99. *De bono conjugali* 11 (PL, 40:382); *De nuptiis et concupiscentia* 11.20 (PL, 44:456–57). In the case of the latter, note that although the citation of Rom. 1:27 constrains Augustine to recognize homosexual behavior, it could hardly be given less attention: the passage relating to women is specifically taken as referring to heterosexual intercourse, and the thrust of the chapter is a *rejection* of the Pelagian argument that Paul meant to stigmatize homosexual as opposed to heterosexual relations. He meant, Augustine retorts, to stigmatize *any* nonprocreative intercourse, even between husband and wife. (In *De bono conjugali* it is *especially* between husband and wife.)

any standards, and many Christians made it their duty to adopt such foundlings.[100]

Given the moral dilemma that a moment of careless pleasure might produce, it is hardly surprising that ethical systems in the economically depressed cities of late antiquity insisted vehemently on acknowledgment of and concern over the procreative aspects of heterosexuality. Heterosexual Christians were faced with a harsh dilemma: either run the risk of bringing children, with their attendant difficulties, into the world each time they indulged in vaginal intercourse, or consciously choose to prevent conception or birth, and take active steps to do so. Christian marriage was thus regulated by the early church largely with an eye to precluding the production or abuse of unwanted children and to preventing adultery and divorce, which were clearly prohibited in the New Testament. Under such circumstances, it is not surprising that many Christians retreated to asceticism. Exploration of nonvaginal sexual outlets, which might have circumvented the difficulty, was precluded for many not by scriptural injunction or any specific teachings of the early church but by the incorporation into later theology of already well-established taboos of an entirely social nature.[101] Oral-genital contact, for instance, is not prohibited in either the Old Testament or the New but was widely execrated by certain elements of pre-Christian Greek and Roman society as degrading,[102] and this prejudice was unquestioningly retained by some Greek and Roman theologians, although it can be shown to antedate Christianity and to have had nothing to do with concepts of "natural morality" or procreative purpose. (To Romans, it was merely a matter of taste and aesthetics.) The impact of this and other social or class-related

100. See Noonan, esp. pp. 85–86, 136.

101. An examination of taboos regarding heterosexual activity within marriage would require a volume at least as long as the present one. Although research on this area is still preliminary, it is already apparent that such taboos are more closely related to socioeconomic status than to any other single factor. Persons with lower incomes and less education regard far more sexual activity as forbidden; often they consider intercourse in the nude to be perverse and immoral and disagree dramatically with wealthier and more educated persons on such seemingly inconsequential matters as the propriety of use of the tongue in kissing or the position assumed by the partners in heterosexual coitus. (Note that such differences relate to approval, not incidence.) The most thorough analysis of such phenomena has been made on the basis of data from the modern West (see, e.g. Kinsey et al., *Sexual Behavior in the Human Male*, esp. "Social Level and Sexual Outlet"—the pioneer study in the area—and Weinrich, pt. 1), but other studies indicate similar patterns in non-Western cultures: e.g., H. K. Malhotra and N. N. Wig, "Dhat Syndrome: a Culture-bound Sex Neurosis of the Orient," *Archives of Sexual Behavior* 4 (1975): 519–28.

102. Investigation of this subject is badly needed; no adequate studies exist. For Greece, Henderson is useful, esp. pp. 51–55, but there is no comparable analysis of Roman attitudes, despite a huge amount of accessible data. See, e.g., Martial on fellatio (2.33, 47, 89; 9.4; 10.31; 11.30, etc.) or even against kissing (e.g., 11.98). Other Roman prejudices are discussed in chap. 3 above.

sexual taboos was profound but cannot rightly be ascribed to the eventual triumph of the "Alexandrian rule"; on the contrary, the success of the latter, at least at the popular level, was doubtless due in some measure to the pre-existence in many areas of virulent prejudice against specific acts which were, incidentally, nonprocreative.

None of these circumstances applied to gay people. They had neither to take any steps to prevent conception nor to cope with unwanted pregnancy. Even the most hostile critics of homosexual behavior admitted that no one was harmed by it but the participants, and if gay people did not share the feeling of some members of their society that such acts were inherently repulsive and degrading, they probably found themselves in no moral difficulty whatever.

It is indeed too often overlooked that just as there was a pagan ascetic and antierotic tradition, so was there a Christian tradition of tolerant and positive attitudes toward love and eroticism, represented by such figures as Ausonius, Sidonius Apollinaris, Saint John Damascene, Marbod of Rennes, Saint Aelred of Rievaulx, et al. It is almost fatally tempting for the historian, like the moral theologian, to pick out those fathers and doctrines which eventually gained universal acceptance as orthodox and to point to these as crucial in the development of Christian attitudes on particular points. Because the modern Catholic church traces its doctrines back in an unbroken chain to specific opinions of early fathers, the historian is apt to accept the notion that a particular opinion triumphed because this or that influential thinker espoused it, disregarding the fact that many equally prominent theologians, some of whom the church regarded as worthy of sainthood, may have held contrary views or that the authority in question may have himself held other views on the same subject which are not incorporated as dogma. Teachings now central to Catholic doctrine were often no more than casual observations of those who first enunciated them, and opinions which seemed crucial to the fathers of the church must frequently be brushed aside by later Catholics as embarrassments. It may be discomfiting to some modern Christian opponents of homosexual behavior that none of the major patristic objections to it rested on or was a logical outgrowth of the teachings of Jesus or the Apostles, and that the earliest and most influential objections were based on fundamental misunderstandings of natural history and Christian Scripture; it may be convenient for canonists to overlook the naiveté of Clement's reliance on the animal history of Barnabas and to concentrate on those opinions of his which are still accepted within the Catholic community; but the historian cannot justify doing so. There is no reason to believe that it was his reference to the incipient "Alexandrian rule" which influenced Clement's disciples rather than his invocation of the Epistle of Barnabas.

There is in fact little reason to assume that the specific objections of influential theologians played any major role in the development of antihomosexual feelings in Christian society. The fact that an opinion was held or taught in some quarters is no proof that it was generally believed: it is hardly likely that Clement of Alexandria and Saint John Chrysostom insisted so vehemently on the sinfulness of homosexual acts because this was the majority opinion in their day; the reverse would be a more cogent inference. The attitude of Ausonius is probably a better index of general Christian feelings: the casual indifference and candor with which he alludes to the subject suggest that he felt no need to defend his opinions.

One must be careful, moreover, not to confuse hostility to same-sex eroticism in particular with hostility to eroticism in general. Augustine, Jerome, Origen, and many other prominent early theologians (along with many pagan philosophers) explicitly rejected eroticism as a positive human experience,[103] insisting that sexuality should be divorced from pleasure in a moral life and linked only to the function of procreation. "Either we marry to have children, or, refusing to marry, we live in continence for the rest of our lives" (Justin Martyr 1 *Apology* 29). The most popular manual of moral doctrine in the Middle Ages cited both Pythagoras and Saint Jerome as insisting that "a man who loves his wife very much is an adulterer. Any love for someone else's wife or too much love for one's own is shameful. The upright man should love his wife with his judgment, not his affections."[104] Pleasure, even during an act aimed at procreation, was sinful in the opinion of many members of the early church.

Such a philosophy, in which human relationships are justified solely by their function, might denigrate homosexuality, but not necessarily. At many points in Christian history even ascetics have valued homosexual feelings as conducive to the sort of love which Jesus evinced toward his followers, and the vast majority of Christian ascetics have viewed heterosexuality as the chief danger to the soul. "There is nothing," Augustine wrote, "which degrades the manly spirit more than the attractiveness of females and contact with their bodies."[105]

103. Many Greeks, for instance, considered it nobler to resist than to succumb to a pleasure which they regarded as particularly distracting from the loftier pursuits of the mind. Others feared erotic impulses as external, almost demonic forces which possessed weaker souls. Little systematic analysis of ancient sexual attitudes in a social context has been attempted, but the works cited above are of some assistance. Note that the Latin word from which "passion" is derived means "to suffer." Even in English the word originally had this connotation, as is evident in some surviving uses like the "passion" of Christ.

104. Vincent of Beauvais *Speculum doctrinale* 10.45: "Adulter est in sua uxore ardentior amator. In aliena quippe uxore omnis amor turpis est, et in sua nimius. Sapiens iudicio debet amare coniugem, non affectu."

105. *Soliloquia* 1.40 (PL, 32:878): "Nihil esse sentio quod magis ex arce dejiciat animam virilem quam blandimenta foeminea corporumque ille contactus."

It is crucial to remember that even where such authorities explicitly condemned homosexuality, they also categorically rejected the majority of human erotic experience. The extreme asceticism of Augustine and others not only rejected erotic love between husband and wife—the basis of modern Christian marriage—but also condemned most sexual acts performed by married couples (i.e., every act not undertaken with procreative intent). And it did so consciously. Augustine admitted that no married persons of his acquaintance engaged in intercourse solely for the purpose of procreation (*De bono conjugali* 13 [15] [PL, 40:384]), and yet procreation, he insisted, was the only truly moral use of sexuality. (Saint Thomas Aquinas did not even consider that it was procreation but "the legitimacy of the offspring" which was the "chief good of marriage.")[106]

This position has not by any means maintained a uniform supremacy. Except in theological disputation, Christian society has in the main ignored it and at many points rejected it openly. Selective inference on this point has, however, allowed historians—and Christians—to overlook its significance in regard to gay people. It will seem to some, for instance, that the open toleration or even approval of gay sexuality by Christians which is depicted at various points in this study must represent a decline in Christian morality rather than a change. But these same persons would probably not argue that the acceptance of erotic heterosexual love between husband and wife represented a decline in Christian morality, although by the same criterion it does, in the sense that it is a relaxation of the most rigid position of some of the fathers.

If, on the other hand, one concludes that the antierotic feelings and doctrines of the most extreme of the fathers were an excess rather than a base point of Christian ethics and that Christian orthodoxy has not necessarily always consisted of rigid adherence to a completely functional approach, then one must also abandon the doctrinaire conclusion that acceptance of homosexuality represents a decline in Christian morality simply because it departs from such a position. One must begin to examine whether toleration of gay sexuality in fact accompanies moral decadence within the Christian community and is associated with the abandonment of Christian ethics in general, or whether it is simply part of a softening of an extreme functionalism in Christian sexual ethics, perhaps within a context of conscientious Christian reform.

Further, it is important to bear in mind in this context that the same fathers of the church—a very vocal minority—who censured homosexual behavior also censured, no less severely, behavior which is today universally

---

106. *Summa contra gentiles* 3.124: "Certitudo prolis est principale bonum quod ex matrimonio quaeritur."

accepted by Christian communities. Lending at interest, sexual intercourse during the menstrual period, jewelry or dyed fabrics, shaving, regular bathing, wearing wigs, serving in the civil government or army, performing manual labor on feast days, eating kosher food, practicing circumcision—all were condemned absolutely by various fathers of the church, the same who condemned homosexual behavior and many other activities, due to personal prejudice, misinformation, or an extremely literal interpretation of the Bible. None of these practices is today a matter of controversy within the Christian community, and it seems illogical to claim that it was the opposition of a few influential Christian theorists which caused homosexual practices alone, out of hundreds of proscribed actions, to incur such a powerful and permanent stigma in Western culture. Obviously some more sophisticated analysis is required.

III Shifting Fortunes

7 The Early Middle Ages

By the beginning of the sixth century, the process of urban decline begun by the disintegration of Roman government and greatly hastened by barbarian invasions had profoundly altered the social structure of much of western Europe. Although it is easy to exaggerate the collapse of Roman civilization and overlook the many ways in which it survived and continued to exert influence on the barbarian kingdoms which supplanted it, it is probably safe to say that at no time after the rise of the Roman state was western European society more predominantly rural than during the period between the fourth and eighth centuries. The transformation of the urban culture of antiquity into the agricultural society of the Middle Ages had an ambivalent effect on gay people.[1] The decay of great cities like Rome—in A.D. 500 a crumbling ruin twice sacked by barbarians, protected from the Byzantine and Ostrogothic forces squabbling over it only by the bishop who now presided over the remnant of its population—appears to have reduced to insignificance (or at least invisibility) the gay subculture so prominent in many ancient urban centers. Extremely little gay literature survives from this period, and such public manifestations as gay marriages or prostitution appear to have been completely unknown. Their disappearance from public view in most places strengthened the position of those hostile to gay people by removing any evidence which would contradict claims about the bizarre, "unnatural," or socially harmful character of gay sexuality. Although only

1. Studies of homosexuality in the Middle Ages are to date extremely few and for the most part unsatisfactory. In addition to the general works mentioned above, one might note Douglass Roby, "Early Medieval Attitudes toward Homosexuality," *Gai Saber* 1, no. 1 (1977): 67–71, a creative but extremely brief analysis; Arno Karlen, "The Homosexual Heresy," *Chaucer Review* 6, no. 1 (1971): 44–63, a largely useless and inaccurate treatment; and Michael Goodich, "Sodomy in Medieval Secular Law," *Journal of Homosexuality* 1, no. 3 (1976): 295–302, and "Sodomy in Ecclesiastical Law and Theory," ibid., no. 4 (1976): 45–52, both of which are useful but marred by an uncritical and excessively legalistic approach. Goodich's book, *The Unmentionable Vice: Homosexuality in the Later Middle Ages, ca. 1000–1350 A.D.*, announced by Clio (Santa Barbara) for 1978, had not appeared when this text went to press.

rarely singled out for special derogation during this period, homosexuality was even more rarely defended, and in the less sophisticated, less cosmopolitan West of the early Middle Ages its mere statistical oddity probably roused suspicion against it. In the Roman cities which survived (e.g., Constantinople or Saragossa), autocrats often made life very difficult for minorities they happened to dislike, such as Jews or gay people, and an overwhelmingly "rural" ethos outside the remaining urban centers may have discouraged most erotic relations outside tribal or extended-family structures.

On the other hand, except in a few areas governmental control had become so ineffective that enforcement of oppressive laws or attitudes was difficult or impossible, and even when totalitarian regimes wished or attempted to restrict expressions of gay sexuality they could do so only in haphazard and inefficient ways. Contrary to popular opinion, moreover, gay people were not generally the subjects of proscriptive legislation during this period, although there had been a gradual narrowing of social attitudes toward all forms of sexuality outside marriage from the third through the sixth century, with gay people suffering the same general restraints on personal freedom as others.

Male prostitution had been officially banned in the Western Empire as early as the third century,[2] though with little effect, and other forms of gay sexuality remained legal in the West. In the East even male prostitution was legal, but at the beginning of the sixth century the tax on it was abolished. This tax had been collected by every emperor—Christian and non-Christian —since Constantine. Indeed Evagrius, who records the abolition of the tax, goes to considerable lengths to defend Constantine from the charge laid against him (by Zosimus) of actually devising it.[3] Evagrius states explicitly that there was no law regulating such relations and that the tax itself constituted a legal safeguard for the acts upon which it was levied, so that those who wished to could engage in them legally and "with impunity."[4] He does not specify what change, if any, occurred in their legal status after

2. The increasing hostility to male prostitution of the later Empire may indicate decreasing distinction in status between citizens and noncitizens, or simply the reduction in number of noncitizens resident in the Empire: formerly Romans had justified male prostitution largely on the grounds that it involved only slaves and foreigners, but by the late fourth century such a rationalization was no longer effective. Christianity and Stoicism had considerably altered the common view of slavery and had raised public consciousness regarding the dignity of the human person regardless of social standing. Caracalla granted citizenship to most of the Empire in 212, and it was becoming increasingly difficult to limit slavery and prostitution to noncitizens.

3. Evagrius *Ecclesiastical History* 3.40–41.

4. "'Ὡς ἀντὶ νόμου τινὸς τὴν ἐσκομιδὴν βοᾶν ἐπ᾽ ἀδείας εἶναι τὴν τοιαύτην ἀθεμιτουργίαν τοῖς βουλομένοις," ibid. 39, as printed in L. Permentier and J. Bidez, eds., *The Ecclesiastical History of Evagrius* (London, 1898), p. 137.

the tax was done away with, although it is possible to interpret his comments as meaning that the suppression of the tax only removed imperial *protection*, leaving the acts "licit for those inclined to engage in them." [5]

Not until 533 did any part of the Empire see legislation flatly outlawing homosexual behavior, even though Christianity had been the state religion for more than two centuries. In that year, following what had been standard ecclesiastical opinion since the fourth century, the emperor Justinian placed all homosexual relations under the same category as adultery and subjected them for the first time to civil sanctions (adultery was at the time punishable by death.) [6]

In 538 and 544 the emperor issued further laws, [7] largely of a hortatory nature, urging all those who had fallen into such sins to seek forgiveness through penance. No new penalties were inflicted, although the obdurate were specifically assigned to the jurisdiction of the city prefect.

Some have seen these laws as the response of a superstitious ruler to the earthquakes of 525 and the plague in Constantinople in 543; and Justinian himself mentioned that the laws were necessary "at this time, when in various ways we have provoked Him to anger on account of the multitude of our sins. . . . For because of such crimes there are famines, earthquakes, and pestilences." [8] Since, however, the first of the laws was passed thirteen

5. In the PG edition by Valesius, this line is punctuated so as to imply something different from the interpretation offered in most translations: Valesius inserts a stop (·) between "εἶναι" and "τὴν τοιαύτην," suggesting that he understood the sense of the passage to be something like "so that he declared the collection against some law, the disgraceful deed itself remaining legal" (86:2680). Although this interpretation would have been much better served by inserting a comma between "βοᾶν" and "ἐπ᾽ ἀδείας," Valesius may have been inspired to do this by considering that the clause beginning "ὡς ἀντί" was intended as the result of "ἀνεῖλε," with the long period beginning "ἐπέκειτο" being simply a parenthetical description of "that" ("ὅ") which Anastasius abolished. If indeed the clause is intended to elucidate what Anastasius did rather than what previous emperors had done, this is the only possible interpretation, and Evagrius does seem to be implying that the "deed itself remained legal" even after the tax was abolished. Most translators, however, have assumed punctuation along the lines of that published by Permentier and Bidez. Thus Louis Cousin paraphrased the line as "Cette imposition sembloit tenir lieu d'une loi, qui autorisoit cette détestable brutalité" (*Histoire de l'église, écrite par Théodoret et par Evagre* [Paris, 1676], p. 505); the Latin translation provided by Valesius himself reads, "Adeo ut collatio ista vice legis proclamaret, licere cuivis incestam illam libidinem perpetrare" (PG, 86:2679); and T. Shorting (?) rendered it "In so much that, this Tax, instead of a Law, made loud proclamation that those who had a mind, might securely and with impunity commit such abominable Leachery" ("The Ecclesiastical History of Evagrius Scholasticus Epiphaniensis," in *The History of the Church* [London, 1709], p. 471).

6. *Institutes* 4.18.4. For an English version of the text, see the complete translation of the Justinianic Code by Samuel Scott, *The Civil Law* (Cincinnati, 1932). There is considerable controversy about the death penalty for adultery. It is almost certainly a Christian accretion to the Julian law, but it is difficult to identify its origins more precisely. Some have opined that Constantine was responsible, but this is far from certain.

7. *Novellae* 77, 141 (Scott, 16:288–89, 17:160–61). Also translated by Bailey, pp. 73–79.

8. Bailey's translation (p. 74).

years after the earthquakes and eight years before the plague, this does not seem a particularly likely explanation.

The emperor expressed his opposition to homosexuality in religious terms, but Byzantine emperors justified most of their enactments—and their very authority—with Christian rhetoric; appeal to scriptural injunction was the standard currency of abuse and oppression in matters political and social as well as religious. It is extremely difficult to imagine that Justinian's legislation on this matter represented an effort to make Christian moral principles into civil law, since one of the constitutions citing biblical authority against gay people is immediately preceded by his edict permitting the dissolution of marriage by common consent—a concession not only at odds with all previous Christian marriage legislation (including Justinian's own) but absolutely contrary to the unanimous teaching of the fathers of the church.[9]

There is no indication that any church official suggested or supported the emperor's action against gay people. On the contrary, the only persons known by name to have been punished for homosexual acts were prominent bishops.

Among these were Isaiah of Rhodes, who had been the *prefectus vigilum* of Constantinople, and Alexander, the bishop of Diospolis in Thrace. They were brought to Constantinople by imperial order and were tried and deposed by the city prefect, who punished them, exiling Isaiah after severe torture and exposing Alexander to public ridicule after castrating him.

Shortly after this, the emperor ordered that all those found guilty of homosexual relations[10] be castrated. Many were found at the time, and they were castrated and died. From that time on, those who experienced sexual desire for other males lived in terror.[11]

Justinian was born in a rural village near Naissus, and it is likely that these measures either reflected his personal hostility toward urban sexual mores

9. *Novellae* 140 (Scott, 17:158–60): "Nam si mutua affectio matrimonia contrahit, merito eadem contraria sententia ex consensu solvit, repudiis missis quae eam declarent."

10. Several terms are used in this account for "homosexuality" and "homosexual" (e.g., "παιδεραστία," "ἀρσενοκοιτοῦντες," "ἀνδροκοῖται"). In better Greek they would have more specific and distinguishable meanings, but it is clear that they are all used here loosely and interchangeably.

11. Joannes Malalas *Chronographia* 18.168 (PG, 97:644). Bailey (p. 78) rightly points out that Theophanes (*Chronographia* 151 [PG, 108:408]) places the punishment of two bishops for homosexual offenses before the reign of Justinian, in A.D. 521, but he was apparently unaware of this account by Malalas, who attributes it to Justinian. Malalas (ca. 491–568) was contemporary with the occurrence; and Theophanes, two and a half centuries later (ca. 758–817), clearly drew on his account of the incident, simply misdating it. Although Theophanes is a major source for later Byzantine history, he is often inexact about dates.

or simply provided an excuse to attack his enemies. Procopius of Caesarea, a contemporary of the events and the best historian of the era,[12] states specifically that Justinian did not concern himself with offenses committed after the passage of the laws but, rather, sought out and prosecuted persons caught in such acts long before, using the law as a pretext against those of the opposite circus faction, the Greens,[13] "or possessed of great wealth, or who happened to have done something else which offended the rulers" (*Anecdota* 11.34–36).[14] The empress Theodora also employed the new laws against her personal enemies: when a young Green made uncomplimentary remarks about her, she had him indicted as homosexual, forcibly removed from the church in which he had taken refuge, hideously tortured, and then castrated without benefit of trial (16.18–22).

It does not appear that the population of Constantinople (or other imperial cities) sympathized with the opinions of Justinian and Theodora on the matter.[15] Procopius records the criminalization of homosexuality as one of several programs the emperor undertook chiefly to get money from

12. The *Anecdota*, or *Secret History*, in which the following comments occur evinces a strong bias against Justinian and even more against Theodora. But it accords in every detail with the other evidence about this matter (some of it from authors who approved the emperor's action), not only in terms of the passage and tenor of the law but even in the details of the punishments inflicted. (E.g., compare Procopius 11.36 with the account by Malalas above.) Even friendly testimony, moreover, admits the unfair enforcement of the law: Malalas relates that Isaiah and Alexander were punished first; then the law requiring castration was passed.

13. Through much of the Middle Ages citizens of Eastern cities belonged to one of two factions, the Blues and the Greens, which sat on opposite sides of the circus and rooted for their particular charioteers. The rivalry between them was violent and transcended all religious and political loyalties, often causing severe political disturbances, enormous social unrest, and profound consequences for many individuals when an emperor of the rival party came to power. Justinian was an ardent Blue and devoted a great deal of energy to harassing Greens. For a recent study of circus factions, see Alan Cameron, *Circus Factions: Blues and Greens at Rome and Byzantium* (Oxford, 1976).

14. For some reason Bailey, who admits the testimony of Procopius in related matters, ignores his discussion of Justinian's motivation and rejects as "unsubstantiated" Gibbon's belief that the law was a perversion of justice under which "paederasty became the crime of those to whom no crime could be imputed" (p. 78). Gibbon was obviously following Procopius, whose testimony on the point seems credible in spite of his hostility to the emperor; perhaps Bailey simply failed to read the relevant sections of the *Anecdota*: he does not impugn their authority.

15. Procopius observes that Theodora could find nothing worse to charge Diogenes with than homosexual affairs ("οὐδέν τι ἧσσον γάμων ἀνδρείων συκοφαντεῖν ἐν σπουδῇ εἶχε"), implying that most people would regard it as at worst a peccadillo (16.23). This is missed or disguised by the translator of the LC edition (Cambridge, Mass., 1919), H. B. Dewing. The interesting phrase "γάμων ἀνδρείων" could refer to homosexual marriage, but I have rendered it as "affairs" because it is plural (although the Greek for "marriage" is often plural) and because this is the most conservative translation. Procopius's terminology for gay sexuality is, like that of most urban Greeks, either neutral or complimentary and in stark contrast to the rhetoric of imperial legislation.

the persecuted and lists it among the oppression of the Samaritans, the pagans, unorthodox Christians, and astrologers (11.13ff.). Theodora ignored the efforts of "the whole populace" to intercede for the young man she had dragged from the church (16.20, 22) but was unable to convict another (also a Green) whom she attempted to prosecute on the same charge, because so many prominent people came to his aid. When the judges refused to hear the charges, in spite of her bribing witnesses and torturing one of his friends, the whole city celebrated a holiday in his honor (16.23–28).

This pattern is typical of the Middle Ages. Almost without exception the few laws against homosexual behavior passed before the thirteenth century were enacted by civil authorities without advice or support from the church. Occasionally ecclesiastical councils or authorities ratified such enactments, often under duress, but purely ecclesiastical records usually stipulate either no penalty at all or a very mild one. The fact that the civil laws in question were frequently aimed at the clergy obviously played a large part in this tendency.

The earliest surviving civil enactments against homosexual behavior in the West exemplify this tendency. Around 650 the ruler of the Spanish Visigoths passed legislation against homosexual acts, stipulating castration for those committing them.[16] As in the case of Justinian's legislation, the edict is phrased in terms of Christian morality, but it is a purely civil law. The church took no part in its passage, although bishops were instructed by the text of the law to oversee the penances of those convicted under its provisions. Only in the most ironic way could the law be viewed as a reflection of the influence of the Old Testament: the same code which proscribed homosexuality stipulated stoning or burning alive for observance of circumcision, the foundation of the Mosaic law.[17]

Both the scope of such laws and the severity of the punishment they imposed were decided anomalies in early medieval justice; their influence was negligible,[18] and they can only be understood in the general social

16. *Leges Visigothorum* 3.5.4, ed. K. Zeumer, in MGH, *Leges*, 1,1 (Hanover, 1902), 1:163. This and subsequent edicts are translated in Samuel P. Scott, *The Visigothic Code* (Boston, 1910), and discussed by Bailey (pp. 92–94), who unfortunately completely fails to grasp the unusual historical situation in which the laws were drafted.

17. Prohibited at 12.2.7 ("Ne Judei carnis faciant circumcisiones"); penalty prescribed in 12.2.11. As in the case of antigay laws, there is strong likelihood that such provisions were not enforced: cf. 12.2.12.

18. The spurious law discussed below, p. 177, n. 30, appeals to "Roman law" as justification for the penalty of burning for "sodomites." The Theodosian Code mentions burning, but in a somewhat different context, and it is distantly possible, in view of the association of Benedict's compilation with various Spanish sources, that this is a reference to the harsh Visigothic enactments of two centuries before. There are a number of references to Visigothic law in Benedict's collection, for which see Emil Seckel's posthumous article, "Studien zu

context of Visigothic Spain. The Visigoths were a barbarian minority of Arian heretics who had conquered and ruled the Hispano-Roman majority of Spain by sheer military superiority. They were not assimilated into urban centers but remained outside in rural areas of strategic importance and did not become Catholic until 589, when the ruling Visigothic families espoused Catholicism precisely to promote greater unity with the Roman Catholic majority.[19] Not only their private mores but even their theological approaches were substantially at odds with the Catholic population, the vast majority of whom were natives of Spain's ancient Roman cities.

In their efforts to establish a unified Spanish Christendom, the Visigoths went to unparalleled lengths to enforce conformity, and they singled out the Jews and gay people as scapegoats for broad social tensions caused by the ethnic and religious disparity of the populace. Increasingly oppressive legislation was passed against these and other groups throughout the sixth and seventh centuries.[20] The Catholic hierarchy cooperated with the Visigothic aristocracy on some matters,[21] resisted them on others, and tried to avoid some conflicts by silence.[22] The greatest of Spanish churchmen of the time, Saint Isidore of Seville, protested vigorously against Visigothic efforts to force conversion upon the Jews, and two church councils absolutely condemned such practices (Toledo IV and VIII). But it was difficult for the

---

Benedictus Levita. VIII," ed. J. Juncker, *Zeitschrift der Savigny-Stiftung für Rechtsgeschichte, kanonistische Abteilung* 55, no. 24 (1935): 105. If this is such a reference, it is the sole allusion to Visigothic antigay legislation known to me in later law.

19. Since the Visigoths first entered the country there had been constant tension with the Catholic majority of the populace, especially since the urban nobility was exclusively and staunchly orthodox. During the sixth century ten of the eighteen Visigothic monarchs were assassinated.

20. A brief but judicious comparison of Visigothic and Frankish enactments regarding Jews may be found in Walter Ullmann, "Public Welfare and Social Legislation in the Early Medieval Councils," in *Councils and Assemblies*, ed. G. I. Cuming (Cambridge, Mass., 1971), 7:23–35. For broader studies see esp. Bernard Bachrach, *Early Medieval Jewish Policy in Western Europe* (Minneapolis, 1977), and Bernhard Blumenkranz, *Juifs et chrétiens dans le monde occidental, 430–1096* (Paris, 1960). The most comprehensive treatment of the Jews in Spain is that of Yitzhak Baer, *A History of the Jews in Christian Spain*, rev. trans. (Philadelphia, 1961–66). Greater detail on the Visigothic period is provided by Solomon Katz in *The Jews in the Visigothic and Frankish Kingdoms of Spain and Gaul* (Cambridge, Mass., 1937), and A. K. Ziegler's *Church and State in Visigothic Spain* (Washington, D.C., 1930). Bachrach's "Reassessment of Visigothic Jewish Policy, 589–711" (*American Historical Review* 78 [1973]: 11–34) reaches conclusions very similar to my own in regard to the relative unimportance of religious fervor in Visigothic anti-Semitic policies.

21. E.g., the edict of the Fourth Council of Toledo (633) requiring deposition and immediate incarceration of priests who supported popular unrest (PL, 84:377, chap. 45).

22. The question of the relative dominance of church and state in Visigothic Spain is the subject of considerable debate. The issue is discussed in detail, but very defensively, by Ziegler; for more general discussion, see Bachrach, Baer, Katz, and Blumenkranz.

unarmed clergy to decline to accede to the fervent desires of the Visigothic conquerors, and many councils enacted legislation hostile to the Jews.

The church failed to cooperate in the oppression of gay people for forty years (and six national church councils) after the promulgation of the civil legislation, but finally, under direct orders from the monarchy to enact ecclesiastical legislation on the subject,[23] it issued a conciliar decree stipulating degradation from holy orders and exile for clerics convicted of homosexual behavior—a dramatic mitigation of the penalty under civil law—and excommunication, 100 stripes, and exile for a lay person (also a mitigation, though less striking). The monarchy promptly issued a civil statute nullifying the modification by establishing that the penalties recently ordained by the Council of Toledo were to be inflicted *in addition to* those already established in civil law, regardless of whether the accused was a cleric or a layman.[24]

It is doubtful that the laws were consistently enforced. In the Roman cities of Spain, Visigothic law probably never had much effect, and the constant repetition of royal decrees against the acceptance of bribes by judges suggests that most people could avoid prosecution by judicious use of cash. When the Muslims invaded Spain some sixty years after the most oppressive anti-Jewish legislation, they found many Jews living in Spain, and it is probable that the same was true of gay people, although since no Muslim writer would have considered homosexual preferences a matter of note, no mention is made of this.

Outside Spain, laws against homosexual relations were rare.[25] Law codes survive from most of the Germanic peoples who settled in Europe. Some, like those of the Lombards, were drafted contemporaneously with the Visigothic codes;[26] others were compiled gradually. By the ninth century almost every area of Europe had some sort of local law code. Although sexuality occupies a considerable portion of such legislation and Christian teachings regarding rape, adultery, incest, illegitimacy, marriage, forni-

23. "Inter cetera tamen obscenum crimen illud de concubitoribus masculorum extirpandum decernite, quorum horrenda actio et honestae vitae gratiam maculat et iram caelitus superni vindicis provocat," *Leges Visigothorum*, Suppl. (MGH, p. 483, "Tomus Egicani regis concilio oblatus"), translated in Bailey, p. 93.

24. *Leges Visigothorum*, 3.5.7 (MGH, pp. 165–66). The text of the conciliar decree can be found ibid. and in Mansi, 12:71.

25. Melchior Goldast, *Constitutiones imperiales* (Frankfurt, 1673) 1:125, prints an "edict of Otto I, promulgated at Rome in 966," which prescribes strangulation and burning for some homosexual act. The passage seems to be an epitome of the edict of 390, although the literal tenor of its wording very strongly suggests that the crime in question is the rape of one man by another: "Qui tanto obscoenitatis furore et licentia abripitur, ut nec corporibus hominum ingenuorum parcendum putet, propter criminis foeditatem strangulatus flammis e medio populi Dei auferatur." It is wanting in modern compilations such as the MGH.

26. *Leges Langobardorum*, ed. F. Bluhme, in MGH, *Leges*, 4 (Hanover, 1868).

cation, etc., receive the sanctions of the civil authorities which promulgated the codes, homosexual relations are not proscribed in any of them.[27]

Charlemagne, who considered himself personally responsible for the creation of a Christian Europe, appears to have been quite shocked upon hearing that some of the monks in his kingdom were "sodomites,"[28] since, as he put it, "the life and chastity of the monks is the greatest hope of salvation for all Christians." He besought the monks "to strive to preserve themselves from such evils," since he "dared not permit such ills any longer in any part of the realm, much less among those who should be especially chaste and devout," and even threatened unspecified punishments for subsequent offenders;[29] but no civil legislation against homosexuality was enacted. The only surviving Carolingian civil statute regarding homosexuality is a forgery.[30]

27. See, e.g., *Lex Salica, 100 Titel-Text*, ed. K. A. Eckhardt (Weimar, 1953); *Lex Ribuaria*, ed. R. Sohm, in MGH, *Leges*, 1, 5 (Hanover, 1875–79); *Leges Burgundionum*, ed. L. R. de Salis, in MGH, *Leges*, 1, 2, 1 (Hanover, 1892); *Lex Baiuvariorum: Lichtdruck Wiedergabe der Ingolstädter Handschrift des bayerischen Volksrechts*, ed. K. Beyerle (Munich, 1926; this edition is preferable to that by E. von Schwind, in MGH, *Leges*, 1, 5 [Hanover, 1926]); the *Leges Alamannorum*, ed. K. Lehmann, in MGH, *Leges*, 1, 5, 1 (Hanover, 1888; reissued and re-edited by K. Eckhardt in 1966; also available in Eckhardt's Göttingen edition, 1958, 1962); and the *Leges Saxonum und Lex Thuringorum*, ed. K. F. Freiherr von Richthofen, in MGH, *Leges*, 1, 5 (Hanover, 1875–79).

28. Although *sodomita* could refer to many types of sexual behavior, the context of the remarks strongly suggests homosexual behavior.

29. *Capitulare missorum generale* sec. 17; in MGH, *Leges*, 2, *Capitularia regum Francorum*, ed. Alfred Boretius, pt. 1 (Hanover, 1883), no. 33, pp. 94–95.

30. The fourth *Additio* of the collection of documents made by Benedict Levita in the latter half of the ninth century contains a spurious "Capitulary of Charlemagne of 779," in which chap. 160 condemns homosexual relations and invokes the example of "Roman law" to justify burning "sodomites" (text in MGH, *Leges*, 2, 2, *Pars altera: capitularia spuria*, pp. 156–57; or PL, 97:909). Much of the capitulary is derived from the genuine *Capitulare Haristallense* (Mansi, 12:893, and MGH, *Leges*, 2, 1, pp. 46–51), but the chapter dealing with homosexuality is an invention by Benedict, who fabricated or forged about three-fourths of the whole collection for various political and ecclesiastical purposes. (The collection also contains some of the famous "Isidorian decretals.") The portions of the antihomosexual passage from "diversarum pollutionem patratores" to "hoc vitium extet" are extracted, with omissions, from the Council of Paris of 829 (MGH, *Leges*, 3, *Concilia*, 2, 2, pp. 634–35). The sentence beginning "Scimus enim" is a paraphrase of a sentence of the same council, substituting "Roman law" for the "law of God," which the council invoked as an example, but not as authority for punishment (ibid.); the section from "Tempus namque est" to "miseris animabus satiantes" is taken word for word from a letter of Saint Boniface to Ethelbert of Mercia. This letter, which did not refer to homosexuality at all, is discussed below. It is tempting to speculate on exactly why Benedict should forge a law severely punishing homosexual acts. Etienne Baluze, in *Capitularia regum Francorum* (Paris, 1677), apparently unaware of the quotation from Boniface, suggested that the portion from "Scimus enim" was an "addition of Louis the Pious" (to the Council of Paris?) (2:1257; text at 1:1226). Goldast published the capitulary as genuine, immediately following the *Capitulare Haristallense* (3:123–25), along with a capitulary of Louis the Pious (pp. 238–39) containing a similar enactment, minus the reference to burning and the quotation from Boniface, and with broader application. On Benedict Levita, see F. L. Ganshof, *Recherches*

An edict was issued exhorting priests and bishops to "attempt in every way to prohibit and eradicate this evil," but it recommended no penalties and was manifestly only an ecclesiastical admonishment.[31] Subsequent Frankish enactments against homosexual practices were almost uniformly based on the mild provisions of this "general admonition,"[32] which cited no biblical or ecclesiastical authority except a canon from the little-known Council of Ancyra—a canon, it might be noted, which had not originally referred to homosexuality at all but was imagined to do so because it was known in the West only through an inaccurate Latin translation.[33]

---

sur les capitulaires (Paris, 1958), p. 71, with the bibliography cited there. (The long promised critical edition of Benedict's collection, begun by Emil Seckel, has not yet appeared.) Benedict also interpolated a vague threat against anyone guilty of "sodomy" into canons quoting the Council of Ancyra: "Si ei vita concessa fuerit . . ." (8.356 in Benedict; published in Baluze, 1:1101). Genuine canons influenced by Ancyra do not include this provision, but the first portion of this canon, as far as "Quisquis autem," is quoted directly from the Isidorian ("Antiqua") version of the Council of Ancyra, which defines "sodomy" as including bestiality, homosexuality, and incest.

31. "Admonitio generalis," in *Capitularia regum Francorum*, pt. 1, no. 22: "Capitulum 49, Sacerdotibus. In concilio Acyronense inventum est in eos qui cum quadrupedibus vel masculis contra naturum peccant: dura et districta penitentia. Quapropter episcopi et presbyteri, quibus iudicium penitentiae iniunctum est, conentur omnimodis hoc malum a consuetudine prohibere vel abscidere." This long capitulary (82 chaps.) consists largely of extracts from the canons of various councils, derived most immediately from the Dionysio-Hadriana canonical collection of 774. Boretius dates it in the year 789, but on questionable grounds. For a more authoritative analysis, see F. L. Ganshof, "The Impact of Charlemagne on the Institutions of the Frankish Realm," *Speculum* 40 (1965): 47–62. Alcuin had something to do with the drafting of the "Admonitio" (see Friedrich-Carl Scheibe, "Alcuin und die Admonitio generalis," *Deutsches Archiv für Erforschung des Mittelalters* 14 [1958]: 221–29), and it is conceivable that his own inclinations disposed him to treat homosexuality leniently.

32. E.g., in Mansi, 17 (suppl.): 230, 368, 412, 526, 829, 1055, 1101, 1143, 1259. Note that these are all ecclesiastical rather than civil enactments.

33. Canon 16 prescribes penances for the ἀλογευσάμενοι, literally, "those who have abandoned reason." The fact that the penances take into account the age and marital status of the sinner does suggest that the offense is a sexual one, but there is no more specific evidence about the nature of the offense. Early Latin translations recognized the ambiguity of the phrase (e.g., the canons attributed to Isidore of Seville: "In hoc titulo Graeca verba haec sunt: Περὶ τῶν ἀλογευσαμένων ἢ καὶ ἀλογευομένων, quae nos latine possumus dicere: De his qui irrationabiliter versati sunt sive versantur," PL, 84:107), but most later versions simply stated that the canon stigmatized this or that sexual act, depending on the whim of the translators. The *Apostolic Constitutions* had designated bestiality "ἡ [ἁμαρτία] πρὸς ἄλογα" (28), and it may have been this which made bestiality one of the most common sins proposed as the subject of this canon; incest and homosexuality were only slightly less common. The best Greek text of the original canons is published in R. B. Backham, "The Texts of the Canons of Ancyra," *Studia biblica et ecclesiastica* 3 (1891): 139–216; Mansi's text, cited by Bailey and others, is less reliable. The various Latin translations are published in Cuthbert Turner, *Ecclesiae occidentalis monumenta iuris antiquissima*, vol. 2 (Oxford, 1907), pt. 1, pp. 1–144; and discussed by Bailey, pp. 86–89. Backham provides English translations or paraphrases of Syriac and Armenian versions apparently unknown to Bailey. The former renders the word in question as a reference to both homosexuality and bestiality; the latter

The relative uninterest of Frankish synods and rulers in this issue is more significant than may be immediately apparent. Frankish social legislation set the tone for civil and ecclesiastical programs in regard to the treatment of Jews, lepers, the poor, clerical incontinence, divorce, work on the Sabbath, etc., well into the Reformation period, not only because the decrees of Frankish councils were major sources of later penitential and canonistic collections but also because they represented the decisions of clerics responding to familiar problems in their own dioceses, for which they had to provide realistic and practical solutions. The correspondence between the relatively mild attitude of Carolingian theologians toward homosexuality and the notable restraint of contemporary legal enactments—indeed the virtual absence of civil statutes regarding it—argues very strongly that the Christian hierarchy in the seventh through tenth centuries considered homosexual behavior no more (and probably less) reprehensible than comparable heterosexual behavior (i.e., extramarital). Even purely ecclesiastical regulations regarding homosexual activities were generally moderate and often surprisingly sympathetic. The first official efforts of the church against any forms of gay sexuality had been cautious: probably influenced by Latin translations of the *Didache*,[34] the Spanish Council of Elvira in 305 denied communion even at the hour of death to men who "defiled" boys but made no effort to regulate sexuality between consenting adult males or between women of any age.[35] This action in fact only brought the church into line with the opinions of Roman jurists of the previous century, who had extended the *Lex Julia de adulteriis coercendis* to protect minors.

Ecclesiastical legislators during the fourth and fifth centuries tended almost unanimously to regard the married state as inevitable for adult males (including most of the clergy) and hence to view homosexual relations

to bestiality alone. An English translation of the entire council is available in Henry Percival, *The Seven Ecumenical Councils of the Undivided Church* (New York, 1800); note his comments on λεπρώσαντες (p. 70). It should be noted that the Council of Ancyra *had* imposed penalties for homosexual acts: these ranged from fifteen years' exclusion from the sacraments (for penitents under the age of twenty and unmarried) to exclusion until death (for those married and over fifty).

34. Although in the East the actual significance of "παιδοφθορήσεις" in the *Didache* (2.2) had been lost by the fourth century, the Latin translation popular in the West rendered it "non puerum violaveris"—a wholly unambiguous reference to forced relations with minors. See *The Teaching of the Apostles*, ed. Harris, p. 16.

35. "Stupratoribus puerorum, nec in fine dandam esse communionem" (71), Mansi, 2:17. The council apparently considered fourteen the age of consent. Whether "defiled" refers to rape or seduction or both is not clear. This council is noted for the severity of its provisions: it was the first to insist on clerical celibacy, assigned a three-year penance to matrons who wore attractive clothing, denied even deathbed communion to clerics who would not divorce adulterous wives, and prohibited freedmen from becoming clerics during the lifetime of their masters.

simply as a form of adultery.[36] As late as the eighth century, Saint John Damascene lumped the Levitical proscriptions against "sodomy" with advice to the married and responded to the question "How may I not fornicate?" with the assumption of Chrysostom: "You have a wife. You have pleasure with impunity."[37] There is little penitential guidance regarding homosexual relations specifically among the unmarried until centuries later, and it is clear that at the practical level the early medieval church was largely unconcerned about exclusively homosexual behavior. For the married, penances for homosexual acts were almost uniformly equal to those for other types of adultery (e.g., see Basil *Epistles* 217; but cf. Gregory of Nyssa *Epistula canonica* 4), and gay sexuality was rarely singled out for special derogation.

Some authors have inferred from the elaborate prescriptions regarding homosexual relations in the "penitentials" that the early medieval church was obsessed with punishing homosexual behavior. This conclusion is unwarranted. The penitentials were collections of penances to be assigned for sins by confessors; they were designed both as guides for priests uncertain about appropriate penances and as efforts at standardization of the severity of such penalties. As such they were necessarily detailed: their aim was to specify a penance for every sin a priest might hear mentioned in the confessional. Homosexuality is given no greater attention than other sins and, viewed comparatively, appears to have been thought less grave than such common activities as hunting.

The eighth-century penitential of Pope Saint Gregory III, for example, specified penances of 160 days for lesbian activities and as little as one year for homosexual acts between males.[38] In comparison, the penance for a priest's going hunting was three years.[39]

36. The LSJ considers a fourth-century word for a male lover, "μυχός," to be a variant of "μοιχός," "adulterer" (see *Oxyrhynchus papyri*, vol. 8 [London, 1911], 1160.26).

37. "῎Εχεις γυναῖκα· ἔχεις μετὰ ἀσφαλείας ἡδονήν," John Damascene *Sacra parallela* 2.11 (PG, 96:256).

38. "Si qua mulier cum altera coitum fecerit, quatuor quadragesimas poeniteat. Molles unum annum poeniteant," Mansi, 12:295, sec. 30. "Molles" would ordinarily refer to those who practiced masturbation, but the context suggests homosexuality. "Quatuor quadragesimas" may mean "four Lents" rather than 160 days, but this would be such a mild penance (everyone fasted during Lent anyway) that I have favored the more unusual interpretation of the word. More severe penances for homosexual acts range from a maximum of ten years to seven (characterized as "more humane") and go as low as three years, for those "unaware of the gravity of this vice"—a suggestion that there was limited popular objurgation of such behavior. Note that in the section which prescribes only a year's penance for the *molles* a seven-day penance is imposed on those who eat fish found dead in a pond (rather than catching live ones?).

39. Ibid., 30, "De diversis minoribusque culpis": "Si quis clericus venationes exercuit unum annum poeniteat, diaconus duos, presbyter tres." In some areas clerics could not

What constituted a year's penance was determined at the discretion of the confessor. In the older tradition of John Cassian, remission of sins was obtained simply through "tears and affliction of the heart,"[40] but even those obliged to follow a penitential of some sort could substitute some spiritual duty, such as prayers or attendance at mass, for the theoretical regimen of bread and water. There is good reason to believe that in a great many cases penances were reduced to fines. Penitential guidelines established for England in the tenth century state as a general principle that one day's fast may be replaced by an offering of a penny or the recitation of various prayers. A whole year's fast could be "redeemed" with thirty shillings or thirty masses.[41]

---

perform ordinary penances because the clerical state was regarded as a permanent condition of penitence. In such places a pilgrimage was sometimes imposed on clerics who committed the sin of "sodomy": see Cyrille Vogel, "Le pèlerinage pénitentiel," in *Pellegrinaggi e culto dei santi in Europa fino alla Ia crociata*, Convegni del Centro di Studi sulla Spiritualità Medievali, no. 4 (Todi, 1963); see also his "Discipline pénitentielle en Gaule des origines au IXe siècle," *Revue des sciences réligieuses* 30 (1956): 1–26, 157–86. This practice should not be regarded as a sign of enormity: Hilarius of Arles excommunicated the bishop of Besançon for marrying a widow (*Acta sanctorum*, May, 2.32), which was hardly generically sinful; and Gallus was excommunicated by Saint Columban for refusing to follow him to Italy (MGH, SS.RR.MM., 4, pp. 251–52). Obviously a much higher standard of conduct was expected of the clergy.

40. *Collationes* 20.8 (CSEL, 13:563): "Item etiam per lacrimarum profusionem conquiritur absolutio peccatorum."

41. "Fasting" did not of course mean going without food altogether but, rather, limiting the quantity or nature of the food consumed or abstaining for specific periods of time (frequently evenings, or days when Christians were required to fast anyway). Early medieval practice varied extravagantly from place to place but was generally not so severe as is popularly imagined. For a good general treatment of the issue, see John McNeill and Helena Gamer, *Medieval Handbooks of Penance: A Translation of the Principal "Libri Poenitentiales" and Selections from Related Documents* (New York, 1938). A seven-year fast could be accomplished in one year's time by reciting psalms and vespers each evening. These provisions are in Mansi, 18:525, under the heading *Canones editi sub Edgardo rege* (18–19), but it is highly unlikely that Edgar actually had anything to do with their drafting (see F. Liebermann, *Die Gesetze der Angelsachsen* [Halle, 1903–6], vol. 2, pt. 2, p. 357; T. P. Oakley, *English Penitential Discipline and Anglo-Saxon Law in their Joint Influence* [New York, 1923], p. 135; and McNeill and Gamer, p. 409). In the edition used by Mansi the commutation to fines is subtitled as if it referred to an indulgence for the ill, but this is clearly not the case. The sick are nowhere mentioned in the text, which clearly states that *any* man may make these substitutions: "Quilibet homo potest unius diei jejunium redimere." The following section stipulates similar substitutions based on wealth. A rich man, for instance, could accomplish seven years' fast in three days by persuading 840 men "by any means whatsoever" to fast with him for three days, thus fulfilling the canonical requirement for days fasted (the mathematics are not exact: the provision is generous). Similar provisions occur in most penitentials. See "Irish Canons," 2:1–12; the "Penitential of Egbert," 15; the "Canon of Egbert," sec. 2; the "Pseudo-Cummean Penitential," chaps. 1–2; the "Penitential of Silos," secs. 14–15 (all in McNeill and Gamer); the Icelandic penitential of Thorlac Thorhallson (ibid., pp. 357–58); and Regino of Prum, as below, 2:447–53.

Although penitentials were known and used on the Continent, they originated and reached their most elaborate development in England[42] and could scarcely be considered universal or uniform in either composition or application. Even where they were applied they reached a rather small audience and hardly constitute an index of medieval morality. Their extensive use by some scholars[43] results not so much from their importance as from their accessibility: they are among the very few medieval works generally organized topically and hence relatively easy to consult on a particular subject such as sex.

In fact, however, many penitentials contained provisions, especially regarding marriage and sexuality, which were heretical, and the church officially discouraged their use at least from the ninth century. The Council of Châlons in 813 "absolutely prohibited those books called penitentials, whose errors are as certain as their authorship is uncertain,"[44] and the Council of Paris of 829 specifically prohibited priests from referring to penitentials for penances for homosexual acts (probably in the hope of instituting greater severity of punishment).[45]

Regular confession and spiritual direction were in any case not widespread in the Middle Ages outside areas directly controlled by cathedral chapters or religious orders. Except for the clergy, few people made regular confessions more than once a year. Nor is there any reason to assume that gay people in the early Middle Ages were any less ingenious at avoiding censure than they have been in other ages. Saint Peter Damian later complained bitterly about the widespread practice of gay priests confessing to each other in order to avoid detection and obtain milder penances, and he alleged that spiritual advisers commonly had sexual relations with those entrusted to their care, a circumstance which would presumably render confessions for the advisee considerably less awkward (*Liber Gomorrhianus* 6, 7 [PL, 145:166–68]). The very same practice is described two centuries later by Caesar of Heisterbach.[46]

A few early penitential works did enjoy widespread authority and exert lasting influence. One of these was the collection of canons of Regino of

42. On the complicated question of the authority of the penitentials in England, see the early but still useful study by Oakley.

43. Bailey, e.g., discusses them at considerable length on pp. 100–110. While his discussion is interesting, it gives a misleading impression of the importance of the English penitentials.

44. "Repudiatis ac penitus eliminatis libris, quos poenitentiales vocant, quorum sunt certi errores, incerti auctores," Mansi, 14:101, chap. 38.

45. MGH, *Leges*, 3, *Concilia*, 2.2. p. 635.

46. Caesar of Heisterbach *Dialogus miraculorum* 3.24, ed. Joseph Strange (Bonn, 1851), pp. 139–41. There is no indication that Caesar was familiar with the *Liber Gomorrhianus*.

Prum (d. 915). His approach to sexuality and sexual sins—like that of most of his contemporaries—was largely gender blind. To Regino it was the act, not the parties involved, which constituted the sin: the penalty for anal intercourse (three years) was exactly the same for two males as for a married couple, and no more severe than that for simple heterosexual fornication.[47] If any difference can be noted in his attitude toward heterosexual and homosexual failings, it is a somewhat more sympathetic approach to the latter. If two men had sex interfemorally, their penance (one year) was considerably less than that for heterosexual fornication.[48] Boys and young men incurred even lighter penances (2.248). Regino was well aware of an earlier tradition of harsher penalties—he subjoined a number of more severe canons from earlier writers as addenda to his own (254–59)[49]—but he avoided such severity in his own prescriptions.

It can hardly be maintained that the relatively indulgent attitude adopted by prominent churchmen of the early Middle Ages toward homosexual behavior was due to ignorance of it. It is in the first place not ignored but treated lightly. In the second place, there is evidence of gay sexuality throughout the period, despite the disappearance of a subculture.

The barbarians themselves were not necessarily strangers to gay sexuality. Aristotle observed that the Celts publicly honored homosexual relations, Strabo that they considered it a dishonor to decline a homosexual liaison, and Diodorus Siculus that they were "absolutely addicted to homosexual intercourse."[50] Similar observations were made about other groups.[51] Germanic literature suggests very strongly that homosexuality was familiar and accepted, possibly even institutionalized. As in most military societies in

---

47. *De ecclesiasticis disciplinis libri duo* 2.249, 246 (PL, 132:332).

48. Heterosexual fornication received a mild penance only if committed by an adolescent.

49. These include penances prescribed by "others" for anal intercourse, ranging from one to ten years; the provisions of the Council of Ancyra supposed to relate to homosexual acts; the Carolingian paraphrase of these; a canon attributed to Saint Basil regarding the seduction of boys or adolescents by monks, specifying an extravagant but short penance (public beating, being spat upon, chains, bread and water for six months); two warnings against clerics' "playing with" boys; and a garbled version of the edict of 390, mentioning the penalty of burning. Since the state was not to burn anyone at the stake for several hundred years, and since the church claimed never to burn anyone, it is almost impossible to regard these opinions as anything but curiosities to Regino, whose own opinion was clearly stated earlier in the work.

50. Aristotle *Politics* 2.6.6, "῎Εξω Κελτῶν ἢ κἂν εἴ τινες ἕτεροι φανερῶς τετιμήκασι τὴν πρὸς τοὺς ἄρρενας συνουσίαν"; Strabo *Geography* 4.4.6; Diodorus 5.32.7: "Πρὸς τὰς τῶν ἀρρένων ἐπιπλοκὰς ἐκτόπως λυττῶσιν." Athenaeus (13.603) repeats Diodorus's comments in a slightly garbled form.

51. E.g., Sextus Empiricus *Outlines of Pyrrhonism* 3.199. R. G. Bury holds that "Γερμανοί" here refers not to "Germans" but to a Persian tribe: see LC edition (Cambridge, Mass., 1933), p. 460, note c. He adduces no proof for this opinion.

which courage, strength, and physical aggressiveness were prized, the Germanic peoples considered passivity in warriors to be shameful. No man could be sexually passive with another and retain the respect accorded a fighting adult male. This does not mean, however, that younger males, slaves, captives, or men with no desire to enjoy warrior status could not be sexually passive and meet with acceptance. An entire genre of Germanic literature revolves around ceremonial insults (*nið* and *ergi*) in which one warrior accuses another of having been sexually passive with him or others.[52] The persistence of this custom over many centuries, its dissemination among tribes as distant from each other as the settlers of Iceland and the Germans in southern France, and its extraordinary impact on Germanic life—affecting language, laws, even pictorial art—argue strongly for its correspondence to some actual practice. It would hardly seem that a mocking reference could have such power if the practice to which it alluded were very rare among the peoples who employed it. It seems probable from the sum of the evidence that among some of the Germans certain men fulfilled a role similar to that of the *berdache* among American Indians, adopting feminine social roles and being sexually passive to another male, and such relationships may have been institutionalized as "marriages" among them. Gregory of Tours recounts with no surprise an incident in which the Count of Javols insulted a bishop by asking him in front of King Sigibert, "Where are your husbands, with whom you live in shame and disgrace?"[53]

It is at any rate agreed upon by scholars in the field that the derogatory import of the accusation of *nið* or *ergi* derived from the suggestion not of same-gender sexuality but of passivity; active homosexuality was not reprehensible. Neither seems to have been unfamiliar.

Among the Roman populace attitudes varied widely. In some areas homosexual behavior seems to have excited wonder as prodigious: a sixth-century treatise on bizarre people and animals[54] opens with an astonished description

---

52. This subject has been explored in a series of articles begun by Bo Almqvist, *Norrön niðdiktning: traditionshistoriska studier i versmagi. 1. Nid mot furstar, Nordiska Texter och Undersökningar*, 21 (Uppsala, 1965), English summary, pp. 206–39; furthered by T. L. Markey, "Nordic *nídvísur*: An Instance of Ritual Inversion," *Medieval Scandinavia* 5 (1972): 7–19; and most recently treated by Joaquín Martínez Pizarro, "On Nið against Bishops," ibid. 12 (1979) (in press).

53. *Historia Francorum* 4.39, ed. Bruno Krusch and Wilhelm Levison (Hanover, 1951), in MGH, SS.RR.MM., I, I, p. 172: "Cum . . . diversa sibi invicem obiectarent, mollem episcopum, effeminatum Palladius vocitaret: 'Ubi sunt mariti tui, cum quibus stuprose ac turpiter vivis?'" The punishment which befalls the count is clearly the result of the falseness of the accusation but does not demonstrate the unlikelihood of such practice. Cf. Martínez Pizarro. Even in this reference to homosexual behavior "mollem" and "effeminatum" do not necessarily connote sexual characteristics.

54. Variously titled *Liber monstrorum de diversis generibus* or *De monstris et beluis liber*, this

of a man who is sexually passive with other men. "First I record having known a man who was of both sexes: although his face and torso looked more like a male than a female and he was thought a male by the unknowing, he preferred the female role [in intercourse] and seduced unwary men like a harlot. This is said to happen frequently among humans."[55] Despite the misleading description, the person in question was almost certainly a homosexual male rather than a hermaphrodite, since two subsequent chapters deal separately with hermaphroditism ("Androgynae" and "Mulieres barbatae"), and since the only evidence of "femaleness" adduced is his preference for a "female role."

The same idea is expressed—rather crudely—about a woman in a contemporary poem:

> You, strange mixture of the female gender,
> Whom driving lust makes a male,
> Who love to fuck with your crazed cunt,
> Why has a pointless desire seized you?
> You do not give what you get, though you service a cunt.[56]
> When you have given that part[57] by which you are judged a woman,
> Then you will be a girl.[58]

work has received extremely little critical attention. It has been edited by Jules Berger de Xivrey in *Traditions tératologiques* (Paris, 1836); by M. Haupt in *Opuscula* (Berlin, 1876), 2:218–52; and by Douglas Bitturff in "The Monsters and the Scholars: An Edition and Critical Study of the *Liber monstrorum*" (Ph.D. Diss., University of Illinois, 1968). M. L. W. Laistner (*Thought and Letters in Western Europe* [Ithaca, N.Y., 1966], p. 178) praises its Latin; and L. G. Whitbread comments on its relation to Beowulf in "The *Liber Monstrorum* and *Beowulf*," *Mediaeval Studies* 36 (1974): 434–71.

55. "De quodam homine utriusque sexus" (Berger de Xivrey, p. 5): "Me enim quemdam hominem, in principio operis, utriusque sexus cognosse testor: qui tamen ipsa facie plus et pectore virilis quam muliebrus apparuit; et vir a nescientibus putabatur; sed muliebria opera dilexit, et ignaros virorum, more meretricis, decipiebat; sed hoc frequenter apud humanum genus contigisse fertur."

56. Conjectural translation: the text is difficult.

57. Or possibly, "When you have played the part": the same ambiguity is present in both Latin and English.

58. Published from Codex Parisiensis 10318 in AL, vol. 1, no. 317, p. 221:
Monstrum feminei bimembre sexus
Quam coacta uirum facit libido,
Quae gaudes futui furente cunno,
Cur te ceperit inpotens uoluptas?
Non das, quod pateris, facisque cunnum.
Illam, qua mulier probaris esse,
Partem cum dederis, puella tunc sis.
Although titled "In puellam hermaphroditam," there is no suggestion of physical oddity in the text, and the poem is certainly about lesbianism. Its language, tenor, and tone all closely resemble epigrams of Martial on the same subject. *Hermaphroditus* often signified "homosexual" in the Middle Ages.

In neither example is there any hint of moral reproach: only surprise in the one case—attenuated by the assertion of frequent occurrence—and personal disapproval in the other.

Latin poetry of the sixth, seventh, and eighth centuries sometimes describes homosexual behavior disparagingly, but rarely in terms of sin.[59] As one might expect, there is some correlation between the quality of the language in such literature and the attitude evinced. The vulgarity of the language of sixth- and seventh-century verse, for instance, contrasts dramatically with the elegant Latin in which poets of the "Carolingian Renaissance" of the eighth and ninth centuries penned verses in praise of gay eroticism, e.g., the rather explicitly erotic relationship represented by the ninth-century author of one of the best-known poems of the early Middle Ages.[60] This poem was composed in one of the few areas of Europe which could be described as "urban" in the ninth and tenth centuries: northern Italy, where commerce and city life were making a dramatic reappearance and where classical learning and urban sophistication may have created a demand for literature celebrating gay love. The verses are notable not only for their romantic tone and the richness and subtlety of the classical elements informing them but also because they may have been composed as a song.[61]

O wondrous idol of Venus,
Of whose substance there is nothing imperfect,
May the creator protect you, he who made the stars and skies
And established the sea and the earth.
May you never feel the sting of the Fates' designs:
May Clotho, who spins the thread of life, cherish you.

59. E.g., from a manuscript of the seventh or eighth century (Cod. Par. 10318, in AL, vol. 1): "De Marte cinaedo" (no. 129, p. 115), "In advocatum effeminatum" (no. 295, p. 212), "In cinaedum" (no. 321, p. 222). A favorable poem is printed in the same manuscript: "In spadonem regium" (no. 298, p. 213).

60. Originally published by G. B. Niebuhr (1829), but better edited by Ludwig Traube in *O Roma nobilis, Abhandlungen der Königliche Bayerische Akademie der Wissenschaft*, Philosophisch-philologischen Classe, vol. 19, pt. 2 (1891), pp. 301–8, and most conveniently available in OBMLV, no. 103. Besides a German translation by Samuel Singer (*Germanisch-romanisches Mittelalter* [Zurich, 1935], p. 124), there is an English version by H. M. Jones in P. S. Allen, *The Romanesque Lyric* (Chapel Hill, N.C., 1928). This was reprinted in Ernst R. Curtius, *European Literature and the Latin Middle Ages*, trans. Willard R. Trask (Princeton, N.J., 1953), p. 114. In addition to this poem, see "De puero amato" (AL, no. 439, p. 279), and "De amico mortuo" (ibid., no. 445, p. 281).

61. It was at any rate clearly put to music at some point. The melody is published (with a translation of the first stanza of this and another poem sung to the same music) by R. S. Lopez in *The Tenth Century: How Dark the Dark Ages?* (New York, 1966), p. 57, following the transcription of Adler (*Handbuch der Musikgeschichte* [Frankfurt, 1924], p. 131).

I hail you, youth; not merely rhetorically
But in the most heartfelt way I implore Lachesis,
The sister of Atropos, not to be careless with you.
May you have as companions Neptune and Thetis
While you are carried on the River Athesis.[62]
Shall I love you wherever you go, since I have loved you [until now]?
Or what shall I do in my misery, when I no longer see you?

Hard marrow from mother's bones
Created men from thrown stones:[63]
Of which one is this young boy,[64]
Who can ignore tearful sobs.
When I am heartbroken, my rival will rejoice;
I shall weep as the doe whose fawn has fled.

The poem was sufficiently popular to be included a century later in a German collection compiled for a member of the clergy;[65] it seems unlikely that its subject matter or tone struck educated contemporaries as indecorous.

There is in fact a considerable body of evidence to suggest that homosexual relations were especially associated with the clergy. Some Christian authors have rather defensively rejected this idea,[66] but with little supporting documentation. Martínez Pizarro rightly points out that barbarians may have considered the educated Roman aristocrats who occupied the higher ranks of the clergy during much of the period "effeminate" simply because of their sophistication and refinement,[67] but this argument does not account for comments on "sodomy" among the clergy by admirers of clerical learning, like Charlemagne, or the constant efforts of the church itself to curtail sexuality between clerics.

The immediate forerunner, for instance, of the Rule of Saint Benedict (the code by which most medieval monks regulated their existence) stipulated

62. Previous editors of the poem have not identified this river. Strecker publishes the opinion that the name should be understood in its Greek sense of "mobile" or "unfixed" (*Die Cambridger Lieder*, ed. Karl Strecker [Berlin, 1926], p. 106). But surely it is the Athesis mentioned by Paul the Deacon (*Historia Langobardorum* 3.23)—i.e., the Adige near Verona. Cf. OBMLV, p. 473.

63. Deucalion and Pyrrha, the only survivors of the deluge that destroyed mankind, restored the human race by throwing stones over their shoulders. In accordance with the promise of an oracle that the new race would spring from "the bones of your mother" (i.e., earth), these stones became men and women of a new human race.

64. In the Latin as in my English there is a poetic ambiguity about whether the "which" in this line refers to the men created from the stones or the stones themselves.

65. Strecker, *Die Cambridger Lieder*, pp. 105–6.

66. E.g., Bailey, pp. 99–100.

67. "On Níð against Bishops."

that all monks were to sleep in the same room, with the abbot's bed in the center.[68] This already argues for efforts to discourage unofficial nocturnal activities, but Benedict's refinement of the previous rule carried these safeguards considerably further: a light had to be kept burning in the dormitory all night, all the monks had to sleep with their clothes on, and the young men were to be "mixed in with the older men and not allowed to sleep side by side."[69] While there are certainly alternative explanations for some of these provisions, their coordination argues strongly for an antisexual interpretation of their purpose.[70] This sort of precaution was already a tradition in the Eastern church, where its purpose was explicitly to forestall homosexual relations.[71] As in the case of public legislation, however, it is crucial to bear in mind that the regular clergy[72] were bound by vows of celibacy, and efforts to prevent sexual activity among them do not necessarily indicate hostility to the sexual activities themselves.

During the early Middle Ages the type of "passionate friendship" familiar to the early church was common and comprised the subject matter of much clerical writing, including almost all of the love poetry of the period. In a society in which there was strong pressure for celibacy, particularly among theologians and regular clergy, and in which communities of celibates occupied the same small space—sometimes the same beds—for life, it is hardly surprising that literature celebrating passionate, if not erotic, friendships would gain a powerful hold on the imagination. The loving relation of teacher and student in religious communities was very much a medieval ideal, despite its obvious parallel to Greek homosexuality, and many of the greatest teachers of the period were known especially for the intensity of their love for their students.

A distinctly erotic element, for instance, is notable in the circle of clerical

---

68. Chaps. 29–30 regulate sleeping arrangements in the *Regula magistri* (most conveniently edited in PL, 88:943–1052, but better in A. de Vogüé, *La règle du maître* [Paris, 1964]). For a summary of arguments on the greater antiquity of the Rule of the Master, see David Knowles, "The *Regula magistri*," in *Great Historical Enterprises* (New York, 1964).

69. Chap. 22: "Adolescentiores fratres iuxta se non habeant lectos, sed permixti cum senioribus." How young the "younger monks" were varied according to century: by the tenth century the practice of oblation (i.e., parents offering their children to monasteries) resulted in the presence of many children in monasteries. This caused even more elaborate prescriptions and efforts to prevent sexual contact between older and younger monks as well as between the younger ones themselves.

70. Mary McLaughlin ("Survivors and Surrogates: Children and Parents from the Ninth to the Tenth Centuries," in *A History of Childhood*, ed. L. de Mause [New York, 1974], pp. 130–31) cites similar provisions from several rules of later periods; all are similar to if not derived from Benedict or Basil. See also Ilene Forsyth, "The Ganymede Capital at Vézelay," *Gesta: International Center of Medieval Art*, 15, nos. 1–2 (1976): 241–44 and nn. 14–18.

71. Especially notable in the writings of Saint Basil, pp. 159–60 above.

72. Those living under *regula* (i.e., monastic clergy).

friends presided over by Alcuin at the court of Charlemagne.[73] This group included some of the most brilliant scholars of the day (Theodulf of Orléans, Angilbert, Einhard, et al.),[74] but the erotic element subsisted principally between Alcuin and his pupils. Intimates of this circle of masculine friendships were known to each other by pet names, most of them derived from classical allusions, many from Vergil's *Eclogues*. (It can hardly have escaped Alcuin's notice that the *Eclogues* contain blatantly homoerotic elements, since he bestowed on a favorite student the name of one of a pair of lovers— Alexis and Corydon—from the second eclogue.)[75] A particularly famous poem is addressed to a pupil whom Alcuin calls "Daphnis"[76] and laments the departure of another young student, "Dodo," who is referred to in the poem as their "cuckoo":

Let us lament, O sweetest Daphnis, our cuckoo,
Whom an evil stepmother has stolen away from his own. . . .[77]

The prominence of love in Alcuin's writings, all of which are addressed to males, is striking. In one poem he writes, "You, sweet love, are the most welcome guest of all."[78] Another is addressed to someone older:

Love has pierced my heart with its flame . . . ,[79]
And love always burns with fresh fire.
Neither land nor sea, hills nor woods nor mountains
Can impede or block the path to him,
Loving father, who ever licks your breast

73. Heinrich Fichtenau (*The Carolingian Empire*, trans. Peter Munz [Oxford, 1957]) reluctantly admits the presence of this eroticism (pp. 93–94). Most scholars have ignored it.

74. Theodulf was a theologian, bishop of Orléans, and probably the outstanding Carolingian poet; Angilbert was abbot of Saint-Riquier and known as "Homer" within the circle; it is to Einhard that we owe the most famous life of Charlemagne.

75. MGH, *Poetae Latini medii aevi*, 1, p. 249; discussed by Adolf Ebert in "Naso, Angilbert, und der Conflictus Veris et Hiemis," ZFDA 22 (1878): 328–35.

76. Daphnis was the Sicilian shepherd believed to have invented bucolic poetry (Ovid *Metamorphoses* 4.277).

77. MGH, *Poetae*, 1, 269–70 (excerpted in OBMLV, no. 79, p. 107); Waddell provides a beautiful translation (omitting the lines above), pp. 79–81. The evil stepmother is generally thought to be wine, to which Dodo was much addicted. Later the poet observes how terrible it would be for him "if Bacchus should drown the cuckoo in his waves, / He who seizes youths in his noxious whirlpool." This could be the source of the second stanza of the "Idol of Venus" (see above), although it can hardly be proven. Alcuin uses a similar figure in another poem ("Si non Neptunus pelago demerserit illos," MGH, *Poetae*, 1, p. 221). Marlowe seems to have borrowed such images (though possibly from another source) for the attempted homosexual "rape" in *Hero and Leander*, st. 11. Perhaps the *noverca* is a "dark lady" on the order of the figure in the Shakespearean sonnets: such triangles are common in gay literature.

78. "Tu iam dulcis amor, cunctis gratissimus hospes," "Conflictus veris et hiemis," MGH, *Poetae*, 1, p. 272.

79. A word is missing from the manuscript.

And who washes, beloved, your chest with his tears.
. . . All joys are changed into sad mournings,
Nothing is permanent, everything will pass.
Let me therefore flee to you with my whole heart,
And do you flee to me from the vanishing world. . . .[80]

One expects hyperbole in poetry, but even in Alcuin's prose correspondence there is an element which can scarcely be called anything but passionate. He wrote to a friend (a bishop and possibly the recipient of the poem quoted above),

I think of your love and friendship with such sweet memories, reverend bishop, that I long for that lovely time when I may be able to clutch the neck of your sweetness with the fingers of my desires. Alas, if only it were granted to me, as it was to Habakkuk [Dan. 14:32–38], to be transported to you, how would I sink into your embraces, . . . how would I cover, with tightly pressed lips, not only your eyes, ears, and mouth but also your every finger and your toes, not once but many a time.[81]

80. MGH, *Poetae*, 1, p. 236:
Pectus amor nostrum penetravit flamma . . .
Atque calore novo semper inardet amor.
Nec mare, nec tellus, montes nec silva vel alpes
Huic obstare queunt aut inhibere viam,
Quo minus, alme pater, semper tua viscera lingat,
Vel lacrimis lavet pectus, amate, tuum.
. . . Omnia tristifico mutantur gaudia luctu,
Nil est perpetuum, cuncta perire queunt.
Te modo quapropter fugiamus pectore toto,
Tuque et nos, mundus iam periture, fugis. . . .
In Alcuin's poetry the terms "beloved," "sweetest son," "love," etc., are used in conjunction with the terms "father," "son," etc. This filial/lover-like relationship in which Alcuin is sometimes the father, sometimes the son, is typical of passionate clerical friendship.

81. Epistle 10, translated in part from Fichtenau, p. 94, q.v. The text is in the MGH, *Epistolae*, 4, p. 36. Alcuin was only a deacon, and the recipient of the poem was a bishop; hence the rather formal address ("sanctissime pater"). Neither the formality of address nor the fact that some of the expressions are borrowed from the Bible argue against the erotic nature of the passion expressed; indeed both these objections beg the real question by posing larger ones. Many portions of the Bible may be considered blatantly erotic, although scholarly opinion regarding such passages (the Song of Solomon, for instance) constantly changes. Nor is there any reason to suppose that inequality in a relationship (ecclesiastical or other) hinders eroticism: the weight of historical and psychological evidence would suggest the contrary. Dronke (*Medieval Latin*, 1:198–99) sees this letter as squarely in the tradition of Christian *amicitia* and attributes its ostensible passion to the influence of Jerome. Granting for the sake of discussion that passion was utterly wanting in Jerome's own feelings, this in no way demonstrates that later writers would not use the same words with passionate overtones: Dronke himself points out that the very same lines are borrowed in a correspondence between two nuns whose relationship he characterizes as "passionate" and

In a letter upbraiding one of his students for what appears to be a homosexual indiscretion, the cleric registers no shock or outrage, simply annoyance. He does not suggest that the young man has violated any civil or ecclesiastical laws or that he faces any penalty other than eventual judgment for his sins. In fact his primary objection to the behavior in question is that it is puerile, unbecoming to a scholar, and apt to lead to a bad reputation. The last charge is particularly interesting; Alcuin says that these deeds have come to his attention not from overhearing someone whispering in a corner but from listening to "everyone giggling in public." This hardly suggests moral outrage on the part of those from whom he heard the story. For his own part, Alcuin simply threatens the youth with the prospect of losing his place in the cleric's affections, where he is now first. It is notable that he implies that the young man—whom he calls "sweetest son, brother, and friend"—is famous throughout England for his beauty.[82]

In his old age Alcuin bitterly regretted the "sins of his youth" and entrusted to his old friend Angilbert the task of explaining them to the pope in person, since Angilbert had committed "the very same sins."[83] A number of interpretations of this reference are plausible; possibly Alcuin had given physical expression to his ardent love and regretted his indulgence as he faced death. Since he felt personally obligated to a life of celibacy, his remorse would not indicate any misgivings about homosexual relations per se.

In contrast to Alcuin's classical effusions to his favorites, the affection of Walafrid Strabo for his friend Liutger was expressed in highly spiritual, purely Christian terms. Walafrid, the abbot of Reichenau, spent nearly all his life behind monastery walls. He wrote poems of praise for contemporaries and friends, works on gardening, saints' lives, and accounts of visions; his works were imbued with a tranquil spirituality and a delicacy of feeling rare in the early Middle Ages. Although he wrote an affectionate poem to the influential monk Gottschalk, his most touching verses were two love poems to Liutger, suggestive of Elizabethan love sonnets in their lofty claims for love's permanence and in the depth of feeling expressed in them.

Dearest, you come suddenly, and suddenly, dearest, you depart:
I hear, I do not see, yet inwardly I see, and inwardly
I embrace you, fleeing in body, but not in love.

"physical" (p. 482). It is quite obvious that such phrases could later be used in an erotic context regardless of their original setting. See below, pp. 220–22.

82. Epistle 294, in MGH, *Epistolae*, 4, pp. 451–52: "Et latior est fama nominis tui quam notitia faciei tuae."

83. Ibid., epistles 94, 97, discussed in Fichtenau, p. 97.

For as certain as I have been, I am and shall always be
That I am cherished in your heart, and you in mine.
Nor shall time persuade me, nor you, of anything else. . . .

When the splendor of the moon shines from the clear heaven,
Stand in the open air, and see in the wondrous mirror
How it grows light in the pure brightness from the moon
And with its splendor embraces two lovers,[84]
Divided in body, but linked in spirit by one love.
If we cannot see each other face to loving face,[85]
At least let this light be our pledge of love . . . .[86]

An equally poignant love poem was written by Gottschalk, while in exile
on an island, to a young monk who was probably at Reichenau.[87] The
younger man had asked Gottschalk to send him a poem, and in responding
to him the poet poured out his grief and anguish in lines redolent of tender
affection.

Why do you order, little lad,
Why do you command, little son,
That I sing a sweet song,
When I am far away in exile
In the middle of the sea?
O why do you bid me to sing?
More likely, sad little one,

84. "Lovers" may be too specific for "caros," but it is difficult to render it satisfactorily
otherwise. "Amantem," in the following line certainly justifies inclusion of the term "lover"
in the poem.

85. Literally, "if face has not been able to see loving face."

86. The texts of both are conveniently published in Laistner, 2d ed. (1966), pp. 344–45,
with translations on pp. 392–93, which the reader may wish to compare with mine. I have
omitted a few lines in each poem, since translations are available and my aim here is simply
to characterize. Waddell publishes a lovely translation of the second one in *Medieval Latin
Lyrics*, pp. 116–17.

87. This is suggested by Bernhard Bischoff in "Gottschalks Lied für den Reichenauer
Freund," *Medium aevum vivum: Festschrift W. Bulst* (Heidelberg, 1960), pp. 61–68, where he
publishes three stanzas not edited in the standard version of the poem. Although Bischoff
admits the poem suggests a rather passionate friendship and is part of a genre of such
literature among the medieval clergy, he rejects the notion that it is comparable to the "Idol
of Venus." Laistner (p. 347) maintains that "in it we hear that same passionate note that we
have already remarked in three poems of Walahfrid." He publishes three stanzas of the poem,
the first two and the last (p. 347), with a translation (p. 393) of exceptional grace and beauty.
It is a shame that he did not use his talents on the entire poem. I disagree, however, with his
rendering of "misercule," since nowhere else is the friend included in Gottschalk's
"Sündenbewusstsein."

Should I weep, little boy,
And lament rather than sing
A song such as you demand,
    Dear love.
O why do you bid me to sing?[88]

It is virtually impossible to translate the affection suggested by the series of diminutives at the end of the lines of this poem: the Latin words "pusiole," "filiole," "puerule" evoke a wealth of associations secular and religious, erotic and spiritual, paternal and lover-like.[89] They are part of a tradition of erotic address between men which has no standard terms of relation and has thus elicited the ambiguities of the Greek "lover, inspirer, hearer," the Roman "friend, brother, dear," the monastic "brother, son, friend, beloved brother," and many other terms of endearment for relationships without real parallel in heterosexual contexts. The same ambiguity courses throughout the poem's content: the pagan theme of lover subject to the behest of the beloved ("Why do you *command*?"), well known in classical poetry and revived in Arabic and Provençal love lyrics, is woven seamlessly into the fabric of a prayer to God that the poet be delivered from his suffering.

Passionate friendships were also known among the laity. The story of Lantfrid and Cobbo relates the extraordinary love between two unmarried young men; "the two were as one."[90] When Cobbo proposes to return to his homeland across the sea, Lantfrid is desolate and insists on accompanying him, but Cobbo, to test his love, urges him to stay behind and asks to be given the wife Lantfrid has acquired[91] for the trip, "so that he might freely enjoy her embrace."[92]

---

88. The standard text is available in the OBMLV, no. 92, pp. 126–28. In addition to Laistner's partial translation, a translation by Howard Mumford Jones appears in Allen's *Romanesque Lyric*, pp. 150–51. This translation lacks the inspiration of Laistner's and is unfortunately set in the context of Allen's opinion that the poem was written to a son of Gottschalk's. The claim that it is addressed to the infant Jesus is more credible, though hardly convincing.

89. Note, e.g., that *pusio* very frequently has overtly sexual connotations, not only in classical literature (Juvenal 6.34) but in medieval poetry as well (e.g., "Ganymede and Helen," line 38, app. 2 below).

90. "Quasi duo unus esset," line 30. The classic form of this tale occurs in an incomplete poem included in Strecker's *Cambridger Lieder*, but it is certainly older than the manuscript. Strecker discusses other versions (pp. 16–17) and reprints one (pp. 18–20). The poem is most conveniently available in OBMLV, no. 119, pp. 163–66, from which this quotation is taken.

91. The Latin suggests that he purchased her ("uxorem quam tibi solam vendicasti," lines 59–60).

92. "Ut licenter fruar eius amplexu," lines 71–72.

Not hesitating for a moment, [Lantfrid] cheerfully places her hand in his:
"Enjoy her as you will, brother,
And let it never be said
That I have held back anything which I possess."[93]

After sailing off out of sight, Cobbo is satisfied with his friend's devotion and returns to Lantfrid to give him back his wife "untouched and with no knowledge of love."[94] No ending to the story survives, but it is hard to imagine a marriage begun under such circumstances mattering much to Lantfrid. Clearly his affection for Cobbo is the primary emotional focus of his life.

Idealization of intense relationships between persons of the same gender was even more notable in the one area of Europe in which a dynamic and influential urban culture survived throughout the early Middle Ages. The Muslims who invaded Spain in the early eighth century had reversed the trend toward ruralization initiated with the barbarian invasions and erected a society centered in great cities invigorated and refurbished by demographic and economic imports from the now Muslim-controlled Mediterranean. Ancient Roman cities like Barcelona, Cordoba, Saragossa, Valencia, and Merida were not only preserved but greatly enhanced by the Muslims. Cordoba was the largest city in the West in the ninth and tenth centuries, and its wealth and sophistication dazzled not only the Muslim but also the Christian world.

Not unexpectedly, gay people flourished in the cities of Spain. To a certain extent, this may be attributed to the attitudes of Islamic culture generally. Although the Qur'an and early religious writings of Islam display mildly negative attitudes toward homosexuality, Islamic society has generally ignored these deprecations, and most Muslim cultures have treated homosexuality with indifference, if not admiration.[95] Almost without

93. Nihil hesitando manum
    manui eius tribuens hilare:
    fruere ut libet, frater, ea.
    ne dicatur, quod semotim
    nisus sim quid possidere. [Lines 63–67]
94. "Intactum ante amoris experimentum," lines 84–85.
95. It is generally assumed by Western Orientalists that the Arabic words "lūwat" ("sodomite" or "sodomy") and "lūtī" ("sodomite") are derived from the Arabic for "Lot," but this seems extremely curious, since in all of the Qur'anic passages relating to Lot and the Sodomites it is made pellucidly clear that Lot was the one male in the city who did *not* involve himself in the sexual abuse of the angels. Moreover, Muslims have generally regarded Lot as a righteous prophet; some have realized that Jews and Christians imputed sexual indiscretions to him, but of a heterosexual nature (see, e.g., Samau'al al-Maghribi, "Ifḥām al-Yahūd," *Proceedings of the American Academy for Jewish Research* 32 [1964]: 58–60). Derivation from "lāta," "to stick," seems more likely: see the EI, s.v. "Lūt," where it is suggested that the name itself may derive from this verb. The persistence of "lūtī" as a term

exception the classic works of Arabic poetry and prose, from Abu Nuwas to the *Thousand and One Nights*, treat gay people and their sexuality with respect or casual acceptance. Hostile statements are rare, except as attitudes of partisan sexuality in literary debates about the types of love, where hostile statements about heterosexuality occur as well. The Arabic language contains a huge vocabulary of gay erotic terminology, with dozens of words just to describe types of male prostitutes.[96] Erotic address by one male to another is the standard convention of Arabic love poetry; even poems really written to or for women frequently use male pronouns and metaphors of male beauty: it is not uncommon to find poetry addressed to a female in which the object of the poet's affections is praised for "a dark mustache over pearly white teeth" or the "first downy beard over damask skin."[97] Poems about the physical allure of a young man's first beard constitute an entire genre of Arabic poetry.[98] That such literary and social phenomena do not simply reflect social strictures against public exposure and admiration of women is demonstrated by the practice in many areas of the Muslim world (especially Spain) of dressing pretty girls to look like pretty boys by cutting their hair short and clothing them in male attire: the women who participated in this unusual form of transvestism were obviously available to be appreciated as females.[99]

---

of derogation in Arabic literature should not be taken to reflect general social attitudes: its force in hostile comments is often more like that of "cinaedus" than "sodomite," with its moral implications, and it is used by gay Muslim writers themselves with defiance, if not pride (as in the use of the sobriquet "il Sodoma" by the Italian Renaissance painter Bazzi to describe himself). In rejecting the interpretation of Ibn Khaqan's nickname as "pederast," R. Dozy, the foremost lexicographer of Hispano-Arabic literature, comments that "pederasty was so common among the Arabs at this time that it could not have been used as a term of reproach" (*Supplément aux dictionnaires arabes* [Leiden, 1881] 1:346). For the importance of Christian understanding (or misunderstanding) of the Qur'anic and legal traditions on this matter, see below, pp. 279–83 and n. 30.

96. See Henri Pérès, *La poésie andalouse en arabe classique* (Paris, 1953), p. 341 and notes. Although both Pérès and A. R. Nykl (*Hispano-Arab Poetry and its Relations with the Old Provençal Troubadours* [Baltimore, 1946]) translate words and poetry dealing with gay sentiments or sexuality with reasonable accuracy and frankness, neither is willing to admit the obvious implications of the texts he translates, and both express disgust at the thought that the literature could actually refer to the activities or feelings implied. Spanish translations of Arabic verse almost invariably disguise or suppress homosexual allusions.

97. See, for one of many examples, the poem quoted by Ibn Khaldun in the *Muqaddimah*, trans. F. Rosenthal (New York, 1958), 3:463 and n. 1895. Note that nearly all the love poetry on pp. 440–80 is written by one man to another.

98. Pérès, p. 341 and n. 6. Such poetry is often a major constituent of Arabic debates about gay love, as it was in similar Hellenistic debates.

99. Nykl, p. 55; Pérès, pp. 372, 400; A. Mez, *Die Renaissance des Islams* (Heidelberg, 1922), pp. 336–37. Ibn Shuhaid describes such a girl: "Having cut off her hair, she approaches with a long and slender neck on the body of a boy [shabī]" (text in A. Daif, *Balaghat al-ʿArab fi-l-Andalus* [Cairo, 1924], p. 46; cited in Pérès, p. 372).

In early medieval Spain this tendency was if anything exaggerated. Every variety of homosexual relationship was common, from prostitution to idealized love.[100] Erotic verse about ostensibly homosexual relationships constitutes the bulk of published Hispano-Arab poetry.[101] Such verses were written by every sort of person of every rank. Kings wrote love poems to or about their male subjects and received erotic poetry in return. Poets wrote love verses to each other or to those of humbler station. The common people as well repeated, if they did not compose, songs celebrating gay love and sexuality. When al-Mutamid, eleventh-century king of Seville, wrote of his page that "I made him my slave, but the coyness of his glance has made me his prisoner, so that we are both at once slave and master to each other,"[102] he was expressing a feeling with which his subjects could not only empathize but about which they themselves probably composed or recited similar verses.

Al-Mutamid also fell in love with the poet Ibn ᶜAmmar, from whom he could not bear to be parted, "even for an hour, day or night," and whom he made one of the most powerful men in Spain.[103] Earlier in the century the kingdom of Valencia had been ruled by a pair of former slaves who had fallen in love and risen together through the ranks of the civil service until they were in a position to rule by themselves.[104] Their joint rule was characterized by admiring Muslim historians as a relationship of complete trust and mutual devotion, without any trace of competition or jealousy, and their

100. Male prostitutes abounded in Andalusian cities: see "Le traité d'Ibn Abdun," ed. E. Lévi-Provençal, *Journal Asiatique* 224 (1934): 241, or in his French translation, *Séville musulmane au début du XIIᵉ siècle* (Paris, 1947), sec. 170. Cf. Abu ᶜAbd Allah as-Saqati, *Kitāb fi ᶜAdabi 'l-Hisba*, ed. G. S. Colin and E. Lévi-Provençal (Paris, 1831), p. 68, and "Vocabulaire," s.v. "khanatha." (N.b., this work is sometimes cited in French as *Un manuel hispanique de Hisba*, although the text is only in Arabic; it is vol. 21 of the *Publications de l'Institut des Hautes Etudes Marocaines* of Rabat.) "Khanatha" could also mean "hermaphrodite," as in the contemporary medical treatise by Abū 'l-Qāsim az-Zahrāwī, "fī alāj al-khanathī," chap. 70 (See Albucasis, *On Surgery and Instruments*, ed. and trans. M. S. Spink and G. L. Lewis [Berkeley, 1973], pp. 454–55). Ad-Damiri and others also use this term for "hermaphrodite."

101. See Pérès; Nykl; Ibn Quzman, *Cancionero*, ed. Nykl (Madrid, 1933), pp. 335–441; and the *Muqaddimah*, 3:440 ff. for modern translations of such poetry. The chief source of Hispano-Arab poetry in the original is the work of al-Maqqarī published by R. Dozy et al. as *Analectes sur l'histoire et la littérature des arabes d'Espagne* (Leiden, 1855–60), 2 vols. Nykl discusses other sources in his introduction to *Hispano-Arab Poetry*, esp. p. xvii, n. 12, and Pérès lists sources for each poem he translates; but many such sources have been edited since Pérès and Nykl completed their works.

102. ᶜAbd al-Wahid al-Marrakushi, *Al-Muᶜjib fi talkhīs ta'rīkh al-Maghrib* (Cairo, 1906), p. 73; French translation by E. Fagnan in *Revue africaine*, 36 (1892): 41.

103. Ibid., pp. 81–83; in French, pp. 51–53; cf. Nykl, pp. 154–62.

104. Lisan ad-Din Ibn al-Khatib, *Histoire de l'Espagne musulmane (Kitab Aᶜmal al-Aᶜlam); texte arabe publié avec introduction et index*, ed. E. Lévi-Provençal (Beirut, 1956), pp. 222–27. Pérès (p. 258), Ahmad al-ᶜAbbadi (*As-Saqālabat fi Isbanīya* [Madrid, 1953], pp. 17–19), and Antonio Prieto y Vives (*Los reyes de Taifas* [Madrid, 1926], pp. 37, 39) all describe Mubarak

love for each other was celebrated in verse by poets attracted to their court from all over Spain.[105]

Hispano-Muslim society combined the freewheeling sexuality of Rome with the Greek tendency to passionate idealization of emotional relationships. Its most intense erotic literature might celebrate relationships which were either sublimated or sexual, but in either case they were as apt to involve same-sex relations as heterosexual ones, if not more so.

It would be a mistake to imagine this cultural predilection for homosexual eroticism as the result of secularization or religious decline: Spanish Islam was noted for its rigidity in legalistic and moral matters, produced outstanding jurists and theologians, and was generally ruled by Muslims considered fanatics in the rest of the Islamic world. Homosexual love imagery was a standard currency of Islamic mystical writings both in and out of Spain. Many of the authors of gay erotic poetry on the Iberian peninsula were teachers of the Qur'an, religious leaders, or judges;[106] almost all wrote conventional religious verse as well as love poetry. Ibn al-Farra', a teacher of the Qur'an in Almería, addressed amorous verse to his pupils in class and wrote a poem about taking a reluctant lover to court, where the *qadi* ruled that the youth must give in to the teacher's advances:

> Then [the judge] indicated to the flowers that they were to be taken,
> And to the mouth that it should be tasted.
> And when my beloved saw him on my side,
> And there was no longer any controversy between us,
> He abandoned his resistance, and I enfolded him
> As if I were a *lam* and my lover an *alif*.[107]
> I continued reproaching him for his unkindness,
> And he said, "May God forgive a past mistake!"[108]

---

and Mudhaffar as "eunuchs," although there is nothing in the text of the *A^cmal* to suggest this. Wilhelm Hoenerbach's partial translation into German (in *Islamische Geschichte Spaniens* [Zurich, 1970], pp. 408–10) more accurately refers to them simply as "youths."

105. Al-Khatib gives one such poem (*tawil*) by Ibn Darrāj on pp. 223–25. Hoenerbach and Pérès each translate two stanzas of the poem, in neither case particularly interesting or crucial ones.

106. E.g., al-Waqqashi, the *faqi* of Valencia supposed to have composed the famous lament over the city's fall to the Cid (incorporated into the *Primera crónica general*). It is especially interesting that, depending on how one reads the Arabic, one of his poems seems to suggest that while wine is prohibited by Allah, kissing his lover is prevented only by the latter's coyness. (For an English version, see Nykl, p. 309).

107. An image of graphic sexual import: the Arabic letters *lam* and *alif* are written together in a way that is here taken to suggest the insertion of one into the other. The *lam* (Ibn al-Farra') is written ل, the *alif* (the youth) ا ; when they occur together, they appear as لا.

108. *Analectes*, 2:260.

Positive attitudes toward gay sexuality in Spain, however, were not limited to Islamic culture. Large numbers of Christians lived in Spanish cities conquered by the Muslims, and cultural contact between Muslims and Christians all over the peninsula was constant and pervasive. Christian warriors like the famous Cid fought for the Muslims as often as against them; Christian kings imitated Muslim dress, kept Muslim doctors and teachers at their courts, entered into treaties with Muslim rulers against other Christians, and even married their children into Muslim families.

In view of what is commonly supposed to have been the general Christian attitude toward homosexual relations, some Christian reaction against Muslim sexual manners might have been expected, but laws of the Christian communities and kingdoms during the period are strikingly silent on the issue of homosexual behavior, even though they legislate in detail on other aspects of sexuality such as bestiality.[109] In some areas Christians sought martyrdom in order to avoid any "contamination" of the faith by Muslim assimilation,[110] but even the most hostile of Christian complaints about Muslim influence fail to mention "sodomy." Some Muslim sources, on the other hand, criticize the *Christian* clergy for their particular addiction to the practice.

It is not likely that Muslim customs simply escáped the notice of Christians: as far away as Germany the homosexual proclivities of Spanish Muslims elicited comment from Christian writers. Hroswitha, a German nun who lived in the tenth century, composed verses embodying a tale she had heard of Pelagius, a young Christian from Galicia, martyred by the caliph of Cordoba for refusing to submit to his advances.[111] The martyrdom of

109. E.g., the Council of Coyanza in 1055, which mentioned "adulteros, incestuosos, sanguine mistos, fures, homicidas, maleficos, et qui cum animalibus se inquinant" (chap. 4, in Tomás Muñoz y Romero, *Colección de fueros municipales y cartas pueblas* [Madrid, 1847], p. 210, or Mansi, 19:785). A somewhat later document, the "Penitential of Silos," repeats verbatim the provisions of the "Roman Penitential" regarding "sodomy": see Francisco de Berganza, *Antigüedades de España* (Madrid, 1719–21), app. 3, p. 669. The date of this material cannot be specified; it is almost certainly twelfth century or later, and its mention of "sodomy" at all is probably due to the change in attitude of the later twelfth century.

110. See the writings of Eulogius of Cordoba: *Memoriale sanctorum libri iii, Liber apologeticum martyrum*, etc., in PL, 115:731–870. These events are conveniently but somewhat uncritically treated in Joseph O'Callaghan, *A History of Medieval Spain* (Ithaca, N.Y., 1975), pp. 107–11. There is controversy over the charges made by Eulogius of "decay" within the Christian community and "oppression" by the Muslims, which O'Callaghan ignores. For a more detailed analysis, see E. Colbert, *The Martyrs of Cordoba: A Study of the Sources* (Washington, D.C., 1962); Isidoro de las Cagigas, *Los mozárabes* (Madrid, 1948–49); and James Waltz, "The Significance of the Voluntary Martyr Movement of Ninth-Century Cordoba," *Muslim World* 60 (1970): 143–59, 226–36.

111. *Passio sancti Pelagii* (PL, 137:1093–1103). The text is also published with an adequate translation into English by Gonsalva Wiegand, in *The Non-dramatic Works of Hroswitha* (St. Louis, 1936), pp. 128 ff.

Christian virgins—of either sex, though females predominate—victimized by the evil lust of pagans was a favorite theme of medieval hagiography, and there is no reason to give undue credence to Hroswitha's poem. But it is interesting to note some of the attitudes evinced by a German contemporary toward the Hispanic interaction of Islam and Christianity, and by a woman to male homosexuality.

Hroswitha does not suggest that homosexual acts are either praiseworthy or especially despicable. She refers to the Muslim ruler, who is depicted in extremely derogatory terms, as "corrupted by the vice of the Sodomites" ("corruptum vitiis . . . sodomitis"), but beyond this there is no indication that what he desires from Pelagius is sinful in itself. She portrays the principal men of the city, "moved by kindness," as urging the king to let the youth out of prison so can enjoy his beauty. When the king tries to kiss Pelagius, the youth does not expatiate on the evils of "sodomy" but, rather, argues against the carnal union of a Muslim and a Christian, suggesting that the king might righly ("licito corde") seek such favors from other Muslims:

> Jestingly he turns his ear to the royal mouth and with a great laugh diverts
>   the kiss declined,
> Observing with his own beautiful mouth,
> "It is not right for a man washed in the baptism of Christ
> To offer his pious neck for the embrace of a barbarian;
> Nor should a Christian, anointed with holy oil,
> Accept a kiss from a servant of the filthy demon.
> Embrace with a clear conscience the stupid men
> With whom you worship idiot clay gods." [112]

The difficulty appears to have subsisted not in the acts but in the faiths, and the king accordingly addresses himself not to the propriety of the kiss but to the necessity of Pelagius's keeping his religion to himself and not maligning that of the Saracens. Pelagius is not to be silenced, and when the king bends to kiss him again he punches him in the nose, upon which the enraged king has him executed.

112. Non patitur talem Christi nam miles amorem
regis pagani, luxu carnis maculati,
aurem regali ludens sed contulit ori,
magno ridiculo divertens ora negata,
fatus et egregio dicebat talia rostro:
Non decet ergo virum, Christi baptismate lotum
sobria barbarico complexu subdere colla,
sed nec christicolam sacrato chrismate tinctum,
daemonis oscillum spurci captare famelli.
Ergo corde viros licito complectere stultos,
qui tecum fatuos placantur cespite divos. [Col. 1099]

Hroswitha meant to make no theological statement about homosexual acts, but her casual tone is revealing. She recognizes that Muslims are more given to such behavior than Christians but seems to feel that the major issue in her story is that of bearing witness to the Christian faith and not cooperating with lustful pagans. The same plot with a female Christian and a Roman male was standard fare in early Christian martyrology. It is all but explicitly stated that among Saracens homosexual relations would not be sinful. It was not "unnatural" for men to relate sexually to men but simply "unseemly" for Christian men to relate in any personal way to pagan men.

Spanish sources, on the other hand, do not suggest that Christians drew the line at physical relations with Muslims. Much of the most popular gay erotic poetry is written in a vulgar Arabic dialect containing many Romance words and expressions, suggesting that it was composed in a milieu familiar with if not consisting partly of Christians.[113] Many Muslims had Christian lovers. Al-Mutamin, the eleventh-century Muslim king of the kingdom of Saragossa, was in love with his Christian page;[114] and ar-Ramadi, one of the most outstanding poets of the tenth century, not only began to wear the distinctive clothing of the Christian minority when he fell in love with a Christian youth but was even converted to Christianity, embracing his lover in front of the priest after the ceremony.[115]

Several factors may be cited as contributing to the relative indifference of early medieval Christians toward homosexual behavior. A general lack of governmental control throughout Europe left most persons free to regulate their own sexual mores. Although the predominantly rural and family-regulated ethos of the time doubtless discouraged homosexuality as a public phenomenon and certainly terminated any distinctive gay subculture outside of Spain, individuals were probably limited in expressing their sexuality only by private circumstances.

The intellectual climate of the period, moreover, was ambivalent in its effect on attitudes toward gay sexuality. Erotic pleasure and romantic passion were deplored by Western fathers of the church, and human relations based on such values found no place in Western theological development after contact with less ascetic Eastern theology ceased. Such feelings did not disappear—clerical writings bear witness to their survival among male monastics, and it is difficult to imagine a period in which the laity uniformly

---

113. This is especially true of the *Cancionero* of Ibn Quzman: see Nykl's edition, pp. xxvii–xxviii.

114. Pérès, p. 342.

115. *Analectes*, 2:443 (discussed in Pérès, p. 279, and less fully in Nykl, p. 59).

failed to fall in love—but they ceased to occupy the attention of philosophy and theology.

On the other hand, the effect of late Roman and Hellenistic idealizations of "nature" and the negative inferences which might be drawn from them in regard to sexuality also disappeared. Although the expression "contra naturam" continued to be employed in describing nonprocreative sexuality, its semantic force was vitiated by the fact that in the intensely rural West of the early Middle Ages no theologian would have cared to invoke "nature" as a moral standard. Increased familiarity with "natural" phenomena unmediated by human artifice reduced to a minimum ideas about the rectitude and beneficence of *natura* in the abstract, and daily contact with animals reversed the tendency of some classical authors to idealize barnyard sexuality. Although fanciful late antique notions about animal behavior survived as entertainment at the popular level, most scholars strove to adopt a more realistic approach. Isidore of Seville, writing in the early seventh century, flatly rejected the alleged sexual irregularities of the weasel and did not even mention the hyena or hare.[116]

By the eighth century animals were an entirely negative example of sexuality: Saint Boniface described adulterers and fornicators as "horses and donkeys,"[117] and the church absolutely forbade intercourse in "the animal position."[118] Many animals became symbols of incontinence and depraved sexual practices.[119]

The most influential definition of "nature" well into the High Middle Ages was that of Boethius (d. 525), generally regarded then as now as the last classical author of the West. Boethius was conversant with much Greek philosophy and formulated an essentially "realistic" definition of "nature": (1) everything that is, (2) all that acts or is acted upon, (3) the principle of motion, or (4) the inherent quality of something.[120]

116. *Etymologiae* 12.3.3; English translation in E. Brehaut, *An Encyclopaedist of the Dark Ages: Isidore of Seville*, Columbia Studies in History, Economics, and Public Law, no. 48 (New York, 1912), p. 226.

117. *Die Briefe des heiligen Bonifatius und Lullus*, ed. Michael Tangl (Berlin, 1916), no. 74; published in English by Ephraim Emerton, *The Letters of Saint Boniface* (New York, 1976), no. 58, p. 131.

118. E.g., Burchard of Worms, in his *Corrector* 19 (PL, 140:959).

119. Ibid., where the rabbit is used as symbolic of intercourse during pregnancy.

120. Boethius *Liber de persona et duabus naturis. 1. Natura quid sit* (PL, 64:1341–42): (1) "Omnis vero natura est"; (2) "Natura est vel quod facere, vel quod pati possit"; (3) "Natura est motus principium, secundum se, non per accidens"; (4) "Natura est unamquamque rem informans specifica differentia." The first definition is self-explanatory and is one of the most common senses of "nature" today. The second and third relate to cosmological and physical questions: in modern terms, (2) is intended to define "natural" as opposed to the "supernatural," or the physical as opposed to the spiritual, since it is the physical which moves or is moved; (3) attempts to include in the "natural" the principles

None of the meanings elaborated by Boethius could be "violated" by sexual behavior, and meanings (1), (2), and (3) would seem necessarily to include homosexuality, since it exists and entails physical change and movement. The fourth would also encompass gay people wherever their predilections were considered innate, and the literature of the time suggests very strongly that this was the case, since homosexual inclinations were often confused or associated with genetic conditions such as hermaphroditism.

The most extensive early medieval treatment of nature was the *Periphyseon* ("On the Divisions of Nature") of Eriugena, composed about the middle of the ninth century.[121] The work is far too complex to be easily characterized, but it seems extremely unlikely that any of the definitions of "nature" provided in it could have been construed as excluding homosexual behavior.[122] "Nature," the author observes, "is the general name for everything which is and is not.... Nothing at all can be conceived of which would not be comprised by this term."[123]

The thrust of the relatively rare theological objections to homosexual acts in the early Middle Ages could not therefore be traced to concepts of "nature," and such objections were generally predicated on the idea of the "impurity" of semen and the undesirability of releasing it except under absolute necessity. "Sodomy" came to refer to any emission of semen not directed exclusively toward the procreation of a legitimate child within matrimony, and the term included much—if not most—heterosexual activity. Around the middle of the eighth century, for instance, Saint Boniface, an English missionary working among the pagans of Germany, wrote back to England that "if, indeed, the people of England—as it is rumored in these provinces and charged against us in France and Italy, being considered scandalous even by pagans—have rejected legal marriages and are living foul lives of adultery

---

of motion—i.e., what are today called "forces," like gravity or electromagnetism. Definition (4) is primarily semantic, a recognition of the base meaning of the word. Of the four, however, it was most crucial, since it underlay the most important theological disputes of the early Middle Ages dealing with the "nature" of Christ. "Secundum ultimam definitionem [i.e., 4], duas in Christo naturas esse constituunt...." The point of the treatise in question was to examine the "nature" of Christ in sense (4).

121. Most recently edited (with translation) by I. P. Sheldon-Williams, *Johannis Scotti Eriugenae Periphyseon (De divisione naturae)*, Scriptores Latini Hiberniae, no. 7 (Dublin, 1968).

122. The "genus" nature is subdivided by Eriugena into four "species": (1) that which creates and is not created; (2) that which is created and also creates; (3) that which is created and does not create; (4) that which neither creates nor is created. Neither these nor any other divisions (e.g., the five modes of comprehending "nature") suggest any means of classifying homosexuality as "unnatural."

123. "Est igitur natura generale nomen ... omnium quae sunt et quae non sunt.... Nihil enim in universo cogitationibus nostris potest occurrere, quod tali vocabulo valeat carere," PL, 122:444 (Sheldon-Williams, p. 36).

1. Paired statues of Harmodius and Aristogiton. Roman, first or
second century A.D. Harmodius and Aristogiton were Attic lovers
who died trying to overthrow the tyrants Hippias and Hipparchus
in the sixth century B.C. Famous throughout the ancient world as
models of faithful affection and patriotic zeal, they were com-
memorated in art and literature for centuries after their deaths.
These Roman marbles, showing them clutching sword hilts, were
copied from statues erected by a grateful Athens. *(Courtesy of
Museo archeologico nazionale, Naples)*

2. Hadrian. Roman, second century A.D. The last of the "five good emperors," Hadrian ruled the Roman Empire from 117 to 138. A veteran general, he is depicted in this lifelike bust in military garb. Hadrian's love for Antinous (following illustration) captured the imagination of his contemporaries and made the latter a common subject of imperial art. *(Courtesy of Museo archeologico nazionale, Naples)*

3. Antinous. Roman, second century A.D. (?). One of the best of many surviving statues of the young man from Bithynia loved by the Emperor Hadrian. Antinous was drowned in the Nile in 130 A.D., and the grief-stricken emperor honored his memory by founding cities, establishing games, and erecting statues in his name throughout the empire. *(Courtesy of Museo archeologico nazionale, Naples)*

4. Ganymede. Roman copy of Hellenistic original. The dog in
this grouping is probably a reference to the popular legend that
the Trojan prince was hunting on Mount Ida when carried off
by an eagle to serve as cup-bearer to Zeus (see, e.g., *Aeneid* 5. 255;
Ovid, *Metamorphoses* 10. 155 ff.), but the scene as a whole suggests
tranquillity and acquiescence rather than abduction. *(Courtesy of
Museo archeologico nazionale, Naples)*

5. End of Apocalypse and beginning of the Epistle of Barnabas, from the Codex Sinaiticus. Fourth century A.D. Comments about the alleged sexual aberrations of the hyena, hare, and weasel in the Epistle of Barnabas were an important source of early Christian misgivings about homosexual behavior. The Epistle forms part of the text of the most famous of early Bible manuscripts, the Sinaiticus, and had a great influence on later thought through the *Physiologus* and other bestiary texts. *(Courtesy of British Museum: Add. ms 43725, fol. 334)*

6. Ganymede with eagle. Roman, fourth century A.D. This depiction of Ganymede with an eagle suggests mutual fascination rather than abduction, perhaps reflecting a tendency of later artists to idealize the relationship between the Trojan prince and Zeus. The eagle is stylistically similar to later representations of the eagle that symbolized Saint John the Evangelist. *(Courtesy of Museo archeologico nazionale, Naples)*

7. Ganymede capital from the church of La Madeleine at Vezelay,
France. Twelfth century. This sculpture is apparently based on
classical accounts of the rape of Ganymede by an eagle: the
hunting dog, the terrified youth, the gaping onlookers, all suggest
the scene related by Vergil and Ovid. The grinning gargoyle is a
twelfth-century addition. *(Bildarchiv Foto Marburg)*

8. Bearded acrobats from the church of La Sauve-Majeure, Gironde, France. Twelfth century. These figures may represent only acrobats or wrestlers, but the position of the bodies and the expressions on the faces could be indications that more intimate contact is involved. Other figures in the series include pairs of men with fingers inserted into each other's mouths, and the area in which the sculpture originated was noted in the twelfth century as a center of homosexual activity. *(Courtesy of the Metropolitan Museum, New York: Gift of George Blumenthal, 1934)*

Pars hominem pingit asinus ps altera pingit:
Morib; infernus notat hȳ pec atq; incordes.

gine tenet. atq; musicū qd̄ dī dulcissimū melodie carm
canunt. pqd̄ homines nauigantes decipiunt ita ut psepe an
dmū demulcentes sensūq; delinentes insopore uertuntur: ti
tē ille uidentes eos cē sopitos. in nadium ẏ laniant carnes eox.
Sic ẏ decipiunt illi ẏ diabolicis pompis ẏ theatralib; uolup
tatib; delectari. I tragœdiis musicis solum ẏ uelut somno
mitis ẏ quam efferunt adaduse uirtuti audissima pda. Co
modo onocentaurus duab; naturis constat. ut phisiolog
asserit. Na supior pars hominī. similis ē posteriorq; asino
similis ẏ nata eū ualde agrestis. P hine assimilant necox
des ẏ bilingues homines. morib infromes. habentes
speciē pietatis ūtutē eā abnegantes sic septū ē. Si ho
mo cū inhonore eet ñ intellex coparat ē immtas
insipientib; ẏ similis factē ē illis. De hiena.

Est aliud animal qd̄ grece dicunt hiena de ẏ
lex dic. Ñ manducabis hienā neq; qd̄ simile eī ē.
Hiertū ē pesaū ppheta. Speluncer hiene heredtas mea.
Phisiologus hine narrat qd̄ duas naturas habeat.
aliqñdo quidē masculus ẏ aliqñdo qd̄ femina ē
ẏ ideo immundū animal ē. Cui similes estimati s
filii isrl: ẏ pmū dm̄ suū coluere. pea luxurie ẏ uolup
tatib; dediti idola coluer: Vel ẏ ñc auaricie student. qd̄
ē simulacrox seruit. coparant bestie huic. Sic ẏ immunda sulica
ẏ nec uir nec femina eē dicit. id ē nec fidelis nec pfidus. Sic
salemon dic. uir duplex corde inconstans ē in oīb; De Onag.

Est ẏ animal aliud qd̄ dicit.   uulf sijs.
Onager. Phisiologus dic de eo ita. Ỹa xx v. die
insis faminolit ẏ ē martius duo decies in nocte
ruget similiter ẏ die. Tunc cx cognoscit qd̄ eẏ
noctuū sit ẏ dies noctisẏ; ex numero horarū ad ecpit. Ona
ger ẏ figurā diaboli gerit. ẏ eū sciret noctes cocquaut hoc
ē cū uideret qd̄ gentium populus ẏ ambulabat in tenebs

9. Hyenas embracing. Twelfth century. The center illustration
of this Latin bestiary depicts two hyenas embracing, a common
artistic reference to the animal's alleged homosexuality. The text—
which is unusual—relates that the hyena "is an unclean animal,
. . . sometimes male and sometimes female," and that "the children
of Israel are thought to be similar to this animal, since they first
worshiped their Lord and then, abandoning themselves to pleasure
and lust, venerated idols and now pursue avarice, which is service
to idols." Although Jews and gay people were often tacitly linked
in later medieval law and literature as nonconformists threatening
the social order, such explicit comparisons were relatively rare.
(Cf. figure 12.) (Courtesy of the Pierpont Morgan Library: ms 832,
fol. 4)

ft animal quod dicitur ster duo cornua habens. qua
rum tanta uis est ut si ab alto mortas ad ima demisf
sit fuerit. corpus eius totum his duobz cornibz sustentur
illesum. Significat autem eruditos homines. qui duorum
testamentorum consonantia quicquid eis aduersi acciderit
quasi quodam salubri temparmento temperare solet. & ueld
duobz cornibz sustibona q ppetuc ueteris testamti accunglice
lectionis attestatione sustentant.

10. Hyena devouring a corpse. Twelfth century. The
unsavory association of hyenas with homosexual
activity was accentuated by other popular allegations
about the hyena, such as the claim that it robbed graves
and devoured corpses, graphically represented here in
the lower picture. *(Courtesy of the British Museum:
Harl 4751, fol. 10)*

11. Weasels mating through the mouth and bearing
through the ear. Fourteenth century. The illustrations
in the margins of this psalter are taken from popular
bestiaries. This page shows two weasels mating
through the mouth and one giving birth through the
ear. Such stories had been popular since the beginning
of the Christian era but reached a wider audience in
the later Middle Ages, when they were illustrated and
translated into vernacular languages. *(Courtesy of
the British Museum: Royal 2B vii, fol. 112)*

De hyena·

Onocentaur⁹

12. Hyenas embracing. German, fourteenth century. The unusual (and unpublished) text of this bestiary's account of the hyena is almost identical to that of figure 9, linking the supposed sexual aberrations of the hyena to the infidelity of the Jews. The drawings in the two manuscripts, however, do not seem to be directly related, and it is striking that, while neither work specifically states that male hyenas mate with each other, both dramatically illustrate this ancient part of the hyena legend in pictures. *(Courtesy of the Bayerische Staatsbibliothek, Munich: clm 6908, fol. 79)*

13. Christ and Saint John. German, fourteenth century. This very sentimental representation of an older Christ and a youthful Saint John is strongly evocative of the tradition of passionate friendship common among the monastic clergy of the Middle Ages and romanticized earlier by writers like Saint Aelred of Rievaulx. *(Courtesy of the Staatliche Museen Preussischer Kulturbesitz, Berlin)*

and lust like the people of Sodom, one can only assume that from such filthy unions will be engendered a degenerate and ignoble people, burning with lust."[124] Previous commentators have certainly been mistaken in assuming any reference to homosexuality in this letter:[125] not only would it be highly unusual for homosexual unions to produce offspring of any sort, but in this and a subsequent letter Boniface defines exactly what he meant by "sodomitical lust": "despising lawful marriage and preferring incest, promiscuity, adultery, and impious union with religious and cloistered women."[126] Homosexuality is neither mentioned nor implied.

Hincmar of Reims, one of the most influential theologians of the Carolingian era,[127] both confirmed and followed prevailing usage in his day in applying the term "sodomy" to all nonprocreative and some potentially reproductive sexual acts. His treatment of such relations prefigured (and probably determined) most subsequent canonistic and theological discussions.[128] He defined as "against nature" any sexual release of semen with a nun, a relative, the wife of a relative, a married woman, any woman in a way which precluded conception, an animal, or by oneself, whether through manipulation or any other means. "Therefore let no one claim he has not committed sodomy if he has acted contrary to nature with either man or woman or has deliberately and consciously defiled himself by rubbing,

124. "Si enim gens Anglorum—sicut per istas provincias devulgatum est et nobis in Francia et in Italia inproperatur, et ab ipsis paganis inproperium est—spretis legalibus conubiis, adulterando et luxoriando ad instar Sodomitanae gentis foedam vitam vixerit, de tali commixtione meretricum, aestimandum est, degeneres populos et ignobiles et furentes libidine fore procreandos," A. W. Haddan and W. Stubbs, Councils and Ecclesiastical Documents relating to Great Britain and Ireland (Oxford, 1871), 3:354. For a translation, see Emerton, Letters, pp. 124–30.

125. Notably Bailey, p. 110, where the quotation is abbreviated in a way that distorts its meaning.

126. Haddan and Stubbs, pp. 35–54, 358–60; citation from p. 359: "In triplo vel in quadruplo Sodomitamam luxoriam vincens, ut ... despiciat legitima matrimonia, et adhereat incestis, luxoriis, adulteriis, et nefanda stupra consecratarum et velatarum feminarum sequatur."

127. For Hincmar's life and importance, see the massive biography by Jean Devisse, Hincmar, archévêque de Reims, 845–82 (Geneva, 1975–76), 3 vols.

128. The discussion occurs in Hincmar's treatise on the divorce of King Lothair of Lorraine from his wife Theutberga (De divortio Lotharii et Tetbergae, interrogatio XII [PL, 125:689–95]), in the context of a question about the possibility of a woman's conceiving through anal intercourse, having an abortion, and remaining technically a virgin (and whether this would constitute grounds for annulment of the marriage of such a woman). He resolves the issue almost in passing by commenting that only one woman in history has ever given birth and remained a virgin (col. 694). Questions about the physical process by which Mary bore a child and remained a virgin exercised the imagination of many of Hincmar's contemporaries and some of his friends. Saint Radbertus wrote a treatise on the subject, the De partu virginis (for which see Edith Ann Matter, "The De partu virginis of Paschasius Radbertus: Critical Edition and Monographic Study" [Ph.D. diss., Yale University, 1976]).

touching, or other improper actions."[129] Hincmar's objection to "sodomy" does not seem to have any relation to the "Alexandrian rule," which certainly could not be invoked to justify classifying as "against nature" intercourse with a nun, relative, the wife of a relative, or someone else's wife. In none of these cases is conception necessarily precluded, and in all it could conceivably be the motivation for the act. Rather, his concern seems to arise from a belief that human seed is "impure,"[130] and its release can only be tolerated under the two circumstances where it is presumably unavoidable: nocturnal emission[131] and procreation.

Homosexuality is thus reduced to a simple form of fornication, i.e., the release of seed in an improper way. This had two important consequences. Since Hincmar believed that women too could release "seed" improperly, logic constrained him to become one of the few medieval writers to comment specifically on lesbianism: "They do not put flesh to flesh in the sense of the genital organ of one within the body of the other, since nature precludes this, but they do transform the use of the member in question into an unnatural one, in that they are reported [n.b.] to use certain instruments of diabolical operation to excite desire. Thus they sin nonetheless by committing fornication against their own bodies."[132] Second, homosexual acts were in effect demoted from the position of unique enormity to which a few influential early fathers had promoted them and joined the ranks of common failings with which almost anyone could empathize. Hincmar is very insistent on this point in regard to the Bible. He lists homosexual acts as *one* of the sins committed by the Sodomites, along with sloth and gluttony. He insists that Paul's Epistle to the Romans condemns all forms of illegitimate sexuality, regardless of gender: "Whence it follows, as the Apostle says to the Romans, that if any commit uncleanness in any way, whether men with men, women with women, men with women, or all by themselves, it is an indecency

---

129. "Nemo igitur dicat, non perpetrare eum peccatum sodomitanum, qui contra naturam in masculum vel in feminam turpitudinem, et attritu, vel attactu, seu motu impudico, ex deliberatione et studio immundus efficitur," col. 693.

130. He refers to it as "lutum," "filth," and "fluxus," a word of principally negative connotation.

131. "Hence Saint Prosper in his book on 'Virtues and Vices' noted, 'Thus it is that bodily emission which is experienced inculpably while sleeping occurs only through sin to those who are awake. In the former case an excess of fluid [*plenitudo humoris*] is expelled naturally; in the latter concupiscence is indulged sinfully.'"

132. "Quae carnem ad carnem, non autem genitale carnis membrum intra carnem alterius, factura prohibente naturae, mittunt: sed naturalem hujusce partis corporeae usum in eum usum qui est contra naturam commutant: quae dicuntur quasdam machinas diabolicae operationis nihilominus ad exaestuandam libidinem operari; et tamen fornicantes in corpus suum peccant," cols. 692–93.

which separates the guilty party from the kingdom of God."[133] Hincmar cited 1 Corinthians 6:9 in a context suggesting both homosexuality and prostitution.[134] (In the popular pre-Scholastic manual of biblical exegesis called the *Glossa ordinaria* even the severe proscriptions of Leviticus 20:13 are given a spiritual interpretation devoid of any real sexual reference.)[135]

When Burchard, bishop of Worms (d. 1025), promulgated his famous decretals—the forerunner of the great collections of canon law of the twelfth and thirteenth centuries—he followed Hincmar in classifying homosexual acts as a variety of fornication.[136] But Burchard apparently considered homosexual behavior somewhat less serious than comparable heterosexual activity.[137] Only anal intercourse with a married man seemed to Burchard a grave sin, but even if committed habitually this sin did not incur a penalty as severe as for a single instance of heterosexual adultery.[138] Other forms of

133. "Unde constat, quia sicut idem dicit Apostolus ad Romanos, cum masculi in masculos, vel feminae in feminas, sive masculi in feminas, vel quilibet per se ipsos modo quolibet turpitudinem operantes, immunditia est, quae separat operantem a regno Dei, et in inferna demergit," col. 692.

134. "Similiter et masculi in masculos turpitudinem operantes . . . qui ab Apostolo masculorum concubitores appellantur, et molles, qui huic turpitudini voluptuose succumbunt. Sed et qui tollit membra Christi facit membra meretricis, adhaerens meretrici," ibid. On the other hand, he was one of the first medieval moralists to quote Joel 3:3 as a homosexual reference (perhaps unwittingly—he gives no source) and seems to have understood Eph. 5:12 as an allusion to homosexual practices as well.

135. "Spiritually we must beware of weakening [*effeminare*] someone who is strong and masculine mentally (in Holy Scripture someone is designated a man if he is perfect in virtue) by base words or actions, lest we be emasculated with him and perish together." ("Spiritualiter autem eum qui fortis est animo et masculus [vir enim in divina scriptura, perfectus in virtutibus nominatur] verbis pravis vel actionibus effeminare caveamus, ne cum ipso dissolvamur et simul moriamur," PL, 113:354).

136. *Decretorum libri XX*, Liber 19 (PL, 140:967–68). For Burchard's sources, see Paul Fournier, "Etudes critiques sur le decret de Burchard de Worms," *Nouvelle revue historique du droit français et étranger* 34 (1910): 41–112, 213–21, 288–31, 564–84. Bk. 19, chap. 5, from which the following are extracted, appears to be original.

137. I have based my discussion on bk. 19 both because its treatment of homosexual acts is more systematic than the brief recapitulation of the provisions of the "Roman Penitential" in 17.56, and because the nineteenth book was the most influential section of the decretals, being circulated separately under the titles *Medicus* and *Corrector* as manuals for priests as well as a basis for subsequent canons. The summary of the "Roman Penitential" in bk. 17 is clearly identified as an earlier approach and moreover suffers from inconsistencies which cast considerable doubt on the text (e.g., the penance for voluntary nocturnal pollution is less than half as long as that for *involuntary* pollution). In general even these earlier penances parallel or are smaller than those for comparable heterosexual offenses.

138. For a single offense of heterosexual adultery by a married man, the penance was eighty days of bread and water, followed by fourteen years of fasting (PL, 140:957); for habitual anal homosexual activity by a married man, the penance was forty days of bread and water, followed by twelve years of fasting (967); for only one or two such acts by a married man, the penance was only ten years of fasting (ibid.). As in the case of other penitential guides, there were numerous ways to circumvent fasting in each of the cases cited.

homosexual intercourse, judging from the penances assigned, were about as serious as challenging a friend to a drinking bout or having intercourse with one's own spouse within two weeks of receiving communion[139] (or at any time during Lent). All of the penances assigned to homosexual acts seem to apply only to married men.[140] It is possible, although silence alone does not constitute proof, that Burchard did not consider homosexual behavior between single persons sinful at all. It seems at least fair to infer that he was not sufficiently concerned about it to assign a specific penance for such activity. In the civil legislation promulgated by Burchard to regulate family matters in his diocese (divorce, rape, inheritance, etc.), there is no mention of homosexual behavior.[141]

Indeed the evidence suggests that despite considerable local variation, attitudes toward homosexuality grew steadily more tolerant throughout the early Middle Ages. The centuries during and immediately after the fall of Roman urban culture witnessed the most hostile period of ecclesiastical thought on all sexual matters, due to shifts in social patterns, the influence of ascetic philosophies, and a Christian revulsion against Hellenistic hedonism. But this reaction seems never to have affected the majority of Christians and was significantly vitiated even at the theological level during the period from the eighth to the tenth century.

139. For interfemoral intercourse, forty days; for mutual masturbation, thirty days—the same as for challenging someone to a drinking bout (ibid., 963); having intercourse with one's spouse within two weeks of communicating incurred a penance of twenty days (ibid.).

140. The penances cited are prefaced with the proviso "si uxorem habuisti." In other cases Burchard appends a specific section for the unmarried with the proviso "si uxorem non habuisti"—e.g., in the immediately following section on bestiality. It is difficult to view his failure to do so in this case, where marital status would seem so obviously relevant, as a careless oversight.

141. *Constitutiones et acta publica imperatorum et regum*, in MGH, *Leges*, 4, 1 (Hanover, 1893), no. 438, pp. 639–44.

8   The Urban Revival

"Invigorated, transformed and launched upon the route of progress, the new Europe resembled, in short, more the ancient Europe than the Europe of Carolingian times. For it was out of antiquity that she regained that essential characteristic of being a region of cities."[1]

Between the tenth and fourteenth centuries, the economy of western Europe, fragmented, rural, and generally depressed since the breakup of the Roman Empire, underwent a dramatic expansion and transformation. The causes of this expansion—increased domestic security; stabilization of economic, social and political institutions; trade; technological advances; changes in climate and agricultural techniques; population growth—are neither fundamental to the present study nor fully understood by historians. But the effects of the change are well documented and were profoundly important to gay people in the eleventh and twelfth centuries. Chief among these was a dramatic acceleration in the rate of urban growth.[2] During the period between 1100 and 1250, many European cities increased in population

1. Henri Pirenne, *Medieval Cities: Their Origins and the Revival of Trade*, trans. Frank Halsey (Princeton, N.J., 1952), p. 103.

2. Although urban growth is universally agreed upon as a characteristic of this period, there are few general surveys of the phenomenon. Good introductions can be found in Leopold Génicot's "On the Evidence of Growth of Population in the West from the Eleventh to the Thirteenth Century" (with useful bibliography), in *Change in Medieval Society*, ed. Sylvia Thrupp (New York, 1964) (originally published in French in *Cahiers d'histoire mondiale* 1 [1953]: 446–62); and in the collection of articles in *La città nell'alto medioevo*, in *Settimane*, no. 4 (1959). But it is probably most useful to consult texts according to place and time for details: e.g., for Italy, E. Sestan, "La città comunale italiana dei secoli XI–XIII nelle sue note caratteristiche rispetto al movimiento comunale europeo," in *Report to the Eleventh International Congress of Historical Sciences* (Stockholm, 1960), vol. 3, or G. Luzzatto, "L'inurbamento delle popolazioni rurali in Italia nei secoli XII e XIII," in *Studi di storia e diritto in onore de E. Besta* (Milan, 1939), vol. 2; for France and Belgium, F. O. Ganshof, *Over stadsontwikkeling tusschen Loire en Rijn gedurende de Middeleeuwen* (Brussels, 1944); for Catalonia, J. M. Font Rius, *Orígenes del régimen municipal de Cataluña* (Madrid, 1946). Many individual cities have also received valuable and extensive investigation: e.g., for Barcelona, José E. Ruiz Domeneq, *La sociedad barcelonesa en los siglos XI y XII* (Barcelona,

five- or sixfold,[3] and some increased in area by almost 800 percent.[4] Many villages grew into towns, and new villages and towns grew up where there had been no urban settlement before.

The influence of urban centers on Europe increased even more rapidly than their physical growth would suggest. Not only did thriving trade in many great cities draw merchants and tradespeople to urban centers, but many social services previously provided locally or not at all became concentrated in city centers—law courts, hospitals, welfare systems, markets, universities, etc.—and these often drew even the peasant landowner into the city's orbit.

Although cities had always been associated with democracy and self-government, an equation in the popular mind between urban life and personal freedom became dramatically prominent during this period.[5] Many cities were communes and, although scarcely democratic, afforded opportunities for self-government unavailable anywhere else in the medieval world. Even in cities under royal or ecclesiastical control, municipal government often included social classes not admitted to power anywhere else, and the lower and middle classes were able in many ways to make their wishes felt in urban environments. Escaping to the city was escaping to freedom for peasants in most of Europe, and residence of a year and a day in a city was often claimed to constitute emancipation from any feudal obligation. "Die Stadtluft macht frei" ("City air makes one free") ran the proverb, and urban dwellers of the eleventh and twelfth centuries consciously developed an atmosphere of liberty and tolerance in which individual rights and personal freedom were of paramount importance. The reemergence of a distinct gay subculture in southern Europe is almost exactly coetaneous with the revival of major urban centers, and the relation between the two was obvious even to contemporaries. It was also during this period that erotic passion—which had been almost totally absent from Western literature since the fall of Rome—suddenly became the subject of a large proportion of

1973)—English excerpt trans. John Boswell in *Speculum* 52 (April 1977) 265–86; for Geneva, that of L. Blondell, "Le développement urbain de Genève à travers les siècles," in *Cahiers de préhistoire et d'archéologie* (Geneva, 1946), vol. 3.

3. See Gino Luzzatto, *Storia economica d'Italia* (Rome, 1949), 1:241.

4. Génicot, p. 18.

5. The most convenient discussion of this subject in English is probably the chapter on "Municipal Institutions" in Pirenne's much controverted but still indispensable *Medieval Cities* (first published in 1925). The more recent work by Ernst Werner, *Stadtluft macht Frei: Frühscholastik und bürgerliche Emanzipation in der ersten Hälfte des 12. Jahrhunderts* (Berlin, 1976), is chiefly a Marxist interpretation of early Scholasticism. The more intrepid may wish to consult Pirenne's massive *Villes et les institutions urbaines* (Brussels, 1939), 2 vols. In English there is little, but one might mention F. Rörig's *Medieval Town* (London, 1967) and Joseph and Frances Gies's *Life in a Medieval City* (New York, 1969).

literature and seemingly the major preoccupation of feudal society. There could hardly be a more dramatic contrast than that afforded by tenth- and twelfth-century literatures in regard to love. Apart from the monastic clergy, love does not appear to have been a concern to tenth-century Europeans in any context: theological, moral, sexual, or emotional. Twelfth-century Europeans, especially in urban areas, do not seem to have been able to think of much else. Religious tracts are suffused with romantic imagery and expressions of ecstatic love; theological speculation centers on divine and human love; popular writings are obsessed with all aspects of human erotic and romantic feelings, from the impassioned hedonism of the *Carmina Burana* to the lofty passion of the knightly lover for distant ladies (or other knights).[6] The twelfth-century "revival" of love included gay people and their passions no less than others. "Courtly love" occurred between women and between men just as between women and men; statistically, the proportion of gay literature surviving from this period is astonishing.

Also characteristic of the period was the reform and revitalization of the church. Some of the particular ways in which this may have related to gay sexuality are discussed below. In a more general way, one may observe that this reformation was accompanied and to a certain extent fomented by monastic renewal and the ascendance of the regular clergy throughout Europe. Such clerics, always officially celibate, tended to regard love as valuable in spiritual contexts other than marriage and frequently idealized personal relationships based on love which occurred outside the family.

Moreover, learning was so highly prized during the period and achieved such remarkable advances that many scholars refer to "the Renaissance of

---

6. Although the issue of "courtly love" and its social and literary ramifications obviously bears on the present discussion, its history is so complicated, its literature so vast, and its existence outside artistic conventions so justly disputed that it would be counterproductive to include it in the present discussion. Where the controversy surrounding it is most penetrable and of greatest relevance to the issues at hand, it has been cited, but no more general treatment could be attempted without doubling the size of this volume. It is difficult even to give bibliographical indications for so vast and complex a subject. L. T. Topsfield, *Troubadours and Love* (Cambridge, 1975) is perhaps the most recent overview, although not entirely successful; Joan Ferrante, ed., *In Pursuit of Perfection: Courtly Love in Medieval Literature* (London, 1975) is better, though focused on more literary aspects; Roger Boase, *The Origin and Meaning of Courtly Love: A Critical Study of European Scholarship* (Manchester, 1977) treats the academic controversies raging about this topic; efforts at broader analysis include John Chydenius, *Love and the Medieval Tradition* (Helsinki, 1977), and Erich Köhler, *Sociologia della "fin'amor" saggi trobadorici* (Padua, 1976). Literally hundreds of older studies on similar topics may be traced through the bibliographies of these works, and more specialized treatments (e.g., transmission through Spain, antecedents in Latin literature, or relations with Catharist heretical movements) are cited elsewhere in this study.

the Twelfth Century." [7] Although few of the endeavors of the time left so monumental a testimony as Gothic architecture, twelfth-century Europe leaped forward in many fields. Biblical scholarship, the study of medicine, law and classical literature, architecture, science, economics, agriculture—almost every aspect of human life underwent new and unprecedented scrutiny during this period. Contact with the rest of the Mediterranean world was both a cause and effect of this cultural efflorescence: the crusades and the Spanish *reconquista* brought Christians into closer contact with Islam, and as Europeans became more and more aware of the classical learning preserved by Islamic society, more and more of them traveled to find the wisdom of Athens and Rome in Spain and Sicily.

Renewed and intensified contact with the achievements and attitudes of the ancient world contributed greatly to tolerance, if not admiration, of gay people and their sexuality. Wherever Ovid was enjoyed, Vergil quoted, Plato read, there gay passions and sentiments were known and studied and often respected.

At the official level, the indifference of the early medieval church toward gay people began to dissipate and was replaced by two opposite approaches. A small, vociferous group of ascetics revived the violent hostility of Chrysostom, claiming that homosexual acts were not only sinful but gravely so, more comparable to murder than to gluttony or fornication. Throughout the period these few men struggled to interest the institutional church in their crusade to change both public and theological opinion on the subject, but ecclesiastical authorities categorically and repeatedly refused to impose penalties for homosexual behavior or even enforce those in effect, and the majority of churchmen simply turned a deaf ear to the few complaints they received from antigay Christians. Meanwhile, another party within the church began to assert the positive value of homosexual relations and celebrated them in an outburst of Christian gay literature still without parallel in the Western world.

Around the year 1051 Saint Peter Damian composed a long treatise called *The Book of Gomorrah* in which he declaimed vituperatively against the evils

7. The classic exposition of this approach is the marvelously erudite study by Charles Homer Haskins, *The Renaissance of the Twelfth Century* (Cambridge, Mass., 1927), still unsurpassed in the breadth of its vision. For a more recent analysis, see Sydney Packard, *Twelfth Century Europe: An Interpretive Essay* (Amherst, Mass., 1973); and see also Gaines Post, ed., *Twelfth-Century Europe and the Foundations of Modern Society* (Madison, Wis., 1961). The eleventh century, in many ways the equal of the twelfth in cultural brilliance, has received less scholarly attention, but there is the superb overview of the tenth and eleventh centuries by R. W. Southern, *The Making of the Middle Ages* (London, 1953). On "medieval humanism" in this period, see the essays by Southern in *Medieval Humanism and Other Studies* (New York, 1970), esp. pp. 29–135.

of sexual relations between males, particularly among the clergy.[8] He
described in lurid detail several varieties of homosexual intercourse and
charged that they were extremely common. He accused priests of having
sexual relations with their spiritual advisees and stated that many clerics
avoided ecclesiastical penalties by confessing to other gay clergy. His
comments are reminiscent of Chrysostom's diatribes against practices which
his contemporaries seemed reluctant to condemn.

> Absolutely no other vice can be reasonably compared with this one,
> which surpasses all others in uncleanness. For this vice is in fact the death
> of the body, the destruction of the soul; it pollutes the flesh, extinguishes
> the light of the mind, casts out the Holy Spirit from the temple of the human
> breast, and replaces it with the devil, the rouser of lust; it removes truth
> utterly from the mind; it deceives and directs it toward falsehood; it sets
> snares in a man's path and, when he falls into the pit, blocks it up so there
> is no escape; it opens the doors of hell and closes the gates of heaven; it
> makes the citizen of the heavenly Jerusalem the heir of infernal Babylon.[9]

It is a telling comment on the indifference of the early medieval church
in this regard that for support of his hostility to such practices, Saint Peter
could produce no more recent ecclesiastical enactment than the Council of
Ancyra (of 314), which Latin writers wrongly assumed to have legislated
against homosexual behavior.[10]

In response to this impassioned polemic, Peter received from Pope Saint
Leo IX a polite acknowledgment, assuring him that he had demonstrated
himself to be an enemy of carnal pollution and agreeing somewhat coldly

8. For the historical accuracy of Peter's comments on this subject, see Joseph Ryan, *St.
Peter Damiani and His Canonical Sources* (Toronto, 1965), p. 155, n. 107, where he praises the
"discernment" of L. Kühn (*Petrus Damiani und seine Anschauungen über Staat und Kirche*
[Karlsruhe, 1933]) in "judging Damiani's tract as an historical source." The major modern
biography of Peter is that of Jean Leclercq, *Saint Pierre Damien, ermite et homme de l'église*
(Rome, 1960); see also J. Gonsette, *Saint Pierre Damien et la culture profane* (Louvain, 1956),
and F. Dressler, *Petrus Damiani: Leben und Werk*, in *Studia Anselmiana*, vol. 34 (Rome, 1954).
Unfortunately, Hans P. Laqua, *Traditionen und Leitbilder bei dem Ravennater Reformer Petrus
Damiani, 1042–1052* (Munich, 1976) is not helpful in this context.

9. Chap. 16 (PL, 145:175): "Hoc sane vitium nulli prorsus est vitio conferendum, quod
omnium immanitatem superat vitiorum. Hoc siquidem vitium mors est corporum, interitus
est animarum, carnem polluit, mentis lumen exstinguit, Spiritum Sanctum de templo
humani pectoris ejicit, incentorum luxuriae diabolum introducit, mittit in errorem, sub-
trahit deceptae menti funditus veritatem, eunti laqueos praeparat, cadenti in puteum, ne
egrediatur oppilat, infernum aperit, paradisi januam claudit, coelestis Jerusalem civem
tartareae Babylonis facit haeredem." Ralph Hexter and I are preparing a translation of this
work, with commentary.

10. Saint Peter lived in Italy and was presumably unaware of Carolingian legislation on
the subject.

to interpose his apostolic authority in the matter. Leo declined to accede to Peter's demand that all clerics guilty of any sort of homosexual offense be removed from office and insisted, rather, that clerics who had not engaged in such activities "as a long-standing practice or with many men" should remain in the same rank they held when convicted, and that only those in the most severely sinful states might be degraded from their rank.[11] Although too much has sometimes been made of Leo's reply,[12] it is unquestionably the response of a pontiff more concerned with maintaining stability within the clergy than with punishing homosexual relations and suggests a rather low estimation of the seriousness of homosexual offenses generally: Leo's comment to Peter that "you have written what seemed best to you" suggests that the pope's own feelings in the matter were not necessarily identical with those of his correspondent.

It is particularly striking that Saint Leo should have disagreed with Saint Peter on this matter since, according to the latter, the pope agreed that prostitutes who serviced priests should be enslaved—a surprisingly severe penalty for a very common activity.[13] Several of Peter's biographers have regarded their difference on this point as sufficiently great to have been the major cause of the eventual rupture between the two.[14]

11. The text of this letter is translated in app. 2.

12. Bailey, for instance, distorts this incident almost beyond recognition (influenced, it would seem, by K. H. Mann, *Lives of the Popes* [London, 1925], 4:51–52): "Leo IX himself . . . began to have second thoughts. Further reflection . . . convinced him that Peter had gone too far, and he felt bound to administer a check to the reformer's zeal. After commending, therefore, the motive behind his courageous and forthright defence of chastity and condemnation of clerical vice, the pope went on to rebuke his harsh and unyielding spirit" (p. 114). In the letter to which Bailey and Mann allude there is no passage suggesting reproof. On the contrary, the letter is filled with praise for Peter and his work. Leo does prescribe lighter penalties for clerics than Saint Peter did, and he implies that he is not wholly in agreement with Peter about the matter in general, but he also states that "justice and my own opinion" demand the sort of penalty Peter had prescribed. The sentence that Bailey translates as if it were a warning to Peter Damian ("And if anyone should dare to criticize or carp at this decree . . . let him know that *he* is in danger of his order," ibid.) refers not to Peter at all, as is perfectly clear from the context, but, rather, to those who recommend *not* punishing such offenses. Bailey and Mann may be confused about the later disagreement between Leo and Peter, but if so they are seriously misled, since the evidence for this rests not on Leo's letter to Peter but on a letter from Peter to Leo.

13. Cited from a letter to the bishop of Turin by André DuChesne, *Histoire des papes et souverains chefs de l'église* (Paris, 1645), 2:504–5. Enslavement of unlicensed prostitutes was common in Spain at a later date; see Boswell, *The Royal Treasure*, pp. 348–51.

14. Ryan (*St. Peter Damiani*, pp. 154–55) opines that the disfavor was unrelated to the *Liber Gomorrhianus*, rightly pointing out that the principal evidence for Leo's displeasure, Peter's epistle 1.4 (PL, 144:208–9), does not prove any such connection. On the other hand, it is difficult to disagree with an authority like A. Fliche (*La réforme grégorienne* [Paris, 1924–37], 1:178 ff., 231), who maintains that Leo was angered by the work because of the bad press it gave the clergy. This is the more traditional point of view: but cf. Franz Neukirch, *Das Leben des Petrus Damiani* (Göttingen, 1875), p. 55.

Peter in fact had no luck in convincing anyone that gay sexuality deserved hostile attention, although he was extremely influential in the reform movements of the day. The Lateran synod of 1059 (Mansi, 19:897–99) issued a series of canons which responded to Peter's demands for clerical reform on every matter but homosexuality.[15] Pope Alexander II (Anselm of Lucca), an ardent and determined reformer of clerical mores (but also a pupil of Lanfranc, famous for his passionate devotion to younger monks),[16] actually stole the *Liber Gomorrhianus* from Peter and kept it locked up: "He knew that he would not be able to get it from me in any other way, so he handed it over to the abbot of San Salvatore in my presence, requesting that a copy be made. But at night, without my knowledge, he carried it away and locked it in his office. . . . And when he is confronted with this, he laughs and tries to placate me with the unctuous humor of urbanity."[17]

About fifty years later efforts were made to interest another pope—Urban II, the reformer who launched the first crusade—in the case of high-ranking prelates who were well known to be involved in homosexual activities. This effort, although mounted by one of the most prominent churchmen of the day, Ivo of Chartres, failed even more completely than Peter Damian's. Ivo informed the papal legate and the pope himself that Ralph, the archbishop of Tours, had prevailed upon the king of France to install as bishop of Orléans a certain John, whom Ivo knew to be the archbishop's lover (and to have had sexual relations with the king, since the latter had boasted of it to Ivo). In fact John had also shared his favors with the previous bishop of Orléans (Ralph's brother) and was generally so accommodating with his person that he was popularly known as Flora, in reference to a celebrated courtesan of the day.[18] For all this, Ivo, who strenuously opposed the election

15. See L. K. Little, "The Personal Development of Peter Damian," in *Order and Innovation in the Middle Ages* (Princeton, N.J., 1976), esp. pp. 333–34.

16. For Lanfranc and his love for his pupils, especially Saint Anselm, see below, and R. W. Southern, *St. Anselm and His Biographer* (Oxford, 1963).

17. "Sciebat enim hoc se a me aliter impetrare non posse; domno abbati S. Salvatoris me praesente tradidit, praecipiens ut transcriberet. Nocte vero, me nesciente, tulit suisque scriniis insarcivit. . . . Ex his tamen cum expostulatur arridet caputque meum tanquam oleo jocosae urbanitatis suavitate demulcet," epistle 2.6 (PL, 144:270). Little (p. 334) assumes without question that the book at issue is the *Liber Gomorrhianus*, and this view, first expounded by A. Capecelatro (*Storia de San Pier Damiano e del suo tempo* [Florence, 1862], p. 166), seems to me the correct one. Ryan (p. 155) follows Neukirch (p. 55) in arguing that it was some other work of Peter's, but he presents little evidence to support his position and fails to take account of the very loving description of the stolen volume, which seems to me applicable only to the *Liber Gomorrhianus*. (Nor is there any inherent unlikelihood of Peter's having had this work with him in Rome fifteen years after its composition, since he was still trying to interest the papacy in reform in this matter.)

18. For the details, see the *Corréspondance* of Ivo of Chartres, ed. and trans. Jean Leclercq (Paris, 1949), vol. 1, nos. 65–66, and also the rather cautious account in *Gallia Christiana*

of John, seems to have objected much less to his promiscuity than to his youth, and he explained that the principal cause of his opposition was his fear that the young man would prove to be merely a puppet of the archbishop of Tours, giving the latter in effect two bishoprics instead of one.[19]

Urban II was a Cluniac and a reformer; he came from France himself and cared ardently about the state of the church there; he already had reason to dislike Ralph for siding with King Philip of France against the papal legate Hugh; and he had received complaints about Ralph's activities from others, including Geoffrey the abbot of Vendôme, to whom he may have been indebted in some measure for his own position as pope.[20] In spite of this, Urban declined to take any action whatever against the election of Ralph's lover, who was consecrated on March 1, 1098.

The life-style of Archbishop Ralph was widely known but apparently did not diminish his prestige or power: although popular songs were composed about his homosexuality, close friends of popes feared his influence in ecclesiastical circles.[21] Nor did the circumstances surrounding his election and consecration affect John of Orléans adversely; contrary to Ivo's fears, he ruled long and effectively as bishop, retiring with honor almost forty years later.[22]

8.1441–46, and 14.71–72. The incident was briefly noted by Charles Petit-Dutaillis, *La monarchie féodale en France et en Angleterre* (reprint ed., Paris, 1933), p. 90; Auguste Fliche, in *Le règne de Philippe I*[er] (Paris, 1912), mentioned it at greater length, pointing out that the pope declined to intervene against Ralph (pp. 436–37). The incident is distorted by H. C. Lea in *The History of the Inquisition in the Middle Ages* (New York, 1906–7), 1 : 9, who provides erroneous citations (apparently misreading Fliche) and misrepresents the details of the relationships: it was not the previous archbishop of Tours with whom John had had relations but John, Ralph's brother. Both Lea and Ivo probably gave a slanted view in calling John a youth: at the time of his retirement he was described as "aged" ("senex"); he could hardly have been less than twenty-five or so at the time of his consecration, about thirty-five years before. Arno Karlen ("The Homosexual Heresy," p. 50) compounded Lea's distortions, claiming that "two successive Archbishops of Tours were homosexuals." This may be true, but not in this particular case.

19. Ivo, *Corréspondance*, no. 65. This is not surprising in view of Ivo's theological opinions; see pp. 226–27.

20. Geoffrey claimed to have helped Urban recover Rome from the antipope Guibert of Ravenna by selling his own baggage train upon his arrival in the holy city and donating the proceeds to Urban.

21. E.g., Geoffrey of Vendôme, who described Ralph as one who "pene universo mundo clamante, sed nullo adhuc vindicante, multa inhonesta et perversa operatur," epistle 1.17 (PL, 157:57), yet was extremely upset to learn that Ralph had spoken against him publicly and went to considerable lengths to defend himself.

22. *Gallia Christiana* 8.1445–46. Orléans was subsequently the butt of many satires on clerical homosexuality. In one poem of twelfth- or thirteenth-century origin accusing Chartres, Sens, and Paris of being particularly rife with homosexuality, the poet observes, "You are more depraved than all of these, Orléans; / You perish holding the title for this crime"; and "The men of Orléans are first among boy lovers" (Ernst Dümmler, "Briefe und Verse des neunten Jahrhunderts," *Neues Archiv der Gesellschaft für ältere deutsche Geschichtskunde* [1888]: 358–63; discussed at more length below).

The marked disinclination of the papacy to prevent the installation as bishop of a person known in both ecclesiastical and lay circles to engage in homosexual activity, or to take action against his lover, already an archbishop, can scarely be considered the result of carelessness or general indifference: not only did the incident occur during a period of intense effort on the part of the Holy See to upgrade the morality of the clergy, but Urban II was hardly the sort to ignore a matter about which he felt any personal outrage. Moreover, it was only four years later that Pope Paschal II intervened directly to depose a known adulterer, Etienne de Garland, from another French bishopric,[23] while both Ralph and John remained in office.

At almost the exact same time, efforts were made to introduce ecclesiastical legislation in England designating homosexual behavior as sinful. (There had been no statutes against it previously.)[24] The Council of London of 1102 took measures to see that the general public was informed of the impropriety of such acts and insisted that in the future "sodomy" be confessed as a sin.[25] That the average Englishman was not already aware of this is not only implied by the wording of the conciliar edict but stated explicitly by Saint Anselm, the archbishop of Canterbury, in a letter to the archdeacon William, prohibiting publication of the decree and observing that "this sin has hitherto been so public that hardly anyone is embarrassed by it, and many have therefore fallen into it because they were unaware of its seriousness."[26]

It is likely that Anselm's reservations about publishing the prohibition were partly due to his realization that its stipulations regarding the degradation of clerics violated the papal decree of Leo IX forbidding extreme measures of this sort in dealing with homosexuality among the clergy,[27] but he

23. See Fliche, *Le règne*, pp. 441–42.

24. I exclude the incorrect Latin translation of canon 16 of the Council of Ancyra, which was included in some "ecclesiastical laws" enacted under Edgar in the tenth century (*Canones editi sub Edgardo rege* 3.16, in Mansi, 18:525–26), since these seem to have constituted no more than advice to confessors and were not included in Edgar's official royal legislation (*Ancient Laws and Institutes of England* [London, 1840], pp. 109–18). Percival (above, p. 179, n. 33) cites this incorrectly.

25. Mansi, 20.1152. "28. Sodomiticum flagitium facientes, et eos in hoc voluntarie juvantes, in hoc eodem concilio gravi anathemate damnati sunt: donec poenitentia et confessione absolutionem mereantur. Qui vero hoc crimine publicatus fuerit, statutum est, si quidem fuerit persona religiosa, ut ad nullum amplius gradum promoveatur, et si quem habet, ab illo deponatur. Si autem laicus, ut in toto regno Angliae, legali suae conditionis dignitate privetur. Et ne hujus criminis absolutionem, his qui se sub regula vivere non voverunt, aliquis nisi episcopus deinceps facere praesumat."

26. "Considerandum etiam est quia hactenus ita fuit publicum hoc peccatum, ut vix aliquis pro eo erubesceret; et ideo multi magnitudinem ejus nescientes, in illud se praecipitabant," PL, 159:95. Cf. Bailey, pp. 124–25 and following notes.

27. The stated reasons for the suppression of the decree were that it had been drafted hastily and needed revision. For the text of Leo's statement, see app. 2.

may also have had personal reasons for suppressing the council's decree. He was, like Alexander II, a pupil of Lanfranc (his predecessor as archbishop); "love and friendship," in the words of his most illustrious modern biographer, "had been the dominant feature of his early and middle years."[28]

In fact the edict was apparently never published: John of Salisbury, writing fifty years later, invoked only the prohibitions of "the emperor" (presumably Justinian) against "sodomy" and failed to mention any ecclesiastical legislation on the subject.[29] John was a cleric himself and doubtless would have been aware of any injunctions from episcopal councils within memory.[30]

The apparent indifference to homosexual behavior of the institutional church during this century is all the more remarkable because it was precisely during this time that the most strenuous efforts were made to enforce clerical celibacy. The very same Leo IX who evinced such lack of interest in punishing homosexual practices is noted as the first pontiff to take decisive action against the marriage of the clergy, which had been only erratically opposed in the Western church for most of the preceding millennium. It was during this time that the tide turned irreversibly against clerical marriages (the First Lateran Council of 1123 declaring them all invalid). Alexander II, who actually suppressed the *Liber Gomorrhianus*, not only prevented Emperor Henry IV from divorcing his wife but forced his own patron to come to Rome twice to do penance for small infractions of clerical discipline. The hundred years following 1050 in fact represent the zenith of papal moral

28. Southern, *Medieval Humanism*, p. 13. For Anselm's loves, see below.

29. Bailey observes that since a council called at Westminster in 1108 did not make any further enactments against "sodomy," the statute in question "seems to have been immediately successful" (p. 125). Not only does it defy credulity that a practice known in every society could be eliminated in six years by conciliar decree; but Bailey has overlooked the facts that (*a*) the edict—as pointed out by him only lines above—was not promulgated at all, and (*b*) the Council of Westminster (by his own description) "dealt fully with breaches of the rule of chastity." Is one to believe that the clergy went on committing every sin of the flesh but "sodomy" and that somehow the never-published edict of 1102 wiped out this single practice?

30. See *Polycraticus* 3.13 or the English translation by J. B. Pike, *The Frivolities of Courtiers and Footprints of Philosophers* (Minneapolis, 1938), p. 200. The passage is a pastiche of classical quotations and most probably does not represent John's personal feelings about gay relations, which may have been quite different. In the *Metalogicon* (4.42) he describes his relationship with Pope Hadrian IV, whom he visited in Rome, in terms reminiscent of those used by chroniclers of Richard Lion Heart's love affair with Philip of France: "'Cum enim matrem haberet et fratrem uterinum, me quam illos artiori diligebat affectu. Fatebatur etiam publice et secreto quia me pre omnibus mortalibus diligebat. . . . Et cum Romanus Pontifex esset, me in propria mensa gaudebat habere conuiuam; et eundem ciphum et discum sibi et michi uolebat et faciebat, me renitente, esse communem," John of Salisbury, *Metalogicon libri IIII*, ed. Clement Webb (Oxford, 1929), 4:217 (trans. Daniel McGarry in *The Metalogicon of John of Salisbury* [Berkeley, 1962], pp. 274–75).

prestige and a period of unparalleled spiritual reform and vigor within Roman Catholicism. It can hardly be argued that indifference to gay sexuality was simply the consequence of apathy.

On the other hand, it might be argued that there was more than a coincidental relation between gay sexuality and some of the reforms effected during this century. Contemporaries, at least, were quick to note that gay priests would be more willing than heterosexual ones to enforce prohibitions against clerical marriage.[31] A satire against a reforming bishop specifically accuses him of hostility to clerical marriage because of his own homosexual disposition:

> The man who occupies this [episcopal] seat is Ganymedier than Ganymede.
> Consider why he excludes the married from the clergy:
> He does not care for the pleasures of a wife.[32]

There is some evidence of a power struggle between gay and married clergy over whose predilections would be stigmatized. A married cleric demands of the hierarchy,

> You who pass new laws and enact harsh statutes
> To wound us, first correct that evil
> Which is more seriously damaging and further from the law.
> Why do you fail to afflict the sodomites with any serious penalty?
> This type of sickness (through which a somber end might come upon the
>   race)
> Ought by rights to be rooted out first.[33]

Satirical literature of the time is filled with references to gay priests, more apt, in the phrase of Walther of Châtillon, "to love gods than goddesses."[34] Even

---

31. See the long poem "We Married Clergy" in app. 2 below. The monastic clergy also fell under suspicion: see Peter the Venerable *De miraculis* 1.14 (PL, 189:878).

32. From a manuscript in Zurich of uncertain provenance, published in J. Werner, *Beiträge zur Kunde der lateinischen Literatur des Mittelalters* (Aarau, 1905), p. 26:
Qui sedet hac sede ganimedior est Ganimede;
Cur uxoratos a clero separat omnes,
Audiat: uxoris non amat officium.

33. In *The Anglo-Latin Satirical Poets and Epigrammatists*, ed. Thomas Wright (London, 1872), 2:209:
Qui nova paras et leges ponis amaras,
Et sic nos mordes, prius illas corrige sordes,
Que gravius ledunt et plus a lege recedunt!
Quid pena vitas urgere gravi sodomitas?
Hec species morbi (qua mors gravis imminet orbi)
Si bene res isset, prius extirpanda fuisset.

34. See *Moralisch-satirische Gedichte Walters von Châtillon, aus deutschen, englischen, französischen und italienischen Handschriften*, ed. Karl Strecker (Heidelberg, 1920), p. 102.

popes were not above such accusations, and in some areas the mere fact of having taken orders seems to have rendered one liable to the suspicion of being a "sodomite."

Some justification for these suspicions is eloquently provided by the astounding amount of gay literature which issued from the pens of clerics during this period. Although these writings varied in tone from the grossly sensual to the loftily idealistic, almost all were composed by priests and bishops in good standing, as orthodox as the opponents of gay love. Most of the writings of such individuals dealt with spiritual and theological matters; only a few wrote mostly secular poetry. But almost all were intellectually influential, and some were among the major Christian thinkers of the day.

This extraordinary flowering of gay love was not limited to expressions of personal sentiment or experience. The same period witnessed the first efforts to formulate a theology which could incorporate expressions of gay feelings into the most revered Christian life-style, monasticism. Saint Anselm, prior of Bec, the most influential monastery of the period, and later archbishop of Canterbury, was probably the most imposing intellectual figure of his day. It was he who brought the tradition of passionate friendship among monks into the limelight of medieval society (as he also prevented the promulgation of the first antigay legislation in England).

Although Anselm was devoted to the monastic ideal of celibacy, he had extraordinary emotional relationships, first with Lanfranc and then with a succession of his own pupils. He frequently addressed letters to his "beloved lover" ("*dilecto dilectori*," e.g., epp. 1.4, 14, 75), and many of his epistles strikingly echo the passions of Saint Paulinus and Walafrid.

> Wherever you go my love follows you, and wherever I remain my desire embraces you. . . . How then could I forget you? He who is imprinted on my heart like a seal on wax—how could he be removed from my memory? Without your saying a word I know that you love me, and without my saying a word, you know that I love you. [Ep. 1.4; PL, 158:1068–69]

> What will a letter of mine show you that you do not already know, my other soul? Go into the innermost chamber[35] of your heart and look at the devotion of your true love; then you will know the love of your true friend. [Ep. 1.14; PL, 158:1079–80]

Erotic interest appears not to have been the primary component of most of Anselm's relationships, and it was probably the strength of his character that

---

35. Literally, "Go to your bedroom": "Intra in cubiculum tuum"; a biblical paraphrase (see Matt. 6:6).

invested such passion in relations which might have seemed casual to an outside observer.[36]

On the other hand, some of his epistolary output appears erotic by any standards. The expression of his sorrow at one Gilbert's absence could pass for a letter between lovers in any society:

> Brother Anselm to Dom Gilbert, brother, friend, beloved lover . . . sweet to me, sweetest friend, are the gifts of your sweetness, but they cannot begin to console my desolate heart for its want of your love. Even if you sent every scent of perfume, every glitter of metal, every precious gem, every texture of cloth, still it could not make up to my soul for this separation unless it returned the separated other half.
>
> The anguish of my heart just thinking about this bears witness, as do the tears dimming my eyes and wetting my face and the fingers writing this.
>
> You recognized, as I do now, my love for you, but I did not. Our separation from each other has shown me how much I loved you; a man does not in fact have knowledge of good and evil unless he has experienced both. Not having experienced your absence, I did not realize how sweet it was to be with you and how bitter to be without you.
>
> But you have gained from our very separation the company of someone else, whom you love no less—or even more—than me; while I have lost you, and there is no one to take your place. You are thus enjoying your consolation, while nothing is left to me but heartbreak.[37]

Because of his personal prestige and importance and the very large numbers of persons touched by his affections, Anselm's version of monastic love was more influential than the erotic friendships which had previously appeared in small literary circles or the more widespread affections which had flowered and passed away unrecorded among anonymous monks and nuns. This love was not divorced from spirituality; on the contrary, Anselm combined his theological insights with his human affections: "From these friendships, and the discussions which cemented them, came the theological treatises."[38]

---

36. Brian McGuire ("Love, Friendship, and Sex in the Eleventh Century: The Experience of Anselm," *Studia theologica* 28 [1974]: 11–52) concludes that Anselm was not gay but apparently means only that he lacked an "obsession with male sexuality."

37. Epistle 1.75; PL, 158:1144–45. The last few sentences of this letter rely heavily on paronomastic uses of Latin which cannot be rendered accurately in English.

38. Southern, *Medieval Humanism*, p. 13.

Many twelfth-century clerics, monastic and secular, were involved in and wrote about passionate friendships like Anselm's. Some of these—e.g., Saint Bernard of Clairvaux, doubtless the most influential religious leader of the day—were certainly not aware of any erotic elements in their feelings. Others, however, were clearly consciously romantic. A twelfth-century manuscript from the monastery of Tegernsee in Bavaria includes at least two distinctly erotic verse letters from one religious woman to another.[39] The first is highly reminiscent of Anselm's lament over his absent friend: "I am weighed down with grief, / For I find nothing / I would compare to your love, / Which was sweeter than milk and honey, / And by comparison to which the gleam of gold and silver seems tawdry." But the writer goes further than Anselm in speaking of the intimacy and exclusiveness of their relationship, declaring that "it is you alone I have chosen for my heart"; "I love you above all else, / You alone are my love and desire"; / "Like a turtledove who has lost her mate / And stands forever on the barren branch, / So I grieve ceaselessly / Until I enjoy your love again."

The next letter, perhaps the outstanding example of medieval lesbian literature, deserves to be quoted in its entirety:

To G., her singular rose,
From A.—the bonds of precious love.
What is my strength, that I should bear it,
That I should have patience in your absence?
Is my strength the strength of stones,
That I should await your return?
I, who grieve ceaselessly day and night
Like someone who has lost a hand or a foot?
Everything pleasant and delightful
Without you seems like mud underfoot.
I shed tears as I used to smile,
And my heart is never glad.
When I recall the kisses you gave me,
And how with tender words you caressed my little breasts,
I want to die
Because I cannot see you.
What can I, so wretched, do?
Where can I, so miserable, turn?
If only my body could be entrusted to the earth

39. Published in Dronke, *Medieval Latin*, 2:476–82: nos. 6 and 7 are clearly written by and to women; 5, similar in tone, is addressed to a woman, but the author's gender is not explicit. Dronke characterizes 6 and 7 as "love letters" and considers that 7 "seems to presuppose a passionate physical relationship" (p. 482).

Until your longed-for return;
Or if passage could be granted me as it was to Habakkuk,
So that I might come there just once
To gaze on my beloved's face—
Then I should not care if it were the hour of death itself.
For no one has been born into the world
So lovely and full of grace,
Or who so honestly
And with such deep affection loves me.
I shall therefore not cease to grieve
Until I deserve to see you again.
Well has a wise man said that it is a great sorrow for a man to be without
    that
Without which he cannot live.
As long as the world stands
You shall never be removed from the core of my being.
What more can I say?
Come home, sweet love!
Prolong your trip no longer;
Know that I can bear your absence no longer.
Farewell.
Remember me.[40]

But it was Saint Aelred of Rievaulx who gave love between those of the same gender its most profound and lasting expression in a Christian context. Aelred was the abbot of the Cistercian monastery of Rievaulx in England, a friend of King David of Scotland (the son of Saint Margaret), and adviser to Henry II of England. In his treatises, *The Mirror of Charity* and *On Spiritual Friendship*,[41] Aelred developed a concept of Christian friendship which, in its

40. Text in Dronke, pp. 480–81; readers may wish to compare the author's translation with Dronke's.
41. The texts edited in the series Corpus Christianorum (*Aelredi Rievallensis opera omnia*, ed. A. Hoste and H. Talbot [Turnhout, 1971]) are preferable to those in PL, vol. 195. The *De spirituali amicitia* is also edited with French translation by J. Dubois in *L'amitié spirituelle* (Paris, 1948). Two older English translations (M. F. Jerome, 1948; H. Talbot, 1942) have been superseded by Mary Laker's *Spiritual Friendship*, Cistercian Fathers Series, no. 5 (Washington, D.C., 1974), with an introduction by Douglass Roby, including a chapter on "Aelred in the Tradition of Monastic Friendship." For the *Speculum caritatis* there is only the incomplete and bowdlerized (see n. 58 below) version of A. Walker and G. Webb, *The Mirror of Charity* (London, 1962), and a rather arbitrary paraphrase of bk. 1 in E. Colledge, *The Medieval Mystics of England* (London, 1962), pp. 105–21. For Aelred's life, see the biography by his disciple Walter Daniel, trans. F. M. Powicke, *The Life of Aelred, Abbot of Rievaulx* (London, 1969), esp. chap. 6; and Roby, "Early Medieval Attitudes toward Homosexuality," pp. 69–70.

emphasis on human affection, surpassed any earlier theological statements and explicitly expressed in prose much of the implicit correlation between human and spiritual love long characteristic of clerical love poetry. It was Aelred who specifically posited friendship and human love as the basis of monastic life as well as a means of approaching divine love, who developed and promulgated a systematic approach to the more difficult problems of intense friendships between monks. In his treatise on spiritual friendship Aelred remarks that "he who abides in friendship abides in God, and God in him" and represents another character in the same dialogue as stating that "God is friendship."[42]

There can be little question that Aelred was gay and that his erotic attraction to men was a dominant force in his life. This was true, by his own account, from the beginning of his emotional life: "While I was still a schoolboy, the charm of my friends greatly captivated me, so that among the foibles and failings with which that age is fraught, my mind surrendered itself completely to emotion and devoted itself to love. Nothing seemed sweeter or nicer or more worthwhile than to love and be loved."[43] For a period, at least, Aelred even gave himself over to casual sexuality; he later referred to it as the time when "a cloud of desire arose from the lower drives of the flesh and the gushing spring of adolescence," and "the sweetness of love and the impurity of lust combined to take advantage of the inexperience of my youth."[44] That these experiences involved overt sexuality is unquestionable: in writing to his sister Aelred speaks of this as the time when she held on to her virtue and he lost his.[45]

Apparently settling down to a more stable relationship, Aelred was still

42. "Dicamne de amicitia quod amicus Jesu Joannes de charitate commemorat: Deus amicitia est? Aelredus: Inusitatum quidem hoc, nec ex Scripturis habet auctoritatem: quod tamen sequitur de charitate, amicitiae profecto dare non dubito, quoniam: Qui manet in amicitia, in Deo manet, et Deus in eo," *De spirituali amicitia* 1 (Hoste and Talbot, p. 301; PL, 195:669–70).

43. Ibid., prologue (Hoste and Talbot, p. 287; PL, 195:659): "Cum adhuc puer essem scholis, et sociorum meorum me gratia plurimum delectaret, et inter mores et vitia quibus aetas illa periclitari solet, totam se mea mens dedit affectui, et deuouit amori; ita ut nihil mihi dulcius, nihil iucundius, nihil utilius quam amari et amare uideretur."

44. *De institutione inclusarum* 32 (Hoste and Talbot, p. 674): "Exhalaretur nebula libidinis ex limosa concupiscentia carnis et scatebra pubertatis"; "Conuenientesque in unum affectionis suauitas et cupiditatis impuritas rapiebant imbecillem adhuc aetatem meam." There are references to Aelred's voluptuous past scattered throughout his writings; his attitudes toward his previous life-style range from detachment to hostility and are not susceptible of easy generalization. His conversion to monastic life is recorded in the *Speculum caritatis* 1.28 (not translated by Walker and Webb but available in Colledge, pp. 119–20).

45. "Quam miser ego tunc qui meam pudicitiam perdidi, tam beata tu, cuius uirginitatem gratia diuina protexit," *De institutione inclusarum* 32 (Hoste and Talbot, p. 674). Cf. Daniel, p. 76.

not spiritually satisfied and for a long time felt torn between his desire to devote himself more completely to God and his attachment to the world, particularly his love for his family and "most of all, the knot of one particular friendship, sweeter to me than all the sweet things of my life."[46] Eventually he decided to abandon his other loves for God, not because they were less good or satisfying but because they could not last forever, whereas his relationship with God could.

Having accepted the habit of monastic life, Aelred accepted with it the vow of celibacy and subsequently considered overt sexuality off limits to him.[47] This applied equally to gay and nongay sexuality, which he always discusses as complementary, although he seems to be aware that there is more popular prejudice against the former.[48]

But celibacy did not alter Aelred's emotional life, nor did his difficult decision to abandon worldly pleasures incite him to the sort of antiphysical reaction which earlier Christians like Augustine (whom he much admired) had adopted. He fell in love with two monks of his order. When he first entered the order he noticed one Simon ("The rules of our order forbade us to speak, but his face spoke to me, his bearing spoke to me, his silence talked," *De speculo caritatis* 1.34.107 [Hoste and Talbot, p. 60]),[49] and their friendship was the mainstay of his life until Simon's death. Although at first tormented by jealousy because on his deathbed Simon had called for another monk, Aelred eventually poured out his heartbroken grief in a paean of devotion to his beloved, without whom, he lamented, he could hardly be said to live (ibid., pp. 58–65).

Aware that the intensity of his passions might suggest a less than spiritual relationship, Aelred either considered such concern beneath comment or simply did not care. "But some may judge by my tears that my love was too

46. "Vinciebat amor sanguinis mei, stringebant uincula socialis gratiae, maxime nodus cuiusdam amicitiae, dulcis mihi super omnes dulcedines illius vitae meae," *De speculo caritatis* 1.28 (Hoste and Talbot, p. 47), translated in Colledge, pp. 120–21.

47. Aelred's more personal writings (e.g., the *Oratio pastoralis*) are filled with his own struggle against carnal desire, which he carried on with fasting and the aid of a bath he had constructed near a spring so that it would be filled with icy water and "quench the heat . . . of every vice" (Daniel, p. 25).

48. "Nec sic hoc dictum aestimes, quasi non vir sine muliere, aut mulier sine viro possit foedari, cum detestandum illud scelus, quo vir in virum, vel femina in feminam, omnibus flagitiis damnabilius judicetur" (*De vita eremitica* 22; PL, 32:1459). That Aelred himself considers sexual license to be gender blind is manifest throughout this treatise, where gay and nongay sexuality are casually juxtaposed as equal threats to celibacy (e.g., 26: "Inter pueros et puellas conversari et non tentari"; 32: "Sed vitiorum materias gulam comprimamus, requiem corporis, feminarum et effeminatorum familiaritatem atque convictum intra metas necessarias cohibeamus.").

49. "Simul quidem loqui Ordinis nostri prohibebat auctoritas, sed loquebatur mihi aspectus eius, loquebatur mihi incessus eius, loquebatur mihi ipsum silentium eius."

carnal. Let them think what they wish. . . . Others see what is done outwardly; they cannot perceive what I suffer inwardly" (1.34.112 [p. 163]).[50] After the death of Simon, Aelred became attached to a younger monk and left a careful record of the development of their love, which, in contrast to his passion for Simon, grew slowly and cautiously

> until we attained that stage at which we had but one mind and one soul, to will and not to will alike. . . . For I deemed my heart in a fashion his, and his mine, and he felt in like manner towards me. . . . He was the refuge of my spirit, the sweet solace of my griefs, whose heart of love received me when fatigued from labors, whose counsel refreshed me when plunged in sadness and grief. . . . What more is there, then, that I can say? Was it not a foretaste of blessedness thus to love and thus to be loved?[51]

In discussing love with his monks, Aelred stressed that friendships could not simply be intellectual. "Feelings," he observed, "are not ours to command. We are attracted to some against our will, while towards others we can never experience a spontaneous affection."[52] Neither attraction nor reason alone should constitute love but, rather, the conjunction of both. Physical beauty was in Aelred's view a completely legitimate inspiration of love, as long as it did not obscure a vicious character.[53] Carnal relationships were not desirable for monks committed to a life of celibacy, but even in these Aelred could see some good: they did afford the joy felt by lovers,[54] and they could be used as stepping-stones to a loftier relationship involving the two lovers and God.[55] Even for celibates Aelred did not discourage physical

50. "Sed forte judicant nunc aliqui fortes lacrimas meas, nimis carnalem existimantes amorem meum. Interpretentur eas, ut uolent; . . . vident alii quid exterius agitur, quid interius patiar non attendunt."

51. *De spirituali amicitia*, 3.124–27; trans. Laker, pp. 120–29. Aelred himself contrasted the two relationships: the first, he observed, was based mainly on emotion and the second on reason (ibid.); but this does not mean that reason was lacking in the first or emotion in the second.

52. I have cited the translation by Walker and Webb (pp. 109–10) as clearly conveying the idea, although not the literal tenor, of Aelred's comment here. The text has "Nam cum affectus isti nequaquam in nostro arbitrio collocentur cum quibusdam aliquando inuisissimi moueamur, nec quoddam, etiamsi uelimus, experiri ualemus," *De speculo caritatis* 3.19.47 (Hoste and Talbot, pp. 127–28).

53. Ibid. 3.27.65 (Hoste and Talbot, p. 136): "De affectu carnali, quod nec omnino respuendus, nec plene sit admittendus" (3.25, in Walker and Webb, p. 119).

54. "Since in the sort of friendship which lust defiles . . . such great joy is experienced," *De spirituali amicitia* 1.36 (Hoste and Talbot, p. 295; "cum in hac tali amicitia, quam uel libido commaculat . . . tanta ac talis experiatur dulcedo"; cf. Laker, p. 59).

55. "This type of friendship is carnal and most common among adolescents. . . . Yet excepting trifles and lies, it should be allowed as long as there is no element of dishonesty in it, in the hope of more abundant grace and as the beginning of a holier friendship," ibid.

expressions of affection. As abbot he allowed his monks to hold hands and otherwise express affection, unlike other abbots who, in the words of Aelred's admiring biographer, "if a monk takes a brother's hand in his own, . . . demand his cowl, strip and expel him." [56]

Aelred's idealization of love between men was a dramatic break with the traditions of monasticism, which had urged since the time of Basil and Benedict that particular friendships of any sort—especially passionate ones— were a threat to monastic harmony and asceticism. Although his views were enormously popular in the twelfth century—he composed his *Mirror of Love* for Saint Bernard—he was conscious of their novelty. But Aelred felt he could invoke an authority higher than that of Benedict, Basil, or even his hero Augustine, in justifying the sort of love which had dominated his life. That authority was the example of Jesus and John, and in giving his description of the perfect love, Aelred even refers to their relationship as a "marriage."

> It is in fact a great consolation in this life to have someone to whom you can be united in the intimate embrace of the most sacred love; in whom your spirit can rest; to whom you can pour out your soul; in whose delightful company, as in a sweet consoling song, you can take comfort in the midst of sadness; in whose most welcome friendly bosom you can find peace in so many worldly setbacks; to whose loving heart you can open as freely as you would to yourself your innermost thoughts; through whose spiritual kisses—as by some medicine—you are cured of the sickness of care and worry; who weeps with you in sorrow, rejoices with you in joy, and wonders with you in doubt; whom you draw by the fetters of love into that inner room of your soul, so that though the body is absent, the spirit is there, and you can confer all alone, the more secretly, the more delightfully; with whom you can rest, just the two of you, in the sleep of peace away from the noise of the world, in the embrace of love, in the kiss of unity, with the sweetness of the Holy Spirit flowing over you; to whom you so join and unite yourself that you mix soul with soul, and two become one.
>
> We can enjoy this in the present with those whom we love not merely with our minds but with our hearts; for some are joined to us more intimately and passionately than others in the lovely bond of

---

3.87 (Hoste and Talbot, pp. 335–36: "Amicitia haec carnalium est et maxime adolescen-tium. . . . Quae tamen, exceptis nugis et mendaciis, si nulla intercesserit inhonestas, spe uberioris gratiae toleranda est, quasi quaedam amicitiae sanctioris principia"). Cf. Laker, pp. 113–14; "dishonorable" for "inhonestas" is probably misleading; the juxtaposition of "mendaciis" suggests that the issue is actually deceit, not "impurity."

56. Daniel, p. 40.

spiritual friendship. And lest this sort of sacred love should seem improper to anyone, Jesus himself, in everything like us, patient and compassionate with us in every matter, transfigured it through the expression of his own love: for he allowed one, not all, to recline on his breast as a sign of his special love, so that the virgin head was supported in the flowers [sic] of the virgin breast, and the closer they were, the more copiously did the fragrant secrets of the heavenly marriage impart the sweet smell of spiritual chrism to their virgin love.[57]

Although all the disciples were blessed with the sweetness of the greatest love of the most holy master, nonetheless he conceded as a privilege to one alone this symbol of a more intimate love, that he should be called the "disciple whom Jesus loved."[58]

In marked contrast to the theological innovations of Aelred in regard to homosexual attraction, the development of theological argument among those hostile to gay sexuality came to a standstill during the hundred years between 1050 and 1150. Ivo of Chartres gathered together nearly 4,000 ecclesiastical opinions in his *Decretum* in an effort to establish standard orthodox positions on all matters of Christian morals and ecclesiastical discipline. Of these, four might be considered to have some relation to homosexuality in a modern context,[59] but only one had been intended originally as a comment on homosexual behavior, and probably none were thought by Ivo to address gay sexuality. A passage from the Council of Elvira about "violating boys" was clearly understood by Ivo's readers as a reference to the unlawful seduction of minor children, as is evidenced by Gratian's substituting for it a statute from Roman civil law even more specific in this regard,[60] and two of the three passages mentioning "unnatural" use had been written and traditionally used in the context of

---

57. "Ut uirgineum caput uirginei pectoris floribus fulciretur, ac thalami caelestis odorifera secreta fragrantiam spiritalium unguentorum uirgineis affectibus quanto uicinius, tanto copiosius instillarent," *De speculo caritatis* 3.110.11 (Hoste and Talbot, p. 159). "Marriage bed," or by analogy "marriage" or "marriage contract," are the only possible translations for "thalamus" in twelfth-century Latin.

58. Ibid. 3.109–10 (Hoste and Talbot, p. 159). Cf. Walker and Webb, pp. 139–40, where the language of this passage is considerably softened, and the striking sentence about the "heavenly marriage" is omitted altogether.

59. Ivo of Chartres *Decretum* 9.105, 106, 109, 115 (PL, 161 : 685–688).

60. Ibid. 9.109 (PL, 161 : 686), from the Council of Elvira of 305. Gratian substituted for this a passage by the imperial jurist Paulus, without question addressed to the corruption of minors (*Decretum* 2.33.3.1.15): "Qui puero stuprum (abducto ab eo, vel corrupto comite) persuaserit, aut mulierem, puellamve interpellaverit, quidve impudicitiae gratia fecerit, donum praebuerit, pretiumve, quo is persuadeat, dederit, perfecto flagitio, punitur capite, imperfecto, insulam deportatur. Corrupti comites summo supplicio afficiuntur." Cf. 2.33.3.1.12, also from Roman law and also applicable to either gay or nongay offenses.

heterosexual relationships.[61] Only a brief statement from the *Confessions* of Augustine could be assumed to refer to homosexuality in general, but when Ivo came to organize the data in his *Decretum* into a systematic scheme of canon law (the *Panormia*), he omitted even this, leaving no reference to homosexual relations whatever, although sexual incontinence of various sorts was discussed at considerable length.[62]

In the later *Decretum* of Gratian (ca. 1140), the foundation of the canon law of the Roman Catholic church, Ivo's texts were inserted into a discussion of adultery[63] and were almost certainly intended to be applied to heterosexual relations only, as both Gratian's own organization and contemporary glosses demonstrate.[64]

Although some of the canonists' materials were later used in ecclesiastical laws against homosexual relations, it is quite clear that the compilers themselves did not understand them to be so directed. This seems extremely curious in light of the generally thorough and comprehensive coverage of their collections, the prevalence of homosexual behavior among their contemporaries, and the specific attention paid to the question by earlier decretists. Canonists before and after them specifically distinguished homosexual acts from "unnatural" heterosexual ones, and it does not seem likely that this distinction could not have occurred to them. Moreover, it is certain that Ivo at least could not have been ignorant of gay sexuality, since he wrote to the pope about the sexual relationship between two bishops well known to him. One cannot but consider the possibility that twelfth-century decretists consciously omitted discussion of an issue which they either considered of little moral import or better left vague in light of contemporary mores.

Indeed, whether it was deliberate or not, the approach to sexuality adopted by early twelfth-century theologians effectively "decriminalized" homosexual relations altogether. When Peter Lombard, writing at the height

61. Especially by Hincmar. They are cited by Ivo as Ambrose 1 *De Abrahamo* 6; Augustine *Confessions* 3.8 and *Contra Julianum* 5, but for the latter cf. the corrector's comments in the *Decretum* of Gratian (*Corpus juris canonici* 2.32.7.14).

62. E.g., the incontinence of priests (PL, 161 : 84–115), lapses of clerics in general (ibid., 133–52), sexual sins relating to marriage (the whole of bk. 4). Note that previous canonists had regularly incorporated at least a discussion of "sodomy" in all discussions of marital sexuality.

63. In *Corpus juris canonici* 2.32.7.12 (Ivo 9.115), 13 (Ivo 9.105), 14 (Ivo 9.106); cf. n. 60 above.

64. E.g., in the *Summa* of Alexander III (*Summa Magistri Rolandi mit Anhang incerti auctoris quaestiones*), ed. Friedrich Thaner (Innsbruck, 1874), where the discussion of Causa 32, Quaestio 7, concerns heterosexual marriage exclusively (Thaner, pp. 183–88), or the *Summa* of Paucapalea (*Die Summa des Paucapalea über das Decretum Gratiani*), ed. Johann von Schulte (Giessen, 1890), pp. 128–29.

of positive attitudes toward gay people, composed what was to become the standard moral text for all of Europe's Catholic universities for the next century, he made no mention of gay sexuality whatever. "The sin against nature" is discussed in his extensive section dealing with marriage and adultery and is defined as the illicit use of a woman by a man, with reference to Augustine's curious principle that such actions were more reprehensible between husband and wife than between a married man and a prostitute.[65]

Despite the preponderance of ecclesiastical literature on the subject, it does not seem likely that the twelfth-century changes in attitude toward gay sexuality were limited to churchmen. The clergy were by and large the only literate class during the Middle Ages. Many individual nobles and some commoners could read and write—especially during this century—but their number was so insignificant compared with the number of literate clerics that statistical considerations alone would favor an extreme disproportion between surviving clerical and lay comments on any particular subject. There is no more reason to assume, on the basis of literary evidence, that only clerics felt or expressed homosexual feelings than to infer, on the basis of the same evidence, that only the clergy experienced delight at the approach of spring.

Clerical literature itself, moreover, suggests that gay love was by no means limited to the ranks of the ordained. Hildebert of Lavardin said specifically of homosexuality that "no walk of life escapes it."[66] Walther of Châtillon observed that in his day "princes turned this crime into a habit."[67] Charges of homosexuality or comments about it occur in purely secular literature such as the *Lai de Lanval*; in the *Roman d'Enéas* both Lavinia and her mother accuse Aeneas of homosexuality.[68] It hardly seems likely that in a society which tolerated open homosexual relations among the highest-ranking prelates of the church there should have been any greater hostility to or less frequent occurrence of gay sexuality among the laity.

65. Peter Lombard, *Sententiarum libri quatuor* 4.38.4 (PL, 192:933). The "sentences" were not only memorized by students of moral theology but had to be commented on in most universities as a precondition for obtaining a license to teach. There are, as a result, commentaries on the "sentences" by almost every major late medieval theologian.

66. "Nullaque conditio cessat ab hoc vitio," Barthélémy Hauréau, *Les mélanges poétiques d'Hildebert de Lavardin* (Paris, 1882), p. 69.

67. "Principes in habitum verterunt hoc crimen," Strecker, pp. 69–70. The same quatrain is attributed to Walther Mapes: see *The Latin Poems Commonly attributed to Walter Mapes*, ed. Thomas Wright (London, 1841), p. 161, lines 41–44. The stanza immediately preceding this one, no. 10 in Mapes's poem, corresponds to the second stanza of Walther of Châtillon's poem. Neither editor comments specifically on the borrowing, and the two poems are otherwise independent.

68. For a discussion see Edmond Faral, "Ovide et quelques autres sources du *Roman d'Enéas*," *Romania* 40 (1911): pp. 212–13 and n. 1. See also Alwin Schultz, *Das höfische Leben zur Zeit der Minnesänger* (Leipzig, 1879–80), 1:456, n. 1.

Indeed some of the most prominent laymen of the age were noted for their homosexual interests, although it cannot be assumed that their reputations were in every case deserved. Sexual foibles involving either gender are favorite sources of humor or derogation for public figures, and one must exercise extreme caution in assessing accounts of homosexual behavior on the part of controversial medieval monarchs or nobles.[69] Many medieval Latin writers shared with their literary ancestors the Romans a tendency to express disapproval of unconventional behavior in terms of gender identity and sexual vice. At least since Freeman first suggested it, for instance, William Rufus (r. 1087–1100) has been commonly assumed to have been homosexual on the basis of numerous comments about his private life in contemporary chronicles, which speak of "effeminacy," "shameful behavior," "moral abandon," "immorality," a "vicious life-style," etc.[70]

It is true that monkish chroniclers after William Rufus unanimously charge him with addiction to sins of the flesh and claim that he introduced into England sins which had not previously been common ("Any sin which had only sprouted before now blossomed fully, and those which had not occurred previously now appeared"), but only Ordericus Vitalis mentions homosexual relations specifically, and he does so only in passing.[71] His

69. What is one to make, for example, of the comments of Giraldus Cambrensis about Richard's chancellor, William Longchamp, bishop of Ely? It is quite obvious that the chronicler hated the Norman bishop intensely, largely on the basis of his national origin. He recounts how Longchamp used "English" as a term of ultimate derogation, saying, "I should be worse than an Englishman if I did such and such" (*De vita Galfredi archiepiscopi Eboracensis* 2, in *Opera*, ed. J. S. Brewer [London, 1873], 4:424); and the sort of tales he relates about the bishop's character are so caricatured and exaggerated that one is inclined to reject them out of hand. Of his homosexuality Giraldus claims that the more outrageous the sexual act, the more William liked it; that he made homosexuality so common that heterosexuals were ridiculed at court—"If you don't do what courtiers do, what are you doing in court?" ("Si ea quae sunt curiae non agis, quid in curia quaeris?" ibid., p. 423); that a woman brought her daughter to him dressed as and trained to imitate a young man, but when the bishop undressed her and found she was a girl he would not touch her ("although she was very beautiful and ripe for the pleasures of the marriage bed," ibid.); and that his reputation was so great that even descendants of his family were suspected of homosexuality. Quite possibly William was gay: it is striking that Giraldus does not accuse him of every sort of sexual license, as many English chroniclers do in denigrating Normans, but insists only on his homosexuality. The account as it stands, however, is obviously an effort to besmirch his memory and cannot be taken at face value. If homosexuality was popular at court, it was not the doing of Longchamp alone.

70. E. A. Freeman, *The Reign of William Rufus* (Oxford, 1882), 1:157, 2:502–3. App. G in vol. 2 collects by topic all of the unflattering references to William in Latin chronicles. Except where otherwise noted, all subsequent material is taken from this collection. For the words translated in the text, see esp. pp. 491 ff. C. Brooke's comments on William's sexuality in *The Saxon and Norman Kings* (London, 1963), p. 179, are sensible.

71. "Tunc effeminati passim in orbe dominabantur, indisciplinate debacchabantur, Sodomiticisque spurcitiis foedi catamitae, flammis urendi, turpiter abutebantur," *Historia, ecclesiastica* 3.8.10 (PL, 188:587). There is no doubt what Ordericus Vitalis means here,

principal objection is to the new styles of clothing introduced at William's court, to the outlandish shoe styles devised by the courtiers, and to their excessive grooming. These are the reasons for labeling the court "effeminate" and "debauched" by all of the writers,[72] and the capriciousness of their antipathy is amply illustrated by the fact that they object equally to beards and long hair, the former of which could hardly be considered "effeminate." Nor did the fact that the designer of one elaborate shoe style (Count Fulk) devised the footwear to disguise a congenital deformity spare him from charges of "immorality" in dress.[73]

Where the chroniclers comment specifically on William's sexual excesses they do not mention homosexuality; he is said to have "committed adultery with violence and impunity" and to have been "given insatiably to obscene fornication and frequent adultery."[74] His followers—the ones Vitalis claims were "effeminate catamites"—are charged with violating the wives and daughters of the Anglo-Saxon nobility; no mention is made of sons.[75]

Against such testimony the charges of Ordericus Vitalis cannot be trusted. He seems to have been obsessed with homosexuality and imputed it to most prominent Normans. In the case of William Atheling, son and heir of Henry I, for instance, although his charges are repeated by other historians, they must be viewed with suspicion (whether or not William was in fact gay). Henry of Huntingdon, William of Nangis, Gervase of Canterbury, and numerous modern historians[76] have all claimed that William's tragic drowning after the sinking of his ship, the *Blanche-Nef*, was the result of God's judgment on the boatload of "sodomites" and "intemperate and foppish youths." This charge is questionable not only on historical grounds[77] but on

---

although the feminine gender of *catamite* is provocative: it is invariably masculine in Latin. In general it seems that Ordericus did not attach very specific connotations to "sodomiticus," however: in 8.4 he refers to "the Venus of Sodom" but seems to clarify it by explaining further that "maritalem thorum publice polluebant adulteria." It would be difficult to demonstrate that "adulterium" here refers to homosexuality.

72. See Freeman, 2:499–502. Some of the charges against the Normans, such as their spending the night drinking and the day sleeping, have an extremely familiar ring to them: see the comments of Boadicea in chap. 3.

73. *Historia ecclesiastica* 3.8.10 (PL, 188:586); discussed sanely by Freeman, 2:502.

74. Henry of Huntingdon: "Adulteria violenter et impune committerent" (quoted in Freeman, 2:495); Ordericus Vitalis: "Obscoenis fornicationibus et frequentibus moechiis inexplebiliter inhaesit" (*Historica ecclesiastica* 3.8.10; cf. other similar comments on these pages).

75. Eadmer, quoted by Freeman, 2:499.

76. E.g., Schultz, 1:454, n. 3.

77. It is refuted specifically by Matthew Paris; and Henry of Huntingdon, one of the originators of the tale, contradicts himself on the point in another work. See *Dictionary of National Biography*, s.v. "William, Son of Henry I." Bailey discusses the incident, but somewhat unclearly, and he overlooks the presence of Henry (pp. 125–26).

grounds of common sense as well. William was in fact not traveling alone on the ill-fated voyage; he was in the party of his father, who had embarked at the same time in an accompanying vessel. Is it likely that William could have loaded his boat with such obvious "sodomites" under his father's watchful eye or that, if they were not "obvious" to his father, they would have been so to the chronicler who was not even present?[78]

Moreover, William actually survived the sinking of the ship, having been put into the water in a small vessel, and nearly reached shore when he decided to go back for his sister. The small boat was then so overloaded with frantic survivors that it sank. If any "moral" cause could be assigned to William's death, it would have to be fraternal concern.

In contrast, it is difficult to question the unanimity and equanimity with which chroniclers allude to the sexual orientation of Richard Lion Heart, the crusading king whose valor became the symbol of chivalric idealism. As a young man Richard had fallen in love with the king of France.

> Richard, [then] duke of Aquitaine, son of the king of England,
> remained with Philip, the king of France, who so honored him for so
> long that they ate every day at the same table and from the same dish,
> and at night their beds did not separate them. And the king of France
> loved him as his own soul; and they loved each other so much that
> the king of England was absolutely astonished at the passionate love
> between them and marveled at it.[79]

Richard gave every indication of being profoundly Catholic: he heard mass daily for much of his life and was the driving force behind the third crusade, remaining in the Holy Land long after the other leaders had returned wearily to Europe. He was constantly in the company of prelates and spiritual leaders, favored the church in his lands, and often made spectacular gestures of piety.

On several occasions he repented of "that sin" ("peccatum illud") and

---

78. On the other hand, Henry was not above siring numerous illegitimate children, and possibly he did not mind his son's inclinations. It was under his reign and presumably with his approval that Anselm quashed the antigay legislation of the Council of London in 1102.

79. "Ricardus dux Aquitaniae, filius regis Angliae, moram fecit cum Philipo rege Franciae, quem ipse in tantum honoravit per longum tempus quod singulis diebus in una mensa ad unum catinum manducabant, et in noctibus non separabat eos lectus. Et dilexit eum rex Franciae quasi animam suam; et in tantum se mutuo diligebant, quod propter vehementem dilectionem quae inter illos erat, dominus rex Angliae nimio stupore arreptus admirabatur quid hoc esset," *Gesta regis Henrici Secundi Benedicti abbatis,* ed. William Stubbs (London, 1867), 2:7. See also Hovedon *Annals* 362,A.6 (*The Annals of Roger of Hovedon,* trans. Henry Riley [London, 1853], 2:63–64).

resolved to lead a holier life, but there is no indication that he regarded it as any more serious than the types of high living—from wine and women to extravagance in dress—for which all religious monarchs (and most writers) of the Middle Ages occasionally did penance.[80] Five years after his first such resolution (on the eve of the crusade), he completely ignored a hermit who harangued him about his well-known proclivities, but when he subsequently fell seriously ill he followed standard medieval practice in promising to adopt a more ascetic life-style in return for a cure.[81] Whether he fulfilled his promise is unclear: he was married but died without legitimate offspring, and so few people even knew about his wife that she had to sue the pope after his death to be recognized as his heir. All his biographers agreed that "it was no marriage."[82]

As in most centuries, the majority of surviving literature of the period dealing with erotic themes concerns the upper class, but there is no more reason to imagine that gay feelings or actions were limited to an upper elite at this time than in any other age. The fact that the writings in question were composed by the upper classes to be read by the upper classes is sufficient explanation for their preoccupation *with* the upper classes. Both accusations and admissions of homosexual behavior occur in literature which comes as close as any twelfth-century writings to constituting popular culture—e.g., the *Carmina Burana*—as well as in works intended for a private audience. Even allowing for poetic hyperbole, contemporary claims for the extreme frequency of homosexual behavior were impressive. Bernard of Morlaix observed that gay people "are as numerous as grains of barley, as many as the shells of the sea, or the sands of the shore." The cities, the countryside, even holy places were "awash," he complained, with flagrant and un-

---

80. Public confession of even minor failings was an ancient tradition of the church which persisted through the Middle Ages in the West (see, e.g., Vogel, "La discipline pénitentielle," pp. 20–26, 163–65) and into modern times in the East. As a literary phenomenon of the twelfth century, among writers like the Goliardic poets such "confessions" were almost certainly insincere; among older writers regrets about the follies of youth may have represented real conviction, although they must still be read cautiously. Such regrets occur as frequently among heterosexual writers as gay ones, and some authors specifically equate both kinds of love in their remorse (e.g., Baudri, Marbod). The very same *topos* is common among Muslim writers in Spain during the twelfth century, like Ibn Quzman (see his *Cancionero*, trans. Nykl), whose verse shows influence either of or on romance themes. Such writers could not have been affected by Christian misgivings about gay sexuality.

81. Hovedon, as translated by Riley, 2:356–57.

82. E.g., Kate Norgate, *Richard the Lion Heart* (London, 1924); Philip Henderson, *Richard Coeur de Lion* (London, 1958); and James Brundage, *Richard Lion Heart* (New York, 1974). Henderson observes (p. 243), "He left no children by his marriage, which appears, in effect, to have been no marriage." Of the many biographies of Richard, only Brundage is frank about his homosexuality, although he discusses it in highly derogatory terms. Norgate's biography remains the best, despite her reticence on this subject.

abashed gay sexuality.[83] The author of verses directed "Against Intercourse with One Sex Only" laments that the "entire universe—alas!—is addicted to this sordid practice."[84]

Nor should the fact that a very large percentage of extant writings from the period by or about gay persons originated in France be given more weight than it deserves. France during this time underwent a literary renaissance of such proportions and produced a volume of poetry of such unprecedented magnitude that it would be more remarkable if its influence, especially in a matter of love, were not disproportionate.[85] In both Italy and Spain poets of courtly love learned Provençal and wrote their verses in it, but this should hardly be taken to indicate that concepts of passionate love between men and women had not occurred to anyone outside of Provence before troubadour lyrics made their way from there to other countries. What it does indicate is that the particular form of expression and specific literary motifs regarding heterosexual love in Provence charmed writers in other countries and were voraciously imitated; the same is probably true of expressions of homosexual love, which were unusually refined in France.

Homosexuality is well attested in England, Italy, Germany, Spain, the Scandinavian countries, even the Holy Land during this time. Muslim writers of twelfth-century Spain considered the Christian clergy peculiarly prone to homosexuality,[86] and Jewish poets wrote gay erotic verse: Moshe

83. Bernard of Morlaix (or Cluny) *De contemptu mundi*, in Wright, *Anglo-Latin Satyrical Poets*, 2:79–80:
Nemo scelus premit, aut tegit, aut gemit esse scelestus.
Ad fera crimina claudite lumina quotquot adestis . . .
Lex Sodomae patet, innumerus scatet heu! Ganymedes.
. . . Quot seges hordea, pontus et ostrea, littus arenas . . .
. . . Castra, suburbia quippe sacraria non minus undant
Hac lue sordida. . . .
84. "Scelus fedum . . . cui—pro dolor—orbus adhesit," "Dissuasio concubitus in uno tantum sexu," lines 22–23, in Werner, *Beiträge*, p. 89. Lines 1–17 of this poem are printed as a poem of Marbod's in PL, 171:1669, and anonymously by Wright, p. 158. The last seven stanzas occur only in the manuscript reproduced by Werner.
85. This is at least partly due to the simple fact that the urban revival of the eleventh and twelfth centuries was centered in France: "In Gaul, in fact, the important place held in the twelfth century by ancient cities such as Orleans, Bordeaux, Cologne, Nantes, Rouen, and others, was much superior to what they had enjoyed under the emperors," Pirenne, *Medieval Cities*, p. 104.
86. E.g., Ibn Abdun: "Inna al-qasisina fasaqat, zanāt, lūatat," p. 239; sec. 154 in the French translation. At least one Hispanic monarch of the time, Alfonso I, may have been gay: see E. Lourie, "The Will of Alfonso I," *Speculum* 50 (1975): 639. I think Lourie draws too much from the French translation of Ibn Athir which she cites: "L'homme qui se voue a la guerre a besoin de la société des hommes, et non des femmes," from the *Recueil des historiens des croisades: historiens orientaux* (Paris, 1877), 1:414; in the original Arabic the verb "ᶜashara" clearly denotes social companionship as opposed to erotic relationship. On the other hand,

ibn Ezra,[87] Ibn Sahl, Ibn Ghayyath, Ibn Sheshet, Ibn Barzel, and Abraham ibn Ezra all wrote love poetry to youths.[88] Judah Halevi, one of the most prominent Jews in Christian Spain, an outstanding Hebrew poet and an influential religious leader,[89] wrote poetry and epigrams to beautiful boys and even transformed a heterosexual Arabic poetic jest into a homosexual one.[90]

A German collection of Latin poems made by an anonymous twelfth-century monk contains many explicitly gay poems, plus a number containing homosexual allusions ("Many the girls and women I have loved, both lad and man; many the boys and men I have loved, both lad and man").[91] There are a few hostile poems as well, although the most vehement of these is probably addressed to a rival in love and motivated by jealousy.[92] Clearly the subject of homosexual feelings and behavior was socially if not personally familiar to the compiler of the manuscript; it appears as a variety of erotic expression worthy of attention—both sympathetic and satirical—like any other.

Information about Scandinavia is difficult to date, but vernacular literature of the High Middle Ages suggests that homosexual relations were sufficiently common that warriors were at pains to avoid a reputation for being passive in such liaisons. Laws in fact regulated the use of the words for "catamite" and "effeminate."[93] Common Icelandic proverbs equate male sexual passivity with failure to defend oneself in battle, and a law in

---

her general arguments are compelling, and Alfonso's favoring the Templars in his will (over a local military order) may in fact relate to their reputation for love between males: see below, chap. 10.

87. Moshe ibn Ezra, *Shira ha-Hol*, ed. H. Brody (Berlin, 1935), 1:11, 147, 159, 179, 246, etc.

88. See J. Schirmann, "The Ephebe in Medieval Hebrew Poetry," *Sefarad* 15 (1955): 55–68, on p. 60.

89. See Baer, *The Jews in Christian Spain*, 1:67 and passim.

90. See Schirmann, p. 60.

91. "Dilexi multas parvas puer et vir adultas; / Dilexi multos parvos puer et vir adultos," "Dissuasio intempestivi amoris," no. 201 in Werner, *Beiträge*, p. 89. For the Germanic author of the collection, see the comments by Werner, p. 1; and A. Wilmart, "Le florilège de Saint-Gatien: contribution à l'étude des poèmes d'Hildebert et de Marbode," *Revue bénédictine* 48, no. 2 (1936): 174. Poems dealing with homosexuality in some form occur throughout Werner's collection: e.g., nos. 8, 9, 60, 61, 198–201. It is possible that the many poems in this collection reminiscent of Marbod are actually unrecognized works of his, though more probably they are imitative of him.

92. No. 9, "Obiurgatio amatoris puerorum," contains no real hint of moral outrage but is simply an exercise in name calling, a sort of *sirventès*. Line 13 ("Exponam, quare te nullus debet amare...") suggests it was written to such a rival. Wilmart classifies it as one of Marbod's poems; it does not occur in the PL edition of Marbod's works. Several manuscripts include it among poems which can be attributed to Marbod with greater certainty; see e.g., Wright, *Anglo-Latin Satirical Poets*, 2:158.

93. See sources cited above, p. 184, n. 52.

Iceland prohibited depicting one's enemies in carvings of homosexual intercourse, presumably because of this association;[94] it is clear that the subject
was by no means unfamiliar. In the *Saga of Harald Hardradr* a favorite of King
Harald admires the king's axe. Harald asks the skald,

> "Have you seen a better axe?"
> "I don't think so," says Halli;
> "Will you let yourself be sodomized for the axe?" asks the king.
> Halli says no. "It seems to me that you should rather dispose of the axe in
> the same way that you acquired it."[95]

This casual banter regarding homosexual relations inserted into a popular
epic indicates that they were a familiar matter of little consequence, even
if the whole exchange is entirely facetious.

Numerous twelfth-century English manuscripts contain gay literature[96]
(much of it unpublished), including both original poetry and copies
of poems by Marbod and other gay poets. Attitudes in this literature
range from absolute indifference to vituperative hostility, but it is
notable that the latter almost never seems to be prompted by purely
religious concern.[97] This is hardly surprising, considering the attitudes of
prominent churchmen of the time such as Saints Anselm and Aelred
or the well-known life-style of Richard, one of England's most colorful
rulers.

That such positive attitudes toward homosexuality were not simply the
rationalizations of gay poets is demonstrated by the writings of contemporaries who clearly were not gay. The satirist Walther of Châtillon did not spare
the gay literati in his attacks on the mores of his time. All the young nobles, he
observed, learn gay behavior when they are sent to France "to become

---

94. E.g., "þraellni hefnir, en argr aldrig" (*Grettir's Saga*), cited in Richard Styche,
"Homosexuality in the Icelandic Republic from the Age of Settlement until 1262," unpublished paper, p. 11; for the likeness in wood, see *Grágás, the Arnamagnaean Legate* (Copenhagen, 1829), 2:147, sec. 105; and *Gisli's Saga*, 2, in *Vestfirðinga sogur*, ed. Bjorn Thórólfsson
and Guðni Jónsson in *Íslenzk fornrit*, no. 6 (Reykjavik, 1943).

95. "Hefir þu sied betri auxi. Eigi ættla ek seigir Halli. Villttu lata serdaztt til auxarennar
seigir konungr. Eigi seigir Halli. en vorkun þiki mier ydr ath þier vilid suo selia sem þier
keypttud," *Haralds saga harðráða* 67 ("Snegluhalla þáttr"), in *Flateyjarbók, en Samling af
Norske Konge-Sagaer*, ed. G. Vigfússon and C. Unger (Christiana, 1860–68), 3:427 (trans. in
Styche).

96. E.g., BM, Add. 24199, Cotton, Vitellius A.XII; Bodleian, Digby 65, Rawlinson
G. 109.

97. E.g., for indifference, Wright, *Anglo-Latin Satyrical Poets*, 2:119, no. 115; p. 121, no.
121; see also no. 122, which seems to have a double meaning in a similar context. Secular
hostility completely unrelated to Christian morality is exemplified in poem 234 of the same
collection (p. 145).

doctors."[98] "Many clerics have I known who were sodomites."[99] But when he came to comment on the actual moral gravity of such behavior, he pictured God as simply "laughing at" clerics guilty of it[100]—a rather casual reaction to behavior which would within a hundred years be considered second only to murder.

Hildebert of Lavardin was one of the greatest men of letters of his day and a prominent clergyman as well, being successively archdeacon and bishop of Mans and archbishop of Tours. There is no reason to believe that he himself was gay, but he maintained friendships with some of the most famous gay men of his day. He was an admirer of Marbod of Rennes and at least acquainted with Baudri of Bourgueil.[101] He had been consecrated by the notorious Ralph, archbishop of Tours, and succeeded him in that office.[102] In a couple of his poems Hildebert repeats standard moralist objections to "the plague of Sodom" and implies that such practices are extremely common.

> Numberless Ganymedes cultivate countless shrines,
> And Juno misses what she alone used to receive.
> Both man and boy are sullied by this vice, the young with the old,[103]
> And no way of life escapes it.[104]

But there is a familiar ring to these complaints: not only does Hildebert himself use similar metaphors in other poems ("Many a house is said to have

---

98. *Moralisch-satirische Gedichte Walters von Châtillon*, pp. 69–70:
Filii nobilium, dum sunt iuniores,
mittuntur in Franciam fieri doctores,
quos prece vel precio domant corruptores;
sic pretextatos referunt Artaxata mores.
Et quia non mutuunt anime discrimen,
principes in habitum verterunt hoc crimen,
virum viro turpiter iungit novus hymen,
exagitata procul non intrat femina limen.

99. Ibid., p. 102: "Ex hiis esse novimus plures Sodomeos, / deas non recipere set [*sic*] amare deos."

100. Ibid.: "Set quotquot invenerit huius rei reos, / qui in celis habitat, irridebit eos." Many of Walther's phrases and some of his opinions are derivative—there are a number of quotations from Juvenal—but this one seems to be original.

101. Baudri's poem 149 is apparently dedicated to him: see Abrahams, pp. xxviii–xxix; Hauréau, *Mélanges*, pp. 107–8. There are also echoes of Baudri in poems of Hildebert's (or vice versa?—one cannot be sure).

102. For Hildebert's consecration, see *Gallia Christiana* (Paris, 1856), vol. 14, col. 74.

103. Or possibly "the panderer with the respectable": the Latin "cum sene laeno" is ambiguous.

104. Hauréau, *Mélanges*, p. 69:
Innumeras aedes colit innumerus Ganymedes,
Hocque, quod ipsa solet sumere, Juno dolet.
Hoc sordent vitio puer et vir cum sene laeno,
Nullaque conditio cessat ab hoc vitio.

many Joves, / But do not therefore expect heaven for the sin of Ganymede"),[105] but they are almost identical with poems of Baudri's (especially
no. 139). It is probable that these mythological allusions were considered
obligatory in declamations against the mores of the times and may have been
entirely facetious. Even ignoring the possibility that Hildebert was consciously
mimicking the double standard of Baudri and rejecting his proposed authorship of the gay poem "Ganymede" translated in app. 2, there is still ample
reason to suspect his sincerity in such lines. Another poem, whose authenticity
is much better attested,[106] states outright that calling male homosexuality a
sin is a mistake and that "the council of heaven" has erred in doing so:

> When Jupiter seeks a boy, and Iphis seeks Ianthe,
> The council of heaven says, "It is a crime."
> I say this is a mistake, since they prohibit crime, while laughing at the
>   games of men:
> One of the women was made into a youth, but neither of the men was
>   made into a woman.
> If it were really a crime, the sentence of the gods
> Would have transformed one of the men and neither of the women.[107]

Hildebert's verses reveal several interesting aspects of contemporary opinion.
Gay sexuality is represented as at worst a lamentable form of carnality

105. Ibid., pp. 187–88: "Multa domus multo fertur habere Joves. / Non tamen expectes
Ganymedis crimine coelum."

106. It occurs in two of the best manuscripts of Hildebert's poetry (BN, Baluze 120; and BM,
Add. 24199), and Wilmart classifies it as unquestionably genuine (p. 181), despite Hauréau's
misgivings (*Mélanges*, pp. 177–78). The latter's arguments against the poem's authenticity
are unconvincing ("The distinction made by the poet and his attenuating decision—'I call
this a mistake'—are so revolting that the poet could not be Hildebert. . . . These loves are
sharply stigmatized in two poems of which Hildebert is the most likely author"): from the
literary point of view, there is no more reason to suppose that the antigay poems are
Hildebert's than that the progay ones are, while from the historical perspective progay verses
seem much more likely. Even if he did not write the celebrated poem on the hermaphrodite
(Hauréau suggests there is doubt, pp. 141–47; but Wilmart accepts it absolutely, "Le
florilège," pp. 180, n. 4; 160), he certainly embellished the old tale of the Master and the
Servant (Hauréau, p. 178), whose morality is in no way more orthodox than that of "Iphis
and Ianthe," even if its heterosexual theme was less offensive to Hauréau.

107. Hauréau, p. 177:
Cum peteret puerum Saturninus, Iphis Iantha,
Coetus ait superum: "Scelus est." Illud voco culpam.
Quo prohibente nefas, ludum ridente virorum.
Altera fit juvenis, fit femina neuter eorum.
Si scelus esset idem, sententia coelicolarum
Alterutrum transformaret, neutramve duarum.
Iphis was a Cretan girl brought up as a boy and changed into one when she fell in love with
another girl, Ianthe; The "it" of lines 2 and 5 must refer to male homosexuality; Ovid also
seems to condemn female homosexuality in his account of Iphis and Ianthe, although he was
alternately indifferent and positive about male homosexuality.

among the married; in each of the antigay poems the example of Jupiter and Juno is invoked, suggesting that marital infidelity is a primary (if not the sole) issue. In the progay poem Juno is not mentioned, and there is no sense of infidelity or of anyone being wronged by the act in question.

Increased familiarity with and tolerance of gay people and their feelings by persons who were not themselves gay is nowhere more poignantly illustrated than in the use of the theme of David and Jonathan by Peter Abelard. No medieval figure is better known for heterosexual interests than Abelard, yet in his sixth *planctus* he explored with great sensitivity and feeling the nature of the love between the two men. Whether or not he intended to portray the relationship as sexual,[108] he certainly used erotic vocabulary to invest it with pathos.

More than a brother to me, Jonathan,
One in soul with me . . .
How could I have taken such evil advice
And not stood by your side in battle?
How gladly would I die
And be buried with you!
Since love may do nothing greater than this,
And since to live after you
Is to die forever:
Half a soul
Is not enough for life.
Then—at the moment
of final agony—
I should have rendered
Either of friendship's dues:
To share the triumph
Or suffer the defeat;
Either to rescue you
Or to fall with you,
Shedding for you that life
Which you so often saved,
So that even death would join

108. Dronke (*Poetic Individuality*, p. 116) speaks of "a shared agony of guilt of which the Bible knows nothing," basing this on the lines "que peccata, que scelere / nostra sciderunt viscera" (47–48). These words seem to me to imply nothing more than that the separation of the two ("nostra sciderunt viscera") was effected by wickedness and evildoing. On the other hand, the overall tone of the poem is markedly more erotic than that of any of the other *planctus*.

Rather than part us.

I can still my lute,
But not my sobs and tears:
A heart too is shattered
By the plucking of stricken hands,
The hoarse sobbing of voices.[109]

Since there is reason to believe that gay poetry was studied in many twelfth-century schools, especially in France, it is possible that Abelard's interest in this subject was academic. On the other hand, he could have been acquainted personally with gay sentiments through his pupil Hilary the Englishman (see p. 249) or other friends in Paris of similar persuasion. The very least that can be said is that Abelard in the first half of the twelfth century could choose and treat as erotic the relationship of David and Jonathan in a formal lament poem just as easily as he could the relationship of Dinah and Sichem.

Even apparently heterosexual characters were often depicted in popular fiction as passionately attached to persons of their own gender. During this century, for example, a story of extraordinary devotion between two knights became immensely popular.[110] Amis and Amile not only loved each other ineffably but resembled each other in every particular, including physical appearance, to the extent that Amis could stand in for Amile at a tournament to free him from suspicion of treachery and win for him the hand of a princess. They were constantly separated from each other in the stories about them by an endless series of misadventures and tragedies; their reunions, albeit short-lived, were ecstatic; their love was repeatedly tested by circumstances which demanded enormous sacrifice by one for the other. The story bears a striking similarity to Hellenistic "romances" in Greek and Arabic literature, without necessarily deriving from them.[111]

109. Text in OBMLV, no. 172, pp. 246–50, lines 45–46, 69–92, 105–10; commentary in Dronke, as above. Waddell translates most of the same lines with characteristic grace and beauty, though quite loosely: *Medieval Latin Lyrics*, p. 169.

110. In the introduction to his edition of *Amis and Amiloun* (London, 1937), MacEdward Leach discusses the various types and divisions of the story, which appeared first in Latin but quickly made its way into most European vernaculars. The bibliography on the subject is vast; Leach gives the major sources. For a more recent treatment, see R. J. Hexter, *Equivocal Oaths and Ordeals in Medieval Literature* (Cambridge, Mass., 1975), pp. 27–37 and the notes and bibliography.

111. For a standard treatment of the sources of the legend, see Gédéon Huet, "Ami et Amile: les origines de la légende," *Moyen Age* 30 (1919): 162–86; and Leach's introduction. To my knowledge no one has considered the possibility of Hellenistic influence through Muslim Spain. On the potential for such transmission, see "Greece in the Arabian Nights," in Gustav von Grunebaum, *Medieval Islam* (Chicago, 1971); and chap. 9 below.

There is no hint of sexual interest between the knights, but their love for each other explicitly takes precedence over every other commitment.[112] In one of the most poignant episodes, Amis is striken with leprosy and cruelly mistreated by almost everyone.[113] His wife tries to strangle him, so his knights have to take him home to his ancestral castle. There soldiers throw him out of the cart on which he lies helpless and threaten his knights with violence. Finally he is taken to Rome, but a terrible famine forces his knights to abandon him. As a last gesture, they carry him to the castle of Amile and leave him outside. Amile discovers the identity of the dying leper by a token given him at their joint baptism, and he and his wife bring Amis into their home and care for him. One night when the two men are sleeping in the same room, the angel Gabriel comes to Amis to tell him that he can be cured of his leprosy if Amile will slay his children and wash him in their blood. Amis is horrified and at first refuses to repeat to Amile what the angel said. At length he is persuaded to reveal the angel's message. Amile, though heartsick, does not hesitate to murder his children for the love of his friend. The children are restored to life just as Amis recovers his health, and the obvious moral is that Amile has acted rightly in obeying the angelic message and subordinating all else to his love for his friend.

The fact that in the twelfth century fervently Christian literature could celebrate a personal affection which explicitly transcended all other relationships and obligations—legal, moral, or familial—is evidence of a far-reaching and profoundly important social change in European society. This change was occasioned by the complex interaction of many factors outside the scope of this study and affected nearly every aspect of life in the High Middle Ages, but its impact was nowhere more dramatic than in the realm of love. As if from nowhere, love in a thousand guises invaded the landscapes, townships, and monasteries of Europe in the eleventh and twelfth centuries, and its warmth revived from long hibernation the fiery passions of ancient Europe. It transformed the ascetic spirituality of the desert fathers into the passionate mysticism of Saint Bernard, breached the barriers of Basil's isolated monastic cells with the tender friendships of Saints Anselm and Aelred, dissolved patristic theology of purely functional sexual relations into the Christian romance which seemed to sweep all before it in the High Middle Ages.

This elevation of love from despised mental disturbance to the animating force of most Christian life-styles was accompanied, if not produced, by a

112. Amis's turning his wife over to Amile recalls the legend of Lantfrid and Cobbo.
113. I have summarized from the thirteenth-century Old French prose version of the tale published in *Nouvelles françoises en prose du XIIᵉ siècle*, ed. L. Moland and C. d'Héricault (Paris, 1856), pp. 35–82. A charming translation of this version is available in William Morris, *Old French Romances* (London, 1896), pp. 27–58.

great efflorescence of urbanity, both demographic and cultural, which brought with it veneration of the humanism of antiquity in social as well as artistic matters and a renewed respect for personal freedom, values, and feelings. These circumstances were conducive not only to public tolerance of idiosyncratic individuals but to the flourishing of minority cultures, many of which made lasting contributions to the cultural values of the majority.

9 The Triumph of Ganymede:

Gay Literature of the High Middle Ages

What is perhaps most striking about the years from 1050 to 1150 is the re-appearance for the first time since the decline of Rome of evidence for what might be called a gay subculture. The most obvious manifestation of this was gay literature, the general range and extent of which has been considered in the preceding chapter. Individual writers recording their personal feelings in isolation, no matter how numerous, probably do not constitute a "sub-culture" in its most common sense; but a network of such persons, conscious of their common difference from the majority and mutually influencing their own and others' perceptions of the nature of their distinctiveness, does in-dicate the sort of change at issue here. A body of gay literature of the pro-portion and types analyzed below had not been seen in Europe since the first century A.D. and would not be encountered again until the nineteenth.

As with so many matters relating to the subject at hand, the type of analysis possible at present must be largely unsatisfactory. The causes of this efflorescence of gay culture remain partly mysterious. They may be related to other cultural currents of the period, such as the rise of what has come to be called "courtly love," but such trends, although more studied, are not much better understood than the gay culture itself, and it would hinder rather than assist the discussion to try to establish correlations between such undefined concepts. Nor is it apparent that increases in tolerance alone would have had the effect of producing such cultural manifestations; they may be more directly related to the great increases in general literary output of the period or even to learning itself. Certainly familiarity with the gay artistic conventions of antiquity had much effect on those of the eleventh and twelfth centuries, and it is evident that increases in literacy and prosperity will result generally in artistic reflection of a greater range of social phenomena. On the other hand, the literacy rate probably continued to rise at least through the fourteenth century, whereas evidence of a gay subculture disappears almost entirely after the twelfth. Advances in knowledge in many disciplines will probably be necessary to clarify the nature of so large and complex a development; the most that can be attempted here is a description of it.

It is worth reiterating as preface to this material that although the concern here is with the aspect of their lives which distinguished such writers from the majority—their romantic interest in persons of their own gender—they were at the same time members of and participants in the larger culture which surrounded them. The bulk of their literary output dealt with standard religious themes of an entirely orthodox nature. Most of them were prominent churchmen in positions of considerable ecclesiastical authority; none was accused of entertaining unorthodox opinions, either during his lifetime or subsequently.

Baudri of Bourgueil (1046–1130), abbot of the French Benedictine monastery of Saint Peter and later archbishop of Dol, epitomizes the transition from the ascetic passions of the monastic love tradition discussed in the previous chapter to the baldly erotic poetry more characteristic of the eleventh and twelfth centuries. Much of his poetry is in the older style of passionate but spiritual affection, like the poem to Godfrey of Reims,[1] whom he offers to immortalize in verse, or that written to his friend Galo,[2] so like Walafrid's lyric to Liutger ("Now is there nothing for you from me except a simple pledge of love").[3] Echoes of Walafrid—or at least the tradition he represented—are also present in his poem to Ralph the monk, whom he calls his "Other self, or myself, if two spirits may be one / And if two bodies may actually become one."[4] In many of these verses the passion implied is

---

1. All quotations are taken from the critical edition of Baudri's poetry, *Les oeuvres poétiques de Baudri de Bourgueil*, ed. Phyllis Abrahams (Paris, 1926). The poem to Godfrey is n. 161. Unfortunately, little critical work has been done on Baudri or his poetry. Otto Schumann, in "Baudri von Bourgueil als Dichter," in *Studien zur lateinischen Dichtung des Mittelalters: Ehrengabe für Karl Strecker* (Dresden, 1931), characterized Abraham's edition as "höchst unzulänglich." Schumann believed that Baudri's poems to men were insincere imitations of the writings of his model, Ovid, and cited as evidence of this his *Confessio poenitentialis* (184), in which he confessed in the same breath to "sodomy," and to theft, perjury, murder, etc.— all sins which one can feel reasonably certain Baudri never committed (p. 165). Schumann overlooks the fact that Baudri himself drew a distinction between those sins he had committed "only insofar as I was able" ("in quantum potui")—theft, sacrilege, perjury, robbery, murder—and others of which he was presumably quite capable—lying, vanity, "sodomy" (active and passive), adultery, insobriety, etc. (Deicide is mentioned ambiguously—it could have been intended to fall under either the first category or the second.) Whether or not Baudri intended the reader to understand "sodomy" as a sin which he had actually committed, both the fact that he mentioned it and the context in which he did so are revealing: two centuries later "sodomy" could hardly have been classified on a level with "pomposity" and "drunkenness."

2. On the identity of this Galo, see the note by Abrahams on pp. 376–77.

3. 231: "Nunc tibi nil ex me nisi tantum pignus amoris."

4. 48: "Alter ego, vel ego si sunt duo spiritus unus, / Sique duo fiant corpora corpus idem."

clearly not related to physical attraction. In writing to Galo, for instance, he says, "I love you intensely, because you are intensely lovable" but goes on to explain that "it is your talent which makes me love you."[5] In others there is no pretence of spiritual affinity. "Nor do the rose and the violet adorn the season of spring more / Than you grace, all by yourself, the ranks of young men" was written to a youth whom he had not even met; he had heard of the young man's extraordinary beauty and could hardly wait, he said, to judge this comeliness in person.[6]

Other poems fall just short of the candor of the "Idol of Venus." There is an eighty-line set of verses (38) addressed to a very beautiful boy[7] whose haughtiness is a particular annoyance to Baudri and a rebuke to a young man who had written him in veiled allusions, eliciting from Baudri the demand, "If you wish to be my boy, clarify these allusions."[8]

Among the many love poems to a certain John, there is his complaint about the youth's fickleness:

I wonder and cannot express my amazement
That my John has not hurried back to me,
Though he is forever promising that he will return.
Either the boy is sick, or he has forgotten me.

. . . .

The boy is fickle, like everything young.

5. 231: "Te vehementer amo, cum sis vehementer amandus, / Ut vehementer amem te tua musa facit."

6. 45:
Nec rosa nec viola plus tempora verna decorat
Quam juvenum solus agmina condecoras.

. . . .

Ignotum facie te tota colligo mente,
Et faciem rutilam saepe figuro mihi.

. . . .

Si locus est mihi fac ignotus cognita signa,
Et formae judex sim Paris alter ego.

7. References to "boys" in gay erotic literature of the High Middle Ages must be read with caution; as noted, portraying objects of erotic attention in terms of youthful beauty is a standard convention of Western erotic imagery, and this tendency received further impetus during the period in question from the use of "Ganymede" as a synonym for "gay." Baudri may really have been romantically interested in boys, but in many cases such language is clearly conventional: Marbod refers to himself as a "boy" in a poem to his lover, although he was certainly an adult at the time, and Hugh Primas designates an adult monk as the "Ganymede" of an evil chaplain (translated in George Whicher, *The Goliard Poets* [New York, 1949], pp. 90–101; portions of the text appear in OBMLV, pp. 251–54, where the editor seems to have made a deliberate effort to delete the verses suggesting homosexuality).

8. 250: "Si meus esse velis puer, hoc expone subaudis"; see also 178.

. . . .
A man is never secure, it [*sic*] can never come fast enough.[9]

Baudri was twice driven from office by mysterious scandals,[10] but there is no evidence that these scandals were related to his erotic preferences. On the other hand, as a bishop he was convinced that a front had to be maintained for the public ("The prudent lover disguises the deeds of love")[11] and he wrote at length to his beloved Peter—whose comb he carried always as a memento of their love—on the subject of discretion in "the game." "If you can, keep your deeds above reproach, but if you cannot, at least keep your confidences to yourself."[12]

In a few places Baudri even tried to disclaim his love poetry, saying that he had written *as if* young love were goading him:

> But neither young love nor serious sin has ever led me astray;
> A playful muse just amuses me, as I am a playful person.[13]

"No evil love," he claimed, "has ever touched me."[14]

9. 177:
Miror nec valeo mirari sufficienter,
Quare non properus rediit meus ille Johannes
Qui se continuo jurans pepigit rediturum.
Vel puer aegrotat, mihi vel subducitur amens.

. . . .
Inconstans puer est, inconstans quaeque juventus.

. . . .
Nusquam tutus homo, nusquam satis acceleratur.
10. First as abbot, then as archbishop. No evidence survives as to the nature of the charges involved: see Abrahams, pp. xx–xxvi.
11. 156: "Quisquis amat, cautus celet amoris opus."
12. 207:
Si potes et tua mens splendescat semper et actus,
Sin autem, saltem te tibi solus habe.
. . . Ludens ludenti quisquis consentit amico,
Et ludum improperat jure negatur homo.
While this metaphor makes sense at the literal level of a game such as backgammon or dice, in which both parties are complicit and neither could take the other to law, it is probably also a reference to the "game" of love: "ludus" is used in the same way by the author of "Ganymede and Helen."
13. 231:
Tamquam torruit me juvenilis amor.
Nec juvenilis amor, nec me malus abstulit error,
Sed mihi jocundo musa jocunda placet.
14. 147: "Nullus amor foedus mihi quidlibet associavit." If it is true that the erotic poems were written to amuse and that the ostensible speaker in them is not Baudri himself, then this is even truer of his poems purporting to attack gay love, of which one is written as if by Paris to Helen (he warns her about the nasty habits of the Greeks, including anal intercourse, 42), and the other survives only in fragments of mythological verse (216). On the other hand, Baudri seems to be expressing his own opinion in 139, where he denigrates both gay and

Even Baudri's disclaimers reveal profoundly altered attitudes toward gay people and feelings. The crucial issue was obviously the propriety of a bishop writing erotic poetry, not the gender of the parties addressed. Baudri frankly admits that the poetry was written to both sexes: "I write to boys, nor do I neglect girls"; "I wrote to please both boys and girls"; "Both sexes have been pleased by my verses."[15]

Baudri may have been troubled about the reaction of the laity to his erotic relationships and poetry, but for his own part he clearly accepted love as good in and of itself and had no difficulty in addressing his love to a person of the same gender. In Baudri's poetic reconstruction of correspondence between Florus and Ovid, Florus is obviously defending the author himself when he exclaims,

It is not you who teach the age but the age which instructs you:

. . . .

Venus knew how to love without your verses.
God made our natures full of love;
Nature teaches us what God taught her.

. . . .

What we are is a crime, if it is a crime to love,
For the God who made me live made me love.[16]

Most of Baudri's gay contemporaries were less defensive. Marbod of

---

nongay sexuality in urging a young man to consider the monastic life. Although he echoes standard theological arguments against homosexual behavior, he also includes a more personal note which may reveal more than the rest of the episcopal advice: "What will you do when your youth is gone?" The ambisexual milieu in which this advice is offered is clearly indicated by Baudri's comment that "many an altar still has Ganymede running about it, / and many a lusty man still wishes to be Jupiter" and by his concluding equation of gay and nongay love in recommending that no one "seek the enjoyment of either girls or boys." It could hardly have occurred to Baudri that this letter, of a distinctly public and official character, would be published in a collection with his own private love poems, giving an impression of hypocrisy. The advice may be heartfelt and indicative of Baudri's sense of failure (as a cleric) to live up to an ideal of celibacy.

15. "Ergo quod pueros demulceat atque puellas / scripsimus" (147); "Carminibus meis sexus uterque placet" (161); "Ad pueros scribo, nec praetermitto puellas" (231).

16. 159:

Non tu saecla [*sic*] doces, sed saecula te docuerunt.

. . . .

Novit amare Venus versibus absque tuis.
Naturam nostram plenam deus egit amoris,
Nos natura docet quod deus hanc docuit.

. . . .

Quod sumus est crimen, si crimen sit quod amamus.
Qui dedit esse deus praestat amare mihi.

Rennes,[17] a teacher of Baudri's, was master of the extremely influential
school of Chartres, chancellor of the Diocese of Angers, and bishop of Rennes.
His poetry, like that of nearly all gay poets of the time, deals mostly with
standard religious themes. He also includes verses bitterly satirizing a boy
who will not yield:

> Surely he is wicked, cruel and wicked,
> Who by the viciousness of his character denies the beauty of his body.
> A fair face should have a wholesome mind,
> Patient and not proud but yielding in this or that.[18]

Possibly this is the same youth about whom Marbod wrote a poem involving a threesome: a boy whom he loved ("that spectacular youth, whose
beauty is my fire") was in love with a very beautiful girl, who was herself in
love with Marbod; none of the three seems to have achieved his or her desire.[19]
It is at any rate clear that the bishop did have a lover, to whom he sent an
urgent demand to return from a distant city where he was on business if he
wished Marbod to remain faithful to him, since strenuous efforts were being
made to woo him away.[20]

Marbod's position as master of the school at Chartres, which trained many
of the most important churchmen of the day, made his attitudes toward gay
sexuality extremely influential.[21] Copies or imitations of his gay poems occur

17. Extremely little critical attention has been paid to Marbod's poetry. F. J. E. Raby
discusses his work superficially and with characteristic bias (*Secular Latin Poetry*, 2d ed.
[Oxford, 1957], 1:329–37). Wilmart has at least begun the task of establishing an authentic
corpus of his poetry ("Le florilège de Saint-Gatien: contribution à l'étude des poèmes
d'Hildebert et de Marbode. III. Les mélanges poétiques de Marbode," *Revue bénédictine*,
48, nos. 3–4 [1936]: 235–58). A French translation of a meager selection of the poems was
published by Sigismond Ropartz, *Poèmes de Marbode, évêque de Rennes* (Rennes, n.d.). The
lack of scholarly attention to Marbod is the more unfortunate as his poetry was widely copied
and occurs in many twelfth- and thirteenth-century collections of verse: see chap. 8, nn.
91, 92 above.

18. PL, 171:1718; translated in full in app. 2: "The Unyielding Youth."
Impius ille quidem, crudelis et impius idem,
Qui vitio morum corpus vetat esse decorum.
Bella bonam mentem facies petit, et patientem,
Et non inflatam, sed ad haec et ad illa paratam.

19. PL, 171:1655. Marbod may have found women attractive as well: in one of several
poems expressing disillusionment with the delights of love he observes that now "the
embrace of either sex is unappealing to me" ("Desplicet amplexus utriusque quidem mihi
sexus," PL, 171:1656).

20. PL, 171:1717–18, translated in app. 2: "To His Absent Lover." Wright (*Anglo-Latin
Satirical Poets*, 2:257) publishes this poem from a British manuscript as one of a number of
Poemata Serlonis. See commentary in Wilmart, "Les florilèges," p. 246; and for "Serlo,"
Jan Öberg, *Serlon de Wilton, poèmes latins* (Stockholm, 1965).

21. The cathedral school at Chartres has traditionally been regarded as the major center
of scholarship in Europe prior to the rise of universities. Southern (*Medieval Humanism*,

in manuscripts all over Europe, from England to Germany (see. chap. 8, nn. 91, 92). It seems likely, in fact, that he used his poetry as teaching material.

A pupil of Abelard's, Hilary the Englishman, explored the theme of the unyielding youth at length in his poetry. In a series of verses addressed to English young men, he praised their beauty extravagantly and complained again and again of their aloofness.[22] Such lines do not seem to be simply imitations of classical sources or idle exercises of literary bent. Sentiments like "Oh, how I wish you wanted money!"[23] are distinctly at odds with classical prejudices and hardly the sort of literary motif which would be common in religious schools.

Hilary's gay verses in fact seem decidedly personal. In one poem he expresses his anxiety over the conflict between his feelings for a youth and his commitment to a woman:

The moment I saw you,
Cupid struck me, but I hesitate,
For my Dido holds me,
And I fear her wrath.[24]

Despite this "Dido," nearly all scholars who have studied the poems have concluded that the writings to women are characterized by an "utter lack of real emotion," while those to boys have struck most as personal and sincere.[25]

---

pp. 61–85) has questioned the existence of a continuous school at Chartres, but there is no disagreement about the role of prominent students from Chartres in disseminating learning in the later eleventh and early twelfth centuries.

22. *Hilarii versus et ludi*, ed. J. J. Champollion-Figeac (Paris, 1838); examples are given in app. 2. I have quoted from the Champollion-Figeac edition because it is more faithful to the manuscript than the later one by John Fuller, *Hilarii Versus et Ludi* (New York, 1929). Fuller provides partial English translations or paraphrases at the beginning of his work but has been criticized for both edition and interpretation: see notes below and in app. 2. Hilary also wrote religious verse, e.g., a resurrection play about Lazarus and plays about Daniel and Saint Nicholas.

23. "O quam vellem, ut velles pretium!" App. 2: "To a Boy of Anjou," line 25.

24. *Hilarii versus et ludi*, no. 13,
Ut te vidi, mos Cupido
Me percussit; sed diffido;
Nam me tenet mea Dido
Cujus iram reformido.
But cf. ibid., "Ego preda tuque predo: / Me predoni tali dedo."

25. Fuller, p. 15; cf. Dronke, *Medieval Latin*, p. 218. There is general agreement that the poems to boys are "the outpourings of a passionate love" (Fuller, p. 15). For a good rebuttal to Fuller's secondary misgivings on this point, see the review of this book by Hans Spanke in *Zeitschrift für französische Sprache und Literatur* 56 (1932): 250–51. Spanke sensibly points out that such lines as "O quam vellem, ut velles pretium!" hardly seem like simple "poetic effusion" to a fellow student. In his satire on the pope Hilary pillories the pontiff's bisexuality ("The pope's organ misses nothing: boys and girls please the pope, / Old men and old women please the pope," no. 14; Champollion-Figeac, p. 42).

Indeed the argument that the apparently gay content of twelfth-century poetry simply represents classical allusions or "echoes of Ovid" will not stand close scrutiny. It is true that such lines as Baudri's "I wrote to please both boys and girls" strikingly parallel classical models, but they also strikingly resemble contemporary writings by Hispanic Jews and Muslims,[26] who were certainly not simply copying Ovid. Sexual attraction can be expressed only in terms of the two available genders; it is fatuous to leap at similarities of phrasing in such cases as demonstrating derivation.

More to the point, whether imitative or not, the simple expression of homosexual attraction by bishops and priests was a novelty in the twelfth century. Alcuin, Hrabanus Maurus, Walafrid, and scores of earlier medieval poets also referred to gay classical models but did not adopt overtly sexual attitudes or terminology. The common use of frankly gay sexual themes and language by clerics of high standing, who also wrote conventional religious verse, is evidence of a remarkable social trend, one suggestive of a more profound change than the introduction of a new literary style.

Most of the gay poetry of the age, however, is not based on classical traditions and demonstrates both the sincerity and the variety of gay relationships among the clergy of the time. One of the most unusual poems of the popular *Carmina Burana* collection relates an affectionate argument between two clerics who are lovers.[27] One is sick and offers to become a monk if God will only grant him recovery. His horrified lover begs not to be abandoned. The ailing cleric is moved by his pleas but retains his resolve. A lengthy dispute follows, in which the lover tries every argument to dissuade his friend from entering a monastery, pointing out the rigors of monastic observances, the dreadful quality of the food, the sadness he would cause his relations if he abandoned them. All to no avail: the ailing cleric is determined. Finally the lover bursts out,

O Art of Reasoning,
I wish you had never been discovered!
You who make so many
Lonely, miserable clerics,

and points out to the monk-to-be that they will be separated forever. At this his companion begins to have second thoughts: "I am already changing my mind," he declares, and he resolves never to become a monk.

Another manifestation of the emergence of a gay subculture during the period 1050–1150 was the rise of a variety of specifically gay *topoi* which

26. For Jews, see Schirmann, "The Ephebe;" for Muslims, see above, chap. 7, nn. 96, 101.
27. Translated in app. 2; "I Am Already Changing My Mind."

found their way into literature all over Europe, nongay as well as gay. The most prominent of these was the figure of Ganymede, the beautiful son of the king of Troy who was carried off by Jove to be a cupbearer in heaven.[28] In late imperial literature Ganymede had become synonymous with what the ancient world called "the beloved" in a homosexual relationship, but he appeared in many different guises in the High Middle Ages, usually as the representative of gay people in general.[29] In several debates of the period he is the spokesman for the gay side, and is very frequently used as the archetype of a beautiful male.[30]

Use of the Ganymede figure was not necessarily a sign of participation in or even approval of the gay subculture, but in view of the widespread adoption of "Ganymede" as a name for a gay person and the general familiarity of all educated persons of the time with his legend, artistic references to Ganymede during the period must be regarded as potential allusions to this subject.[31]

There can be little doubt, for instance, that a capital from this period in the church of La Madeleine at Vézelay depicting the abduction of Ganymede by an eagle[32] is some sort of comment on the issue, although it is much more difficult to ascertain what sort of statement is intended, and for whom. The representation of the terrified Ganymede in the clutches of the ravishing eagle has been interpreted, perhaps rightly, as suggesting a negative attitude on the part of the iconographer toward some aspect of homosexuality during the period, perhaps a derogation of possible sexual abuse of oblate children

28. The accounts of the rape of Ganymede most familiar to medieval authors were probably those of Vergil (*Aeneid* 1.28, 5.255–57) and Ovid (*Metamorphoses* 10.155, 11.756). A brief overview of the artistic tradition relating to Ganymede may be found in Forsyth, "The Ganymede Capital at Vézelay," pp. 241–46; for an older but more exhaustive treatment, see PW, s.v. "Ganymede."

29. Examples of the use of the figure of Ganymede in twelfth-century literature are far too numerous to be cataloged; almost all of the gay authors cited in this and the preceding chapter occasionally allude to the story or character of Ganymede, and many hostile writers do so as well (e.g., Primas, as cited above, and Bernard of Morlaix, in his *De contemptu mundi*, discussed below).

30. E.g., by Baudri of Bourgueil (Abrahams, p. 24) and Hildebert (see chap. 8, nn. 104, 105, above).

31. On the other hand, the subject may have pleased some writers simply as a classical allusion, and they may have been indifferent to its sexual overtones. In the long poetic treatment of the subject by Godfrey of Reims, e.g., there is neither erotic content nor any sign of reticence about the subject. But since Godfrey was a friend of Baudri of Bourgueil, it is rather difficult to believe that he was unaware of gay people or of the significance of Ganymede in this context. For the poem, see A. Boutémy, "Trois oeuvres inédites de Godefroid de Reims," *Revue du moyen âge latin* 3 (1947): 335–76; and for Godfrey's life, see M. Williams, "Godfrey of Rheims, a Humanist of the Eleventh Century," *Speculum* 22 (1947): 29–45.

32. See Forsyth, "The Ganymede Capital," and the bibliography cited therein.

in monasteries.[33] It is at least worth considering, however, that the incident had always been regarded as an abduction, if not a rape, even in Rome, and that the sculpture in question may be simply a vivid portrayal of this. Surprise, even terror, would seem quite natural under the circumstances, and the details of the sculpture correspond exactly to the description of the event in the *Aeneid,* save only the addition of a devilish gargoyle in a corner of the capital. It would not be surprising if the sculpture were intended simply as a mythological allusion, but even if the depiction is taken as derogatory, it is clear evidence of the prominence and openness of the subject at the time: in the fourteenth century the abduction of a male for the sexual use of another would hardly have been considered a fit subject for ecclesiastical sculpture.[34]

Other gay conventions included the unyielding youth, occasionally mentioned at other times in the Middle Ages, but much more common during the period under discussion, and the love between David and Jonathan, which became the biblical counterpart of the pagan Ganymede as a symbol for passionate attachment between persons of the same gender. The latter theme found its way into writings ranging from the monastic asceticism of Aelred[35] to the secular humanism of Abelard.

33. So Forsyth; her treatment of the subject is judicious and admirable, although it seems to me that she devotes insufficient attention to the fact that the eagle—unquestionably the dominant figure in the group—might evoke in contemporaries' minds the image of Saint John the Evangelist, depicted in medieval art as an eagle. The significance of this in a later age has been commented on by Erwin Panofsky, as Forsyth notes (see, e.g., *Renaissance and Renascences in Western Art* [Stockholm, 1965], p. 78; cited by Forsyth, p. 246, n. 20), and she herself points out that the resemblance in this particular case might be more than coincidental: the eagle in question is artistically quite similar to the symbol of Saint John in the main tympanum of the abbey church at Cluny (p. 245, n. 5). La Madeleine is now in the diocese of Sens, named as a site of homosexual prostitution in a contemporary poem (translated below), but at the time the capitals were effected and the poem written it was in the diocese of Autun (or independent of diocesan jurisdiction). Sens was, nonetheless, a more prominent city in the same area, and there may be some connection between the two works.

34. Artistic monuments are particularly susceptible of debate over interpretation. Another sculpture of arguable relation to the present subject, dating also from the twelfth century, is now in the Cloisters in New York (see James Rorimer, *The Cloisters* [New York, 1963], pp. 46–47): a corbel originally from the Benedictine church of La Sauve in southwest France has traditionally been characterized as "bearded acrobats," a description which is doubtless superficially accurate. The position in which the two possibly nude men are portrayed, however—the buttocks of one resting on the groin of the other—the extremely prominent, wide open mouth of one of the men, and the intense expression on the other, all suggest the possibility that more might be going on than simple acrobatics. See pl. 8. For information on the provenance and dating of the corbels, see Jacques Brosse, ed., *Dictionnaire des églises de France,* vol. 3, *Sud-Ouest* (Paris, 1967), s.v. "Sauve-Majeure."

35. *De spirituali amicitia* (PL, 195:692); *De speculo caritatis* 1.34.104; see also Dronke, *Medieval Latin,* 2:345, 351–52.

Like that of the modern West, the gay subculture of the High Middle Ages appears to have had its own slang, which gradually became diffused among the general population. The equivalent of "gay," for example, was "Ganymede." The similarity of this word to "gay" in its cultural setting is striking. In an age addicted to classical literature, the invocation of Greek mythology to describe homosexual relationships not only tacitly removed the stigma conveyed by the biblical "sodomita," the only word in common use before or after this period, but also evoked connotations of mythological sanctions, cultural superiority, and personal refinement which considerably diminished negative associations in regard to homosexuality. Although "Ganymede" was also used derisively, it was basically devoid of moral context and could be used by gay people themselves without misgivings.

The term was used as an adjective as well as a noun. Its significance was assumed to be obvious in literary references. Even obscure classical variants of the name (such as "Frix") or arcane eponyms (like "Erichthonius") became common. Occurrences of "sodomita" are correspondingly rarer in the eleventh and twelfth than in the tenth or fourteenth centuries, even in hostile literature.

The word "ludus" ("game") also seems to have acquired a specialized meaning in certain circles: its use in oblique or punning references to homosexuality in many different literary contexts suggests that it was widely used with specifically gay connotations.[36] "Hunting" and terminology related to it figure prominently in poetry by or about gay people, and it is possible that it represented what "cruising" describes in the gay subculture of today, although as a metaphor it is obvious enough not to require any special explanation. The rich irony of Ganymede having been hunting himself when the eagle swooped down upon him doubtless added to the effectiveness of the metaphor,[37] as did the residual association of hares with homosexuality.[38]

Many other gay expressions are now lost or indecipherable: "wood" may have had some sexual significance at the time,[39] and the Roman "mule"[40]

36. Of countless examples which could be cited, see, e.g., Marbod, poem 207 (n. 12 above); "Ganymede and Helen," lines 165–68 (app. 2); and Godfrey, epigram 115 (in Wright, *Anglo-Latin Satirical Poets*, 2:119, and below, p. 263, n. 70).

37. John of Salisbury (*Polycraticus* 1.4 [PL, 199:390]) and others specifically moralized on the significance of Ganymede's association with hunting.

38. A decidedly progay poem, for example, uses the image of a "hare hunting hares" in reference to Ganymede's abduction: see discussion below and text in app. 2 ("Ganymede and Hebe"). This may be simply a repetition of derisive statements of the day, but it is conceivable that "rabbit" was either adopted by gay people in self-defense (as "nigger" is by some blacks) or that it took on connotations like those of "bird" or "chick" in a heterosexual context (or "chicken" in modern gay slang).

39. See below, n. 66.

40. See above, chap. 3 (Juvenal and Virro).

is contrasted in one poem with a "horse,"[41] a distinction with no discernible analogy to gay slang before or after.

A further indication of a distinct subculture was the reemergence of male prostitution, possibly due in part to demographic and/or economic shifts. Much poetry of the period alludes to the possibility of youths selling their favors, a subject which had disappeared from Western literature after the fall of Rome.[42] This genre includes verses by gay writers such as Hilary as well as by nongay ones, like the author of the poem "Why Does My Lady Suspect Me?" The speaker in the poem, trying to convince his mistress that he is *not* gay, suggests that if he wished to do so, selling his favors would profit him greatly:

> Though a lord may promise much,
> And abject poverty constrain me . . . ,
> I am not one of those inclined to do
> What is profitable rather than proper . . .
> I prefer to remain poor and pure
> Than to live wealthy and debauched.[43]

In the most popular poem of the period on the subject, there are numerous references to prostitution. The opponent of gay relations argues that a boy "sells his charms heedless of his sex,"[44] and the gay side concedes,

> The fragrance of profit is pleasing; no one avoids gain.
> Wealth, if I should speak plainly, does have a certain appeal.
> Anyone who wishes to grow rich is willing to play this game:
> If a man desires boys, he is willing to reward them.[45]

41. "Quod sequeris pueros," no. 234 in Wright, *Anglo-Latin Satirical Poets*, 2:145: "Et meus in fortem cessit asellus equum." This entire poem is to say the least opaque, although it is a good example of the type of gay poetry which might carelessly be taken as antigay polemic, since it is a satire on a lover of boys. It is clearly delivered, however, by another lover of boys (or at least one boy) and strongly suggests a distinct gay subculture with its complicated jargon and references to such gay conventions of the day as "hunting" ("simplicis aucupium est").

42. In addition to the examples cited below and the poetry of Hilary, see Buecheler, p. 249, n. 781.

43. "Cur suspectum me tenet domina?" From the *Carmina Burana*, no. 211 in OBMLV, pp. 317–18.

44. "Puer sexus inmemor, sua vendit crura" ("Ganymede and Helen," line 156; translated in full in app. 2).

45. Ibid., lines 165–68:
Odor lucri bonus est, lucrum nemo vitat;
Nos, ut verum fatear, precium invitat.
Hunc, qui vult ditescere, ludum non dimittat!
Pueros his evehit, pueros hic ditat.
See also Wright, *Anglo-Latin Satirical Poets*, 2:145.

Another poet tersely observes of the object of his satire, "You enjoy the defilement itself more than the money to be made from it," [46] and Alain de Lille has Nature complain that "many of those youths whom I have favored with the grace of beauty are so obsessed with the love of money that they have exchanged their hammers of love for the duties of the anvil." [47]

One anonymous poem mentions male brothels in Chartres, Orléans, Sens, and Paris; another preserved in the same manuscript hints that such brothels employed only those with large genitals. The application of such a criterion of discrimination could scarcely be possible unless there were both a large demand for such services and a large class of those willing to provide them. The mere mention of such establishments is astonishing; such references (positive or negative) are wholly wanting in Christian literature up to the eleventh century and disappear immediately after the thirteenth.

One of the most interesting results of the reemergence of a gay subculture was the appearance for the first time in Latin literature of debates about homosexual versus heterosexual love. [48] Although such debates were common in Greek literature through the fourth century, they had disappeared altogether during the early Middle Ages, and no Latin equivalents are known before the twelfth century. Moreover, aside from the similarity of the premises—an argument over which type of love is superior—there is no demonstrable connection between the *dubbii* of antiquity and the poetic controversies of the High Middle Ages.

The earliest, most important, and longest of these was the "Debate between Ganymede and Helen." Modern scholarship has largely ignored this poem, but it was extremely popular in the Middle Ages: it survives wholly or in part in manuscripts all over Europe, from Italy to England, [49] and it

---

46. No. 6 in Werner, *Beiträge*, p. 5: "Mavis stuprari quam que solet inde lucrari." Also in Wright, 1:258.

47. *De planctu naturae*, Prose 4: "Multi etiam alii juvenes, mei gratia pulchritudinis honore vestiti, si debriati amore pecuniae, suos Veneris malleos in incudum transtulerunt officium" in Wright, 2:463.

48. A similar, though apocopated, gay response to heterosexual feelings may be recorded in the margin of an eleventh-century Viennese manuscript containing the popular poem "Iam dulcis amica, venito," where a contemporary hand has written in the left margin, "Iam dulcis amice, venito, quem sicut cor meum diligo" (see Strecker, *Die Cambridger Lieder*, pp. 69, 137). It is possible, however, that the correction is related to the confusion of speakers in stanzas 6–8.

49. Known manuscripts are listed in Rolf Lenzen, "Altercatio Ganimedis et Helene: Kritische Edition mit Kommentar," *Mittellateinisches Jahrbuch* 7 (1972): 161–86; such wide geographical and temporal distribution is notable. For the memorization of the poem, see Barthélémy Hauréau, "Notice sur un manuscrit de la Reine Christine à la Bibliothèque du Vatican," in *Mémoires de l'Académie des inscriptions et belles lettres* (Paris, 1878), 29:274–76. Since Hauréau published his comments several manuscripts of the poem have come to light

was recited aloud to students and known by heart by many educated persons. Its influence on subsequent literature was profound.[50]

Although there is probably no connection between "Ganymede and Helen" and the Hellenistic controversies on this subject,[51] the poem may not be entirely original. Debates were a staple of the literary diet of the twelfth century.[52] There were poetic arguments about whether clerics or knights were better lovers (the clerics always won: they wrote the poems),[53] whether spring or summer was the lovelier season, the niceties of good manners, which monastic order was superior in virtue, even matters of doctrine. While it is entirely possible that "Ganymede and Helen" was a spontaneous variation on this tradition in response to the increasingly prominent gay minority of the day (or composed by one of its members?), there are striking resemblances between it and a similar debate in the *Arabian Nights* which deserve consideration. In "The Dispute between the Man and the Learned Woman from Baghdad concerning the Relative Excellence of Girls and Boys," the speakers conduct a dispute much like that between Ganymede and

---

which strongly support his conclusion: a thirteenth-century English copy occurs with the language textbook of John of Garland (Cambridge, Gonville and Caius College MS 385); a twelfth-century French version follows the text of Hugh of St. Victor on the sacraments and precedes a primer of the Greek alphabet (Paris, BN, Lat. 2920); and a Vatican copy from the thirteenth century is bound with Priscian's *Institutiones grammaticae* (Biblioteca Apostolica Vaticana, Lat. 2719).

50. See Hauréau, "Notice"; Hans Walther, *Das Streitgedicht in der lateinischen Literatur des Mittelalters* (Munich, 1920), pp. 141–42, 203–6, with further bibliography. See also J. Schreiber, *Die Vagantenstrophe der mittellateinischen Dichtung* (Strasbourg, 1894), pp. 88 ff. The debate *De Clarevallensibus et Cluniacensibus*, attributed to Walther Mapes (Thomas Wright, *The Latin Poems Commonly Attributed to Walter Mapes* [London, 1841], pp. 237–42; cf. *Anglo-Latin Satirical Poets*, 2:83–87), also shows the influence of "Ganymede and Helen."

51. Despite the opinions of W. Wattenbach ("Ganymed und Helena," ZFDA 18, n.s., 6 [1875]: 124–36), Karl Praechter ("Zum Rhythmus Ganymed und Helena," ibid. 43, n.s., 31 [1899]: 169–71), and Curtius, there is not even a "distant connection" with the Pseudo-Lucian, with the exception of similar animal arguments, but it is unlikely that these represent literary borrowing. Animal arguments are common in any discussion of homosexuality, including modern scientific and political discussions, and literary influence cannot be assumed. The dialogue by John Katrarios, "Ἑρμόδοτος ἢ περὶ Κάλλους," ed. Antony Elter (Bonn, 1898), is the first work even in Greek to show any influence of the Pseudo-Lucian in the later Middle Ages, and it postdates "Ganymede and Helen" considerably (see Franz Schumacher, *De Ioanne Katrario Luciano imitatore* [Bonn, 1898]). Moreover, it is not a debate about types of love but a discussion about the propriety of attraction to physical beauty. Although it is predicated on a homosexual situation, gender is not an issue. Cf. n. 56.

52. Walther provides the broadest coverage of this complicated subject. F. J. E. Raby's chapter on "The Poetical Debate" (in *Secular Latin Poetry*, 2d ed. [Oxford, 1957]) is adequate as an introduction.

53. Discussed in Walther and Raby; an interesting variant on this—a debate among a convention of nuns—is mentioned in Lewis, *The Allegory of Love*, pp. 18–21.

Helen.[54] The use of a female disputant is especially significant; no antecedent examples of this genre involve women as disputants. This alteration of the classical format reflects a profound change in the position of women in the milieux in which the later debates were written; instead of appearing in the literature of love as simple objects, preferred by one male and rejected by another, in these discussions of gay love women take part on their own behalf, as intellectual equals of the males involved and as persons whose own sexual rights deserve equal time in the arena of debate.

Although the Arabic debate is not written entirely in verse, the majority of the arguments are quotations from poetry. The tone is acerbic, and misogyny plays a large part, just as in "Ganymede and Helen." The arguments range over many subjects; their facile ingenuity parallels those in "Ganymede and Helen." Both disputes are initiated by the female, and in both she seems to win, but on rather unconvincing notes. At several points the similarities between the objections of the two women are striking: both criticize homosexual relations on the basis of the stains they leave, and both finally protest the debate on the pretext of offended modesty.[55]

It is extremely unlikely that the Arabic tale in its present form could antedate "Ganymede and Helen," but it is not at all improbable that a prototype of it could have been known to the authors of both.[56] All scholars

54. In Richard Burton's translation this dispute begins in the 419th night (1st ed., 5:154–63). A clearer English translation is provided by Powys Mathers from the French of J. C. Mardrus, *The Book of the Thousand Nights and One Night* (London, 1972), in which the dispute occurs as tales 390–93 (2:409–15). Homosexuality occurs so frequently in the *Nights* that it would be impossible to cite even the major instances. Lesbianism is also specifically mentioned, which is rare in medieval literature of any language. For an interesting but fragmentary treatment, see de Becker, pp. 61–68. A slightly more sophisticated résumé is provided in Bullough, *Sexual Variance*, chap. 9. It is a great pity that no Arabist has dealt with this subject, since a thorough knowledge of the language is essential for an understanding of literary nuances.

55. Burton, 5:162–63; Mardrus, 2:414–15; "Ganymede and Helen," lines 193–96, 209–12, 241–44.

56. Whether or not the *Nights* existed in any set form in the twelfth century, many of the stories eventually included in them were in circulation. The *Kalila-wa-dimna*, e.g., translated into Castilian in the thirteenth century, was already known at the court of Eugene the emir of Sicily in the twelfth: see Charles H. Haskins, "The Greek Element in the Renaissance of the Twelfth Century," *American Historical Review* 25 (1920): 603–15. The earliest documentable European version of any of the *Nights* in their present form occurs in an Italian tale by Giovanni Sercambi (1347–1424), but manuscripts of parts dating from the thirteenth century or earlier have been discovered in Constantinople (see the EI, s.v. "Alf layla"). Moreover, debates on this subject in Arabic survive from as early as the ninth century, although only one has been published (and only in Arabic): al-Jāḥiẓ, *Kitāb mufākharat al-jawārī wa'l-ghilmān*. Arguments about gay love occur elsewhere in the *Nights*; e.g., in the tale of Budur (Mardrus, 5:60 ff.) in which, ironically, a woman in disguise tries to convince her husband that homosexuality is now the only fashionable form of love (see also the 329th night and following). That such discussions occur in precisely those tales which most suggest

are agreed that the Latin debate must have been composed in the twelfth century or later, and it is entirely possible that its composer could have known an Arabic story along similar lines, especially if he lived in southern France, as has been suggested.[57] Though its precise nature and range is still debated, there is now little opposition to the idea that Islamic literary traditions from Spain exercised some influence on southern French poetry.[58] "Ganymede and Helen" may bear the marks of that influence.

On the other hand, the poem is certainly original in many ways and deserves to be considered on its own merits. It is too important to be summarized here and is translated in its entirety in appendix 2. A few points deserve clarification. The apparent victory of Helen should be viewed cautiously. A disclaimer at the end of works celebrating sensual themes such as erotic passion (of any type) is common in literature of the High Middle Ages. Poetry dealing exclusively with heterosexual themes includes such "surprise endings" as well. The real sympathies of the writer in such cases must be read between the perfunctory opening and closing, but in the case of "Ganymede and Helen" this is not easy. Both sides are allowed to score

---

Greek influence argues for the possibility of some borrowing from Hellenistic *dubbii*, though the arguments themselves are dissimilar. For Greek influence on the *Arabian Nights*, see von Grunebaum, pp. 294–320.

57. However, there is little agreement about the home of the author. Curtius believed the poem was written by Bernard Sylvestris (p. 116) but made light of Wattenbach's suggestion that the author must have been of southern French origin because of the mention of olive trees: olive trees could reflect either Islamic or Italian influence as well. Lenzen notes much classical influence on the poem, suggesting that the author was quite well educated, in spite of the rather unsophisticated form of the lines. He overlooks the paraphrase of Suetonius's joke about Nero in lines 113–16 and the apparent reference to a Greek poem (now in AP, 13:17) in lines 133–36. I think southern French provenance overwhelmingly likely.

58. The question of the extent and means of influence of Arabic literature on Provençal and other vernacular literary traditions is too vast and unsettled a question to be treated here. A judicious and extremely erudite overview of the recent works on the subject may be found in Juan Vernet, *Literatura árabe* (Barcelona, 1966), pp. 215–27, with a bibliography on pp. 246–49. See also S. M. Stern, "Esistono dei rapporti letterari tra il mondo islamico e l'Europa occidentale nell'alto medio evo?" *Settimane* 12, no. 2 (1965): 639–66; or the much longer and more detailed treatment by Emilio García Gómez in *Las jarchas romances de la serie árabe en su marco* (Madrid, 1965). This process probably began earlier and was more important than has been implied by scholarship concentrating on literary aspects. See, e.g., Allan Cutler, "Who Was the 'Monk of France,' and When Did He Write?" *Al-Andalus* 28 (1963): 249–69; and J. W. Thompson, "The Introduction of Arabic Science into Lorraine in the 10th Century," *Isis* 12 (1929): 184–93. Failure to take cognizance of known channels of the dissemination of Arabic learning has led a number of scholars into errors. R. W. Southern made a point in his *Western Views of Islam in the Middle Ages* (Cambridge, Mass., 1962) of characterizing Gerbert's mathematical insight as derived exclusively from Latin translations of Greek originals, apparently unaware that Gerbert had studied in Spain, probably at Ripoll, a monastery now almost universally accepted as a center for the study of Arabic science.

points against each other, and both make good and bad arguments. The beauty of Helen and Ganymede is described without much hint of the author's preference, and most of the arguments result in a draw; Helen's arguments from "nature" cannot have been taken very seriously in a poem of this sort, nor were Ganymede's misogynistic parries apt to excite a twelfth-century audience used to antifeminist polemics. The narrator scores a point in her favor by commenting on the fertility of heterosexual coupling—a popular ploy in contemporary literature—but her own best attack is against the boy's avarice, which is especially interesting: she implies that she would find his behavior less reprehensible if it were motivated by love. This is probably an indication of the absolute value of love in the society which produced the poem. The argument ("waste of seed") with which she purportedly wins has been expressed earlier in the debate without effect and would be irrelevant in the sort of ambience which could produce a work of this sort.[59]

Several of Ganymede's points are telling. Helen apparently yields to his claim that gayness is common among the most important and influential people of the day and that the very people in a position to declare it a sin are involved in it. Some of his most superficial arguments do the most damage, e.g., his comments about Jupiter's interest in him as opposed to Juno, verified by the opening of the debate. Regardless of his personal sympathies, it is clear that the writer had more fun with Ganymede's arguments and was more inspired in penning them. His argument about the superiority of same-sex coupling on the basis of grammar was so clever and so felicitously phrased that it was quoted for more than a century after in the major works on homosexuality, whether for or against.[60]

59. But part of her argument may be missing; see app. 2, n. 71.

60. See, e.g., Gautier de Coinsi, "Seinte Léocade," in *Fabliaux et contes de poètes françois des XI, XII, XIII, XIV, et XV siècles*, ed. Etienne de Barbazan (Paris, 1808), 1:310:

La grammaire hic à hic acouple,
Mais nature maldit la couple. . . .
Nature rit, si com moi sanble,
Quant hic et hec joignent ensanble;
Mais hic et hic chose est perdue. . . .

See also *Gilles de Corbeil*, ed. C. Vieillard (Paris, 1909), p. 362:

Res specie similes in sexu dispare jungit;
Articulos genere sexus paritate coequat
Sintasis, ex toto cupiens concinna videri. . . .

The argument is repeated several times in slightly different forms in this long poem. Alain de Lille seems to echo the same idea in his *Complaint of Nature* 4 ("Eorum siquidem hominum qui Veneris profitentur grammaticam, alii solummodo masculinum, alii femininum, alii commune, sive genus promiscuum, familiariter amplexantur. Quidam vero, quasi heterocliti genere") and responds to it specifically and in great detail in prose 5, insisting that the elegance of a grammatical analogy cannot justify the error of homosexual relationships and formulating a counterargument based on the female organ as a noun and the male organ as an adjective.

What is probably most significant about the poem is not who won or lost or what the writer's feelings were but the tolerant ambience in which it must have been written. It parallels the gender blindness of Hellenistic poetry strikingly; the gods themselves comprise both factions: "Some are drawn by Helen, others by Ganymede" (line 66). There is no punishment or penance at the end for the defeated Ganymede, only rejoicing as love draws him to Helen and they are married.[61] In some versions the poet's last line is pointedly double-edged: "God, if ever I should perform this [i.e., "sodomy"], ignore me!" ("Deus, hoc si fecero, sis oblitus mei!"); in others (including what may be the best copy), the author adopts a somewhat more revealing tone: "God, if ever I should perform this, have mercy on me."[62]

"Ganymede and Helen" was the product of a society in which gay people were an important segment of the population, where defenses of gay love were sufficiently common to have taken on a defiant rather than apologetic tone and to have inspired poetic genius in representing them. The poem's extreme popularity in many areas of Europe may be due either to the fascination it exercised on less tolerant societies or to the ubiquity of the sort of circumstances which gave rise to it.

A similar debate of which only a single copy survives[63] may have been influenced by "Ganymede and Helen"; it involves a vitriolic controversy between Ganymede and Hebe before the council of heaven. If its author knew the earlier poem, however, he borrowed little but this situation. "Ganymede and Hebe" is far more erudite than its predecessor; a metrical rather than rhythmic poem, its ninety lines are filled with classical allusions and language, and it was probably inspired by a passage in Servius's commentary on the *Aeneid*,[64] where Juno is portrayed as outraged by Ganymede's arrival to take Hebe's place as cupbearer to the gods.[65]

61. This might suggest that active and passive roles were not regarded as very fixed: Ganymede would have had to play a more active role (technically, at least) with Helen.

62. A manuscript in the Houghton Library at Harvard University (MS Lat. 198) reads "Deus, hoc si fecero, miserere mei," and under this the reading of other extant manuscripts. A Vatican manuscript (Cod. Regin. Lat. 344) has "vel misertus" above "oblitus."

63. This poem has never been edited, probably due as much to its difficulty as to its subject matter, and it is published for the first time in app. 2. For its location, see app. 2, n. 91; it is incorrectly catalogued as including what is actually a separate poem in defense of married clergy (also translated and published for the first time in app. 2: "Married Clergy"). Neither poem has received scholarly notice before now.

64. Ovid *Metamorphoses* 10.155–61, where Juno's ire is only slightly less prominent, might also have been the inspiration. Servius, a commentator of the fourth century, profoundly influenced medieval appreciation of Vergil.

65. Servius, 2:31, "Ergo irascitur Iuno quod non ob hoc tantum raptus sit, ut pocula ministraret, sed quod ideo violatus sit, ut divinos honores consequeretur."

In the poem Juno is afraid to reproach Jove herself and persuades Hebe to speak out against Ganymede before the gods and to ask that he not be allowed to usurp the honors rightly enjoyed by goddesses. Unlike the author of "Ganymede and Helen," the author of this poem makes no pretense of neutrality; he is clearly and openly on the side of Ganymede, who, he says, eclipses Hebe in beauty "as the sun outshines the moon" (51–52).

Although it evinces classical influence, "Ganymede and Hebe" is thoroughly original and seems to represent some sort of personal statement rather than literary exercise. Hebe does not invoke traditional moral strictures against homosexual acts, nor is "nature" given more than passing mention; instead, she laments the success of his heavenly venture and asks that his dangerously potent effect on the gods be somehow brought under control. Ganymede's rejoinder is acerbic and bitter, part misogyny and part elliptical allusions which may have had some meaning as contemporary proverbs or perhaps as conventions of speech among the gay subculture. It is certainly a less telling defense of homosexuality than the response of Ganymede in the earlier poem, but probably no less sincere. The final parry—"Either I rightly enjoy the ruler in heaven, or one must regard as a crime / Something which the providence of fate has made necessary" (89–90)—is highly reminiscent of Baudri's eloquent defense of his nature and suggests a belief among gay people of the time that their preferences were innate and thus inculpable. This idea, if widespread, could account for the nearly total absence of negative moral theology on the subject during this period; it is at any rate certain that in the following century Aquinas was quite prepared to accept Aristotle's belief that homosexual inclinations were innate and therefore "natural."

A much less erudite but in some ways more interesting dispute over gay love may have been invented without the knowledge of the heterosexual partisan. A unique manuscript now preserved in Leiden contains separate verses attacking gay love and homosexual practices, naming Chartres, Sens, Orléans, and Paris as preeminent in the practices described and denigrating a flourishing and well-developed gay subculture of prostitution and highly specialized erotic interests.[66]

66. Dümmler, "Briefe und Verses des neunten Jahrhunderts," pp. 358–60. Dümmler dates the hand in which the poetry is written as twelfth- or thirteenth-century. Historical considerations make the former more likely. The manuscript formerly belonged to the scholar Peter Daniel of Orléans. These verses do not seem to be the work of one person; they have apparently been collected from various writings and juxtaposed in a little primer of objections to homosexuality. Stanzas 12–14 are notably more sophisticated than the earlier ones; the last suggests the sort of objection to all nonstandard (i.e., nonprocreative) sexuality which characterizes the Scholastic theology of the later twelfth and early thirteenth centuries. Stanzas 5–8 were probably not intended as references to homosexuality in their original

Let Chartres and Sens perish, where Adonis sells himself
  According to the law of the brothel, where males are prostituted.
A noble city, a unique city infected with these evils,
  Paris rejoices to wed a young master.
You are more depraved than all of these, Orléans;
  You perish holding the title for this crime.

Up to now Chartres and Paris have reveled
In the vice of Sodom; now the Paris of Sens also becomes an Io.[67]

The men of Orléans are preeminent—if you think well
Of the manners of this type—at sleeping with boys.

By the counsel of Venus my girlfriend sends me a call boy:[68]
With this member she wants to keep her womb for herself.

        .   .   .   .

Enemy of nature, who cares not to engender,
  You spill your seed into the forbidden lap of Erichthonius.[69]

----

context, so I have deleted them from the text, but I translate them here for the interest of
readers:

  While your purse jingles, a crowd of friends crowns you:
  When the sound stops, you start to be your own companion.

  The bed is wooden, but not cut from any tree:
  Whoever will pay, let him pay and it will be his.

  There is a certain river which has a remarkable name:
  If you subtract the head, it is a soldier; the tail, a bird;
  If you take away the mid-part, it is that from which a scar comes.

  If the blind lead the blind, justice is equalized,
  So that both fall at once if they go off the path.

Stanza 5 may refer to masturbation, but cf. J. A. Schmeller, *Carmina Burana: Lateine und deutsche Lieder und Gedichte einer Handschrift des XIII Jahrhunderts aus Benediktbeuern*, in *Bibliothek des literarischen Vereins in Stuttgart*, vol. 16 (1847), no. 170A. I can shed no light on the odd use of "wood" in st. 6: possibly wood had a sexual significance in the later Middle Ages comparable to that of leather in the modern West. Petronius (119) also makes oblique comments about wood with moralistic overtones, and Burchard describes a technique of masturbation involving wood (*Decretorum* 19.5 [PL, 140:968]). Stanza 7 is a riddle: the answer is "Vulturnus," from "Turnus," a soldier; "vultur," a bird; and "vulnus," a wound, whence one gets a scar. I can suggest no reason for the inclusion of the puzzle here except that it is similar to one written by Baudri of Bourgueil, a gay poet. Perhaps there is some arcane sexual allusion in it. Cf. Dümmler, p. 358, n. 4. Stanza 8 is a biblical *topos*: Matt. 15:14. The same image occurs in poetry with heterosexual themes: e.g., see Lluís Nicolau d'Olwer, "L'escola poètica de Ripoll en els segles X–XIII," *Institut d'estudis catalans* 6 (1923): 70.

  67. In the first line "Paris" is a city; in the second, the prince of Troy. Cf. Öberg, *Serlon*, pp. 106–7.

  68. The manuscript has "Sabelum," which could be Sabine or more probably a reference to the Sabellus of Martial's epigrams, esp. 3.98 and 6.33.

  69. Eponym for a Trojan, probably in reference to Ganymede.

Scorch, God, with a blow of your thunderbolt, the enemy of nature,
Who wastes the labor of creation in the lap of a male.

He should die shamefully who, coupled in shameful love,
Gives the thigh of a boy what he owes the mouth of the womb.
Sweet companion, henceforth despise the legions of Gomorrah,
And be mindful, I implore you, of the fact that such
Cities have time and again passed into ruin by fire.
When you are supine, while you recline on the altar of death,
You make roosters hens and boys girls.

Small in body, be assured they are giant in the crotch,
  For each little one has a long member.
Though he himself be small, nonetheless the measure of size
  Is taken at the groin, which must be long.[70]

A man who is free to sin sins less; the freedom
  Renders feeble the seeds of evil.
Who is less free to sin the rare ability
  Drags more vehemently into every occasion of sinning.

The greedy woman provides a receptacle in three places,
Whence the crime of Sodom is rendered easy to imitate by many,
Since all it requires is the young and beautiful.

Appended to these verses in the same manuscript, but in a different
handwriting, is an incomplete collection of verses in favor of gay love,
obviously intended as a refutation of those which precede it.

The indiscriminate Venus grasps at any remedy,
But the wise one rejoices with the tender Ganymede.

I have heard it said that he plays Venus more than she,
But Venus is happy, since he only stuffs boys.[71]

Nothing is more certain than this, that Venus would
Be devoid of every sweetness if she lacked Ganymede.

---

70. Cf. Wright, *Anglo-Latin Satyrical Poets*, no. 115, 2:119:
Qui vidit te, Grosphe, duos deprendit in uno,
A retro puerum videt, ab ante, virum.
Si ludis, puer es; da posteriora, probatur,
Ludum defendis; vertere, liber eris.
71. "Garcifarizat": one of many romance vulgarisms in the poetry. The translation is in
many places approximate, since the verses were either poorly transcribed or written in
substandard Latin. This line is especially puzzling.

For his face smiles, his complexion shines, his legs are soft,
His lap[72] is sweet, his heart gentle and his beauty charming;
His demeanor is open, suppressing shyness, his spirit
Is ready for the boyish sin, and his body prepared
To undergo anything his seducer should ask:
This boy surpasses all treasure; nothing is more blessed than he.

Many you will find for whom the boyish sin is execrable in words
But who do not dislike the deed.
The more they detest it with their words—to hide what they love and
    freely do—
The more they indulge it in their acts.

Venus kindles all fires, but the greatest heat
Is in sex with males; whoever has tried it knows it.

Often you will see old men whose youths were so sordid. . . .[73]

The phraseology and form of this "debate" bear little relation to those discussed above, but it is evocative of similar social conditions, i.e., the existence of a gay subculture of sufficient self-consciousness to pen literary defenses for itself and to make claims for the superiority of homosexual eroticism.[74]

Another pastiche debate follows a declamation against the evils of women, in which the poet sneers at procreation-based arguments for heterosexual love:

A woman's love is not love but poison.
It tastes like honey, but it is deceptive: it is pus, full of rot.
If anyone should ask, Why then do we honor them?
We honor women because offspring issue from them,
And they are the watchdogs of the home like wolves in their dens.[75]

72. Literally, "groin."

73. The text is incomplete. The *topos* of the old man ridiculously pursuing love as if still a youth is common to twelfth-century poetry and is applied in gay as well as nongay contexts: e.g., see A. Wilmart, "Le florilège mixte de Thomas Bekynton," *Medieval and Renaissance Studies* 4 (1958): 63, no. 12.

74. The use of the word "sin" in a gay response is interesting, as it suggests a certain casual cynicism about the attitude of hostile theologians: obviously the writer does not consider the behavior sinful in any worrisome sense. Possibly in certain social circles the word had a force comparable to the modern English "vice," which describes activities as disparate in moral gravity as selling narcotics and overindulging in sweets.

75. Munich, Bayerische Staatsbibliothek, clm 6911, fol. 128. (thirteenth or fourteenth century):

Nec muliebris amor amor est. Est imo uenenum.
Mel sapit in ludo; pus est putredine plenum.
Si quis erit, qui quesierit, "Cur ergo coluntur?"
Exit ab hiis proles, ideo colimus mulieres;
Et sunt heredis custodes ut lupus edis.

It is followed by a couplet predicting eternal damnation for "sodomites":
"Let them perish and go to hell, never to return, / Who prefer young men as
wives."[76] But this in turn is answered by another couplet, apparently (though
obliquely) upholding the "naturalness" of nonprocreative sexuality:
"Against you, Nature, who are more beautiful than all, / No one has sinned
unless he has created something mortal."[77]

This extraordinary efflorescence of gay subculture, with a highly developed
literature, its own argot and artistic conventions, its own low life, its elaborate
responses to critics, did not survive far into the thirteenth century. The
society which produced it—a society of ebullient expansion and intense
devotion to the humane values of antiquity, a brilliant urban culture consciously tolerant of human variation—was radically changed during the
thirteenth century by forces which are discussed in the following chapter.

Given the complexity of the political scene at the time and the infinite
variety of human response, it is startling how completely and dramatically
the gay artistic tradition was broken off. A few poems exemplifying this
tradition survive from the first half of the thirteenth century,[78] including
what may be the sole extant example of medieval love poetry written in a
vernacular language by one woman to another.[79] But by the end of the
century such literature and apparently the subculture it represented were
utterly gone. Even hostile comments about homosexuality take on a different
tone. No longer do they seem to be partisan opposition to a large social

76. "Intereant et eant ad tartara non redituri, / Qui teneros pueros pro coniuge sunt
habituri." This couplet comprises the final lines of the Paris redaction of "Quam pravus
mos": see app. 2, "A Perverse Custom."

77. "In te, natura, que pulchrior omnibus una / Es, nil peccavit, nisi quod mortale
creavit." It is by no means clear that the juxtaposition of the cited lines was intended to
constitute argumentation on the subject of homosexuality. Many unrelated lines occur
sequentially in the collection. The survival of poems derogating a procreative justification of
love, however, is quite interesting, whatever their relationship to the more typical thirteenth-
century lines about "sodomites." Dronke (*Medieval Latin*, 2:490) interprets the lines quite
differently, translating thus: "In creating you—who alone are more beautiful than all—
Natura has been faultless, save that she made you mortal." The context in the manuscript
(which Dronke does not discuss, since he is interested only in these and the two following
lines), the placement of "natura" and "que," and the use of "quod mortale" all seem to me
to argue against this interpretation. "Nisi quod mortale creavit" is an awkward reference
to "te," but not inappropriate in a more general sense.

78. One such poem, about Ganymede, is translated in app. 2. However, it may have been
written in the twelfth century.

79. The poem is published with an English translation by Meg Bogin, *The Women
Troubadours* (New York, 1976), pp. 132–33. The text was first published by Oscar Schultz-
Gora, *Die provenzalischen Dichterinnen* (Leipzig, 1888), p. 28, from a manuscript now in Paris.
For the identity of the author, whose gender is disputed on the basis of extremely scanty
evidence in either direction, see Bogin, pp. 176–77.

element; now they are harsh condemnations of individual and seemingly isolated sinners.

The change was as far-reaching as the phenomenon itself and terminated the artistic effusions not only of gay Christian clerics and laymen but even of non-Christians; the last Jewish poet to continue the tradition of gay Hebrew poetry in Spain wrote in the thirteenth century.[80] After his death the voice of Europe's gay minority was stilled, not to be heard again for centuries, and not until the present century with the variety and profusion of the eleventh and twelfth.

80. Todros Abulafia: see Schirmann, "The Ephebe," pp. 61–62. Of course, some of the gay literature already composed doubtless continued to be read and copied, as the many manuscripts containing poems by Marbod and others indicate. For a fascinating example, see the letter (obviously influenced by "Ganymede and Hebe") requesting sexual favors from a boy, included in the thirteenth-century collection of model letters published by Léopold Delisle, "Notice sur une *Summa dictaminis* jadis conservée à Beauvais," in *Notices et extraits des manuscrits de la Bibliothèque Nationale et autres bibliothèques* 36 (Paris, 1899): 199–200 (and the boy's negative reply, p. 200).

IV The Rise of Intolerance

10 Social Change:

Making Enemies

Most of the attitudes of fanaticism and intolerance which are today thought of as characteristically "medieval" were in fact common only to the later Middle Ages. The early Middle Ages, with a few exceptions, had accommodated a great many beliefs and life-styles with relative ease. In many areas of Europe Catholics managed to coexist peacefully with Arians, Donatists, or Manicheans, and when trouble erupted between such groups it was often the non-Catholics who initiated it. Outside of Spain Jews and gay people not only lived quietly among the general population but often rose to positions of prominence and power. Prosecutions for heresy were unknown after the decline of Roman power until the rise of new secular states in the High Middle Ages. Nor did what civil authority existed undertake to regulate personal morality in any detailed way during the early Middle Ages. Civil laws regulating sexuality or marriage were rare, of limited application, and weakly enforced. For all its credulity, poverty, ignorance, and deprivation, the early Middle Ages was not a period of consistent oppression for most minorities.

Almost all historians are agreed that the late eleventh and early twelfth centuries were periods of "openness" and tolerance in European society, times when experimentation was encouraged, new ideas eagerly sought, expansion favored in both the practical and intellectual realms of life.[1] And most historians consider that the thirteenth and fourteenth centuries were ages of less tolerance, adventurousness, acceptance—epochs in which

1. Although none refer to gay people specifically, the most useful studies of the later Middle Ages in relation to this chapter are probably those of John Mundy, *Europe in the High Middle Ages, 1150–1309* (New York, 1973), an excellent survey of the social and legal changes of the period; J. K. Huizinga, *The Waning of the Middle Ages*, trans. F. Hopman (New York, 1924), a now famous essay about the social catastrophes which befell west central Europe in the final medieval centuries; and Friedrich Heer, *The Medieval World: Europe, 1100–1350*, trans. Janet Sondheimer (New York, 1962), which advances the idea that the twelfth century was an "open" one and the thirteenth the beginning of a period of "closing." Heer's chap. 13, on "Jews and Women," is particularly relevant. More specialized bibliography can be found in these works, and by topic below.

European societies seem to have been bent on restraining, contracting, protecting, limiting, and excluding. Few scholars, however, are in exact agreement about why this change took place.

Even in the specific case of intolerance of gay people it is mysterious. It does not seem, for instance, to have had any relation to the "urban/rural" dichotomy mentioned earlier in this study. Although demographic analysis of medieval populations is, as noted, notoriously difficult, and there may have been factors such as an increase in the number of rural immigrants to cities which affected later medieval sexual tolerance, on balance it seems very unlikely that the population of Europe was any less "urban" in the thirteenth or fourteenth century than it had been in the twelfth. If any change occurred, it was probably in the direction of further urbanization; it may in fact have been increasing urban predominance which generated or aggravated some of the severe social tensions of the later Middle Ages.

On the other hand, another factor discussed previously almost certainly played a large role in the narrowing of social tolerance during the period: the rise of absolute government. Perhaps the single most prominent aspect of the period from the later twelfth to the fourteenth century was a sedulous quest for intellectual and institutional uniformity and corporatism throughout Europe. This trend not only resulted in the strengthening and consolidation of civil and ecclesiastical power and administrative machinery but left its mark on less concrete monuments of European culture as well. Theology was fitted into systematic formulas and collected in comprehensive compendia—summas—of such formulas. The Inquisition arose to eliminate theological loose ends and divergences of opinion. Secular knowledge was gathered into uniform approaches, encyclopedias, which attempted to unite all of contemporary learning in one book or system. Secular and ecclesiastical concerns were melded in the interests of uniformity, as in the collections of canon law which joined Roman civil law with Christian religious principles in an effort to standardize clerical supervision of ethical, moral, and legal problems.

Probably nothing so exemplifies the later medieval fascination with order and uniformity as the astronomical increase in the amount of legislation of all sorts enacted from the thirteenth century on. The total of royal edicts and enactments for all the ruling houses of Europe during the twelfth century would probably come to not more than 100 volumes. By the fourteenth century the output from a single monarch in a small kingdom might run to 3,000–4,000 registers of documents.[2] The rediscovery of the political works of

2. The number of papal legal rescripts also increased by a factor of 10 or more during the same two centuries; the fourteenth-century pope John XXII left about 65,000 papal bulls

the ancients—particularly the compilation of Roman law effected by Justinian—occasioned a great increase in theoretical as well as practical interest in lawmaking. Probably at no time since the reforms of Diocletian had there been so dramatic a change in the legal structure of Europe as in the latter half of the thirteenth century, when new law codes were drafted or old ones revised for almost every area of the European mainland.

Much of this codification and consolidation of power entailed loss of freedom for distinctive or disadvantaged social groups. Although it is extremely difficult to generalize about such things, it seems that women steadily lost power after the twelfth century, as admission to the organizational hierarchy of both church and state became more and more fixed and inflexible and required qualifications—such as ordination or a university education—which were difficult or impossible for women to attain. Some groups became real minorities for the first time. The poor, who rarely appeared in documents before the thirteenth century except as abstract objects of ethical concern, increasingly troubled the authorities of the later Middle Ages and were very frequently cited—rightly or wrongly—as the cause of the social unrest of the thirteenth and fourteenth centuries.[3] They became the objects of massive legislation and considerable antipathy on the part of the establishments of various countries.

Pressure for conformity and corporate unity was not limited to institutions. It appeared in all classes. Indeed legal regulations imposed on Jews and Muslims during this period were often designed to prevent popular uprisings against them. Some bishops protected heretics from the mob, and many kings undertook to punish violence against Jews. The later medieval increase in popular hostility to previously tolerated minority groups is no easier to explain than growing institutional rigidity. It was certainly aggravated by social tensions related to changing agricultural and economic

---

(Mundy, p. 6). The demand created by such enormous legal machinery not only gave rise to a huge class of notaries and lawyers throughout Europe but changed the whole fabric of the educational system from one devoted almost exclusively to the pursuit of religious and philosophical concerns to one very largely directed toward the production of bureaucrats for church and state.

3. A brief but judicious account of the treatment of the poor in the early Middle Ages may be found in Ullmann, "Public Welfare and Social Legislation"; and F. J. Niederer, "Early Medieval Charity," *Church History* 21 (1952): 285–96. For the poor in general and in the High Middle Ages, see *Etudes sur l'histoire de la pauvreté*, 2 vols., ed. M. Mollat, Publications de la Sorbonne, Etudes, no. 8 (Paris, 1974). In English, see Brian Tierney, *Medieval Poor Law: A Sketch of Canonical Theory and Its Application in England* (Berkeley, 1959), or "The Decretists and the Deserving Poor," *Comparative Studies in Society and History* 1 (1958–59): 360–73; and F. Graus, "The Late Medieval Poor in Town and Countryside," in Thrupp, *Change*.

patterns, but it is not clear how to separate cause from effect in analyzing such developments, and specific reasons for public hostility toward one group are probably only a small part of the explanation for an intolerance which encompassed minorities of very different social status, economic importance, and distinctiveness from the majority. The indebtedness of hard-pressed peasants (or embarrassed monarchs) to Jewish moneylenders, for instance, doubtless played a role in the rise of anti-Semitism in increasingly cash-based economies, but it is notable that in anti-Semitic propaganda of the day Jews are no more apt to be associated with usurers than with Muslims, heretics, traitors, "sodomites," or other groups disliked by the majority for entirely different reasons. During the decades surrounding the opening of the fourteenth century, the Jews were expelled from England and France; the order of the Templars dissolved on charges of sorcery and deviant sexuality; Edward II of England, the last openly gay medieval monarch, deposed and murdered; lending at interest equated with heresy and those who supported it subjected to the Inquisition; and lepers all over France imprisoned and prosecuted on charges of poisoning wells and being in league with Jews and witches.[4] There was certainly no single cause for such varied expressions of public hostility, but it is difficult to view them as wholly unrelated. However different the immediate circumstances which produced them, they all drew support from widespread fears of alien and disruptive social elements, fears which could easily be focused on vulnerable or little-understood minority groups.

If the ultimate origins of late medieval intolerance are at present indeterminable, the proximate causes are a little more accessible. One of the most obvious of these was the xenophobia which induced, accompanied, and resulted from the crusades. It is somewhat ironic that religious and secular leaders had at first hoped the crusades would reduce internal conflict in Europe by deflecting internecine hostilities and chronic feudal warfare onto a common external enemy. Once roused to fervor against the enemies of Christendom, however, crusading armies showed less discrimination in venting their aggressive feelings than pious leaders had anticipated. The first crusading armies got no further than Germany before they turned their

4. This last phenomenon has received scant scholarly attention, although it resulted in loss of property and autonomy for many leprosaria and life for some lepers. In 1322 Charles IV ordered all lepers in France incarcerated forever; the order was never carried out, but it effectively terminated the popular upheaval. I am grateful to Susanne Roberts for making available to me her unpublished paper on this subject, "The Leper-Scare of 1321 and the Growth of Consular Power," based on her research in southern French municipal archives. Her paper effectively demonstrates the complex interactions of popular fear, royal greed, and local jealousy over juridical prerogatives that operated to the disadvantage of many minorities during the later Middle Ages.

combative energy on the helpless Jews of the Rhineland and murdered them by the thousands.[5]

The Jews were in fact one of the first casualties of the intolerance of the later Middle Ages. For centuries they had lived among European Christians quietly and with little difficulty. Few popes or bishops had objected to their presence, and they had become integral parts of urban economies through commerce and finance. During the later eleventh and early twelfth centuries Jews had been among the intellectual leaders of the "twelfth-century renaissance," contributing not only many of the translations of Graeco-Arabic science and philosophy which filtered into the rest of Europe from Spain but also the content of much religious and philosophical thinking of the time.

During the latter half of the twelfth century, however, an increasingly conformist European society found the persistent distinctiveness of the Jews more and more irritating. Tracts and derogatory writings about Jews began to appear. By 1173, when Thomas of Monmouth published his account of the ritual murder by Jews of a Christian child (William of Norwich, subsequently Saint William of Norwich),[6] both the story and the veneration of the child supposedly martyred by the Jews easily gained wide popularity in England and France. Accusations of the ritual murder of Christian children became commonplace throughout Europe and had disastrous consequences for the Jews. No charge against a minority seems to be more damaging than the claim that they pose a threat of some sort to the children of the majority.

Only a few years later, the Third Lateran Council of 1179 issued a series of statutes designed to curb Jewish economic and civil authority and to limit Jewish-Christian social interaction.[7] Although Jews continued to prosper

5. Mundy's account (pp. 81–108) of the persecution of the Jews in the later Middle Ages is particularly lucid. In addition to the other works cited in n. 1, see E. A. Synan, *The Popes and the Jews in the Middle Ages* (New York, 1965); Jacob Marcus, *The Jew in the Medieval World* (New York, 1972); Solomon Grayzel, *The Church and the Jews in the Thirteenth Century* (Philadelphia, 1933); and articles by G. I. Langmuir, e.g., "The Jews and the Archives of Angevin England: Reflections on Medieval Anti-Semitism," *Traditio* 19 (1963): 183–224, or "'Judei nostri' and the Beginning of Capetian Legislation," ibid. 16 (1960): 203–69. See also the bibliographical essays by Ivan Marcus ("The Jews in Eastern Europe: Fourth to Sixteenth Century") and Kenneth Stow ("The Church and the Jews: from St. Paul to Paul IV") in *Bibliographical Essays in Medieval Jewish Studies*. More specialized bibliography can be traced through these studies.

6. See translation and discussion in Jacob Marcus, *The Jew in the Medieval World*, pp. 121–26. Note also the use of alleged threats to children in derogating Muslims and gay people. Europeans and some Americans well into the twentieth century believed that gypsies would steal children.

7. Neither twelfth-century Jewish-Christian relations (which were generally good) nor the Third Lateran Council have received much scholarly attention. The decrees of this

in parts of Europe—the papal household was managed by Jews throughout the century[8]—Philip Augustus of France capitalized on burgeoning intolerance by imprisoning the Jews on his lands and demanding a heavy ransom for their release (1180), annulling all loans made to Christians by Jews (1181), and finally (1182) expelling the Jews from his domain.[9] He subsequently readmitted them, but the accusations of ritual murder he used to justify his actions greatly inflamed popular passions. By the thirteenth century Jews appeared in French literature in the same category as "thieves, kidnappers, usurers, assassins, murderers, and traitors,"[10] and Christians who had sexual relations with Jews were equated with those who had intercourse with animals.[11]

The Fourth Lateran Council, meeting in 1215,[12] forbade Jews to hold any public office, restricted their financial arrangements, prohibited them from going outdoors during the last days of Holy Week, and ordered them to wear clothing which distinguished them from Christians. The last measure began the process of legal ostracism which was to culminate in violence and expulsion throughout Europe. In areas like Spain, where Jewish communities were large and influential, where religious variety was commonplace and many social systems interacted (and where—most important—prominent Christians undertook to defend the Jews), wearing the "Jewish badge" was not enforced.[13] In areas of greater homogeneity like England, where social uniformity could be realized without substantial economic loss or public disruption, Jews were forced to wear it. Inevitably, it only aggravated popular hostility. In 1290 the Jews were permanently expelled from England. In France, although inveighed against by the lower clergy and despised by such prominent and beloved figures as Saint Louis,[14] they were able to hold on

---

council (Mansi, 22:209–468) dealing with the Jews are summarized in general texts such as that of Grayzel. A convenient summary of the historical framework of each of the Lateran Councils and translations of their decrees may be consulted in Raymonde Foreville, *Latran I, II, III et Latran IV* (Paris, 1965).

8. Synan, pp. 79–80.

9. Marcus, *The Jew in the Medieval World*, pp. 24–27.

10. See, e.g., Jacques de Vitry *Historia occidentalis*, ed. John Hinnebusch (Fribourg, 1972), chap. 3, p. 80: "et ideo fures, raptores, sacrilegos, feneratores, iudeos, sicarios et homicidas, et seditiosos homines." Note that de Vitry feels that all such persons should be not only severely punished but "extirpated" ("Quos graviter punire et penitus exstirpare et de medio tollere debuerunt").

11. See below, p. 292 and n. 70.

12. Discussed in Foreville, pp. 277 ff. Text in Mansi, 22:953–1086. The decrees of both Third and Fourth Lateran Councils in regard to Jews and gay people (as well as other minorities) were incorporated into canon law in the thirteenth century.

13. Discussed in Grayzel, pp. 61–70, with bibliography.

14. Joinville records Louis's suggestion that Jews who spoke against Christian theological tenets be slain on the spot by any Christian present: see *The Life of Saint Louis*, trans. M.

until the beginning of the fourteenth century; in Germany to the fifteenth. They lasted longest in Spain but suffered repeatedly at the hands of fanatical mobs; many were forced under threat of death to convert to Christianity and became liable to the Inquisition after they had done so. Those who remained openly Jewish—although an enormous number—were finally expelled en masse at the close of the Middle Ages in 1492.[15]

Long before this, crusading fervor had spilled over onto other Europeans who were neither Jewish nor Muslim. In the early thirteenth century France became the first Christian nation to declare a crusade against other Europeans on the basis of differing religious views. A particularly popular constellation of heretical movements in the south of France, loosely called the "Albigensian heresy,"[16] had attracted so much attention and become so threatening to many that a crusade was declared against it, and a great army of northerners descended on the area. Modern historians have generally regarded the purely religious issues as a small part of the origins of the conflict; even the pope who had declared the crusade eventually tried to stop it, and many orthodox Christians—like Peter "the Catholic" of Aragon, who died fighting on the heretical side[17]—saw it as political aggression on the part of the northern French. Like most examples of thirteenth-century pressure for conformity, the "Albigensian Crusade" was a complex mixture of religious, economic, and political motivations; simple greed and the masses' great fear of disruptive elements (external or internal) were also crucial.

Many other groups felt the weight of pressure to conform. The Franciscans came perilously close to being declared heretical before their final acceptance by the church; and fear of the poor, increasingly perceived as members of an alien element rather than the victims of circumstance, reached such a

---

Shaw (London, 1969), pt. 1, chap. 1, p. 175. William of Chartres said that Louis so hated the Jews that he could not even look upon them (see Mundy, p. 95). But cf. Michel Riquet, "Saint Louis, roi de France, et les Juifs," in *La septième centenaire de la mort de St. Louis* (Paris, 1976), pp. 345–50.

15. For the best account of the Spanish Jews in the later Middle Ages, see Baer, *The Jews in Christian Spain*.

16. The literature on the Albigensians is vast. Particularly useful to the English-speaking reader are J. Strayer, *The Albigensian Crusades* (New York, 1971); and W. Wakefield, *Heresy, Crusade and the Inquisition in Southern France, 1100–1259* (London, 1974). In French, Michel Roquebert, *L'épopée cathare* (Toulouse, 1970–77); and Christine Thouzellier, *Catharisme et valdéisme en Languedoc à la fin du XIIe et au début du XIIIe siècle* (Paris, 1966) are useful. See also the general works on heresy cited below.

17. Ironically, Peter had gained his reputation fighting—and defeating—the Muslims in Spain. He was not sympathetic to heresy but hostile to northern intervention in southern France, where the Aragonese had dynastic interests.

pitch by the early fourteenth century that the papacy forbade too zealous an adherence to the ancient ideal of apostolic poverty as heretical.[18]

Lending at interest, although always officially deplored, had been tacitly allowed during most of the Middle Ages, but during the thirteenth century those who engaged in the practice, "usurers,"[19] suddenly found themselves the objects of the most drastic penalties. At the beginning of the century, Philip II of France was content merely to regulate the rate of interest demanded on loans,[20] but by 1254 increasing hostility to usurers induced Louis IX to forbid the taking of interest altogether.[21] The church's tolerance also gave way: laymen who lent at interest were first excommunicated and then, when this failed of effect, denied Christian burial. Usury became a reserved sin, absolvable only by a bishop or papal delegate. Servants of usurers became excommunicate, as did by 1274 priests who administered sacraments to them or allowed them Christian burial. A whole area could incur interdict for failure to expel usurers, and cemeteries in which usurers were buried were interdicted until the body was exhumed. Those who borrowed at interest and did not denounce the usurer within a month were excommunicate. The Council of Vienne in 1311 solemnly declared that anyone who maintained that lending at interest was not gravely sinful was guilty of heresy and liable to the Inquisition.[22]

In such an atmosphere it is scarcely surprising that gay people found themselves the objects of increasing mistrust and hostility on the part of the heterosexual majority.

---

18. *Cum inter nonnullos 1323*; see M. D. Lambert, *Franciscan Poverty* (New York, 1961), pp. 235–36; cf. E. W. McDonnell, "The *Vita apostolica*: Diversity or Dissent?" *Church History* 24 (1955): 15–31.

19. "Usury" applied not to excessive interest but to the taking of interest at all, except under highly circumscribed conditions. The best short analysis of ecclesiastical attitudes and rulings on usury during this period is still that of T. P. McLaughlin, "The Teaching of the Canonists on Usury (XII, XIII, and XIV Centuries)," *Mediaeval Studies* 1 (1939): 81–147, and 2 (1940): 1–22; see also J. T. Noonan, *The Scholastic Analysis of Usury* (Cambridge, Mass., 1957); John T. Gilchrist, *The Church and Economic Activity in the Middle Ages* (New York, 1969); and the older but still interesting treatment of B. N. Nelson, *The Idea of Usury*, 2d ed. (Chicago, 1969). Texts of medieval economic history are of course useful on this topic (e.g., Carlo Cipolla, *Money, Prices and Civilization in the Mediterranean World, Fifth to Seventeenth Century* [Princeton, N.J., 1956]), as are more general texts (e.g., Mundy, pp. 174–89).

20. E. de Laurière, *Ordonnances des roys du troisième race* (Paris, 1723–1849), 1:36, 44.

21. "De christianis vero . . . prohibemus districte, quod nullas usuras haberi faciant Barones, Senescalli nostri, vel alie quecumque persone eisdem. Usuras autem intelligimus quidquid est ultra sortem," ibid., "Grande ordonnance," sec. 33. The textual tradition of this legislation is extremely uncertain. The critical edition promised by L. Carolus Barré ("La grande ordonnance de 1254 sur la réforme de l'administration et la police du royaume," in *La septième centenaire*, pp. 85–96) has not appeared.

22. This decree was incorporated permanently into canon law: *Clementinarum* 5.5.1.

The first records of such pressures against gay people and their sexuality occur in popular tracts objurgating the mores of the times, like Bernard of Morlaix's "Contempt of the World."[23] Homosexual acts are usually represented in such writings not as peculiarly reprehensible but simply as symptoms of the hedonism and sensuality of the day, like heterosexual fornication, greed, venality, and the arrogance of the wealthy.

A few social critics, however, did single gay people out for special attack. In opposition to most previous exegesis, for instance, Peter Cantor (d. 1197) interpreted Romans 1 : 26–27 as referring exclusively to gay people and applied nearly a dozen other biblical passages to the sinfulness of homosexuality.[24] Using the word "sodomy" to refer solely to homosexual acts (again against theological precedent), he argued that it was not merely a violation of chastity but on a par with murder as one of two sins that "cry out to heaven for vengeance." He did not hesitate to invoke the law of Leviticus as precedent for the physical punishment of "sodomites," though it had been ignored or treated allegorically by most writers since the Council of Jerusalem. Peter was distressed that there were no general ecclesiastical sanctions against behavior which had, in his view, incurred the destruction of five cities. "Why is it," he demanded, "that what the Lord punished severely the church leaves untouched?"[25] Since there were no legal penalties for homosexuality in effect in France at the time, Peter appealed to the Roman civil enactment of 342 as precedent for secular prosecution of homosexuality.

As if in direct response to Peter's urging, Lateran III of 1179 became the first ecumenical ("general") council to rule on homosexual acts. Reacting to growing European intolerance of all forms of nonconformity, the council imposed sanctions against moneylenders, heretics, Jews, Muslims, mercenaries, and others, including those committing homosexual acts: "Whoever shall be found to have committed that incontinence which is against nature, on account of which the wrath of God came upon the sons of perdition and consumed five cities with fire, shall, if a cleric, be deposed from office or confined to a monastery to do penance; if a layman, he shall suffer excommunication and be cast out from the company of the faithful."[26]

23. Wright, *Anglo-Latin Satirical Poets*, II: 3–102, and in H. C. Hoskier, *"De contemptu mundi": A Bitter Satirical Poem of 3,000 Lines upon the Morals of the Twelfth Century by Bernard of Morval, Monk of Cluny* (London, 1929); English translation, "The Scorn of the World," by H. Preble, *American Journal of Theology* 10 (1906); 72–101, 286–308, 496–16.

24. This passage is transcribed in its entirety in app. 2 ("On Sodomy").

25. "Sed nunc quomodo abierunt haec in desuetudinem, ut quae graviter punit Dominus, intacta relinquat Ecclesia?" *Verbum abbreviatum* 138 (PL, 205:335). Note that Peter is not suggesting that the church has become generally lax but that it has altered its values, as is evident in the clause succeeding: "Et quae leviter punit, ipsa gravissime puniat."

26. "Quicumque in incontinentia illa quae contra naturam est, propter quam venit ira Dei in filios diffidentiae, et quinque civitates igne consumpsit, deprehensi fuerint laborare, si

Although the literal tenor of this canon could be interpreted as referring to all nonprocreative intercourse, and during the transition period which followed it was often so construed, its social context suggests strongly that it was aimed at homosexual practices. It passed into the permanent collections of canon law compiled in the thirteenth century (e.g., *Decretalium* 5.31.4).

Such measures were not easily enforced or widely accepted. The Fourth Lateran Council, meeting some thirty-six years after the Third, seemed to retreat somewhat from the position of its predecessor in regard to gay people, although it passed even more stringent legislation regarding Jews, Muslims, and other minorities. The laity were not mentioned at all in its decree, which was only concerned with maintaining clerical celibacy, and although it suggests that clerics should "especially" avoid "sodomy" (which is not defined), it stipulated that the most severe penances be reserved to married clerics who committed sexual sins, "since they could make use of legitimate matrimony."[27] Moreover, the council found it necessary to issue a special provision against prelates who sheltered or supported priests guilty of sexual irregularities.[28] Doubtless primarily a reference to the many who opposed the termination of clerical marriages, it may also have been intended to obviate resistance on the part of clerics to measures against gay people—including, in many cases, themselves.

There is indeed some evidence that accusations of homosexuality against prelates attempting to enforce clerical celibacy may have taken on the aspect of a smear campaign in the thirteenth century,[29] and a defensive reaction against such charges could be partly responsible for the increasing severity of the church.

Gay people, like other groups, were also affected by the animosities

---

clerici fuerint, ejiciantur a clero, vel ad poenitentiam agendam in monasteriis detrudantur; si laici, excommunicati subdantur, et a coetu fidelium fiant prorsus alieni," Mansi, 22:224–25.

27. Now part of canon law (*Decretalium Gregorii Papae IX* 3.1.13): "Ut clericorum mores et actus in melius reformentur, continenter et caste vivere studeant universi, praesertim in sacris ordinibus constituti, ab omni libidinis vitio praecaventes, maxime illo, propter quod venit ira Dei in filios diffidentiae.... Qui autem secundum regionis suae morem non abdicaverunt copulam conjugalem, si lapsi fuerint, gravius puniantur: cum legitimo matrimonio uti possint."

28. Ibid.: "Praelati vero, qui tales praesumpserint in suis iniquitatibus sustinere, maxime obtentu pecuniae vel alterius commodi temporalibus, pati subjaceat ultioni."

29. See, e.g., the long and caustic poem on this subject translated in app. 2: "Married Clergy." Although some poetry of this sort survives from the twelfth century, it appears to become much more acrid in the thirteenth. Many earlier poems attacking clerical celibacy emphasized the "naturalness" of heterosexual liaisons without imputing homosexual interests to fomenters of reform: see, e.g., the collection of such poems attributed to Walther Mapes and published by Wright, *The Latin Poems*, pp. 171 ff.

connected with the crusades.[30] Serious early polemics against Islam had
sometimes criticized Muslim marital practices but did not focus on Islamic
tolerance of homosexuality.[31] From the time of the first crusade, however,
accounts of Muslim sexual mores increasingly concentrated on behavior
which was atypical or repugnant to the majority of Christians.[32] Doubtless
such efforts were not intended as derogations of homosexuality per se, and
significantly, the earliest examples used homosexual rape—not consensual
homosexual acts—as instances of Muslim immorality. But the regular
association of minority sexual preferences with the most dreaded of Europe's
enemies inevitably increased popular antipathy toward the minority as well
as the Muslims.

An "appeal from the Eastern emperor" for aid against the pagans over-
running the Holy Land, which was forged and circulated in the West to
arouse popular support for the first crusade,[33] concentrated its attention
not on theological or political differences between Christians and Muslims
but on extreme violations of sexual and ethnic taboos sure to evoke horror and
disgust among Europeans. Thinly veiled anti-Semitism underlay the charge
that the infidels circumcised Christian youths over the baptismal fonts of

30. Of the various surveys dealing with European antipathy toward Islam and Islamic
countries during the period of the crusades, Southern's *Western Views of Islam in the Middle
Ages* is probably the best. Cf. Norman Daniel, *Islam and the West: The Making of an Image*
(Edinburgh, 1960), and W. M. Watt, *The Influence of Islam on Medieval Europe* (Edinburgh,
1972), in Islamic Surveys, no. 9. The Mongols had a somewhat similar effect on European
society in the thirteenth century; see, e.g., Gian Bezzola, *Die Mongolen in abendländischen
Sicht (1220–1270): Ein Beitrag zur Frage der Völkerbegegnungen* (Bern, 1974), but less was
known about their personal habits, and their impact was more political and eschatological.

31. See, e.g., Peter the Venerable *Summa totius haeresis sarracenorum*, in James Kritzeck,
Peter the Venerable and Islam (Princeton, N.J., 1964), pp. 207–8.

32. A few writers attempted to distinguish between the more familiar Muslims of Western
areas like Sicily and Spain and those of the Middle East by suggesting that the climate of
the torrid Middle East affected the morals of those who lived there. Jacques de Vitry, for
example, claimed that "in the East, especially in hot regions, bestial and wanton people, to
whom the austerity of the Christian religion seems intolerably burdensome, . . . easily
embark on the path which leads to death" ("in partibus Orientis, et maxime in calidis
regionibus bruti et luxuriosi homines, quibus austeritas Christiane religionis intolerabilis
et importabilis videbatur, . . . viam que ducit ad mortem, facile sunt ingressi"), *Libri duo,
quorum prior orientalis, siue Hierosolymitanae: alter, occidentalis historiae nomine inscribitur* (Douay,
1597), vol. 1, chap. 6, pp. 25–26.

33. Nearly all modern scholars are agreed that this letter (translated in app. 2), purporting
to be addressed to Count Robert of Flanders by Alexius I Comnenus, is a forgery, probably
composed in the West shortly before the first crusade. There is much less agreement about
who composed it and whether or not there may actually have been a letter from the emperor
to the count which formed the basis of the surviving version, but the arguments are far too
complex to be taken up here. I have used the text provided by C. Du Cange in his notes to
the *Alexiad*, PG, 131:563–68; it is also available in *Recueil des historiens des croisades: historiens
grecs* (Paris, 1875–81), 2:52–54.

churches, allowing the "blood of circumcision" to run into the fonts.[34] The invaders not only ravished Christian virgins and matrons but forced the mothers to sing lewd songs while observing the rape of their daughters and vice versa. "But what next? We pass on to worse yet. They have degraded by sodomizing them men of every age and rank: boys, adolescents, young men, old men, nobles, servants, and, what is worse and more wicked, clerics and monks, and even—alas and for shame! something which from the beginning of time has never been spoken of or heard of—bishops! They have already killed one bishop with this nefarious sin."[35]

The letter and the tales of infidel sexual atrocities were immensely popular and effective and found their way into crusade literature of every sort.[36] In Guibert of Nogent's contemporary history of the first crusade (*The Work of God Performed by the Franks*), the account of the fatal rape of the bishop is followed by the implication that such behavior was characteristic of Muslims and is subtly linked to the famous Middle Eastern incident which gave "sodomy" its name: "Although it is allowed the wretches, in their opinion, to have many women, this is accounted little by them unless the value of such filth is also sullied by uncleanliness with men. Nor is it surprising that God has impatiently borne their ancient evil and the cry against it and that the land has vomited forth such execrations from its dead inhabitants."[37]

34. "Nam pueros et juvenes Christianorum circumcidunt super baptisteria Christianorum, et circumcisionis sanguinem in despectum Christi fundunt in eisdem baptisteriis," PG, 131:365.

35. Ibid.: "Sed quid adhuc? Veniamus ad deteriora. Totius aetatis et ordinis viros, id est pueros, adolescentes, juvenes, senes, nobiles, servos, et, quod pejus et impudentius est, clericos et monachos, et heu proh dolor! et quod ab initio non dictum neque auditum est, episcopos Sodomitico peccato deludunt. et etiam unum episcopum sub hoc nefario peccato jam crepuerunt."

36. At least three complete manuscripts of the letter survive from the early twelfth century (Angers, Brussels, and Paris), and it was incorporated within decades into the works of Robert the Monk and Guibert of Nogent; the influence of the letter is easily discernible in William of Tyre's reconstruction of Urban II's harangue at Clermont (PL, 201:231–34). For a recent summary of the controversy surrounding this letter (with a somewhat imperfect translation), see Einar Joranson, "The Problem of the Spurious Letter of Emperor Alexius to the Count of Flanders," *American Historical Review* 55, no. 4 (1950): 811–32. I do not find convincing Joranson's argument (first advanced by Carl Erdmann in *Die Entstehung des Kreuzzugsgedankens* [Stuttgart, 1935], p. 365, n. 7) that the letter was actually intended to excite hostility to Alexius himself, but even if he is right, this does not affect the importance of the incendiary use of homosexual atrocities, or the ultimate effect on gay people.

37. "Et quum sit miseris permissa suo ipsorum arbitrio multiplicitas feminarum, parum est apud eos nisi et dignitas tantae spurcitiae volutabro commaculetur marium. Nec mirum si Deus exoletam eorum nequitiam et in clamorem versam impatienter tulerit, tantaque funestorum habitatorum execrementa, more antiquo terra vomuerit," Guibert de Nogent *Gesta dei per francos* 1–5, in *Recueil des historiens des croisades: historiens occidentaux* (Paris, 1879), 4:131–32. The Latin is unusual; "excrement" may be closer to what Guibert intended by "execrementa," but it is difficult to be sure.

Throughout the thirteenth century, wanton and violent sexuality were prominent and regular attributes of Muslim society in most Western literature. Jacques de Vitry informed readers of his *Oriental History* that Muhammad,

> the enemy of nature, popularized the vice of sodomy among his people, who sexually abuse not only both genders but even animals and have for the most part become like mindless horses or mules . . . .

> Sunk, dead, and buried in the filth of obscene desire, pursuing like animals the lusts of the flesh, they can resist no vices but are miserably enslaved to and ruled by carnal passions, often without even being roused by desire; they consider it meritorious to stimulate the most sordid desires.[38]

The earliest and most drastic legislation against gay people enacted by any government of the High Middle Ages was passed in the nascent kingdom of Jerusalem by Europeans attempting to create a Western feudal society in the Muslim Middle East. These laws, drafted only decades after the first crusade, specified death by burning for "sodomites," and it is quite clear that the word in this case referred to homosexual males.[39]

Although this legislation was not imitated in the West for more than a century, the feelings which produced it were only slightly less powerful there. Crusaders who remained in the Holy Land were accused by Western propagandists of adopting the "effeminate" ways of the Muslims, and those who returned were rumored to have brought back with them the filthy customs of the pagans.[40]

38. "Per hoc latenter vitium Sodomiticum hostis nature in populo suo introduxit. Unde ipsi ex maxima parte non solum in utroque sexu, sed etiam in brutis turpitudinem abusiue operantes, facti sunt, sicut equus et mulus quibus non est intellectus," *Libri duo*, vol. 1, chap. 5, p. 18. "Unde more pecudum post carnis concupiscentias abeuntes, in luto voluptatis obscoene infixi, mortui, et sepulti, nullis vitiis resistere norunt, sed carnis passionibus miserabiliter subiecti et suppeditati, plerumque non provocati ab appetitu, credunt esse meritorium foedos appetitus provocare," 6:25. The English translation of this work by A. Stewart, *The History of Jerusalem* (London, 1896), is particularly unreliable in sexual matters; many passages are bowdlerized or omitted. The French version of M. Guizot, *Histoire des croisades* (Paris, 1825), in Collection des mémoires rélatifs à l'histoire de France, vol. 22, is preferable.

39. Text in Mansi, 21 : 264; translated in Bailey, p. 96. This council also dealt severely with other sexual matters: adulteresses were to be punished with death, and if a husband forgave an adulterous wife, both were to be exiled (see Jean Richard, "Le statut de la femme dans l'orient latin," in *La femme*, Recueils de la Société Jean Bodin, no. 12 [Brussels, 1962], 2:387). On the other hand, there is evidence that this stricture was not enforced (see, e.g., William of Tyre, *A History of Deeds Done beyond the Sea*, trans. E. A. Babcock and A. C. Krey [New York, 1943], 2:76–77); possibly the antihomosexual ones were not either.

40. For example, see the comments of Ordericus Vitalis about Robert, Duke of Normandy (*Historia ecclesiastica* 10.16, 8.4), but his objectivity in the matter, as noted, is questionable.

As crusade after crusade failed, the "sodomitical" Muslims came to seem a greater and greater threat to Europe, and accounts of Muslim wickedness reached even higher pitches in their efforts to rouse European antagonism.

According to the religion of the Saracens, any sexual act whatever is not only allowed but approved and encouraged, so that in addition to innumerable prostitutes, they have effeminate men in great number who shave their beards, paint their faces, put on women's clothing, wear bracelets on their arms and legs and gold necklaces around their necks as women do, and adorn their chests with jewels. Thus selling themselves into sin, they degrade and expose their bodies; "men with men working that which is unseemly," they receive "in themselves" the recompense of their sin and error.[41] The Saracens, oblivious of human dignity, freely resort to these effeminates or live with them as among us men and women live together openly.[42]

Christians, it was charged, cooperated in beautifying and selling hapless Christian youths for this purpose, "feed[ing] them with sumptuous meals and delicate beverages to make them pinker and rosier and more voluptuous, and thus more alluring and apt to satisfy the lust of the Saracens. And when the libidinous, vile, and wicked men—the Saracens—corrupters of human nature, see the boys, they immediately burn with lust for them and, like mad dogs, race to buy the boys for themselves . . . so that they can have their evil way with them."[43]

41. This sentence is paraphrased from the Vulgate version of Rom. 1:27; I have used the KJV where the quotation is direct.

42. "Apud sectam sarracenorum actus quicumque venereus non solum est improhibitus, sed licitus et laudatus. Unde, preter meretrices innumerabiles, que apud eos sunt, homines effeminati sunt plurimi, qui barbam radunt, faciem propriam pingunt, habitum muliebrem assument, armillas portant ad brachia et ad pedes, et ad collum torques aureos, ut mulieres; et ad pectus monilia circumponent, et sic sub peccato venumdant contumeliis afficiunt sua corpora et exponunt, et masculi in masculum turpitudinem operantes, mercedem iniquitatis et erroris recipiunt in seipsis. Sarracenis ergo, humane dignitatis obliti, se ad illos effeminatos impudenter inclinant, vel cum eisdem habitant, sicut hic inter nos publice habitant vir et uxor," William of Ada, *De modo sarracenos extirpandi*, in *Recueil des historiens des croisades: documents armeniens* (Paris, 1869–1906), 2:524.

43. Ibid., pp. 524–25: "Et cum aliquem puerum aptum corpore invenire possunt, christianum vel tartarum, ut premittitur, ad vendendum, nullum precium est eis carum dandum pro hiis quos vident ad hujusmodi complendam nequiciam aptiores. Quos, postquam emerunt, ut statuam, ornant sericis et aureis indumentis, corpus eorum et facies lavant sepius balneis et aliis lavamentis, et eos pascunt lautis cibariis et potibus delicatis. Et hoc faciunt ut pinguiores et rubicundiores et delicaciores, et per consequens magis apti et allectivi ad sarracenorum complendum libidinem videantur. Quos ut vident libidinosi, scelerosi et nefandi homines, sarraceni videlicet, humane nature perversores, statim in eorum concupiscenciam exardescunt, sed ut canes insani, ad istos pueros, diaboli laqueos, sibi emendos festinant currere, ut possint cum eis suam impudiciciam exercere."

The implication that infidel homosexual interest posed a threat not only to adult Christians but to their children, like comparable accusations against Jews, was particularly effective.[44]

Gay people were also sometimes associated—to their manifest disadvantage—with the most despised of all minorities of the later Middle Ages, heretics.[45] The push for conformity was nowhere more pronounced than in matters of faith, and the great theological discussions of the twelfth century had resulted by the mid-thirteenth in the establishment of rigid and exacting standards of faith to which all Christians must adhere or face the powers of the Inquisition, recently given to the order of Dominicans (whose severity in enforcing orthodoxy earned them the sobriquet "domini canes," "the hounds of the Lord"). Although the excesses of the Inquisition are often exaggerated, especially in regard to physical abuses and capital punishment, there is no doubt that its indefatigable prosecution of intellectual nonconformity profoundly altered the intellectual climate of Western Europe and created an ambience of fear even among the perfectly orthodox. Under the cloud of suspicion generated by inquisitiorial concerns, the orthodoxy of no less a figure than Saint Thomas Aquinas, later considered the ultimate standard of Dominican orthodoxy, had come under question.

Numerous heretics of the twelfth and thirteenth centuries and some whole movements, like the Albigensians, were accused of practicing "sodomy," often (though not always) in the specific sense of homosexual intercourse.[46] Civil and ecclesiastical records of trials dealing with heresy mention

44. Jacob of Verona (fl. ca. 1335) proclaimed that Muhammad had taught that no sexual act was sinful, including acts "against nature," and reported that the "sultan" had a retinue of some 500 youths brought for his pleasure from the Baltic, Greece, and Italy and sold at Cairo (Liber peregrinationis, ed. Ugo Monneret de Villard [Rome, 1950], pp. 98, 102); his contemporary Ludolf of Sudheim tersely commented that Muslims are "weak and lustful and sexually abuse males" (De itinere terrae sanctae, ed. G. A. Neumann, Archives de l'orient latin, vol. 2, pt. 2 [Paris, 1884], p. 372). Such ideas were still common about Muslims as late as the fifteenth century. Panormitanus mentions in several places that Sicilian Muslims were known for raping Christian women and boys (Commentaria in quintum decretalium librum [Venice, 1642], vol. 7, fols. 146v, 180r) and that the king of Sicily commissioned archbishops to supervise punishment of such offenses.

45. It would be impossible in a work of this scope to provide even the broadest overview of writings on medieval heresy. The questions of heresy and the oppression of sexual nonconformity are so obviously related that few books dealing with one will not touch upon the other. A particularly good picture of the difference between the early and later Middle Ages in this regard is provided by the contrasting data in J. B. Russell, Dissent and Reform in the Early Middle Ages (Berkeley, 1965); and Robert Lerner, The Heresy of the Free Spirit in the Later Middle Ages (Berkeley, 1972), each with additional bibliography.

46. See, e.g., W. Wakefield and A. Evans, Heresies of the High Middle Ages (New York, 1969), pp. 103, 109, 212–15, 254–55; J. C. S. Runciman, The Medieval Manichee (Cambridge, 1947), pp. 176–79; and Lerner, pp. 20–25 ("Heresy and Fornication: A Topos of the Thirteenth Century") and chap. 1, passim.

"sodomy" and crimes "against nature" with some regularity. It became a commonplace of official terminology to mention "traitors, heretics, and sodomites" as if they constituted a single association of some sort. "Bougre," a common French word for heretics, even came to refer to a person who practiced "sodomy" or, more particularly, "a homosexual male."[47]

It is now impossible to determine the accuracy of such associations. The only materials which survive for investigating the practices of heretical groups are those left by the church authorities who prosecuted them, and these are for obvious reasons suspect. Both common sense and the wildly exaggerated and fanciful nature of many of the charges argue strongly against their reliability, and the frequency with which exactly the same accusations appear against different heretical movements in widely separated geographical areas suggests that specific charges against heretics may often have been standard formulae rather than actual observations.

An association of homosexuality with heterodoxy could have been partly the result of analogy with the Muslims, especially in southern France, where Muslim practices had been familiar since before the crusades; or it may simply have been an effective way to characterize heretics as alien and disruptive.

Despite an almost total lack of reliable evidence, at least three possible explanations for the association of homosexuality and heresy deserve to be considered: (1) many heretics actually were gay; (2) heretical movements may have been more sympathetic toward homosexuality than was orthodox Catholicism; (3) some gay people may have been branded heretics for refusing to renounce their erotic preferences.

1. As the position of gay Catholics grew less and less comfortable, perceptive gay people may well have felt disaffected from the church and could have sought spiritual satisfaction in unorthodox movements with more flexible sexual attitudes. The fact that heretics in southern France, where gay literature had been especially prominent for several centuries, should have been particularly suspect in this regard offers at least speculative corroboration for inquisitorial accusations. Moreover, in some cases heresy was most common among precisely those people (e.g., the nobles of southern France) whom one would expect to have the most tolerant attitudes toward homo-

---

47. Bailey, p. 147, cites a law of 1533 which refers to "the detestable and abominable Vice of Buggery committed with mankind or beast." It is nonetheless certain that the French "bougre" for a long time simply referred to adherents of heresies believed to be of Eastern ("Bulgarian") origin. The point at which it came to mean "sodomite" is at present indeterminable. It is possible—though no previous commentator seems to have considered this—that it never actually denoted "sodomy" in French but was merely sufficiently vague to be interpreted sexually: cf. below, pp. 290–91. The word survives in modern French with no sexual meaning whatever.

sexuality, and it occurred in precisely those areas (e.g., the highly urban centers of the low countries) where the most people might think of themselves as "gay."

2. It is known that many heretical movements influenced by Eastern dualism and Manichean philosophies disapproved of procreation, since it entrapped souls in evil matter. Disapprobation of this sort might well lead to tacit or even explicit encouragement of homosexual practices as substitutes for objectionable heterosexual ones. The Albigensians in particular were thought to preach that homosexual relations were not only sinless but a desirable means of foiling the devil's efforts to ensnare souls in matter. Some heretical groups rejected concepts of nature then being revived as Christian values; others, particularly black magic and witchcraft-related sects, appear (at least in the records left by their persecutors) to have modeled their theories and practice to some extent on Islam. (Muhammad was by this time the Antichrist for most Europeans.) If they, like their contemporaries, associated homosexual practices with Islam, they may have consciously explored gay sexuality as part of their religious beliefs.

However, it is almost impossible to separate accusations from fact in this context and to discern what cults or groups may actually have been affected by non-Christian sexual mores and which simply suffered derogation on such grounds by those who wished to discredit them. More than six centuries of acrid debate, for instance, have failed to resolve the mystery surrounding the dissolution of the Templars on charges which included homosexuality, heresy, and black magic.

3. It is not likely that many people were prosecuted by the Inquisition simply for homosexual behavior, which by the thirteenth century had come to be regarded by much of the church as a carnal sin but not a heresy per se. Some gay people, however, may have taken stands against the relatively recent theological rejection of homosexual acts, either as the result of familiarity with an older tradition or simply in defiance of an ecclesiastical attitude which they considered unjust. Such people would have come under the jurisdiction of the Inquisition and been severely punished if they refused to alter their stance. But few if any cases are known in which a defense of homosexuality was the sole offense of a heretic. Much more typical are cases like that of Arnald de Vernhola, who was tried by the bishop of Pamiers in 1323 for various crimes of heresy, including his belief that homosexual acts were no more serious than fornication (a belief, it might be noted, which would have been completely orthodox only 200 years before). Although Arnald, a subdeacon, had impersonated a priest and even gone as far as hearing confessions, his homosexual activities and beliefs about them seem to have attracted more attention from ecclesiastical authorities and occupy a

very large percentage of his trial record, the conclusion of which is translated in appendix 2.[48]

On balance, the most reasonable inference would seem to be that, while heretical movements might attract nonconformists of all sorts and might have some reason to deal with homosexuality more flexibly than the Catholic church, most of the charges of sexual deviation leveled against heretics were formulaic, either the consequence of fear and prejudice or conscious fabrications for propaganda purposes. Many heretical movements of the time were noted for extreme asceticism, even among their critics, and the indulgence and moral looseness of the Catholic clergy was one of the major complaints of those abandoning the organized church. It does not seem likely that persons willing to suffer gruesome deaths for the sake of restoring Christianity to its early purity would have preached sexual license of any sort, homosexual or heterosexual, and there is no reliable evidence that most heretics' sexual mores differed from those of their Catholic contemporaries except in the direction of greater restraint. There is, on the other hand, considerable reason to suspect ecclesiastical officials of wishing to portray heretics in the most damaging light possible, and sexual peculiarities were singularly useful for this purpose in the changing climate of opinion of the thirteenth century.

The widely held belief that both of the greatest threats to Christian Europe's security (the Muslims from without, the heretics from within) were particularly given to homosexual relations contributed greatly to the profoundly negative reaction against gay sexuality visible at many levels of European society during this period. Since they left few records, one can only speculate about effects of this reaction among the lower classes, but the upper classes and the bourgeoisie—the latter just now coming into prominence in most of Europe—wrote their reactions into textbooks, theology, and law in the course of the century.

Only two of the most important law codes of the century failed to institute severe penalties for homosexual behavior, and these were atypical not only in predating most of the others but in reflecting the attitudes of areas traditionally more tolerant of social nonconformity.

As noted above, Germanic legislation outside Spain had never penalized gay sexuality, and even thirteenth-century German law codes continued this tradition: neither the *Sachsenspiegel* compiled around 1233 nor the later *Schwabenspiegel*[49] suggested penalties for homosexual acts. Since German

48. This incident is summarized by Emmanuel Le Roy Ladurie in his minute analysis of Fournier's inquisitorial records, *Montaillou, village occitan de 1294 à 1324* (Poitiers, 1975), pp. 209–15. Note that he has misread Arnald's estimate of the number of gay people in Pamiers as 1,000 instead of 3,000. His extrapolations about the "causes" of Arnald's homosexuality are rather naive.

49. Both ed. August Eckhardt in *Deutschenspiegel*, MGH, Fontes (Hanover, 1930).

ecclesiastics and theologians were affected by many of the antigay intellectual currents of the time, and since homosexuality was well known in Germany, this silence must be due in some measure to an unwillingness to enforce conformity in private matters. The laws in question are in fact notable for their concentration on matters of clear public interest, like land disputes and violent conflict, and avoidance of matters of individual conscience.

The *Constitutions of Melfi* (*Liber Augustalis*) promulgated by the German emperor Frederick II for the kingdom of Sicily in 1231[50] are widely regarded as among the most enlightened legislation of the Middle Ages. An attempt to put the niceties of Roman law into realistic use in a feudal society, they regulate many aspects of personal life, including matters of faith and morals. There is no question of their orthodoxy: heresy is condemned absolutely, under penalty of death with no appeal;[51] the violation of nuns is a capital offense; and usury is made a crime. But prosecution of usury is reserved to the civil courts, where Frederick himself could oversee it, and Jews are specifically exempted from any legal action on this account. Although marriage is protected and adultery punished, the *Constitutions* pointedly stipulate that this is a religious matter, not a civil one, and should be reserved to ecclesiastical courts. Pimping and prostituting one's daughter are severely punished, but prostitutes themselves are specifically protected in several statutes, and failure to assist any woman being attacked is punishable under the law.[52]

Although the antigay provisions of later Roman law were certainly known to the authors of the *Constitutions of Melfi*, homosexual acts are conspicuously absent from its sexual legislation, and even more notably missing from its regulations against the standard coterie of miscreants penalized in other codes of the day: forgers, poisoners, arsonists, perjurers, blasphemers, et al.[53] This is doubtless due in some measure to the fact that the code was

50. Usually cited in the Carcani edition (Naples, 1786), but better edited by Jean Huillard-Bréholles (H-B), *Historia diplomatica Friderici II* (Paris, 1852–61), vol. 4, pt. 1, pp. 1–178. There is now an excellent English translation of the latter by James Powell, *The Liber Augustalis or Constitutions of Melfi* (Syracuse, N.Y., 1971). For a convenient summary of the sources of the *Constitutions*, see Hermann Dilcher, "Die sizilische Gesetzgebung Friedrichs II, eine Synthese von Tradition und Erneuerung," in *Probleme um Frederick II*, ed. Josef Fleckenstein, Vorträge und Forschungen: Konstanzer Arbeitskreis für mittelalterliche Geschichte, vol. 16 (Sigmaringen, 1974).

51. *Constitutions* 1.1 (H-B, 1:2; Powell, pp. 7–9). On Frederick's attitude toward heresy, see the comments by Selger in Fleckenstein.

52. 1.6 (H-B, 1:8, 9; Powell, pp. 11–12); 1.20 (H-B, 1:23; Powell, p. 23); 1.6 (H-B, 1:9; Powell, pp. 12–13); 3.83 (H-B, 3:60; Powell, pp. 147–48); 3.84–85 (H-B, 3:61–62; Powell, p. 148); 1.21 (H-B, 1:25; Powell, p. 24), 3.77 (H-B, 3:55; Powell, p. 146); 1.23 (H-B, 1:27; Powell, p. 26).

53. Ibid., 3.61 (H-B, 3:39; Powell, p. 141), 64 (H-B, 42; Powell, p. 142), 69 (H-B, 47; Powell, p. 143), 70 (H-B, 48; Powell, ibid.), 87 (H-B, 64; Powell, p. 149), 91 (H-B, 68; Powell, p. 151), 92 (ibid.), etc.

drawn up for the unusually tolerant Frederick,[54] but it is probably as much the result of the more liberal atmosphere of those highly urbanized areas of Europe where several Mediterranean cultures interacted. The *Constitutions* are also notable, for example, for the complete absence of derogatory references to or restrictions upon Jews or Muslims and for their unusual concern with the rights of women.

Most thirteenth-century law codes, however, were drawn up outside the cosmopolitan trade capitals of the Mediterranean and during the latter half of the century, when pressures against nonconformists were more pronounced. A Castilian royal edict of the middle of the century forbidding monks to leave their orders subjoined the following law concerning homosexual acts:

> Although we are reluctant to speak of something which is reckless to consider and reckless to perform, terrible sins are nevertheless sometimes committed, and it happens that one man desires to sin against nature with another. We therefore command that if any commit this sin, once it is proven, both be castrated before the whole populace and on the third day after be hung by the legs until dead, and that their bodies never be taken down.[55]

This law is remarkable not only for its severity[56] but also for its reference to "nature": no European civil law prior to the thirteenth century had either prescribed death for homosexual acts or related their gravity to "nature." The influence of Justinian's law (now popular everywhere in Europe), popular antagonism to nonconformity, and intellectual fascination with "nature" are all discernible in this unprecedented enactment.

54. Contemporary popes accused Frederick himself of "sodomy" (see, e.g., Ernst Kantorowicz, *Kaiser Friedrich der Zweite* [Berlin, 1936], p. 288, and *Ergänzungsband*, p. 137) but had political reasons for doing so. What is more significant than Frederick's own sexuality is his familiarity with and equanimity about foreign or nonconformist elements of Christian society. Both Frederick and Louis IX, for instance, influenced by Roman law, forbade gambling with dice and frequenting taverns; in the same statute Louis also prohibited chess—a Muslim contribution to European leisure—but Frederick admired Islamic culture and permitted chess in his realms.

55. "Maguer que nos agravia de fablar en cosa que es muy sin guisa de cuidar, e muy sin guisa de facer; pero porque mal pecado alguna vez aviene, que home codicia a otro por pecar con el contra natura: mandamos, que qualesquier que sean, que tal pecado fagan, que luego que fuere sabido, que amos à dos sean castrados ente todo el pueblo, e despues, a tercer dia, sean colgados por las piernas fasta que mueran, e nunca dende sean tollidos," *Fuero real* (promulgated by Alfonso X) 4.9.2, in *Los códigos españoles* (Madrid, 1847), 1:409.

56. The Visigothic laws stipulating castration for those guilty of homosexual offenses had survived in some areas of Spain in the vernacular *Fuero juzgo*. It is striking that even this penalty—the most severe of any European government of the early Middle Ages—did not suffice for the thirteenth century. In the *Fuero juzgo* see 3.5.5 and 6 (*Los códigos españoles*, 1:130). The passages are more or less exact translations of the Latin.

In the ideal law code drafted for Alfonso the Wise (1252–84), "nature" received even more attention, and the dangers to the state of tolerating sexual deviance were repeatedly emphasized.

Regarding Those Who Commit Sexual Sins against Nature
"Sodomy" is the sin which men commit by having intercourse with each other, against nature and natural custom. And because from this sin arise many evils in the land where it is perpetrated, and it sorely offends God and gives a bad name not only to those who indulge in it but also to the nation where it occurs, . . . we wish here to speak of it in detail. . . . Sodom and Gomorrah were two ancient cities, inhabited by very bad people, and so great was the wickedness of their inhabitants that because they engaged in that sin which is against nature, our Lord despised them to the point of destroying both cities with all their occupants. And no one escaped except Lot and his companions, who had not participated in this evil. From that city, Sodom, where God worked this miracle, the sin took its name and is called sodomy. And every man should be on guard against this failing, because many evils are born from it, including ill fame and bad repute for those who practice it. For such crimes our Lord sent upon the land guilty of them famine, plague, catastrophe, and countless other calamities.

Anyone can accuse a man of having committed a crime against nature before the judge of the district in which the crime was committed. If it is proved, both of those involved should be put to death. However, if one was forced or is under the age of fourteen, he should not suffer this penalty, because those who are forced are not guilty, and minors do not understand how serious a crime they have committed. This same penalty shall apply to a man or woman who has intercourse with an animal. And the animal also shall be killed to obliterate the memory of the deed.[57]

This code was not put into effect until the fourteenth century, and it is doubtful that any provisions of this sort were regularly enforced. But it is eloquent testimony to the shift in attitude on the part of the rising power structure of western Europe during the period in question.

At almost the exact same time in France, the legal school of Orléans issued a code containing a synthesis of both Spanish laws, requiring for the

57. Translated from *La setena partida*, 21, in *Los códigos españoles* (Madrid, 1848) 4:424–25. For a complete English translation of the *Siete partidas*, see Samuel Parsons Scott, *Las siete partidas* (Chicago, 1931). For the sections dealing with the Jews, a comparable minority, see Marcus, *The Jews in the Medieval World*, pp. 34–40.

first offense by a male castration; for the second, dismemberment; for the third, burning.[58] This provision, unlike almost all other legal approaches of the thirteenth century, specifically mentions female homosexuality as well, stipulating dismemberment for the first two offenses by a woman and burning for the third.[59]

In both cases a provision is made for the aspect of all such laws which would have more effect than any other consideration on their enforcement: all the goods of those convicted were to be confiscated for the king. Such a stipulation was an open invitation to monarchs in financial difficulties to eliminate nonconformity from their lands and relieve their fiscal embarrassment simultaneously.

The *Coutume de Touraine-Anjou* contains a law,[60] repeated almost verbatim in the influential *Etablissements* of Saint Louis,[61] requiring that those proven guilty of heresy or "bougrerie" be burned and their property given to their lord. Even if, as some have maintained, "bougrerie" in this statute did not originally refer to homosexuality,[62] little time elapsed before it was taken

58. *Li livres de jostice et de plet* 18.24.22, ed. Pierre Rapetti (Paris, 1890), pp. 279–80: "Cil qui sont sodomite prové doivent perdre les c . . . [*sic*]. Et se il le fet segond foiz, il doit perdre menbre. Et se il le fet la tierce foiz, il doit estre ars." Note that this and several other codes alluded to subsequently were issued privately and are taken as indicative not of legal practice but of changes in the attitudes of lawmakers, particularly as contrasted with earlier codes (also often private law) which did not evince such antipathies. It should be remarked, however, that this distinction is of questionable import: royal statutes were often based on or took cognizance of private law codes, and officially enacted codes may have had far less efficacy than comparable modern legal texts.

59. "Feme qui le fet doit a chescune foiz perdre menbre, et la tierce doit estre arsse. Et toz leur biens sont le roi."

60. No. 78: "Se aucuns est soupeçonneus de bougrerie, la joutise le doit prandre et envoier à l'evesque: et se il en estoit provez, l'en le devroit ardoir: et tuit se mueble sunt au baron. Et, en tel maniere doit l'en ouvre d'ome herite, por coi il en soit provez. Et tuit si mueble sunt au baron" *Coutume de Touraine-Anjou*, ed. Paul Viollet, in *Les établissements de Saint Louis accompagnés des textes primitifs et de textes dérivés* (Paris, 1883), 3:50.

61. *Etablissements* 1.90 (ibid., 2:147). See discussion in introduction, vol. 1, s.v. "sodomie."

62. Both Bailey (pp. 141–44) and Bullough (p. 391) attempt to demonstrate that "bougrerie" would not have meant "sodomy" to thirteenth-century writers, but in addition to the legal considerations cited below, one may note Matthew Paris's comment that the French of his day called usurers *bougres* ("usurarii, quos Franci Bugeros vulgariter appellant," *Chronica majora*, ed. Henry Luard [London, 1872], 5:513), very strongly suggesting that the term had much broader meaning than "heretic." It seems quite likely, in fact, that it was used for miscreants and nonconformists in general and might thus have been applied to gay people even when not originally intended as a reference to them. At least by the sixteenth century "buggery" was used in English law to designate homosexuality, and the powerful French influence on English law makes it likely that this was in some way related to earlier French statutes. Bailey correctly points out that in several sections of the *Livres* "bougrerie" can hardly mean anything but heresy in the most general sense, and "sodomite" is used to designate a person guilty of homosexual offenses. He could in fact have pursued his argument much further: in 10.19.7 of the *Livres*, for instance, the text alone might lead one to conclude

as such a reference, and its original ambiguity may have been a conscious effort to afford the government broad powers of regulation. By 1283, when the code of Philippe de Beaumanoir was drafted, the ambiguity had been removed, and the law stipulated that these penalties be enforced against heretics and those who committed "sodomy."[63]

In Italy various cities had begun campaigns against intellectual and sexual nonconformity apparently as early as 1233,[64] and by the latter half of the century there were civil laws against gay sexuality in at least Bologna (1265) and Siena (1262). In the latter, "sodomy" was specifically related to heresy, and the usual incentive was offered for accusation and successful prosecution: confiscation of the offender's property. By the mid-fourteenth century such laws existed in Florence and Perugia as well.[65]

In Norway the law of the Gulathing compiled around 1250 required the permanent outlawing of men convicted of "sodomy."[66] Although this code incorporated material much older than the thirteenth century and few of its provisions can be dated with accuracy, there is some reason to conclude that the prohibition of "sodomy" was an addition of the period in question. The contemporary Icelandic code *Grágás* was derived from the same prototype—brought to Iceland in the tenth century—but did not forbid homosexual behavior. It seems more likely that Norwegians would have added such a

---

that homosexuality is precisely what is at issue, since the discussion surrounding a spouse's freedom to remarry if the other partner falls into "bougrerie" recalls Visigothic legislation absolving the wives of "sodomites" from conjugal obligations. But the passage is simply a translation into the vernacular of a decree of Innocent III (incorporated into canon law: *Decretalium* 4.19.7) relating, in the Latin, to "heresy" plain and simple. Neither Bailey nor Bullough notes that the disputed passage in the *Etablissements* is also taken from canon law and that the Latin text of this relates to "heresy" rather than to any sexual failing (*Decretalium* 5.40.26, "Super quibusdam"). It is not, however, impossible that French authorities interpreted "heresis" as applying to deviant behavior in a broader sense than "heresy" or that they borrowed the wording of canon law for their own purposes. Bailey and Bullough also fail to take into account the code of Beaumanoir and its obvious relationship to the law in question.

63. Philippe de Beaumanoir, *Coutumes de Beauvaisis* 30.833, ed. A. Salmon (Paris, 1899), p. 431: "Qui erre contre la foi comme en mescreance de laquele il ne veut venir a voie de verité, ou qui fet sodomiterie, il doit estre ars et forfet tout le sien si comme il est dit devant."

64. A convenient, if superficial, account of secular law with special reference to Italy can be found in Michael Goodich, "Sodomy in Medieval Secular Law," as noted above. Goodich's otherwise useful summary suffers from three salient defects: (1) he does not assess what "sodomy" meant to the lawmakers who used the term; (2) he assumes that religious prejudice alone would account for the rise of antihomosexual legislation; (3) he does not analyze his material chronologically but lumps it all together as "late medieval."

65. Ibid., pp. 298–301.

66. "If two men practice sodomy and are accused and convicted of it, they shall both suffer permanent outlawry," *The Earliest Norwegian Laws*, trans. Laurence Larson (New York, 1935), p. 60.

provision in compiling their thirteenth-century version than that the Icelanders would have deleted it.[67]

Neither of the two most important twelfth-century English legal compilations—*The Laws of Henry the First*, drawn up in the century's first decades, or Glanvil's *Treatise on the Laws and Customs of the Kingdom of England*, written in its latter half—mentioned homosexuality, although the former had much to say on other private sexual issues (fornication, adultery, abortion, etc.),[68] and the latter was strongly influenced by Roman law, which later jurists were to use as precedent for enactments against gay sexuality. About a century later, however, just as the Jews were being expelled from the country, a new legal text was drawn up in which various types of social and religious deviance were severely punished. The same article of this code condemned to gruesome deaths arsonists, sorcerers, those who abandoned the Christian faith, those who dared to sleep with the wife of their feudal lord (or even the nurse of his children), and those who had intercourse with Jews, animals, or persons of their own gender (note the juxtaposition).[69] Those guilty of the last three offenses were to be buried alive;[70] the others drawn and/or burned. The provisions of this law were repeated almost verbatim in a subsequent vernacular compilation known as *Britton*.[71] The inclusion of homosexual acts as criminal offenses in both these works is all the more

---

67. Especially since the Icelandic code (e.g., *Staðarhólsbók* 105), like the Norwegian one (in Larson, pp. 143, sec. 196; 356, sec. 35), does include references to punishment for false accusations of homosexual passivity: it is quite obvious that homosexuality was not simply unknown in Iceland. It is unlikely that, as some editors of the *Grágás* have suggested, this omission is due to a reservation of such cases to ecclesiastical courts. The counterexample of Norwegian law argues against this, as does the fact that civil legislation often mentions homosexual behavior without any suggestion that it violates a law, civil or religious. Penalizing either false accusations of or passive homosexual behavior itself without prohibiting homosexual liaisons absolutely is not unheard of: Assyrian laws dating from the twelfth century B.C.—or earlier—appear to do so: see J. C. Miles, *The Assyrian Laws* (Oxford 1935), p. 391. Indeed, in several of the American states where homosexual acts are not illegal a libel case might arise based on a false accusation of homosexuality.

68. *Leges Henrici Primi*, ed. and trans. L. J. Downer (Oxford, 1972); see, e.g., 12.3, 70.16.

69. *Fleta* 1.35, ed. H. G. Richardson and G. O. Sayles (London, 1955), p. 90. Cf. *Siete partidas* 7.24.9.

70. *Fleta* ibid.: "Contrahentes vero cum Iudeis vel Iudeabus, pecorantes et sodomite in terra uiui confodiantur, dum tamen opere capti, per testimonium legale vel publice conuicti." Note that they are not to be burned, as Goodich wrongly states (p. 297), possibly confusing this law with that of *Britton*, although he unaccountably denies that *Britton* even contains a reference to "sodomy."

71. *Britton*, ed. Francis Nichols (Oxford, 1865), vol. 1, bk. 1, chap. 10(9): "De Arsouns: . . . et ceux qi de ceo serount atteyntz soint ars. . . . Et meymes tiel jugement eynt sorciers et sorceresces, et renyez, et somodites [sic], et mescreauntz apertement atteyntz." Both the date and attribution of this code are in doubt, but it probably should be regarded as early fourteenth century. Sorcerers are not mentioned in *Fleta*, but "renyez" is almost certainly the vernacular for "traditores."

striking because the lists of miscreants in the relevant articles are otherwise strikingly similar to those in the earlier *Laws of Henry the First*, where gay people, however, are not mentioned.[72]

Between 1250 and 1300, homosexual activity passed from being completely legal in most of Europe to incurring the death penalty in all but a few contemporary legal compilations. Often death was prescribed for a single proved act. Could such a sudden change in morality actually be imposed by law? Were any gay people really put to death for "sodomy"?

Legal records for the Middle Ages are completely inadequate to answer this question. Very little is actually known about infliction of the death penalty for any crimes, and what is known—e.g., in the case of heresy—is vehemently disputed, with figures often varying by a factor of 1,000. Extremely few instances of capital punishment for the simple crime of "sodomy" are known from published sources.[73] Unpublished materials may some day yield more information, but there seems little reason to imagine that they will dramatically alter present understanding.[74]

Erratic enforcement of laws may have been due at least partly to the general feeling on the part of most Europeans that matters of sexual morality were primarily ecclesiastical and should be handled by clerics. Did the church, then, act against gay people in response to popular hostility or pressure from princes?

The evidence again is meager. Despite the edicts of the Third and Fourth Lateran Councils and a dramatic change in theological attitudes, there is little noticeable change in church practice throughout the thirteenth century. It is clear that in some areas "sodomy" became a "reserved sin"— i.e., one which could be absolved only by the pope or a delegated bishop.[75] If consistently enforced, such a policy would doubtless have made life difficult for actively gay Catholics. There is every reason to believe, however, that such policies were observed indulgently, if at all, and it is clear that in

---

72. Cf., e.g., the cited passages from *Fleta* and *Britton* with *Leges* 10.1, 12.1a, 47.1, 64.2, etc.

73. For a published instance, see the *Annales Basileenses*, in MGH, SS, vol. 18, sub anno 1277.

74. The unusually detailed trial records of the Crown of Aragon, e.g., do not record a single instance of proceedings on charges of "sodomy" prior to 1500, in spite of the fact that the Crown during this period employed the standard clause of reservation in pardons "excepting traitors, heretics, and sodomites." Moreover, I failed to encounter any mention of "sodomy" in the more than 2,000 extant Crown registers for the period 1355–66, although many other sexual matters (rape, adultery, infidelity, miscegenation) appear. Leopoldo Piles Ros, *Estudio documental sobre el Bayle general de Valencia* (Valencia, 1970), p. 288, n. 750, does publish such an instance, but since the case involved a Muslim, the interference in personal sexual mores may not be typical: see Boswell, *The Royal Treasure*, pp. 133, 343 ff.

75. A letter of Honorius III to the archbishop of Lund (in what is now Sweden) in 1227 makes clear that "sodomy" was reserved in the latter's diocese. This letter is translated in app. 2 below.

most of Europe "sodomy" did not occupy a position of singular enormity until considerably later. The *Book of Excommunications* written by the French cardinal Bérenger Frédol at the end of the thirteenth century does not even mention homosexual acts, although it does mention other types of non-conformity stigmatized by clerics of the day, such as usury.[76] In some areas rather severe penances—by the standards of the High Middle Ages—were imposed,[77] but as in every age there were many ways to avoid ecclesiastical penalties, especially for the wealthy.[78]

Except in Italy,[79] even campaigns specifically directed against sexual minorities do not seem to have employed practical methods as harsh as their rhetoric. Gregory IX sent the Dominicans to root out homosexuality in Germany, which he had heard was "so ridden with unnatural vice . . . that some parts, especially Austria, are thought of as if infected with the foulness of leprosy."[80] The pontiff drew a terrifying picture of the fate that awaited gay people in the next world:

> For if the just Lord will punish those whom the frailty of weakness may
> in some way excuse, what will the arbiter of eternal salvation and
> damnation provide for the enemies of nature, who falsify its custom?
> When these abominable persons—despised by the world, dreaded by
> the council of heaven, who have become more unclean than animals,
> more vicious than almost anything alive, who have lost their reason
> and destroyed the kindness of nature, who are deprived of interior
> light and do not discriminate one sex from the other—when they come
> to that terrible judgment, will he not command that they be tortured
> in hell with some unimaginable type of pain worse than that given to
> all the other damned souls?[81]

76. *Le "Liber de excommunicacione" du Cardinal Bérenger Frédol*, ed. Eugène Vernay (Paris, 1912), 4:14.

77. At the end of the twelfth century the penance for relations between two males in Iceland was nine or ten years (see *Diplomatarium Islandicum*, ed. Jón Sigurðsson [Kaupmanna-höfn, 1856–76], 1:240: "IX vetr eda X firir hordom þann er karlmenn eigozst uith"), which was a stiff penance for the day (the same as that for heterosexual rape). But there were many commutations (p. 241), and it was doubtless preferable to the outlawry demanded only a little later in Norway or a visit to Rome, theoretically required of Danes guilty of the same offense.

78. Alexander III, e.g., granted to bishops the right to absolve from excommunication those who were "noble and delicate and unable to bear hardship" ("qui sunt nobiles et delicati ita quod laborem non possunt sustinere," cited in Vernay, *Le "Liber,"* p. 112).

79. See Goodich, pp. 298–301.

80. "Regio Teutonie . . . innaturali vitio, . . . ita in quibusdam partibus, et Austria precipue, maculata dicitur, quod quasi lepre perfusa turpitudine reputatur," *Bullarium ordinis fratrum praedicatorum* 54, ed. Thomas Ripoll (Rome, 1729–40), 1:39–40.

81. Ibid., 53: "Sed si tales, quod quodammodo inconstantia fragilitatis excusat, justus Dominus judicabit, de hostibus nature usum falsantibus naturalem, quid salutis, et damna-

But to remedy such practices in this world, he simply directed the Dominicans to act as "doctors of the soul" and bring them back to the "observance of reason, a life of cleanliness, and the state of celibacy or chaste marriage" through prayer, sacrifice, and good example.

Alterations in the status of gay people evident in records of the late twelfth and thirteenth centuries probably subsisted more at the level of rhetoric and declamation than of actual punishment, but they were no less profound for that. During the 200 years from 1150 to 1350, homosexual behavior appears to have changed, in the eyes of the public, from the personal preference of a prosperous minority, satirized and celebrated in popular verse, to a dangerous, antisocial, and severely sinful aberration. Around 1100, the efforts of prominent churchmen liked and respected by the pope could not prevent the election and consecration as bishop of a person well known to be leading an actively gay life-style, and much of the popular literature of the day—often written by bishops and priests—dealt with gay love, gay life-styles, and a distinct gay subculture. By 1300, not only had overtly gay literature all but vanished from the face of Europe, but a single homosexual act was enough to prevent absolutely ordination to any clerical rank, to render one liable to prosecution by ecclesiastical courts, or—in many places—to merit the death penalty.

This shift of popular opinion could be hazardous to many groups other than gay people themselves, as is evident in the celebrated historical controversy surrounding the Templars.[82] The Templars were the wealthiest and in many

---

tionis eterne arbiter providebit? nonne ipsos ad tremendum judicium abominabiles accessuros, mundo contemptibiles, et horribiles collegio supernorum, qui brutis immundiores effecti et fere quibus que viventibus nequiores, rationi sensu carentes, indulgentiam nature pretereunt, et interno privati lumine, sexu differentiam non attendunt, inscrutabili penarum genere prae aliis perditis praecipiet in inferis contorquere?"

82. The literature on the Templars and their downfall is vast and of uneven quality. Recent studies (e.g., Alejandro Vignati and Peralta, *El enigma de los Templarios* [Barcelona, 1975]) have not surpassed, in documentation or wisdom, the classic treatment by Heinrich Finke, *Papsttum und Untergang des Templerordens* (Münster, 1907), published with a volume of invaluable materials from Aragonese archives. A bibliographical summary to 1927 may be found in M. Dessubré, *Bibliographie de l'ordre des Templiers* (Paris, 1928); Guillaume Mollat, *Les papes d'Avignon*, 9th ed. (Paris, 1949), pp. 562–65, updates this. Probably the most judicious brief summary, published with an interesting contemporary letter in defense of the Templars, is C. R. Cheney's "Downfall of the Templars and a Letter in Their Defense," in *Medieval Texts and Studies* (Oxford, 1973). Mundy attributes the debacle of the Templars to the need of Europeans to find a scapegoat: see *Europe*, pp. 73–74. For more extended studies in English, see Edith Simon, *The Piebald Standard: A Biography of the Knights Templars* (Boston, 1959); E. J. Martin, *The Trial of the Templars* (London, 1928); and G. A. Campbell, *The Knights Templar: Their Rise and Fall* (New York, 1937). A provocative collection of conflicting opinions is provided by *The Guilt of the Templars*, ed. C. Legman (New York, 1966); Legman's own essay, arguing that the charges against them were based on fact, is revealingly set in the context of strident hostility to homosexuality, which he sees as the underpinning of all of Christianity. The essay by H. C. Lea, inveterate critic of Catholicism, is more credible.

ways the most powerful religious order in Europe at the opening of the fourteenth century. Founded shortly after the first crusade to defend the areas of the Holy Land reconquered from the Muslims, the Poor Knights of the Temple prospered amazingly during the following centuries, due both to their own fervor and organization and to the fact that they combined in their life-style the two most popular passions of the day: sectarian (i.e., anti-Muslim) Christianity and knightly valor. The enormous amounts of money donated to foster their labors, their protection by the papacy and independence of civil authority everywhere in Europe, and their rigid international structure all imparted to the order such an aura of stability, success, and wealth that it became the "bank" of much of Europe, probably disposing of real capital only somewhat less than the imagined treasure it possessed in the minds of envious princes.

Although their wealth increasingly excited the envy of secular authorities and other churchmen, it did not significantly diminish their effectiveness, and throughout the thirteenth century Templars died—possibly by the thousands—fighting for Christianity in the Middle East. By the final decades of the century, however, the Holy Land had been irrevocably lost, and this fact not only undermined the prestige of all those involved in its defense but rendered the crusading orders in some measure superfluous.

It was about this time that Philip the Fair acceded to the throne of France, desperate for money and land, and cast his eye hungrily upon the prosperous order of the Knights Templar, whose international treasury sat in mysterious splendor in the midst of his capital city. In October of 1307 Philip ordered all the Templars of France (probably about 2,000) arrested and began a campaign to discredit them with such success that within five years what was once the most powerful order in Christendom was dissolved by the papacy[83] and disappeared into ignominy, leaving its wealth to other orders and the secular authorities which cooperated in effecting its demise.

The charges leveled against the Templars were brilliantly calculated to raise public indignation: they involved sacrilege, heresy, and various types of obscene ritual and homosexual behavior. The Templars' meetings had always been secret; although many other orders also kept their internal affairs secret, in the case of a group as powerful as the Templars such secrecy was bound to give their enemies ammunition, and it enabled fervid imaginations to exploit every thirteenth-century anxiety in exciting public

83. Probably more out of fear of the trouble Philip could cause than conviction regarding the guilt of the Templars: Clement V was hardly the man to stand up to Philip and was fearful that the French king would insist on pursuing an inquiry against his predecessor, Boniface VIII, whom Philip had hated passionately. The suppression of the Templars was probably Clement's bribe to Philip to leave Boniface's memory alone.

hatred and fear. The Templars were said to be in league with the devil, to worship Muhammad, to parody the Mass, to sodomize new recruits regularly, to indulge in homosexual acts during their sacred ceremonies. The fact that the charges were the same sort of formulaic denigrations which any thirteenth-century antagonist hurled at his opponent—strikingly similar, for instance, to those leveled against Pope Boniface VIII by the same Philip—did not arouse suspicion on the part of the masses, who either supported or passively accepted the suppression of their erstwhile heroes.

Opinion is still divided on the question of the Templars' guilt, although the majority of modern historians tend to regard them as innocent. That tribunals appointed to investigate them everywhere outside France—England, Scotland, Ireland, Castile, Aragon, Germany—found them innocent of all charges; that the Council of Vienne of 1311 voted over-whelmingly against abolition of the order, since the prelates did not consider any of the charges against the Templars substantiated; that up to the very moment of their incarceration much of Europe's nobility and Philip himself had trusted the Templars with their personal fortunes and the revenues of their kingdoms; and that many members who had confessed to crimes under the most extreme torture recanted and upheld the complete innocence of the order in the face of imminent death—all these facts argue strongly for the Templars' innocence. Indeed the courageous death of the grand master, Jacques de Molay, even softened the popular animosity Philip had stirred up against the knights.

Almost all historians agree that whether or not the charges had any foundation, Philip himself acted from personal jealousy of the order's power and wealth. What is significant in the context of attitudes toward gay people is the fact that, as part of a deliberately conceived and well-executed campaign of character assassination against a powerful and previously orthodox group, one of the most effective accusations which could be made was the charge of "sodomy." Only a century before in the same European cities, a cleric convicted of habitual sodomy would have suffered at worst demotion and a religious penance. Now "sodomy" could be used as a charge carrying the death penalty and justifying—in the minds of some—the dissolution of an entire order of Christian knights. Mere suspicion of the act was considered sufficient to warrant such torture that many of the knights died under it. After his interrogation by French officials, Jacques de Molay showed papal legates his broken and fleshless arms, "on which nothing remained but bones and nerves," and revealed his skinned back, belly, and testicles: the legates were so appalled that they "wept bitterly and could say nothing."[84] It is

84. Finke, *Papsttum*, 2:117, no. 75: "e va mostrar los brasos, que totç los ach trencatç e descarnatç, que parech, que atans (?) [sic] fos escapatç, que noy ac romas mas los ossos els

also striking that although many Templars confessed under torture to sacrilege and heresy, extremely few would sign confessions of "sodomy"—a charge they apparently feared more than that of spitting on the cross and renouncing Jesus.

Kings themselves were no longer safe. In the twelfth century the king of France could elevate to the episcopate a man thought to have been his bed partner, and the future king of England could fall head over heels in love with another monarch without losing support from either the people or the church. But by the fourteenth century all this was changed, and its opening decades witnessed first the downfall of the Templars at the hands of Philip IV and then the execution (at the hands of his daughter Isabella) of the last overtly homosexual monarch of the Middle Ages, Edward II of England.[85] Enormous controversy still obscures the nature of Edward's troubles not only with Isabella, his wife, but also with the kingdoms of England and Scotland, which he inherited in debt and turmoil from his father, Edward I. There is little doubt, however, that his wife and the barons of England were violently hostile to Edward's sexual proclivities, although he more than fulfilled his royal duties by fathering four children with Isabella.

Edward's first lover, Piers Gaveston, had been exiled by Edward I (who actually liked Piers but objected to the relationship). Edward II recalled him after his accession, but Gaveston was twice exiled by Parliament,[86] which resented the king's attachment to him, and he was finally murdered by hostile barons.

Although there is no way to assess how the populace in general felt about

---

nervis, que tota la carn e la peil ne fo levada del esquena e del ventre e de les cuxes. . . . E con los cadernals viren la gran error e la gran malvestat, ploraren fot agrament, que no podian res dir."

85. Most biographers before the last few years have ignored Edward's sexuality, but both Harold Hutchison's *Edward II: The Pliant King* (London, 1971) and the more popular *Life and Times of Edward II* (London, 1973) by Caroline Bingham are open-minded and frank on the subject. Charles Wood ("Personality, Politics, and Constitutional Progress: The Lessons of Edward II," *Studia Gratiana* 15 [1972]: 521–36) stresses the importance Edward's sexual feelings may have had in a historical context, but his treatment is marred by a hypercritical and inconsistent approach. He rejects, for example, the statement of the *Chronicle of Melsa* about Edward's predilections with the argument that "this view is no more than the opinion of one writing over half a century after the king's death" (p. 524) but relies heavily on the account of Edward's captivity and murder by Geoffrey le Baker (*Chronicon Angliae temporibus Edwardi II et Edwardi III*, ed. J. A. Giles [London, 1847]) written only twenty years earlier than the former and some thirty after the events it recorded. It is difficult to see what recommends the extravagant and emotional chronicle of le Baker over that of Melsa when they are closer to each other in time than either is to the events in question.

86. This point is well made by Wood, especially on pp. 527–28, where he observes that many general complaints about the king's behavior seem to camouflage the real conflict over his attachments to Gaveston and Hugh le Despenser, Edward's second lover.

their gay monarch, there can be no doubt that his erotic preferences were widely known and generally regarded as the cause of his downfall. The most restrained of all his biographers noted that Edward's love for Gaveston, like David's for Jonathan, went "beyond love of women."[87] The *Chronicle of Melsa* tersely observed that "Edward in fact delighted inordinately in the vice of sodomy and seemed to lack fortune and grace throughout his life."[88] Ralph Higden eloquently linked Edward's affections to his troubles. "He was ardently in love with one of his friends, whom he exalted, enriched, advanced, and honored extravagantly. From this cause came shame to the lover, hatred to the beloved, scandal to the people, and harm to the kingdom."[89]

It has frequently been suggested that it was not the nature but the intemperateness of Edward's love that roused the ire of his subjects. Whether or not this is true, it deserves to be noted that Edward was scarcely wanton or frivolous about his passions: his relationship with Gaveston lasted thirteen years and appears to have been steadfast and faithful until the very end. Edward had been in love with Gaveston for a decade before he was married at twenty-three: that he continued to love him after his marriage is scarcely surprising. The inordinateness of the favors and promotions he bestowed upon him has been exaggerated by historians, both then and now, often as a mask for disgust at the nature of the relationship. Gaveston was not a commoner, as one might suppose from the bitter comments of his contemporaries, but an aristocrat of charm and enormous martial skill and valor. His rapid rise to power was no more "immoderate" than that of dozens of royal servants of the later Middle Ages trusted precisely because they were not part of the most powerful baronial families. Edward's relationship with Hugh le Despenser, who had been in his service since both were young men, developed quite gradually and does not appear to have become intimate

---

87. "In planctu Dauid super Jonatan amor ostenditur, quem dicitur super amorem mulierum dilexisse. Fatetur et sic rex noster," *Vita Edwardi Secundi*, ed. N. Denholm-Young (London, 1957), p. 30.

88. "Ipse quidem Edwardus in vitio sodomitico nimium delectabat, et fortuna ac gratia omni suo tempore carere videbatur," Thomas of Burton *Chronica monasterii de Melsa*, ed. Edward Bond (London, 1867), 2:355. The use of "nimium" here was probably not intended to suggest that moderation was possible in the case of "sodomy." It should be taken to imply that Edward's interest in such activities was, in the writer's eyes, *inherently* inordinate —a common use of "nimium" and a characteristic objection to homosexuality at the time.

89. "Ad unum aliquem familiarem ardenter affectus, quem summe coleret, ditaret, praeferret, honoraret. Ex quo impetu provenit amanti opprobrium, amasio obloquium, plebi scandalum, regno detrimentum," Ralph of Higden *Polychronicon* 7.41, ed. Joseph Lumby (London, 1882), 8:298, repeated in the *Chronicle of Melsa* under "Abbot Roger," chap. 31 (Bond, pp. 280–81).

until long after Gaveston's death. The two men were so discreet about their relationship that some authorities have regarded it as purely political.[90]

The image of the wronged Isabella seeking redress for the violations of her marriage rights is sometimes evoked to explain Edward's fall, but it will not stand close scrutiny. As regards her person, she had been treated no worse than many of England's most noted queens—far better than Eleanor of Aquitaine, for example—and as regards her marriage, at the time she led the barons of England in revolt against her husband she was living in open and notorious adultery with Mortimer of Wigmore.[91]

Moreover, the reported manner of the deaths of Edward and le Despenser makes pellucidly clear the nature and origin of the animosity directed against them: Hugh's genitals were cut off and burned publicly before he was decapitated,[92] and Edward was murdered by the insertion into his anus of a red-hot poker.[93]

90. There is no doubt that both Hugh and his father were politically useful to Edward, but this does not reduce the likelihood of a romantic relationship between the two younger men. Popular rumor, comments by nobles, the actions of Parliament, the reaction of the queen, and Hugh's death all suggest that his union with the king was of the same sort as Gaveston's. Froissart (*Chroniques*, in *Collection des chroniques nationales Françaises*, ed. J. A. Buchon [Paris, 1824], vol. 11, bk. 1, chap. 24, p. 52) states explicitly that Hugh had committed "sodomy" with the king and was the cause of Edward's abandoning Isabella. The *Vita Edwardi Secundi* recounts the words of Earl Aylmer at the parliament of 1321, when Edward was resisting baronial demands for Hugh's exile: "Do not therefore lose your kingdom for someone else. He perishes on the rocks who loves another more than himself" ("Noli ergo pro aliquo uiuente perdere regnum tuum. Alpibus ille perit qui plus se diligit ullum"; Denholm-Young, p. 113).

91. See Charles Wood, "Queens, Queans, and Kingship: An Inquiry into Theories of Royal Legitimacy in Late Medieval England and France," in *Order and Innovation in the Middle Ages*.

92. Froissart, vol. 11, bk. 1, chap. 24: "Quand il fut ainsi lié, on lui coupa tout premier le . . . et les . . . pour ce qui'il étoit hérite et sodomite, ainsi que on disoit mêmement du roi, et pour ce avoit le roi déchassé la reine de lui et par son ennort. Quan le . . . et les . . . lui furent coupés, on les jeta au feu pour ardoir" (ellipses in original). Froissart is hardly the last word in accuracy, but it is notable that the penalty he describes was in fact the common French punishment for "sodomy." Whether or not the description of le Despenser's end is accurate, however, is not crucial; what is significant is that Froissart represents a common view of the time about his and Edward's erotic preferences and the fate deserved by those who engaged in such practices.

93. "Cum veru ignito inter celanda confossus ignominiose peremptus est," Higden 7.44 (Lumby, 8:324). No aspect of Edward's life has excited more controversy than its end. I have adopted Higden's account because in my judgment it accurately represents attitudes toward the king and because it was widely believed and repeated throughout the fourteenth and subsequent centuries (e.g., by le Baker, p. 95; see Hutchison, p. 142, for other sources). There will probably never be agreement on the subject. T. F. Tout's study, *The Captivity and Death of Edward of Carnarvon* (Manchester, 1920; reprinted from the *Bulletin of the John Rylands Library* of the same year), was inconclusive, despite its wealth of detail and scholarship; and more recent students seem to have obscured rather than clarified the matter. Hutchison, for instance, argues for the credibility of Higden's account on the basis of its

"Humanity," wrote C. S. Lewis, "does not pass through phases as a train passes through stations; being alive it has the privilege of always moving yet never leaving anything behind."[94] It would be wrong to imagine that the social changes discussed in this chapter were any more complete or absolute than any other shifts in social values and mores. Alterations of popular attitudes are not neat and do not observe sharp chronological divisions. Old prejudices overlap new ones, visceral convictions resist intellectual changes, group intolerance is mitigated by individual forebearance, and what appears in the literature of a society may be far behind or long in advance of the attitudes of ordinary citizens. Especially during periods lacking rapid and effective transport and communication, new attitudes and beliefs travel slowly and take hold haphazardly, and all these reservations restrict the accuracy at a more specific level of the general picture presented here.

It remains nonetheless clear that a considerable transformation of public attitudes toward homosexual behavior took place during the later twelfth and thirteenth centuries. It is not possible to analyze the causes of this change satisfactorily, although many contributing factors have been considered, nor can one easily discover how great an effect such a transition had on the daily lives of most people. Celebrated cases such as those of the Templars and Edward II may be anomalous, and historical records do not suggest efficient enforcement of new laws against homosexual behavior. But literature of the day does indicate profoundly altered ideas on the part of the public about the gravity of homosexual acts, the acceptability of homosexual persons, and the nature of gay sexuality. The fear engendered by increasing hostility is widely evident in the defensive reactions of those charged with homosexual activities and the devastating use made of such accusations in political contexts. Such fear doubtless played a large role in the disappearance of nearly all manifestations of a gay subculture by the mid-thirteenth century, and this in turn facilitated the success of exaggerated and fanciful claims about the harmful and dangerous nature of gay sexuality. As it had been safe and effective to denigrate gay people in the declining cities of the late Roman Empire, where Jews, religious dissidents, and many who did not conform to majority or governmental standards were ostracized or oppressed, so was it

---

inclusion in the English translation of John of Trevisa, who was vicar of Berkeley castle, where Edward died; but Trevisa in fact omits any mention of Edward's murder, observing simply that "he deyde aboute the feste of seynt Matheu the evangeliste" (Lumby, 8:325). The English statement commonly credited to Trevisa (e.g., by Bailey, p. 170)—"He was sleyne with a hoote broche putte thro the secrete place posterialle"—actually comes from an anonymous fifteenth-century translation now contained in BM Harleian MS 2261, printed by Lumby along with that of Trevisa. Cf. the recent study by G. P. Cuttino and T. W. Lyman, "Where Is Edward II?" *Speculum* 53 (1978): 522–44.

94. *Allegory of Love*, p. 1.

in the cities of the later thirteenth century, where similar conditions increasingly prevailed. The contrast with the climate of opinion in the same cities only two centuries earlier—when saints wrote of gay love in the cloister, bishops celebrated it in verse, Muslim, Jewish, and Christian poets made it the coinage of an international subculture, and debates about it were copied into school texts—is remarkable.

Moreover, whatever its effect on individual lives, the change in public attitudes had a profound and lasting impact on European institutions and culture as a result of the permanent and official expression it achieved in thirteenth-century laws, literature, and theology, all of which continued to influence Western thought and social patterns long after the disappearance of the particular circumstances which produced them.

11 Intellectual Change:

Men, Beasts, and "Nature"

Although the "natural" arguments of Barnabas and Clement of Alexandria exercised some influence on subsequent Christian attitudes toward homosexual behavior, especially at the popular level, they could never fully take root in the intellectual soil of the early Middle Ages, and scholarly appeals to animal behavior were rare through the tenth century. Among people struggling to keep alive in the face of the destructive powers of "nature," not only familiar with but dependent upon animals for labor and sustenance of every kind, prey to real wild beasts and terrified of imaginary ones, animal morality was not apt to be an effective philosophical construct. As late as the twelfth century in less urbanized areas, "realistic" approaches to "nature" predominated among the educated. Saint Aelred used animals as a decidedly negative example in regard to general sexuality,[1] and although he recognized that homosexual behavior occurred among animals, he viewed this not as a moral indication pro or con, but simply as a matter of fact.[2]

By the time of the High Middle Ages, however, the climate of opinion was highly conducive to moral arguments based on zoological example, and under its beneficent skies the seeds sown by early Christian moralists not only took root and grew but eventually overshadowed almost every other approach to the subject. As southern Europe became more and more urban and cultural centers more removed from daily contact with agricultural life-styles, "nature" came to seem a more and more important and benevolent force and

---

1. "... More sordid, if not morally worse, than those [involved in vanity and worldly pomp] are those in whom there is scarcely anything human left, whom obscene lust has transformed into animals" ("Alii etsi non deteriores, certe sordidiores, quibus pene de homine nihil est, quos obscoena turpitudo transformauit in bestias," *De speculo caritatis* 3.40.111 [Hoste and Talbot, p. 160]). The translation of this line by Walker and Webb (p. 140) is particularly loose and misleading. Cf. *De institutione inclusarum* 32 (Hoste and Talbot, p. 674).

2. *De sanctimoniali de Wattun* (PL, 195:793): "Sicut equus et mulus quibus non est intellectus irruit in virum quem feminam esse putabat."

increasingly preoccupied Christian thought.[3] The rediscovery of the zoological texts of Aristotle in the thirteenth century accelerated this tendency—
both stimulating and satisfying an enormous demand for biological knowledge
throughout the scholarly communities of Europe—but a demand had existed
centuries before, when there was little to fill it except bestiaries, based on
classical sources (especially the *Physiologus*) and medieval legends. By the
twelfth century bestiaries were among the more popular forms of literature in
western Europe and were being copied and illustrated all over the continent.[4]
The illustrations often made such works accessible to the common man, but
their influence extended as well to kings and bishops, who commissioned
them, and they were effective among all classes as sources of moral allegory.
Saint Peter Damian wrote to the monks of Montecassino that

> the natural behavior of animals can be perceived in human acts
> through spiritual insight, just as some things may be observed among
> humans which belong to the sphere of the angels. As the almighty
> creator, God, established all earthly things for the use of humans, so he
> took care to enlighten man through the individual natures and
> instinctive behavior he bestowed on lower animals: from animals
> people may learn what behavior should be imitated, what avoided;
> what may wisely be borrowed from them, and what should rightly
> be avoided.[5]

3. On the subject of "nature" in the later Middle Ages, see the essays in *La filosofia della
natura nel medioevo: atti del terzo Congresso internazionale di filosofia medioevale* (Milan, 1966), esp.
T. Gregory, "L'idea di natura nella filosofia medievale prima dell'ingresso della fisica di
Aristotele—il secolo XII," and F. van Steenberghen, "La philosophie de la nature au
XIIIe siècle"; Brian Stock, *Myth and Science in the Twelfth Century* (Princeton, N.J., 1972);
M.-D. Chenu, *Nature, Man and Society in the Twelfth Century*, trans. J. Taylor and L. K. Little
(Chicago, 1968), and *La théologie au douzième siècle* (Paris, 1957); Curtius, *European Literature*;
Dronke, *Medieval Latin*; George Economou, *The Goddess Natura in Medieval Literature* (Cam-
bridge, Mass., 1972); R. Klibansky, *The Continuity of Platonic Tradition during the Middle Ages*
(London, 1950); E. C. Knowlton, "The Goddess *Natura* in Early Periods," *Journal of English
and Germanic Philology* 19 (1920): 224–53; Pellicer, *Natura, étude sémantique*; F. J. E. Raby,
"*Nuda Natura* and Twelfth-Century Cosmology," *Speculum* 43 (1968): 72–77; see also
the works on "natural law" cited below, n. 41, and Nicole Grévy-Pons, *Celibat et nature:
une controverse médiévale—à propos d'un traité du début du XVe siècle* (Paris, 1975).

4. Despite their well-known popularity and great influence, relatively little scholarly
attention has been focused on the bestiaries. Probably the most convenient single study is that
of Florence McCulloch, *Mediaeval Latin and French Bestiaries* (Chapel Hill, N.C., 1962),
which might be supplemented by Francis Klingender, *Animals in Art and Thought to the End of
the Middle Ages* (Cambridge, Mass., 1971), and P. A. Robin, *Animal Lore in English Literature*
(London, 1932). Shorter but less general treatments may be found in M. James, "The
Bestiary," *History*, n.s., 16, no. 61 (1931): 1–11; and G. Cronin, "The Bestiary and the
Medieval Mind: Some Complexities," *Modern Language Quarterly* 2 (1941): 191–99.

5. "Nam et naturales actus pecorum per spiritualem intelligentiam reperiuntur in
moribus hominum; sicut et in hominibus aliquid invenitur, quod ad officia pertineat

The long letter of pastoral advice to which this paragraph serves as introduction consists entirely of elaborate moral inferences from the animal and
mineral lore contained in contemporary bestiaries and comparable works of
"natural history." Stones called *pyroboli* from "a mountain in the Orient,"
for instance, serve as a warning to the monks to avoid contact with anything
"feminine": the stones are male and female, and if brought into proximity
they burst into flame and destroy each other.[6] Although the weasel (labeled
a reptile) receives more or less favorable treatment in Peter's letter, the
hyena's sex changes again earn it derogation as a "dirty animal" whose
example should be avoided by all Christians.[7]

Prior to the advent of Aristotelian biological texts, almost all Western
zoological information of whatever sort was derived from late classical
sources which regarded the hare, hyena, and weasel as sexually aberrant, and
one finds negative allusions to these animals in all types of medieval literature in addition to bestiaries,[8] from popular medical treatises for women[9] to
the "treasure books" written by Brunetto Latini,[10] the mentor of Dante.

Serious writers in Latin were at first limited to such sources as the *De
bestiis*, which offered the hyena legend in summary form,[11] but throughout

---

angelorum. Rerum quippe conditor omnipotens Deus, sicut terrena quaeque ad usum
hominum condidit; sic etiam per ipsas naturarum vires, et necessarios motus, quos brutis
animalibus indidit, hominem salubriter informare curavit. Ut in ipsis pecoribus homo
possit addiscere quid imitari debeat, quid cavere, quid ab eis mutuari salubriter valeat,
quid rite contemnat," *De bono religiosi status et variarum animantium tropologia* 2 (PL, 145:767).

6. Ibid., 5 (769–70).

7. Ibid., 17 (777–78), 19 (780).

8. It would be impossible to provide a listing here of all the bestiaries containing allusions
to these animals and their sexuality. The entries in McCulloch will be of some help to the
general reader. In addition to those works cited below, see, for the hyena, the important
twelfth-century English bestiary translated by White, *The Bestiary*, pp. 31, 32; the thirteenth-
century vernacular bestiary of William of Normandy, *Le bestiaire: Das Thierbuch des nor-
mannischen Dichters Guillaume le Clerc*, ed. R. Reinsch (Wiesbaden, 1967), pp. 290–93; and the
Italian bestiary in M. Goldstaub and R. Wendriner, *Ein tosco-venezianischer Bestiarius* (Halle,
1892), pp. 183–85, with notes. For the weasel, see the discussion and notes in Goldstaub
and Wendriner, pp. 291–93; and Richard of Fournival, *Bestiaire d'amour*, ed. Cesare Segre
(Milan, 1957), pp. 26, 115; *Libellus de natura animalium*, ed. J. Davis (London, 1958), s.v.
"mustela"; the Cambrai bestiary, ed. E. B. Ham, *Modern Philology* 36 (1939): 225–37, esp.
sec. 1, p. 233; the Provençal bestiary, "Aiso son las naturas d'alcunas auzels e d'alcunas
bestias," in Karl Bartsch, *Provenzalisches Lesebuch* (Elberfeld, 1855), p. 163; and Thomas of
Cantimpré *Liber de naturis rerum*, Cambridge, Mass., Houghton Library MS Lat. 125, fol.
44, s.v. "mustela," where the idea that it conceives through the mouth is attributed to
"Clemens papa." For the hare, see nn. 15–17 below.

9. In the writings of Trotula, for instance, the testicles of the weasel are a contraceptive:
see *On the Diseases of Women*, trans. Elizabeth Mason-Hohl (Los Angeles, 1940), p. 18.

10. *Li livres dou trésor de Brunetto Latini*, ed. F. J. Carmody (Berkeley, 1948), 188, p. 166.

11. *De bestiis et aliis rebus* 61–62; authorship presently disputed; probably late eleventh or
early twelfth century (PL, 177).

the twelfth and thirteenth centuries more and more material became available from the Latin tradition and from the translations of Arabic works being effected in areas of Spain and Sicily recently conquered from the Muslims.[12] To make such knowledge widely available, encyclopedias, or digests of information arranged topically, were compiled. These works, although far more comprehensive and scholarly than the more popular bestiaries, often drew the same conclusions about the "immorality" of sexually atypical animals. Alexander Neckam (d. 1217), an early and widely quoted encyclopedist, dealt at length with the peculiarities of the hare and its ethical implications:

> They say that the hare of the nobler sex [i.e., the male] bears the little hares in the womb. Can it be that a bizarre nature has made him a hermaphrodite? They also say that in the mother's womb, along with the tiny little hares, larger babies, previously conceived, are carried; in this one can perceive an affront to the law of [her] inferior nature.[13] Effeminate men who violate the law of nature are thus said to imitate hares, offending against the highest majesty of nature. Not unjustly is Tiresias considered to have incurred the wrath of Juno and been deprived of the light of sight.[14] For those who follow the unlawful law of the Phrygian youth [Ganymede] provoke the wrath of the divine power, and when they have been deprived of the light of grace they are assured of being cast into the outer darkness.[15]

12. Of many works which could be cited on this subject, the most recent summary can be found in Dorothee Metlitzki, *The Matter of Araby in Medieval England* (New Haven, 1976), esp. pp. 10–13, 13–49; a more circumscribed but admirably concise treatment is that of Richard Walzer, "Arabic Transmission of Greek Thought to Medieval Europe," *Bulletin of the John Rylands Library* 19 (1945–46): 160–83. For Aristotle, S. D. Wingate's *Medieval Latin Versions of the Aristotelian Scientific Corpus* (London, 1931) is indispensable.

13. I.e., in addition to the male's violation of the "law of nature" by bearing the young, the female violates even the law of her "inferior nature" by superfetation. Note that "nature" is used in this paragraph in several different senses.

14. Neckam either misunderstands or deliberately distorts the traditional series of events in the story of Tiresias. Cf. Ovid *Metamorphoses* 3.316 ff.

15. *De naturis rerum* 134, ed. Thomas Wright (London, 1863), pp. 215–16: "Ferunt leporem characterem sexus nobilioris habentem lepusculos in utero gestitare. Numquid eum hermaphroditum prodigiosa natura fecit? Addunt etiam in utero materno cum lepusculis tenellis grandiusculos tempore priori conceptos contineri, in quo derogari videtur legi naturae inferioris. Lepores imitari dicuntur qui jus naturae offendunt effoeminati, majestatis summae naturae rei. Non immerito Tiresias indignationem Saturniae sensisse perhibetur, lumine privatus. Divinae enim potentiae indignationem incurrunt, exlegem legem adolescentis Phrygii sequentes, et, dum lumine gratiae privantur, in tenebras exteriores mitti promerentur." This passage is probably derived from Pliny *Natural History* 8.81.218–19, although the dependence is not perfectly clear, and other sources are possible. Barnabas and Novatian both suggested homosexuality as a failing or association of the rabbit, but neither

The philosophical difficulties created by claiming that men "offend the highest majesty of nature" by imitating behavior determined by the same "nature" do not seem to have troubled Neckam, but they may have played a role in the reluctance of some scholars of the period to draw moral inferences from animal behavior. In the most influential encyclopedia of the later Middle Ages, *On the Properties of Things,* by Bartholomaeus Anglicus, the sexual legends about the weasel, hyena, and hare are all treated in greater detail than in Neckam's (or any other previous) treatise, but ethical implications are conspicuously absent.[16]

The legends themselves nonetheless continued to be incorporated into serious zoological works throughout the Middle Ages and doubtless inspired many to draw the same moral conclusions Christians had drawn since the time of Barnabas. These influences were by no means limited to a credulous lower class: Vincent of Beauvais's encyclopedia, the *Speculum majus,* which included the stories about the hare and the weasel,[17] was one of the most widely employed scholarly sources in Europe well into the Renaissance.

These particular animals, however, were not the only "natural" objections

---

was well known in the West in the twelfth century. Neither Aristotle nor the *Physiologus* accused the hare of hermaphroditism, although Aristotle did mention the hare's tendency to superfetation. Timothy of Gaza's treatment of the hare had passed into Muslim animal lore at least by the ninth century (e.g., in Ibn Qutayba ʿUyun al-Akhbār 4.28.2 [Cairo, 1925], 2:93), and there is no doubt that Neckam had access to Arabic sources (see George Sarton, *Introduction to the History of Science* [Baltimore, 1927], pt. 2, 1:385–86; also Metlitzki). It is especially interesting that the hare should have come under attack in later English animal lore (see White, p. 10, for another example), since there was an influential English tradition of medicinal use of hares: see the "Penitential of Theodore" 11.5 (McNeill, p. 208): "The hare may be eaten, and it is good for dysentery; and its gall is to be mixed with pepper for pain." See also O. Cockrayne, *Leechdom, Wortcunning, and Starcraft of Early England* (London, 1864), 1:343–47. In his discussion of the weasel (123) and the hyena (151), Neckam relies on the sober accounts of Isidore and Solinus, respectively, rejecting or ignoring the traditional sexual association of these creatures.

16. Bartholomaeus was an English Franciscan who composed his *De rerum proprietatibus* in the first half of the thirteenth century. Like the *Speculum majus* of Vincent of Beauvais, it was copied and read voraciously all over Europe, but being about one tenth the length of Vincent's encyclopedia, it enjoyed even greater popularity. Almost every major European library contains manuscripts of the *De rerum* (Paris alone has more than eighteen), which was translated in its entirety into French, English, and Spanish. Bartholomaeus accepts the sex changes of the hyena (18.59), although he is aware that Pliny followed Aristotle in denying this. He repeats both medical and sexual lore regarding the hare (18.66), deriving the latter entirely from Pliny. For the weasel (18.72) he relies on Isidore's realistic and restrained information (supplemented by Pliny and Aristotle) and rejects the alleged sexual foibles of the animal.

17. Hare (*lepus*): "Speculum doctrinale" 15.90; "Speculum naturale" 18.61–62. Weasel (*mustela*): "Speculum doctrinale" 15.96; "Speculum naturale" 19.34. These ideas survived in serious English zoological works nearly into modern times: see Izaak Walton's *Compleat Angler,* chap. 5.

to homosexual behavior among writers of the day. "Nature's intent," as interpreted by the observer, was explored at length on the basis of "natural" principles ranging from grammatical constructions[18] to alchemical theories. In the "Dream of Arisleus,"[19] for instance, the hero is transported in a dream to a land where the natives practice exclusive homosexuality. Arisleus informs the country's king that such unions will not produce offspring but will always be sterile, and that only male-female unions will be fruitful.[20] The treatise is an alchemical allegory: two of the principal characters are apparently allegorical representations of sulfur and mercury.[21] The confusion of moral and "natural" laws in the work is striking; Arisleus urges the king to abandon homosexuality in favor of incest, which will be more productive, and counters the king's objections to incest with the biblical example of Adam's children.[22]

By a curious paradox, the same centuries which fostered the revival and promulgation of the notion that certain animals were innately homosexual also witnessed the rebirth of the contrary idea: that the absence of such behavior among animals constituted proof of its "unnaturalness." One satirist declaims,

A perverse custom it is to prefer boys to girls,
Since this type of love rebels against nature.

. . . .

Animals curse and avoid evil caresses,
While man, more bestial than they, approves and pursues such things.[23]

Late Latin and Hellenistic culture had managed to accommodate these seemingly irreconcilable beliefs largely by dint of their enormous variety and geographical expanse. Few early Christians claimed that homosexuality was at once unknown among animals *and* practiced by hyenas and hares. The *Physiologus* appealed to an audience unfamiliar with Ovid's description of homosexual behavior as unknown among animals, and probably relatively few people would have read both Augustine and the *Physiologus* before the eleventh or twelfth century.

18. See above, p. 259, n. 60.
19. A Latin compilation of Arabic alchemical lore interpolated into the *Turba philosophorum*, printed in *Quellen und Studien zur Geschichte der Naturwissenschaften und der Medizin,* ed. Julius Ruska (Berlin, 1931), vol. 1.
20. Ibid., p. 326.
21. See explanation by Ruska, p. 324. The king's son is named Cabritus, which Ruska takes to be the Latin translation for the Arabic "kibrit," "sulfur"; he is persuaded to marry his sister Beua, which Ruska interprets as a garbled form of the Arabic "baida," "mercury." Metlitzki accepts Ruska's interpretation (pp. 84–85).
22. Ruska, p. 327.
23. Translated in its entirety in app. 2, "A Perverse Custom."

By the end of the latter century, however, the two ideas were common-places of the same culture at the same time. Their successful coexistence for centuries thereafter is evidence of the ability of the human mind to entertain paradoxes with equanimity. Although most writers who treated the subject can be shown to have embraced both beliefs only by implication, a few did so explicitly. Within the same thirty lines of poetry, for instance, Bernard of Morlaix castigated gay people for imitating hyenas and for indulging in behavior unknown to animals.[24] In Vincent of Beauvais's widely read "Speculum doctrinale" the argument that animals do not practice homo-sexual behavior is followed immediately by the accusation that men who indulge in such acts are like hares.[25]

Nonetheless, the claim that gay sexuality was reprehensible because unknown among animals did not win immediate acceptance. Early in the twelfth century, for instance, the author of "Ganymede and Helen" had Helen maintain that the heterosexuality of "birds, wild animals, and boars" should be an example to humans, to which Ganymede could still respond that humans were hierarchically superior to animals and should not imitate them: "But man should not be like birds or pigs: / Man has reason."[26] In his influential poem on the "community of the world,"[27] Bernard Silvestris agreed with Ganymede that "brute animals obviously have dim perceptions: with downward looks they keep their faces pointed to the ground";[28] heaven and its inhabitants should provide the models for humanity, "which alone turns its holy head to the stars."[29] But Bernard contributed greatly to an idealization of "nature" which was to undermine this idea. The heroine of his poem is the goddess Natura, who laments that the world is in chaos and

24. *De contemptu mundi*, p. 80, line 4: "Mas maris immemor, of furor! o tremor! est ut hyena." Line 28: "Nescit ea pecus, aut canis, aut equus, ast homo totus." Cf. p. 81, line 3: "Bestia non sapit. . . ."

25. 4.162: "Inter quae animalia cuncta, / Foemina foeminea correpta cupidine nulla est" ; "Vir facie, mulier gestu, sed crure quod ambo. / Es lepus. . . ." The quotations are from Ovid *Metamorphoses* 9.733–34 and Ennodius *Epigrammata* 52 (PL, 63:344). In bk. 15 of the same work Vincent accepts as fact the legend which gave rise to Ennodius's jibe (sec. 90: "Lepus autem sexum suum per annos singulos mutat"), so it is hardly likely that he failed to grasp its meaning. The apparent self-contradiction is all the more striking because in the "Speculum morale" attributed to Vincent and printed as part of the *Speculum majus* (or *Bibliotheca mundi*) the arguments of Aquinas about the "unnaturalness" of homosexuality are adduced (3.9.2: "De speciebus luxuriae").

26. 34.1–2: "Non aves aut pecora debet imitari / Homo, cui datum est ratiocinari" (Lenzen, p. 177).

27. *Bernard Silvestris De mundi universitate libri duo sive megacosmus et microcosmus*, ed. C. S. Barach and J. Wrobel (Innsbruck, 1876).

28. "Bruta patenter habent tardos animalia sensus, / Cernua deiectis vultibus ora ferunt," 10.27–28 (Barach, p. 55).

29. "Tollet homo sanctum solus ad astra caput," ibid., 30. Cf. Ovid *Metam.* 1. 84–86.

should be restructured into a more harmonious and just whole.[30] Bernard was not hostile to gay people, and his goddess has nothing to say on the subject, but she was the inspiration for a longer and even more influential poem by Alain de Lille, *The Complaint of Nature*, in which Natura complains specifically and at great length about the violations of her sovereignty practiced by twelfth-century society in sexual matters.[31] Most of her harangue is concerned with heterosexual or nonsexual offenses, but Alain, who condemned homosexual behavior, directs Natura's attention to homosexual activity in numerous places, directly rebutting some of the points scored against her in "Ganymede and Helen," and capitalizes on the twelfth-century revival of Roman law by obliquely quoting the long-forgotten law of 342 against homosexual marriages.[32]

No specifically Christian theology informs *The Complaint of Nature*; the arguments are theistic but entirely philosophical. In an age preoccupied with effecting a union of theology and philosophy, however, the absence of specifically Christian referents only strengthened Alain's case. Nothing so charmed the tastes of the age as non-Christian "proofs" of Christian moral principles, and the pagan figure of Natura employed by Alain and others provided just such reinforcement for those who wished to denigrate homosexual activity. This may have been deliberate. It would be a mistake to think of writings like *The Complaint of Nature* as literary exercises in invective, like the satires of Juvenal or Martial's epigrams. Alain was very much influenced by the hostility to nonconformity which was sweeping Europe in his day, and he consciously tried to erect an intellectual structure which could support it. He wrote treatises against heretics, Jews, infidels, and Muslims,[33] and he took part in the Third Lateran Council of 1179, which condemned or restricted the freedom of these and other nonconformist groups (as noted above, Lateran III was the first "ecumenical" council to condemn homosexual behavior). Alain was a celebrated and influential teacher, often called the "Universal Doctor," and his philosophical support for popular hostility provided effective ammunition against gay people for later theologians.[34]

30. For discussion, see Stock, *Myth and Science*; Economou, *The Goddess Natura*, provides a summary of the poem on pp. 151–58.

31. *De planctu naturae* (PL, 210:451–82; or in Wright, *Anglo-Latin Satirical Poets*, 2:429–522; translation by Douglas Moffat in *The Complaint of Nature by Alain de Lille*, Yale Studies in English, vol. 36 [1908; reprint ed., Hamden, Conn., 1972]). For the relationship between Alain's and Bernard's works, see Stock, esp. pp. 282–83.

32. In Wright, 2:414: "Conqueruntur jura; leges armantur, et ultore gladio suas effectas injurias vindicari." The use of the indicative rather than the jussive employed in the original implies that Alain thought measures were being taken to outlaw such behavior. Cf. Peter Cantor's more accurate citation.

33. *Ars fidei catholicae, Tractatus contra haereticos*, and *Theologicae regulae* (PL, 210).

34. In his treatise *De virtutibus et vitiis* Alain defined "peccatum contra naturam" as any

The thirteenth-century Scholastic effort to rationalize the Christian faith in accordance with principles of Greek philosophy drew heavily on concepts of "nature" popularized in the twelfth century by writers like Alain de Lille and often incorporated their more personal prejudices as well.

Ironically, the popular fascination with the goddess Natura may also have been due to her ostensible irrelevance to traditional Christian morality. The extreme idealizations of love in many forms during the late eleventh and early twelfth centuries rendered the sexual ethics characteristic of early Christian morality—formulated with complete disregard for erotic passion—either unacceptable or irrelevant to many Christians. There was no Christian moral guidance on the subject of erotic passion, within or without marriage, and in an age hungry for literature and moral authority on the subject, the goddess Natura was a godsend.[35] The expressed romantic ideals in the most advanced areas of Europe during this period revolved very largely around types of love (primarily adultery) which directly violated traditional Christian sexual morality. In societies which glorified erotic relations of this sort, almost any traditional moral premises which could have been invoked to oppress gay people would also have reflected very badly on the most popular and appealing fantasies, if not realities, of the heterosexual majority. But in the hands of a clever writer, like Alain de Lille or Marie de France, the goddess Natura could by her own authority encourage and approve those forms of sexuality, traditional or not, which the writer wished to favor and discourage or condemn any forms the writer happened to dislike. She might bless any sexual unions which were heterosexual and fruitful or only those which occurred within marriage, but in either case it was her own authority which justified her opinion—not the teachings of the church. Throughout the twelfth and thirteenth centuries, the goddess gained in stature and familiarity,[36] here supporting popular prejudices, there creating new opinions, everywhere appearing as a beneficent and universally admired figure, until she was one of the most established and pervasive parts of the European intellectual apparatus—a position she has retained to the present day. By the opening of the thirteenth century, her authority was virtually

---

emission of semen outside the vessel appointed for it (i.e., the vagina: "Peccatum contra naturam est quando extra locum ad hoc deputatum funditur semen," art. 1, published in O. Lottin, *Psychologie et morale aux XIIe et XIIIe siècles* [Gembloux, 1960], 6:75), but in the majority of his writings he clearly employs it in reference to homosexual behavior.

35. Natura's popularity was due in some measure to contemporary fascination with idealized semidivine female figures—the Fates, Reason, "the Lady Poverty," etc.: see Joan Ferrante, *Woman as Image in Medieval Literature from the Twelfth Century to Dante* (London, 1975).

36. Economou's *Goddess Natura* is the best general description of this process; see also Curtius, pp. 106–27, 444 ff.; Dronke, *Poetic Individuality*, 17, 21, 159ss; etc.

unquestioned; she reigned supreme in almost every intellectual sphere. And in the moral sphere she represented, thanks to the efforts of Alain de Lille and others, an exclusively heterosexual constituency.

The popular acceptance of the goddess Natura as the champion of heterosexual fecundity clearly had a profound impact on the development of moral theology in the thirteenth century. By a strange irony, a popular literary figure of decidedly pagan origin speaking on her own authority for the sexual preferences of the majority had come to dominate even dogmatic theology. Which, if any, of the many competing philosophical or theological meanings of "nature" could the goddess be said to represent? Throughout the twelfth century the most popular definitions of "nature" remained those based on Boethius. Gilbert de la Porrée and other Scholastics of the day glossed, commented on, or simply appropriated Boethius's definition with very few changes.[37] Boethius's "nature" made no appeal to animals, suggested nothing about human sexuality, and certainly did not preclude homosexual relations; even the goddess Natura could hardly derive her objections from it. Alain de Lille himself based his theological definitions of "nature" on Boethius,[38] and of the nine definitions he provides, none excludes homosexual relations.[39] It was not until the thirteenth century that actual definitions of "nature" were formulated to exclude homosexual activity, and in the beginning these were only tenuously related to even the most general meanings of "nature." A gloss on the *Sentences* of Peter of Poitiers, for instance, notes four meanings of "natural," of which the last is explicitly calculated to exclude homosexual behavior: "Sometimes 'natural' refers to what is not unusual [*contra usum*], like intercourse between man and woman, 'unnatural' [*innaturale*] to what is unusual."[40] This means of removing gay sexuality from the realm of the

---

37. *Gilberti Porretae commentaria in librum De duabus naturis et una persona Christi*, "De natura" (PL, 64:1359–68). Cf. John of Salisbury *Metalogicon* 1.8.

38. *Distinctiones dictionum theologicalium*, s.v. "natura" (PL, 210:871).

39. Ibid.: (1) all that is known ("omne illud quid quo modo potest intelligi"); (2) all that exists physically ("acts or is acted upon": "quidquid agere vel pati potest"); (3) the property by which something is defined (the divine and human "natures" of Christ); (4) a quality inherent from the time of origin (e.g., the ability to sin is "natural" to angels); (5) the native characteristics of a thing; (6) inherent defectiveness ("vitium inolitum"), as when one is said to die of "natural causes" ("de natura"); (7) something characteristic of or conducive to life (e.g., body heat); (8) what is common to all humans, as a concept of good and evil; (9) reproducible form (Alain finds the Incarnation "unnatural" here). Boethius is cited as the origin of nos. (1)–(3); Plato of the fourth. (Chenu finds eleven definitions in the passage rather than nine: *Nature*, p. 20.)

40. "Quandoque naturale, quod non est contra usum, ut coitus maris· cum femina; innaturale, quod est contra usum," from MS Erfurt, Amplon., Cod. Q, 117, cited in Chenu, *Nature*, p. 20, n. 41. Abelard too had equated "nature" and "use" but—possibly because of his recognition of the frequency of homosexuality—had then paranomastically related the

"natural" presupposes something few subsequent theologians were willing to admit: that Christian society equates the "good" with the "common." Although to a certain extent this was true, it was not a position which the church wished to espouse officially, and the influence of Aristotle was already convincing most Scholastics that mere statistical deviance could not be held sinful, since "heroic virtue," sainthood, superior intellect, and even sexual continence were statistically deviant. Certainly according to the glossator's definition celibate clergy would be "unnatural."

Another means of excluding gay sexuality from the "natural," however, providentially appeared in the twelfth century and proved ultimately decisive in formulating theological objections, although it was not originally a theological concept. Late Roman law had embraced the principle that there was a "natural law" known to mankind apart from legislation enacted by particular nations.[41] Justinian's *Digest*, which *was* Roman law to the later Middle Ages, opens with a discussion in which the "natural law" known to all sentient beings is contrasted with the "law of nations" enacted by humans alone (1.1.1.1–4). This discussion was drafted by the Roman jurist Ulpian, in the third century of the Christian era, at the height of Roman idealization of "nature": "Natural law is what nature has taught all animals. This law is not unique to the human race but common to all animals born on land or sea and to birds as well. From it comes the union of male and female which we call marriage, as well as the procreation of children and their proper rearing [*educatio*]. We see in fact that all other animals, even wild beasts, are regulated by understanding of this law."[42]

---

latter to design: "Qui est contra naturam, et ideo magis abusio dicendus est quam usus. Contra naturam, hoc est contra naturae institutionem, quae genitalia feminarum usui virorum praeparavit, et e converso, non ut feminae feminis cohabitarent," *Expositio in Epistolam Pauli ad Romanos* 1 (PL, 178:806). The argument from design triumphed in some Catholic circles but was derided as "moral plumbing" in others. It was rejected by Aquinas and is very rarely explicit in subsequent medieval authors. It is interesting that Abelard limited his comments to female homosexuality.

41. For discussion of the development of the concept of "natural law" in the High Middle Ages, see, in addition to works cited earlier in this chapter, Odon Lottin, *Le droit naturel chez Saint Thomas d'Aquin et ses prédécesseurs*, 2d ed. (Bruges, 1931); and R. M. McInery, "The Meaning of 'Naturalis' in Aquinas's Theory of Natural Law," in *La filosofia della natura*, pp. 560–66.

42. 1.1.1.3: "Ius naturale est, quod natura omnia animalia docuit. nam ius istud non humani generis proprium: sed omnium animalium, quae in terra, quae in mari nascuntur: avium quoque commune est. Hinc descendit maris atque foeminae coniunctio, quam nos matrimonium appellamus: hinc liberorum procreatio, hinc educatio. videmus etenim cetera quoque animalia, feras etiam, istius iuris peritia censeri." In contrast, the *ius gentium* "est quo gentes humanae utuntur. quod a naturali recedere facile intelligere licet: quia illud omnibus animalibus, hoc solis hominibus inter se commune sit," ibid., 4. Among other difficulties with Ulpian's definition, one might note that he had previously defined law (*ius*)

This concept of law was not popular during the early Middle Ages, when most writers entertained a less flattering image of animal morality, and Saint Isidore of Seville revised it when he offered his definition of "natural law" in sixth-century Spain:

> Natural law is common to all nations, because it is maintained by natural instinct rather than legislation. Under it are comprised the union of male and female; care and rearing of children; common possession of all things; individual liberty for all; [free] acquisition of all things on land, sea, or sky; return of goods borrowed or owed; repelling violence with force. For these things and those like them are never considered unjust but always natural and right.[43]

Animals are conspicuously absent from Isidore's adaptation. The "natural instinct" which dictates the return of borrowed goods could hardly be inferred from animals. "Nature" is still present, but what constitutes "natural law" seems to be a curious combination of utopian ideals and empirical observation, with little relation either to reality or Christian teaching.[44]

By the opening of the twelfth century, "natural law" had been transformed from a force of "nature" to a specific and highly refined ethical precept. According to Gratian, "Natural law is what is contained in the law and the Gospels, according to which everyone is commanded to do to others what he would have done to himself and is forbidden to do anything to someone else which he would not have done to himself."[45]

Had this definition of natural law triumphed in Scholastic circles, it would have been extremely difficult to prove that consensual homosexuality violated "natural law." But Roman law, urbanization, and interest in biology were just beginning to dominate Europe when Gratian wrote his

---

as the *art* of goodness and justice ("Ius est ars boni et aequi"; introduction). Given the classical distinction between "nature" and "art," it is hard to understand how Ulpian could consider law to be both "natural" and an "art."

43. *Etymologiae* 5.4.1–2 (PL, 82:199): "Jus naturale est commune omnium nationum, et quod ubique instinctu naturae, non constitutione aliqua habeatur, ut: viri et feminae conjunctio, liberorum susceptio et educatio, communis omnium possessio, et omnium una libertas, acquisitio eorum quae coelo, terra marique capiuntur. 2. Item depositae rei vel commodatae restitutio, violentiae per vim repulsio. Nam hoc aut siquid huic simile est, nunquam injustum, sed naturale, aequumque habetur."

44. No secular society known to Isidore allowed "common possession of all things" or free "acquisition of all things on land, sea, or sky"; and yet if Isidore simply described an ideal state, why did he include the repelling of violence with force—a violation of both the direct command (Matt. 5:39, Luke 6:29) and the clear example of the author of "nature" in Christian philosophy?

45. *Decretum, Distinctio prima*: "Jus naturale est, quod in lege et evangelio continetur, quo quisque jubetur alii facere, quod sibi vult fieri, et prohibetur alii inferre, quod sibi nolit fieri." Cf. ibid., c.7, for Isidore's definition.

Decretum. As Justinian's law code swept Europe in the twelfth and thirteenth centuries and became the principal legal text of universities, Ulpian's definition increasingly displaced later ones; and as European society during the same period became increasingly urban, it was easier and easier for Christians to accept legal and ethical premises based on idealized animal behavior.

In the end, the same ideas about "nature" and animals which had given rise to the bestiaries came to predominate in legal circles as well. Already noticeable among canonists like Huguccio at the end of the twelfth century, the trend was all but universal by the early thirteenth. The ideas of Isidore and Gratian continued to be mentioned, but they were clearly secondary to concepts of "natural law" which based their appeal on animal behavior. "What nature has taught all animals" was cited by some, like William of Auxerre,[46] as the major and most inclusive definition of "natural law" and by others, like Saint Bonaventure, as the "most appropriate" of the three basic meanings.[47] Tacitly it underlay almost all Scholastic discussions of "nature" and the "natural," and it was referred to by Thomas Aquinas—the ultimate authority for "natural morals"—as if it were the only definition of the concept (*Summa theologiae* 2a.2ae.57.3.Resp.).

By the middle of the thirteenth century, as the church began the synthesis of theology and canon law which was to stand almost unchallenged into the twentieth century, and as most European states were incorporating theological principles into secular law codes, opposition between "nature" and homosexual behavior was a common assumption of Europeans. Few questioned exactly what this "nature" was, and even fewer were able to explain it; but the average thirteenth-century reader was apt to encounter it in so many different guises that it probably came to seem self-evident. In part "nature" was a beneficent and lovable goddess appearing in the most popular literature of the day and generally speaking for the sexual prejudices and desires of the majority; in part it was the source of a law which was assumed to be universal and which appeared to provide the foundation for all civil and much canon law; in part "nature" was a complex philosophical construct inherited from Boethius and the twelfth-century naturalists and now being expanded with knowledge gained from new translations of Plato and Aristotle.

---

46. "Ius naturalis universalius est quod omnia naturalia animalia dictat [*sic*]," *Summa in aurea in quattuor libros sententiarum a subtilissimo doctore magistro Gillermo Altissiodorensi* (Paris, 1500), fol. 287r.

47. "Tertio modo dicitur ius naturale propriissime, quod 'natura docuit omnia animalia,'" *Bonaventurae commentaria in quatuor libros sententiarum Magistri Petri Lombardi* 33.1.1, Conclusio (Quaracchi, 1889), 4:748.

Albertus Magnus was the first of those responsible for the final synthesis to comment extensively on homosexual behavior.[48] Almost inevitably, his writings evince a certain confusion and inconsistency in regard to the "naturalness" of homosexual acts. In his *Summa theologiae* Albertus condemned homosexual acts as the gravest type of sexual sins because they offended "grace, reason, and nature."[49] (Next after these would be those acts that offended "only grace and reason," e.g., adultery.)[50] Albertus offered no explanation of the precise way in which *sodomia*—which he defined as the carnal union of persons of the same gender—violated nature, but he did cite Romans 1:26–27 as an authority for his opinion.[51]

In other writings, however, Albertus described homosexuality as a contagious disease which passed from one person to another and was especially common among the wealthy.[52] In his commentary on Luke he cited a biblical text suggesting that it was innate[53] and observed that those who had it scarcely ever got rid of it, but in his treatise on animals he described a relatively easy cure: the fur from the neck of an Arabian animal he called "alzabo," burned with pitch and ground to a fine powder, would "cure" a

48. Numerous thirteenth-century writers mention homosexuality in passing, and most relate it to popular concepts of "nature": Vincent of Beauvais's *Speculum doctrinale* (10.49) treats (in addition to the matters discussed above) the "crime of sodomy" entirely in terms of the natural. It consists, however, of a simple grouping of the standard canonist statements, excerpted for the most part from treatments of heterosexual intercourse, along with the assertion that "sodomy" (defined as any emission of semen outside the "appropriate vessel") is more serious than incest with one's mother (these comments are obviously addressed only to males), and claims that such acts are on a par with murder as sins that "cry out to heaven for vengeance." Cf. the comments of Peter Cantor above. No effort is made to analyze the precise import of "nature" in the materials employed. This would have been difficult, since the four texts use the word in widely divergent senses.

49. "Dicendum, quod deformitas omnium peccatorum mensuratur tribus, scilicet gratia, ratione, et natura. Et illud quod est contra gratiam, rationem et naturam, maximum est, sicut est sodomia," 2.18.122.1.4 (in *Alberti Magni Ratisbonensis episcopi, ordinis praedicatorum opera omnia*, ed. A. Borgnet [Paris, 1890–99], 33:400–401).

50. "Quod autem est contra gratiam et rationem, post hoc majus est, sicut adulterium," p. 401.

51. "Sodomia est peccatum contra naturam, masculi cum masculo, vel foeminae cum foemina," p. 400. In his commentary on Luke, Albertus interpreted a number of other biblical passages as applying to homosexual relations, often through the most extreme casuistry: see *In evangelium Lucae* 17.29 (Borgnet, 23:488).

52. In the commentary on Luke Albertus argued that homosexual behavior is "more abominable" than other sins because of four characteristics: (1) its ardor, which overthrows the order of nature; (2) its "stink," which rises to heaven ("And well is it said that its stink rises, since this execrable vice is known to prevail more among the upper classes than the lower ones"); (3) its persistence, "because when it afflicts someone, it almost never leaves him"; and (4) its communicability, "because it is said to be a contagious disease and to spread from one person to another."

53. "Right from the womb these wicked men have gone astray," JB, Ps. 58:3, cited by Albertus, ibid., as Ps. 57:4: "Peccatores a vulva, erraverunt ab utero."

"sodomite" to whose anus it was applied.[54] (Note that this suggests that a "sodomite" is a homosexual male who engages in anal intercourse.)

There is considerable irony to the supposed animal-fur cure: Albertus was aware of but rejected the vulgar tradition that the hyena was homosexual[55] (it would not have strengthened his claim that homosexual acts were "against nature"). He was apparently unaware, however, that "alzabo" is simply a transliteration into Latin of the Arabic "al-ḍabᶜ," which means "hyena." The curative properties of the hyena's fur (particularly around the anus) were a commonplace of Arabic animal lore[56]—though "sodomy" was not considered a disease among Arabs—and it is clear that Albertus derived his information from a Latin version of an Arabic animal treatise, ignorant of the actual meaning of "alzabo."[57]

54. *De animalibus* 22.2.1.10, ed. Hermann Stadler, in *Beiträge zur Geschichte der Philosophie des Mittelalters: Texte und Untersuchungen* (Münster, 1920), vol. 16, pt. 2, p. 1360, sec. 23: "Alzabo ut in libro sexaginta Animalium dicitur, animal est multum valens medicinae in desertis Arabiae conversans. . . . Dicunt etiam quod pili in collo huius animalis accepti et misti pulverizati combusti cum pice, unctum in ano sodomitam curant a vitio." The *alzabo* section is not included in older editions of the *De animalibus*, including that of Borgnet (vols. 11–12), where sec. 12.2.1.10 deals with the *asinus* (sec. 1.7. in Stadler). There is no doubt that the Cologne manuscript employed by Stadler for his edition is the best of all those extant. Some scholars—including George Sarton—have considered it an autograph.

55. "Jorach etiam dicit quod aliquando [huaena] est mas et aliquando femina. . . . Sed iste Iurach frequenter mentitur," *De animalibus* 22.2.1.56 (Stadler, p. 1405, sec. 106). It is curious that Albertus should cite the mysterious Jorach (for whom see G. Sarton, *Isis* 15 [1931]: 171–72) as authority for an opinion given by Pliny and the authors of most Western zoological treatises. Pauline Aiken has shown ("The Animal History of Albertus Magnus and Thomas of Cantimpré," *Speculum* 22 [1947]: 205–25) that Albertus actually made little if any direct use of Pliny: almost all the material in the *De animalibus* is taken directly from the *De naturis rerum* of Thomas of Cantimpré, in many cases including rather crude misinterpretations of Pliny. In this particular case, however, Albertus clearly did not follow Thomas, who does not cite Jorach and accepts the dual sexuality of the hyena: "Hyena animal est sepius in sepulchris habitans mortuorum. Duas habet naturas, maris et femine," *Liber de naturis rerum*, Cambridge, Mass., Houghton Library MS Lat. 125, fol. 25r, s.v. "hyena." Neither Albertus's material on the *alzabo* nor that on the hyena is derived from Thomas of Cantimpré.

56. See, e.g., Kamal ad-Dīn ad-Damīrī, *Ḥayāt al-Ḥayawān al-Kubrā* (Bulak, 1875), 2:89–90, where similar properties are suggested. Ad-Damīrī says that the curative properties of the hyena's anal fur are agreed upon by physicians ("ᵓaṭbaqa ᶜalayhi al-ᵓatbāᵓ," p. 92) and cites as sources for his general material on this subject al-Jāḥiẓ, ar-Rāzi, az-Zamakhshāri, al-Qazwīni, et al. (p. 89). Ad-Damīrī's treatments of the hare, hyena, and weasel were profoundly influenced by Greek legends and Christian "ideal" natural attitudes: see ibid., s.v. "ḍabᶜ," "ᵓarnab," and "ibn ᵓirs."

57. Of the 113 animals listed in bk. 22.2 of the *De animalibus*, only two—*alzabo* and *alfech*—were not derived from an identifiable Western source. No other Scholastic zoological treatises mention *alzabo*. Although I have not been able to identify the exact Arabic source of Albertus's information, I consider it most likely that he derived it from a garbled Latin translation of an Arabic zoological encyclopedia rather than from a medical treatise of ar-Rāzi, as Stadler suggests. Albertus introduces the animal as occurring in the sixtieth book of Aristotle's *Animalium*, although the Latin version of the *Animalium* had only twelve books

This seems even more ironic in view of the fact that the Arabic legends were derived from the same early Christian animal fables which had justified and partly produced antihomosexual prejudice in the first place: Scholastics thus unwittingly incorporated as separate data the antigay fables of the Clementine/*Physiologus* tradition and the Arabic medical/zoological lore based on them.[58]

The moral authority of "ideal" nature reached its most influential and in many ways its final development at the hands of Albertus's most famous pupil, Saint Thomas Aquinas (d. 1274), whose *Summa theologiae* became the standard of orthodox opinion on every point of Catholic dogma for nearly a millennium and permanently and irrevocably established the "natural"[59] as the touchstone of Roman Catholic sexual ethics.[60]

Since Aquinas's teachings represent to a large extent the final synthesis of high medieval moral theology, they merit particularly detailed attention. It

---

and did not mention the Arabic *alzabo*. The number sixty may be the section of the Arabic encyclopedia from which Albertus derived the material in question, or the Latin translator may have simply mistaken the Arabic "sitta" ("six"—the number of the book in the *Animalium* where the hyena actually occurs) for "sittūn" ("sixty"). Moreover, both "alzabo" and "hahane" disrupt the alphabetical order of the Cologne manuscript. This curious circumstance would be the logical result of the addition to the Latin text of the "alzabo" entry from a Latin translation of an Arabic encyclopedia, also alphabetical, in which "hahane" occurred within the article on *aḍ-ḍab*ᶜ as an effort to reproduce in Arabic the Greek word "ὕαινα" actually used by Aristotle (the basis of most Arabic zoological works).

58. The *Physiologus* itself was translated into Arabic in the early Middle Ages and included the traditional account of the hyena and its sex changes: see Land, pp. 139–40, s.v. "al-ḍab*ᶜ*". Cf. al-Jāḥiẓ, *Kitāb al-Ḥayawān*. For another example, see Vincent of Beauvais *Speculum naturale* 10.62: "De medicinis ex hyaena: Etiam si viri mulierum coitus oderint, spinae illius articulum primum in remediis habent comicialem"; this is almost identical with the relevant passage in ad-Damīrī.

59. Almost all studies of Saint Thomas and his theology treat his concept of "nature" to some degree. For more specific studies see Lottin; and the several articles on the subject in *La filosofia della natura* (e.g., J. I. Alcorta, "El concepto de naturaleza en Santo Tomás") and in *St. Thomas Aquinas, 1274–1974: Commemorative Studies*, ed. A. Maurer et al. (Toronto, 1974), vol. 1, esp. V. J. Bourke, "The *Nicomachean Ethics* and Thomas Aquinas," and M. B Crowe, "St. Thomas and Ulpian's Natural Law."

60. Saint Thomas's positions did not triumph easily or immediately. His writings were controversial during his lifetime and for some time thereafter. His teachings on "nature" and "natural law," for example, appear to have been vigorously opposed by some (e.g., Duns Scotus: see E. Piernikarczyk, "Das Naturrecht bei Johannes Duns Scotus," *Philosophisches Jahrbuch* 43 (1930): 67–91; and M. B. Crowe, "Nature and Natural Law in John Duns Scotus," in *La filosofia della natura*) and simply ignored by others (e.g., Ramon Lull *Liber de natura* 100, in *Raymond Lulle, philosophe de l'action*, ed. A. Llinarès [Grenoble, 1963]; briefly discussed in R. D. F. Pring-Mill, "La estructura del 'Liber de natura' del Beato Ramón Llull," in *La filosofia della natura*). Since the discussion in this chapter is intended only to elucidate the concepts of the "natural" upon which Aquinas grounded his condemnation of homosexual behavior, no effort is made to discuss "natural" philosophy subsequent to the *Summa theologiae*. For these the reader is referred to the general bibliography in n. 3 above.

may be worth repeating here that the aim of such analysis is not to engage in polemics on moral issues but to investigate the extent to which such positions reflect logical or consistent application of traditional Christian principles, and where they do not, to suggest other ways of accounting for their development. It is difficult to see how Aquinas's attitudes toward homosexual behavior could even be made consonant with his general moral principles, much less understood as the outgrowth of them. Despite his absolute conviction in every other context that humans were morally and intellectually superior to animals and therefore not only permitted but obliged to engage in many types of activity unknown or impossible to lower beings, Aquinas resorted again and again to animal behavior as the final arbiter in matters of human sexuality. Even granting the illogic of the premise, such an undertaking was no mean task for a mind of Thomas's acuity. In condemning promiscuity ("fornication"), for instance, he had to come to grips with the fact—well known in spite of the recent ascendance of animals as models of sexual propriety—that promiscuous sexuality was common among familiar animals like dogs and cats; so common, in fact, that even the most devoted adherents of "nature" compared humans given to obsessive or wanton venereal pursuits to animals. If animals could "naturally" pursue lives of such carefree and expansive sexuality, why could not humans "naturally" do likewise?

To answer this question, Aquinas had to stretch considerably the Platonic tradition of selective inference from birds, arguing that there is some inherent distinction among animals on the basis of postnatal requirements for the offspring:

> We see in fact that among all those animals for whom the care of a male and a female is required for the upbringing of the offspring, there is no promiscuity [*vagus concubitus*] but only one male with one female, or several females: this is the case among all birds. It is different, however, among those animals for whom the female alone is sufficient for the upbringing of the offspring, among whom there is promiscuity, as is evident in the case of dogs and other similar animals.[61]

61. *Summa theologiae* 2a.2ae.154.2.Resp.: "Videmus enim in omnibus animalibus in quibus ad educationem prolis requiritur cura maris et foeminae, quod in eis non est vagus concubitus, sed maris ad certam foeminam, unam vel plures, sicut patet in omnibus avibus; secus autem est in animalibus in quibus sola foemina sufficit ad educationem foetus, in quibus est vagus concubitus; ut patet in canibus et hujusmodi aliis animalibus." This argument is repeated almost verbatim from an earlier (and less influential) work, the *Summa contra gentiles* (3.122), discussed below. The idea that humans should *not* imitate dogs was certainly not original to Aquinas; if nowhere else, he would have known it from the *Summa* of Alexander III (*Magistri Rolandi*), where it is introduced in commentary on Gratian's *Decretum*, Causa 27, Quaes. 1 (Thaner, p. 125).

Although judged by the standards of the time this argument evinces remarkable biological insight, it presents a great many moral and philosophical difficulties. Aside from the fundamental paradox of this whole line of reasoning, that man, the paragon of the great chain of being, should have to follow the example of lower animals in matters of morality; and overlooking the factual error in the premise that all birds are monogamous,[62] one is still struck by the many crucial questions left unanswered in Aquinas's "answer."[63]

62. Saint Bonaventure, in a similar context, had limited his claims regarding aviary monogamy to turtledoves (*Commentaria* 33.1.1.Concl., p. 748): "Quaedam animalia bruta sunt—licet non omnia—quae coniunguntur in individuam copulam, ut sint turtures. . . ." In his earlier treatment of the subject (*Summa contra gentiles* 3.122), Saint Thomas had also observed that only certain birds are monogamous ("sicut patet in quibusdam avibus") but apparently decided to broaden his claim in the more influential *Summa theologiae*.

63. E.g., (1) how is it known that human offspring require two parents? Do not widows and widowers rear children "naturally"? Is it sinful for only one parent to rear children? Certainly there is no biblical authority on the subject: the command to be "fruitful and multiply" suggests nothing particular about the duties of parenthood; Hagar had to raise her son alone; Esther appears to have been brought up by her uncle; New Testament comments on sexuality did not emphasize procreation, much less dual parenthood—a case could be made, in fact, that the discouragement of remarriage for widows and widowers constitutes a negative injunction in this regard. In the *Summa theologiae* Aquinas contents himself with observing that "it is obvious that for the upbringing of a human there is need not simply for the mother who nourishes but much more for the father who instructs and defends and who watches out for both interior and exterior well-being" (2a.2ae.154.2.Resp.); but in the *Summa contra gentiles* he had explained more explicitly that the male is needed for the proper care of the human child because the male is "more perfect in reason, to give instruction," and "stronger in virtue, to offer correction" (3.122). As in the case of arguments about homosexuality, it was the position of the *Summa theologiae* which influenced later moralists: see the *Speculum morale* attributed to Vincent of Beauvais, 3.2. (2) Why should "fornication" necessitate the absence of a father in any case? Many bastards know their fathers, and it was particularly common in the Middle Ages for men to acknowledge with some pride what were (ironically) called "natural" children. In the fifteenth century both ruling houses of Spain traced their descent through illegitimate offspring, and the same could be observed of many European ruling families. Aquinas is either mistaken or devious in answering this question—the only one of those listed here which he addresses directly. "It does not matter," he says, "if someone who commits fornication should provide for the upbringing of the child, because that which falls under the cognizance of the law is determined according to what commonly happens, not according to what might happen in a particular case" (*Summa theologiae* 2a.2ae.154.2.Resp.). Even in regard to civil law this would not be a cogent argument, since Aquinas has already stated that civil law should not attempt to restrain all vice but only those acts which actually harm others (1a.2ae.96.2) and since the entire concept of "natural law" is predicated on what should happen rather than what does happen. The issue in this article, however, is not law at all but morality: what Saint Thomas purported to be discussing was not why the law might restrain fornication in general but why fornication would be mortally sinful to the individual committing it. His argument here is manifestly irrelevant to this consideration, since it ignores the intent—the crucial determinant of sin—and addresses itself only to statistical probabilities and physical

It is difficult to believe, moreover, that animal behavior actually suggested this position to Saint Thomas: he can only appeal to birds, a tiny minority, as monogamous—elsewhere he qualifies his example even further as only some birds—and the analogy between the parental duties of birds and those of humans is questionable, to say the least. The invocation of "nature" is significant, however, as an indication of the lengths to which Scholastic apologists for Christian ethics would go to demonstrate that "nature" was at the foundation of Christian society's sexual taboos. Even granting the selective inference from monogamous species of birds, sexual promiscuity ought to have been no more reprehensible in "natural" ethics than gluttony, which also prescinds from the supposedly "natural" tendency of animals to eat only what is necessary for sustenance. Indeed, Aquinas concedes, heterosexual promiscuity would be no more serious than gluttony if it were not for its potentially harmful effects. While one excessive meal has no permanent consequences, a single act of heterosexual fornication may ruin the life of a human being: that of the illegitimate and (Thomas assumes) uncared-for child produced by it (*Summa theologiae* 2a.2ae.154.2 ad 6).

One would surmise from this argument that Aquinas would regard homosexual acts as no more serious than gluttony. He could argue that they did not fulfill any requirement of nature, but hardly that they produced unwanted or neglected children. The only argument which prevented his "natural" ethics from accepting heterosexual promiscuity as mere intemperance could not be applied to homosexual acts. This left gay sexuality in the position it had occupied in the minds of earlier theologians like Burchard, i.e., at the very worst comparable to drunkenness, and considerably less serious than heterosexual fornication.

But Aquinas could not pursue his logic this far out of the mainstream of thirteenth-century popular morality and public intolerance, and he struggled instead to construct a philosophical justification for classifying homosexual acts as not only serious but worse than comparable heterosexual ones; in fact he promoted them to a position of unique enormity unparalleled since the time of Chrysostom.

In an early work (*Summa contra gentiles* 3.122) Saint Thomas had predicated his objection to homosexual activity not on animal sexuality but on an argument which many later theologians were to seize upon in regard both

---

consequences. (3) If the future interest of the offspring is the determinant of the morality of a particular act of intercourse, then would not producing a child for whom one could not adequately provide be as gravely sinful as producing a child one did not wish to care for? This position has in fact been adopted reluctantly and somewhat obliquely by twentieth-century Catholicism but was completely ignored by Aquinas himself.

to contraception and "unnatural" sex acts—that semen and its ejaculation were intended by "nature" to produce children, and that any other use of them was "contrary to nature" and hence sinful, since the design of "nature" represented the will of God. Unlike later writers, however, Saint Thomas realized that this argument had fatal flaws. He himself raised the question of other "misuses" of "nature's" design. Is it sinful for a man to walk on his hands, when "nature" has clearly designed the feet for this purpose? Or is it morally wrong to use the feet for something (e.g., pedaling an organ) which the hands ordinarily do?[64] To obviate this difficulty, he shifted ground and tacitly recognized that it was not the *misuse* of the organs involved which comprised the sin but the fact that through the act in question the propagation of the human species was impeded.[65]

This line of reasoning was of course based on an ethical premise—that the physical increase of the human species constitutes a major moral good—which bore no relation to any New Testament or early Christian authority and which had been specifically rejected by Saint Augustine. Moreover, it contradicted Aquinas's own teachings. Nocturnal emissions "impede" the increase of the human race in precisely the same way as homosexuality—i.e., by expending semen to no procreative purpose—and yet Aquinas not only considered them inherently sinless but the result of "natural" causes.[66] And voluntary virginity, which Aquinas and others considered the crowning Christian virtue (*Summa theologiae* 2a.2ae.151, 152), so clearly operated to the detriment of the species in this regard that he very specifically argued in its defense that individual humans are *not* obliged to contribute to the increase or preservation of the species through procreation; it is only the race as a whole which is so obligated.[67] Because of this, Aquinas found it necessary to shift ground again in formulating theological opposition to sexual nonconformity in his major and most influential moral treatise, the *Summa theologiae*.

64. "Ut si quis, verbi gratia, manibus ambulet, aut pedibus aliquid operetur manibus operandum: quia per huiusmodi inordinatos usus bonum hominis non multum impeditur."

65. "Inordinata vero seminis emissio repugnat bono naturae, quod est conservatio speciei. Unde post peccatum homicidii, quo natura humana iam in actu existens destruitur, huiusmodi genus peccati videtur secundum locum tenere, quo impeditur generatio humanae naturae."

66. *Summa theologiae* 2a.2ae.154.5, Resp.: "patet quod nocturna pollutio nunquam est peccatum."

67. "A duty may be of two sorts: it may be enjoined on the individual, and such a duty cannot be ignored without sin. Or it may be enjoined upon a group; in this case no individual in the group is obligated to fulfill the duty. . . . The commandment regarding procreation applies to the human race as a whole, which is obligated not only to increase physically but to grow spiritually. It is therefore sufficient for the race if some people undertake to reproduce physically," ibid., 2a.2ae.152.2ad 1.

There are three substantive comments on homosexuality in the *Summa*.[68] In the last and best known of these Aquinas discusses under two headings (1) whether "vices against nature" constitute a species of lust (he concludes they do) and (2) whether they are the most sinful species of lust (they are). "Vices against nature" include masturbation, intercourse with animals,[69] homosexual intercourse, and nonprocreative heterosexual coitus.

Although nature is defined elsewhere in the *Summa* in many different, sometimes conflicting ways, ranging from "the order of creation" to "the principle of intrinsic motion,"[70] no definition is provided here for the "nature" these sins are against, and all common conceptions of "nature" are missing from or excluded by the particulars of the discussion. "Animal" sexuality is opposed to the "natural" at one point,[71] and no other sense of "nature" suggested[72] would apply any more to homosexual acts than to procreative extramarital sexuality. Although at one point he does remark

68. 1a.2ae.31.7; 1a.2ae.94.3 ad 2; 2a.2ae.154.11–12. Of these, only the last has received scholarly attention in the context of Scholastic attitudes toward homosexuality. The first was briefly touched upon by McNeill, in *The Church*, p. 97, but unfortunately the location of the passage was cited incorrectly in the notes.

69. Aquinas uses "bestiality" ("bestialitas") in three distinct senses but does not define or distinguish them explicitly. In some contexts the word refers to "base" or "primitive" behavior: what Aristotle called "bestial" in the *Nicomachean Ethics* because of its similarity to the behavior of animals. In other contexts he uses the same term to designate human intercourse with animals, and in one place the related adjective appears to refer to the way in which animals copulate with each other (11 Resp.; this extreme inconsistency gives rise to a logical absurdity in the organization of article 11: in 1 "vices against nature" are classified as a subspecies of "bestiality," but in the response to the arguments "bestiality" appears as a subspecies of "vices against nature"). This confusion not only persisted but grew more pronounced under later Thomists. Giles of Rome (Aegidius Romanus, d. 1316) argued in his *Commentary on Romans* that homosexual behavior was a form of "bestiality" ("Sufficiat scire coitum masculinum cum masculis et foemininum cum feminis bestialitatem esse") but adduced as proof of its sinfulness the fact that it was unknown among animals (*Aegidii Romani archiepiscopi Bituricensis in Epistolam beati Pauli Apostoli ad Romanos commentarii*, in *Operum D. Aegidii Romani* [Rome, 1555], vol. 1 chap. 1). Giles's position is the more complicated because he maintains that homosexual acts are against the "nature" not only of the species but also of the genus and the individual (ibid.). For ramifications in literature, see, e.g., Alfred Triolo, "'Matta bestialità' in Dante's 'Inferno': Theory and Image," *Traditio* 24 (1968): 247–92.

70. "Natura est principium motus intrinsecum," 3a.32.4.3.

71. 11 Resp.: "Si non servetur naturalis modus concumbendi ... quantum ad alios monstruosos et bestiales concumbendi modos." Aquinas does not explain the principle by which he determines which aspects of animal sexuality should be avoided by humans (e.g., the position they adopt in coitus, as here) and which imitated (e.g., ornithological monogamy, as above).

72. These are many and inconsistent, ranging from the "nature" of the venereal act to the "order of nature." "Human nature" is the most prominent: this is reminiscent of Augustine (as above, chap. 6), who doubtless influenced Aquinas on the matter, but Thomas's position is markedly different.

that the potentially procreative types of lust discussed earlier under "fornica-tion" and "adultery" do not "violate human nature," this is directly contradicted by his assertion in the treatment of "fornication" that "it is against human nature to engage in promiscuous intercourse."[73] Indeed, as he subsequently admits, not only are all sexual sins "unnatural," but all sins of any sort are "unnatural."[74] The "natural" in this section is in fact simply the "moral";[75] and it seems circular, to say the least, to argue that homosexual acts are immoral because they are immoral.

In an earlier part of the *Summa*,[76] however, in a discussion of whether there can be "unnatural" pleasures (the answer is yes), Aquinas does offer more explicit ideas about "nature" and "natural" in relation to homo-sexuality. In fact, he provides some surprising definitions. "It should be observed that a thing is called 'natural' when it is according to 'nature'. . . . 'Nature,' in the case of man, may be taken in two senses. On one hand the 'nature' of man is particularly the intellect and reason, since it is in regard to this that man is distinct as a species."[77] This first definition appears to refer to the "nature" *of* something, in this case man, but its use is paradoxical because what Aquinas here takes to comprise the "nature" of man is exactly what most adherents of "ideal" nature exclude: his reason. It is indeed very difficult to see how homosexuality violates "nature" in the sense of man's reason. It was precisely the reason of man which proponents of gay sexuality had recently used to defend themselves against "ideal" nature,

73. 2a.2ae.154.2. Resp.: "Ideo contra naturam hominis est quod utatur vago concubitu."

74. See n. 89 below.

75. This is the obvious import of many other discussions of "nature" and "natural law" in the *Summa*, e.g., 1a.2ae.91.2: "It is clear that natural law is nothing other than the participation of rational creatures in eternal law." Cf. the discussion at 2a.2ae.153.2 Resp., where "reason" occupies the very same position as "nature" in 154: "It must be observed that in human affairs a sin is whatever is against the order of reason, which must order all things according to their ends." Aquinas's mentor, Aristotle, had also conflated "nature" with "reason" and morality: note, e.g., *Politics* 1.5, where it is asserted that it is "contrary to nature" for the body to rule the mind, and this is considered proven by the fact that this condition occurs only in "immoral" men.

76. 1a.2ae.31.7. The extent to which this discussion is indebted to *Nicomachean Ethics* 7.5 is often overlooked by editors. It is important to note, however, that Aquinas seriously mis-represents some of Aristotle's comments. Despite the *Summa*'s assertion to the contrary ("Philosophus dicit quod quaedam delectationes sunt aegritudinales et contra naturam"), Aristotle does not characterize the behavior treated in this section as "unnatural"; the actions discussed are classified as "unhealthy" ("νοσηματώδης"), "wretched" ("μοχθηρός"), or "bestial" ("θηριώδης"). Aquinas also alters Aristotle's meaning for "bestial." On the general issue of Aquinas's use of the *Ethics*, see Bourke. Aquinas's commentary on this portion of the *Ethics* (lecture 5, commentary 1368–84) is less informative than the treatment in the *Summa*.

77. "Dicendum quod naturale dicitur quod est secundum naturam. . . . Natura autem in homine dupliciter sumi potest. Uno modo, prout intellectus et ratio est potissime hominis natura, quia secundum eam homo in specie constituitur."

arguing that it is man's "nature" to rise above what is "natural" to animals and to love regardless of the physical compulsions of procreation (e.g., in "Ganymede and Helen," which Aquinas might have known). Aquinas would not have had to alter his commitment to procreation as the function of sexuality in any way to have recognized that "natural" affection, which in animals exists of "necessity" between mates and relatives, is transferred by "human nature" to relations where there is no "necessity" for affection— e.g., voluntary friendships—without moral defect, and that an analogous argument could be used to justify sexual relations among humans where no "necessity" compels. In the immediately preceding section, for instance, he distinguishes between "natural" and "unnatural" desires: the former are those which animals experience as a consequence of necessity. The latter are unique to humans, "who alone can recognize as good and fitting something which is beyond the requirements of nature."[78] These desires "beyond the natural" are characterized by Aquinas not only as "rational, individual, and acquired" but as appertaining to things which are "good and fitting," despite their exceeding the "natural" and being unknown to animals.

As his second definition of "nature" Saint Thomas then offers a meaning which directly contradicts the first: "On the other hand, 'nature' in man may be taken to mean that which is distinct from the rational, i.e., that which is common to men and other beings, particularly that which is not subject to reason."[79] This appears to be the ever popular concept of "animal nature," a meaning not just peripheral to but ostensibly rejected in the treatment of homosexuality above, but here providing the only substantiation for the claim that homosexual acts are "unnatural." Things are "natural" to both men and animals when they pertain to the preservation of the individual or the species: the examples of food, drink, sleep, and sex are cited. They have nothing to do with thought but are the responses *necessary* for the existence of either the individual or the species. Homosexuality and celibacy might be "against nature" in this sense if one took the simplistic view that indulgence in them somehow precluded the reproduction of the human race;[80] certainly they do not diminish the existence of the individual.[81] Aquinas does not, however, show that homosexuality would preclude the reproduction of the

78. "Sed secundae [i.e., nonnaturales] concupiscentiae sunt propriae hominum, quorum proprium est excogitare aliquid ut bonum et conveniens, praeter id quod natura requirit," 1a.2ae.30.4. Resp.

79. "Alio modo potest sumi natura in homine secundum quod condividitur rationi, scilicet id quod est commune homini et alias, praecipue quod rationi non obedit," ibid.

80. But note that this would directly contradict the opinion of Augustine that such an eventuality would be in accord with the divine will.

81. Actually Aquinas implies that it does affect the individual's own survival, though it is extremely difficult to imagine how this could be.

race; he could only do so if there were a logical compulsion that if any humans were to engage in homosexual acts, all would then be exclusively homosexual. Otherwise the position of homosexuality could be considered the same as "unnatural" desire (or celibacy): unnecessary, but not evil.

This difficulty pales, however, beside the startling revelation following the second definition that homosexuality may in fact be quite "natural" to a given individual, in either sense of the word. "Thus it may happen that something which is against human nature, in regard either to reason or to the preservation of the body, may become natural to a particular man, owing to some defect of nature in him."[82] The "defect" of nature mentioned here should not be taken as implying some contravention of "natural laws." Aquinas compares this sort of "innate" homosexuality to hot water: although water is not "naturally" hot, it may be altogether "natural" for water under certain circumstances to become hot.[83] Although it may not be "natural" for humans in general to be homosexual, it is apparently quite "natural" for particular individuals.

This circumstantial etiology of homosexuality cannot be taken as indicating in itself moral inferiority. Aquinas also believed that women were produced by "defective" circumstances (1a.92.1): if conception took place under completely "natural" circumstances, males would always result ("for the active force of the male seed intends to produce something similar to itself, perfect in its masculinity"),[84] but if some peculiarity intervened—a defect in sperm or seed or the prevalence of a moist south wind at the time of con-

82. "Ita igitur contingit quod id quod est contra naturam hominis, vel quantum ad rationem, vel quantum ad corporis conservationem, fiat huic homini connaturale, propter aliquam corruptionem naturae in eo existentem," ibid. "Connaturale" does not in general have a meaning distinct from "naturale"; if there is any difference, it is that the former more often refers to what is "natural" to a particular individual—i.e., blue eyes—or to a group (white skin) than to what is "natural" to a species (lungs) or all of the observable world (the effect of gravity). Of course what is "natural" to an individual is also, as part of the individual, "natural" to the whole. Aquinas's uses of "nature" and related terms, however, are so inconsistent that it is impossible to generalize about terminological subtleties without context; the interested reader should consult the relevant entries in the *Index Thomisticus* (Stuttgart, 1974–) s.v. "connaturalis."

83. The choice of heat as a point of comparison is striking: the metaphor is not taken from Aristotle and must be understood as Aquinas's own idea. Heat had been for earlier theologians not only "natural" but part of the very essence of "nature": one of Alain de Lille's definitions of "nature" was "heat"—"Dicitur naturalis calor, unde physicus dicit esse pugnam inter morbum et naturam, id est naturalem calorem" (*Distinctiones*, s.v. "natura" [PL, 210:871]; this is definition 7 in n. 39 above); and Thierry of Chartres envisioned heat as the "creative power and efficient cause" of everything—*De sex dierum operibus*, ed. N. Haring, in *Archives d'histoire doctrinale et littéraire du moyen âge* 22 (1955): 184–200; also John of Salisbury, *Metalogicon* 1.8 (McGarry, p. 29).

84. "Quia virtus activa quae est in semine maris intendit producere sibi simile, perfectum secundum masculinum sexum," 1a.92.1. ad 1.

ception—females would be born (here quoting Aristotle). Although Aquinas did believe that females were in this sense "defective" males and although he certainly considered women inferior to men in many practical ways,[85] it cannot be argued that he considered the condition of femaleness to be morally reprehensible, nor would he have argued that behavior which is the result of a female "nature" is morally inferior to behavior dictated by the more "natural" male condition. Neither homosexuality nor femaleness can be shown to be "immoral" simply because it does not represent the primary intent of "nature," and both are in fact "natural" to the individuals in question.

In Aquinas's view, moreover, everything which is any way "natural" has a purpose, and the purpose is good: "Natural inclinations occur in things because of God, who moves all things. . . . Whatever is the end of anything natural cannot be bad in itself, since everything which exists naturally is ordained by divine providence to fill some purpose."[86] Since both homosexuality and femaleness occur "naturally" in some individuals, neither can be said to be inherently bad, and both must have an end.[87] The *Summa* does not speculate on what the "end" of homosexuality might be, but this is hardly surprising in light of the prejudices of the day.

If, then, the "nature" of man in general is to desire some things which are not "naturally" required or enjoyed by animals (1a.2ae.30) and if the "nature" of some individuals is to desire homosexual intercourse (1a.2ae.31), in what sense could homosexual acts be "unnatural"? In his third comment on homosexuality, although he refers again to the "animal nature" which he has admitted should not limit human behavior, Aquinas gives a clue to the

---

85. "Woman is naturally [*naturaliter*] of less character [*minoris virtutis*] and dignity than man," ibid., 2.

86. *Summa contra gentiles*, 3.126: "Naturales inclinationes insunt rebus a Deo, qui cuncta movet. . . . Illud autem quod est finis aliquarum naturalium rerum, non potest esse secundum se malum: quia ea quae naturaliter sunt, ex divina providentia ordinantur ad finem." See Aristotle *Politics* 1.2: "Nature does nothing without a purpose"; ibid., 8: "Nature makes nothing without a specific function, nothing without a purpose."

87. It is not necessary for God to effect the change from potential heterosexuality to actual homosexuality for it to be "natural": no active force is required for "natural" mutation, which may be entirely passive (3a.32.4 ad 3). Later in the same section of the *Summa* in which he accepted Aristotle's definition of homosexuality as "natural" (in a "real" sense), and *immediately following* the description of homosexuality quoted above, he observes, "In fact, because of the diverse conditions of humans, it happens that some acts are virtuous to some people, as appropriate and suitable to them, while the same acts are immoral for others, as inappropriate to them" (1a.2ae.94 ad 3; see ibid., 3: "What is virtuous for one person is sinful for another"). It would seem that Saint Thomas would have been constrained to admit that homosexual acts were "appropriate" to those whom he considered "naturally" homosexual.

real origin of his attitude toward the "unnaturalness" of homosexual behavior:

> It must be noted that the nature of man may be spoken of either as that which is peculiar to man, and according to this all sins, insofar as they are against reason, are against nature (as is stated by Damascene);[88] or as that which is common to man and other animals, according to which certain particular sins are said to be against nature, as intercourse between males (which is specifically called the vice against nature) is contrary to the union of male and female which is natural to all animals.[89]

In the end Aquinas admits more or less frankly that his categorization of homosexual acts as "unnatural" is a concession to popular sentiment and parlance. Since theologically sins are necessarily "unnatural," it is simply redundant to argue that homosexuality is sinful because it is "unnatural"; homosexual acts would have to be shown to be sinful *apart from* their "unnaturalness" to be immoral from a theological point of view; but Aquinas could bring to bear no argument against homosexual behavior which would make it more serious than overeating and admitted, moreover, that homosexual desire was the result of a "natural" condition, which would logically have made behavior resulting from it not only inculpable but "good."[90]

But homosexual acts "are called the unnatural vice," he observes, because they do not occur among animals, and he bows to the speech patterns and zoological notions of his contemporaries. Aquinas was not an innovator; the *Summa*'s position, in this as in many matters, was a response to, not the origin of, popular attitudes. The arguments Aquinas and his contemporaries used

88. *De fide orthodoxa* 2.4, 4.20 (PG, 94:976, 1196).

89. "Dicendum quod natura hominis potest dici vel illa quae est propria hominis, et secundum hoc omnia peccata inquantum sunt contra rationem sunt etiam contra naturam, ut patet per Damascenum; vel illa quae est communis homini et aliis animalibus, et secundum hoc quaedam specialia peccata dicuntur esse contra naturam, sicut contra commixtionem maris et foeminae, quae est naturalis omnibus animalibus, est concubitus masculorum, quod specialiter dicitur vitium contra naturam," 1a.2ae.94.3 ad 2.

90. Possibly biblical strictures played a role in Aquinas's insistence on the extreme gravity of homosexual acts despite the apparent incompatibility of this position with his general ethical schemes. The Bible is not cited in his major moral treatises, however, as the reason for his condemnations, and there are problems with the approaches in his biblical commentaries. In his commentary on Romans 1 (1.8.151), for example, he establishes a connection between homosexuality and temple prostitution on the basis of the Vulgate's mistranslation of 2 Maccabees 4:12 ("et optimos quosque epheborum in lupanaribus ponere": cf. LXX), and in his commentary on 1 Cor. 6:9 he seems to take *molles* as "catamites" (6.2.285: "mares muliebria patientes"), although this is in direct contradiction to the definition of "mollitia" given in the *Summa theologiae* (2a.2ae.154.11). Most later theologians retained the *Summa*'s definition.

to justify categorizing homosexual acts as the gravest of sexual sins (of all sins, according to some) cannot be shown to derive from the previous Western moral tradition, but they had all been brought to bear on the subject of homosexuality in civil legislation and popular diatribe before the *Summa* was written. The popular satirical poem "Quam pravus est mos" predated by more than a century each of Aquinas's major arguments against gay sexuality, derogating it as unknown among animals, a violation of "nature," a departure from reason, and an impediment to the reproduction of the human race.[91] Albertus Magnus, Vincent of Beauvais, and Saint Thomas Aquinas were all writing in societies which had already passed laws against homosexual behavior and in which popular hostility toward gay people was becoming a literary commonplace. The *Summa* was not begun until 1265, after antigay provisions had been incorporated in law codes in Castile, France, and parts of Aquinas's native Italy. And although opposition to homosexual acts based on the "natural" necessity of procreation should have applied to all nonprocreative sexuality, in fact most theologians, like Albertus Magnus, applied their condemnations only to gay people; others, like Saint Thomas, although admitting that all vices were "unnatural," proceeded to use "unnatural" as specifically referring to homosexuality.

The positions of Aquinas and other high medieval theologians regarding homosexuality appear to have been a response more to the pressures of popular antipathy than to the weight of the Christian tradition, but this is not to suggest that the *Summa* itself did not affect subsequent attitudes. It must be recognized that the context of an accusation is often as damning as the charge itself: Aquinas played to his audience not simply by calling on popular concepts of "nature" but also by linking homosexuality to behavior which was certain to evoke reactions of horror and fear. He compared homosexual acts not with other instances of exceeding what is necessary, like overeating or drunkenness, nor with other behavior of which animals are supposed to be incapable, such as telling lies or counterfeiting currency, but with violent or disgusting acts of the most shocking type, like cannibalism, bestiality,[92] or eating dirt. Indeed, by suggesting subliminally to his thirteenth-century readers that homosexual behavior belonged in a class with actions which were either violently antisocial (like cannibalism) or threateningly

---

91. "A Perverse Custom." It is not at all improbable that this poem was familiar to Saint Thomas and other Scholastics. What is probably the earliest copy was written in France, most likely in the twelfth century, and versions survive from as far away as Oxford and Leipzig and as late as the fourteenth century: obviously the work enjoyed a considerable popularity.

92. "Sicut si aliquis delectetur in comestione carnium humanarum, aut in coitu bestiarum aut masculorum," 2a.2ae.142.4.3.

dangerous (like heresy),[93] Aquinas subtly but definitively transferred it from its former position among sins of excess or wantonness to a new and singular degree of enormity among the types of behavior most feared by the common people and most severely repressed by the church.

Moreover, it was particularly significant for gay people that Thomas's ideas about homosexuality triumphed just at the moment when the church began to enforce orthodoxy more rigorously than ever before and to insist that everyone accept in every detail not just the infallible pronouncements of popes and councils but every statement of orthodox theologians. Although the intent was not to eradicate acceptance of homosexuality in particular, the effect was to eliminate all opinion in the church which did not accord with accepted theology on every matter, and since it was Aquinas's authority which ultimately became the rule, acceptance of homosexuality ceased to be a safe option for Catholics liable to prosecution for heresy.

Because of the extraordinarily conservative nature of Catholic theology and the persistence of the prejudices which animated the hostile theological developments of the thirteenth century, the popular opposition to homosexuality given official expression in the writings of Aquinas and his contemporaries continued to influence religious and moral attitudes well into modern times. It must be remembered, however, that intellectual responses to homosexuality generally reflected rather than caused intolerance. It is instructive to note in this regard that there was, by any objective standard, a much more powerful medieval *moral* tradition against usury than against homosexual behavior. Unlike homosexuality, usury had been condemned almost unanimously by philosophers of the ancient world as uncharitable, demeaning, and contrary to "nature," both because it violated the kindness which humans ought to extend to each other in times of need and because it represented an "unnatural" growth of money (the usurer did nothing to earn the increase which accrued to him, and the money therefore increased "unnaturally"). Because they were thought to exploit the poor, who were most in need of loans and least able to afford interest, usurers were looked upon everywhere with disgust. Cicero mentions them in the same breath with child molesters.[94] Early theologians universally regarded Jesus's command to "lend hoping for nothing again" (Luke 6:35) as an extension of Levitical prohibitions of usury among Jews to the entire Christian community.

The ethical case against usury was considerably stronger that that against homosexuality. Many more biblical passages could be claimed to relate to it,

93. "Sicut in speculativis error circa ea quorum cognitio est homini naturaliter indita," 2a.2ae.154.12.Resp.

94. *Pro Sestio* 8: "Despiciens conscios stuprorum ac veteres vexatores aetatulae suae puteali et faeneratorum gregibus inflatus."

including, with only a little stretching, Jesus's constant condemnations of the rich.[95] "Natural law" forbade it. The fathers of the church forbade it. The very same theologians influential in condemning homosexuality forbade absolutely and in no uncertain terms lending money at interest: Peter Cantor, Albertus Magnus, and Saint Thomas Aquinas.[96] Many more church councils had condemned it, beginning with Nicea, the most famous of all, and including dozens of others before the steady and severe proscriptions of the First, Third and Fourth Laterans.

By the fourteenth century usury incurred more severe penalties in church law than "sodomy" did and was derogated in exactly the same terms. The most famous of the commentators on canon law, Panormitanus, equated it explicitly with "unnatural" sexuality: "Whenever humans sin against nature, whether in sexual intercourse, worshiping idols, or any other unnatural act, the church may always exercise its jurisdiction. . . . For by such sins God Himself is offended, since He is the author of nature. This is why Jean Lemoine felt . . . that the church could prosecute usurers and not thieves or robbers, because usurers violate nature by making money grow which would not increase naturally." [97]

Because usurers were almost necessarily well-to-do, they were at first even more eagerly prosecuted under civil law than gay people. The same thirteenth-century laws which penalized gay people—the Coutumes of Touraine-Anjou, the Etablissements, etc.—stipulated that the property of anyone who had practiced usury within a year of his death was to be confiscated to the king automatically. Many local statutes empowered nobles to exact the same lucrative penalty. Less judicious proceedings were also employed: the crusade against the Albigensians named usurers as well as heretics as the

95. Jean LeMoine commented that "usury is condemned in both Old and New Testaments as well as in canon law, and its punishment therefore belongs to the founder of the canons and to the vicar of Christ" ("Usura est peccatum inductum ex veteri et novo testamento et ex lege canonica et ideo punitio spectat ad conditorem canonum et ad vicarium Christi"), Panormitanus Commentaria 7.231.

96. For Peter Cantor, see Verbum abbreviatum (PL, 205:144–47); for Albertus Magnus, In III librum sententiarum 37.3 ad 3 (Borgnet, 28:702); for Aquinas, Summa theologiae 2a.2ae.78, where the practice is declared an absolute evil even for Jews, regardless of any laws to the contrary.

97. Panormitanus Commentaria 7.180: "qualitercunque homines peccent contra naturam, vel in actu venereo, vel adoranda idola, vel alio modo contra naturam, semper ecclesia potest iurisdictionem suam exercere in laicos. . . . Nam ex hoc peccato laeditur ipse Deus, qui est author naturae. Et per hanc rationem sensit Joannes Monachus . . . quod ideo ecclesia punit usurarios, et non fures seu latrones, quia usurarii delinquunt contra naturam facientes germinare pecuniam, quae naturaliter non germinat." Cf. 241: "Judei peccant contra legem suam et contra naturam exercendo usuras." Panormitanus quotes Innocent as observing that the church's jurisdiction in this matter could be extended even to pagans (180).

objects of its enmity. The former were presumably even more tempting to northern nobles short of cash.

But theology, ethics, law, and even crusades were powerless against a practice which increasingly met the needs of the age and which soon ceased to derive support from widespread popular antipathy. As long as most usurers were Jews, prejudice provided a visceral impetus to prosecution for usury, but by the fourteenth century interest banking more and more frequently involved the Christian majority as well, and the emotional basis of opposition to the practice was steadily eroded by its manifest utility and increased familiarity. As a part of the everyday life of the majority culture, its erstwhile objectionableness eventually came to seem so distant that the ethical tradition against it was sidestepped altogether by the ingenious expedient of declaring ancient prohibitions against it to apply only to the demanding of *excessive* interest.

There were few popular reasons for reinterpreting thirteenth-century strictures against gay people, Jews, witches, or other groups who remained objects of suspicion or hatred on the part of the general population. The prejudices which had been largely responsible for ecclesiastical condemnations continued to animate them, and most of them stood unchallenged at least through the Reformation. There was of course great variation in the fortunes of such groups and their individual members in varying locales and times; this story remains to be written. But there was little change, for a very long time, in public and institutional attitudes toward them, and the history of these attitudes in regard to gay people—at least in its broadest outlines—has already been told here. Religious sanctions and intellectual support created by later medieval theology crystallized public and official expression of such attitudes in the thirteenth century and prolonged their effects for centuries thereafter; such expression both inspired and drew life from the vehement antipathy of the masses. Only when and where the latter abated did such groups experience a general amelioration of their fortunes. In the case of gay people, such changes were relatively rare and lie far beyond the scope of this study.

12 Conclusions

"Conclusions" may be too strong a term for the type of generalization or summary which can be made on the basis of this study; early treatments of any historical phenomena, no matter how thoroughly effected, must be regarded as provisional. Only a few themes emerge clearly from what has preceded. Roman society, at least in its urban centers, did not for the most part distinguish gay people from others and regarded homosexual interest and practice as an ordinary part of the range of human eroticism. The early Christian church does not appear to have opposed homosexual behavior per se. The most influential Christian literature was moot on the issue; no prominent writers seem to have considered homosexual attraction "unnatural," and those who objected to physical expression of homosexual feelings generally did so on the basis of considerations unrelated to the teachings of Jesus or his early followers. Hostility to gay people and their sexuality became noticeable in the West during the period of the dissolution of the Roman state—i.e., from the third through the sixth centuries—due to factors which cannot be satisfactorily analyzed, but which probably included the disappearance of urban subcultures, increased governmental regulation of personal morality, and public pressure for asceticism in all sexual matters. Neither Christian society nor Christian theology as a whole evinced or supported any particular hostility to homosexuality, but both reflected and in the end retained positions adopted by some governments and theologians which could be used to derogate homosexual acts.

During the early Middle Ages gay people were as a consequence rarely visible. Manifestations of a distinctive subculture are almost wholly absent from this period, although many individual expressions of homosexual love, especially among clerics, survive. Moral theology through the twelfth century treated homosexuality as at worst comparable to heterosexual fornication but more often remained silent on the issue. Legal enactments were very rare and of dubious efficacy.

The revival of urban economies and city life notable by the eleventh

333

century was accompanied by the reappearance of gay literature and other evidence of a substantial gay minority. Gay people were prominent, influential, and respected at many levels of society in most of Europe, and left a permanent mark on the cultural monuments of the age, both religious and secular. Homosexual passions became matters of public discussion and were celebrated in spiritual as well as carnal contexts. Opposition to gay sexuality appeared rarely and more as aesthetic partisanship than as moral censure; exceptions to this were ignored by religious and civic leaders.

Beginning roughly in the latter half of the twelfth century, however, a more virulent hostility appeared in popular literature and eventually spread to theological and legal writings as well. The causes of this change cannot be adequately explained, but they were probably closely related to the general increase in intolerance of minority groups apparent in ecclesiastical and secular institutions throughout the thirteenth and fourteenth centuries. Crusades against non-Christians and heretics, the expulsion of Jews from many areas of Europe, the rise of the Inquisition, efforts to stamp out sorcery and witchcraft, all testify to increasing intolerance of deviation from the standards of the majority, enforceable for the first time in the newly emerging corporate states of the High Middle Ages. This intolerance was both reflected in and perpetuated by its incorporation into theological, moral, and legal compilations of the later Middle Ages, many of which continued to influence European society for centuries.

Beyond these modest conclusions and the facts which support them, little can be asserted with confidence. The social topography of medieval Europe is so unexplored that the writer on this subject cannot hope to avoid leading his readers down many wrong paths or, occasionally, coming to a dead end. His comfort must subsist in the belief that he has at least posted landmarks where there were none before and opened the trails on which others will reach destinations far beyond his own furthest advance.

1 Lexicography and Saint Paul

It is not readily apparent to modern English speakers with little knowledge of classical languages that the passage of thousands of years obscures, sometimes beyond recovery, the exact meaning of words in the languages of cultures with experiences and life-styles very different from their own.[1] A variety of translations for the same phrase in Jeremiah are reproduced below. Although the passage is of little doctrinal import, it is obviously quite difficult to establish any consensus about its precise meaning. Some of the renderings are relatively similar, but there could hardly be more difference between "mad after females" (LXX) and "fed in the morning" (KJV).

When the word or passage in question is controversial, the difficulties are apt to be aggravated by ambiguities on both sides of the linguistic barrier. It is significant in this context that Greek—the language of early Christian theology—is particularly ill suited to express the sexual attitudes of the Christian religion, since crimes of a sexual nature in classical Greece were designated in terms unrelated to the considerations which made some sexual practices reprehensible in Christian ethics. This problem is exacerbated by the fact that there is often equal imprecision in the languages into which the Greek is being translated, especially English. The strict definitions of such

1. For the context of this discussion, see chap. 4, pp. 106–7. The following abbreviations for versions of the Bible are employed in this appendix: c = The Confraternity Edition of the New Testament, 1941 (published with the Reims-Douai Old Testament, q.v. below); GN = Good News for Modern Man, 1966; JB = Jerusalem Bible, 1966; JBF = Bible de Jérusalem, 1955; JBG = Bibel: Deutsche Ausgabe mit den Erläuterungen der Jerusalemer Bibel, 1968; JBI = Bibbia di Gerusalemme, 1973; JBS = Biblia de Jerusalén, 1967; KJV = King James or Authorized Version, 1611; LB = Luther's Bible, 1522–45; LS = Sainte Bible, trans. Louis Segond; LXX = Septuagint; NAB = New American Bible, 1970; NEB = New English Bible: New Testament 1961, Old Testament 1970; RDV = Reims-Douai Version, 1609; RSV = Revised Standard Version: New Testament 1946, Old Testament 1952.

Translations of Jeremiah 5:8

Masoretic text: סוּסִים מְיֻזָּנִים מַשְׁכִּים הָיוּ

LXX	Ἵπποι θηλυμανεῖς ἐγενήθησαν[2] [They became horses mad after females][3]
Vulgate	Equi amatores et emissarii facti sunt [They have become passionate and wandering horses]
LB	Wie die vollen müßigen Hengste [Like full, idle stallions]
RDV	They are become as amorous horses and stallions
KJV	They were as fed horses in the morning
RSV	They were well-fed, lusty stallions
JBF	C'étaient des chevaux repus et bien membrés [They were well-fed and well-endowed horses]
JBS	Son caballos lustrosos y enteros [They are shiny and robust horses]
JB	They were well-fed, lusty stallions
JBG	Feiste, wohlgebaute Hengste sind sie [Fleshy, well-built stallions they are]
NEB	Like a well-fed and lusty stallion
NAB	Lustful stallions they are

words as "fornication" and "adultery" observed in moral theology are considerably blurred in common usage, and words such as "prostitute" and "whore" are virtually indefinable. For example, "prostitute" is used to describe, with increasing imprecision, persons who sell their bodies for money, persons who lend their bodies to others for ceremonial purposes ("temple prostitutes"), those whose standards of sexual conduct the speaker considers too loose, and those whom the speaker simply wishes to denigrate.

Salient examples of this sort of semantic difficulty are the Greek words "πορνεία" and "μοιχεία." In Attic Greek πορνεῖα were houses of male prostitution, in which πόρνοι practiced their trade quite legally and with little stigma, as long as they paid the tax on prostitution, the πορνικὸν τέλος. In the LXX "πορνεύων" clearly has the sense of a male prostituting himself (e.g., Deut. 23:18), but in the Koine of the New Testament "πορνεία" is a

2. The Hebrew text from which the LXX was effected may not have been identical with the Masoretic text.

3. Although the context suggests that "mad after females" refers to concupiscence, the expression in question does not always imply sexual interest: cf. the use of the equivalent word "γυναικομανῶ" in Aristophanes *Thesmophoriazusae* 576. The idea of stallions "mad with lust" is of course common in sexual comedy (see, e.g., the prologue to *Sodom*, formerly attributed to the Earl of Rochester).

feminine singular and no longer applies to male brothels. What it does apply to is less clear: many English translators content themselves with the vague word "immorality."[4] This is safe enough, since whatever else "πορνεία" may be, it is certainly "immoral," but the term is misleadingly general. Since "πόρνη" retains the older meaning of "prostitute," there is little justification for excluding this sense from "πορνεία," especially when the two words are linked by context, as in 1 Corinthians 6.[5] "Πορνεύων" and "πόρνος" are left completely ambiguous by the uncertainty surrounding "πορνεία," being rendered by such varied terms as "whoremonger," "fornicator," or "immoral male."

Similarly, "μοιχεία" is widely assumed to be the Greek equivalent of the modern term "adultery," even though in Attic it could refer to the seduction not only of the wife of a citizen but of his widowed mother, unmarried daughter, sister, or niece as well[6] and though it is used by New Testament writers (e.g., Matt. 12:39) with connotations obviously broader than "adultery" in its modern sense. Like "ὑβρίζειν," "stuprum," and other classical words for sexual offenses, "μοιχεία" was originally related to proprietary and status considerations irrelevant to the Christian concept of chastity; pinpointing the time and nature of the transition to more recent associations is far more difficult than many translations imply.

If such ambiguities regarding matters of grave import to the majority of the Christian population can be overlooked or distorted in translation, it is hardly surprising that terms which affect only small minorities may be interpreted with carelessness or imprecision. English translations of the lists of sinners at 1 Corinthians 6:9 and 1 Timothy 1:10 appear to the non-specialist to be precise and concrete renderings of specific Greek words, but in fact there is very considerable uncertainty about the meaning of many of the words involved. For the Greek "πλεονέκται" English versions give translations as varied as "covetous" (KJV, C), "greedy" (RSV, GN), "grabbers"

4. The other common translation of the word is "fornication," but this is equally if not more misleading, since (a) popular use of this word is considerably at variance with its technical meaning in moral theology, and (b) it too originally meant prostitution—a fact which was known to Latin writers throughout most of Christian history and influenced their understanding of Paul's attitudes in ways in which it does not affect modern readers unaware of the etymology of the term. Exactly when and to what extent "fornicatio" ceased to mean simply "prostitution" and came to refer to recourse to prostitutes or general extramarital sexuality has never been closely analyzed but is obviously important in the context of early Christian understanding of Pauline sexual teachings.

5. A few very recent translations have taken cognizance of this: the NAB observes that in 1 Cor. 6:12–20 "the fornication referred to is probably that of religious prostitution, an accepted part of pagan culture in Rome"; but most older versions give the impression that any sort of extramarital sexuality is being condemned.

6. See, e.g., Demosthenes *Prosecution of Aristocrates* 53–55; see also the discussion of this in Dover, *Greek Popular Morality*, p. 209, and "Classical Greek Attitudes," p. 62.

(NEB), "usurers" (JB), and "misers" (NAB); for "ἅρπαγες" interpretations range from "extortioners" (KJV) to "swindlers" (NEB, JB) to "robbers" (NAB, RSV) to "the greedy" (C) to "lawbreakers" (GN). For "μαλακοί" and "ἀρσενοκοῖται" English versions unanimously give some reference to homosexual behavior, but the best foreign translations do not.[7]

Translations of "μαλακοί" and "ἀρσενοκοῖται" in the major English versions of the Bible[8]

Greek	I Cor. 6:9: οὔτε μαλακοὶ οὔτε ἀρσενοκοῖται	I Tim. 1:10: ἀρσενοκοίταις
Wyclif	lecchouris or men that done synne of sodom	them that trespassen with malis aȝenes kynde
Tyndale	abusars of themselves with the mankynde	them that defile themselves with mankynde
RDV	the effeminate, liars[9] with mankind	them who defile themselves with mankind
KJV	effeminate, abusers of themselves with mankind	them that defile themselves with mankind
RSV	homosexuals	sodomites
C	the effeminate, sodomites	sodomites
JB	catamites, sodomites	those who are immoral with boys or with men
NEB	who are guilty of homosexual perversion	perverts
NAB	sodomites	sexual perverts

7. There is no direct reference to homosexuality in the translation of this passage into French by Louis Segond or in the French original of the Jerusalem Bible, published in 1955 with worldwide critical acclaim. The latter renders the passages as "ni dépravés, ni gens de mœurs infâmes" (1 Cor. 6:9) and "les gens de mœurs infâmes" (1 Tim 1:10). Luther interpreted "ἀρσενοκοῖται" as "Knabenschänder" and "μαλακοί" as "Weichlinge." The former is an impossible construction of the Greek. Translations of this passage are particularly revealing of the paramount influence of cultural attitudes on religious beliefs. The French original of the Jerusalem Bible, as noted, followed Louis Segond in departing from an earlier French tradition of translating these words as references to homosexuality (e.g., the translation of Martin of 1728). But the German edition of the Jerusalem Bible interpreted the words as "sissies" and "child molesters" (following Luther), and the Spanish Jerusalem Bible translated them as "effeminates" and "homosexuals," as did the English Jerusalem Bible, although both of the latter were prepared in collaboration with the same scholars who failed to see any clearly homosexual referent in the French version.

8. Because some English versions translate the negative "οὔτε" and some do not, all negatives have been omitted from the English passages to avoid confusion.

9. This spelling occurs in all editions with this translation, but some editions translate "sodomites."

The range of meanings offered for the words in various translations is wide indeed: the exclusion of the "ἀρσενοκοῖται" from the kingdom of heaven is taken by some (RSV, NEB, JBS) to refer to "homosexuals," by some to "perverts" (JBI), by others to "sodomites" (C, NAB, JB), by others to "child molesters" (LB, JBG), and by still others to "people with infamous habits" (LS, JBF); the "μαλακοί," according to the translation one consults, range from "catamites" (JB) to "the effeminate" (KJV, C) to "sissies" (LB, JBG). Such disparity inspires skepticism, and close examination suggests that no modern translations of these terms are very accurate.

The enormous range of meaning associated with the word "μαλακός" in patristic literature has been noted above, along with the oldest and most widespread meaning accorded it in specifically Christian contexts—masturbation. Its regular use in this sense by those familiar with the Pauline writings and its complete absence from civil and ecclesiastical texts dealing with homosexuality ought to preclude its association with homosexuality in the minds of modern translators, but since this is apparently not the case, it may be worth commenting here on three specific lexical errors made in the literature on this subject.

1. The idea that the association of the word "μαλακός," with "effeminacy" links it to homosexuality is a misprision. Gay men were not viewed as "effeminate" in the ancient world unless they happened to exhibit feminine characteristics *in addition to* being gay. Many heterosexual males were called "effeminate" by ancient writers, and there is no essential connection between inappropriate gender behavior and sexual preference in any ancient literature. Patristic sources do not in any case use "μαλακός" for "effeminate" but, rather, employ terms like "θηλύδριος,"[10] "ἀνδρόγυνος,"[11] or "τῶν ἀνδρῶν οἱ γυναικώδεις,"[12] since "μαλακός" was associated with masturbation or general moral laxity.

Furthermore, what constitutes "effeminacy," particularly in a moral context, is highly questionable. Dionysius of Halicarnassus describes Aristodemus of Cumae, a courageous, daring, and powerful ruler whose nickname was "μαλακός," "either because he had been 'effeminate' [θηλυδρίας] as a child and had undergone the things associated with women, as some say, or because he was gentle by nature and unruffled [μαλακός] by anger, as others claim" (8.2.4). The second of these descriptions could hardly have anything to do with homosexuality, and the fact that contemporaries

10. Tatian *Adversus Graecos* 29; Clement *Paedagogus* 3.3.76.

11. Justin Martyr 1 *Apology* 27; Tatian *Adversus Graecos* 29; Clement *Paedagogus* 3.2.41 (cf. 45).

12. Clement *Paedagogus* 2.10 (PG, 8:536); also "μαλθακώτερος," 3.3.56. Cf. "γυνίδας" and "τεθηλυμμένη," ibid.

were so uncertain about the connotations of the word would, one might suppose, give modern translators some pause. Even the first meaning, however, need not relate to homosexuality. To those predisposed to believe that all cultures have shared modern prejudices, it may seem obvious that what Aristodemus "suffered" was sexual use by males, but this is neither stated nor implied.[13] On the contrary, in a subsequent chapter Dionysius explains very specifically what would constitute "effeminacy" in a youth, and it has nothing at all to do with sexuality (7.9ff.).

It is crucial to bear in mind how different attitudes on these subjects were in Hellenistic cities during the centuries preceding and following the birth of Christ. Hercules could engage in any number of homosexual liaisons without the slightest loss of prestige or any hint of decreased manliness, but the simple act of wearing a woman's garment or performing tasks traditionally reserved to females would be considered irredeemably degrading. Concepts of "effeminacy" have varied so widely through time and were certainly so different in Paul's time from those prevailing today that even if "effeminate" could be justified as a translation for "μαλακός," it would be a totally ambiguous one.

2. The fact that "μαλακός" is sometimes applied to obviously gay persons in classical literature is no more proof that the word actually means "gay" or "homosexual" (or even "sexually passive") than the application of "proper" to "Englishman" is proof that "proper" means "English."[14] There is no reason to suppose that gay people should have been spared any particular derogatory epithet, and unless it can be shown that the obloquy in question has some inherent relationship to homosexuality, no necessary connection can be assumed. So many people are denigrated as "μαλακοί" in ancient literature, for so many reasons, that the burden of proof in this case must be on those who wish to *create* a link with gay people. In the absence of such proof, the soundest inference is that "μαλακός" refers to general moral weakness, with no specific connection to homosexuality.

13. Given prevailing attitudes in Hellenistic cities, it is in fact almost inconceivable that merely participating in homosexual activities as a youth—passively or actively—would have earned Aristodemus a particular sobriquet. If his nickname did relate to sexual behavior, it must have been intended to pillory some lack of restraint or the adoption of some feminine characteristic in the performance of the actions in question.

14. Lucian, e.g., describes the blood of some priests he pillories for passive homosexual behavior as "μαλακός" (*Lucius* 37), but this can hardly be taken to indicate anything about the sexuality of the individuals in question. If it means anything more than "flowing" or "sickly," it is simply "weak willed" or "unrestrained." Obsessive passivity may be part of the unrestraint in question, but since they are priests who spend their time seeking group sexual encounters, this can hardly be taken to comprise the sum of the objection. Mere homosexual interest could not be an issue, since it is specifically characterized in the same work as typical of humans (33: "ἔρωτας ἀνθρωπίνους ἐρᾷ ἐπὶ γυναῖκας καὶ παῖδας οἰστρούμενος," cf. 32: "ἐπὰν γυναῖκα ἢ παῖδα").

3. The argument that in 1 Corinthians 6:9 the two words "*μαλακοί*" and "*ἀρσενοκοῖται*" represent the active and passive parties in homosexual intercourse is fanciful and unsubstantiated by lexicographical evidence. The second term does imply an active role, though not necessarily in homosexual intercourse, but there is no more reason to take "*μαλακοί*" as its passive than to assume it to be the passive of the preceding word, "*μοιχοί*." Indeed, if context is to be admitted as evidence, the juxtaposition of "*ἀρσενοκοῖται*" and "*πόρνοι*" in 1 Timothy suggests very strongly that prostitution is what is at issue, in one case presumably (male) heterosexual prostitution and in the other, homosexual (although it could be argued that the distinction intended is between the prostitute and the client). "*Πόρνοι*" occurs in both passages where "*ἀρσενοκοῖται*" is found, unlike "*μαλακοί*," which is only in one.

Moreover, prostitution was manifestly of greater concern to Saint Paul than any sort of homosexual behavior: excluding the words in question, there is only a single reference to homosexual acts in the Pauline writings, whereas the word "*πόρνος*" and its derivatives are mentioned almost thirty times. If one is simply to pick a likely context from which to derive the meaning of "*μαλακοί*," prostitution (or whatever is meant by "*πορνεία*") is by any reasonable standard a much better candidate for the honor.

"*Μαλακοί*" does not occur in 1 Timothy 1:10, and the two terms are never juxtaposed in this way elsewhere in patristic literature dealing with homosexual intercourse, although "*μαλακός*" sometimes occurs independently in its broad sense of "morally weak."[15] Philo, a Hellenized Jew almost exactly contemporary with Paul, several times (and with various phrases) makes exactly the active-passive distinction sought by adherents of this line of thought, but he uses neither of the words from 1 Corinthians. Instead, he describes the active and passive parties respectively as "*δρῶντες*" and "*πάσχοντες*," or "*παιδερασταί*" and "*παιδικά*."[16] Clearly "*μαλακός*" had no necessary or particular relation to homosexuality in the literature of Paul's time.

The second word, "*ἀρσενοκοῖται*," is more difficult to deal with. Saint Paul appears to have been the first author to use the word, and it appeared very infrequently after him.[17] The authors of most lexica, including all the

15. It is striking that in the *Problems* attributed to Aristotle a lengthy discussion of the origins of homosexual passivity employs the word "*μαλακός*" only in its general sense of "unrestrained," not in any particularly homosexual context (4.26).

16. See *De vita contemplativa* 7; *De legibus specialibus* 3.7. The former dichotomy is the most common one in Greek literature on the subject; it is also employed by the author of the *Problems*.

17. J. H. Moulton and G. Milligan (*The Vocabulary of the Greek Testament* [London, 1952], p. 79) opine that the word first occurs "among the imperial poets" and cite as authority an

standard English ones, have traditionally contented themselves with corroborating the inference of biblical translators by giving the definition as "sodomite." There is a double irony to this since—as is now generally recognized—the Sodomites were not punished for homosexuality, and since "ἀρσενοκοῖται" had only a tangential relation, if any, to homosexuality.

The claim that this word "obviously" means "homosexual" defies linguistic evidence and common sense. The second half of the compound, "κοῖται," is a coarse word, generally denoting base or licentious sexual activities (see Rom. 13:13), and in this and other compounds corresponds to the vulgar English word "fucker," i.e., a person who, by insertion, takes the "active" role in intercourse. The prefix "ἀρσενο-" simply means "male." Its relationship to the second half of the compound is ambiguous: in bald English the compound means "male fuckers," but it is not clear whether "male" designates the object or the gender of the second half. The English expression "lady killer," when written, conveys the same ambiguity: in speech, emphasis would indicate whether "lady" designates the victim or the gender of the "killer," but in print there is no way to distinguish whether the phrase means "a lady who kills," or "a person who kills ladies." This is a particularly revealing parallel, since a third and largely unrelated meaning (i.e., "wolf," or "Don Juan") is actually the most common sense of the term but could not be deduced from the constituent parts, a telling example of the inadequacy of lexicographical inference unsupported by contextual evidence.

Other Greek phrases, seemingly analogous to "ἀρσενοκοῖται," may be misleading. It might seem, for instance, that if "παιδερασταί" refers to "men who love boys," and "παιδοφθορέω" means "to corrupt boys," then "ἀρσενοκοιτέω" must mean "to sleep with men" and "ἀρσενοκοῖται" designate those who do so; but this sort of facile analogy will not stand close scrutiny. In "παιδοφιλέω" the "παιδο-" is indeed the object of "φιλέω," but in "παιδομαθής" it is the subject (of "μανθάνω"), as it is in "παιδότρωτος" (of "τιτρώσκω"); in "παιδοπόρος" it is neither: it simply functions as modifier without expressing any implicit verbal relation. The "obvious" relationship between the two parts of compounds of this sort is not susceptible of formulation without careful analysis of individual cases. It would certainly be

---

inscription from the AP and Theodor Nägeli, *Der Wortschatz des Apostels Paulus* (Basel, 1904), p. 46. Both citations are erroneous. The inscription dates from the sixth century A.D. Nägeli cites this same inscription, two Christian apologists who wrote well after Paul, and a line from bk. 2 of the *Oracula Sybillina*. Only the latter could by any stretch of the imagination be considered "an imperial poet," but prevailing scholarly opinion regards it as a work of Jewish or Christian origin, very thinly disguised as pagan. Its date is wholly uncertain, and it is far from clear that either this line (which may be interpolated) or the work as a whole predates Paul.

wrong to assume that because "pyromania" refers to an obsession with fire, "nymphomania" must describe an obsession with brides: in fact, it describes the opposite, an obsession with men, and the prefix "nympho-" ("bride"), although a noun, acts as the modifier of "mania" rather than its object.

Similarly in the case of compounds of "ἀρσενο-": "ἀρρενοποιός," "making men," combines a verbal second part with an objective first, as do "ἀρρενογαμέω," "ἀρρενογονέω," "ἀρρενόομαι," "ἀρρενοτοκέω," etc. In these and many other words the "ἄρρενο-" functions as the object of the activity described or implied by the second half of the compound. But in many other compounds of the word this is not the case. "Ἀρσενόμορφος" does not mean "forming a male" but "of masculine form": the "ἀρσενο-" functions as an adjective modifying "μόρφος," as it does in "ἀρσενογενής," "ἀρσενόθυμος," "ἀρσένωμα," etc.[18]

In general, moreover, those compounds in which the form "ἄρρενο-" occurs employ it objectively; those in which "ἀρσενο-" is found use it as an adjective. This tendency can be seen in the lists above as well as in many other words; the few exceptions are generally words in which no confusion between adjective and object could arise, such as "ἀρρενόπαις,"[19] or in which the semantic import of the word would be the same regardless of the grammatical relation of the constituent parts, such as "ἀρρενοφανής."[20] The origin of this distinction and its relation to the general orthographic shift from Attic "ἄρρην" to Hellenistic "ἄρσην" (Old Attic) have not been carefully examined.[21] That it is not merely historical accident in this case is suggested by the fact that the two forms exist contemporaneously over long periods of time and that some words do not undergo this shift, as well as by

18. Uses of the corresponding feminine form, "γυναικο-," parallel those for the male in their variability (e.g., "γυναικάδελφος" means "wife's brother," but "γυναικάνηρ" does not mean "wife's man"), but there is overwhelming preference for adjectival use, as in "γυναικόθυμος," "γυναικοκρασία," "γυναικόμορφος," "γυναικόφωνος," "γυναικόψυχος," etc.

19. In such cases both forms are frequently known: e.g., both "ἀρρενόθηλυς" and "ἀρσενόθηλυς" occur. A number of compounds of similar form occur in 1 Tim. 1:10, but in each case the objective character of the prefixed noun stem is obvious from the form of the word (e.g., "ἀνδρο-," "πατρο-," "μητρο-"). Paul's preference for such forms in the objective case might well justify the assumption that he would have written "ἀνδροκοῖται" (a form used by other Koine writers) rather than the ambiguous "ἀρσενοκοῖται" had he intended to stigmatize those who were simply sexually active with men, especially since "ἀνδροφόνοι," an extremely similar word, is separated by only one word in the text from "ἀρσενοκοῖται."

20. "Ἀδελφοκοιτία" is a germane example. "Ἀδελφός" could be either the subject or the object of the "κοιτία"; the meaning would be the same either way, and related words might argue in either direction. In "ἀδελφοκτονέω" the "ἀδελφός" is the object; in "ἀδελφομιξία" it is probably adjectival. (The word is extremely rare: the LSJ does not list it, but Theophilus uses it in Ad Autolycum 1.9 [PG, 6:1023].)

21. See Robert Browning, Medieval and Modern Greek (London, 1969), p. 31.

the semantic division noted. In no words coined and generally written with the form "ἀρσενο-" is the prefix demonstrably objective; overlap occurs on a small scale in words containing "ἀρρενο-," possibly because it represents both a regional and a temporal variation on older usage.[22]

"Ἀρσενοκοῖται," then, means male sexual agents, i.e., active male prostitutes, who were common throughout the Hellenistic world in the time of Paul. That such a designation existed in the Latin of the time is well known: the *drauci* or *exoleti* were, as discussed previously, male prostitutes capable of the active role with either men or women. "Ἀρσενοκοῖται" is the Greek equivalent of "drauci";[23] the corresponding passive is "παρακοῖται."[24] "Ἀρσενοκοῖται" was the most explicit word available to Paul for a male prostitute, since the words "πόρνος" and "πορνεύων," used for this purpose in Attic and Old Testament Greek, had been adopted in the Koine Greek in which Paul wrote to refer to men who resorted to female prostitutes or who simply committed "fornication" (as in the very passage in question).[25]

There can be no doubt that Paul was familiar with male prostitution, through the Old Testament if nowhere else, or that he would have viewed it with the same horror with which he regarded female prostitution. It would not be surprising if he considered active prostitution more reprehensible

22. There is contextual evidence for the adjectival quality even of "ἀρρενο-." An inscription to Basil I on a gate in Thessalonica specifies the object of the activity performed by the ἀρρενοκοῖται: "Βάρβαρον οὐ τρομέεις, οὐκ ἄρρενας ἀρρενοκοίτας" (AP, 9.686). The word "ἄρρενας" in this line, unless it is purely pleonastic—which would be odd in an inscription, where one would ordinarily expect terseness—makes sense only in the light of the coarse ambiguity described above: the phrase must mean "male fuckers of men." That the object of the activity is specified thus makes clear that it is not contained in the word itself. Were the sense otherwise—i.e., if the ambiguity involved the subject of the activity—the Greek would have had to clarify the subject with an adjective rather than the object with a noun, and one would expect something like "οὐκ ἀρρενικοὺς ἀρρενοκοίτας." This would of course confirm that there might be female ἀρσενοκοῖται, at least in theory, and that the objectionableness of ἀρσενοκοιτία lies elsewhere than in the gender of the parties involved. Indeed, whichever way one takes it, the insertion of "ἄρρενας" into this line really precludes taking "ἀρρενοκοῖται" as a reference to male homosexuality, since it is apparent that the genders of the parties involved in ἀρσενοκοιτία, whatever it is, cannot be assumed.

23. "Ἀρσενοκοῖται" thus expresses both common Attic words for male prostitutes, "ἡταιρηκώς" (male courtesan, or prostitute of higher caliber) and "πόρνος" or "πεπορνευμένος" (an ordinary prostitute, or male whore), but it adds a new distinction, active vs. passive, which was unknown in Attic designations for prostitutes. It was only toward the beginning of the Christian era that adult men would be sufficiently open about a desire to be passive that active prostitutes would be a subject of discussion.

24. See, e.g., Diodorus Siculus 5.32.7. Cf. the ironic pun on this and its similarity to "παράκοιτις" ("wife") in AP, 5.207.

25. "Πορνεύων" is found at 1 Cor. 6:18; "πόρνος" at 1 Cor. 5:9–11, 6:9, Eph. 5:5, 1 Tim. 1:10, Heb. 12:16, 13:4, Rev. 21:8, 22:15.

than passive,[26] but it is not necessary to assume that he understood the precise nuance of "ἀρσενοκοῖται" in terms of sexual roles. Since it was unambiguous in its reference to male prostitution (as opposed to male recourse to female prostitution), he may well have intended it generically.[27]

Perhaps the most extensive evidence that "ἀρσενοκοῖται" did not connote "homosexual" or even "sodomite" in the time of Paul is offered by the vast amount of writing extant on the subject of homoerotic sexuality in Greek in which this term does not occur. It is extremely difficult to believe that if the word actually meant "homosexual" or "sodomite," *no* previous or contemporary author would have used it in a way which clearly indicated this connection.

Herodotus referred to homosexual attachments with the phrase "παισὶ μίσγονται" (1.35). Plato, in his numerous dialogues on love between men, never once used the word in question, even though in several works he specifically distinguished between men who love men and those who love women and in his later years went so far as to characterize sexual relations between persons of the same sex as "παρὰ φύσιν," a phrase employed by Paul in Romans 1:27. Aristotle discussed homosexual relations at length and with medical detachment but never used the word "ἀρσενοκοῖται"; he called such relations "ἡ τῶν ἀφροδισίων τοῖς ἄρρεσιν." Plutarch paralleled not only the "παρὰ φύσιν" of Romans but even the "ἀσχήμων," yet he used all sorts

26. Especially if, as seems likely, he intended to derogate prostitutes who serviced women: although the ancient world was familiar with women who played an active sexual role with men, there is no record of passive male prostitutes who serviced such women, and a condemnation of male prostitution in both a heterosexual and a homosexual context would require "ἀρσενοκοῖται". Even in a purely homosexual context Paul probably would have considered passive prostitution less reprehensible than active. Talmudic opinion tended to condemn the active partner in a homosexual relationship more than the passive one (see, e.g., Bailey, p. 62) even in nonmercenary relations, and the sexual exploitation of enslaved males was so common in the ancient world that many people regarded passive prostitution as a calamity rather than a moral failing. At least by the fourth century Christians took Joel 3:3 as a reference to the forced prostitution of Hebrew youths by their enemies ("Et posuerunt puerum in prostibulo"). (The expression is ambiguous in the Hebrew; the LXX seems to imply that the boys were given *to* prostitutes—"Καὶ ἔδωκαν τὰ παιδάρια πόρναις"— perhaps to be used by them?) At Rome it was the active prostitutes (*exoleti*) who were the first object of legal repression, and laws against passive prostitution were directed at those who organized and oversaw the trade, not the prostitutes themselves.

27. It is conceivable that the word also applies to females who take an active sexual role with men, especially for money. Many ancient writers, Christian and pagan, wrote with disdain about women who played an active role in intercourse with men: e.g., Clement of Alexandria *Paedagogus* 3.3, "Τὰ γυναικῶν οἱ ἄνδρες πεπόνθασι, καὶ γυναῖκες ἀνδρίζονται παρὰ φύσιν"; Martial 1.90, "At tu, pro facinus, Bassa, fututor eras," 7.67, "Pedicat pueros tribas Philaenis," 7.70, etc.; Seneca *Epistles* 95.21; Caelius Aurelianus *Tardarum passionum* 4.9 (Drabkin, pp. 900–905); etc. If it could be shown that "ἀρσενο-" were the object rather than the gender of "κοῖται," it would certainly refer to this sort of gender inversion rather than to homosexuality in general.

of other terms to designate homosexual relations—"ἡ παρὰ φύσιν ὁμιλία πρὸς ἄρρενας," "παιδικὸς ἔρως," "ἀφροδισίων παιδικῶν κοινωνία," "ἡ ἄρρενος πρὸς ἄρρεν μίξις"[28]—without ever mentioning "ἀρσενοκοῖται."

Josephus and Philo were both Greek-speaking Jews writing in Greek close to the time of Paul. Philo, in fact, was almost exactly contemporary. Both discussed Sodom, both believed—following a Jewish apocryphal tradition of their day—that the Sodomites were punished for homosexuality, and both had vocabularies highly similar to Paul's, yet neither mentioned the word "ἀρσενοκοῖται" or any resembling it. (Philo called the Sodomites "ἄνδρες ὄντες ἄρρεσιν ἐπιβαίνοντες," De Abrahamo 26.134–38.) The Pseudo-Lucian Affairs of the Heart was written long after the use of such a word would have been widespread in the Hellenistic world and dealt at great length with homosexual love and behavior. The author used terms like "ὁ ἄρρην ἔρως," "τὰς ἄρρενας ἐπιθυμίας," and "ἐρώτων τοὺς ἄρρενας." "Ἀρσενοκοῖται" does not occur. Sextus Empiricus knew and used a word which came closer than any other classical noun to meaning "homosexuality," but it was "ἀρρενομιξία" (1.152), not "ἀρσενοκοιτία." Libanius, a Greek writer contemporary with Saint John Chrysostom who deplored the homosexuality prevalent among his peers, does not appear to have known a word for "homosexual," since he used phrases like "ἡ περὶ τοὺς ἄρρενας νόσος" to describe homosexuality (Oratio de festorum invitationibus 53.10).

One would certainly expect to find such a word among other Christian writers in Greek, yet one looks for it in vain among all the discussions of homosexual relations. Almost immediately after prohibiting homosexual activities, The Teaching of the Twelve Apostles quotes much of the list of sinners in 1 Corinthians 6:9; conspicuous by their absence are the words "μαλακοί" and "ἀρσενοκοῖται."[29] Tatian uses "παιδεραστία" in describing the Romans' homoerotic practices (e.g., Adversus Graecos 19 [PG, 6:843]); Justin Martyr rails against homosexual abuses but calls them "κιναιδία," "ἔρωτες ἀρσένων," "τῇ ἀθέῳ καὶ ἀσεκεῖ καὶ ἀκρατεῖ μίξει," "ἀνδροβατεῖν," etc., never once employing "ἀρσενοκοῖται" (1 Apology 25, 27; 2 Apology 12.5). Eusebius quotes Romans 1:26–27 almost verbatim, excoriating homosexual relations in all their manifestations, yet nowhere does he employ the word which supposedly means "homosexual" in Paul's writings.[30] Clement of Alexandria uses at least thirteen different expressions for "homosexual,"

28. In the dialogue Bruta animalia, female homosexuality is included as well: "Οὔτ' ἄρρενος πρὸς ἄρρεν οὔτε θήλεος πρὸς θῆλυ μῖξιν," 990D.

29. 5.1–2: "μοιχεῖαι, . . . πορνεῖαι, κλοπαὶ, εἰδωλολατρίαι, . . . ἁρπαγαί," etc.

30. Demonstratio evangelii 4.10: "Εἶτα πάντα ἀπαγορεύσας ἀθέμιτον γάμον καὶ πᾶσαν ἀσχήμονα πρᾶξιν, γυναικῶν τε πρὸς γυναῖκας, καὶ ἀρρένων πρὸς ἄρρενας μίξεις, ἐπιλέγει."

"sodomite," and "sodomy," but none of them is "ἀρσενοκοῖται."[31] Yet he clearly knew the word, since he quoted the passage from Corinthians (in a different context) in several of his works.[32] Gregory of Nyssa knew and used the word "ζωοφθορία," an extremely rare word for sexual relations with animals, yet when he discussed homosexual relations he had to call them "ἡ κατὰ τοὺς ἄρρενας λύσση" (Epistula canonica 4).

Saint John Chrysostom probably wrote more about the subject of same-sex sexuality than any other pre-Freudian writer except Peter Damian. In dozens of works he discusses or mentions it. Greek was his native language, the patristic Greek of the later Empire, thoroughly imbued with the Koine of the New Testament. His writings abound with New Testament references, and he quotes from all the Pauline epistles with accuracy and facility. Yet among the dozens of words and phrases used by Chrysostom to name, describe, or characterize homosexual relations, neither "ἀρσενοκοῖται" nor any derivative of it occurs in any of these writings.[33] This absence is particularly notable in several instances where the use of the word would seem almost inevitable if it were indeed related to homosexuality: in his commentary on Romans 1:26, for instance, where he quotes 1 Corinthians 6:18 in a discussion of Roman homosexual behavior but does not refer to the place in the text only nine verses before where homosexuality is allegedly mentioned by name (see text in app. 2). It is even more striking that in discussing the supposedly homosexual activities of the people of Sodom, he quotes directly from the list of sins in 1 Corinthians 6:9 and 1 Timothy 1:10,[34] yet he does

---

31. E.g., in Paedagogus 2 and 3, passim: "ἀρρενομιξία," "κατόπιν εὐνάς," "ἀσυμφυεῖς ἀνδρογύνους κοινωνίας," "ὀπισθοβατικόν," "παιδοφθορία," "μίξις ἀφροδισίων τοῖς νέοις," "περὶ τὰ παιδικὰ ἐκμανῶς ἐπτοημένοι," "λίχνος πόρνος," "παῖδες ἀρνεῖσθαι τὴν φύσιν δεδιδαγμένοι," "κίναιδος," "ἀνδρογύνων συνουσίαις," "ἐπικιναίδισμα," "ἀνδρῶν μίξις ἄθεσμος," "ἀπ' ἄρρενος ὕβρις."

32. Paedagogus 3.11 (PG, 8:660); Stromata 3.18 (PG, 8:1212).

33. Some of the expressions he uses are "παιδεραστεῖν," "ἡταιρηκώς," "ἄνθρωπος πεπορνευμένος," "μίξις τῶν ἀνδρῶν," "ἀνὴρ πεπορνευμένος," "ἡ μίξις παρὰ φύσιν" (In Epistolam ad Romanos, homily 4); "τὰ παράνομα," "τὴν παράνομον πονηρίαν," "ἄθεσμος μίξις," "τὴν φύσιν παραδειγματίζειν" (In capitulum XIX Genesis, homily 43); "ἄρρενες ἐν ἄρσεσιν τὴν ἀσχημοσύνην κατεργάζειν," "τῶν ὑβριζομένων παίδων," "οἱ ἀκόλαστοι," "ἔρως καινός τις καὶ παράνομος" (Adversus oppugnatores vitae monasticae 3.8); "παῖδας ἐσφάζειν," "παισὶν ἐπιμαίνεσθαι" (In Epistolam ad Titum, homily 5); "τοὺς κοινοὺς τῆς φύσεως ἀνατρέψαντας νόμους" (De fato et providentia 4); cf. De perfecta caritate 8 and In acta apostolorum 12.4. He does use a related word once in a different context: see below, p. 351.

34. De perfecta caritate 8 (PG, 56:290). It is unlikely that it could be coincidence rather than quotation for such unusual words as "πλεονέκται" and "ἅρπαγες" to occur together with "μοιχοί." Note that in his commentary on Titus he quotes the whole list of sins from 1 Cor. 6:9 verbatim in the same paragraph in which he discusses the homosexual excesses of the Sodomites: but he does not use the word "ἀρσενοκοῖται" or any form of it to name these excesses, contenting himself instead with the circumlocution "παισὶν ἐπεμαίνοντο," and

not mention the one word which translators would have us believe refers specifically to homosexuality.

All this is convincing enough, but the final proof lies in the fact that after writing so copiously on the subject of homosexual relations in every exegetical work where the text could possibly suggest a connection—e.g., Genesis 19, Romans 1—and even some which do not—Titus, for instance—Chrysostom does not mention so much as one word about homosexuality when expounding on the very places where "ἀρσενοκοῖται" occurs; in his commentaries on 1 Corinthians 6:9 and 1 Timothy 1:10 there is not a hint about sexual activity between persons of the same sex. In fact on several occasions Chrysostom copied out the list of sins from Corinthians and actually omitted the one word which is claimed to mean homosexual;[35] considering his feelings on the subject, abundantly evidenced in many works, it is virtually inconceivable that he would have done so had he understood the term to refer to what he had elsewhere called "the worst of all sins."

The Latin fathers also concerned themselves with homosexual relations. Owing to the somewhat misleading translation of "ἀρσενοκοῖται" as "masculorum concubitores,"[36] one might have expected to find the passages from Corinthians and Timothy at least mentioned in relation to homosexuality, even though to a Latin speaker the phrase would clearly imply acts of prostitution rather than sexual inclination. Yet they are not mentioned.

---

establishing no connection between the ἀρσενοκοῖται and the Sodomites (*In epistolam ad Titum* 3.5 [PG, 62:693]). Cf. homily 43 on Genesis 3 (PG, 54:399–400) and 42 on Matthew 3 (PG, 57:449).

35. E.g., homilies 16 and 37 (PG, 61:135, 317).

36. Jerome, following the older Latin translations, rendered the Greek "ἀρσενοκοῖται" into Latin as "masculorum concubitores," a vague phrase suggestive of multiple interpretations. Most obviously, it would be the active counterpart of the *concubinus*, a passive male concubine. This would correspond almost exactly to the Greek, and it is not unlikely that Jerome's chaste pen would have preferred the more clinical "concubitor" to the vulgar "exoletus." Other authors who use the phrase include Pseudo-Quintilian, who employs it in reference to prostitution which is either passive or nonspecific ("[quem,] si quis masculorum erat concubitorum, sine cunctatione subegisse potuerat," *Declamationes maiores* 3B.5; cf. 3B.3: "Quis enim inter tot milia bellatorum vel prostituentis obscenos vidit amplexus vel vocem audiit prostituti?"). This text, however, cannot be dated even approximately and is not necessarily indicative of opinion in Jerome's time. Constantin Ritter (*Die Quintilianischen Declamationen* [Freiburg, 1881], p. 25) believed that 3B was much later than the rest of the work and proposed the tenth century as the date of composition. It is obviously later than the bulk of the *Declamationes*, but the tenth is hardly the likeliest of centuries for its composition. Cf. Yngve Englund, *Ad Quintiliani quae feruntur Declamationes maiores adnotationes* (Uppsala, 1934); and S. F. Bonner, *Fifty Years of Classical Scholarship* (Oxford, 1954), esp. p. 373. Like other sexual phrases, "concubitor" gained a wide range of connotations in the Middle Ages. A seventh-century Visigothic statute used it to describe all those engaging in homosexual acts: see p. 176. It retained, however, the sense of male prostitution well into the twelfth century; see, e.g., Dümmler, "Briefe und Verse," p. 358.

Arnobius does not mention them in castigating the homosexual behavior of the pagan gods (*Adversus gentes* 4.26). Tertullian's discussions of homosexuality in *Ad nationes* (1.16) do not mention them, nor does the long poem on the sins of Sodom formerly attributed to him.[37] Lactantius discusses at some length "those men who prostitute their bodies to lust and forget what they were born to be, contending with women in passivity" (*Institutiones divinae* 5.9 [PL, 6:578ff.]; cf. 6.23); in the very same place he quotes at length from the list of sins in 1 Corinthians 6:9, yet he excludes any mention of a word for "homosexual" and fails to invoke the passage as apostolic authority against the practices he is condemning (ibid. [PL, 6:576]).

Augustine discusses homosexuality both independently and in relation to biblical texts. Nowhere does he quote the word from the Pauline epistles or use any words similar to Latin translations of Corinthians or Timothy. Instead, he uses circumlocutions like those mentioned earlier: "stupra in masculos," "immunditas," "masculi in masculos nefanda libidine accensi," etc.[38] Other Latin writers—Ausonius, Cyprian, Minucius Felix, et al.— discuss homosexual relations in considerable detail and with large vocabularies. None quotes from Corinthians or Timothy. None invokes Paul as authority against such practices. None uses phrases like Jerome's.[39]

As late as the twelfth century, when the original meaning of "ἀρσενο-κοῖται" had long been lost in the West, Peter Cantor ransacked the Scriptures for all possible references to homosexuality; he came up with every one accepted as such today—Genesis 19, Leviticus 18 and 20, Romans 1, Jude— plus many rather fanciful inferences (e.g., from Ezekiel, Isaiah, Joshua, Titus, Colossians), but he did not cite 1 Corinthians 6:9 or 1 Timothy 1:10.[40]

No laws passed against homosexual behavior under Christian influence designate the object of their proscription as "ἀρσενοκοῖται."[41] Even

37. This poem, which is almost certainly not genuine, is reprinted in the Migne (PL) edition of Tertullian's works with the cautious comment that it is "attributed to Tertullian."

38. Note that the last phrase is simply a telescoping of Rom. 1:26–27. It would be tedious to cite all the brief references to this subject in the Augustinian corpus; the phrases listed are taken from *Contra mendacium* 9.20, 17.34; *De mendacio* 7.10; *De natura et gratia* 22.24; and *De civitate Dei* 16.30. Cf. epistle 211.14 for lesbianism.

39. See Ausonius *Epigrams* 59; Cyprian *Epistles* 1.9; Minucius Felix *Octavius* 28. For a later period, see Gregory *Dialogues* 4.37 and *Moralia* 14.19.

40. *Verbum abbreviatum* 148 (PL, 205:333–35). He did mention 1 Tim. 1, but only in a general way, as invocation against licentiousness; neither "masculorum concubitores" nor verse 10 is cited. But cf. notes below.

41. A typical legal proscription (of 533) is against those "qui cum masculis nefandam libidinem exercere audent." It is interesting that although seventh-century secular legislation against homosexuality in Visigothic Spain employed the phrase "masculorum concubitores," ecclesiastical legislation enacted contemporaneously and in response to it did not, referring instead to those "qui contra naturam masculi in masculos hanc turpitudinem operaverint."

ecclesiastical legislation does not invoke the phrase but limits itself to references to Sodom or more general circumlocutions (e.g., the *Apostolic Constitutions* refer to "ἡ Σοδόμων ἁμαρτία"). When Saint Basil—writing in the fourth century—established penances for sexual relations between persons of the same gender (epistle 217), he quoted directly from Romans 1:26 ("τὴν ἀσχημοσύνην ἐν τοῖς ἄρρεσιν") but did not use the words from the later epistles.

Some sources roughly contemporary with Paul (i.e., within two or three centuries) do employ the word "ἀρσενοκοῖται" or derivatives of it ("ἀρσενοκοιτέω" and "ἀρσενοκοιτία"); these occurrences offer further evidence that the word did not connote homosexuality to Paul or his early readers. Although Polycarp, Theophilus, and Nilus only quote from the Pauline texts without providing any context for the specific failings of the ἀρσενοκοῖται,[42] Aristides and Eusebius (and possibly Origen)[43] do provide some contextual evidence. Aristides describes in great detail in his *Apology* (second century A.D.) the corruption of the pagan gods and argues from this that either the laws of classical nations were wrong to prohibit adultery, rape, etc., or else the gods were themselves criminals, since they customarily violated these laws. Among the crimes the gods had committed was ἀρσενοκοιτία (9.13). In no city within the Roman Empire in the second century were there laws in effect against homosexual relations per se, least of all in Aristides' native Athens.[44] Christian writers were acutely aware of this, especially Clement of Alexandria, an Athenian contemporary of Aristides.

42. Polycarp *To the Philippians*; Theophilus *Ad Autolycum* 1.2, 2.14; Nilus *Epistularum libri quattuor* 2.282. In this category also fall the references by Cyril of Alexandria (*Homiliae diversae* 14) and the *Oracula Sybillina* (2.13). Though neither is a quotation from Paul, neither gives any contextual evidence whatever: the first simply mentions those "μὴ θρηνοῦντες διὰ [τὸ πέταυρον τῆς ἀρσενοκοιτίας]" (brackets in published text), and the latter offers the prohibition "μὴ ἀρσενοκοιτεῖν, μὴ συκοφαντεῖν, μήτε φονεύειν." The authorship and dating of both works is in considerable doubt, and their testimony would contribute little in any event.

43. The *Expositio in Proverbia*, though somewhat ambiguous, strongly implies an equation of "ἀρσενοκοῖται" with "γυναῖκες ἄτιμοι," i.e., female prostitutes: "Ἀλλ' ἐὰν ἴδῃ τινὰ ἑαυτὸν ἐπιδιδόντα ταῖς ἡδοναῖς εὐθὺς συναντᾷ αὐτῷ τὸ εἶδος ἔχουσα πορνικόν, ἢ ποιεῖ τὰς νέων ἐξίπτασθαι καρδίας. Οἱ μὲν ἐν ταῖς πλατείαις ῥεμβόμενοι, μοιχείας καὶ πορνείας καὶ κλοπῆς λαμβάνουσι λογίσμους· οἱ δὲ ἔξω τούτων ῥεμβόμενοι, τὰς παρὰ φύσιν ἡδονὰς μετέρχονται, ἀρσενοκοιτεῖν ἐπιζητοῦντες, καὶ ἄλλων τινῶν ἀπαγορευομένων πραγμάτων φαντασίας λαμβάνοντες· ὅρα δὲ μὴ κατηγόρημα εἴη τοῦτο καὶ ἁγίων ἀνδρῶν· καὶ τις μὴ ἡσυχάζων ἀλλὰ ῥεμβόμενος, τοῖς κατηγορήμασι κοινωνήσει τῆς ἀτίμου γυναικός" (PG, 17:181). There is very little chance that this document is genuine: see Eugène de Faye, *Origène* (Paris, 1923), p. 213. It is most probably the work of later hands and therefore not useful for determining the earlier use of the word.

44. In his *De legibus specialibus* Philo contrasts Mosaic prohibitions of homosexual acts with their complete acceptance by Hellenistic society (3.37).

Prostitution, on the other hand, while legal for slaves and freedmen, was prohibited to the upper classes in most of the Hellenistic world, and it is clear that this is the charge Aristides is laying against the gods, in the tradition of Aeschines against Timarchus.[45] That the gods had no need of money is not to the point: many wealthy men and women were prostitutes in the ancient world, apparently for psychological reasons. The word, moreover, may have had the dual connotation of the English "whore"; if so, the exchange of money would not be necessary to justify the charge.

That the ἀρσενοκοῖται did not necessarily engage in any homosexual activities in discharging the duties of their sinful trade is made clear by Eusebius, who distinguishes between the ἀρσενοκοῖται and those who commit "sins against nature": "Moses prohibited adultery, ἀρσενοκοιτία, and indulgence in pleasures against nature."[46] There can indeed be no question of homosexuality here, since the sentence immediately following makes it obvious that the entire discussion concerns the proper attitude of Christian men toward *women*: "I, however, would have my disciples not even look at a woman with unchaste desire."[47] Apparently Eusebius understood "ἀρσενοκοιτεῖν" to apply to prostitution of men directed toward women rather than other men.

This is presumably the distinction intended by Chrysostom as well when he separates the ἡταιρηκώς from the ἀρσενοκοῖτος[48] in his commentary on 1 Corinthians (homily 16 [PG, 61:135]), although at least two other dichotomies are possible: between prostitutes of higher and lower class (this is suggested by the word "ἡταιρηκώς," but Chrysostom elsewhere fails to make such a distinction) or between active and passive prostitution. Of the two, "ἡταιρηκώς" more implies passivity, and hence necessarily homosexual

45. Note that the other charges laid against the gods clearly are violations of Roman law: ἀνδροβατής = *stuprator*, i.e., one guilty of the rape (statutory or violent) of a free citizen; ἀρρενομανής = a woman given to adultery or fornication, both severely punished under Rome's inequitable laws regarding chastity in marriage. Prostitution, rape, and adultery, moreover, are the standard charges of Christians against pagan morals: see, for prostitution, Minucius Felix *Octavius* 28; for rape of males by males, Justin Martyr 1 *Apology* 12.5 ("Διὸς δὲ καὶ τῶν ἄλλων θεῶν μιμηταὶ γενόμενοι ἐν τῷ ἀνδροβατεῖν"), and Chrysostom *In epistolam ad Titum*, homily 5.4; for "ἀρρενομανία"—a word used in classical Greek primarily of males, but in patristic almost exclusively of females—see Caesarius Nazianzenus *Dialogi* 139 (cf. LXX usage, also of females).

46. *Demonstrationis evangelicae* 1 (PG, 22:65). The reference to Moses could apply to "ἀρσενοκοιτεῖν" as an allusion to Deut. 23:18, which was inaccurately rendered in the LXX. Eusebius did not know Hebrew.

47. "'Ἐγὼ δὲ μηδ' ἐμβλέπειν γυναῖκα μετ' ἐπιθυμίας ἀκολάστου τοὺς ἐμοὺς βούλομαι μαθητάς."

48. *Sic*: a hapax legomenon; no lexica list this variant.

connections, although both words connote prostitution rather than sexual object choice.[49]

The fourth century marks a sort of dividing line between the Greek-oriented period of the Western church and its Latin phase. It was during the fourth century that the Latin versions of the Bible circulating in the West began to be supplanted by the standard edition collected and translated from the Hebrew and Greek by Saint Jerome (383–92). The increasingly concrete division between the Eastern and Western Empire, the decline of familiarity with Greek among the Western aristocracy, theological distinctions between East and West, and a great many other factors combined to incline European Christianity to rely almost exclusively on Latin from the fourth century on, while Greek continued to be the ecclesiastical language of the East. Few of the most prominent Christian writers in the West knew Greek in the fifth century, and even fewer in the sixth.

As a consequence of this change, the precise meanings of unusual Greek words were rapidly lost in the West. Even in the East there had been a decline in precision and usage of terms for sexual activities due to rapidly changing social patterns and increasing public reticence. The word "παι-δοφθορέω," for instance, could have meant only "child molesting" to an Attic speaker but by the second century A.D. was used by some Greek writers as synonymous with homosexual activity.

In the case of translations into Latin, the loss of accuracy was more profound. The word "ἀλογευσάμενοι" ("having lost reason") was widely misunderstood from the fourth century on and translated into Latin as referring to such disparate sins as bestiality, homosexuality, and incest. For a thousand years or more Christians were prosecuted for "sodomy" and bestiality under canons which probably had not even mentioned the former and may not have named the latter for the reasons generally assumed.[50]

---

49. The passage is admittedly strange, since here as elsewhere Chrysostom omits the word "ἀρσενοκοῖται" from its place in 1 Cor. 6:9, in this case mentioning it in the next line in a variant form. It is reasonably clear, however, that "ἡταιρηκώς" and "ἀρσενοκοῖτος" are amplifications of the "μαλακοί" in the sentence preceding ("Καὶ ὁ Παῦλος ἐνταῦθα, Μὴ πλανᾶσθε· οὔτε πόρνοι [τὸν ἤδη καταδικασθέντα πρῶτον τίθησιν], οὔτε μοιχοὶ, οὔτε μαλακοί, οὔτε μέθυσοι, οὔτε λοίδοροι βασιλείαν Θεοῦ κληρονομήσουσι"), since in the sentence where they occur the sense requires that the same list be repeated minus the words "μέθυσοι" and "λοίδοροι"—which are the matters under discussion—and "πόρνοι," which has been parenthetically removed in the previous sentence ("This he places first as having been already condemned"); this leaves only the μοιχοί and the μαλακοί to be compared in gravity of sin with the μέθυσοι and λοίδοροι: "Πολλοὶ τούτου ἐπελάβοντο τοῦ χωρίου, ὡς σφόδρα τραχέος, εἴ γε τὸν μέθυσον καὶ λοίδορον μετὰ τοῦ μοιχοῦ καὶ τοῦ ἡταιρηκότος καὶ τοῦ ἀρσενοκοίτου τίθησι." Since the μοιχοί are specifically mentioned again, the words in question must be an expansion on "μαλακοί."

50. E.g., canons 15–17 of the Council of Ancyra as erroneously interpreted by numerous subsequent Latin councils.

It was also during the fourth century that the word "ἀρσενοκοῖται" became confused and lost its original significance, so that by the sixth century it was used to designate activities as different as child molesting and anal intercourse between husband and wife.[51] To the extent that they concerned themselves with the Greek at all, Latin writers generally accepted Jerome's translation as the best equivalent but attached a wide variety of meanings to the phrase.[52] It manifestly had no bearing on the rise of antigay feeling among Christians in the West. The Carolingian theologian Hincmar of Reims was the first medieval moralist to make use of 1 Corinthians 6:9 in writing about homosexuality, and even he seems to have understood the Vulgate's reference as involving prostitution as well. The passage was not cited again by a major theologian for four centuries.[53] Saint Thomas Aquinas, in the thirteenth century, was the first really influential theologian to use the passage from 1 Corinthians as scriptural basis for hostility to homosexual behavior, and he did so chiefly in a work addressed to the Muslims of Spain.[54]

However modern translators may choose to render the words in question, the historian should not be led to imagine that they played a role in the development of European attitudes toward homosexuality. There is no reason to believe that either "ἀρσενοκοῖται" or "μαλακοί" connoted homosexuality in the time of Paul or for centuries thereafter, and every reason to suppose that, whatever they came to mean, they were not determinative of Christian opinion on the morality of homosexual acts.

51. The homily falsely attributed to Macarius Aegyptus is probably the earliest instance of the use of the word in a context other than prostitution, but since the work is spurious, it is impossible to be certain of its provenance or date (the earliest would be the fourth century). It implies a connection between sodomy and ἀρρενοκοιτία (4.20.22). The change in this instance to "ἀρρενο-" may indicate that the writer had conflated the biblical "ἀρσενοκοῖται" with the more common "ἀρρενομιξία." Cyril of Alexandria also employs this form in the fifth century (PG, 77:981; or Aubert Cyrilli opera, "Homiliae diversae" 14.5.414), whereas Theodoret, quoting from 1 Cor. 6:9 in the same century, uses the older form, "ἀρσενοκοῖται" (Historia ecclesiastica 4.20 [PG, 82:1169]). In the sixth century it is used in authentic works by Malalas, who employs it to describe illicit relations with boys on the part of bishops (PG, 97:644); and it occurs in a work attributed to Joannes Jejunator (d. 596) which provides clearer context than any other ancient text, at least in regard to the genders of the parties involved: "Τὸ μέντοι τῆς ἀρσενοκοιτίας μύσος πολλοὶ καὶ μετὰ τῶν γυναικῶν αὐτῶν ἐκτελοῦσιν" (PG, 88:1895). Note that insistence that "ἀρσενοκοῖται" means "homosexual" results in a totally nonsensical reading of this sentence: "And many even practice the vice of homosexuality with their wives." See app. 2, p. 364 below.

52. For a ninth-century Greek-Latin glossary which includes "ἀρσενοκοίτης" [sic: although this form does not occur in the NT], see M. E. Miller, "Glossaire grec-latin de la Bibliothèque de Laon," Notices et extraits des manuscrits de la Bibliothèque nationale 29, no. 2 (1880): 64.

53. Peter Damian cited 1 Tim. 1:10 but not 1 Cor. in his Liber Gomorrhianus 4 (PL, 145:165), but as noted, this work had little effect.

54. Summa contra gentiles 3.122. Cf. p. 328, n. 90 above.

Appendix
2   Texts and Translations

Clement of Alexandria (d. ca. 215)
Paedagogus 2.10

The end [of marriage] is good breeding of children [εὐτεκνία], just as the reason for the farmer's scattering seed is the provision of nourishment, since the purpose of a man of agriculture is the gathering of fruits. . . . All land is not suitable for cultivation, and even if it were, it would not all be for the same farmer. For there can be no sowing upon rocks, nor should seed be wasted,[1] since it is the source of generation and comprises both the substance

---

1. "Καθυβριστέον," a pun on various senses of "ὕβρις" and its derivatives. This passage is filled with paranomastic device, very little of which is translatable.

355

of procreation and the design of nature. It is surely impious for the natural [κατὰ φύσιν] designs to be irrationally perverted into customs which are not natural [παρὰ φύσιν]. Consider, for instance, how the all-wise Moses somewhat symbolically repudiated fruitless sowing, saying, "You shall not eat the hare or the hyena." For he did not wish men to partake of the qualities of these or to taste such wickedness themselves, since these animals are quite[2] obsessed with sexual intercourse.

The hare, for example, is said to grow a new anus each year [see Barnabas 10; Pliny 8.55; etc.], so that he has the same number of openings as the number of years he has lived. Hence the prohibition against eating the hare represents a rejection of pederasty. The hyena, on the other hand, is alternately male and female in succeeding years—by which [Moses] suggests that those who abstain from the hyena will not be very prone to adultery.[3] While I agree that the all-wise Moses meant that we should not become like these animals on account of the prohibition laid equally against them, I do not concur with the interpretation of those who treat them symbolically.[4]

Nature is never constrained to change, and that which is once formed cannot simply will to reverse itself wrongly, since desire is not nature. Desire can alter the character of something already formed, but it cannot remake its nature. It is true that many birds change with the seasons both their colors and their voices, as, for instance, the blackbird is said to change from white to a gold color and to a strident from a soft voice, and as the nightingale changes its color and its song with the seasons. But they cannot change a whit of their actual nature. . . . Nor can it be believed that the hyena ever changes its nature or that the same animal has at the same time both types of genitalia, those of the male and the female, as some have thought, telling of marvelous hermaphrodites and creating a whole new type—a third sex, the androgyne, in between a male and a female. They are certainly wrong not to take into account how devoted nature is to children, being the mother and begetter of all things.

Since this animal [the hyena] is extremely lewd, it has grown under its tail in front of the passage for excrement a certain fleshy appendage, in form very like the female genitalia.[5] This design of the flesh has no passage leading to any useful part, I say, either to the womb or to the rectum. It has, rather, only a great cavity, whence it derives its fruitless lust, since the passages

2. There is a pun here, almost certainly intentional, on the double sense of the word "κόρος" in "κατακόρως," "extremely." "Κόρος" means "boy" as well as "surfeit."

3. "Adultery" ("μοιχεία") here probably has a broader sense than its modern English connotations: see chap. 4 and app. 1. It is nonetheless distinct from "πορνεία" (extreme or mercenary promiscuity) here as elsewhere in the literature of this period.

4. I.e., Barnabas and his followers.

5. Cf. Aristotle *Historia animalium* 6.32.

intended for the procreation of the fetus are inverted. This same thing occurs in the case of both the male hyena and the female, because of their exceptional passivity. The males mount each other, so it is extremely rare for them to seek a female. Nor is conception frequent for this animal, since unnatural insemination is so common among them. It seems to me on this account that Plato in the *Phaedrus* deprecates pederasty, calling it "bestial," because those who give themselves up to [this] pleasure "take the bit" and copulate in the manner of quadrupeds, striving to beget children [thus].[6] "The ungodly, moreover," as the Apostle says [Rom. 1:26–27], "he gave up unto vile affections: for even their women did change the natural use into that which is against nature; and likewise also the men, leaving the natural use of the woman, burned in their lust one toward another, men with men working that which is unseemly and receiving in themselves that recompense of their error which was meet."

Nor did nature concede to these very libidinous animals [the right] to mount the passage for waste matter. Urine flows to the bladder, undigested food to the stomach, tears to the eyes, blood to the veins, earwax to the ears; mucus is carried to the nostrils. And there is a fundament placed next to the end of the intestine through which excess material is carried away. Only in the case of the hyena has nature devised this superfluous part for their excessive[7] copulations, and it is consequently hollow, up to a point, for the use of the libidinous parts; but for the same reason the hollow is a blind alley, since it was not designed for procreation. It is manifestly clear to us from this that physical relations between males [ἀρρενομιξίας], fruitless sowings, coitus from the rear [τὰς κατόπιν εὐνάς], and incomplete, androgynous unions [τὰς ἀσυμφυεῖς ἀνδρογύνους κοινωνίας] all ought to be avoided; and nature herself should, rather, be obeyed, who discourages [such things] through an arrangement of the parts which makes the male not for receiving the seed but for sowing it.

When Jeremiah—or the Spirit speaking through him—used to say, "The cave of the hyena has become my home" [Jer. 12:9; cf. 7:11], loathing the food of the dead bodies, he was referring in a subtle parable to idolatry; for the house of the Lord should truly be free of idols. Again, Moses forbade eating the hare because the hare copulates in every season and does so from the rear, with the female consenting. That is, it is one of those animals which mount from the rear. [The female] conceives monthly and gives birth, copulates and begets children, and as soon as she has given birth, she is immediately mounted by any nearby hare (for they do not limit themselves to one mate), conceives again, and gives birth yet again.

6. Or, "and they try to inseminate children."
7. "Πέριττος"; the same word is used for the preceding "superfluous."

She has in fact a double womb, and it is not enough for only one of the cavities of the womb to be stimulated by intercourse, since every vacuum seeks to be filled; it happens that when they are pregnant the other part of the womb is seized with desire and becomes passionate. Hence they are constantly pregnant. The point of this parable is to advise abstinence from excessive desire, mutual intercourse [ἐπαλλήλων συνουσιῶν], relations with pregnant women, reversal of roles in intercourse [ἀλληλοβασίας],[8] corrupting boys, adultery, and lewdness. Moreover, Moses himself prohibited [these] quite plainly, dispensing with metaphor and putting a bare face on it: "You shall not fornicate; you shall not commit adultery; you shall not corrupt boys."[9] The decree of the Word must be observed by everyone, and no part of it may ever be violated; nor can the Commandments be undermined.

The name for an evil desire is *hybris* [ὕβρις],[10] and Plato called the steed of evil desire *hybriste* [ὑβριστήν; *Phaedrus* 254C] when he read, "You have become to me as stallions obsessed with females" [Jer. 5:8].[11] The angels who came to Sodom make known to us the punishment attendant upon *hybris*. For they burned those who were trying to dishonor them right there in the city, demonstrating with a clear sign that this—the fire—is the fruit of lust [cf. 3.8 (PG, 8:616)]. The experiences of those before us, as I said above, have been recorded for our instruction, so that we may not be corrupted by the same things but may, rather, guard against falling into equal [sins]. For young men must be viewed as sons and the wives of others protected as if they were one's own daughters.

The greatest government is the ruling of the passions and the control of the womb and the things yet within it. For if reason does not permit a wise man to move even his finger randomly, as the Stoics assert, how much more ought the sexual part to be controlled by those in pursuit of wisdom? This is the reason, it seems to me, that it is called "the private," because it is essential to use this part of the body with more modesty than any other part. For nature allows us the enjoyment of lawful unions just as of foods, insofar as [such enjoyment] is appropriate, useful, and decent; that is, it permits a desire for procreation. But those who pursue excess fall into that which is

8. This and "mutual intercourse" seem to be reflections of Clement's disgust at the idea of a woman taking an active role in heterosexual intercourse.

9. Only the second of these is actually from Exodus (20:14), despite le Nourry's misleading citation in the PG edition. The third is pure invention on Clement's part. Παιδοφθορία is not mentioned in either the Old or New Testament.

10. Another pun on "ὕβρις," which referred to rape in its original Attic sense—a meaning it retains here initially in the discussion of Sodom—but which Clement extends to all nonprocreative sexuality by analogy with "useless" ("καθυβριστέον") seed.

11. Clement believed that Plato had read the OT; see p. 140 above.

unnatural,[12] harming themselves with unlawful intercourse [cf. Rom. 1:27].

But the best course of all is never to have sexual intercourse with boys as one would with a woman. On account of this the Philosopher, [instructed] by Moses, says,[13] "Do not inseminate rocks and stones, since a fruitful nature is not obtainable from their roots." Moreover, the Word has commanded as clearly as possible through Moses [that] "you shall not lie with a man as with a woman. It is an abomination."[14] He adds, "Also abstain from every female field" which is not your own. The good Plato, culling the Holy Scriptures and inferring from them what is lawful, has advised, "Thou shalt not lie carnally with thy neighbor's wife, to defile thyself with her."[15] For the sowings of concubinage are illegitimate and adulterous. Sow not where you do not desire to reap, nor touch anyone at all besides your own wife,[16] with whom alone it is licit for you to enjoy the pleasures of the flesh for legitimate succession. These things alone are lawful according to the Word. . . .[17]

Saint John Chrysostom (d. 407)
Commentary on Romans, Homily 4
(*In Epistolam ad Romanos*)

For this cause God gave them up unto vile affections: for even their women did change the natural use into that which is against nature: and likewise

12. "Πταίουσι περὶ τὸ κατὰ φύσιν." One would normally read this "They fall into the *natural*," especially as Clement himself used "τὸ κατὰ φύσιν" only shortly before this to mean "the natural" as opposed to "the unnatural." Possibly it retains this meaning here, in which case either (a) "περί" should be taken as "outside" or "beyond" (a somewhat unusual reading, which would render the phrase "they fall outside the natural"); or (b) Clement uses "natural" in two inconsistent senses, one positive and one negative. Obviously the "natural" arrangement of the hyena's sexual apparatus as he understands it is deplorable, so this is not inconceivable.

13. Plato *Laws* 8.912; cf. discussion in chap. 1.

14. Lev. 18:22. The succeeding quotation ("Also abstain . . .") is a paraphrase of the *Laws* of Plato and does not occur in the Bible.

15. Lev. 18:20, KJV. The LXX has, literally, "You will not give to your neighbor's wife the intercourse of your seed, to defile yourself with her," which might be taken as a somewhat narrower proscription (i.e., only against illegitimacy, not against all extramarital erotic pleasure). Cf. the JB: "You must not give your marriage bed to your neighbor's wife; you would thereby become unclean." Clement cites the Greek text incorrectly, reading "σπέρματος, τοῦ ἐκμιανθῆναι" for "σπέρματός σου ἐκμιανθῆναι."

16. Note that here and throughout this treatise Clement assumes that the males to whom he writes are married.

17. Text in PG, 8:497–505. A nineteenth-century translation of this work in vol. 2 of *The Ante-Nicene Fathers*, ed. Alexander Roberts and James Donaldson (Edinburgh, 1885), was bowdlerized by translating into Latin the passages dealing overtly with homosexuality; the translation by Simon Wood, *Christ the Educator*, in vol. 23 of the series The Fathers of the Church (New York, 1954), is very much better. For a discussion of this document, see esp. pp. 139–40 above.

also the men, leaving the natural use of the woman, burned in their lust one toward another [Rom. 1:26–27, KJV].

The passions in fact are all dishonorable, since the soul is more damaged and degraded by sins than the body is by illness, but the worst of all is a mania for males.[18] Notice how in this passage [Paul] deprives them of any excuse, as he did in the case of their beliefs, observing of their women that they "did change the natural use." No one can claim, he points out, that she came to this because she was precluded from lawful intercourse or that because she was unable to satisfy her desire she fell into this monstrous depravity. Only those possessing something can change it, which is what he says in his comments on their beliefs: "They have *changed* the truth of God into falsehood."

Again, he points out the same thing about the men, in a different way, saying they "left the natural use of the woman." Likewise he casts aside with these words every excuse, charging that they not only had [legitimate] enjoyment and abandoned it, going after a different one, but that spurning the natural, they pursued the unnatural.

Sins against nature, however, are more difficult and less rewarding, so much so that they cannot even claim to provide pleasure, since real pleasure is only in accordance with nature. But when God has abandoned someone, everything is inverted. Because of this, not only were their beliefs satanic, but even their lives were diabolical. When, therefore, he referred to their beliefs, he pointed to the physical world and the human mind, saying that with the judgment given them by God they could have been led by the hand to the Creator by the visible world, but since they refused, they were unpardonable. Here before the world, moreover, he has put legitimate pleasure, which they could have enjoyed freely and with more sense and thus have been freed from shame. But they refused and for this reason are excluded from any pardon, since they have outraged nature herself. And it is even more shameful that the women should seek this type of intercourse, since they ought to have more modesty than men. . . . Having first discoursed on women, he goes on to the men, saying, "Likewise also the men, leaving the natural use of the woman." This is the sign of ultimate depravity, when both sexes are corrupted, and the one designed to be the teacher of the woman and the one called to become the helpmate of the man both behave toward each other as enemies. Notice how emphatically he phrases his comments. He says

18. This awkward phrase ("ἡ κατὰ τῶν ἀρρένων μανία") could mean "frenzy against males" but is apparently Chrysostom's effort to cope with the absence in Greek of a term corresponding to "homosexual behavior"; he obviously intends it to refer to relations between women as well, although at the literal level it would necessarily describe heterosexual women.

not that they had fallen in love [ἠράσθησαν] and were drawn to each other by passion but that they "burned in their lust for each other." You can see [or, "Do you see"] that all such desire stems from a greed which will not remain within its usual bounds.

People who transgress the laws established by God desire bizarre things rather than what is lawful, just as sometimes some people, abandoning desire for foodstuffs, desire earth and small stones, and others, seized by extreme thirst, have sometimes even desired mud. Just so, these people are driven to this illicit passion. You ask, "Where does this excess of desire come from?" From the sin of those who abandon Him: "men doing unseemly things with other men."

II. . . . In ancient times this practice appears to have been the law, and one legislator forbade household slaves to use unguents or to love boys, conceding this prerogative—or, rather, vice—only to the freeborn.[19] But then they regarded the matter not as a vice but as something honorable, to be restricted to the free citizenry as being too good for household slaves. This was the attitude of the wisest of peoples, the Athenians, and of their hero Solon. And one could find many other works of the philosophers full of this evil. We should, however, not say that because of this the action is lawful but, rather, that those who accepted such a law are pitiable and worthy of compassion [literally, "many tears"]. . . . For I tell you that such people are even worse than murderers, and it would be better to die than to live dishonored in this way. The murderer only separates soul from body, but these people destroy the soul within the body. Whatever sin you mention, you will not name one which is the equal of this. And if those who suffer it really perceived what was being done to them, they would rather die a thousand deaths than undergo this.

III. There is nothing, absolutely nothing more demented or noxious than this wickedness. If in speaking of fornication Paul said, "Every sin which man commits is outside the body, but when someone fornicates he sins against his own body" [1 Cor. 6:18], what shall we say of this insanity, which is inexpressibly worse than fornication? For I maintain that not only are you made [by it] into a woman, but you also cease to be a man; yet neither are you changed into that nature, nor do you retain the one you had. You become the betrayer of both and are worthy of being driven out and stoned by both men and women, since you have wrought injury upon both sexes. Just to demonstrate my point, suppose that someone came up to you and offered to change you from a man into a dog. Would you not try to get away from such a degenerate? Yet [by this sin] you have changed yourselves

19. See *In Epistolam ad Titum* 3.5.4 (PG, 62:693).

from men not into dogs but into a much more loathsome animal than this. A dog, at least, is useful, but a male prostitute [ἡταιρηκώς]²⁰ is good for nothing.

What, I ask [literally, "tell me"], if someone threatened to force men to carry and give birth to children? Would we not be filled with rage? But note that those who rave after these things are already doing even worse things to themselves: for it is not the same thing to be changed into the nature of a woman as it is to become a woman while yet remaining a man or, rather, to be neither one nor the other.²¹

Saint John Chrysostom
Against the Opponents of the Monastic Life 3
(Adversus oppugnatores vitae monasticae)

What then is this evil? A certain new and illicit love has entered our lives, an ugly and incurable disease has appeared, the most severe of all plagues has been hurled down, a new and insufferable crime has been devised. Not only are the laws established [by man] overthrown but even those of nature herself. Fornication will now seem a small matter in the reckoning of sexual sins, and just as the arrival of a more burdensome pain eclipses the discomfort of an earlier one, so the extremity of this outrage [ὕβρεως] causes lewdness with women, which had been intolerable, to seem so no longer. Indeed to be able to escape these snares [in any way] seems desirable, and there is some danger that womankind will become in the future unnecessary, with young men instead fulfilling all the needs women used to.

And this is not even the worst, which is that this outrage is perpetrated with the utmost openness, and lawlessness has become law. For no one fears, no one any longer shudders. No one is ashamed, no one blushes, but, rather, they take pride in their little joke; the chaste seem to be the ones who are unbalanced, and the disapproving the ones in error. If [the chaste or disapproving] happen to be insignificant, they are beaten up; if they are powerful, they are mocked, laughed at, refuted with a thousand arguments. The courts are powerless, the laws,²² instructors, parents, friends, teachers—all are helpless. Some are corrupted with money, and some are only out to get what they can for themselves. As for those more honorable, who have

---

20. The introduction of the idea of prostitution into a discussion of ostensibly non-mercenary sexual relations is not at all unusual, in either ancient or modern sexual diatribes, and does not suggest any unusual meaning of "ἡταιρηκώς."

21. See pp. 156–57 above. Text in PG, 60:417–22. A somewhat stilted nineteenth-century translation is available in vol. 11 of The Nicene and Post-Nicene Fathers, 1st ser., The Homilies of Saint John Chrysostom (Oxford, 1841).

22. Chrysostom is probably referring to laws protecting minors.

some concern for the welfare of those entrusted to them, they are easily fooled and gotten around, for they fear the power of the debauched.

It would be easier, in fact, to escape a suspicion of tyranny than to get free from their clutches after having tried to save anyone from these disgusting activities. Right in the middle of cities men do these unseemly things to each other, just as if they were in a vast desert. Even if some escape these snares, they will be hard put to avoid the evil reputation of those who revel in such vices, first of all because they are very few and might easily be lost in the great throng of the wicked. . . .

There is among some animals a powerful sex drive [οἶστρος], an irresistible urge no different from madness. Even so, they do not experience this type of love but remain within the bounds of nature. Although roused ten thousand times, they never transgress the laws of nature. But seemingly rational humans, the beneficiaries of godly learning, those who instruct others in what should and should not be done, those who have heard the Scriptures brought down from heaven—these do not consort with prostitutes as fearlessly as they do with young men. Just as if they were not men, as if God's justice did not wait, as if there were no final judgment, as if darkness covered all and no one could see or hear such things, they dare all this with absolute frenzy. The parents of the abused youths[23] bear this in silence and neither sequester their sons nor seek any remedy for the evil.[24]

John the Faster (?) (d. 595)
Penitential

The priest stands by [the penitent's] side and questions him as cheerfully and kindly as possible, and if he can, he kisses him and puts the penitent's arms around him, especially if he sees that he is overcome with grief and shame, which might wrongly dominate his thoughts, and he speaks to him in a soft and serene voice:

"In what way, my brother, did you first lose your virginity? By fornication, lawful wedlock, masturbation [μαλακία], or one of those sins which are against nature [παρὰ φύσιν]?" When he has confessed and said thus and such, [the priest] questions him further: How many women had he had when he was married, and how many of these were slaves, how many were widows, how many were married, how many were nuns—for some who wear

23. "Ὑβριζομένων παίδων." This whole passage does seem to be concerned with the seduction of boys, although the sense of "παῖς," as noted above, must be viewed with caution.

24. See pp. 131–32 above. Text in PG, 47:360–62. A Latin translation accompanies the Greek text, and there are two French versions, one in *Saint Jean Chrysostome: œuvres complètes*, ed. M. Jeannin (Bar-le-Duc, 1874), vol. 2, and one by P. E. Legrand, *Saint Jean Chrysostome: contre les détracteurs de la vie monastique* (Paris, 1933).

the habit indulge in such things—and so forth. It is a small matter if the women were whores [πόρναι] but a great one if they were married. . . . Before all else the number of persons should be ascertained, and the types of person. There are six types: it is one penance if they were slaves, another if freeborn; one if they were whores, another if virgins; one thing if they were widows, another if married; one thing if they were nuns, and another if they were married to priests.

Likewise one must inquire about ἀρσενοκοιτία,[25] of which there are three varieties. For it is one thing to get it from someone, which is the least serious; another to do it to someone else, which is more serious than having it done to you; another to do it to someone and have it done to you, which is more serious than either of the other two. For to be passive only, or active only, is not so grave as to be both. One must inquire into which of these [practices] the penitent has fallen, and how often, and for how long, and if it happened before marriage or after, if before the age of thirty or after.

It must be ascertained further whether he has penetrated an animal, of which sin there is only grade.

Likewise there are two types of masturbation [μαλακία]: one wherein he is aroused by his own hand and another by someone else's hand, which is unfortuate, since what the parties begin by themselves ends up also harming others to whom they teach the sin.

One must also ask about the perplexing, beguiling [πολυμαγγάνου], and shadowy sin of incest, of which there are not just one or two varieties but a great many very different ones. One type is committed with two sisters of the same father or mother (or both). Another involves a cousin; another the daughter of a cousin; another the wife of one's son; another the wife of one's brother. It is one thing with a mother-in-law or the sister of a mother-in-law, another with a stepmother or a father's concubine. Some even do it with their own mothers, and others with foster sisters or goddaughters. In fact, many men even commit the sin of ἀρσενοκοιτία with their wives.[26]

25. Apparently this word is here used to mean "anal intercourse," but as this is an impossible construction of its constituent parts and as its meaning is of some importance, I have refrained from translating it and left it to the reader to infer its exact sense from the context. That it does not refer to homosexual activity generically is obvious from the facts that (a) other types of homosexual activity—e.g., mutual masturbation and the seduction of boys—are discussed separately, and (b) the same word is used subsequently to refer to relations between husband and wife.

26. "Τὸ μέντοι τῆς ἀρσενοκοιτίας μῦσος πολλοὶ καὶ μετὰ τῶν γυναικῶν αὐτῶν ἐκτελοῦσιν." This sentence would seem to preclude absolutely interpreting this word as referring to homosexual intercourse. Preconception can, however, triumph over deduction, as is evident in the nonsensical rendering of the phrase into Latin in the PG volume: "Scelus quidem masculorum concubitus multi etiam cum mulieribus ipsis perficiunt" ("Many men even commit the sin of sleeping with men with their own wives").

[The priest] should also inquire in this way about murder, voluntary or involuntary, and then about whether [the penitent] has injured his parents, either physically or with harsh words, and whether he has taken communion after eating or drinking, has defiled himself during Lent, or has received communion indifferently after having sex with a woman. Has he contracted a secret marriage or indulged in kissing and fondling without going all the way?[27] Has he seduced a boy [ἐπαιδοφθόρησεν], prevented someone from receiving his pay, spoken against someone, or injured someone wrongly? Has he eaten blood, or something strangled, something killed by an animal [Lev. 5:2], a carcass [Lev. 11:8], or something slain by birds? Or has he been involved with divination, magic, or potions . . . ?[28]

Pope Saint Leo IX
We More Humanely (*Nos humanius agentes*, 1051)
Response to Saint Peter Damian's *Liber Gomorrhianus*

The book which you have published, my son, against the fourfold pollution of carnal contagion, frank in style and even more direct in reasoning, provides indisputable evidence of the intention of your mind to enter the holy fray on the side of the splendid might of shining modesty. You have indeed smitten wantonness of the flesh by thus striking with the arm of the spirit against obscene desire, clearly delineating the execrable vice by the authority of virtue, which, since it is itself immaculate, allows no uncleanness. Nor could it ever be the sort of thing which would lend itself to sordid vanities. Indeed these clerics concerning whose disgusting lives your wisdom has discoursed mournfully, fairly, and reasonably are rightly—altogether rightly—excluded from [literally, "do not belong to"] the bond of its inheritance, from which they have cut themselves off with voluptuous pleasures. Because if they lived chastely, they might be called not only the holy temple of God but also the sanctuary, in which the Lamb of God is sacrificed in shining glory, through whom the horrid filth of the whole world is cleansed. Such clerics of course reveal by the testimony of their deeds, if not

27. Or, "not finishing the job": "τὸ δὲ ἔργον οὐκ ἐτέλεσε."

28. See pp. 107, 353 above for discussion. This penitential, one of the earliest in Greek, has traditionally been ascribed to John the Faster ("Jejunator"), patriarch of Constantinople from A.D. 582 to 595, whose name appears on several manuscripts of the work. Although this attribution is vigorously contested (not without reason), no resolution of the issue has been possible, and scholarly opinion on the subject ranges from acceptance of John's authorship to a belief in composition as late as the tenth century. A complex summary of the various points of view may be found in Emilio Herman, "Il più antico penitenziale greco," *Orientalia Christiana periodica* 19 (1953): 71–127. For the text as cited, see PG, 88:1893–96. There is no English translation, and the Latin provided in the PG edition is particularly loose and misleading.

their words, that they are not what they are thought to be. For how could anyone be or even be called a cleric when he has not feared to do evil through his own will?

About these things, since you have written what seemed best to you, moved by holy indignation, it is appropriate that as you wish, we interpose our apostolic authority, so that we may remove any scrupulous doubt among those reading [this], and that it may be clear to all that the things contained in this little book, like water thrown on the fires of hell, have met with our approval. Therefore, lest the unpunished license of filthy desire should spread, it is essential to combat [it] with appropriate measures of apostolic severity and moreover to give some evidence of strictness.

Even though all those polluted by the filth of any of the four types [of this sin] mentioned are excluded from all rank in the spotless church by the just censure of equity—both that of sacred councils and by our own judgment—yet we, acting more humanely, desire and ordain that those who elicited their seed either with their own hands or mutually with someone else, and even those who spilled it interfemorally, if it was not a long-standing practice or performed with many men and if they have restrained their desires and atoned for these shameful sins with a suitable penance, should be admitted to the same rank which they held while in sin (though they must no longer remain so), trusting in divine mercy. But there may be no hope of recovering their rank for those who are tainted with either of the two types of sin you have described—alone or with others—for a long time or with many men even for a short time, or—what is horrible to mention as well as to hear—who have fallen into the last category.[29]

If anyone shall dare to criticize or question this decree of apostolic direction, let him know that he is himself acting in peril of his rank. For he who does not attack vice encourages it; such a one is rightly accounted guilty [and worthy] of the [same] end as he who perishes through sin.

But, beloved son, I rejoice inexpressibly that you demonstrate with the example of your life just what you have taught with the gift of your words. For it is greater to instruct by deed than by word. Wherefore, God willing, you shall earn the branch of victory and rejoice with the Son of God and the Virgin in the abode of heaven, and for every one of that crowd saved by you from the fires of the devil you shall be crowned and rewarded with graces.[30]

29. Or, "who have moved on to the rear"—a more literal reading of the words "in terga praelapsi sunt"—but this seems inconsistent with the euphemistic terminology which otherwise characterizes the epistle.

30. See pp. 211–12 above. Text in Mansi, 19:685–86. The ponderous complexity of the Latin text, characteristic of official papal letters, is reflected in the somewhat awkward translation.

Spurious Letter of Alexius Comnenus to Count Robert of Flanders Imploring His Aid against the Turks
(Late Eleventh–Early Twelfth Century)

To the noble and glorious Count Robert of Flanders and to all rulers of all realms, both lay and clerical, who are devoted to the Christian faith, the emperor of Constantinople sends greetings and peace in Our Lord Jesus Christ and His Father and the Holy Spirit.

O incomparable count, great defender of the faith, it is my desire to bring to your attention the extent to which the most holy empire of the Christian Greeks is fiercely beset every day by the Pincinnatti [Patzinaks?] and Turks, and how it is ceaselessly preyed upon and despoiled, and how massacres and unspeakable murders and outrages against Christians are perpetrated. But since the evils committed are so many and, as we said, so unspeakable, we shall mention but a few, which are nevertheless horrible to hear and disturb the very air [in which they are spoken].

For they circumcise Christian boys and youths over the baptismal fonts of Christian [churches] and spill the blood of circumcision right into the baptismal fonts and compel them to urinate over them, afterward leading them violently around the church and forcing them to blaspheme the name of the Holy Trinity. Those who are unwilling they torture in various ways and finally murder. When they capture noble women and their daughters, they abuse them sexually in turns, like animals. Some, while they are wickedly defiling the maidens, place the mothers facing, constraining them to sing evil and lewd songs while they work their evil. We read of a similar act perpetrated in ancient times against the people of God, whom they mocked after humiliating them in various ways by demanding, "Sing us one of the songs of Sion!" [Ps. 136:3, Vulgate].

Likewise, while defiling the daughters, they compel the mothers to sing wicked songs; the mothers' voices must, we imagine, produce more laments than songs, as it is written regarding the death of the holy innocents: "In Rama was there a voice heard, lamentation, and weeping, and great mourning, Rachel weeping for her children, and would not be comforted, because they are not" [Matt. 2:18]. The mothers of the innocents represented by the figure of Rachel could not be consoled for the death of their children, but they take consolation regarding the salvation of their souls. These mothers, however, so much the worse, have no consolation whatever, since [their daughters] perish in both body and soul.[31]

---

31. The text has "animalibus" for "animabus."

But what next? We pass on to worse yet. They have degraded by sodomizing them men of every age and rank—boys, adolescents, young men, old men, nobles, servants, and, what is worse and more wicked, clerics and monks, and even—alas and for shame! something which from the beginning of time has never been spoken or heard of—bishops! They have already killed one bishop with this nefarious sin.

They have polluted and ruined the holy places in innumerable ways and threaten even worse things. In the face of all this, who would not weep—Who would not be moved? Who would not shudder? Who would not pray? Nearly the entire territory from Jerusalem to Greece, and all of Greece with its upper regions (Cappadocia the Greater and Lesser, Phrygia and Bithynia and Phrygia the Lesser),[32] and many other areas as far as Thrace—too many to mention here—have all been invaded by them, and hardly anything remains except Constantinople, which they threaten soon to take from us unless we are speedily relieved by the help of God and the faithful Latin Christians. They have even invaded the Propontis [Sea of Marmora] (which is also called Aridus and runs from the Black Sea next to Constantinople itself into the Mediterranean) with 200 ships which captured Greeks made for them and oarsmen they shanghaied, and they threaten to take Constantinople, as we said, at any moment either by land or from the Propontis itself.

These few among countless evils wrought by this most impious race we have mentioned and written down for you, the count of Flanders and a lover of the Christian faith. The rest we pass over as too unpleasant to be read. For the sake of the name of God and the piety of all those who uphold the Christian faith, we therefore implore you to lead here to help us and all Greek Christians every faithful soldier of Christ you can obtain in your lands, great, small, or middling, that they might struggle for the salvation of their souls to free the kingdom of the Greeks, just as in past years[33] they have liberated, to some extent, Galicia and other western kingdoms from the yoke of the unbelievers. For although I am emperor, no remedy remains to me, nor do I know where to turn next, but I am, rather, constantly fleeing from the Turks and Pinemaci [sic: Patzinaks?] and am reduced to waiting in a single city for their imminent arrival. And since I prefer to be subject to you, the Latins, rather than have Constantinople taken by them, you should fight courageously and with all your strength so that you might receive in bliss a glorious and indescribable reward in heaven. It is better that you should have

32. I.e., Troy, Pontus, Galatia, Libya, Pamphylia, Isauria, Lycia, and the major islands of Chios and Militina.

33. Or perhaps, "last year."

Constantinople than the pagans, since in it are preserved the most precious remains of the Lord: the pillar to which He was bound, the whip with which He was flogged, the scarlet robe with which He was clothed, the crown of thorns with which He was crowned, the reed He held in His hands instead of a scepter, the robe taken from Him at the cross, the greater part of the wood of the cross on which He was crucified, the nails used to crucify Him, the linens found in the sepulcher after the resurrection, the twelve baskets of the crumbs of the five loaves and two fishes, the head of Saint John the Baptist with the hair and beard intact, the remains of bodies of many of the innocents, of several prophets, of apostles, of martyrs (most notably that of Saint Stephen, the first martyr), and confessors and virgins, too many to be named here individually. All of these things the Christians rather than pagans ought to possess, and it will be a great boon to all Christians if they are kept, but a shame and a judgment on them if they are lost.

If they are unwilling to fight for these, and if they love gold more, they will find in Constantinople more gold than in all the rest of the world. Just the treasures of the churches of Constantinople—silver, gold, precious gems, and silks [i.e., vestments]—would be enough for all the churches of the world, and the treasures of the mother church, Sancta Sophia [Holy Wisdom], are immeasurably greater than all these and can without doubt be compared with the treasure of the temple of Solomon.

And what shall I say of the infinite treasure of the nobles, since no one can even estimate the wealth of the ordinary merchants? What may be found in the treasuries of the previous emperors? I say with certainty that no tongue could describe it, since not only the treasure of the emperors of Constantinople but also that of all the ancient Roman emperors has been brought here and hidden in the palace. What more need I say? What appears openly before the eyes of men is nothing compared with what lies hidden. Hurry, therefore, with all your people and fight with all your strength, lest such treasure fall into the hands of the Turks and Pincinnatti. For they are infinite in number, and 60,000 of them are expected any day, and I fear that soon they may corrupt our greedy soldiers with this great treasure, as Julius Caesar once did when he invaded the kingdom of the Franks through greed. And thus it will happen that the Antichrist will capture the whole world at the end of time.

Act therefore while you have time, lest you lose the kingdom of the Christians and, what is worse, the sepulcher of the Lord, and so that you may earn a reward rather than a punishment hereafter. Amen.[34]

---

34. Translated from PG, 131:565–68. See pp. 279–80 above.

Marbod, Bishop of Rennes (d. 1123)
Poems

An Argument against Romance

A rare face, perfectly hued:
Whiter than snow, pinker than blushing roses in spring;
A heavenly glance, a smile promising sweetness;
Flame red offerings of full lips;
Shining white teeth in perfect array;
Limbs with strength, charming manners without pretense—
All these the girl possesses who yearns to unite herself to me;
And that spectacular youth, whose beauty is my fire,
Loves her, catches her, does everything to please her.
But she spurns him and wants me; she orders me to love her,
Entreats me, and all but dies when I refuse.

To His Absent Lover

If there is something you love in the city you inhabit, something you do not
    wish to lose,
And if you love it truly, stop worrying about the court.
End all delays. Your fault increases by the hour.
And this fault, being irreparable, is grave.
Put aside everything which keeps you in Calonne [?]—
You are losing more in this city than you are gaining in that one.
What can there be of as much value as a boy faithful to his lover?
[But] any more delay, and he who is now loyal may become unfaithful,
Since he is being tempted even now with much flattery—
And when someone is tempted, there is reason to fear he may fall.
Hurry back if you want to keep what you love.
Abandon the castle if you want to hold on to the city [?].[35]

The Unyielding Youth

Horace composed an ode about a certain boy
Whose face was so lovely he could easily have been a girl,

---

35. The text reads, "Desine castellum, si vis retinere citellum." There are no English
translations of Marbod's poetry, nor is there a critical edition. The three poems translated
here are taken from PL, 171:1635, 1717–18. See pp. 247–49 above.

Whose hair fell in waves against his ivory neck,
Whose forehead was white as snow and his eyes as black as pitch,
Whose soft cheeks were full of delicious sweetness
When they bloomed in the brightness of a blush of beauty.
His nose was perfect, his lips flame red, lovely his teeth—
An exterior formed in measure to match his mind.

. . . . .³⁶

This vision of a face, radiant and full of beauty,
Kindled with the torch of love the heart of whoever beheld him.
But this boy, so lovely and appealing,
A torment to all who looked upon him,
Was made by nature so cruel and unyielding
That he would die rather than yield to love.
Harsh and ungrateful, as if born of a tiger,
He only laughed at the soft words of admirers,[37]
Laughed at their vain efforts,
Laughed at the tears of a sighing lover.
He laughed at those whom he himself was causing to perish.
Surely he is wicked, cruel and wicked,
Who by the viciousness of his character denies the beauty of his body.
A fair face should have a wholesome mind,
Patient and not proud but yielding in this or that.[38]
The little flower of age is swift, of surpassing brevity;
Soon it wastes away, vanishes, and cannot be revived.
This flesh so fair, so milky, so flawless,
So healthy, so lovely, so glowing, so soft—
The time will come when it is ugly and rough,
When this youthful skin will become repulsive.
So while you bloom, adopt a more becoming demeanor.[39]

36. Two lines have been omitted here; they are difficult to render satisfactorily in English and add little to the poem.

37. Cf. Dronke, *Medieval Latin*, 2:341, no. 2a, lines 15–20: "Gaudet lamentis, / gaudet querelis, / ridet et ex[an]gues / miseros amantes, / ridet et precordia / trahere suspiria."

38. See Tacitus *Annals* 15.21.4: "Some virtues themselves are hated: the strictness that never relaxes, the strength of soul that never yields to favor."

39. This poem is entitled in the PL edition "Satyra in amatorem puelli sub assumpta persona" ("A satire on the lover of a boy under an assumed identity"), but it does not seem likely that Marbod actually intended to satirize the lover rather than the boy, and no "identity" is assumed. The advice at the end seems rather clearly to represent the sincere opinion of Marbod himself.

Hilary the Englishman
Love Poems
(Twelfth Century)

7. To a Boy of Anjou

Beautiful and singular youth,
Kindly inspect, I implore you,
These writings which are sent by your admirer;
Look at them, read them, and profit by what you read.

Prostrate at your knees,
On bended knee, with clasped hands,
As one of your suppliants,
I spare neither tears nor prayers.

I am afraid to speak face to face;
Speech escapes me, I am held speechless,
So I admit my sickness in writing,
Confident that I shall merit healing.

Enough, wretch! I barely bore it
When I tried to hide my love;
Now that I can no longer dissemble,
I finally extend my hands, bound together.

As a patient I demand a doctor,
Holding out my hands in supplication.
You alone have the only medication;
Therefore save me, your clerk.

Long held in a dreary jail,
I found no one who would have mercy on me;
Since I cannot be set free with a gift,
I must lead a life worse than death.

Oh, how I wish you wanted money!
Mine is the pain! Mine the suffering!
It is ignorant of you[40] to have decided
Such commerce constitutes vice.

---

40. Reading "es nescius" (with Herkenrath) instead of the "sed melius" printed by
Champollion-Figeac.

Surely, youth, this is foolishness,
To be so unyielding,
. . . . .⁴¹

A solemn resolve of chastity
Ruined the fair Hippolytus;⁴²
Joseph nearly met his end
When he spurned the queen's desire.⁴³

9. To an English Boy

Hail, fair youth, who seeks no bribe,
Who regards being won with a gift as the height of vice,
In whom beauty and honesty have made their home,
Whose comeliness draws to itself the eyes of all who see him.

Golden haired, fair of face, with a small white neck,
Soft-spoken and gentle—but why do I praise these singly?
Everything about you is beautiful and lovely; you have no imperfection,
Except that such fairness has no business devoting itself to chastity.⁴⁴

When nature formed you, she doubted for a moment
Whether to offer you as a girl or a boy,
But while she sets her mind's eye to settling this,
Behold! You come forth, born as a vision for all.

Afterward, she does finally extend her hand to you
And is astonished that she could have created anyone like you.
But it is clear that nature erred in only this one thing:
That when she had bestowed on you so much, she made you mortal.

No other mortal can be compared with you,
Whom nature made for herself, as if an only child;
Beauty establishes its home in you,
Whose sweet flesh shines as brightly as the lily.

41. Two lines are omitted here; the first is missing from the manuscript, leaving the next ("Qui sit pulcris ex pudiciciae") ambiguous.

42. The account in Seneca's *Phaedra* might have been familiar to Hilary.

43. Gen. 39:7 ff. Dronke translates this stanza only. The numbers of the poems correspond to the texts in *Hilarii versus et ludi*, ed. Champollion-Figeac, from which the translations were made and which is more faithful to the manuscript than Fuller, who has been criticized for both edition and interpretation. See p. 249 above.

44. For "nequid" I read "nequit," as does Fuller. Trask, translating the line in Curtius, *European Literature*, p. 116, renders it "Save—protesting chastity jars with forms so fair!" He translates only sts. 2 and 6.

Believe me, if those former days of Jove should return,
His handservant would no longer be Ganymede
But you, carried off to heaven; by day the sweet cup
And by night your sweeter kisses you would administer to Jove.

You are the common desire of lasses and lads;
They sigh for you and hope for you, because they know you are unique.
They err or, rather, sin who call you "English":
They should add letters and call you "angelic."[45]

13. To an English Boy

Beautiful boy, flower fair,
Glittering jewel, if only you knew
That the loveliness of your face
Was the torch of my love.

The moment I saw you,
Cupid struck me; but I hesitate,
For my Dido holds me,
And I fear her wrath.[46]

Oh, how happy would I be
If for a new favorite
I could abandon this love[47]
In the ordinary way.

I will win, as I believe,
For I will yield to you in the hunt:
I am the hunted, you are the hunter,
And I yield to any hunter like you.

Even the ruler of heaven,
Once the ravisher of boys,
If he were here now would carry off
Such beauty to his heavenly bower.

Then, in the chambers of heaven,
You would be equally ready for either task:
Sometimes in bed, other times as cupbearer—
And Jove's delight as both.

45. A pun on "anglicus" and "angelicus," doubtless copied from Bede (p. 144 above).
46. This stanza was translated in a footnote to Dronke, p. 218.
47. I.e., if I could leave my "Dido" for you, as other men leave one woman for another. The Latin is tortuous.

Peter Cantor (d. 1192)
On Sodomy
(*De vitio sodomitico*)

The sin of Sodom was "abundance of bread and proudness of life and excess of wine."[48] In condemning this sin[49] the Lord says, "But the men of Sodom were very evil, and sinned greatly before the Lord." And the Lord said, "Because the cry of Sodom and Gomorrah is great, and because their sin is very grievous, I will go down now, and see whether they have done altogether according to the cry of it, which is come unto me" [Gen. 18:20–21, KJV]. The novelty of a sin so great and unheard of evokes astonishment and wonder in the hearer. Whence the Lord is introduced as if marveling and amazed at such a crime, saying, "I will go down and see. . . ."

In fact it seems incredible to me that men could have perpetrated such a crime. A sin "speaks" when it involves an action which is barely noticeable; it "cries out" when it is perpetrated openly with the clear commission of a crime. Of only two sins is it said that their gravity "cries out" to heaven from earth: murder and sodomy. Thus, it is written, the Lord complains that he "created them male and female for the multiplication of men," but murderers and sodomites destroy and slay them as mortal enemies and adversaries of God and the human race, as if to say, "You have created men that they might be multiplied, but we shall strive to undermine and wreck your labor."

Furthermore, when the Lord assigns the punishments to be inflicted for various sins, he seems to abandon his native patience and kindness with this one, not waiting for the Sodomites to come to justice but, rather, punishing them temporally with fire sent from heaven, as he will ultimately exact justice through the fires of hell.

The Lord formed man from the slime of the earth on the plain of Damascus, later fashioning woman from his rib in Eden. Thus in considering the formation of woman, lest any should believe they would be hermaphrodites,[50] he stated, "Male and female created he them," as if to say, "There will not be

48. Ezek. 16:49. I have rendered many of Peter's biblical quotations into English myself, since his passages from the Vulgate often rely on idiosyncrasies of the Latin which do not appear in English translations made from the Hebrew or Greek. In the cases where the KJV conforms to the Latin, I have used it, with the indication [KJV].

49. Presumably homosexuality, although—strikingly—the immediately preceding biblical description of the sins of the Sodomites makes no mention of any sort of sexual behavior.

50. "Androgynos": confusion or conflation of the concepts of and terminology for hermaphroditism and homosexuality is ancient. Although it was to reemerge in the thirteenth and fourteenth centuries as awareness of gay people declined (see, e.g., Dante's portrayal of "sodomites" crying, "Nostro peccato fu ermafrodito" in *Purgatorio* 26.82), this sort of inaccuracy was rare in Peter Cantor's day, when general familiarity with gay people and

intercourse of men with men or women with women, but only of men with women and vice versa." For this reason the church allows a hermaphrodite— that is, someone with the organs of both sexes, capable of either active or passive functions—to use the organ by which (s)he[51] is most aroused or the one to which (s)he is more susceptible.

If (s)he is more active [literally, "lustful"], (s)he may wed as a man, but if (s)he is more passive, (s)he may marry as[52] a woman. If, however, (s)he should fail with one organ, the use of the other can never be permitted, but (s)he must be perpetually celibate to avoid any similarity to the role inversion[53] of sodomy, which is detested by God.

Furthermore, in Romans we read, "Wherefore God gave them over to the desires of their hearts, to uncleanness, so that they might afflict their own bodies with disrespect, in ignominious passions. For their women changed the natural use into that which is unnatural. Likewise the males, abandoning the natural use of the female, burned in their lusts, males doing evil with males, abandoned to reprobate sensibilities, so that they do things which are unbecoming" [paraphrase of Rom. 1:26–27].

Similarly Jude 7: "Even as Sodom and Gomorrah and the cities about them in like manner, giving themselves over to fornication and going after strange flesh," males doing evil with males, women with women.

The flesh of a man and wife is one; so [the sodomites] are made an example, sustaining the penalty of eternal fire in the present. Compare Leviticus 18[:23]:[54] "You shall not lie with a male as with a female, for it

---

lively scientific interest in hermaphrodites enabled even those hostile to both to distinguish between them. Concern over medical aspects of hermaphroditism was common in early medieval Islamic science (see, e.g., Albucasis *On Surgery and Instruments* 70.454–55); Maimonides engaged in elaborate moral speculations on the position and obligations of hermaphrodites: see *The Code of Maimonides, Book 4: The Book of Women*, trans. Isaac Klein, Yale Judaica Series, no. 19 (New Haven, 1972), pp. 13, 14, 26, 303–5, 349, 493. Peter Cantor was, however, one of the few Scholastics to comment on the moral aspects of hermaphroditism as opposed to homosexuality. He apparently assumed that whereas the former was an inculpably experienced "condition," the latter represented willful choice. Such a distinction has been upheld by some modern theologians but would have been rejected by Aquinas, who regarded homosexuality as congenital.

51. "(S)he" is used here to suggest the ambiguity regarding the gender of the hermaphrodite which Peter achieves by using Latin verbs with no expressed pronominal subject. The English translator has no comparable option.

52. Text has "et" for "ut."

53. "Alternitatis": note the similarity to John Chrysostom's horror at sex-role inversion. Although he regards their condition as inculpable, Peter is apparently willing to restrict the sexual expression of the hermaphrodites merely to avoid the semblance of homosexuality.

54. Peter provides chapter references for some of his biblical citations, but no verse numbers (the latter had not been standardized in his day). I have supplied those in brackets; where none is provided, the passage cannot be identified due to Peter's carelessness in transcription.

is an abomination," ignominious and unspeakable. Intercourse with a male incurs the same penalty—death—as intercourse with an animal. Whence Leviticus 20[:13]: "If a man also lie with mankind, as he lieth with a woman, both of them have committed an abomination: they shall surely be put to death; their blood shall be upon them" [kjv].

But how is it that these have fallen into disuse, so that what the Lord punished severely the church leaves untouched, and what he treated lightly she punishes harshly? I fear that one may result from avarice and the other from the coldness of charity. These enemies of man are like Onan, who spilled his seed on the ground, refusing to raise children to his brother, and was struck by God. These, as Isaiah says in Chapter 1 [Isa. 1:9?], are as Sodom and Gomorrah, silent in the praise of God and hardened in the enormity of their sins. Likewise in 1 Timothy 1 and Colossians 3[:5]: "Mortify therefore your members which are upon the earth" [kjv]. And Joshua 6[:26]: "Cursed be the man before the Lord, that riseth up and buildeth this city Jericho: he shall lay the foundation thereof in his firstborn, and in his youngest son shall he set up the gates of it" [kjv]. Much more cursed is he who raises up the sin of Sodom, thus losing the first and last of his children, i.e., faith and humility, even for wickedness.

In his contempt for this sin God even turned against the land, changing the Pentapolis into the Dead Sea, in which no fish can live and upon which no ship bearing humans may sail. In that land there are trees bearing fruit which crumbles at the touch into dust and ashes. For just one look back at Sodom, Lot's wife was changed into earth and a pillar of salt, as if the Lord were saying, "I wish that no memory of this crime should remain, no reminder, no trace of its enormity."

Such men, spastic and feeble, who change themselves from males to females, abusing feminine coitus, are kept as women by the pharaoh for his pleasure. They are imitators of Sardanapalus,[55] a man who was more corrupt than any woman. Jeremiah also, at the end of the Lamentations, adds to his long lament and sorrow over the ruin and captivity of the city a complaint and groan about sodomy, saying, "They abused the young men indecently, and boys have perished on wood."[56] Such men were struck not only dumb but blind knocking on Lot's door at noon, so that seeing, they did not see. So

55. On Sardanapalus, king of Assyria, see Plutarch *Moralia* 336C; Clement of Alexandria *Paedagogus* 3.11, etc.

56. So the Vulgate: "Adolescentibus impudice abusi sunt, et pueri in ligno corruerunt" (Lam. 5:13). The lxx has "'Εκλεκτοὶ κλαυθμὸν ἀνέλαβον καὶ νεανίσκοι ἐν ξύλῳ ἠσθένησαν." "'Εκλεκτοί" is apparently a misreading of the Hebrew "bachūrīm" ("youths") for "bachīrīm" ("elect"). The kjv is more faithful to the Hebrew: "They took the young men to grind, and the children fell under the wood." In the Hebrew and Greek the reference is certainly to some sort of forced labor; only in the Latin is the sexual innuendo possible.

Isaiah 66[:17]:[57] "Those that sanctify themselves and think themselves pure in gardens behind a gate, or inside behind a door. . . ." So Joel 3[:3]: "They have placed a boy [in a brothel]."[58] So also, "When a man marries as a woman, let the laws be armed, let justice come forth."[59]

I Am Already Changing My Mind
(*Iam mutatur animus*, Twelfth or Thirteenth Century)

[A:] Help me, O God the Father,
    For death is near!
    If you grant me tomorrow,
    I will become a monk.

    Hasten to help me!
    Already [death] is trying to take me!
    Grant, O Father, a respite;
    Give me comfort.

[B:] O my beloved,
    Whatever are you thinking of doing?
    Counsel yourself otherwise!
    Do not abandon me!

[A:] Your sorrow, brother,
    Moves me to tears,
    For you will be an orphan
    When I am a monk.

[B:] Remain for a little, then:
    At least until after the next three days.
    Perhaps this danger
    Will not be a mortal one.

[A:] Such is the anguish
    That runs through my veins
    That I have doubts
    There will be any life tomorrow.

57. Peter alters the Vulgate here by inserting the words "vel post ostium" to echo Gen. 19:6. Cf. the KJV.

58. So the Vulgate: "Puerum posuerunt in prostibulo." This is probably not the sense of the Hebrew, but Peter could not have known this.

59. *Verbum abbreviatum* 138, text in PL, 205:333–35. For the last quotation, see chap. 5, pp. 123–24 above.

[B:] Monastic rules
       Are unknown to you:
       They fast every day
       And keep vigil assiduously.

[A:] Those who keep vigil for God
       Are seeking to be crowned.
       He who thirsts after God
       Merits satisfaction.

[B:] The food is awful—
       Beans and vegetables—
       And after such a feast
       There is little to drink.

[A:] What good are banquets
       Or Dionysian revels
       When [after][60] the feasts
       The flesh falls prey to worms?

[B:] At least be moved
       By the cries of relatives,
       Who would mourn you as a monk
       Just as the living mourn the dead.

[A:] Whoever loves his relations
       And neglects God
       Will be accounted guilty for this
       When the Judge comes.

[B:] O Art of Reasoning,
       I wish you had never been discovered!
       You who make so many
       Lonely, miserable clerics.

       Never again will you see
       Him whom you love so much,
       That most beautiful little cleric,
       ———.[61]

60. Lacuna in the manuscript.
61. The name is omitted in the original. It was common in the Middle Ages to leave a
blank space for a name, especially if a personal poem was subsequently published and
widely distributed.

[A:] Alas! Poor me!
    I do not know what to do.
    I am far away in exile,
    Without any advice.

    O brother, spare your tears!
    Perhaps things will get better.
    I am already changing my mind—
    I shall never become a monk![62]

Pope Honorius III
Letter to the Archbishop of Lund, February 4, 1227

We have received a petition from you requesting that we deign to provide mercifully for the fact that numerous subjects of yours, clerics and laymen, frequently engage in prohibited sexual relations, not only with persons related to them but also by having sinful intercourse with dumb animals and by that sin which should neither be named nor committed, on account of which the Lord condemned to destruction Sodom and Gomorrah; and that some of these on account of the length and dangers of the journey, others on account of shame, would rather die in these sins than appear before us on such charges.

Therefore, since divine mercy is greater than human perverseness and since it is better to count on the generosity of God than to despair because of the magnitude of a particular sin, we order you herewith to reprimand, exhort, and threaten such sinners and then to assign them, with patience and good judgment, a salutary penance, using moderation in its devising, so that neither does undue leniency prompt audacity to sin, nor does unreasonable severity inspire despair.[63]

---

62. See chap. 9, p. 250 above for discussion. From the well-known *Carmina Burana* collection of verses found in a thirteenth-century monastic manuscript from Benediktbeuern. This (probably twelfth-century) poem occurs on fols. 52v–53r and was published by Schmeller in his original edition of the manuscript. It is not, however, reprinted in later editions of the *Carmina Burana*, including the Schmeller edition of 1894. This translation was effected from the much better edition by Otto Schumann, "Über einige *Carmina Burana*," ZFDA 63, no. 45 (1926): 81–99. Some scholars have attempted to discount the apparently homosexual nature of the poem: see comments by Schumann, esp. pp. 92–95.

63. Text in A. Krarup, ed., *Bullarium Danicum*, no. 208 (Copenhagen, 1932), 1:178. See pp. 293–94 above.

Ganymede and Helen
(Twelfth Century)

The sun had entered the House of the Bull,[64] and spring, blossom laden,
Had reared its lovely, flowered head.
Under an olive tree I lay, on a bed provided by the grass,
Amusing myself by recalling the sweetness of love.

The redolent scent of the flowers, the freshness of the season,   5
The gently billowing breeze, the chorus of the birds—
While these caressed my mind, sleep crept slowly up.
Oh, that it had never left my eyes!

For I seem to see Ganymede and Helen
Standing on the summer grass beneath a lovely pine,   10
With regal air and serene faces,
With foreheads that shame the lily and cheeks, the rose.

They seem to sit down together on the ground,
Which smiles up at their faces.
It is said that only the gods bestow such beauty.   15
Each is astonished to have found an equal in loveliness.

They exchange words about many things,
And they contend with each other about their comeliness,
Just as if radiant Phebe and Apollo were arguing.
The impudent youth compares himself to the female.   20

She, already longing for the male and ready for bed,
Has for some time felt the proddings of love.
The singular beauty of Ganymede inflames her,
And already the warmth within proclaims itself without.

64. Cf. Ovid *Metamorphoses* 9.736. The author of this poem is unknown. The text was first published by Wattenbach, and an effort toward a critical edition (collating numerous manuscripts discovered after Wattenbach's edition) was published by Lenzen. The poem is mentioned briefly by Curtius in *European Literature*, p. 116, n. 26, and at greater length by Raby in *Secular Latin Poetry*, 2:289–90. The manuscript tradition is discussed by Walther, *Das Streitgedicht*, p. 141, n. 2; by Wattenbach, pp. 126, 135–36; and by Ingeborg Schröbler, "Zur Überlieferung des mittellateinischen Gedichts von 'Ganymed und Helena,'" in *Unterscheidung und Bewahrung: Festschrift für Hermann Kunisch zum 60. Geburtstag* (Berlin, 1961). Further comment is available in Karl Praechter, "Zum Rhythmus Ganymed und Helena," ZFDA 43, n.s., no. 31 (1899): 169–71; in Charles Langlois, "La littérature goliardique," *Revue bleue* 51 (1893): 174; and in Walther, *Das Streitgedicht*, pp. 141–42. The present translation was made from the Lenzen published text but modified on the basis of readings from Houghton Library MS Lat. 198.

Modesty shrinks from a hospice of love: 25
Nor has the maid still the modesty of a virgin;
And since she is not asked, she asks, and entices,
Offering him her lap, her kisses, her bosom.

Both are stretched out upon the verdant grass,
And might have been blessed with union,   30
But Ganymede, not knowing the role expected of him,
Presses himself against her as if he wishes to be passive.

She senses something is wrong and is astounded.
She pushes him away, rails at him;
She curses nature and rants at the gods   35
That a monster should be clothed with so fair a face.

The matter brings them to a fight:
The more she praises the female, the more he the male.
They agree that Nature and Reason shall be
The judges and determine the issue.   40

Each therefore mounts a steed without delay.
Three dawns see them hurrying on,
Until the face of the rising sun greets them
At the house of Nature, toward which they give rein.

Mother Nature is in the palace of Jupiter,   45
Ruminating over the secrets of things to come,
Weaving thread into countless figures
And creating things with precise scales and balances.

Close by stands her companion, Reason, under whose surveillance
She causes the newborn to grow and sows the seeds of those yet
    to be born.   50
They mix the different sexes, and from this mixture
Of different kinds, fertility arises.

Providence also attends, of loftier stature,
Whom the Creator of nature bore of pure thought.
Neither the past nor the present escapes her;   55
Every visible creation is under her observation.

"Lo," she says, "I behold two humans coming,
Of elegant beauty and astonishing comeliness.
I wonder that earth could have produced them:
Heaven itself would be proud of such offspring.   60

I seem to hear them bringing their accusations against each other.
I understand the argument, but I wish I did not.
Now will you see all the gods gather."
She had spoken, and they saw it happen just so.

The tale arouses Jove and his whole brood;   65
Some are drawn by Helen, others by Ganymede.
The palace is opened, the seats are ready.
The gods fill the heavenly halls with majesty.

Meanwhile Dardanus and Tindaris[65] are called in;
They are already stepping onto the threshold of the palace.   70
They leave their horses; they shine with golden appointments.
As they enter the celestial gateway, they are sighted immediately.

Unexpected, the boy is seen to enter
Like the morning star shining before the dawn.
He seems to scorn all with his eyes,   75
And his face disdains to adorn a mortal.

His hair is like imperial gold cloth,
Which is dyed by the Chinese from pure saffron.
When it tries to reach his eyebrow
It curls back coyly on the smoothness of his forehead.   80

His eyebrows are separated by a comely space;
His wide eyes sparkle with sweet rays;
His mouth invites a kiss almost as a demand—
His whole face glows with sweet charm.

Helen follows, blushing slightly—   85
She has not yet known a man and is still shy—[66]
As Cynthia came from the wave of Thetis.
Nor is she second to the boy in fairness of face.

Her hair is partly loose and hanging free,
Partly bound into an elaborate coiffure,   90
Which is well pulled back from the top of her face;
She holds her head aloft as one unused to fear.

Her brow is proud, but her eye is playful.
Her nose is beautifully shaped;
Venus has seasoned her kiss with her own nectar,   95
And some god polished her chin with his own hand.

65. I.e., Ganymede and Helen; see p. 253 above.
66. Note the discrepancy between this line and line 26.

Lest her hair cover her real beauty,
She moves it away from her face, pushing it up behind each ear,
So her face appears like the dawn,
Mixed, when it comes, with pink and white.   100

Then you could see the gods squirming on all sides,
Apollo growing hot, Mars[67] panting,
Groaning as if he had Venus herself in his arms.
He made no effort to restrain himself; it was disgusting to hear.

Jupiter calls Ganymede without shame,   105
But Nature has prepared a seat for the maiden.
She takes it ill that the boy has entered her home:
She calls him neither son nor heir.

A silence comes over the hall; the boy stands up.
Helen stands also, turning her face away from him.   110
Assuming that she will charge first into the fray of this battle,
The entire assembly turns its eyes to her.

H: "Alas," says Helen, "I am sorry for you.
       You clearly hate the female gender.
       The natural order is overturned and law destroyed through you. 115
       I wonder why, since you will not produce children, your
            father produced you?"

G: "Let the old produce sons, for the enjoyment of the young:
       The young lust to have those in their prime.
       The game we play was invented by the gods
       And is today maintained by the brightest and best."   120

H: "That face of yours is only decoration for the sake of decoration;
       It will pass away with you, since you will never know a wife.
       If you would marry [and beget a son],
       Your son could replace the form of his father."[68]

---

67. Lenzen prefers "Jupiter" ("Iovem") to "Mars" on the basis of the reading in D
(Berlin, Staatsbibliothek Diez B Sant. 28), but this seems highly unlikely in view of line 105.
Jupiter remains on the side of Ganymede up to line 258.

68. This *topos* was a favorite of later literature (e.g., Lorenzo Valla *De voluptate*). Cf.
Shakespeare's sonnet 11:
Let those whom Nature hath not made for store,
Harsh, featureless and rude, barrenly perish:
Look, whom she best endow'd she gave the more;
Which bounteous gift thou shouldst in bounty cherish:
She carved thee for her seal, and meant thereby
Thou shouldst print more, not let that copy die.

G: "I have no interest in replacing my face,   125
      But only in pleasing individuals with my individual being;
      I only hope that beauty of yours fades with age,
      Since I think it causes me to be loved a little less."

H: "Oh, how lovely is love between different sexes,
      When a man favors a woman in a mutual embrace!   130
      He and she are drawn together by natural attraction:
      Birds, wild animals, boars, all enjoy this union."

G: "But humans should not be like birds or pigs:
      Humans have reason.
      Peasants, who may as well be called pigs—   135
      These are the only men who should resort to women."

H: "No love has ever touched the heart of a boy,
      But when the same bed joins a man and a woman,
      This is the correct connection, the proper arrangement,
      For like affections arise only from different sexes."   140

G: "Disparity divides things: it is rather like things that are rightly
          joined together;
      For a man to be linked to a man is a more elegant coupling.
      In case you had not noticed, there are certain rules of grammar
      By which articles of the same gender must be coupled together."

H: "When the creator of men formed man,   145
      He tried to make woman more beautiful than man,
      So that he might attract man to mate with woman,
      And men would not love other men more than women."

G: "I should have agreed that it was decorous to love women,
      If appearance were the same thing as good manners.   150
      But when women are married, they sully the delights of the bed;
      And when they are not married, they make themselves
          public utilities."

H: "Let men blush, let Nature grieve;
      It is not the intention of Nature that men be bound to each other.
      Venus joins men only in a fruitless union: 155
      The boy sells his charms heedless of his sex."

G: "We know this activity is accounted worthy by those worthy
          to be counted;
      The people with power and position in the world—
      The very censors who decide what is sin and what is allowed—
      These men are not immune to the soft thighs of a boy."   160

H: "I am not considering those people who act when driven by frenzy.
No reasonable argument defends you, O youth!
This boy has never felt any desire,
Whence he sins and offends even more gravely."

G: "The fragrance of profit is pleasing; no one avoids gain.   165
Wealth, if I should speak plainly, does have a certain appeal.
Anyone who wishes to grow rich is willing to play this game:
If a man desires boys, he is willing to reward them."

H: "Even if this were not counted a sin for youth,
No rationalization could defend the elderly.   170
I can only laugh when I see some obstinate old man:
A game of this sort is surely a sin in old age."

G: "I do not excuse the elderly, whom age accuses;
It does seem disgraceful, when they can already see white hairs,
To occupy themselves with such matters and usurp the
    activities of the young.   175
But the old should not be a discouragement to the young."

H: "Tell me, youth, when youthful good looks change,
When you grow a beard, when your face gets wrinkles,
When your chest turns bushy, when your hole grows tough,
What anxious stud will dream of you then?"   180

G: "Tell me, maiden, when your virginal charms waste away,
When your lips grow thick, your skin dries out,
When your eyebrows droop and your eyes are tired,
Is not then the most passionate of your lovers also going to
    droop a bit?"

H: "You try to be smooth and hairless below   185
So that your temple there might be like that of a woman,
So that in defiance of nature you might become a girl.
You have declared war on nature with your filth."

G: "I might wish to be smooth and soft below the waist,
But God forbid that I should have the shrine of a woman.   190
This is done precisely so I might repel women, whom I contemn.
How much difference is there between a woman and an ass?"

H: "Oh, if I were not restrained by gentle modesty,
I would not be mincing any words with you.
But it is demeaning to use bad language,   195
And foul words ill become the mouth of a maiden."

G: "But we came prepared to speak of vulgar matters:
     There is no place here for the modest.
     Shame and piety have already been abandoned,
     Nor shall I spare either maidenly airs or the truth."   200

H: "I do not know which way to turn, for if I do not speak on a
          par with the vicious,
     I shall be called the loser;
     But if I strive to equal you in words,
     I shall be thought a whore to have spoken so impurely."

G: "Find someone else to fool, someone who does not know you.   205
     I know whom you have offered your bosom to, lying on
          your back.
     Where was that dovelike innocence then?
     Suddenly Thais has become Sabina."⁶⁹

H: "You males who apply yourselves to men,
     Who rashly emasculate males,   210
     By night you taint both boys and yourselves with vice;
     In the morning—I should really pass over this—the shame
          is on the sheets."

G: "You men in whose bed sleeps a prostitute,
     Whom it delights to be filled with feminine filth,
     When Thais, recumbent, reveals herself to you,   215
     You know what her bilge water smells like."

H: "Thais smells of Thais in the manner of Thais,
     But a girl excels balsam in fragrance.
     There is honey in her kiss, honeycomb in her lips.
     Blessed he who enjoys sleep with a virgin."   220

G: "When Jupiter divides himself in the middle of the bed,
     And turns first to Juno, then to me,
     He hurries past the woman and spends his time playing love
          games with me.
     When he turns back to her, he either quarrels or snores."

H: "Your Venus is sterile and fruitless,   225
     And highly injurious to womankind.
     When a male mounts a male in so reprobate a fashion,
     A monstrous Venus imitates a woman."

69. Thais is an archetypal prostitute of Latin literature; see Dronke, *Medieval Latin*, 2:496, note to line 2. Cf. Martial 6.93 (not cited by Dronke). For Sabina, see Lenzen, p. 182nn.

G: "It is not a monstrous thing, if we avoid the monster:
The yawning cave and the sticky bush,   230
The hole whose stink is worse than anything else in the world,
The cavern which neither pole nor oar should approach."

H: "Hush your foul and unpleasant language!
Converse more modestly, you filthy boy!
If you are not willing to defer to a maiden,   235
At least defer to the gods and to Nature."

G: "If the subject is cloaked with the ornaments of words,
Decorated filth will be able to fool us.
I will not be a party to gilding the dross:
It is only right for the words to fit the subject."   240

H: "I shall throw away the cloak of modesty;
If you feel that way, I shall henceforth speak plainly:
When that impure coupling joins you
And you lose the tear of Venus between your thighs,

Ha! There, if you do not realize it, is the offense to mankind!   245
The words are nasty, but the deed even more so."

When the boy hears the unmentionable crime,
A stupor seizes his tongue, a blush rises to his cheeks.
A warm dew steals furtively from his eyes.
Wanting an argument, he does not defend himself.   250

He is silent. Reason rises to speak.
She prudently limits herself to a few words:
"There is no need of a judge," she says, "the matter speaks for itself.
"I say to the boy, Enough. The boy is conquered."

He replies, "At least I utter no rebuttal.   255
"I recognize error, now that I have learned what it is."
"And I," Apollo adds, "have come to my senses." [70]
Jupiter says, "I am aflame for my Juno."

The ancient heresy is banished by the inhabitants of heaven.
The chorus of virgins rejoices; Juno gives thanks.   260
Reason celebrates with the children of Nature.
The maiden is crowned with public approval.

---

70. Note that Apollo had previously been identified as a partisan of Helen's faction (line 103). This is one of several difficulties of the concluding lines.

> Ganymede asks to be granted her hand in marriage:
> All the attendant gods approve this as fitting.
> The blessed union joins them in bliss,   265
> The voice of joy resounds; my slumber departs.
>
> This vision befell me by the will of God.
> Let the Sodomites blush, the Gomorrhans weep.
> Let everyone guilty of this deed repent.
> God, if I ever commit it, have mercy on me![71]   270

A Perverse Custom
(*Quam prauus est mos*, Twelfth Century)

A perverse custom it is to prefer boys to girls,
Since this type of love rebels against nature.
The wildness of beasts despises and flees this passion.
No male animal submits to another.
Animals curse and avoid evil caresses,   5
While man, more bestial than they, approves and pursues such things.

71. Lenzen and, to a lesser degree, Schröbler overlook the significance of several unique aspects of the Houghton manuscript (H). There is yet no way to date this manuscript accurately, as all are agreed, and the tradition is such that it cannot be shown to have any particular relation to other extant copies (Lenzen, p. 166). On the other hand, it is the only copy which is not part of a collection, and curiously, it is written on a strip of vellum which could not have been part of any larger volume, since it must be reversed vertically rather than laterally. It contains two versions of the final line, in the same hand—suggesting that the writer either composed the poem and changed his mind about the last line or had before him two versions of it. The second version is the same as that found in other copies, but the first seems to be a more revealing comment on the author (see chap. 9, n. 62 above for the two readings; Lenzen does not take note of the variance). Between lines 244 and Lenzen's 245 there is a space for six lines. Throughout the poem the speakers are indicated in the margin by "G" and "H," and beside this space a "G" indicates that four of the missing lines would have been Ganymede's. The other two would be the first two lines of a stanza by Helen which is completed by Lenzen's lines 245–46. As it stands in other copies, the poem consists entirely of four-line stanzas except for st. 61, which has six lines. Schröbler (p. 330) is inclined to think this not so unusual but does not cite any other instances of a single expanded stanza in contemporary verse. Lenzen leaves open the possibility that there are missing lines (p. 163). If H represents the autograph, as its odd form and expanded ending might lead one to suppose, the author clearly intended to give both Ganymede and Helen one more argument, and the poem is missing both Ganymede's response to Helen's "losing the tear of Venus" argument and her final salvo, the one which presumably terminates the discussion (the "ibi fit iactura" of line 245 being simply a reference to this argument, whatever it may have been). Schröbler suggests that the scribe of H may simply have felt that the six-line stanza represented an error of a previous copyist and left what he imagined to be adequate space for a correction. But this explanation does not account for the extra ending. Further textual study and paleographical analysis are needed; possibly more manuscripts will be discovered.

The irrational obeys reason's law;
The rational strays far from reason.
When the Lord blessed the first parents on earth,
He ordered them to be fruitful, to farm and fill the earth.   10
They were not both created men but a man and a woman,
And thus multiplied, filling the earth.
If both had been men and had favored this passion,
They would have died out without posterity.
Although he hates all vices, God despises this one particularly: 15
Of which—if you are doubtful—the destruction of Sodom is proof,
Where we read that sulfur and fire annihilated
The residents of Sodom and that an evil people perished with fit penalties.[72]
Those who follow this heresy had better reconsider now
Or face condemnation to flames and sulfur.   20
Let them perish and go to hell, never to return,
Who wish to have tender youths as spouses.[73]

Three manuscripts of this poem dating from the twelfth or thirteenth century have been published independently;[74] a fourth and later version is here published for the first time. The textual relation of the four is extremely complicated, and no effort will be made here to solve all the difficulties involved. The Paris text, translated here, is the most sophisticated as well as the most complete of the versions, containing twenty-two lines of which all but four (9–12) are attested by other exempla. Its Latin is scholarly and elegant, and it was almost certainly composed in the twelfth century.[75] The

72. Cf. Cambridge University, Gonville and Caius College MS 385/605 (thirteenth century):

Quam male peccauit sodomita ruina probauit.
Comprobat esse reum sulphur et ignis eum.
Fetor fetori fit pena; calorque calori;
Talibus est talis congrua pena malis.

The same lines recur in a fourteenth-century manuscript now in the Bodleian Library, Oxford (MS Laud Misc. 2, fol. 5v).

73. Text in BN, MS 15155, published in Hauréau, *Notices et extraits de quelques manuscrits latins de la Bibliothèque nationale* (Paris, 1892), 4:311–12. For historical commentary on this poem, see chap. 11 above.

74. (1) Paris. (2) Oxford, MS Laud. Lat. 86, fols. 94v–95r (not 96, as Dümmler states below), dated by Walther (*Initia carminum*, no. 15159) as thirteenth-century, but by the Bodleian catalog as "12/11/13"; published by Ernst Dümmler, "Zur Sittengeschichte des Mittelalters," ZFDA 22, n.s., no. 10 (1878): 256–58. (Dümmler erroneously states that in line 6 "homo" is missing from this manuscript; in fact it is written in lightly.) (3) Reims 1275, fol. 190v, dated by Walther as thirteenth century, published by W. Wattenbach, "Beschreibung einer Handschrift der Stadtbibliothek zu Reims," *Neues Archiv der Gesellschaft für ältere deutsche Geschichtskunde* 18 (1892): 519–20.

75. Walther does not date the Paris manuscript (*Initia carminum*, no. 14013), but it is found in a thirteenth-century manuscript containing much twelfth-century material.

final couplet of this redaction is missing from the two other early versions but occurs independently in a thirteenth- or fourteenth-century Bavarian manuscript[76] and in a fourteenth-century Leipzig copy of the poem which, perplexingly, is otherwise closer to the Oxford-Reims versions.

The Oxford and Reims versions comprise, respectively, only eighteen and sixteen of the lines in the Paris poem. They are more closely related in wording than any of the others, although the order of verses in Reims differs dramatically from both the Paris and Oxford copies. The latter differ in wording but are identical in order, save for omissions. The Oxford copy seems in fact to be almost a simplified version of the Paris poem, or one made from a copy so defective that the scribe had to reconstruct the opening of many lines.

Both Oxford and Reims include a couplet lacking in the Paris version: "On sterile ground seed would lack roots, / Nor would it bear fruit, but would always lie fallow."[77] The Leipzig version, reproduced below, also includes

76. Bayerische Staatsbibliothek clm 6911: see chap. 9, nn. 75, 76 above.

77. Lines 11–12 of the Oxford version, 5–6 of Reims: "In sterili terra semen radice careret, / Nec faceret fructus, sed semper inane iaceret." Taking the Paris copy as the original and adding to it these lines after its line 14, the poem then has a maximum of twenty-four lines, disposed thus:

Paris	Oxford	Reims	Munich	Leipzig
1	1	1	...	1
2	2	2	...	2
3	3	...	...	...
4	4	...	...	...
5	5	7	...	7
6	6	8	...	8
7	7	9	...	...
8	8	10	...	...
9	...	...	...	...
10	...	...	...	...
11	...	...	...	...
12	...	...	...	...
13	9	3	...	3
14	10	4	...	4
...	11	5	...	...
...	12	6	...	...
15	13	11	...	5
16	14	12	...	6
17	15	13	...	...
18	16	14	...	...
19	17	15	...	...
20	18	16	...	...
21	...	...	1	11
22	...	...	2	12

Note that this schematization does not take account of variant readings; all lines of similar content are counted as equal, regardless of variations in wording or punctuation.

four lines not found in other copies. They are extremely difficult to render satisfactorily into English but mean, roughly,

I know not if they bear by whom one passes to hell,   [9]
But I know that if they do, they bear through the rear.   [10]
We are not of their number, doing this among them,   [13]
But we are of those who do it to them.   [14]

Quam prauus est mos juuenes preferre puellis,
Cum sit nature veneris mos ille rebellis.
Si patribus vestris veneris mos hic placuisset
Liberis extinctis nulla successio fuisset.
Omne quod vitium Deus hoc specialiter odit,   5
Quod bene si dubites Sodome destructio prodit.
Quod negat et refuit [sic] sceleratos bestia captus,
Hoc probat et sequitur hic plus quam bestia factus.
Nescio si pariunt quibus itur ad inferiora,
Sed scio si pariunt, pariunt per posteriora.   10
Si[c] pereant et eant ad Tarthara, non redituri,
Qui teneros pueros pro coniuge sunt habituri.
Non sumus in illis facientes illud in illis,
Sed sumus ex illis illud facientibus illis.⁷⁸

Ganymede and Hebe (Translation and Text)
(*Post aquile raptus*, Twelfth or Thirteenth Century)

After the abduction by the eagle, after the lovely indiscretion⁷⁹ with the
   boy,
Juno bemoans in her chambers the cup stolen from Hebe.

But she dares not air her grief openly,
So she rouses Hebe to the fight and promises her aid.

78. Leipzig, Karl Marx Universität MS 1029. A colophon to this poem adds, "Hii versus situentur in [?]. Item lex julia de adulteriis s. e[t] contra exercentes nefandam libidinem cum masculis." It is followed by four lines in praise of priestly virtue, which probably bear no relation to the preceding but are published here for the sake of completeness:
   Viri venerabiles, sacerdotes Dei,
   Precones altissimi lucerne diei,
   Caritatis radio fulgentes in spei,
   Auribus papite verba oris mei.
79. "Nefas" usually means something stronger than "indiscretion"; its literal meaning is "unmentionable." But the author of this poem can hardly have meant anything so strongly negative, as its contents make clear.

She arms her beforehand with rhetorical devices,   5
Teaches her sharp words to cut the boy to the quick.

From her mistress the servant learns her part:
What words to use, what arts to employ.

The council is convened and begins to consider the arguments.
When Hebe seeks justice in its midst and begins to speak,   10

Her face reddens, and the hue of her countenance colors her words.
She blushes to speak, and her blush itself says all.

"Immortal race, image of eternal Paris,
Treasure of nature, nature's first source,

You who restrain the unjust by divine law,   15
I seek justice from the just; I ask that rights be restored to the injured.

I was Jove's cup bearer while grace allowed,
With the . . . [?] of Jove, and with the sanction of your blessing.

But a new arrival has occupied my place: a unique enemy.
Should I keep silent, boy? Why? You know all.   20

The Phrygian youth and Troy's shame have invaded the heavens
And founded Trojan strongholds in the skies.

Here a hare hunts hare;[80] he breathes his charm[81]
And the scent of game into the heavens.

A new prey, the boy! Preying on what is mine.   25
Has the abducted come to ravish the rights of goddesses?

But the fates prepare justice, as you, Apollo, urge.
Troy is in ruins, and a woman will render its just deserts.

Already our young man has invaded the marriage rites;
Already the ends of the earth are marked with his name as gifts for him. 30

O houses and seats of virtue! O mindless lust!
In you sounds the dead flute of Troy.

Here with a movement of his side, of his leg, his foot,
Virtue is cast aside and sits and weeps from afar.

He adorns his face and curls his hair with an iron.   35
With Ganymede as master, crime spreads everywhere.

80. Ovid *Ars amatoria* 3.662.
81. A pun: "lepŏrem" would mean "hare"; "lepōrem" means "charm."

With his face he provides reason for a thousand evils;
With such an incentive, let every god beware—

Those thousand deities of land and sea and sky.
A boy—this impure boy—is wed in heaven.[82]   40

The lord summons the Trojan nephew by day
And importunes him by night.

I pass over what Jove's handmaid is about by day,
But this I say: Who sleeps with her at night?

Already, O gods, Nature blushes, and the kindly mother   45
Implores you with tears, let the punishment fit the crime.

This Juno asks, and Pallas, and the other goddesses:
Let the judgment of the goddesses be swift."

She had finished. A murmur begins, and a louder tumult,[83]
But the boy rises: his face commands silence.   50

Night has fled, and the day follows. As the sun outshines the moon,
So the glory of Ganymede surpasses that of Hebe.

Atlas, who bears it, delights in the weight of this star,[84]
And Pallas is moved by him for whom a woman sighed.

Apollo thinks of Hyacinth, Silvanus of Ciparissus;[85]   55
Venus remembers Adonis: such beauty was his.

Mars, as if embracing him, looks with longing eyes
And sighs, seeing the delicate lips, for tender kisses.

Silently his joys conquer Jove; he imagines
He is more of a god because in this even grace yields to him.   60

He raises his eyes from the ground, like a Trojan son,
And seems to spread twin suns in the sky.

Such beauty would implore pardon if he sinned:
His face and body intercede for him with the lord.

His mind is shaken by all this, like a boy in a childhood fright,   65
[But] words of grace flow from his sweet mouth.

82. Vergil *Eclogues* 8.49–50.
83. Vergil *Aeneid* 12.239.
84. Ibid., 8.141.
85. For Hyacinth, see Ovid *Metamorphoses* 10:162 ff; for Ciparissus (Cypress), ibid., 121 ff., and Vergil *Georgics* 1.20.

"The father of Trojans is here, and his whole posterity;
  The people of Teucer are noted among the stars.

What have I done? I did not force my arms into the heavens.
  I was shown the way—not ravished—by my loving friend.   70

'Jove's company,' he said, 'the council of the gods,
  The heavens, the fates—all will welcome you to life in the skies.'

So I accepted the offered glory and enjoy it: Is this the charge against me?
  Was my mixing the nectar a base offer from a base person?

Or was it better for a vile old woman with the hand of a Moor—   75
  A shrew like this—to be the servant of Jove's table?

As long as Jove is Jove, I will be whatever you want.
  Before, a woman reared her haunches; now a man offers his mouth.

Those who assail a particular type of sex[86]—which is approved
    regardless of type—
  Are fools: a thunderbolt will strike the gaping hole.   80

Would you look at the sky during the day to see if the moon is full?[87]
  And do you blush with every wave of the Red Sea?[88]

In a wolf's den the woman sits and spins tales;[89]
  Speaking falsehood with deceit, the pen of her tongue paints evil.

Was it my fault that Ida pleased the hunters?[90]   85
  No woman faithless to herself can be expected to keep faith.

She assails and provokes me with the poison of long speaking,
  But a rare thing is a chaste whore or a peaceful woman.

Either I rightly enjoy the ruler in heaven, or one must regard as a crime
  Something which the providence of fate has made necessary."[91]   90

86. Literally, "the name of sex."
87. I.e., homosexual and heterosexual love are as different as the sun and the moon.
88. Apparently this odd line means "Must everything be just like everything else?" ("Do you have to be the same color as the Red Sea?"). I.e., can there not be two completely different kinds of love?
89. Cf. Bayerische Staatsbibliothek clm 6911, fol. 128: "Et sunt heredis custodes ut lupus edis" (translated above, chap. 9, n. 75).
90. Ganymede was carried off while hunting on Mount Ida.
91. Cf. *Carmina Burana* (Schmeller, no. 84a): "Non est crimen amor, quia, si scelus est amare, / Nollet amore Deus etiam divina ligare" ("Love is not a crime; if it were a crime to love, / God would not bind even the divine with love"). See also above, p. 247. The text of "Ganymede and Hebe," previously unpublished, is from a thirteenth-century manuscript now in Munich, Bayerische Staatsbibliothek clm 17212, fols. 26v–27r.

Post aquile raptus, post dulce nefas puerile,
Hebe rapta sibi flet pocula Juno cubile.

Juno tamen non ausa palam spirare dolorem,
Suscitat in litem Hebem, spondetque fauorem.

Rethoricis illam documentis ante figurat,   5
Emula verba docet, puerum quibus intus adurat.

A domina discit cause vernacula partes,
Quos sermone modos, quos gestiat artibus artes.

Curia contrahitur et ludicra membra reuoluit,
Cum mediis Hebe pacem petit ora resoluit.   10

Ora rubet uultusque color sua uerba colorat,
Effarique rubet et iam rubor ipse perorat.

"Inmortale genus, eterni Paridis imago,
Nature pretium, nature prima propago,

Vos ego qui premitis iniustos iure beato,   15
Iustos iura precor, det iura queror violato.

Illa ego sum pincerna Iovis dum gratia fauit,
Quam Iovis [?] qua[m] sanctio vestra beauit.

In mea iura uenit hospes nouus, unicus hostis.
An sileam, puere? Sed quid? Vos omnia nostis.   20

Hic Phrigius Troieque nefas irrupit in astra,
Et super celos fundauit Troiea castra.

Hic agitat lepores lepus, iste suumque lepōrem,
Et pulpamenti celo spirauit odorem.

O nova preda puer, o rerum predo mearum!   25
An raptus rapere venisti iura dearum?

Vindictam sed fata parant ut Delie suades.
Troia ruit, meritasque dabit sibi femina clades.

Insĕrŭit thalami iam noster pusio uotis,
Iam sibi terra polus signantur nomine dotis.   30

O domus! o sedes virtutis et inscia luxus!
In te postuma lasciuit Troica buxus.

Hic flexu lateris, humero, pede gesticulatur,
Virtus pulsa loco longe sedet et lacrimatur.[92]

Inducit uultum crispatque comas calamistro,   35
Pullulat in multis scelus, hoc Ganimede magistro.

In facie mille fouet argumenta malorum,
Hoc incentivo caueat sibi quisque deorum

Ve maris et terre ve celi numina mille.
Nupsit in astra puer, puer impurus, puer ille,   40

Quem uocitat rex Dardanum de luce nepotem;
Sollicitat Phrigium uere de nocte nepotem.

Sed taceo pincerna Iovi quod luce propinat.
Hoc fabor: quis pincernam de nocte supinat?

Iam, superi, natura rubet, materque benigna,   45
Vos lacrimis orat, sit criminis ultio digna.

Hoc Juno rogat, hoc Pallas, hoc queque dearum,
Ut maturetur sententia celicolarum."

Finierat. Serpit murmur feriusque tumultus,
Sed puer exsurgit, meruitque silentia uultus.   50

Nox abiit, sequiturque dies. Ut uincere Phebem
Phebe soles, Ganimedis honor sic preuenit Hebem.

Sideris huius honus gaudet qui sustinet Atlas,
Et sentit pro quo suspiret femina Pallas.

Jacincti Phebus et Siluanus Ciparissi;   55
Adonis memor est Venus: hoc decus infuit ipsi.

Mars ut in amplexu lasciuis patrat ocellis,
Suspiratque uidens teneris oscilla labellis.

Pertemptantque Iouem tacite sua gaudia; credit[93]
Se magis esse deum quod in hoc sibi gratia cedit.   60

Euocat a pedibus oculos ut Dardana proles;
Est uisus geminos celo diffundere soles.

Ipse decor ueniam siquidem peccauerit orat,
Pro quo suo domino facies et forma perorat.

92. MS: "lacrimantur."
93. Cf. AL, no. 795: "Et se tunc tandem credidit esse deum."

Mens rebus ut puero puerili mota stupore;   65
Gratia uerborum tenero distillat ab ore.

"Dardanus hic pater est, hic linea tota nepotum,
Et Teucri genus est hoc inter sidera notum.

Quid feci? Non inieci mea brachia celis.
Non rapuit, sed iter docuit comes ille fidelis.[94]   70

Inquit enim te cena Iouis, te curia diuum,
Te celi te fata iŭuant super ethera uiuum.

Accessi decus hoc datum, hoc fruor, hoc ego plectar?
Quod turpem dare turpe fuit quod misceo nectar?

Turpis ănus maurique manus, muliercula talis   75
An decuit quod uerna fuit mensē Iovialis?

Sic tibi sim quicquid uis, dum sit Jupiter idem.
Nuper fellat homo; crissauit femina pridem.

Qui nomen sexus agitant sine nomine fultum,
Committunt folles, et cudet fulmen hiulcum.   80

Respicias astra die an sit luna fecunda?
Et rubeas quotiens rubri maris estuet unda?

In fauea uulpis mulier sedet et noua fingit,
Ficta loquendo dolis lingue stilus acra pingit.

Crimen erit mihi quod placuit uenatibus Yda?   85
Nil fidĕi seruit mulier sibimet malefida.

Incitat, irritat me uerbi felle loquacis,
Sed rara est casta meretrix et femina pacis.

Aut duce virtute celo fruor, aut scelus esse
Constet quod fati series facit esse necesse."   90

Married Clergy (Translation and Text)
(*Nos uxorati*, Twelfth or Thirteenth Century)

We married clergy were born to be made fun of,
To be ridiculed, to be criticized by everyone.

94. MS: "o" after "docuit."

If a guiltless man points out the crimes of others,
Those censured can bear the rebuke with patience;
[But] you who attack our sins, have a look at your own.[95]   5
Leave us alone and chastise yourself, sodomite!
You draw up harsh laws, enact bitter statutes,
And make things generally impossible for us.
You deny that it is right to touch a woman's bed
And to consummate the marriage rite in the bridal chamber.   10
But it is the natural right of a man to enjoy his wife.
This is how we were all born, how we multiply,
How each generation follows the preceding one.
Thus survives the human race in its quest for perpetuity.
This response rightly takes account of the laws of nature: 15
If no one propagated, if no man procreated,
Everything would come to an end; the world would be finished.
Coitus precedes birth, as the pregnant woman the child she bears.
No woman would conceive if no man impregnated.
In my judgment the correct opinion   20
Holds the natural sin of the [bridal] bed
To be more venial than that contrary to nature.
I applaud what prostitutes do when it leads to birth,
And whatever nourishes the fruit born of its seed.
Let that seed be damned from which no offspring will follow,   25
Which flows vainly and produces nothing useful.
Vilely and dangerously you sin and plot to destroy
In vain what, rightly expended, would produce life.
Do not waste the material for creating offspring.
A half man, a debauchee, you steal the prostitute's joys: 30
Truly, I say, you have the makings of a murderer.
No dumb animal is drawn to this evil;[96]
No creature's lust is accustomed to abusing its like.
The doe submits to the stag; subdued, the she-goat weds the ram;
The bear lies down with the mate appropriate to it.   35
The rest of the animals mate according to nature's law,
[But] you are driven by a lust which all of nature abhors.[97]

95. Cf. Wright, *Anglo-Latin Satirical Poets*, 2:209.
96. See Ovid *Metamorphoses* 9:731–37.
97. From the same manuscript as "Ganymede and Hebe," also previously unpublished. The syntax and poetic structure of this poem are ragged and erratic; the translation is in many places approximate. For discussion, see pp. 217–18, 278 above.

Nos uxorati sumus ad ludibria nati,
Obprobrioque dati, cuiuslibet ore notati.
Vir qui sorde caret, si sordida facta notaret,
Equa mente pati possent maledicta [98] notati.
Qui nostras mordes proprias circumspice sordes.   5
Tangere nos uita et corrigere sodomita.
Iura seuera paras. Leges decernis amaras,
Et nimium duris nos conditionibus uris.
Esse negas rectum muliebrem tangere lectum,
Et thalami ritum nupte complere maritum.   10
Naturale uiri ius est uxore potiri.
Hinc omnes nati sumus, hinc et multiplicati;
Sic precedenti gens instat postera genti.
Sic hominum durat series, qui soluere curat.
Legem nature notat haec responsio iure: 15
Si generaret [99] nemo, res in fine supremo
Quo pacto staret mundus, ni vir generaret.
Ortum precedit coitus; que feta quem edit.
Non concepisset mulier ni uir generasset.
Hoc intellectum mea censet opinio rectum   20
Qui naturalem lecti culpam uenialem
Amplius esse putat quam quod natura refutat.
Laudo quod scortum quod ... [?] [100] ducit ad ortum,
Quodque suo ductum nutrit de germine fructum.
Semen dampnetur quod proles nulla sequetur,   25
Quodque fluens gratis nil confert utilitatis.
Turpiter et dire peccas, cogisque perire,
Quod recte fusum uite prodiret inusum,
Materiam proli generande tollere noli.
Semiuir et mollis scorto sua gaudia tollis,   30
Certa dico fide tibi inest homicide.
Huius cura mali bruto non est animali.
Nullius bruti socio solet ardor abuti.
Ceruum cerua subit, capro capra subdita nubit;
Subiacet ursa pari cui debet mixta iugari.   35
Cetera nature coeunt animalia iure,
Te uitium torret natura quod omnis abhorret.

98. MS: "madedicta."
99. MS: "generet."
100. Indecipherable.

Ganymede
(Thirteenth Century?)

Eyes, neck, cheeks, curl of golden hair—
These were the flames of Jove for his Ganymede.
When Jupiter was seeking to allow himself a little [pleasure] with the boy,
The god ordained that all things were licit with a boy.
Heedless of the care of the world and the murmurs of the gods,
Of the tongue of his injured wife and of heaven,[101]
He bore the Ilian lad to the heavens, a star to the stars,
And finally even believed that he was a god,
So that the kept boy could please him by touch as well as sight.
In the daylight he bore Jove his cup and at night kisses.[102]

Triangle
(Thirteenth Century?)

Graecinus loved a boy, a maid loved Graecinus,
And the boy loved only the maid.
Graecinus handed her over to the boy,
Who surrendered himself to the man,
And both man and boy got what they wanted.[103]

Arnald de Vernhola
Confession (1323)

Asked if he had ever said to anyone or had himself believed that sodomy was
a lesser sin than simple fornication with a prostitute, and particularly if he
had ever demonstrated to anyone that this was written in canon law, he
responded no to each question.

Asked if he had stated or believed that because his nature impelled him to
satisfy his desires with a man or woman it was not therefore a sin to have
relations with men or women, and [whether he believed such relations] were
slight or venial sins, he responded that although he thought his nature

---

101. "Jovem" here does not seem to make much sense except as meaning "heaven," a
use sanctioned by Cicero, Horace, Vergil, Ovid, and others doubtless familiar to thirteenth-
century writers, but one with which I am somewhat uncomfortable. The entire translation
reflects the awkwardness of the original.

102. Text in AL, no. 795. The editor dates this poem as thirteenth-century on the basis of
the manuscript in which it and the following poem (797) were found (Parisinus 3761).
Baluze attributed it to Hildebert of Lavardin (cf. chap. 8, n. 106 above). Cf. Dronke,
Medieval Latin, 2:393.

103. From the same manuscript, no. 797 in AL. Cf. Marbod, chap. 9, n. 19 above.

inclined him toward the sin of sodomy, he had nevertheless always considered it a mortal sin but thought it was the same as simple fornication, and that the wrongful defloration of a virgin, adultery, and incest were all more serious sins than the sin of sodomy (the carnal knowledge of men by men). And he had said this to Guillem Ros, the son of Peter Ros of Ribouisse, and to Guillem Bernardi, the son of John Joch of Gaudiès, with whom he had committed the sin of sodomy. But he had not said this in order to induce them to consent to an act which they otherwise would not have [committed]. He said to Guillem Ros that the sin of masturbation was equal to the sin of simple fornication or sodomy: they were equal in gravity, he said, . . . if the sin of masturbation was performed deliberately and intentionally.

Asked if he had said to anyone or believed that as a subdeacon he could sacramentally absolve someone who confessed mortal sins to him, and that that person would actually be cleansed of all his sins and would not have to confess the same sins again to a priest, he responded that he had indeed said to certain people that he could absolve them of their sins, and that he had absolved some people as described when he had heard their confessions, even of mortal sins, without instructing them to confess the same sins to a priest. . . . He himself, however, had never believed that he could absolve anyone of mortal sins sacramentally confessed to him . . . but had said these things and heard confessions in order to hear what sins those confessing to him had committed. . . .

Asked if he had said to anyone that he would celebrate mass, or if he had actually said mass or had put on priestly vestments for the saying of mass, and if he believed that in celebrating mass he could actually make [the bread and wine into] the body and blood of Christ, he responded that he had indeed said to some people that he had celebrated mass and that he was a priest, but that he had actually not done it, nor did he believe that he, not being a priest, could do so.

Asked if he had committed the sin of sodomy with anyone else, either with the persons mentioned or with others or in other places, except as he had confessed, he said no.

Asked if he committed any other crimes of heresy or knew of any that anyone else had committed, he said no.

He said nothing else relevant, although diligently examined.

Asked if he regretted that he had believed and stated and taught these errors, insofar as he could, leading others into error, and if he wished to abjure these errors, he said yes. . . .[104]

104. Translated from Vatican MS 4030, fol. 233r-v, published in Jean Duvernoy, *Le régistre d'inquisition de Jacques Fournier, évêque de Pamiers (1318–1325)* (Toulouse, 1965), 3:49–50. See pp. 285–86 above.

Frequently Cited Works

A listing of all the works cited in this study would be uselessly massive. This list includes only items cited frequently and in widely separate contexts; it is intended simply to preclude a search back through many pages to locate the first full reference to a work which appears throughout the book. It does not include sources cited often but in successive (or nearly successive) notes, and it lists only one edition—the *Leges Visigothorum*—comprised in standard reference collections (e.g., PL or MGH editions: see Abbreviations). Classical texts (Aristotle, Ovid, etc.) are cited only when a particular edition or translation has been referred to in more than one chapter.

Bibliography in its proper sense will be found in the notes, particularly near the beginning of each chapter.

Abrahams, Phyllis, ed. *Les oeuvres poétiques de Baudri de Bourgueil*. Paris, 1926.

Aelred of Rievaulx. *Aelredi Rievallensis opera omnia*. Edited by A. Hoste and H. Talbot. Corpus Christianorum. Turnhout, 1971.

Albertus Magnus. *Summa theologiae*. In *Opera*, edited by August Borgnet. Paris, 1895.

Albucasis. *On Surgery and Instruments*. Edited by M. S. Spink and G. L. Lewis. Berkeley, 1973.

Allen, P. S. *The Romanesque Lyric*. Chapel Hill, N. C., 1928.

Aristophanes of Byzantium. *Excerptorum Constantini De natura animalium libri duo: Aristophanis Historiae animalium epitome, subjunctis Aeliani Timothei aliorum eclogis*. Edited by Spyridon Lambros. In *Supplementum Aristotelicum*, 1.1. Berlin, 1885.

Aristotle. *The Nicomachean Ethics*. Translated by H. Rackham. New York, 1926.

Aurelianus, Caelius. *Celerum vel acutarum passionum. Tardarum passionum*. Edited and translated by I. E. Drabkin. Chicago, 1950.

Baer, Yitzhak. *A History of the Jews in Christian Spain*. Philadelphia, 1961–66.

Bailey, Derrick Sherwin. *Homosexuality and the Western Christian Tradition*. London, 1955.

Baluze, Etienne. *Capitularia regum Francorum*. Paris, 1677.

Bellamy, John. *Crime and Public Order in England in the Later Middle Ages*. London, 1973.

Bernard of Morley. *De contemptu mundi*. In *The Anglo-Latin Satirical Poets and Epigrammatists*, edited by Thomas Wright, vol. 2. London, 1872.

Bibliographical Essays in Medieval Jewish Studies. Vol. 2. New York, 1976.

Blumenkranz, Bernhard. *Le juif médiéval au miroir de l'art chrétien*. Paris, 1966.

Borgnet, August. *Alberti Magni Ratisbonensis episcopi, ordinis praedicatorum opera omnia*. Paris, 1890–99.

Boswell, John. *The Royal Treasure: Muslim Communities under the Crown of Aragon in the Fourteenth Century*. New Haven, 1977.

Brandt, Paul: *see* Hans Licht.

Bullough, Vern. *Sexual Variance in Society and History*. New York, 1976.

Cambrensis, Giraldus. *De vita Galfridi archiepiscopi Eboracensis*. In *Opera*, edited by J. S. Brewer. London, 1873.

Carmody, Francis, ed. "Physiologus Latinus versio Y." *University of California Publications in Classical Philology*, vol. 12, no. 7 (1941).

Champollion-Figeac, J. J., ed. *Hilarii versus et ludi*. Paris, 1838.

Corpus iuris canonici. Edited by Emil Friedberg. Leipzig, 1879–81.

Curtius, Ernst R. *European Literature and the Latin Middle Ages*. Translated by Willard R. Trask. Princeton, N. J., 1953.

Daniel, Marc. *Hommes du grand siècle*. Paris, n.d.

de Becker, Raymond. *L'érotisme d'en face*. Paris, 1964. (Translated into English as *The Other Face of Love* by M. Crosland and A. Daventry. New York. 1969.)

de Pogey-Castries, L.-R. *Histoire de l'amour grec dans l'antiquité*. Paris, 1930.

Didache: see Teaching of the Apostles.

Dover, Kenneth. "Classical Greek Attitudes to Sexual Behavior." *Arethusa* 6 (1973): 59–73.

———. *Greek Popular Morality*. Oxford, 1975.

Dronke, Peter. *Medieval Latin and the Rise of European Love Lyric*. 2d ed. Oxford, 1968.

Dümmler, Ernst. "Briefe und Verse des neunten Jahrhunderts." *Neues Archiv der Gesellschaft für ältere deutsche Geschichtskunde* 13 (1888): 358–63.

Economou, George. *The Goddess Natura in Medieval Literature*. Cambridge, Mass., 1972.

The Fathers of the Second Century. Edited by C. Coxe. The Ante-Nicene Fathers, vol. 2. New York, 1885.

La Filosofia della natura nel medioevo: atti del Terzo Congresso internazionale di filosofia medioevale. Milan, 1966.

Forsyth, Ilene. "The Ganymede Capital at Vézelay." *Gesta: International Center of Medieval Art* 15, nos. 1–2 (1976): 241–46.

Fournier, Jacques. *Le régistre d'inquisition de Jacques Fournier, évêque de Pamiers*. Edited by Jean Duvernoy. Toulouse, 1965.

Freeman, E. A. *The Reign of William Rufus*. Oxford, 1882.

Gibbon, Edward. *The History of the Decline and Fall of the Roman Empire*. Edited by Dean Milman, M. Guizot, and W. Smith. London, 1898.

Goldast, Melchior. *Constitutiones imperiales*. Frankfurt, 1673.

Goodich, Michael. "Sodomy in Medieval Secular Law." *Journal of Homosexuality* 1, no. 3 (1976): 295–302.

Grayzel, Solomon. *The Church and the Jews in the Thirteenth Century*. Philadelphia, 1933.

Griffin, Jasper. "Augustan Poetry and the Life of Luxury." *Journal of Roman Studies* 66 (1976): 87–105.

Hauréau, Barthélémy. *Les mélanges poétiques d'Hildebert de Lavardin*. Paris, 1882.

———. "Notice sur un manuscrit de la Reine Christine à la Bibliothèque du Vatican." *Mémoires de l'Académie des inscriptions et belles lettres*, vol. 29. Paris, 1878.

———. *Notices et extraits de quelques manuscrits latins de la Bibliothèque nationale*. Vol. 4. Paris, 1892.

Heer, Friedrich. *The Medieval World: Europe, 1100–1350*. Translated by Janet Sondheimer. New York, 1962.

Henderson, Jeffrey. *The Maculate Muse: Obscene Language in Attic Comedy*. New Haven, 1975.

Henkel, Nikolas. *Studien zum Physiologus im Mittelalter*. Tübingen, 1976.

Hexter, R. J. *Equivocal Oaths and Ordeals in Medieval Literature*. Cambridge, Mass, 1975.

Horapollo Nilous. *The Hieroglyphics of Horapollo Nilous*. Edited and translated by Alexander T. Cory. London, 1840.

Hyamson, M. *Mosaicarum et Romanarum legum collatio*. London, 1913.

Ibn Quzman. *Cancionero*. Edited by A. L. Nykl. Madrid, 1933.

al-Jāḥiẓ, ʿAmr ibn Baḥr. *Kitāb al-Ḥayawān*. Cairo, 1945–47.

———. *Kitāb mufākharāt al-jawārī wa'l-ghilmān*. Edited by Charles Pellat. Beirut, 1957.

John of Salisbury. *Metalogicon libri IIII*. Edited by Clement Webb. Oxford, 1929.

———. *The Metalogicon of John of Salisbury*. Translated by Daniel McGarry. Berkeley, 1962.

Jordan, William; McNab, Bruce; and Ruiz, Teofilo, eds. *Order and Innovation in the Middle Ages: Essays in Honor of Joseph R. Strayer*. Princeton, N.J., 1976.

Karlen, Arno. "The Homosexual Heresy." *Chaucer Review* 6, no. 1 (1971): 44–63.

———. *Sexuality and Homosexuality*. New York, 1971.

Kinsey, Alfred; Pomeroy, Wardell; and Martin, Clyde. *Sexual Behavior in the Human Female*. Philadelphia, 1953.

———. *Sexual Behavior in the Human Male*. Philadelphia, 1948.

Kirsch, John, and Rodman, James. "The Natural History of Homosexuality." *Yale Scientific Magazine* 51, no. 3 (1977): 7–13.

Laistner, M. L. W. *Thought and Letters in Western Europe, A.D. 500 to 900*. 2d ed. Ithaca, N.Y., 1966.

Land, J. *Anecdota Syriaca*. Vol. 4. Leiden, 1875.

A Latin Dictionary. Edited by C. T. Lewis and Charles Short. Oxford, 1879.

Lauchert, Friedrich. *Geschichte des Physiologus*. Strasbourg, 1889.

Leges Visigothorum. Edited by K. Zeumer. Hanover, 1902. (In MGH, Leges, 1.1.)

Licht, Hans [Paul Brandt]. *Sexual Life in Ancient Greece*. Translated by J. H. Freese. London, 1932. (First published in German as *Sittengeschichte Griechenlands*. Dresden, 1925–28.)

McCulloch, Florence. *Mediaeval Latin and French Bestiaries*. Chapel Hill, N.C., 1962.

McLaughlin, T. P. "The Teaching of the Canonists on Usury (XII, XIII, and XIV Centuries)." *Mediaeval Studies* 1–2 (1939–40): 81–147, 1–22.

McNeill, John. *The Church and the Homosexual*. Kansas City, 1976.

McNeill, John, and Gamer, Helena. *Medieval Handbooks of Penance: A Translation of the Principal "Libri poenitentiales" and Selections from Related Documents.* New York, 1938.

Maimonides. *The Code of Maimonides,* Book 5: *The Book of Holiness.* Translated by Louis Rabinowitz and Philip Grossman. Yale Judaica Series, no. 16. New York, 1965.

————. *The Guide of the Perplexed.* Translated by M. Friedlander. New York, n.d.

al-Maqqarī, Abū ʾl- ʿAbbās Aḥmad ibn Muḥammad. *Analectes sur l'histoire et la littérature des arabes d'Espagne.* Edited by R. Dozy, G. Dugat, L. Krehl, and W. Wright. Leiden, 1855–60.

Marcus, Jacob R. *The Jew in the Medieval World.* New York, 1972.

Meier, M. H. E. "Paederastia." In *Allgemeine Encyclopädie der Wissenschaften und Künsten,* edited by J. S. Ersch and J. J. Gruber, 3.9.149–88. Leipzig, 1837.

Metlitzki, Dorothee. *The Matter of Araby in Medieval England.* New Haven, 1976.

Mundy, John. *Europe in the High Middle Ages, 1150–1309.* New York, 1973.

Noonan, John. *Contraception: A History of Its Treatment by the Catholic Theologians and Canonists.* Cambridge, Mass. 1965.

Nykl, A. L. *Hispano-Arab Poetry and Its Relations with the Old Provençal Troubadours.* Baltimore, 1946.

Öberg, Jan. *Serlon de Wilton, poèmes latins.* Stockholm, 1965.

O'Callaghan, Joseph. *A History of Medieval Spain.* Ithaca, N.Y., 1975.

Ovid. *Metamorphoses.* Translated by Frank Miller. 1916; reprint ed., Cambridge, Mass., 1976.

Oxyrhynchus papyri. Edited by B. Grenfell and A. Hunt. London, 1903.

Panormitanus [Nicolò de' Tudeschi]. *Commentaria in quintum decretalium librum.* Venice, 1642.

Pellat, Charles. *The Life and Works of Jāhiẓ.* Translated by D. M. Hawke. London, 1962.

Pérès, Henri. *La poésie andalouse en arabe classique.* Paris, 1953.

Photius. *Photius: bibliothèque.* Edited by Réné Henry. Paris, 1960.

Pirenne, Henri. *Medieval Cities: Their Origins and the Revival of Trade.* Translated by Frank Halsey. Princeton, N.J., 1952.

Pomeroy, Sarah. *Goddesses, Whores, Wives, and Slaves: Women in Classical Antiquity.* New York, 1975.

Raby, F. J. E. *Secular Latin Poetry.* 2d ed. Oxford, 1957.

Reade, Brian, ed. *Sexual Heretics: Male Homosexuality in English Literature, 1850–1900.* New York, 1970.

Robinson, David, and Fluck, Edward. *A Study of Greek Love-Names, Including a Discussion of Paederasty and a Prosopographia.* Baltimore, 1937.

as-Saqati, Abū ʿAbd Allah. *Kitāb fi ʿAdabiʾl-Ḥisba,* ed. G. S. Colin and E. Levi-Provençal. Paris, 1831.

Sbordone, Francesco. *Physiologus.* Milan, 1936.

Schachar, Isaiah. *The "Judensau": A Medieval Anti-Jewish Motif and Its History.* London, 1974.

Schirmann, J. "The Ephebe in Medieval Hebrew Poetry." *Sefarad* 15 (1955): 55–68.

Schmeller, J. A. *Carmina Burana: Lateine und deutsche Lieder und Gedichte einer Handschrift des XIII Jahrhunderts aus Benediktbeuern.* In *Bibliothek des literarischen Vereins in Stuttgart,* vol. 16 (1847).

Schreiber, J. *Die Vagantenstrophe der mittellateinischen Dichtung.,* Strasbourg, 1892.

Schultz, Alwin. *Das höfische Leben zur Zeit der Minnesänger.* Leipzig, 1879–80.

Scott, Samuel Parsons. *The Visigothic Code.* Boston, 1910.

Seneca the Elder. *Controversiae.* Translated by Michael Winterbottom. London, 1974.

Servianorum in Vergilii carmina commentariorum. Edited by E. K. Rand et al. Lancaster, Pa., 1946–65.

Southern, R. W. *Medieval Humanism and Other Studies.* New York, 1970.

———. *Western Views of Islam in the Middle Ages.* Cambridge, Mass., 1962.

Stock, Brian. *Myth and Science in the Twelfth Century.* Princeton, N.J., 1972.

Strecker, Karl. *Die Cambridger Lieder.* Berlin, 1926.

———. *Moralisch-satirische Gedichte Walters von Châtillon, aus deutschen, englischen, französischen und italienischen Handschriften.* Heidelberg, 1920.

Summa Magistri Rolandi mit Anhang incerti auctoris quaestiones. Edited by Friedrich Thaner. Innsbruck, 1874.

Symonds, John Addington. "A Problem in Greek Ethics." In *Studies in the Psychology of Sex,* edited by Havelock Ellis, vol. 1, app. A. 1897; reprint ed., New York, 1975.

Synan, Edward A. *The Popes and the Jews in the Middle Ages.* New York, 1965.

The Teaching of the Apostles (Διδαχὴ τῶν ἀποστόλων). Edited by J. Rendel Harris. Baltimore, 1887.

Theodoret of Cyrus. *Thérapeutique des maladies helléniques* [*Graecarum affectionum curatio*]. Edited and translated by Pierre Canivet. In Sources chrétiennes, vol. 57. Paris, 1958.

van de Spijker, Herman. *Die gleichgeschlechtliche Zuneigung*. Freiburg, 1968.

Vogel, Cyrille. "La discipline pénitentielle en Gaule des origines au IXᵉ siècle." *Revue des sciences réligieuses* 30 (1956): 1–26, 157–86.

von Grunebaum, Gustav. *Medieval Islam*. Chicago, 1971.

Waddell, Helen. *Medieval Latin Lyrics*. New York, 1948.

Wakefield, W., and Evans, A. *Heresies of the High Middle Ages*. New York, 1969.

Walther, Hans. *Das Streitgedicht in der lateinischen Literatur des Mittelalters*. Munich, 1920.

———. *Initia carminum ac versuum Medii Aevi posterioris Latinorum*. Göttingen, 1969.

Weinrich, James D. "Human Reproductive Strategy: The Importance of Income Unpredictability and the Evolution of Non-reproduction: Some Evolutionary Models." Ph.D. dissertation, Harvard University, 1976.

Werner, J. *Beiträge zur Kunde der lateinischen Literatur des Mittelalters*. Aarau, 1905.

Whicher, George. *The Goliard Poets*. New York, 1949.

White, T. H. *The Bestiary: A Book of Beasts*. New York, 1954.

Wilmart, A. "Le florilège de Saint-Gatien: contribution à l'étude des poèmes d'Hildebert et de Marbode." *Revue bénédictine* 48, nos. 2–4 (1936): 3–40, 147–181, 235–258.

Wilson, E. O. *Sociobiology: The New Synthesis*. Cambridge, Mass., 1975.

Wright, Thomas, ed. *The Anglo-Latin Satirical Poets and Epigrammatists*. London, 1872.

———. *The Latin Poems Commonly Attributed to Walter Mapes*. London, 1841.

Index of Greek Terms

General Index